Venice and the Slavs

VENICE
AND THE SLAVS

The Discovery of Dalmatia
in the Age of Enlightenment

LARRY WOLFF

Stanford University Press ⌁ *Stanford, California 2001*

Stanford University Press
Stanford, California
©2001 by the Board of Trustees of the
Leland Stanford Junior University

Printed in the United States of America on acid-free,
archival-quality paper.

Library of Congress Cataloging-in-Publication Data
Wolff, Larry.
    Venice and the Slavs : the discovery of Dalmatia in
the Age of Enlightenment / Larry Wolff.
        p. cm.
    Includes bibliographical references and index.
    ISBN 0-8047-3945-5 (alk. paper)
        1. Dalmatia (Croatia)—History—18th century.
2. Venice (Italy)—Relations—Croatia—Dalmatia.
3. Dalmatia (Croatia)—Relations—Italy—Venice.
I.Title.
    DR1628.W65 2001
    949.72—dc21   00-067121

Original printing 2001

Last figure below indicates year of this printing:
00 09 08 07 06 05 04 03 02 01

Typeset by Shepherd, Inc. in 10/12.5 Galliard

For Peter Stansky
and in memory of Billy Abrahams

Out after the play, in the theatre slung with green glass
beads, onto the black tossing water, so silent, so swaying:
& the poor people asked us not to overpay the traghetto;
& there were cactuses; & a man singing in the morning;
& R. & I went to the Tiepolo church; & the thick yellow
service with the priests weaving a web in incantation,
& the little boys & the reverence & secularity
& ancientness made us say This is the magic we want:
& magic there must be; so long as magic keeps its place.

Virginia Woolf, diary, 18 *April* 1932

Acknowledgments

My research for this book has taken me into areas where I have often felt uncertain about my own background and preparation, and I have, from the beginning, relied upon the kindness of my academic colleagues who have repeatedly and generously helped me to proceed. Someone like myself, whose research involves exploring the misunderstandings and misconceptions of previous centuries, must inevitably be aware of his own susceptibility to the intellectual trap of presuming to have fully mastered the subject under investigation. Without the support and encouragement of other scholars, more knowledgeable than I, it would have been hardly possible to pursue this study with the great excitement that, together with considerable insecurity, may accompany the exploration of new domains.

I am grateful for research support on this project from the American Council of Learned Societies, the International Research and Exchanges Board, and the Gladys Krieble Delmas Foundation. I was greatly assisted by the archival staff of the Archivio di Stato in Venice during my research expeditions and, on shorter visits, by the staffs of the Povijesni Arhiv in Zadar, the Povijesni Arhiv in Dubrovnik, and the Archivio Segreto of the Vatican. I also had the help of the library staff of the Biblioteca Marciana in Venice, while my work in Widener Library and the Houghton Collection at Harvard, as well as at the O'Neill Library at Boston College, reminded me that sometimes there's no place like home.

In presenting portions of this work in progress I had the great good fortune to learn from extremely stimulating groups of colleagues. The Triplex Confinium project, which met in Graz in 1998, permitted me to benefit from the focused academic concerns of Drago Roksandić, Karl Kaser, Hannes Grandits, Zrinka Blažević, and Borna Fürst-Bjeliš; I also rediscovered the world of the Morlacchi in the company of Elisabetta Novello and Alessandro Sfrecola and was lucky enough to find myself back together with Wendy Bracewell at the moment when I had most to gain from her insight. The conferences on European identity in 1998 and 1999, sponsored by the University of Aarhus, gave me the opportunity to learn from the reflections of Uffe Østergård, Peter Bugge, and Kristian Gerner. A conference on integrating Eastern Europe and Western Europe, which took place at Chapel Hill, N.C., in 1998, put me on a panel with Dubravka Ugrešić, Andrei Pippidi, and Jacques Rupnik, allowing me to benefit from their wisdom. I also presented portions of this research at the Central European University in Budapest, at the Remarque Institute of New York University, and at the Georgetown Center for Eurasian, Russian, and East European Studies; speaking at these institutions, I was both hosted and intellectually galvanized in my work by Sorin Antohi, Tony Judt, and Charles King, respectively.

At Boston College I thank Robin Fleming and Matthew Restall for the encouragement they gave me, in our sessions together, to think ambitiously even about small research trips. I am also grateful to the deans at Boston College, who were extremely supportive while I was working on this project, especially Bob Barth, S. J., Joe Quinn, and Mick Smyer. I thank Alan Reinerman for encouraging me to venture into Italian history. Paul Breines has been a model to me in staying cool while relishing a sense of academic adventure. Jim Cronin I thank for his continuing friendship, for his inspirational sense of the humor to be found in the most extraordinary academic circumstances, and finally for his deep understanding of the academic drive to research, write, and publish.

In Venice I received assistance and hospitality from Giovanni Levi and Rosella Mamoli Zorzi. Ivana Burdelez kindly oriented me in Dubrovnik. I thank Marco Cipolloni for our famous encounters by coordinated trains in Bologna, and for finding the Slavic Othello. Gaetano Platania has, once again, given me not only his friendship and encouragement, but a host of references and relevant publications to advance my research; our last meeting at the Hungarian Academy in Rome reminded me forcefully of how much his support has meant to me over the last twenty years.

I am grateful to Brendan Dooley, Franco Fido, and Norman Naimark, who read portions of this work in progress and gave me both encouragement and invaluable criticism. Massimo Donà and Marko Jačov generously made available to me materials from their own research. I thank Ivo Banac, not just for the beer at Kavanagh's, but for the insight and assistance that came along with it. Working on Alberto Fortis, an eighteenth-century natural historian, I needed help with the history of science and found ready assistance from my friends Kathy Ann Miller, Lisbet Koerner, Mario Biagioli, and Steve Gould. Fortis was also an early anthropologist, and I am grateful to Mort Klass for his anthropological guidance. In the crisis of finishing the manuscript, when my ancient computer gave up the ghost, it was Carolyn Fuller and Bill McAvinney who came to the rescue and retrieved the files from my hard disk.

Maria Todorova has been an intellectual guide and inspiration for contemplating the implications of balkanism. Jean-Philippe Belleau has contributed his special anthropological appreciation of the Morlacchi. Jeremy King has helped me think through my perspective on nationality. Andrei Zorin offered me insight into the mystique of Catherine on the Adriatic. Paschalis Kitromilides helped me to appreciate important aspects of the Venetian role in southeastern Europe. Pierre Saint-Amand has profoundly enhanced the excitement of my immersion in the eighteenth century. Svetlana Boym offered Slavic inspiration, and this project always benefited from the fresh air of our walks by the Charles River, to say nothing of the canoe excursion.

I am most deeply grateful to Wayne Vucinich, for the tremendous support and guidance that he has given me, ever since he became my academic adviser and my uncle, when I went to Stanford as a graduate student in 1979. Once again, as I worked on Venice and Dalmatia, I found myself taking advantage of his academic wisdom, and I would not have been able to find my way in this exploration of southeastern Europe without his help. As I come to the end of the project I find that my historical sense of what once lay inland from the Adriatic owes much to his extraordinary memoirs of Bileća, which he read aloud to me on the occasions when I came to visit him at Stanford.

My parents, Bob and Renee Wolff, were magnificently supportive in staying with my kids while I went to Dalmatia; I am grateful for that, as for so much else. My older children Orlando and Josephine were there in Venice with me when I made my first exploratory foray, and Anatol, born soon after, has been part of the special disruption project which superimposes the earliest years of childhood development upon the gradual progress of academic research; eventually he became old enough to lose my pocket Croatian dictionary. Orlando has truly facilitated my work on this book by helping me to become the last person in America to get on the Internet. Josephine has offered me the benefit of her inspirational organizational skills and helped me check off each small academic step toward ultimate completion; I am grateful also for her insight that I can sometimes be difficult to talk to, because I get that look in my eyes, and you know that I'm "thinking about the Slavs." Perri Klass has lived with my academic distraction for a long time, and inevitably turns out to know what I need academically better than I know myself. Though there is no detail of this book, whether of intellectual vision or logistic execution, that does not owe something to her involvement, I especially want to thank her for her profound appreciation of what the archives could and did mean to me in my research, and for accompanying me on what became our own voyage into Dalmatia.

Contents

List of Illustrations   XII

Introduction   1

1. The Drama of the Adriatic Empire: Dalmatian Loyalty and the
   Venetian Lion   25

2. The Useful or Curious Products of Dalmatia: From Natural History
   to National Economy   76

3. The Character and Customs of the Morlacchi: From Provincial
   Administration to Enlightened Anthropology   126

4. The Morlacchi and the Discovery of the Slavs: From National
   Classification to Sentimental Imagination   173

5. Public Debate after Fortis: Dalmatian Dissent and Venetian
   Controversy   228

6. The End of the Adriatic Empire: Epidemic, Economic,
   and Discursive Crises   276

Conclusions and Continuities: The Legacy of the Venetian
Enlightenment in Napoleonic Illyria, Habsburg Dalmatia,
and Yugoslavia   319

Notes   363

Index   393

Illustrations

1. Carta della Dalmazia, Albania, e Levante   4

2. View of the Crypto-Porticus or Front towards the Harbour   23

3. Imperatoris Diocletiani Palatii Ruinae   28

4. La Dalmatina, Atto IV   73

5. La Dalmatina, Atto V   74

6. A Country Woman of the Canal of Zara   94

7. Natural History Specimens   98

8. View of the Inside of the Temple of Jupiter   105

9. Morlacchi Triptych   155

10. Map of the Territories of Trau, Spalatro, and Makarska, the Primorje and Narenta, with the Adjacent Islands   162

11. *Les Morlaques,* title page, by J.W.C.D.U. & R.   210

12. Stanislavo Socivizca   251

13. Carta Geografica della Dalmazia   282

14. Ti con nu, nu con ti   354

Venice and the Slavs

Introduction

The Obscurity and Celebrity of Venetian Dalmatia

In the eighteenth century, when Edward Gibbon surveyed the lands that had once belonged to the ancient Roman empire, he observed that Dalmatia, "which still retains its ancient appellation, is a province of the Venetian state." As Gibbon wrote and published *The Decline and Fall of the Roman Empire* in the 1770s and 1780s, Dalmatia did retain its ancient name as well as some classical ruins, such as the tremendous palace of Diocletian at Split, to testify to the former Roman affiliation. The province's eighteenth-century political importance, however, lay in a different historical drama, the decline and fall of the Venetian empire, then in the final decades of its sovereign survival. Though Venice still clung to its eastern Adriatic empire over "the best part of the sea-coast," the Roman province of Dalmatia, to Gibbon's regret, had not been preserved in its ancient integrity: "The inland parts have assumed the Sclavonian names of Croatia and Bosnia; the former obeys an Austrian governor, the latter a Turkish pasha; but the whole country is still infested by tribes of barbarians."[1] For Gibbon the balance of civilization could be construed from the displacement of ancient appellations by Slavic names, and his reflections on Dalmatia were not objectively neutral when he pronounced the province to be "infested" by barbaric tribes.

On the one hand, he tended to conflate the eighteenth-century circumstances with the ancient drama of the decline and fall, the overrunning of Roman provinces by barbarian invasions. On the other hand, he perfectly reflected the philosophical values of his own century, of Augustan England, of the age of Enlightenment, when he interpreted the map of Europe according to an implicit opposition between civilization and barbarism. Gibbon's eighteenth-century summation appeared curiously relevant again at the end of the twentieth century, when the political situation of Dalmatia was again associated with the names and fates of Croatia and Bosnia, and foreign observers grimaced again, barely concealing the Augustan distaste that the supposedly civilized still feel for the presumably barbarous.

Gibbon's remarks on Dalmatia were followed by a footnote, that emblematic numeral of neutral scholarship, naming the historian's source: "A Venetian traveller, the Abbate Fortis, has lately given us some account of those very obscure countries."[2] The abbé Alberto Fortis, Paduan by birth, when Padua was part of the Venetian republic, published his *Viaggio in Dalmazia* in Venice in 1774, not long before Gibbon published his passing remarks on Dalmatia, in 1776, in the first volume of the *Decline and Fall*. Fortis's work was promptly translated into English and published in London in 1778 as *Travels into Dalmatia*. Fortis, though a priest, was emphatically a man of the Enlightenment, much more interested in natural history, geology, and paleontology than in any religious matters. With his voyage to Dalmatia, and his investigations into the natural resources and economic potential of the province, he set forth the issues of empire before the public of Venice. The great success of his book made the subject of Dalmatia fundamental for the Venetian Enlightenment and much more than a footnote to the Enlightenment all over Europe.

Fortis found in Dalmatia the classical ruins of ancient Rome, studied the "Sclavonian names" that designated contemporary Slavic society, and described the customs of the most notable "barbarians" in the province. These were the Morlacchi: "a race of ferocious men, unreasonable, without humanity, capable of any misdeed." Fortis, however, quoted this conventional Venetian opinion of the Morlacchi for the purpose of rebutting its excessive excoriation, and he went on to attribute to these Dalmatian barbarians a sort of noble savagery, according to the revisionist values of the Enlightenment. Gibbon might have found the presence of barbarians distasteful, but Fortis offered a sympathetic anthropological treatment of "barbarous" customs in Dalmatia and an ambivalent verdict upon "the society that we call civilized." Gibbon was absolutely right, however, to recognize that Fortis's account had illuminated the hitherto "obscure" province of Dalmatia, publicizing its topography and anthropology all over Europe, as the *Viaggio in Dalmazia* rapidly appeared in German, French, and English translations. Obscurity, of course, was a matter of perspective, and, no doubt, Dalmatia always appeared dimmer from the distance of England than from the Adriatic maritime proximity of Venice. Yet the inland mountains of Dalmatia, the Dinaric Alps, where the Morlacchi resided, had been obstacles to Venetian observation, preserving provincial opacity and obscurity; from the perspective of San Marco it was easier to contemplate and comprehend the accessible cities of coastal Dalmatia. There, on the Adriatic, such towns as Zadar and Split, known under their Italian names as Zara and Spalato, were sufficiently influenced by Italian culture for Fortis to pronounce that "the society of Zara is as civilized as one could desire in any notable city of Italy." Fernand Braudel described Dalmatia as "a narrow strip of Mediterranean life," a hilly landscape of "terraced gardens, orchards, vineyards, and fields where the hillside was not too steep," and small towns on the Adriatic—all in the menacing shadow of the "wild mountains," extending almost to the coast.[3] What enlightened Europe came to find most fascinating about Dalmatia in the late eighteenth century was the wildness that lay beyond the Adriatic coast, in the obscure mountainous interior of the province.

Venice was inevitably interested in Dalmatia in the eighteenth century, as the metropolitan capital on the lagoon sought to refashion the rule of centuries across the Adriatic into the form of a modern empire. If London also took an interest in Fortis's travels in Dalmatia, it was because England, even more than Venice, was deeply invested in the importance of empire and the issues of imperial rule. Indeed, Gibbon's epic engagement with the decline and fall of the ancient Roman empire belonged to a contemporary context of excitement and anxiety about the modern British empire. The first volume of the *Decline and Fall* appeared in the same year as the American Declaration of Independence. Edward Said has emphasized the correlations of "culture and imperialism," observing that empire is "supported and perhaps even impelled by impressive ideological formations," that "the enterprise of empire depends upon the idea of having an empire." Anthony Pagden has argued for the importance of "ideologies of empire" in early modern England, France, and Spain, with reference to their respective possessions in North and South America. In the eighteenth century those ideologies of empire were culturally reconceived and reformulated according to the values of the Enlightenment.[4]

The eighteenth-century Venetian empire was miniature by comparison to the British, French, and Spanish dominions. The late medieval

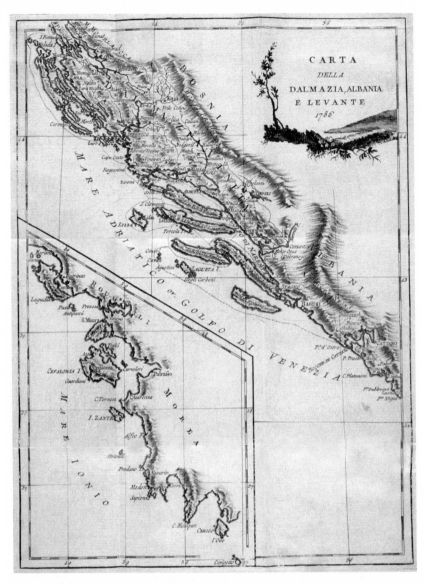

FIGURE 1. "Carta della Dalmazia, Albania, e Levante," from Giulio Bajamonti, *Storia della peste che regnò in Dalmazia,* his history of the plague in Dalmatia, published in Venice in 1786. The map represented the meager remnants of Venice's once farflung imperial domain beyond the sea, the *Oltremare,* which formerly extended all around the eastern Mediterranean. Dalmatia itself was most of what remained in the eighteenth century, with the appendage of Venetian Albania to the south, at the Gulf of Kotor, and, still further south, the several Ionian Greek islands, such as Corfu, Cephalonia, and Zante, inset on the map. *(By permission of Widener Library, Harvard University.)*

empire of Venice, dominating the arrival of Asian trade in Europe, had consisted of many Mediterranean islands, from Negroponte and Naxos to Crete and Cyprus, as well as powerful commercial communities in important ports around the sea, like Acre, Alexandria, and Constantinople. Control of the Adriatic, including the Dalmatian coast, was essential to more remote seafaring enterpises. The decline of Venice's eastern Mediterranean domain followed from the Ottoman conquests of the fifteenth century, but, at the same time, the Republic extended its mainland state—the Terraferma—across northern Italy as far as the River Adda, almost to Lake Como. In the eighteenth century, Venice still ruled over a mainland territory that included several restive Italian cities—Padua, Vicenza, Verona, Brescia, Bergamo—as well as the Friuli region and the Istrian peninsula along the Gulf of Venice. There were also a few Greek Ionian islands like Corfu, Cephalonia, and Zante, just beyond the Adriatic, though the great Greek prizes, the imperial Mediterranean bases, had already been traumatically lost, Cyprus in the sixteenth century and Crete in the seventeeth century. Yet, Venetian Dalmatia, along with its appendage of Venetian Albania, was not only preserved but actually extended by conquest in the early eighteenth century. The province became the focus for Venice's final fantasies of imperial resurgence, as the gondola of state glided toward political annihilation at the century's end. Dalmatia was Venice's America, though small in size and close at hand, just across the Adriatic, replete with savage tribes and civilizing missions; the Venetian Enlightenment fashioned a richly elaborated ideology of empire upon the province's slender territorial base. Gibbon, with his eye on the ancient Roman empire, and perhaps a glance over his shoulder at the modern British empire, failed to observe that Fortis, in redeeming Dalmatia from obscurity, stood forth as the enlightened public spokesman for a renovated Venetian vision of Adriatic empire.

After the decline and fall of the Roman empire, Dalmatia was ruled by the Byzantine emperors from Constantinople, and in the seventh century the migration of the Slavs into southeastern Europe decisively altered the province's ethnographic character. Venice established outposts on the Dalmatian coast as early as the year 1000, though the medieval kingdom of Croatia also extended to the Adriatic during the eleventh century. When the kings of Hungary assumed the Croatian crown in the twelfth century, there commenced a protracted contest between

Hungary and Venice for the eastern Adriatic coast, finally resolved in Venice's favor in the early fifteenth century. Venice ruled Dalmatia thereafter, consolidating naval domination over the Adriatic Sea and establishing a unified administration at the end of the sixteenth century under the governorship of the Provveditori Generali. The eighteenth century, however, brought an important difference in the territorial dimensions of the province, for after the peace of Carlowitz in 1699, when the Ottoman empire ceded Hungary to the Habsburgs, the Venetians managed to obtain an inland extension of Dalmatia at the expense of Ottoman Bosnia. Dalmatia was given further inland depth after the peace of Passarowitz in 1718. These two enlargements of the province, the new and newest acquisitions, *nuovo acquisto* and *nuovissimo acquisto,* meant that Dalmatia no longer consisted only of the old coastal strip, *vecchio acquisto,* whose maritime stations had once marked the route to mercantile destinations in the eastern Mediterranean. With Adriatic control and Mediterranean trade more tenuous and less profitable, and with serious competition from Habsburg Trieste as a free port after 1719, Venice had to reconsider the imperial potential of Dalmatia in terms of both terrestrial and maritime advantages.

During the first half of the eighteenth century, the Provveditori Generali reevaluated Dalmatia's importance to take into account its new lands and especially its new inland inhabitants, the ferocious Morlacchi in the mountains. During the second half of the eighteenth century, these same issues, concerning the new territorial, economic, and anthropological significance of the province, burst forth from the official confines of administrative reports and emerged into the public sphere of the Venetian Enlightenment. Alberto Fortis publicized "those very obscure countries" to the point that even Edward Gibbon in England noted the new level of Venetian interest in Dalmatia. Though Venice's political stake in Dalmatia dated back seven centuries before the time of Fortis's voyage, the Venetian Enlightenment discovered and explored a province that Venice had never really known. There were new and newest acquisitions, of course, but there were also new issues and aspects of empire in the eighteenth century, posing new questions and defining new perspectives. Venice's "discovery" of Dalmatia revealed hitherto obscure aspects of the inland Dalmatians, but also the innermost cultural preoccupations of the Venetians themselves during the final decades of their sovereign independence.

The intellectual history of this discovery of Dalmatia must consider not only how Venice ruled there—the administrative means, economic uses, and political purposes of Adriatic empire—but also how Venice viewed the province, the articulation and elaboration of Dalmatian themes according to the cultural perspectives of the Venetian Enlightenment. The development of an imperial discourse of Dalmatia during the eighteenth century focused on several distinctive concerns. The most fundamental was the construction of an ideology of empire, Adriatic rather than Atlantic in its dimensions and references, mapping the geography of backwardness to justify the imperatives of economic development. Closely related was the formulation of a civilizing mission to redress the supposed barbarism of the Dalmatian Morlacchi, or rather, as it may appear, the formulation of the barbarism of the Morlacchi to establish the importance of Venice's civilizing mission. The ideological importance of the Morlacchi pointed toward an anthropological classification of the Slavic peoples, based on new Venetian knowledge of Dalmatia, in the context of the Enlightenment's contemporary articulation of the idea of Eastern Europe; the philosophical reconception of Europe, as divided between more and less civilized western and eastern domains, perfectly fit the evolution of Venice's imperial perspective on its eastern Adriatic province. The discussion of such concerns conditioned the emergence of an enlightened, imperial public sphere within the Republic, for the reception and consumption of the published discourse on Dalmatia in its ever diversifying forms and aspects; this public sphere eventually came to constitute an Adriatic rather than a narrowly Venetian forum, with bases in Zadar and Split as well as Venice and Padua. Finally, that sphere became the site for the ascriptive formulation of national identity, as the Adriatic Enlightenment contemplated an anthropological constellation of overlapping labels: Dalmatians, Morlacchi, and Illyrians, as well as Albanians and Bosnians, even Serbs and Croats, and especially Slavs, whose name became the taxonomic key to sorting out the ethnographic alternatives. Imperial ideology influenced the negotiation of national identity in Dalmatia, through the meeting of imaginations, in the ruling metropolis and from within the province itself. Thus, the intellectual history of Venice's discovery of Dalmatia in the eighteenth century must focus on the articulation of an imperial imbalance, emphasizing the challenge of backwardness and development, the value of civilization over barbarism, the anthropological classification of the Slavs, the dynamics of discursive domination within the public sphere, and the ascription of national identity in an imperial context.

In addressing these Dalmatian issues the Venetian Enlightenment contributed culturally to an agenda of imperial concerns: the political coherence of the Adriatic empire, the economic development and even exploitation of provincial resources, the cultivation of the patriotic loyalty of the Slavs to the Venetian Republic of San Marco, and the disciplinary administration of the Morlacchi in the name of civilization. The historian Marino Berengo, writing in 1954 about Venetian Dalmatia, offered the designation "semi-colonial" as a suitable label for the government of the province in the eighteenth century: "Here was firmly established a semi-colonial regime that was rendered legitimate and almost inevitable by the fearful backwardness of the region and the continuing Ottoman threat that transformed entire territories into military districts, such that the administrative organization was inspired by criteria still more centralist than those prevailing for the continental state." In the multivolume *Storia di Venezia* of the 1990s, Benjamin Arbel has discussed the *colonie d'oltremare,* the overseas colonies, including Dalmatia, and described the Renaissance imperial pursuit of profit and honor, "ad proficuum et honorem Venetiarum." The relations between ruling Venice, the *Dominante,* and the dominion beyond the sea, the *Oltremare,* according to Arbel, "always preserved their fundamental colonial nature." At the same time, the administrative distinction between the mainland Italian *Terraferma* and the trans-Adriatic *Oltremare*—both ruled by the *Dominante* from metropolitan Venice—remained significant for matters of maritime trade and Ottoman relations.[5] In the age of Enlightenment that distinction was publicly affirmed and culturally elaborated with special reference to Dalmatia.

The perceived asymmetry between the Republic's continental Italian and trans-Adriatic territories was rendered "legitimate" in the eighteenth century by the ideological articulation of difference in Dalmatia, whether as economic backwardness, anthropological barbarism, or alien nationality. Since Dalmatia, however, was made up of mixed Italian and Slavic elements, with different social and economic levels from the coastal cities to the inland mountains, there was a balance of difference and similarity with respect to Venetian Italy. "The Atlantic and the Pacific are seas of distance," Predrag Matvejević has written, "the Adriatic a sea of intimacy."[6] Dalmatia was not America, did not lie beyond the Atlantic, but was located just across the Adriatic and was undeniably in Europe. With its Diocletian remains Split had a more evidently venerable classical pedigree than Venice itself. The Dalmatian mountains, rising immediately to the east of the Adriatic coast—a range of the Alps, after all—could hardly be endowed with the absolute "otherness" of the Orient. Rather, the exoticism of semi-colonial Dalmatia was formulated according to the demi-Orientalism by which the Enlightenment discovered Eastern Europe. The Adriatic divided the dominions of Venice along just the same geographical axis that was becoming increasingly significant for marking the distinction between Eastern and Western Europe. For that reason, the imperial ideology of the Venetian Empire reinforced the broader continental reconception, and, reciprocally, the western and eastern vectors of civilization, as marked upon the map of the European Enlightenment, conditioned the Venetian perspective on Dalmatia.

The Venetian Enlightenment thus cultivated the articulation of Adriatic difference, which vindicated the asymmetrical aspects of imperial rule in Dalmatia. Yet, even if the Enlightenment's formulas of discursive mastery were sometimes inseparable from the political and economic priorities of power, it was also true that imperatives of empire were often accompanied by beneficently enlightened intentions. The Dalmatian historian Giuseppe Praga, after departing from Zadar for Venice, published his *Storia di Dalmazia* in Padua in 1954, writing in counterpoint to Berengo about the eighteenth-century Venetian discovery of Dalmatia: "Little by little it became clear what a chest of hidden treasures Dalmatia could be if properly cared for and administered. It was no longer economic interest alone that stood behind all the activity, but the forces of science and culture also began to take an interest in the problems of renewal."[7] It would be difficult to disentangle the strands of economic and cultural interest that constituted the Venetian perspective in the age of Enlightenment, but the exploration and excavation of the province's "hidden treasures" ultimately turned out to be less fiscally profitable than philosophically rewarding. The intellectual historian may remark that the scant success of the semi-colonial economic and agronomic program, within an empire doomed to imminent extinction, was overshadowed by the abundant wealth of flourishing cultural reflections and representations, inventive Venetian variations on Dalmatian themes.

National Historiography, Imaginary Ethnography, and Cultural Geography

The history of Dalmatia after the abolition of sovereign Venice in 1797 has stimulated a politically and nationally charged historiography of Venetian rule. After Venice, and excluding the brief French interlude of Napoleonic Illyria, Dalmatia was ruled by the Habsburgs from Vienna until World War I. At Versailles Dalmatia was contested, and then divided, between Italy and Yugoslavia, with Zadar assigned to Italian rule as Zara. Mussolini took most of the rest of the Dalmatian coast during World War II, but after the war the whole reverted to Tito's Yugoslavia, inscribed in the constituent republic of Croatia. With the dissolution of federal Yugoslavia in the 1990s, independent Croatia has held the Adriatic coast against federal siege and bombardment, most notably at Zadar and Dubrovnik. These changes of sovereignty under circumstances of military struggle, political contention, and ideological controversy have been divergently interpreted within a deeply politicized historiography. Academic disputation over Dalmatia has thus played a part in Italian pretensions to the province, in competing Serbian and Croatian conceptions of national identity in Dalmatia, and in the challenging ethnographic enigma of the distinction and the extinction of the Morlacchi.

Though the actual population of Italians in Dalmatia was only a small minority at the time of World War I, the Versailles settlement, assigning most of the province to Yugoslavia, was not favorably received in Italy. Diplomatic dissatisfaction was accompanied by historiographical attention to Venetian Dalmatia, cultivated in the context of an Italian historical claim upon the eastern Adriatic coast. Attilio Tamaro published in Rome in 1919, the year of Versailles, a history of "the Italian nation on its eastern frontiers," including Dalmatia. In his account of "Italian intellectual life" in eighteenth-century Venetian Dalmatia, he concluded that "all Dalmatians" cherished "a profound love" for Venice, and "besides their little provincial country they had only one other, Italy, in whose bosom they lived like members of one large family." In Rome in the 1920s, under the Mussolini regime, a journal was published, *Archivio Storico per la Dalmazia,* adorned with an engraving of Diocletian's palace at Split, named by the editors, of course, as Spalato. The journal naturally took a great interest in the history of Venetian Dalmatia and, in spite of its compromising context in the capital of fascist Italy, published much valuable research, such as the articles by Fabio Luzzatto on seemingly neutral subjects like "Dalmatian Writers about Agrarian Politics in the Eighteenth Century" and "Academies of Agriculture in Dalmatia in the Eighteenth Century."[8] In fact, the attentions of the journal to Venetian Dalmatia affirmed by political implication the historical Italian connection.

If the Italian minority among the Slavs in Dalmatia has been the occasion of political and historiographical controversy ever since 1797, the Dalmatian Slavs themselves have also been ethnographically controversial, since the nineteenth century when they began to be sorted, and to sort themselves, into Croats and Serbs. Though this distinction largely followed the religious division between Catholicism and Orthodoxy, it was also complicated by disputed identifications based on medieval historical claims, variations in linguistic dialect, and even the ideological affirmation of unitary Serbo-Croatian Yugoslavism. The Republic of Venice recognized the religious difference, and counted its Orthodox Slavic subjects in Dalmatia as about a fifth of the estimated provincial population of a quarter of a million in the late eighteenth century. The Adriatic empire, however, did not recognize a national distinction between Serbs and Croats among the Slavs, and, in fact, Venice preferred to consider both Italians and Slavs of Dalmatia as amalgamated members of the same Dalmatian nation.

From a Venetian perspective the most striking social contrast was between the more "civilized" coastal Dalmatians and the inland Dalmatian Morlacchi; moreover, the former were mostly Catholic and the latter largely Orthodox in religion, though some Morlacchi were also Catholic. In the eighteenth century it was the coastal Dalmatians who distinguished themselves from the inland Morlacchi, and the Venetians who recognized and validated that difference. The Morlacchi were notably different from other Dalmatians geographically, living in the mountains, and economically, often practicing semi-nomadic pastoralism instead of more settled agriculture. Many Morlacchi were also new Dalmatians, inasmuch as they lived along the Bosnian border, and had recently become Dalmatians either by emigration or through Venice's new and newest territorial acquisitions. Over the course of the century, and under the influence of the Enlightenment, these evident differences were further emphasized as perceptions of the Morlacchi acquired a new intellectual coherence; their social practices were interpreted, sociologically, as uncivilized manners, and, anthropologically, as primitive customs. Linguistically, they were recognized as Slavs, though this did not actually differentiate them from most other Dalmatians. The name Morlacchi was both imprecise and relative, for Dalmatians could use the term rather freely to distinguish themselves from other Dalmatians, supposedly more primitive and less civilized; at the same time, Venetians invested the term with their own civilizing ideology of empire. Eighteenth-century observers did not hesitate to designate the Morlacchi as a "nation," but the early modern meaning of nationality was often obscure, and in this case testifies most clearly to the elusiveness of retrospective ethnography.

Croatia has successfully claimed Dalmatia in the twentieth century, both within Yugoslavia and after its dissolution, but the national affiliation of the Morlacchi has been historiographically contested, the more freely since the denomination of Morlacchi has virtually ceased to exist as a social or national category. In an article published in Zagreb in the 1920s, in the journal *Hrvatsko Kolo,* Marijan Stojković noted that "today one does not speak any more, as one once did, about the Morlacchi," and he went on to make the Morlacchi "nation" parenthetically Croatian: "naroda 'Morlaka' (Hrvata)." In a Yugoslav *History of Yugoslavia,* published in the 1970s, Ivan Božić made a different identification of the Morlacchi—"(actually Orthodox herdsmen who considered themselves Serbs)"—in a similarly parenthetical remark. Marko Jačov, in a book published in Belgrade in the 1980s, *Venice and the Serbs in Dalmatia* (*Venecija i Srbi u Dalmaciji*), suggested that the Orthodox Dalmatians in the eighteenth century should be regarded as Serbs.[9] In the 1990s history brutally outstripped the historians. The Serbs of inland Dalmatia refused to adhere to independent Croatia in 1991; the Croatian government carried out the "ethnic cleansing" of the region in 1995, expelling perhaps 150,000 Serbian inhabitants from the Krajina region where the Morlacchi once lived.

Since the Morlacchi qua Morlacchi disappeared from the rank of nations, or even ethnographic groups, over the course of the nineteenth century, their descendants are presumably Serbs or Croats; yet the assignment of those modern national labels to the eighteenth-century age of Venetian rule would be historically anachronistic. The intellectual history of Venice's discovery of Dalmatia must reevaluate contemporary conceptions of the Morlacchi to appreciate exactly what the name meant, in eighteenth-century terms, to Dalmatians, to Venetians, and to the international public of the Enlightenment. The primitive Morlacchi, after Fortis's travels, became a fully European intellectual sensation, attracting the poetic attentions of both Goethe and Herder in faraway Weimar. In the eighteenth century the Morlacchi first preoccupied the Venetian administration in Dalmatia, eventually enabling Venice to formulate a civilizing mission; they then became the subject of enlightened writers like Fortis who studied the Morlacchi as Venice's noble savages, the better to appraise the significance of "civilization," a newly formulated and already controversial notion within the European Enlightenment.

By the beginning of the twentieth century the encyclopedic ethnographer Jovan Cvijić relegated the Morlacchi to a footnote in his "human geography" of the Balkan peninsula: "In the course of my voyages in the Dalmatian mountains people often remarked to me on the difference between the Dinaric immigrants and the ancient Slavic population, on the one hand, and the Slavicized Vlachs or Morlachs, on the other. These latter, according to my informants, constitute the most primitive populations, besides being very rare."[10] In the eighteenth century the Morlacchi sometimes called themselves Vlachs, but they spoke a Slavic language, and within the Venetian Enlightenment they became the exemplary models of primitive Slavdom. According to twentieth-century ethnography, they were not truly Slavs at all, but Slavicized Vlachs, the herdsmen of the Balkans, of Latin or Illyrian or even Asiatic Turanian descent. The famous eleventh edition of the Encyclopedia Britannica in 1910 made the eccentric claim that the Morlacchi constituted 96 percent of the population of Habsburg Dalmatia, employing the designation to include all the Dalmatian Slavs. An American tourist in Dalmatia before World War I was fascinated to find in Zadar "the Morlacchi—strange, uncouth-looking people from the mountains," their women adorned with "quantities of chains made of shells, beads, and jingling coins, which fittingly completed their barbaric gorgeousness."[11] The modern disappearance of the Morlacchi must send the historian back to the eighteenth-century Venetian discovery of these pastoral people—when they were first made into emblems of barbarism, already adorned with shells and beads—in order to rediscover a lost element from the Enlightenment's imaginative ethnography of Europe's imagined communities.

After 1797 Venice no longer needed the civilizing mission of the Morlacchi, when there was no longer any Adriatic empire in need of ideological vindication. The Dalmatians, however, were not completely forgotten in Venice, in spite of the rupture in political relations. A history of Venice by Fabio Mutinelli, published in 1841, was dedicated, "To the Dalmatians, to you who for so many centuries in the armies and navies of the Venetians shared with them their victories and defeats." Nineteenth-century nostalgia for the Serenissima Repubblica could focus on the the Dalmatians and their near-legendary loyalty to Venice. When Giustina Renier-Michiel, born under the Republic in 1755, published her book on the *Origins of the Venetian Festivals* in 1829, she did not fail to note that the famous Ascension festival, Venice's wedding with the sea, commemorated the medieval moment when the Dalmatians "offered themselves in a transport of joy" to the Venetian dominion.[12] In Venice today the Riva degli Schiavoni, the embankment of the Slavs, already named in the eighteenth century, still indicates where the ships for Dalmatia once embarked. At the Dalmatian School, the Scuola Dalmata of San Giorgio degli Schiavoni, Carpaccio's Renaissance masterpieces cover the walls, celebrating the patron saints of the Dalmatian Slavs, Saints George, Triffon, and Jerome.

In twentieth-century Yugoslavia Dalmatia was, of course, geopolitically important as the country's Adriatic coast; in Europe at large its reputation was based more and more on the popularity of the Adriatic beaches with foreign tourists. Even so, the name of Dalmatia became less recognizable abroad, appearing on the map of Europe as the coast of Yugoslavia or the coast of Croatia. Perhaps the Dalmatian name finds its greatest international celebrity today in the breed of spotted dogs, who are supposed to have come originally from Dalmatia. One cultural critic of canines has argued that the name of the dog is a "dead metaphor," which may call to mind the Disney movie *One Hundred and One Dalmatians* but will never evoke the Adriatic coast.[13] It is possible, in fact, that before the unsurpassable publicity of the Disney film in 1961, the most celebrated previous title that featured the name of Dalmatia was Alberto Fortis's *Viaggio in Dalmazia* in 1774. Its fame spread throughout the eighteenth-century Republic of Letters, which was admittedly less pervasive than the twentieth-century empire of cinema.

Fortis's book was, above all, aimed at focusing Venetian and European attention upon the eastern Adriatic coast. "Travel with me along the banks of a little known river, once frequented by valorous Roman soldiers," wrote Fortis, dedicating a section of his work on the Cetina River to the botanist Giovanni Marsili of the University of Padua. "I invite you to cross the rough mountains that separate the sea from the beautiful interior regions of Dalmatia inhabited in our age by the Morlacchi, but with rather less discomfort than that which I have sometimes suffered in crossing them."[14] This invitation to vicarious voyaging, without the discomfort of real travel, was aimed not only at the distinguished scientist in Padua but at the general readers of Venice, to direct their interest across the Adriatic Sea. Fortis focused the Venetian perspective on and beyond Dalmatia, along the coastal shore, beside the interior river, marking the contours of the geographical horizon. As a matter of orientation, Venice was west of Dalmatia, though not due west, not on the directly opposite shore, like Ancona, the Adriatic port of the Papal State. Rather the lagoon of Venice lay in the northwestern corner of the Adriatic gulf, and Venetians, as well as Paduans, looked southeast toward the Dalmatian coast.

If Venice viewed Dalmatia in the demi-Oriental context of Eastern Europe, it was because the southeastern perspective was, historically, Venice's Adriatic route to the eastern Mediterranean, to Constantinople, to the intermediary stations of Oriental trade. The southeastern perspective on Dalmatia began, just beyond the Istrian peninsula, at the islands of Cres and Losinj, also known as Cherso and Osero, the insular subjects of Fortis's first trans-Adriatic reflections. The view from Venice continued along the coast from Zadar to Split, and then reached the important island towns of Hvar and Korčula, also known as Lesina and Curzola. Thereafter, the imperial Venetian gaze was interrupted by the small independent republic of Ragusa, modern Dubrovnik, which was not joined to Dalmatia until Napoleon abolished Ragusan sovereignty at the beginning of the nineteenth century. Beyond Ragusa, however, Venetians discovered the coastal continuation of their own territories with an enclave around the Gulf of Kotor, the appendage to Venetian Dalmatia described as Venetian Albania. In fact, Kotor today is the port of modern Montenegro; though Venice in the fifteenth century had ruled the coastal Albanian town of Durrës (or Durazzo), by the eighteenth century that was long lost to the Ottomans, along with the rest of Albania. Thus, although the Provveditori Generali in the eighteenth century nominally governed over Dalmatia and Albania, the latter title was the geographical exaggeration or misnomer for a fragment of Montenegro. Fortis did not travel to the enclave of "Venetian Albania," which thus remained marginal in the public imagination of imperial possibilities. Still, he did invoke Albania to argue that the supposed barbarism of the Morlacchi was merely relative; considering the violence of customary vendettas, he noted that "in Albania, from what I've been told, the effects are still more atrocious."[15] Albania was to make an operatic entry into the culture of the Enlightenment, as comedy rather than atrocity, when the Venetian librettist Lorenzo Da Ponte, living in Vienna in 1790, dramatized for Mozart the preposterous mock Albanians of *Così Fan Tutte*.

This southeastern perspective along the eastern Adriatic coast followed the traditional route of the Venetian fleets, making their way to the eastern Mediterranean. On such a coastal course it was geographically logical for the Venetians to encourage their fellow crusaders to subdue the restive town of Zadar in 1202, on their way to the conquest and sack of Constantinople in 1204. The eighteenth-century Venetian view still retraced this historical path, recalling the dramatic manifestations of Venice's former maritime supremacy. Fortis, however, also invoked an alternative perspective, more directly eastern, when he invited his readers to follow with him the course of the Cetina and cross the Dinaric Alps. This inland eastern route, eschewing the coast, brought the traveler to the border between Venetian Dalmatia and Ottoman Bosnia, then overland across the Balkan peninsula to Constantinople. This was, in fact, the path of the eighteenth-century Ottoman caravans, bringing their Oriental trade to Venice by land instead of by sea, arriving with their wares at the lazaretto of Split before the final Adriatic shipment. Frequent fears and occasional outbreaks of plague, like that of 1783 which killed a third of Split's urban population, were a reminder of the intimate inland adjacency between Dalmatia and Bosnia, between the Venetian and Ottoman empires. Fortis recognized that Bosnia, like Albania, lay just beyond the circumscribed domain of his travels, but his scientific curiosity was stimulated as he explored inland Dalmatia. He noted the mineral deposits of Bosnia, "inasmuch as one can conjecture from the reports"; he wished he could confirm the "fossil history of Bosnia," but knew that paleontology depended upon empirical observation and could not be accepted "on the word of others."[16] Even as he redeemed Dalmatia from obscurity, Fortis indicated the inaccessible landscape of Bosnia as the next frontier.

Fortis's invitation into the Dalmatian mountains opened up to the Venetian public a new eastern perspective, across the new and newest acquisitions in Dalmatia, to an array of receding Oriental horizons: the neighboring province of Bosnia, the route of the Balkan caravans, the Turkish capital at Constantinople, and Asia with its profitable products in the far distance. The cultural elaboration of this perspective in the eighteenth century was based on an historically inflected geography, for each eastern horizon was also marked by historical memories, such that Venetians simultaneously looked into the distance and into the chronological depth of Venice's past. At the almost invisible vanishing point of the eastern perspective, Venetians could still discern the figure of Marco Polo saluting their own adventurous spirit from the China of Kublai Khan. In 1755 Gasparo Gozzi put Marco Polo on the stage and delineated his western perspective from China, as he looked longingly back from "these so strange and barbaric shores" toward the "beautiful Adriatic waves." In 1758, Carlo Goldoni put a Dalmatian heroine on the stage in *La Dalmatina* and made her a captive in Moslem Morocco, so that she might better appreciate and celebrate "the fortunate peoples of the Adriatic empire." A minor dramatic confection of the 1790s, *The Dalmatian Hero: or Aurangzebbe King of Siam,* actually activated its Dalmatian protagonist in a Siamese *mise en scène.*[17]

The Venetian Enlightenment was thus engaged in staging the issues of Oriental perspective, which commenced just across the Adriatic in Dalmatia and reached all the way to China and Siam. Venice's discovery of Dalmatia in the eighteenth century must be considered in the context of what Paolo Preto, in his study of Venice and the Turks, has described as Venetian "Orientalism of enlightened derivation."[18] The Venetian perspective on Dalmatia was essential for the ideological clarification of east and west, all the more urgent inasmuch as Venice itself, with its Byzantine aspects and associations, was vulnerable to insinuations of Oriental exoticism. Along the axes of east and west, the Enlightenment proceeded to analyze the balance between civilization and barbarism, and this too was historically sensitive, since the Venetians needed only to consider the Fourth Crusade to see themselves as the barbarians sacking the civilized imperial metropolis of Constantinople. Discovering Dalmatia by the light of the European Enlightenment, Venice insisted upon its own geographical alignment with the alleged domain of civilization, while not altogether suppressing the relevant philosophical reservations to that convenient view. Fortis's sympathetic appreciation of the Morlacchi recognized that civilization and barbarism, like east and west, were matters of perspective.

Dalmatia, Eastern Europe, and the Mediterranean World

The intellectual history of the Venetian discovery of Dalmatia in the age of Enlightenment involves tracing the parallel concerns and increasing interplay of dual perspectives: the official reflections of the provincial administration and the published contributions of enlightened authors, eventually converging in reciprocal public controversy over the condition of Dalmatia. This study follows the different forms of discourse concerning Dalmatia, according to the times and terms of their emergence into the public sphere of critical discussion. The first chapter, which deals with mid-century conceptions of Dalmatia, focuses on the performance and publication of Goldoni's play *La Dalmatina*, set in the context of Venice's political concerns and historical reflections, and counterposed to Carlo Gozzi's earlier experience of military service in Zadar. The second chapter focuses on Fortis's travels and publications, between 1770 and 1774, in the international context of the contemporary Russian-Ottoman war, with its Adriatic implications for nervous, neutral Venice; Fortis's scientific and economic emphases are considered in the cultural context of enlightened Venetian interests in natural history and national economy. The third chapter focuses on the character and customs of the Morlacchi, considering the administrative concerns of the Provveditori Generali, and their closed official domain of relations and dispatches on the subject, before Fortis's transformation of the whole nature of the debate by making the Morlacchi into a public sensation. The fourth chapter considers the identification of the Morlacchi as Slavs and the enlightened appreciation of their South Slavic poetry, first by Fortis, then by Goethe and Herder with their interest in matters *morlackisch*, and, finally, in the visionary Venetian novel *Les Morlaques* by Giustiniana Wynne. The fifth chapter describes the development of public controversy in response to Fortis and, in particular, the articulation of an indigenous Dalmatian dissenting perspective, resistant to Fortis's discursive mastery over the subject of Dalmatia. The sixth chapter follows the final Dalmatian crises of the Adriatic empire, from the plague of Split in 1783 to the mobilization of the Dalmatians in 1797; in that year there also appeared the ultimate tribute to the primitive virtues of the Morlacchi, in an article on the "Morlacchismo" of Homer, written by Fortis's Dalmatian friend from Split, Giulio (or Julije) Bajamonti.

The social, economic, and political history of Venetian Dalmatia in the eighteenth century, as written during the last fifty years, has included important research by numerous scholars, of whom one might especially note Praga, Berengo, and Jačov, as well as Gligor Stanojević and Šime Peričić. The important recent work by Luca Ciancio, concerning Fortis, focuses more on his lifelong geological interests than his particular geographical engagement with the province of Dalmatia. Also invaluable on the subject of Fortis are the many contributions of Žarko Muljačić. The intellectual history of Venice's discovery of Dalmatia dates from the article by Stojković in *Hrvatsko Kolo* in 1929, titled "Morlakizam," an echo of the term "Morlacchismo," already coined by Bajamonti in 1797. In historiographical retrospect "Morlakizam" refers not only to the supposedly primitive character of the Morlacchi, but also to the foreign fascination that they provoked during the late eighteenth century. Further elaboration upon this intellectual history may be found in Arturo Cronia's monumental work on Italian knowledge of the Slavic world. Cronia goes beyond "Morlacchismo" to propose the term "Morlaccomania." Mate Zorić, in his article on "Croatians and Other South Slavs" in eighteenth-century Italian literature, writes in the first-personal plural about "the interests of Italian writers in our people"—including also perspectives on "our Morlacchi."[19] Finally, the most important, and indeed inspirational, work for studying this intellectual history is Franco Venturi's *Settecento riformatore*; in the very first volume Venturi introduces Marco Foscarini as an advocate of Venetian attention to Dalmatia, and in the final volume Dalmatia is treated as a matter of fundamental importance for the Venetian Enlightenment.

Rebecca West, traveling in Yugoslavia in the 1930s, explored Dalmatia in a spirit of passionate appreciation, and her book about her travels, *Black Lamb and Grey Falcon,* still shows intellectual traces of the sentimental "Morlacchismo" of the Enlightenment. "It is strange, it is heartrending, to stray into a world where men are still men and women still women," wrote West. "I felt apprehensive many times in Korchula, since I can see no indications that the culture of Dalmatia is going to sweep over the Western world, and I can see many reasons to fear that Western culture will in the long run overwhelm Dalmatia."[20] Her reverence for the virtues of the Dalmatians rested upon the emphatic assumption that they did not belong to the Western world, that their culture was in marked contrast and opposition to that of the West. Her admiration for the South Slavs went hand in hand with the heritage of demi-Orientalism by which the Enlightenment invented Eastern Europe, defining the difference between east and west. Venice's discovery of Dalmatia in the eighteenth century clearly indicates that such differentiation could assume a variety of aspects, from condescending disparagement to imperial responsibility to sentimental appreciation. For Rebecca West on Korčula in the 1930s the inevitable implication was that Dalmatia belonged to Eastern Europe, according to the cultural coordinates of enlightened geography. Such perception of difference was by no means simply a matter of empirical observation, since travelers were also able to note alternative alignments and resemblances. When Fitzroy Maclean parachuted into Yugoslava as the British liaison to Tito's Partisans during World War II, he too eventually came to Korčula, and proceeded to Partisan headquarters: "Everybody came with us to show us the way, chattering merrily to us as we went, for the Dalmatians have something of the cheerful volubility of the Italians they dislike so much." Partisan headquarters was located in an "old Venetian palace," and Maclean noted that "over the doorway the Lion of St. Mark stood headless, decapitated by some over-zealous Partisan, who celebrated the end of Mussolini's rule by destroying the symbol of an earlier period of Italian domination."[21] Thus, the casual perception of chattering similarity defied the logic of imperial enmities, old and new, and denied any assumption of absolute opposition between Dalmatia and the Western world. However, by the time Maclean's account was published in 1949, Tito presided over Communist Yugoslavia, and the cultural geography of the Cold War underlined the directional vector of the title, *Eastern Approaches.*

When St. Paul recounted in Romans (15:19) that he had preached the gospel of Christ "from Jerusalem, and round about unto Illyricum," Dalmatia, the land of the pre-Roman Illyrians, was located on the Mediterranean map of the ancient world. In eighteenth-century Venetian Dalmatia there was some interest in whether Paul was actually shipwrecked on the eastern Adriatic coast. When Shakespeare set *Twelfth Night* in Illyria, the only important geographical circumstance of the otherwise unspecified setting was its coastal accessibility to the shipwrecked siblings Sebastian and Viola. Renaissance geography still recognized the ancient network of Mediterranean relations. "Knows't thou this country?" inquired Viola in Illyria, but Shakespeare provided very little knowledge to detail the Dalmatian scenario. Its "obscurity" constituted a merely convenient

Adriatic arena for the exercise of his theatrical imagination. Traveling along the Adriatic coast in the 1930s, at the same time as Rebecca West, was Fernand Braudel, visiting the archives to gather materials for his historical masterpiece, *The Mediterranean and the Mediterranean World in the Age of Philip II*. Braudel was the man who might have answered Viola's inquiry most comprehensively, with his archival trove of detailed information about the eastern Adriatic coast in the sixteenth century, the age of Shakespeare as well as Philip II. Furthermore, because Braudel's research was empirically focused on the sixteenth century, his study looked back to before the articulation of difference between Dalmatia and the Western world, back to an era when Venetian Dalmatia was still recognized as an integral part of the Mediterranean landscape. While Rebecca West in the 1930s pursued the sentimental—"heartrending"—discovery of an eastern alternative to the overwhelming West, Fernand Braudel refused that alternative in a spirit of almost sentimental nostalgia for Mediterranean unity. "I have loved the Mediterranean with passion, no doubt because I am a northerner," declared Braudel in the very first sentence.[22] Such passion was premised upon the Renaissance conception of Europe divided between north and south, antedating the Enlightenment's reconception of the continent according to east and west.

Braudel described an age in which Venice was still the reigning "Queen of the Adriatic," policing the passage of ships and ruling that all merchandise upon the sea had to touch port in Venice itself. Such Venetian ambitions depended upon the domination of "the Balkan coast opposite which commanded the Adriatic," that is, the coast of Dalmatia. In Braudel's Mediterranean vision, the Balkan and Italian peninsulas faced one another across the Adriatic gulf in geographical balance, combined in political, economic, and cultural unity. This unity, however, featured the cultural preeminence of "Italianism" as the region's "predominant flavor," in spite of the Slavic population of Dalmatia: "The gulf was Venetian, of course, but in the sixteenth century it was more than this; it was the sphere of a triumphant Italian culture. The civilization of the peninsula wove a brilliant, concentrated web along the east coast of the sea." Braudel evidently felt some personal qualms about this sixteenth-century asymmetry, and, after censuring "apologists of racial expansion" in Mussolini's Italy, he added a footnote to "discount the exaggerations" of Attilio Tamaro concerning the Italian culture of Dalmatia. Seeking to specify the geographical coordinates of the Adriatic region, Braudel observed: "Strictly speaking it is not orientated north-south but north-west and south-east; it was the route to the Levant, with long established trade and relations, open too as we shall see to the illnesses and epidemics of the East. Its civilization was profoundly complex. Here eastern influence could already be felt, and Byzantium lived on." He noted the Venetian development of Split in the late sixteenth century, as the end point for overland caravans from Asia, bringing silk and spices to Venice by way of Dalmatia. Furthermore, the Dalmatians themselves, even the Morlacchi, were often an immigrant presence in Venice: "The Riva degli Schiavoni was not only a point of departure."[23] Clearly, Braudel discerned within the Adriatic unity of the sixteenth century all those social, economic, and cultural elements that would be fashioned into an ideology of difference in the eighteenth century, as the vindication of Venetian empire.

Braudel cited the ethnography of Cvijić on the stability of Dalmatian society but argued that the province could not be altogether stable. "For the Dalmatian strip is linked by the Adriatic to Italy and to the world," observed Braudel. Dalmatia was "wide open to outside influence," and Venice in the sixteenth century not only "dominated it politically," but also "penetrated" the province with Venice's "triumphant civilization, without even trying."[24] In the eighteenth century Venice was already trying; the cultural penetration that had casually accompanied political and economic domination was superseded by the intellectual efforts of the Enlightenment, the purposeful articulation of an ideology of empire aimed at reordering political and economic priorities.

"Before we dismiss the consideration of the life and character of Diocletian," noted Gibbon, "we may for a moment direct our view to the place of his retirement." In 305 A.D. Diocletian abdicated the imperial office and retired to Dalmatia, where he built the "magnificent palace" by the sea at Split. Gibbon described the situation as if he had been there himself: "The views from the palace are no less beautiful than the soil and climate were inviting." The footnotes, however, showed that he was working from the engravings of the palace published by Robert Adam in London in 1764, "an ingenious artist of our own time and country whom a very liberal curiosity carried into the heart of Dalmatia." Gibbon furthermore cited Fortis for a more critical judgment of the stylistic deca-

FIGURE 2. "View of the Crypto-Porticus or Front towards the Harbour," from Robert Adam, *Ruins of the Palace of the Emperor Diocletian at Spalatro in Dalmatia,* published in London in 1764. Before the walls of Diocletian's palace, along the harbor of Split, ships are unloaded, while turbaned merchants weigh and measure. Since the sixteenth century Split was an important commercial entrepôt where the Ottoman caravans from Constantinople, entering Dalmatia from Bosnia, met the merchant fleets of Venice. The lazaretto at the harbor, for purposes of quarantine, was a sometimes insufficient precaution to prevent the epidemic spread of plague accompanying intercontinental commerce, and Split was particularly hard hit in the outbreak of 1783. *(By permission of the Fine Arts Library, Harvard University.)*

dence of the palace: "We are informed by a more recent and very judicious traveller that the awful ruins of Spalatro are not less expressive of the decline of the arts than of the greatness of the Roman empire in the time of Diocletian." Thus, the historian of the *Decline and Fall* was able to satisfy his own "curiosity" and arrange for an unobscured "view" of Dalmatia all the way from England, while sparing himself the discomfort that Fortis endured in the voyage. Madame de Staël was similarly indulgent toward the heroine of her novel *Corinne,* published in 1807; an ascent to the top of the Campanile in the Piazza San Marco permitted Corinne to enjoy a view of Dalmatia, right across the Adriatic. "Let us give another moment to Dalmatia," she enjoined, like Gibbon lingering for a last glimpse of Diocletian's retirement, "for when we go down from this height, we will not be able to make out even the vague delineation of that country."[25] Dalmatia was already returning to obscurity with the passing of the eighteenth century, and though it was always an optical impossibility to perceive the province from whatever height in Venice, Corinne's view testified to the imaginative force of cultural geography. Venice did indeed define an imperial perspective on Dalmatia in the age of Enlightenment, and the intellectual history of that "view" must try to reconstruct what Venetians envisioned when they looked out across the Adriatic.

CHAPTER ONE

The Drama of the Adriatic Empire:
Dalmatian Loyalty and the Venetian Lion

Introduction: Goldoni's Dalmatian Heroine
and the Public of Venice

In the autumn of 1758 the subject of Dalmatia came prominently before the public of Venice, when Carlo Goldoni, already famous as the
foremost dramatist of the city, presented at the Teatro San Luca his
new play, *La Dalmatina*. In the 1750s Goldoni had written a series of
Oriental dramas, featuring a Persian scenario, *La Sposa Persiana* in
1753, and then its sequels *Ircana in Julfa* and *Ircana in Ispaan* in 1755
and 1756; these mingled in Goldoni's dramatic imagination with an alternative exoticism of the Americas, as represented in *La Peruviana* in
1754 and *La Bella Selvaggia*—"The Beautiful Savage," of Guyana—at
carnival in 1758. These "tragicomedies," with their exotic heroines,
whether of Persia or Peru, were far removed dramatically, as well as geographically, from the comedies of Italian and especially Venetian society, which continue to be recognized as Goldoni's masterpieces. The
title of *La Dalmatina* pointed across the Adriatic, but the play was not
actually set in Venetian Dalmatia. Rather, the drama unfolded across
the Mediterranean in Moslem Morocco, where the Dalmatian heroine
found herself a slave, captured by corsairs, awaiting ransom or rescue in
accordance with tragicomic conventions. Her Dalmatian identity was
enough to rank her alongside Goldoni's exotic heroines of the 1750s,
but Dalmatia itself, after centuries of Venetian sovereignty, was not a
sufficiently remote scenario to sustain this sort of dramatic confection.
Goldoni's *La Dalmatina* in 1758 put Dalmatia before the public in a
manner that measured the province's uncertain degree of exoticism
with respect to Venice.

When he wrote his memoirs in Paris in the 1780s, Goldoni recalled the composition of *La Dalmatina* in Venice in the 1750s. "The Venetians," he declared, "make the greatest case ('le plus grand cas') of the Dalmatians, who, bordering the Turk, defend their properties and guarantee at the same time the rights of their sovereigns." Goldoni thus established an identity of interests between Dalmatians and Venetians, so that the former might be recognized as markers for the sovereignty of the latter on the eastern coast of the Adriatic. Indeed the power of the play depended to some extent on the Dalmatian heroine being readily adopted by the Venetian public in a spirit of sympathetic identification. "It is from this nation that the Republic takes the elite of its troops," wrote Goldoni, "and it is from among the women of this courageous people that I chose the heroine of my drama."[1] The sovereign republic was Venice, of course; the Dalmatians, however, were recognized as a nation. The dramatist's self-conscious act of choice—selecting the Dalmatians—constituted the original impulse to represent that nation in the public forum of the Venetian theater. More than a decade before Fortis first crossed the Adriatic, Goldoni's drama was performed in a preliminary moment of public interest in the province, while the indistinctive depiction of Dalmatian characters and concerns revealed the minimal level of knowledgeable representation prior to Fortis's published researches.

Goldoni's Dalmatian heroine was named Zandira, in rhymed relation to Delmira, the beautiful savage of Guyana who had already made her appearance on the stage during the carnival season. Captured by Barbary pirates, Zandira, at the beginning of the play, seemed destined for the harem; the course of the drama was to bring the Dalmatian Radovich to the heroic rescue of Zandira. The cast of characters called for Turkish and Dalmatian combatants, and the fourth act commenced with a naval battle between rival armadas. The contest ended in victory for the irrepressible Radovich, who affirmed his patriotic loyalty to Venice with a poetic allusion to "the Lion in my breast" ("il mio Leone in petto"), the Lion of San Marco.[2] In the end, the Dalmatian hero and heroine departed from Africa together, concluding the play, as Goldoni observed, "to the greatest satisfaction of the public" ("la plus grande satisfaction du Public"). This was no abstract, notional public, however, whose satisfaction might be perfunctorily presumed, and neither was it a narrowly Venetian public, whose members remained aloof from the conflicts enacted by the Dalmatians upon the stage. "The hall that day was full of

Dalmatians," wrote Goldoni, recalling the premiere at the Teatro San Luca. "They were so content with me that they heaped me with praises and with presents."[3] Such an audience, active in its appreciation, may be considered part of the evolving eighteenth-century public sphere, as proposed by Jürgen Habermas. Indeed, it was a mark of Goldoni's modern sense of himself as a playwright that he justified his work with reference to the public sphere. The public of Venice, however, was not homogeneously Italian but reflected the ethnic diversity of the urban population, which included Dalmatians as well as Greeks, Turks, and Jews. The subject of Dalmatia could not be represented to the public of Venice as unequivocally exotic, when the audience in the theater and the population of the city reflected the relative familiarity of the Dalmatians.

On the stage, of course, the Dalmatians spoke their lines in Goldoni's Italian verse, and the Dalmatian heroine was performed by an Italian actress, Caterina Bresciani, who was already experienced in exotic Goldonian roles; she had also appeared in *La Sposa Persiana* and *La Bella Selvaggia*. At the conclusion of *La Dalmatina*, she apostrophized the public in the final Martellian couplet, representing from the stage an eighteenth-century Venetian conception of empire:

> E per mare e per terra siete alla gloria nati,
> Oh dell'Adriaco impero popoli fortunati.

> Both by sea and by land you are born to glory,
> Oh fortunate peoples of the Adriatic empire.[4]

In fact, Venice's prospects on the Adriatic were not altogether glorious in the eighteenth century, a time of economic, political, and social unease. Goldoni's inspirational drama was intended to captivate the public on behalf of an imperial vision. The "Adriatic empire" might mean different things to different peoples, notably to Venetians and Dalmatians, and it was precisely the proposed plurality of fortunate peoples (*popoli fortunati*) that gave Goldoni's appeal its ideological interest. The performance of Dalmatian imperial enthusiasm deployed a political chemistry of combination, association, impersonation, and appropriation.

Putting Dalmatia before the theatrical public of Venice in 1758, Goldoni established a preliminary milestone, anticipating Fortis, for the exploration of imperial issues and the formulation of an ideology of Adriatic empire in the spirit of the Venetian Enlightenment. The decision to choose a dramatic heroine from among the Dalmatians occurred in the

IMPERATORIS
DIOCLETIANI PALATII
RVINAE
PROPE SALONAM

FIGURE 3. "Imperatoris Diocletiani Palatii Ruinae." Frontispiece from Robert Adam, *Ruins of the Palace of the Emperor Diocletian at Spalatro in Dalmatia,* published in London in 1764. Antiquarian artists in tricornered hats have taken up a position before the sphinx to sketch the Roman ruins at Split, but clearly Adam has also taken note of the picturesquely turbaned contemporary figures who seem to be negotiating a purchase of poultry from the cage. The juxtaposition of turban and tricorn suggests that Dalmatia belonged to the domain of "Eastern Europe," an intermediary land where Europe encountered the Orient. According to Adam, "the Venetian governor of Spalatro, unaccustomed to such visits of curiosity from strangers, began to conceive unfavorable sentiments of my intentions, and to suspect that under pretense of taking views and plans of the Palace, I was really employed in surveying the state of the fortifications." *(By permission of the Fine Arts Library, Harvard University.)*

context of increasing administrative attentions to the province, dating from the previous decade; such official matters did not come before the public at large, but remained within the closed political circle of patricians in the service of the Republic. Political concerns and administrative agendas inevitably provoked the inklings of tentative public interest in Dalmatia. In the 1740s the very young Carlo Gozzi went to Dalmatia to serve in the military administration in Zadar, and there his precocious dramatic impersonations produced a different Dalmatian heroine in the decade preceding Goldoni's *La Dalmatina*. In 1747 Marco Foscarini, speaking in Venice in the Maggior Consiglio, recognized serious problems of administration in Dalmatia and urgently called for enlightened political reform. His appeal resulted in an official investigation of the government of the province and eventually led to the agricultural reform of 1755, sponsored by the Provveditore Generale Francesco Grimani. At the same time, in the 1750s, historians of the Venetian republic, like Giacomo Diedo and Vettor Sandi, wrestled with different ways of formulating Venice's historical relation to Dalmatia. Thus, Goldoni's *La Dalmatina* of 1758 constituted the most public expression of an interest in Dalmatia that had already begun to emerge in administrative, political, and historical arenas. The drama explored the political significance of the Adriatic empire, the rhetorical dimensions of Dalmatian patriotism and Slavic loyalty to Venice, the Mediterranean context of the Venetian-Dalmatian encounter, and the delicate balance between an imperial union of fortunate peoples and an ideological asymmetry of perceived exoticism.

Gozzi's Dalmatian Comedy

Goldoni's archenemy in the 1750s was the fiercely conservative literary gladiator Carlo Gozzi. From the perspective of Venetian nobility, and in the name of Italian literary tradition, he denounced Goldoni for bringing about the artistic collapse of the comic theater by the vulgarity of bourgeois values and vernacular rhythms. In 1758, the year of *La Dalmatina*, Gozzi launched one of his most spirited polemical attacks on Goldoni, inventing an allegorical monster, with four faces and four mouths, to represent the manifold monstrosity and benighted bestiality of Goldonian comedy. Gozzi himself cherished the ritualized forms and figures of the Commedia dell'Arte and eventually composed a series of dramatic fables—such as *Il re cervo* (*The King Stag*), *La donna serpente* (*The*

Serpent Woman), and *Turandot*—to challenge the success of Goldoni's comedies and tragicomedies. As it happened, Goldoni's *La Dalmatina* addressed issues of some special relevance to his rival's personal history, for at the age of twenty, in 1741, Gozzi had gone to Dalmatia to spend three years in military service under the Provveditore Generale in Zadar. Those three years gave him considerably more direct experience of Dalmatia than Goldoni could ever have claimed, but Gozzi did not make this a part of his literary record until decades later, in 1780, when he wrote his memoirs; in fact, these were only published in 1797, as *Useless Memoirs* (*Memorie inutili*), at the moment of Venice's political annihilation. Gozzi's story offered a striking counterpoint to Goldoni's drama, inasmuch as the figure of the female Dalmatian was central to both. If Goldoni created the part as a theatrical character on the Venetian stage, Gozzi, in a remarkable instance of national and sexual cross-dressing, acted the part himself on the stage in Dalmatia.

Gozzi's passage to Dalmatia was very much a matter of aristocratic collusion in the allocation of provincial posts: "recommended by my maternal uncle Almorò Cesare Tiepolo to His Excellency Girolamo Quirini elected Provveditore Generale in Dalmatia and Albania." In 1741 such a position required no imperial preparation or special outfitting. "With my little equipage, to which I did not neglect to add the box of my books and my little guitar," recalled Gozzi, "I passed into those provinces as a man of fortune, in order to learn to know the nature of the military and of those peoples."[5] The lighthearted spirit of a young man setting out for military service with his little guitar hardly testified to seriousness of purpose in the administration of Dalmatia. Gozzi contemplated Dalmatia as a "new world" to explore, but he was also continually "laughing and joking about all the adversities and all the sufferings that I experienced during my Illyrian triennium." He complained about the Dalmatian climate, the biting assaults of Adriatic bugs, and the hardship of "sleeping the nights in your boots, often in the open valleys of the Morlacchi country." Such sufferings seem to have been the normal inconveniences of military life in the provinces for someone accustomed to living along the canals of the capital. His first experience of "those peoples" occurred in the context of shipboard inconvenience on the boat to Dalmatia. He told the comic story of his search for the ship's toilet in the middle of the night, including an encounter with the Morlacchi sentinel "with a dark countenance and two span-length moustaches." It was the Morlacchi sentinel's who-goes-there that delayed the young Venetian in his increasingly urgent need, and the scene between them was presented as a kind of stage comedy, with even the moustaches specified as a comic element of costume.[6] By the time he wrote his memoirs, Gozzi was a master of the theater, and his remembrance of himself as a young man with a little guitar in a new world was shaped by his sense of comic drama.

In the same decade, in 1745, another very young man with an important literary future, the twenty-year-old Casanova, sailed from Venice to Corfu, on the way to Constantinople, on a ship that carried "twenty-four canons and two hundred Slavic soldiers." Together with their military chaplain, a Slavic priest, they totaled 201 Dalmatians, and Casanova's shipboard encounter with them was no more edifying than Gozzi's meeting with the Morlacchi sentinel. Casanova particularly disliked the priest, "very ignorant, insolent, and brutal, whom I mocked on every occasion, and who naturally became my enemy." In the middle of a tempest this priest made a great show of exorcising demons for the benefit of the superstitious crew, who consequently neglected to attend to the endangered ship. When Casanova tried to get the sailors to work, it was suggested to them that he was one of the demons who needed to be exorcised, and they found an opportunity to try to push him overboard.[7] This account of ignorant and superstitious Slavic soldiers was very far from Goldoni's tribute to Venice's Dalmatians as "the elite of its troops." Casanova's cavalier contempt in the 1740s, as well as Gozzi's comic disparagement, underlines the political significance of Goldoni's literary "lionization" of the Dalmatians in the 1750s.

When Gozzi sailed across the Adriatic, he recorded that his voyage from Malamocco, the principal port of Venice's Lido, to Zadar, the administrative center of Dalmatia, lasted no less than "twelve very uncomfortable days and twelve nights of annoyance and interrupted sleep." For all its Adriatic proximity, Dalmatia remained at some distance from Venice by the measure of eighteenth-century transport, and Venetian cultural perspective could be adjusted so that the province seemed either quite close or rather remote. Gozzi's first impressions upon arrival registered the theatricality of Venetian rule, as the outgoing Provveditore Generale passed on the baton of imperial command to his successor Quirini. The elaborate ceremonial, as well as the "thundering" of musical instruments and artillery salutes, seemed to Gozzi an occasion that "deserves to be seen by the countless men who have a tickling of curiosity for spectacles."[8] Such was the spectacular representation of Venetian imperial rule in Dalmatia.

Gozzi's official service in Dalmatia left time for him to indulge his "custom as observer" (*costume d'osservatore*) of the province and its people. In fact, he understood the employment of himself and his colleagues to be that of "we courtiers" (*noi cortigiani*), attending the provincial court of the Provveditore Generale. Gozzi was assigned to participate in an engineering study of the fortifications of Zadar, "a most useful study for anyone who wants to be a soldier."[9] He also, however, had literary ambitions, which he pursued alongside his military obligations, such as they were. Gozzi mostly kept his writing to himself, but was disappointed to be overlooked when an opportunity occurred for presentations of poetry in public. The occasion involved the staging of another spectacle, celebrating the Adriatic empire:

> The city of Zara wanted to give a sign of veneration to our Provveditore Generale Quirini, and there was built for only one solemn day in the Forte meadow a great timber hall, decorated with beautiful damasks, and invitations were sent to many people to assemble an academy, on the appointed day, of writers of prose and poetry. Every academic invited had to recite two compositions, in prose or in verse, as he wished. Here is the first: "If he be more praiseworthy the prince who keeps, defends, and cultivates his own estates in peace, or he who seeks to conquer new estates with arms to expand his dominion." Here is the second: "A composition in praise of the Provveditore Generale."[10]

Thus, the provincial administration in Zadar in the 1740s was staging a celebration of the city's "veneration" for Venetian rule. Indeed, just as Goldoni in Venice made a theatrical event out of patriotic speeches in Martellian verse, written for the parts of the Dalmatians, so Quirini in Dalmatia, as Provveditore Generale, presided over an academy of poetic recitations, in praise of himself and of the government he represented.

In the previous decade of the 1730s, the Provveditore Generale Zorzi Grimani had noted some concerns about different levels of loyalty in the *vecchio acquisto,* ruled by Venice for centuries, and the *nuovo* and *nuovissimo acquisto,* which came to Venice only in 1699 and 1718. The former territories seemed to Grimani more reliable in their loyalty: "The inhabitants of the coastal cities and the islands were in the beginning of their subjection of inquiet temper and anxious for innovation, but having grown old under the dominion, with devotion and loyalty already rooted in them, they live at present as vassals in perfect exquisiteness."[11] The new and newer subjects, however, were only now at "the beginning of their subjection," less "rooted" in their loyalty to Venice, and therefore offered more cause for concern. Yet, in spite of Grimani's greater confidence in the *vecchio acquisto,* in the late 1730s there was a revolt against tax contributions in precisely those lands which had "grown old under the dominion." The revolt was put down by military force in 1740, the year before the arrival of Quirini with Gozzi in attendance.[12] Public demonstrations of loyalty in the 1740s were therefore not altogether manifestations of complete imperial confidence.

Gozzi, since he was not invited to participate in the academy, could only disparage the Dalmatian character of the occasion, conducted "with the greatest Italianate Illyrian seriousness" (*serietà illirica italianata*). Such was the idiom of the Adriatic empire—"Italianate Illyrian"—whose "seriousness" of spirit corresponded to the patriotic declamations of Goldoni's Dalmatians. For Gozzi that idiom was an object of mockery, as much for its presumption of solemnity as for its cultural miscegenation, and he would soon have the opportunity to make it into the material of stage comedy. On the occasion of the academy, "the air resounded for three hours with long, erudite, grandiloquent dissertations, and not very sweet poetry," and he himself secretly composed two sonnets on the prescribed subjects. Later, his sonnet in praise of the Provveditore Generale was acknowledged as Quirini's favorite, so that Gozzi was recognized, "in Zaratine opinion," as a poet.[13] His relation of the story in his memoirs, decades later, still saluted this triumph of Venetian talent (his own) over the ridiculous Dalmatian presumption of the "Italianate Illyrian" academy. Gozzi's vindication of himself "in Zaratine opinion," like Goldoni's justification of his play before an audience of Dalmatians in the Teatro San Luca, ratified an imperial mastery of political discourse even in the staging of Dalmatian veneration for the Venetian government. The great theatrical triumph of Gozzi's service in Dalmatia, however, was his own impersonation of a Dalmatian heroine.

"I was in Dalmatia a famous servant girl in the theater, in improvised comedy," he recorded in his memoirs. Gozzi was eventually to become truly famous in Venice as an adamant partisan of the traditional form of improvised comedy, of the Commedia dell'Arte, so this early episode in his dramatic career, performing the part of a servant girl in Dalmatia, fit neatly into the memoirs of his life in the theater. Such a role, however, could only be described by Gozzi in a spirit of heavy irony, recommending the travesty as possibly "efficacious for some other military boy, opening up to him the way to ascend rapidly perhaps to the rank of colonel."[14] The irony reflected not only on the humor of a military man in a cross-dressing female role, but also on the travesty of national identity, a Venetian patrician as a Dalmatian servant girl.

At the court of Quirini in Zadar, there were amateur dramatic performances during the carnival season, and in the comedies the female parts were taken by young men. For Gozzi the key to the role was not just dressing as a woman, but creating a distinctly Dalmatian costume.

> I had myself dressed as a Dalmatian servant girl. My hair was divided and braided with pink silk ribbons. My dresses and clothes were those of the prettiest servant girl of the city of Sebenico. I put aside Tuscan speech, which the servants use in our theaters of Italy, and since I had learned tolerably Illyrian speech, I prepared to express my sentiments in dialogue and soliloquy, improvised with a Venetian dialect altered by pronunciation and by many Italianized Illyrian (*illirici italianizzati*) terms, so that my language was a droll gibberish (*gergone faceto*). I managed to execute my arranged part with a most loquacious courage, and this new unexpected species of servant girl, understood by those nationals no less than by the Italians, was received with joy by my spectators, and generally won over the spirits of everyone.[15]

This representation of the Dalmatian girl drew upon, on the one hand, almost folkloric precision in the details of costume and, on the other hand, the creative adaptation of language to compose an Adriatic combination of "Italianized Illyrian" character which came out sounding like gibberish. Like Goldoni at the Teatro San Luca, Gozzi in Zadar presented his Dalmatian girl to a mixed audience of Venetians and Dalmatians and, again like Goldoni, pronounced himself to be a triumph on both fronts. Where Goldoni gave his Dalmatian heroine the dignity of perfect intelligibility in Italian verse (though in other plays he was noted for his use of Venetian dialect), Gozzi made his character "understood" by both audiences through the comedic strategy of gibbering unintelligibility. In both cases the respective parts of the audience must have received the performance somewhat differently, each according to its place in the dynamics of the imperial relation.

Gozzi's farcical impersonation of a servant girl was altogether different from Goldoni's ideal representation of a Dalmatian heroine. In *La*

Dalmatina the drama was driven by Zandira's danger of losing her Christian virtue in a Moroccan harem, but Gozzi regarded the virtue of his Dalmatian servant girl as merely a matter of comedy.

> My reproaches, my ostentatious chastity, my reflections, my laments, made the Provveditore Generale and all the listeners laugh so much, that I was universally accorded the victory of being considered the most capable and the most clownish servant girl who ever appeared in the theater. Improvised comedies were often called for in order to laugh at the droll chatter and the Italianized Illyrian gibberish of Luce, which means Lucia among us. By this name I was called in the comedies, and not by that of Smeraldina, Corallina, or Columbina.[16]

The impersonation of the Dalmatian servant girl, Luce, was thus Gozzi's earliest contribution to the cause of the Commedia dell'Arte; he invented a new nationally inflected figure for the genre, a figure who could really only be appreciated along the coast of the Adriatic. Dalmatian laments and reproaches were just laughing matters, from an imperial perspective, while the chastity of a Dalmatian girl was undoubtedly a subject of much joking among the Venetian soldiers in Zadar. Gozzi's performance, however, must have been sufficiently sympathetic in its humor to disarm and transmute provincial discontent among the Dalmatians, if they were indeed "won over" in the audience. Gozzi impersonating Luce in Zadar was, of course, no more and no less authentically Dalmatian than Caterina Bresciani performing the part of Zandira in Venice. Indeed, Gozzi seemed to be seeking to represent certain popular and vernacular aspects of the Dalmatian character when he offered "Italianized Illyrian gibberish" as an antidote to the "Italianate Illyrian seriousness" of the poetic academy. Clearly, according to Gozzi's dramatic values, the clownish character of improvised comedy was actually less ridiculous than the pompousness of formally recited sonnets on set themes.

Sexual Relations: Venetians and Dalmatians

Gozzi's performances as Luce made him the toast of the carnival in Zadar, with some consequences for his personal and professional life. Professionally, he was "dispensed from the guard and from other military inspections for the duration of the three carnivals of my triennium."

Personally, he found that his cross-dressing role as a Dalmatian girl in the theater made him a figure of fascination to the Dalmatian women of Zadar: "Many ladies sought in competition to get to know this male Luce, such a joking devil on the stage."[17] Gozzi's account of his own sentimental education in Zadar emphasized the importance of Luce for his earliest affairs. "I can take my oath that I left my father's house at the age of sixteen, on military service in Dalmatia, innocent," he wrote, though in fact he was twenty. "The town of Zara was the rock on which this frail bark of my innocence foundered."[18] This he attributed not to the general character of military service, but rather to the moral environment of Dalmatia, and especially the morals of the Dalmatian girls whose "ostentatious chastity" was only a pretense.

Gozzi lost his virginity to a Dalmatian girl who made his acquaintance after seeing him on the stage: "Her heart had first been touched when she saw me play the part of Luce, the soubrette, in the theatre." He may have expected her to be as "clownish" as Luce herself, for he claimed to be surprised when the girl's overtures to him demonstrated "a finesse I hardly expected from a Dalmatian." She was not a virgin, and he was not her first Venetian; she had already fallen for a "notorious seducer," who exploited for his sexual advantage his "position of authority in the province of Dalmatia." Gozzi was able to appreciate the nature of such exploitation, even as he himself participated in the gendered imperial relations between Venetian men and Dalmatian women. When he left Zadar for six weeks with Quirini, Gozzi returned to find his Dalmatian girl already engaged in an affair with the army steward, who was rumored to have syphilis. Gozzi broke with the girl, and she, weeping, cursed the poverty which led her to sleep with the steward in order to obtain flour for her family.[19] This story of Gozzi's first love affair with a Dalmatian woman demonstrated an imperial pattern of seduction, coercion, and exploitation. He might have recognized himself more easily as one of her several Venetian seducers had he not focused instead on her seduction of him.

Gozzi's second love affair was with a thirteen-year-old girl who helped him dress and arrange his hair for his performances as Luce; she too was supposedly the sexual aggressor and Gozzi merely succumbed to her insistence.[20] Casanova in St. Petersburg in the 1760s enjoyed a sexual relation with a thirteen-year-old Russian girl, purchased as a slave, and told the story in his memoirs to give his readers an idea of the exceptional erotic opportunities that might attend an eastern sojourn.[21] Gozzi and Casanova were Venetian contemporaries, and Gozzi's memoirs advertised romantic encounters in Dalmatia, at an only minimally eastern displacement from Venice, imbued nevertheless with an element of exoticism. When the thirteen-year-old Dalmatian girl turned out to have other lovers as well as himself, Gozzi expressed himself disillusioned and horrified at such depravity in one so young. Her immorality was his to exploit, and at the same time his to deplore, in the morally and imperially asymmetrical context of Venetian Dalmatia.

Gozzi observed in Dalmatia the undercurrents of hostility between Venetians and Dalmatians: "The rivalry of courage between the Italian nation and the Illyrian nation, which always had a hidden bitterness of disapproval, often caused ugly dangers in those lands." The Italians had to put up with "insolences against urbanity" from a "resolute and most peculiar (*strambissima*) nation." Such rivalry between Italian and Dalmatian men became ugliest when it touched upon the relations between Italian men and Dalmatian women. For instance, when one of Gozzi's friends flirted from a window with a closely guarded Dalmatian girl, her intended husband took up the issue with the Venetians:

> One morning this rather rough Illyrian placed himself in conversation with us officials of the court in a little square where we were sitting on some stone benches. He clumsily (*goffamente*) put to a clumsy purpose a clumsy exaggeration of contempt for the customs of the men and women of Italy, with a smile between silly and sour, joking in his fashion. . . . The truth is that that clumsy speech signified in substance, without equivocation, that all Italian men were cuckolds and all Italian women whores.[22]

The reiterated emphasis on the clumsiness of the Dalmatian man made this encounter, in Gozzi's account, both a sort of clownish theatrical comedy and a pointed lesson in urbanity and backwardness. The Venetians nevertheless felt provoked "to defend audaciously the masculine and feminine customs of our nation," and to disparage "that barbarism and masculine tyranny toward women" in Dalmatia.[23] It was, of course, precisely the incidence of sexual relations between Venetian men and Dalmatian women that made this into such a heated subject of national rivalry.

Gozzi told the story of a certain Dalmatian man who armed himself to guard by night the street in Zadar on which lived a certain altogether unworthy Dalmatian woman:

> It has to be known that on this little street resided one of the most beautiful girls of the people that ever human eye did see, called by name Tonina. She had many who longed for her, and her wickedness, her furtiveness, and the bait she knew how to give to some simpletons, made her character so bad that her beauty became venal and cheap, though she knew how to sell it dear.[24]

The violent efforts of her deluded Dalmatian admirer notably failed to keep other men away from her door, and Gozzi presented the whole situation as an episode of Commedia dell'Arte. Indeed, he himself finally introduced the wicked character of Tonina into his improvised comedy performances of Dalmatian girlhood.

It happened during the third and last carnival season of Gozzi's triennium in Dalmatia. He was performing the part of Luce in the theater at the special request of the Provveditore Generale, and expressing her character in readily intelligible gibberish.

> In that farce I was Luce, unhappily married with Pantalone, who was profligate, broke, and bankrupt. I was reduced to extreme indigence and had a baby girl in swaddling, the fruit of my marriage. In a nocturnal scene of my soliloquy I cradled my child. I sang a song to put her to sleep. This song was interrupted by the narration of my misfortunes, with strokes that made the spectators laugh a lot. . . . The description of what a beautiful piece of woman I had been, and what a carcass I had become, caused continual laughs and continual clapping of hands.[25]

In 1744 it was still possible to represent the poverty of Dalmatia as theatrical comedy. In fact, there was poverty to the point of famine in Dalmatia in the 1740s, and Quirini's successor, Giacomo Boldù, had to provide emergency supplies of grain to keep the population from starving.[26] Yet Gozzi did not refrain from the mockery of extreme indigence, and the show was even to be followed, according to the soldiers' plan, by "a dinner and a festive ball in a private hall, to pass a lively night after the performance of the farce."[27] Since this was improvised comedy, however, the farce took an unexpected turn.

The official who played the part of Pantalone was late in arriving at the theater, and until he appeared on the scene, Gozzi had to prolong the monologue of Luce. There was some funny business about the baby crying, about trying to sing the baby to sleep. Then, further improvising the routine, Gozzi unlaced his bosom to nurse the baby: "I attached my little girl to the breasts that I did not have." There was much laughter in the audience when Luce yelped about the "greedy creature" biting the maternal breasts. Pantalone, however, still did not appear, and Gozzi was increasingly at a loss for what to do next. "Accidentally I raised my gaze to the boxes," he recalled, "and I saw in the proscenium that Tonina of evil custom, resplendent in beauty and in luminous gala dress from the fruit of her crimes, who boldly laughed more than anyone at my female jokes." Suddenly Gozzi knew how to prolong his soliloquy:

> On the spot I applied the name of Tonina to my little doll daughter, and directed my speech toward her. I caressed her, and contemplated her features; I flattered myself that my daughter Tonina must grow up to be a beautiful girl. I protested for my part that I would give her a good education, by example, by attention, by precepts, and by scoldings. I therefore exclaimed to the little Tonina that I held in my lap that if, in spite of my maternal cares, she should fall one day into such and such errors, into such and such imprudences, into such and such debaucheries, and should cause such and such disorders, she would be the worst Tonina in the world, and that in such a case I devoutly prayed to heaven to cut short her days while still in swaddling. The such and such errors, the such and such imprudences, the such and such debaucheries, and the such and such disorders were precisely very well known anecdotes relative to the Tonina in the proscenium. I never saw in all my days a greater acclamation for a comic soliloquy of mine. All the spectators turned their faces together toward the box of the beautiful Tonina in gala dress, with the greatest uproar of laughter and fracas of applause ever heard.[28]

It was the comic culmination of Gozzi's career as a Dalmatian girl in the theater, and this ultimate triumph came from creating an emphatic encounter between the Dalmatian impersonation on the stage and the Dalmatian presence in the audience. That the real Tonina was seated in a box at the proscenium already located her, topographically, at the boundary between the stage and the audience, and in Gozzi's improvisations as Luce, as later in Goldoni's *La Dalmatina* at the Teatro San Luca, the performance of Dalmatian character played upon a permeable boundary between the drama and the public.

If Gozzi made Luce appeal to everyone, Dalmatian and Venetian, by balancing his impersonation between sympathy and mockery, when he brought Tonina into the performance he improvised a fine line between tribute and travesty. Luce was herself once a "beautiful piece of woman," and, in the juxtaposition of Luce and Tonina, Gozzi posed the dramatic Dalmatian alternatives of poverty and venality. Such were the subaltern roles envisioned by a Venetian patrician in the 1740s. While Gozzi gave his performance, the real Tonina "fled from the theater blaspheming my soliloquy and my name," but later, at the ball, they danced together as almost reconciled enemies, and she even sought to seduce him by the fondlings and flirtations of "her perverse nature."[29] In this case he claimed to have preserved his already considerably compromised Venetian virtue against her aggressively seductive Dalmatian charms. Such was his script for the drama of the imperial encounter between the sexes. Gozzi was not sufficiently sentimental to imagine that the swaddled Dalmatian doll baby of the 1740s would grow up in the next decade to become Goldoni's Zandira, a patriotic model of every virtue.

Foscarini's Map of Dalmatia

In the seventeenth and eighteenth centuries, as the Venetian empire in the Mediterranean suffered severe setbacks, Dalmatia was not only preserved intact but actually expanded, inland, along the border with Ottoman Bosnia. In 1669, when Venice had to accept the crushing loss of Crete to the Turks by the peace of Candia, the Dalmatian frontier was held at the Nani line. In 1699, when the Ottomans had to accept the peace of Carlowitz, ceding Hungary to the Habsburgs, Venice took the exciting prize of the Morea, the Greek Peloponnesus, as well as a fat further extension of inland Dalmatia, the *nuovo acquisto,* bounded by the Grimani line. Finally, when the Ottomans ended another war in 1718 with the peace of Passarowitz, Venice had to give up the Morea but managed to detach from Bosnia another strip of Dalmatian territory, the *nuovissimo acquisto,* stipulated in the 1720s by the Mocenigo line.[30] The patrician families of Venice thus staked their names to a series of frontier lines, moving farther and farther from the sea, making Dalmatia into a province whose glory or misery would have to be evaluated by sea and by land—"per mare e per terra"—as Goldoni's heroine proclaimed in the concluding couplet of *La Dalmatina.* Those families also sent their sons, like young Gozzi, into the service of the Adriatic empire in Dalmatia.

This expansion of the Venetian empire through the extension of Dalmatia promptly created problems of provincial administration that had to be addressed in the context of more general eighteenth-century currents concerning political reform. Gozzi's experience in the early 1740s was suggestive of the potential tensions between Venetian officials and Dalmatian subjects and furthermore demonstrated that not every young Venetian was a model of imperial dedication in Dalmatia. In fact, the administration of Dalmatia became a central issue in Venetian politics in 1747 when Marco Foscarini seized upon it as a symptom of the need for enlightened reform, addressing the Maggior Consiglio, the Great Council, in a speech on the need for an investigation of administrative abuses in the province. Foscarini had already, as Venice's official historian, made a study of the Republic's political institutions and traditions; the case of Dalmatia in 1747 became for him a test of whether Venice could adapt and reform itself according to the challenges of the eighteenth century. According to Franco Venturi in *Settecento riformatore*, Foscarini sought to demonstrate that Venice still possessed "the necessary, indispensable political will to alter that which had to be reformed, to remedy, for instance, the sad, tragic fortunes of Dalmatia."[31] Fundamentally, Foscarini believed in the viability of Venetian institutions, and, years later, in the political crisis of 1761, he defended the prerogatives of the Council of Ten, arguing for a more moderate "correction" in the face of demands for political reform. Foscarini's triumphant moderation was consummated with his election as doge in 1762, the year before his death in 1763. In 1747, however, his political concerns encouraged a younger generation of Venetians to think critically about their institutions, and by making Dalmatia a serious subject for reformers, he put that province prominently on the agenda of the Enlightenment in Venice.

He appealed to the members of the Maggior Consiglio to send an investigative commission of "inquisitors" across the Adriatic to "the provinces of Albania and Dalmatia, which for many years have longed to recognize in such a magistracy the true paternal image of this most holy principate." Such a commission, he argued, was justified by numerous precedents in Venetian history, as a means for correcting administrative abuses and restoring the supposed perfection of Venice's venerable political constitution. It was the remedy to "the rapacity of whoever pulled at the public patrimony for private comfort," while, if unattended, "evils, increasing from day to day, reach a peak, as unfortunately becomes evident with the example of Dalmatia."[32] The administration of the new and newest acquisitions had predictably created new and newest opportunities for administrative abuse and corruption. The dispatch of inquisitors into Dalmatia became, for Foscarini, the occasion to investigate more generally the mid-century vigor of Venice's political condition.

Foscarini regretted that in "descending to the particulars" of the government of the province, it would be necessary "to touch upon unpleasant things for Your Excellencies to hear, and weighty for me to expound." Nevertheless, he felt compelled to speak, as Dalmatia faced the urgent alternatives of "either salvation or desperation." He presented to the senators the irony that this unhappy state of affairs had come about as a consequence of territorial expansion in Dalmatia: "Who would believe that the present calamities take their origin from the happiest event that concerned the Venetian name in these parts, I mean from the propagation of the borders effected in the last wars?"[33] The recently extended borders of Dalmatia called for new maps, and Foscarini felt that he needed one in order to present his subject properly to the Maggior Consiglio. "For a long time, and in vain, I spent myself in untiring research in the public archives," he related, "and with people who had lived in those parts for many years." Yet an accurate up-to-date map of Dalmatia was so unattainable that it seemed to him "almost miraculous" when one finally came to hand, the work of a public engineer Zuanne Camozzini. One fact, Foscarini noted, would be immediately evident to the senators if they studied the map: "that is, that in the conquests of the last two wars Albania and Dalmatia have increased in quadruple proportion relative to the former measurements, such that in the time of our ancestors the extent of those provinces subject to the Republic did not exceed the fifth part of the present dominion."[34] The map was a mark of imperial mastery over Dalmatia, permitting the Venetians to know their new territories and consider government and administration accordingly.

At the beginning of the century the celebrated Franciscan mapmaker Vincenzo Coronelli was the official cosmographer of the Venetian republic and the presiding figure of the Accademia Cosmografica of the Argonauts, Venice's geographical society. Coronelli did not ignore Venetian expansion in Dalmatia, and even while the Ottoman war was still being waged, before the peace of Carlowitz in 1699, he prepared maps on "The Conquests and Acquisitions made in Dalmatia." After the peace of Passarowitz in 1718 the provincial administration commissioned

further mappings of the Ottoman-Venetian border, motivated by particular concern over contagion and plague; one such map of 1731 included
the ironic remark that "if the old Dalmatians acquired fame on account
of their bellicose valor, the Dalmatians today are becoming famous for
their infirmity."[35] In any event, the Dalmatian territories that had been
wrested from the Ottoman empire were becoming better known to the
mapmakers of Europe. Indeed, it was generally accepted wisdom among
eighteenth-century cartographers that the Ottoman empire was wholly
inadequate to the task of mapping its lands according to modern standards. Robert's *Atlas Universel,* published in Paris in 1757, regretted an
absence of reliable geographical information for the Ottoman empire—
"but the approach to these states is difficult for enlightened people, and
does not permit one ever to hope for sufficient lights to give something
satisfying in geography." The atlas actually included Dalmatia on the
map of "European Turkey," though contemporary cartography was well
aware that the province belonged to Venice and that Venetian mapmakers, like Coronelli, had contributed to improved geographical knowledge
of the region. Indeed, the atlas affirmed as a general principle that there
was always better mapping information about "the lands that have belonged to civilized nations, to the Venetians for instance."[36] Venice's territorial gains in Dalmatia, at the expense of the Ottoman empire, were
codified and consolidated through cartography, and Foscarini in 1747 appreciated this principle even though he could not immediately put his
hands upon the appropriate map. When he finally found it he affirmed its
political importance. "Because I can not put this geographical map in
solemn exhibition," he said, before the Maggior Consiglio, "I have ordered the secretary not to refuse it to any citizen who wants to review it
with his own eyes."[37] Dalmatia was thus made available to the public,
and Foscarini's offering of the province to the public in cartographic
form in 1747 suggests a precedent for Goldoni's presentation of the
province to the public in dramatic form in 1758.

For Foscarini, the new dimensions of Dalmatia were a challenge to
Venice's old political traditions. "If the old people were to arise," he
wondered, rhetorically, invoking past generations, "would they recognize
Dalmatia any more?" In this "new Dalmatia" everything would appear
different to them: "new for acquisitions, new for taxations, new for military and civilian constructions, and new for so many furtive practices and
licentious manners of public administration." Contemporary inquisitors

would have to regard Dalmatia with the righteous and rigorous perspective of Venice's most venerable political principles, making Dalmatia into a test of Venetian integrity, eradicating new abuses in the name of old traditions. The alternative to reform was disaster:

> Good God, what would be in such a case the unhappy fate of our provinces? And what men are those, who will preserve a tempered and civic spirit, far from the official eye (*dall'occhio pubblico*), free from any danger of subsequent censure, and amidst the most improper customs, retaining in themselves the supreme power over all things? If we listen to such insinuations, we will finish by losing, along with the love of the subject people, what little remains of the income; which is to say that we will lose the provinces by our own hand, even as God saves them from Ottoman violence.[38]

The "official eye," *occhio pubblico*, referred to the eye of the republican state, not the modern public opinion cited by Goldoni when his drama excited "the greatest satisfaction of the public." In the eighteenth century both senses of "public" persisted in Venice, referring sometimes to the official domain of the state and sometimes to the modern public sphere of civil society, according to the context. If Dalmatia was "far from the official eye," then clearly that eye was geographically located in Venice, making the province the object of its gaze; when Foscarini offered the map of Dalmatia to the eyes of Venetian citizens he conceded the importance of a broader "public" perspective on the province.

In the climactic peroration of his speech Foscarini dramatized the importance of Dalmatia for Venetian patriotism, paying tribute to "glorious memories" of the province's place in the history of the Republic.

> It is the firstborn province (*provincia primogenita*) of Your Excellencies, for it numbers eight entire centuries of subjection to the Venetian Dominion; and while the successive losses of Cyprus, of Candia, and of the Morea have afflicted three centuries, it alone has seen its own borders expand. Besides, the highest honor in maritime battles, in conquests and vigorous resistances, in competition with all others, always went to Dalmatia's unvanquished peoples and to those neighbors also of the subject Albanian nation.[39]

Foscarini's political interest in Dalmatia was nourished by patriotic sentiment over its special status as the "firstborn" and, eight centuries later, almost the last remaining of Venice's overseas possessions. In a remarkable rhetorical device, Foscarini summoned the Dalmatians to speak for themselves within his own speech:

If they could speak, they would say that they could not resign themselves to seeing those of their own blood defrauded, the expectation of their ancestors disappointed. The latter held as sure that the accomplished acquisitions would become with time the firmest bulwarks (*antemurali*) of the power of the Republic, and together fruitful lands.[40]

Like Goldoni putting the Dalmatians on the stage of the Teatro San Luca, and writing their lines for them, Foscarini brought the Dalmatians into the Maggior Consiglio and made them speak through him of their ancestors' satisfaction in beings subjects of Venice.

By his ventriloquy the Dalmatians also spoke their contemporary grievances: "We suffer hunger amidst abundance. . . . Our fields are made pasture for foreign herds." After such a conjuring of voices, it was not easy to tell whether Foscarini spoke for himself or for them when he presented the ultimate indictment: "Unfortunately it is certain, Serenissimo Mazor Consegio, that an infinite number of families which, having shaken off the yoke of the Turks with arms in hand, and were brought beneath the placid and temperate Dominion of the Republic, for some time since have abandoned the new establishments and houses, to return as tattered beggars under the Ottoman tyranny."[41] Such migrations of Slavs, crossing the borders of Venice and the Ottoman empire, and the Habsburg empire as well, did occur in the eighteenth century; impoverished populations, like the pastoral Morlacchi, followed their flocks to better pastures, responding to slightly more advantageous conditions drawing them in one direction or another.[42] That the threshold of survival was low enough to make the political and religious borders appear as matters of indifference to the population of Dalmatia was alarming to one such as Foscarini who cherished an ideal of Dalmatian loyalty to Venice. Gozzi, only a few years before, had made a comedy out of the "extreme indigence" of Luce, the Dalmatian servant girl. Foscarini insisted on taking seriously the laments of Dalmatian poverty.

After speaking so frankly—"unpleasant things for Your Excellencies to hear"—Foscarini softened the impact with an assurance that such social alienation was by no means usual in Venice's history.

> The manner of the Venetian government has usually been to enamor (*innamorar*) peoples, and by the desire to enjoy it, to cause them to transfer from even the most comfortable and delightful residences: if however we tolerate in Dalmatia the contrary effects, it is necessary to conclude that the old forms are ruined.[43]

For Foscarini, reforms were just the renewal of old forms, and Dalmatia was the occasion for demonstrating that the system still worked for Venice in the eighteenth century. Venice was to prove its own political viability by showing that it could still make itself loved by its subjects. This conservative aspect of Foscarini's political approach would be all the more evident in the moderating role he later played at the time of the Venetian crisis of 1761. In 1747 Foscarini concluded his speech with confidence that the inquisitors in Dalmatia would bring "comfort" to the "afflicted provinces," and would call forth "the acclamations of the peoples."[44] Thus the ending of Foscarini's speech in the Maggior Consiglio in 1747 pointed toward the applause of the Dalmatian audience—"with praises and with presents"—for Goldoni in the Teatro San Luca in 1758.

Venetian Recollections of Dalmatian Acclamations

Foscarini's anticipated Dalmatian "acclamations" were also echoed in the history of the Republic of Venice—"from its foundation up to the year 1747"—written by Giacomo Diedo. While Foscarini began as the official historian of Venice, and then became important in politics, Diedo had a patrician career in politics, going as far as the Council of Ten, and then turned to history. His *Storia della Repubblica di Venezia* coincidentally concluded in 1747, the year of Foscarini's speech on Dalmatia, because Diedo died in 1748, and the four-volume work appeared posthumously in 1751. His first volume examined not only the foundation of the Republic, but also Venice's earliest political relations with Dalmatia. The first formal submission of the Dalmatian cities to Venetian sovereignty, around the medieval millennial year 1000, was of ideological interest to Diedo in the eighteenth century, for it remained fundamental in the mythology of Venice's political culture, commemorated in the annual Ascension festival, the wedding of the city with the sea. Edward Muir has shown the particular importance of the festival as an imperial ritual in Renaissance Venice.[45]

Diedo appreciated the imperial significance of the millennial moment and focused his historical attention upon "the first acquisitions of the Venetians in Dalmatia, which then might serve as a base for further advances." In fact, the coastal cities of Dalmatia did indeed serve Venice as indispensable naval bases for an imperial commercial domain that eventually advanced beyond the Adriatic to the eastern Mediterranean, but for Diedo and his eighteenth-century contemporaries, Dalmatia was also an ideological base on which to construct a culturally convenient vision of the Venetian empire. The Dalmatians, accordingly to Diedo, in order "to secure themselves from the molestations of the barbarians" (the Narentani along the river Neretva), appealed for the protection of Venice at the end of the tenth century, so that the millennial Adriatic armada of the Doge Pietro II Orseolo was welcomed "with acclamations by the inhabitants who saluted him as their liberator."[46] As the armada proceeded along the coast, from Zadar to Split, the peoples of Dalmatia were eager "to resign themselves to obedience to the doge," and, graciously, they "were received with humanity under the republican dominion."[47] Orseolo then assumed the title of Doge of Venice and Dalmatia, to be transmitted to his successors, a dogal dualism that politically bestrode the shores of the Adriatic. Diedo thus demonstrated that the Adriatic empire commenced with acclamations in Dalmatia, just as Foscarini looked for new acclamations as the ratification of imperial reform.

History writing in Venice, from the time of the Renaissance, was civically conceived and officially sponsored; Marcantonio Sabellico had received encouragement from the Republic in the fifteenth century, and the position of official historian was created in the sixteenth century, to be occupied by Andrea Navagero and then Pietro Bembo. The seventeenth-century Dalmatian historian, Joannes Lucius (Giovanni Lucio or Ivan Lučić) of Trogir, in a work published in Venice in 1674, noted that the fourteenth-century chronicle of Andrea Dandolo already gave the story of Orseolo "acclaimed as a liberator by the Dalmatians" and that "the other Venetian historians write substantially the same."[48] Diedo worked within this historiographical tradition, and it was only natural for him to seek to celebrate and legitimize the medieval aggrandizement of the state. His account of the millennial armada was historically accurate enough, but still misleading in its implication that Venetian rule in Dalmatia dated continuously from that time. On the contrary, this was fiercely contested and frequently overturned in the wars and insurrections of the next four centuries. It was not Venetian rule in Dalmatia, but rather the Venetian claim, which was definitively established at the millennium. Diedo celebrated the legitimacy of that claim in the eighteenth century, as did Foscarini when he reminisced on Dalmatia's "eight entire centuries of subjection."

Diedo's history, concluded in 1747, published in 1751, interpreted the foundation of the Adriatic empire as an enlightened drama of liberation, the triumph of humanity over barbarism. Two other works, appearing in Venice in those same years, suggested alternative mid-century visions of Venetian Dalmatia, from Slavic and Roman perspectives. The Dalmatian Filip Grabovac, an army chaplain, published in Venice in 1747 an anthology of verses and stories concerning the legendary and historical past of Dalmatia, *Cvit razgovora naroda i jezika iliričkoga aliti rvackoga* (*The Flower of Conversation of the Illyrian or Croatian Nation and Language*). Such a work, officially approved for publication by the Riformatori of the University of Padua, composed by a Dalmatian poet in a language that he called either Illyrian or Croatian, demonstrated the Republic's plurality of peoples in a different fashion from Diedo's history or Goldoni's drama. The Slavic word *narod* could be translated as "people" or "nation," suggestive of collective identity—whether Illyrian or Croatian—though without the ideological specificity of modern nationalism. Grabovac appealed in poetry to the past and future glory of Dalmatia: "Slava Dalmacije." Yet, in recounting their struggle against the Ottoman Turks, he represented the Dalmatians as part of the domain of the South Slavs, and not simply as subjects of Venice's Adriatic empire. The poems, which included libelous remarks about living Dalmatians, caused some controversy; Grabovac ended up in prison in Venice, and copies of the book were burned in Dalmatia.[49] Another vision of Dalmatia, likewise ambivalently Venetian, emerged from the *Illyricum Sacrum*, the church history of Dalmatia whose first of many monumental volumes appeared in Venice in 1751, composed in Latin by the Jesuit Daniele Farlati. In this ecclesiastical context, Dalmatia appeared as much a religious province of Rome as a secular province of Venice.[50] These alternative contexts, and even languages, for discussing Dalmatia, in the *Cvit razgovora* and the *Illyricum Sacrum*, indicated by contrast the purposefully ideological concerns of Diedo, writing about Dalmatia in his Venetian history, and, soon after, Goldoni, celebrating the Adriatic empire in *La Dalmatina*.

In 1751, the year that Diedo's history was published, the Venetian Senate finally received the finished report from the inquisitors, who had been dispatched to study the problems of Dalmatia after Foscarini's speech in 1747. Foscarini had urged them to investigate administrative abuses, and they returned with a report of "greed and malice" on the part of some officials, contributing to "extreme misery and desperation" among the Dalmatians. The report, however, was not without criticism of the Dalmatians themselves, especially for their inadequacies as farmers. "If we were disturbed by the depravities and disorders in which we found these provinces immersed," wrote the inquisitors, "our spirit was especially distressed at seeing the ineptitude and inertia of the peoples, which, as due to the laziness of their ancestors, leaves the lands desperately idle." The solution that the inquisitors envisioned was land reform, the assignment of state lands from the *nuovo* and *nuovissimo acquisto* in such a fashion as to create incentives for agricultural success. They called for "salutary rules toward an equitable and charitable distribution of lands, for upon this, we frankly can not keep from repeating, depends uniquely the true redemption of these provinces, the true well-being of the peoples, and the interest of the principate."[51] Like Foscarini, who instigated their investigation, the commissioners recognized the alternatives of "desperation" and "redemption" in Dalmatia and formulated a conception of imperial responsibility that combined the interests of Venice and the Dalmatians.

The Provveditore Generale Francesco Grimani instituted in 1755 the agricultural reform recommended by the inquisitors in 1751. According to the Grimani law, uncultivated state lands were assigned to Dalmatian subjects, with particular attention to making farmers out of the pastoral Morlacchi. The assignment of two fields to a farmer, less than two acres, not as property but in usufruct, with heavy levels of tax contribution, undercut the intention of making Dalmatia agriculturally prosperous. The shortcomings of the reform were evident within a generation, and, in historical retrospect, Marino Berengo has judged it to be an "almost total failure," especially because the size of the assignments was inadequate for the cultivation of inland Dalmatia's not particularly fertile soil.[52] Grimani himself, however, with all the confidence of the Enlightenment, believed that he had solved the economic problems of the Dalmatians with the reform that thereafter bore his name. "Satisfying thus their honest conveniences, even to the point of bringing them to call themselves spontaneously content (*chiamarsene spontaneamente contenti*)," he wrote in 1756, "I fixed by my own hand the detail of the assignments."[53] Just as Foscarini conjured the voices of the Dalmatians to speak their grievances, so Grimani had them declare themselves content. Furthermore, just as during Gozzi's service in the 1740s there was an occasion for reciting compositions "in praise of the Provveditore Generale," so in the 1750s the literary academy of Zadar produced orations and poems in Latin and Italian to honor Grimani, the great reformer. A volume of these compositions was published in Venice in 1757, so that the Dalmatians might pay tribute to their Venetian governor before the public of Venice.[54] The next year, in 1758, Goldoni had his Dalmatians celebrate the Adriatic empire from the stage in Martellian verse.

In 1755, the year of the Grimani law, Vettor Sandi published in Venice another history of the Republic, *Principi di storia civile della Repubblica di Venezia*. Franco Venturi has compared Sandi to Foscarini, emphasizing that for both of them, "the political form of the patriciate stands at the center of their vision," but observing that, in Sandi's case, the succession of volumes eventually became "a monument to an immobile past," a sort of "museum" of Venetian history. Sandi's civil history was dedicated to the Serenissimo Maggior Consiglio Veneziano. His discussion of medieval Dalmatia echoed the speech of Foscarini in 1747, and the history of Diedo in 1751, attributing primary importance to the establishment of Venetian rule over the province: "Here then were the first foundations of the power of the Republic in the acquisition of maritime Dalmatia, the firstborn acquisition (*primogenito acquisto*) of Venice." This was the beginning, according to Sandi, of Venetian rule "outside the lagoons," of Venetian domination in the Adriatic gulf.[55]

Just as Diedo cited the "acclamations" that greeted the doge's millennial armada, Sandi also was intent upon demonstrating Dalmatia's voluntary submission to Venetian rule. Harassed on land and sea by Saracens, Croatians, and Narentani, the Dalmatians gave themselves over to Venice: "not by conquests of violence, but by invitations and the spontaneous will of the peoples, who to escape from the ferocity of rapacious invaders or from an oppressive tyranny, appealed for asylum to the free Venetian Signoria, to subject themselves (*assoggetarvisi*)." Such an appeal, according to Sandi's evaluation of human rights and natural law, was justified for the Dalmatians by "the right to seek defense, without violating the laws relative to possessors, who do not wish or do not care any more to save them." The indifferent "possessors" were the Byzantine emperors, who had not reigned in Constantinople since 1453, three centuries before Sandi wrote his history; nevertheless, he was notably concerned to demonstrate that Venice had not appropriated Dalmatia illegitimately from Byzantium.

With the barbarous ways by which at that time the Dalmatian areas were afflicted, incessant were the appeals of those populations to the court of Constantinople, but negligence and circumstances caused them to remain fruit-
less. Abandoned, therefore, and desperate for their salvation, in universal
congress of the nation seeking refuge from their evils, they saw it nowhere
nearer or more secure than with the Venetians. . . . So through legates sent
to Venice they demonstrated that, were they liberated from the cruelty of the
Slavs, they and their cities would subject themselves forever, voluntarily, to
the Venetian Signoria.[56]

While it was safe for Sandi to make insinuations about the negligence of
the Byzantines, who were no longer around to take offense, the "barbarous" character attributed to "the cruelty of the Slavs" was more
fraught with contemporary relevance. After all, the eighteenth-century
inhabitants of the province were themselves recognized as Slavs. Sandi's
historical ethnography implicitly posed the awkward problem of from
whom and for whom Venice "liberated" Dalmatia.

Sandi's "universal congress of the nation" implicitly excluded the
Slavic population of Dalmatia. In fact, at the millennium there may have
been still largely Latin towns on the Dalmatian coast, in contrast to the
Slavic interior, but those towns probably became increasingly Slavic during the following century. By the late twelfth century, the population of
Zadar was reported singing Slavic hymns in honor of the pope, and in
the early fourteenth century a Venetian visitor to Cres needed a Slavic
translator because the islanders did not know Latin. Giovanni Marchisini,
in the fourteenth century, celebrated the birth of three lion cubs in
Venice by dedicating them to the Doge Giovanni Soranzo as emblems of
medieval empire: "a three-fold lineage of races is subject to you, for
Venetian, Slav, and even Greek are under your sway." The Dalmatian
Lucius observed in the seventeenth century that Venetian historians
tended to "confuse the names of the Dalmatians with those of the Slavs,
not distinguishing the particular names of the Croats, the Serbians, and
the Narentani, from the general name of the Slavs."[57] Sandi, in the eighteenth century, illustrated the ideological implications of such confusion.

Diedo dramatized the issue of legitimacy when he gave an account of
the Venetian ambassador before the pope in the thirteenth century, justifying the duties that Venice imposed on shipping in the Adriatic.

The pope was given to understand the foundation of the possession and validity of the imposed duty. The ambassador showed that the dominion of the

Venetians over the waters of the Adriatic was acquired by just reason of war
as far back as remote times, by the victorious arms of the Doge Pietro Orseolo against the Saracens in the time of decadence of the Eastern Empire; the
enjoyment of possession having never been interrupted, it is reconfirmed by
the indefatigable custody provided by the fleet to the common safety against
the infestations of corsairs.[58]

To demonstrate possession of Dalmatia and domination of the Adriatic
was one and the same thing in Diedo's interpretation of medieval history. Diedo and Sandi both agreed that Byzantine rights to the province
had lapsed, whether through "decadence" or "negligence." Diedo earlier recognized the piratical role of the Narentani in provoking the
Venetian assumption of empire, but then, in elaborating a justification of
right by conquest, he preferred to present the hostile corsairs only as
Moslem Saracens. Sandi more frankly recognized the barbarous pirates as
both Saracens and Slavs, though such recognition was of more controversial relevance to the population of Dalmatia. Goldoni resolved the
dilemma when he made his pirates Barbary Saracens and their captives
Dalmatian Slavs.

Diedo, while attesting to legitimate possession and "indefatigable
custody" of the province, could not actually write the medieval history of
Dalmatia without frequent accounts of rebellions against Venice, often
encouraged by the kings of Hungary. In fact, Dalmatia was not ruled
continuously or completely by Venice after the armada of Pietro Orseolo
until the settlement by treaty with Hungary in the early fifteenth century.
During that intermediary medieval period there were competing claims
upon the Dalmatian coast, by Croatia in the tenth and eleventh centuries
and then by Hungary, which ruled Croatia from the twelfth century.
Diedo, however, discerned in these centuries of uncertain sovereignty
Venice's insistent assertion of its rightful rule. For instance, in the
eleventh century the city of Zadar rebelled against the Republic: "It was
suspected that the other towns of Dalmatia might follow the example;
therefore, the doge rushed promptly with an armada, the siege of the
contumacious city was strict, and then having obtained pardon, it was restored to obedience." In another rebellion of the twelfth century, "the
city of Zara was the first to chase out the magistrates of the Republic," so
that Venice in response proceeded to "demolish the walls of several contumacious cities." Furthermore, for the moment, "the Hungarians were
chased out (*scacciati*) not only from Dalmatia, but also from Croatia." In

1202 the Doge Enrico Dandolo prevailed upon the soldiers of the Fourth Crusade to seize Zadar on his behalf, on their way to Constantinople. In the fourteenth century, faced with "insurrections" (*sollevazioni*) at Zadar and the "contumacy (*contumacia*) of the rebels," the reigning doge achieved "the glory of rendering quiet with his gentle manners the whole province of Dalmatia, but perhaps by the gentleness (*dolcezza*) of his means gave inclination and instigation to the ferocious nature (*natura feroce*) of those people to rebel soon after for the seventh time against the dominion of the Republic."[59] In 1782 Casanova wrote an historical novel, unpublished then, about the Hungarian-Venetian struggle for Zadar in the fourteenth century, *Aneddoti veneziani militari ed amorosi;* the story was based on a French novel about the Hundred Years War by Mme de Tencin, *Le Siège de Calais,* transposed by Casanova to the siege of Zadar in 1358. The Hungarians conquered Zadar in the military encounter of the novel, but the amorous plot culminated in a Venetian-Dalmatian marriage, the token of future imperial union.[60] Casanova's historical fiction testified to the persistence of contemporary concern with the past history of Venice's involvement in Dalmatia.

The halls of the Doge's Palace in Venice included painted scenes of Venetian conquests of Zadar, which attracted the artistic interest of Antonio Guardi, around 1730, when he made watercolor studies of them. Guardi produced dramatic renderings of Andrea Vicentino's Renaissance painting of the crusaders' conquest of Zadar in 1202, in the hall of the Maggior Consiglio, and of Tintoretto's painting of the siege of Zadar in 1346, in the hall of the Scrutinio.[61] The subjugation of Zadar was programmatically important in the Renaissance decoration of the Doge's Palace, but the subject was still interesting to Guardi in the eighteenth century, even though his watercolors, like Diedo's history, revealed past relations of bellicose violence between Venice and Dalmatia.

Sandi offered further confirmation of this concern when he recalled that the ancient Romans required five Dalmatian wars to conquer the province, and afterwards Augustus had to take further trouble with the Dalmatians to "tame them (*domarli*)." The reward for ancient Rome was "better and more secure order for the navigation of the Adriatic."[62] Medieval Venice, of course, sought a similar advantage in overcoming so many Dalmatian rebellions. William Bouwsma has demonstrated the exceptional importance of the Venetian historiographical tradition in the Renaissance, for defending Venice's political values and defining Venice's political identity.[63] The work of eighteenth-century historians like Diedo and Sandi, touching on Dalmatian matters, suggests that writing history could also contribute to the formulation of an ideology of empire.

The Venetian history of Dalmatia was an account of incessant insurrections, philosophically explained by the nature of the Dalmatians who were both contumacious and ferocious. The notion of ferocious nature derived from the idea of barbarism in the early Enlightenment; the discourses of Jean-Jacques Rousseau in the 1750s would soon render such a model more controversial by boldly challenging the negative valuation of savage man in the state of nature. That challenge would eventually leave its mark even on the map of Dalmatia, when the Morlacchi were reconceived as Venice's very own noble savages. For Diedo, however, the "gentle manners" of civilization constituted such an unequivocal standard of superiority that he only allowed himself to wonder whether the Venetians in the fourteenth century had already become so excessively civilized that the graces of *gentilezza* rather encouraged the rebellious impulses of ferocity. Foscarini in 1747 believed that Venice's traditional policy was to "enamor" its provincial subjects, but Diedo and Sandi described an imperial history of not entirely enamored adherence in Dalmatia. Grimani in 1756 claimed to have brought the Dalmatians to the point of declaring themselves "spontaneously content," thus presuming to resolve not only the contemporary agricultural crisis but also the historical record of medieval Dalmatian discontent.

Another literary perspective on that same medieval discontent was expressed in a mock epic poem concerning the fourteenth-century Venetian conspirator, Baiamonte Tiepolo, who was supposed to have taken refuge in Dalmatia after having failed to depose the reigning doge in 1310. The poem was composed by Zaccaria Vallaresso, probably in the 1740s, though it remained unpublished for several decades. The second part, entitled *Baiamonte Tiepolo in Schiavonia,* concerned the treasonous protagonist's involvement with insurrections in Dalmatia; it was finally published pseudonymously in Venice in 1770. As in Gozzi's memoirs of Dalmatia in the 1740s, Vallaresso identified the Dalmatians by their preposterous moustaches, and, like Gozzi, he mocked the provincial language as *lingua Illirico-Italiana,* comically misunderstood as nonsense. The Slavonic liturgy, which was controversial in Dalmatia in the tenth century and remained so in the eighteenth century, was cited in the poem as an instance of Dalmatian barbarism:

> Qui fino dell'Altare i Sacerdoti
> Portano due mustacche di sicario,
> Ed all'usanza del paese espressa
> Barbara lingua ha pur la Santa Messa.
>
> > Here even the priests at the altar
> > Wear the moustaches of assassins,
> > And according to the usage of the land
> > Holy Mass is also in a barbarous language.[64]

The image of moustaches at mass was almost enough in itself to convey the Venetian comedy of Dalmatia.

The mock-historical aspect of the poem, however, was sometimes fully consistent with the spirit of serious history, like that of Diedo, composed at the same time in the 1740s. Vallaresso was himself a prominent patrician in Venetian politics, with diverse literary interests. Though it is not known whether he actually spent time in Dalmatia, he certainly had some Dalmatian connections, since Grabovac, in 1747, dedicated to Vallaresso a poem "in Illyrian verse," within the *Cvit razgovora*. In *Baiamonte Tiepolo in Schiavonia*, Vallaresso proposed to narrate an episode suppressed by Venetian history, but nevertheless familiar in its general form: "We will see Dalmatia in revolt." At the end of the epic, rebellious Dalmatia submitted humbly to Venice, following the same formulas employed by the authentic historians.

> Le marine città miglioran stato
> Col soggettarsi al Veneto Senato.
>
> > The coastal cities improve their condition
> > By subjecting themselves to the Venetian Senate.[65]

They raised the standard of San Marco, saluted the Venetian Lion, and surrendered through "pacts of voluntary devotion" (*volontaria dedizione*). Thus, medieval Venice triumphed in Dalmatia, in such a fashion as to be "applauded by the peoples."[66] Mock epic reinforced the messages of solemn history, anticipating the applause of the Dalmatians in the Teatro San Luca for Goldoni's drama, *La Dalmatina*.

Theatrical Representations of Public Patriotism

The first performance of *La Dalmatina* in 1758 secured, according to Goldoni, "the greatest satisfaction of the public," including the Dalmatians in the audience. Goldoni's plays were not only written for the appreciation of the public, but, in some cases, they were also plays about the public sphere, concerning inns and cafes, as suggested in such titles as *La Locandiera* and *La Bottega del caffè*. The setting of *La Vedova scaltra* (*The Shrewd Widow*) specified a variety of public spaces in Venice, including an inn, a cafe, and the street, all Venetian locations that the theater public might also frequent as participants in eighteenth-century public life. Rather less accessible and familiar was the setting of an Oriental drama like *La Sposa Persiana:* "The scene represents Isfahan, capital of the kingdom of Persia, in the house of Machmut, in an atrium that leads to the seraglio of Tamas."[67] The exotic and the familiar, as dramatic settings, exercised different claims upon the interests and sympathies of the Venetian public, and *La Dalmatina* offered the mixed entertainment of an exotic setting with somewhat less exotic characters. The action took place in Tetuan, featuring many Oriental intimations of the seraglio, as if Dalmatia were not quite exotic enough as a dramatic scenario. Yet, the hero and heroine were Dalmatians, subjects of San Marco, like those who were present in the audience at the first performance, recognizable figures to the public of Venice.

When Voltaire published his universal history, the *Essai sur les moeurs,* in 1754, he composed a dedication to the German Elector Palatine Charles Theodore, which was presented as a sort of anti-dedication, deploring the conventional tributes to aristocratic patrons—to their ancestors and their virtues—as tedious for the reading public. "This here is not even a dedication," wrote Voltaire. "It is an appeal to the public that I dare to make before your electoral highness."[68] When Goldoni eventually published *La Dalmatina* in a collection of his plays in 1763, he too composed a dedication—to Gian-Francesco Pisani, Procurator of San Marco—which suggested a complex balance between patron and public. By that time Goldoni was in Paris, having left Venice in 1762 to continue his career at the Comédie Italienne. His last play before leaving was again explicitly concerned with public life in Venice, *Una delle ultime sere di carnevale,* a drama of carnival, concluding with the commencement of a voyage to Moscow. Thus Goldoni himself took leave of "the public," as he remarked in his memoirs: "Here terminates the collection of my pieces composed for the public in Venice."[69] Yet, his plays continued to appear before that public, and *La Dalmatina,* which after the premiere of 1758 returned to the stage in 1759 and 1760, was still performed in the 1760s when Goldoni was in Paris.

The publication of *La Dalmatina* in 1763 took place in Venice, and though Goldoni wrote his dedication from Paris, he reestablished himself within the political culture of the Republic by addressing Pisani:

> The jubilation and the acclamations of the Serenissima Dominante, over the merited election of your excellency to the sublime dignity of Procurator, arrived even in Paris, and I, who interest myself with respectful filial love in the well-being and the honors of my country (*Patria*), have taken consolation with myself, and with all those of our nation (*Nazione*) who find themselves here. This happy occasion has made me desire more than ever to find myself again in my adorable country; I would have wished to be able to kiss the hands of all those who contributed to such a glorious, such a just election; to unite myself with the people (*Popolo*) in the piazzas and the celebratory streets; to sing hymns of praise to the grateful Republic. May your excellency permit me to send from afar to those excellent lagoons my exultation, which I may render public in print, that I may participate in the jubilation of my fellow citizens with the precious acquisition of your supreme protection.[70]

Like Voltaire, who greatly admired Goldoni and enthusiastically endorsed his Italian theatrical reform, the playwright in publishing his work exploited the occasion of the dedication to delineate his own relation to the public. Goldoni further offered a sort of lexicography of patriotism in its constituent concepts—*Patria, Nazione, Popolo, Repubblica*—at the moment of their modern recombination in the passage from Renaissance republicanism into the public sphere of the Enlightenment. In Venice the crisis of 1761 had been surmounted; the republican institutions were vindicated after the criticisms and corrections proposed by the partisans of Angelo Querini, and Marco Foscarini was elected as doge in 1762. Though Foscarini died in 1763, he left behind the dominating idea of his dogedom, what Franco Venturi has called a "dream of continuity" and "harmonic union between culture and liberty."[71] From Paris Goldoni sought to participate in that harmonic union, appearing before the public in the performance and publication of his plays. He affirmed his connection to the Venetian nation ("with all those of our nation who find themselves here") and the Venetian people in their public spaces ("to unite myself with the people in the piazzas"). The patron Pisani served as a sort of statue at the center of the dedication, around which Goldoni theatrically staged a performance of public patriotism, presented to the public in print. The dedication indicated the diverse aspects of the public sphere in the superimposition of theatrical public, reading public, and political public.

These issues, however, were further complicated by the fact that the drama that was being dedicated was, specifically, *La Dalmatina,* which had been first performed in a quite particular relation to the public of Venice, for an audience which included the Dalmatians of the city.

> My *Dalmatina* is one of the comedies that in Venice principally has done me the greatest honor. I saw the people (*Popolo*) interested in receiving it, in celebrating it. It concerns a nation (*Nazione*) loyal and worthy of the Serenissima Repubblica; it concerns in some fashion the glorious name of the Venetians, the valor of the Slavs, and the respect that they both command principally upon the sea. To whom could one better entrust the protection of this theatrical work, founded on truth, crafted in verisimilitude; to whom could one better commend it than to a Pisani, which is as much as to say, to one of the leading supporters of the decorum and honor of the country (*Patria*), whose zeal has sacrificed everything to the well-being, to the splendor, to the tranquillity of the Adriatic empire?[72]

This invocation of empire in the dedication thus echoed the heroine's tribute, within the play, to the "fortunate peoples of the Adriatic empire." The constellation of political concepts—*Patria, Nazione, Popolo, Repubblica*—was flexibly deployed to fit the imperial formula, to accommodate the relation between Venice and Dalmatia. The "people" of Venice who celebrated *La Dalmatina* included the Dalmatians of the audience, who rewarded Goldoni with praise and presents. Just as the people celebrated the election of Pisani, with Goldoni joining them in the piazzas, so the people also celebrated Goldoni himself and his play, *La Dalmatina.* The election of the Procurator of San Marco took place within the Maggior Consiglio and was therefore hardly the work of the "people" of Venice, whose celebration in the piazzas was, constitutionally, little more than an enthusiastic flourish. Goldoni, however, who legitimated his theatrical reform through the approval of the public, could appreciate the significance of applause. The implicit analogy between these sorts of celebration suggest that for Goldoni the theatrical aspects of republican government were related to the political aspects of theater, engaged with the concerns of the Serenissima Repubblica.

Those concerns, as addressed in *La Dalmatina,* were "the glorious name of the Venetians" and "the valor of the Slavs," treated together "in some fashion"—but the fashion was one of suggestive association through the drama rather than any explicit political equation. Goldoni sought to annex the valor of the Slavs to the name of the Venetians, at a moment when the glory of that name was in manifest decline.[73] Berengo has remarked that Dalmatia, in the eighteenth century, represented a "unique glimmering of the ancient paths of Venetian expansion," just the "surviving appendix" of a past Mediterranean dominion.[74] The "splendor" of the Adriatic empire was really a remembered splendor of centuries past, which Goldoni evoked even as he sought to articulate a more modern idea of empire, based on an actively engaged public of associated nations. He proposed an empire of Venetians and Slavs, around the Adriatic, mirrored in the urban population of the metropolis itself and only sentimentally anchored in the exigencies of maritime trade. Habsburg Trieste, an imperial free port from 1719, challenged Venice's domination of the Adriatic by the middle of the eighteenth century, while the "tranquillity" of that sea was ensured by its lesser commercial importance in an age of Atlantic hegemony. The publication of *La Dalmatina* in 1763, the year of the peace of Paris, marking the triumph of England's maritime empire, might have invited an ironic reaction to that supposedly special "respect" commanded by Venetians and Slavs at sea.

Goldoni in 1763 was reliving his own authorial glory of 1758. In a short preface that followed the dedication and targeted the reader— "L'Autore a chi legge"—Goldoni began by distinguishing his reading public from his theatrical public and singling out in particular the audience that was present for the premiere: "Those who were present at the first performance of this comedy will remember what a happy outcome it brought." Goldoni himself left Venice for Rome immediately after that performance, missing those that followed, because "after the pleasure of that evening, nothing was left for me to desire." Thus, addressing the broad reading public of Venice in 1763, he referred his readers to the more intimate, privileged public of the first performance at the Teatro San Luca in 1758. He invited them to crowd into the theater and experience vicariously, retrospectively, the pleasure of that remembered evening, to witness not only the effect of the first performance but also the reaction of the first audience:

> The valorous Signora Caterina Bresciani sustained with such spirit and truth the character of the Dalmatian girl that she merited the applause of all, and especially of the Slavs. Those valorous, most loyal subjects of the Serenissima

Repubblica of Venice, when they heard announced an Illyrian woman on the stage, feared some stroke of poetic license upon the quite respectable character of the nation, and woe to me if I had not rendered the justice it merits; they would have been loath to pardon me, and I don't know if I would have made the voyage to Rome. Thank the Lord no one has ever been able to complain of me on that account, and it was written to me, to console me, that the nationals (*Nazionali*) went in troops with their big swords (*spadoni*) to see their female compatriot, to applaud the honorable Radovich when he boasted of carrying jealously "his Lion in his breast." This is the glorious Lion that I too cherish jealously in my breast, that animated me to write this comedy, that inspired in me the strokes and the sentiments that made the greater pleasure of the comedy.[75]

The Italian Venetian reading public was thus encouraged to consider the conduct of the Dalmatian Slavs at the first performance. Those Slavs were described as both supremely loyal to Venice and, at the same time, intensely suspicious of any Venetian misrepresentation of their character. Gozzi in Zadar in the 1740s, performing the "ostentatious chastity" of Luce, mocking the "such and such debaucheries" of Tonina, represented the character of Dalmatian women as barely respectable. Goldoni, however, suggested that the sensitivity of the Dalmatians in Venice to such and such aspersions actually put his own life at risk; he feared that, had he given offense, he might not have made the voyage to Rome, might instead have been cut down by the troops with their oversized swords. Yet, even as Goldoni flattered himself that he did the Dalmatians justice, there was surely an element of caricature in the way he described them to his readers, as trooping to the theater, swords in hand, overly enthusiastic in matters of dramatic appreciation.

The Dalmatians in Venice, often identifiable like Radovich by their Slavic names, figured prominently in the industry of shipbuilding as well as in naval service manning the ships. Frederic Lane has suggested that at the naval victory of Lepanto, in 1571, "the galleys listed as manned 'from Venice' included some with crews composed largely of Greeks or Dalmatians," and, thereafter, "Dalmatians and Greeks were numerous among the sailors of all ranks." Dennis Romano has demonstrated the significant percentage of servants of Dalmatian origin in Renaissance Venice. Robert Davis has described the participation of Dalmatian soldiers and sailors in the *pugni*, the battles of the bridges, in seventeenth-century Venice, though witnesses thought the Slavs seemed less apt at fighting with their fists than with their weapons. When the faction of the Castellani prepared for battle in 1667, "in coming up the Grand Canal, they also picked up a great many sailors of the fleet and a squad of two hundred Dalmatians." Massimo Donà has studied the soldiers of the Milizia Oltremarina, or transmarine militia, who were recruited in Dalmatia and stationed in the garrisons of the Venetian Terraferma; in 1760 there were two regiments, totaling almost a thousand Dalmatians, guarding the lagoon at the Lido di Venezia.[76] The Dalmatian community in Venice found a social focus, from the fifteenth century, in the Scuola Dalmata at San Giorgio degli Schiavoni, with its famous Carpaccio frescoes. There the resident Dalmatians of Venice gathered to elect their community officers, and in the eighteenth century they took a special protective interest in Dalmatian girlhood, awarding dowries to poor girls in the name of St. George and St. Triffon of the Dalmatian nation (*Nazion Dalmatina*).[77] With this sense of custodial concern for Dalmatian maidens, the members of the Scuola Dalmata might well have taken an enthusiastic interest in the marital fate of Zandira on the stage of the Teatro San Luca. At the same time Dalmatian sailors in Venice might have been flattered to recognize themselves in the heroic figure of Radovich.

Goldoni mentioned that *La Dalmatina* also pleased his friend Stefano Sciugliaga, from Ragusa, who lived in Venice as a member of the Dalmatian nation: "my friend Sciugliaga who does honor to that illustrious nation." Sciugliaga directed a printing press, and in 1757 and 1758 published studies that he had written himself about the shipwreck of St. Paul, perhaps in Dalmatia.[78] Not only were works of Dalmatian interest published in Venice, but there were also important contemporary publications in the language that Grabovac, in 1747, called Illyrian or Croatian. In 1756 Andrija Kačić-Miošić, a Dalmatian Franciscan from Makarska, published in Venice ("U Mleci") his *Razgovor ugodni naroda slovinskoga* (*Pleasant Conversation of the Slavic Nation*), his poems about the heroic history and legends of the Slavs; there was a second edition in 1759. Kačić declared his purpose "to praise, extol, and glorify his own nation (*svoj narod*)," to show "the courage in battle and the renowned prowess of their grandfathers." Writing in Dalmatia and publishing in Venice, he intended for the work to return to Dalmatia to reach "the poor peasants and shepherds, those people who can not speak any other language but Slavic."[79] Though Goldoni composed *La Dalmatina* for an urban Venetian audience, most unlikely to consist of shepherds and peasants, in 1758 he did put his play before a public that included a component community of Slavic Dalmatians.

Almost thirty years later, in 1786, Goethe attended a performance in the Teatro San Luca of Goldoni's *Le Baruffe Chiozzotte* (*Chioggian Brawls*), first performed there in 1762. The play concerned the inhabitants of Chioggia, an island fishing town of the Venetian lagoon. The stage representation of the common people of Chioggia made an immense impression upon the audience in 1786, as reported by Goethe: "I have never in my life witnessed such an ecstasy of joy as that shown by the audience when they saw themselves and their families so realistically portrayed on the stage. They shouted with laughter and approval from beginning to end." Such recognition and identification between audience and *dramatis personae* was precisely the theatrical triumph of *La Dalmatina* in 1758 and was, in fact, an essential component of Goldoni's dramatic reform. Goethe further reported that the actresses of 1786 "imitated the voices, gestures, and temperaments of the people with uncanny skill."[80] This talent for popular impersonation evidently also belonged to Caterina Bresciani in 1758, when she "sustained with such spirit and truth the character of the Dalmatian girl that she merited the applause of all, and especially of the Slavs." If for the popular classes it was something unusual to see themselves represented on the stage in Goldoni's play, for the Dalmatians in Venice it was something unprecedented, and their enthusiasm of identification was all the more intense. Just as Goethe witnessed with fascination the ecstatic recognition between the audience and the actors, so the Venetians in the audience in 1758 found their own dramatic experience enhanced by the meta-theatrical encounter between the Dalmatians in the audience and the Dalmatians in the play.

The sentimental connection between Goldoni and his Dalmatian hero, between the hero and the public, between the public and Goldoni, was the Lion in the breast, "il mio Leone in petto," the totemic expression of Venetian patriotism that inspired the whole conception of the drama. The patriotic purpose of the drama was to affirm the common identity of Venetians and Dalmatians, crossing the Adriatic and transcending the cultural barrier between province and metropolis, between Slavs and Italians. Goldoni composed his drama even as the Enlightenment was formulating the difference between Western Europe and Eastern Europe, and in the *Essai sur les moeurs* in 1754 Voltaire lumped together as uncultivated, uninhabited lands "half of Dalmatia, the north of Poland, the shores of the Don, the fertile country of the Ukraine," where one might go "to seek lands in a new universe at the limits of the old one."[81] Voltaire was evidently aware of the *nuovo* and *nuovissimo acquisto* in Dalmatia, on the eve of the Grimani reform, and mentally associated the uncultivated fields of Dalmatia with those of Poland and Ukraine. For Voltaire Dalmatia was a remote land of Eastern Europe, but for Goldoni it was much closer to home, a Mediterranean land, only just across the Adriatic. Goldoni was sensitive to the intimate tensions between Venice and Dalmatia, implicit in their imperial relation, and he pretended, perhaps in exaggeration, that he put himself at some risk of violence in staging his play. If the patriotic identities of Venice and Dalmatia were to be plausibly combined and consolidated on the stage of the Teatro San Luca, perhaps it was strategically essential to offer the sharp contrast of a setting in Morocco, far from the Adriatic shores.

The Valor and Loyalty of the Slavs

From Diedo's and Sandi's histories to Goldoni's drama, across the decade of the 1750s, a transmutation of values revised the representation of the Dalmatian character. The "cruelty of the Slavs" cited by Sandi, and the "ferocious nature" that Diedo deplored, became the "valor of the Slavs" invoked by Goldoni and dramatized on the stage. The Dalmatians were celebrated by Goldoni as a "courageous people" whose courage made them all the more apt to serve as soldiers and sailors for Venice. While Diedo, however, found them rebellious and contumacious in the Middle Ages, Goldoni presented them as paragons of loyalty in the eighteenth century, "loyal and worthy of the Serenissima Repubblica." Yet, ever since Foscarini's speech in 1747, the issue of emigration from Dalmatia made it impossible to take for granted Dalmatian loyalty. Indeed, in 1758, when *La Dalmatina* was performed in Venice, there was an incident of emigration by Orthodox Slavs from Dalmatia to Russia. Furthermore, in that same year, the Venetian government was concerned about foreign recruitment of Dalmatian soldiers: "The Dalmatian nation is too much esteemed, and such troops too eagerly and fondly sought." Two years before, in 1756, an agent of Frederick the Great was arrested and executed by Venice for recruiting Dalmatian soldiers around Verona for the Prussian army. Paolo Preto has suggested that during the eighteenth century Dalmatia was a particular center for the covert foreign recruitment of soldiers, requiring constant surveillance by the Venetian secret services.[82] Russian recruitment was to become especially pressing at the time of the Russian-Ottoman War of 1768 to 1774.

The celebration of Dalmatian loyalty upon the stage surely betrayed some political insecurity on that point. Berengo has remarked upon Dalmatia's relative loyalty, that is, the absence of those municipal autonomous impulses manifested in Venice's Italian dominions, the loyalty by default that characterized a land of underdevelopment. He has argued that class tensions overrode political discontents, "because here the unique and greatest dissent was created not between subjects and government, but rather between nobles and plebeians, between lords and sharecroppers." The Lion of San Marco was the political beneficiary of these internal Dalmatian divisions. "We see thus reinforced and diffused in all of Dalmatia," concludes Berengo, "from the islands to the most godforsaken corner of the hinterland, from the Morlacchi to the nobles of the city, a loyalty to Venice so profound and so undisputed that neither the misappropriations of functionaries, nor the haughtiness of patricians, nor famine and misery could scratch it."[83] It was this almost archaic loyalty of Venice's most miserable and godforsaken subjects that Goldoni sought to dramatize, playing upon its unscratched surface, so that by poetic transmutation such loyalty seemed to acquire the ideological luster of modern patriotism.

At her first appearance, Zandira was commanded to identify herself before the alcaide Ibraim, who held her fate in his hands. Her forthcoming identification, by which she introduced herself to the Venetian public as well as the Moroccan governor, was a matter of birth and blood.

> In illirica terra nacqui, non lo nascondo,
> Ho nelle vene un sangue noto e famoso al mondo.
> Sangue d'illustri eroi, d'eterna gloria erede,
> Che alla sua vita istessa sa preferir la fede . . .

> In Illyrian land I was born, I do not conceal it,
> I have in my veins blood well-known and famous in the world.
> The blood of illustrious heroes, heir to eternal glory,
> That knows to prefer loyalty over even one's own life . . .[84]

Goldoni rhymed *natio splendore* ("native splendor") with *militar valore* ("military valor"), celebrating the Dalmatian character, and Zandira went on to define the Adriatic relation between Dalmatia and Venice. She too attended to the Lion within her own patriotic breast.

Della Dalmazia in seno ho il mio natal sortito
Dove l'adriaco mare bagna pietoso il lito.
Dove goder concede felicitade intera
Il Leon generoso che dolcemente impera.

> Of Dalmatia in my breast I have my natal origin
> Where the Adriatic sea mercifully bathes the shore.
> Where the enjoyment of complete felicity is granted by
> The generous Lion who gently rules.[85]

Thus, the heroine trumpeted her own patriotism and heroism from the moment she stepped on the stage. Her patriotism was a matter of loyalty, her heroism a matter of valor, but these were generic rather than personal virtues, for they flowed through her veins in the blood of the Dalmatian nation. Indeed, the verses seemed to contrast the gentleness and generosity of Venetian imperialism with the military valor of the illustrious Illyrians. Under Goldoni's Venetian pen, however, such emphatic patriotism not only celebrated itself but also proclaimed its complete contentment within the Adriatic empire.

The alcaide Ibraim wanted Zandira to know that he too knew how to rule gently, for when he invited her to join his harem as a special favorite, he insisted that he would not have her against her will:

Ma volontario il cenno vogl'io dal tuo bel core;
Benché in Affrica nato, la tirannia ho in orrore.

> But voluntary the sign I want from your beautiful heart;
> Though in Africa born, I hold tyranny in horror.[86]

She declined, of course, but not out of bigotry, for she was already in love—and therefore she could not accept, "even if a European asked for my hand." Radovich, the Dalmatian hero, arrived in the very next scene. He had come to ransom Zandira, not knowing, of course, that she was already in love with someone else, and he identified himself in phrases that had to sound familiar to the audience.

Son io quel Radovich, il di cui nome è noto
Del mar che Affrica bagna a ogni angolo remoto.
Son d'illirica patria, patria famosa al mondo,
Che di memorie illustri vanta il terren fecondo . . .

> I am that Radovich whose name is well-known
> In every remote corner of the sea that bathes Africa.
> I am of the Illyrian country, a country famous to the world,
> That boasts a fertile terrain of illustrious memories . . .[87]

In fact, the poor terrain of Dalmatia was not producing a good harvest of anything but illustrious memories, even in these years of agricultural optimism immediately following the Grimani reform. That hardly mattered to Radovich, who was certainly no farmer and went on to rhyme *nostro valore* ("our valor") with *Schiavoni han cuore* ("Slavs have heart").[88] No audience could have failed to observe, after these successive scenes, that Zandira and Radovich, Dalmatina and Dalmatino, spoke the same Illyrian language of hyperbolic heroism and irrepressible patriotism.

They both drew upon the same rhetorical reserve, and, in a striking convergence, they both insisted upon the fame of their nation, famous beyond the Adriatic, supposedly celebrated in every remote corner of the Mediterranean. Goldoni's dramatic genius was, above all, a genius for comedy, and there were perhaps some elements of comic inflection that entered into his rhetorical rendering of Dalmatian patriotism. Radovich and Zandira appear almost as cartoons of national virtue, and the dual audience at the Teatro San Luca in 1758, Venetian and Dalmatian, may have appreciated the drama from slightly different perspectives. Goldoni allowed for an ungenerous element of imperial irony on the part of the Venetians, even regarding the extravagant loyalty of the Dalmatians to Venice itself.

The potential for comedy in patriotic rhetoric was realized as soon as Zandira and Radovich were brought face to face, for his offer to ransom her—"to lead you back to the port of your country"—was rather ungraciously deflected in the very name of Dalmatian patriotism. Zandira, secretly in love, protested that she would rather remain a captive in Morocco, so that "valorous men" of Dalmatia might be ransomed instead of an "unwarlike woman." She would eventually give the lie to her own modest idea of unwarlike womanhood when, in the fourth act, she picked up an axe and challenged the Barbary pirate Ali, who wanted her for his own harem: "Barbarian, surrender your weapon, or I will kill you by my own hand."[89] For the moment, her rhetorical patriotism hid her secret motive.

Zandira was in love with one of her fellow captives, Lisauro, whom Goldoni described as a "perfidious" Greek. Lisauro, however, knew that Zandira could never love a Greek, and, therefore, "forewarned of the national aversion of the Dalmatians for the Greeks, announced himself as a citizen of the town of Spalato."[90] He was therefore a pretend Dalmatian, and, as soon as he appeared on the stage, he too had to declare his Dalmatian identity. "It suits me to pretend (*fingere*)," he commented to himself, for the benefit of the audience, before addressing Radovich:

> Signore, ho anch'io l'onore d'esser di tua nazione,
> Spalatro è la mia patria, civil mia condizione;
> Nel militar mestiere fu noto il padre mio,
> Stiepo Calabrovich; son militare anch'io.

>> Signore, I too have the honor of being of your nation.
>> Spalatro is my country, civil my condition;
>> My father was well-known in the military trade,
>> Stiepo Calabrovich; I too am a soldier.[91]

As soon as he spoke, one of the Moroccans commented quietly, "Bravo, he pretends to be a Slav, but I know he is a Greek."[92] Goldoni thus signaled the audience that they were witnessing a false performance of patriotism, and he underlined the theatrical nature of that performance with an ironically appreciative *bravo*. The dramatist recognized that patriotism could be cartooned with a few rhetorical phrases, and therefore it could be altogether dissimulated. After all, Lisauro's invention of himself as a Dalmatian was closely related to Goldoni's dramatic invention of the "true" Dalmatians, Radovich and Zandira. He had only to write the lines and leave them to the performers—like Caterina Bresciani, an Italian actress playing a Dalmatian role. She had already appeared for Goldoni in Persian persona in *La Sposa Persiana*, declaiming beautifully in her native Florentine accent.[93] If the great performance of *La Dalmatina* was that of Bresciani, representing the Dalmatian character before an audience of Slavs in Venice, the performance within the performance was that of Lisauro, impersonating a Dalmatian soldier in Morocco—also declaiming in Italian. Just as Goldoni understood that Dalmatian identity could be employed as a dramatic property, he recognized that patriotism could be both pretended and performed.

Lisauro invented for himself a Slavic father, named Stiepo Calabrovich, not only Dalmatian but a military hero—even well-known, *noto,* like Radovich himself. Evidently, Goldoni's sense of humor made every invented Dalmatian hero into a famous invented hero; each cherished the conviction of his own celebrity and of the collective celebrity of that somewhat obscure nation. Radovich, seeking to confirm Lisauro's Dalmatian character, could only think to ask, "Do you know who I am?" Lisauro readily replied:

> Conosco de' Radovicci il nome;
> So che i marziali allori ti coronar le chiome.
>
> I know the name of the Radovich family;
> I know that martial laurels crown your locks.[94]

Thus did the Dalmatians recognize each other, by testifying to each other's fame. Radovich now could hardly claim that he had never heard of Stiepo Calabrovich, and one of the Moroccans commented about Lisauro, "He's a perfect flatterer."[95] Goldoni showed himself aware that patriotism was not only susceptible to pretense but also to flattery. Indeed the dramatic complications of the play depended upon the premise that Dalmatian passions were easily misdirected. Eventually, the resolution required that Zandira recognize Lisauro's deception, that she discover true Dalmatian romance in Radovich, and that they both acknowledge the true object of their Dalmatian patriotism, which could only be the Lion of Venice. Goldoni seemed to suggest that the Dalmatians, for all their loyalty and all their valor, might not be altogether reliable as imperial subjects unless their patriotic passions were attentively monitored and artfully directed.

Conclusion: The True Glory of Europe

Goldoni's Dalmatian girl was far from home, her declamations of identity all the more emphatic in the alien context of African Barbary. The Dalmatian drama was meant to be exotic, related to Goldoni's Persian and Peruvian confections, and therefore could hardly be located in a familiar Venetian setting; yet, Dalmatia itself, just across the Adriatic, was perhaps not quite exotic enough as a setting for the Dalmatians, who were therefore dramatically displaced to remote Morocco. Dalmatia, the ostensible subject of the drama, was scenographically effaced in the complex play of Mediterranean perspectives, present only in the hearts of the hero and heroine, like the Lion of Venice that Radovich also carried with him wherever he went: "Ho la mia patria in core, ho il mio Leone in petto." ("I have my country in my heart, my Lion in my breast.")[96] This was the patriotic identity of a seafaring hero, representative of a maritime nation,

and Goldoni allowed himself the liberty of activating his Dalmatian any-
where at all on the Mediterranean. Yet, the formula of "la mia patria in
core"—the country in the heart—also corresponded to the modern idea
of patriotism, which Rousseau consolidated for the Enlightenment in his
Considerations on Poland in 1771, prescribing national survival through
the injunction "to establish the Republic in the heart of the Poles."[97]
The heart's encapsulation of Dalmatian identity not only allowed it to
endure within the Venetian empire, but also enabled it to achieve dramatic expression in a remote Moroccan setting and to proclaim itself
upon the stage of the Teatro San Luca.

When Lisauro was finally forced to reveal himself as a Greek, not a
Dalmatian after all, Radovich denounced the masquerade as an offense
against nationhood:

> Perfido! se mentire il tuo natal pretendi,
> La mia nazion tradisci, la tua nazione offendi.
>
> Perfidious! if you pretend to lie about your birthplace,
> You betray my nation and offend your nation.[98]

This notion of national apostasy as the ultimate betrayal and dishonor
perfectly fit the patriotic agenda that Goldoni pursued from the moment
the Dalmatians stepped on stage and declared their identity. Dalmatians,
Africans, even Greeks had to wrestle with their national reputations when
they encountered each other in the course of the drama. Patriotism became a matter of performance, of representing the nation on an international stage, and Goldoni dramatized the issue accordingly.

Venice, however, was represented as an Adriatic empire of several nations, and its imperial identity transcended the rivalries of its national
components. When Lisauro revealed his true birthplace to be the Ionian
island of Zante, ruled by Venice, Radovich was immediately ready to for-
give all:

> L'isola fortunata ne' lidi suoi felici
> Dell'Adriatico Impero gode qual noi gli auspici.
> Vanne, in te del mio Principe un suddito rispetto;
> Ho la mia patria in core, ho il mio Leone in petto.
>
> The fortunate island within its happy shores
> Enjoys like us the auspices of the Adriatic Empire.
> Go, I respect in you a subject of my prince;
> I have my country in my heart, my Lion in my breast.[99]

The capacity of the patriotic breast was demonstrated as Radovich made room in his own to include even his rival, the perfidious Greek. The sovereignty of Venice was the solvent that reconciled the hearts of nations, transmuting elements of patriotism even as it called into question the political purposes of patriotic identity. Subjects of Venice, "they are all my brothers," declared Radovich in the concluding scene, and the final line of the play was Zandira's tribute to "the fortunate peoples of the Adriatic empire." In such a drama there was obviously no place for Gozzi's comic impersonation of Luce, not only because Gozzi was insufficiently sympathetic, but above all because Luce was miserable and unfortunate.

As the Dalmatians prepared to return to the shores of the Adriatic, Radovich had one last mission in Morocco:

> Pria di spiegar le vele verso il paterno tetto,
> Tutti i schiavi europei di riscattar prometto.

> Before unfurling the sails for the paternal roof,
> I promise to redeem all the European slaves.[100]

As for Zandira, she had only to make clear that she had transferred her affections to Radovich—despising Lisauro now as someone "unworthy to vaunt the name of my country"—and she too was ready to depart:

> Deh Radovich pietoso, che nel mio amor confidi,
> Partiam da queste arene, torniamo ai patrii lidi.

> Merciful Radovich, who trusts in my love,
> Let us depart from these arenas, let us return to the shores of our country.[101]

From the perspective of Morocco the shores of the Adriatic were reasonably remote, and it was unnecessary to distinguish between the western and eastern shores; from far away, Venice and Dalmatia appeared to be very close to one another.

The Dalmatian hero in Morocco represented not only his nation and his empire, but all of Europe, and so Radovich, before leaving Africa, redeemed all the European slaves. Zandira, apostrophizing him, recognized the multiple dimensions of his heroism:

> Ah si, del suol illirico e dell'Europa intera
> Sei, Radovich, l'esempio, tu sei la gloria vera.

> Ah yes, of Illyrian soil and of all Europe
> You, Radovich, are the exemplar, the true glory.[102]

None of the characters in this play ever set foot on the soil of Illyria or the soil of Europe. In fact the glory of the Dalmatians, in Goldoni's conception, was altogether abstracted from the soil—that poor and unproductive soil that frustrated agricultural reform in the 1750s in Dalmatia. Goldoni did not follow the Dalmatians home to their paternal roofs, did not represent their living conditions on stage. In the 1770s Alberto Fortis's scientific expedition to Dalmatia would study, and present to the public of Venice, the backwardness of the Morlacchi. Goldoni wrote about his characters as Dalmatini, never as Morlacchi; for him they were familiar provincial subjects rather than strangely primitive aliens. Conscious as he surely was of the obvious phonological relations between barbarians and men of Barbary (*barbari, barbareschi*) and between slaves and Slavs (*schiavi, schiavoni*), he may have preferred to avoid the near rhyming resemblance between Morlacco and Morocco.

For Goldoni the Dalmatians constituted a nation, one of the constituent nations of the Adriatic empire: "you betray my nation and offend your nation," declared the heroic Dalmatian to the perfidious Greek. Yet, Goldoni's vocabulary of nationality was not rigorous or precise. He casually called his hero and heroine Dalmatians (*Dalmatini*), Illyrians (*Illirici*), or Slavs (*Schiavoni*), depending upon the meter of the verse. Grabovac in 1747 was similarly undecided when he wrote about the "Illyrian or Croatian" nation, while Kačić in 1756 paid tribute to the "Slavic" nation of peasants and shepherds. If the nation is an imagined community, as Benedict Anderson has proposed, it evolves according to the imagination of its members, and, at the same time, it responds to the formulas of foreign ascription. Goldoni practiced a dramatic art of imaginative ascription when he celebrated the Dalmatian nation by writing the lines of nationally articulate Dalmatians. Even when he denominated the Dalmatians as Slavs, he never indicated a national affiliation with lands beyond the sovereignty of Venice. He also never mentioned the religious allegiance of his Dalmatians, Catholic or Orthodox, for in the Moroccan context it was enough to know that they were Christians. Goldoni could not accept the religious perspective of the *Illyricum Sacrum,* which seemed to value Dalmatian devotion to Rome over political loyalty to Venice; neither could he consider the case of Orthodox Dalmatians, with their complicating religious affiliations to Serbs, Russians, and Greeks. The ecumenicism of the Enlightenment offered the ideological background for Goldoni's staging of Dalmatian national identity within the political boundaries of the Adriatic empire. At the mid-eighteenth-century moment of unformed and unassorted identities, Venetian statesmen, officials, historians, and dramatists could still aspire to the ascription of an imperial Adriatic allegiance to the Slavs of Dalmatia.

Gozzi, remembering Dalmatia in the 1740s, noted "the rivalry of courage between the Italian nation and the Illyrian nation," which often provoked "ugly dangers." His own performance as a Dalmatian servant girl was delicately attuned to the rivalry between those nations, dramatically confronting and comically disarming the inevitable tensions. Goldoni in the 1750s preferred to avoid the dangers and evade the rivalry, by eliminating both Italian characters and Dalmatian settings from his drama. The Dalmatians could only engage in rivalry with the Africans, while Italian actors and actresses represented both sides of the encounter. Goldoni dissolved the difference between Dalmatians and Venetians, and in the end Radovich became the exemplar of an even more general idea, representing the true glory of Europe. It is safe to say that such a signification would have seemed rather strange on the stages of almost any other city of Europe in the 1750s, but in Venice Goldoni's public could have considered the thesis with a complex measure of interest and irony. The patriotic public that the playwright invoked in the dedication was defined in relation to the piazzas of Venice, the municipal space that mediated between the provincial soil of Illyria and the continental mass of Europe. Goldoni, deploying the language of the Enlightenment to reformulate the values of the Venetian Renaissance, proposed an imperial hierarchy of intricately related patriotic sentiments, dramatizing the valor of the Slavs of Dalmatia the better to define Venice's Adriatic perspective on Europe.

In 1792, a new edition of Goldoni's plays, published by Antonio Zatta in Venice, featured *La Dalmatina* with elegant illustrations. In the battle scene, beneath palm trees, the Dalmatians appeared fully European with tail coats and tricornered hats, while their Oriental enemies had turbans, and long moustaches, which some Venetians, like Gozzi and Vallaresso, once considered characteristic of Dalmatians. Representing the true glory of Europe, Radovich, in the final scene, wore a waistcoat, knee breeches, and buckled shoes, in striking contrast to the robes, slippers, and turbans of the Moroccan men.[103] Thus, over the course of a genera-

FIGURE 4.   "La Dalmatina, Atto IV." Illustration for the fourth act of *La Dalmatina,* from Carlo Goldoni, *Opere Teatrali,* published in Venice by Antonio Zatta in 1792. In this image from Goldoni's drama, from an edition that appeared a full generation after the play was first performed in 1758, the Dalmatians, in fully European costume, fight for the "true glory" of Europe against their Oriental Islamic opponents. *(By permission of the O'Neill Library, Boston College.)*

tion, from 1758 to 1792, the European aspect of Goldoni's Dalmatians became even more vivid.

In 1793 there was published in Venice a play by Giovanni Greppi, probably recently performed, entitled *The Dalmatian Hero* (*L'Eroe dalmate*) and subtitled "Aurangzebbe, King of Siam." The hero happened to find himself in Siam, rather than Morocco, illustrating an even more emphatic encounter between Dalmatia and the Orient. Marcovich, the captain of a Dalmatian ship, was the only model of manly virtue to

FIGURE 5. "La Dalmatina, Atto V." Illustration for the fifth act of *La Dalmatina*, from Carlo Goldoni, *Opere Teatrali,* published in Venice by Antonio Zatta in 1792. Wearing a bonnet and a tricornered hat, Zandira and Radovich represent Adriatic Europe to the extravagantly turbaned figures of Oriental Barbary. They have vindicated Dalmatian virtue and stand ready to return to their native Adriatic shores. *(By permission of the O'Neill Library, Boston College.)*

appear on the stage in a scenario of Siamese treachery. He lectured to the Siamese on the duty of defending one's country, and demonstratively saluted the flag of San Marco.

> Dell augusto mio Principe il vessillo
> Glorioso, e temuto, il di cui prezzo
> É la salda, ed immobile mia fede,
> Che in faccia a morte sostener saprei.

> The flag of my august prince,
> Glorious and feared, whose value
> Is my firm and immobile loyalty,
> Which I would know how to sustain in the face of death.[104]

Like Radovich a generation earlier in Morocco, now Marcovich upheld in Siam the same principles of Dalmatian patriotism and supreme loyalty to Venice. In the 1790s, the final decade of the Serenissima Repubblica, dramatic Dalmatian heroes had to travel even further afield to affirm their devotion to Venice and to represent the true glory of Europe.

> Né obblio giammai, che nacqui in fortunate
> Terre soggette all'immortal Leone . . .

> I will never forget that I was born in the fortunate
> Lands subject to the immortal Lion . . .[105]

In Greppi's long forgotten play, Venice witnessed, once more, a dramatic vision of the Adriatic empire, the home of fortunate lands and peoples, including especially Dalmatia and the Dalmatians.

CHAPTER TWO

The Useful or Curious Products of Dalmatia: From Natural History to National Economy

Introduction: Adriatic Expeditions

In 1770 the Russian fleet of Catherine the Great completed its circumnavigation of the continent of Europe, to arrive in the eastern Mediterranean, opening a new naval campaign in the ongoing war against the Ottoman empire. Such a dramatic deployment of the fleet created a sensation throughout Europe; Catherine wrote to Voltaire that it would be "a new spectacle this fleet in the Mediterranean," and Voltaire wrote to Catherine that the enterprise was the greatest since Hannibal. In Venice, the journalistic account of the year 1769, *Storia dell'Anno*, remarked on "the difficulty of sailing so far" and "the boldness of the enterprise," provoking "disbelief" so that some "considered it an imaginary or a fabulous event."[1] By 1770 it was no longer possible to disbelieve, and though the principal action of the campaign was in the Aegean, the appearance of some Russian ships in the Adriatic was of particular concern to Venice.

Control of the Adriatic had once meant that Venice refused to allow armed foreign ships to enter, but such claims could no longer be enforced even at the beginning of the eighteenth century. A Russian presence in the Adriatic in 1770 was alarming for more particular reasons. Catherine's manifesto to the Orthodox subjects of the Ottoman empire promised liberation, and she especially encouraged a Greek uprising. This, in turn, produced sympathetic unrest among the Greeks of the Venetian Ionian islands, such as Corfu, Cephalonia, and Lisauro's Zante. At the same time Russian recruitment and mobilization extended along the eastern coast of the Adriatic, appealing to the Orthodox part of the Slavic population of Dalmatia. In 1772 the Provveditore Generale in Dalmatia, Giacomo Da Riva, recorded concern about "the secret seduction of subjects for the service of Russia." The contemporary Venetian account of the war, *Storia della guerra presente,* remarked that for Italian states, "as the closest ones (*come piu prossimi*) to the military expeditions of Russia," it was necessary to bring "all their attention to having their subjects respected." Furthermore, during the period of the war, which was also a time of famine in Dalmatia, there were disturbing incidents of emigration from the province into the neighboring states.[2] From the Venetian perspective, the complications of war threatened to create unrest even among the most supposedly loyal subjects, Goldoni's Dalmatians. In this same context, in 1770, Zaccaria Vallaresso's *Baiamonte Tiepolo in Schiavonia,* the epic poem about medieval insurrection in Dalmatia, was finally published, decades after it was composed.

In 1770, at this moment of elevated Venetian sensitivity, Alberto Fortis crossed the Adriatic to inaugurate the enlightened discovery of Dalmatia with an exploration of the island of Cres. In 1774, the year of the Russian-Ottoman treaty that concluded the war, Fortis published in Venice the full account of his travels, *Viaggio in Dalmazia.* This was followed by German and French translations published in Switzerland, in 1776 and 1778 respectively. Also in 1778, there appeared in London the English translation, *Travels into Dalmatia: Containing General Observations on the Natural History of that Country and the Neighboring Islands; the Natural Productions, Arts, Manners and Customs of the Inhabitants.* In 1758 Goldoni had declined to represent the Dalmatians in the natural setting of Dalmatia, displacing his hero and heroine across the Mediterranean to exotic Morocco. He made the Dalmatians, but not Dalmatia, the subject of his dramatic study. Fortis, however, offered a detailed description of Dalmatia not only to the public of Venice but also to a broader European audience of the Enlightenment, and he scrupulously studied the "inhabitants," especially the Morlacchi, in the context of their Dalmatian environment.

Fortis's expeditions to Dalmatia occurred in the context of Venetian neutrality during the Russian-Ottoman war, and public interest was conditioned by heightened concerns over the loyalty and security of the province. Stimulated by these concerns, Fortis formulated a modern ideology of empire to emphasize the significance of Venetian rule in Dalmatia. His own network of scientific and political patronage was invoked within the book to recommend the importance of Dalmatia to the

Venetian government and the European Enlightenment. His researches in natural history were applied to a vision of imperial economy, while his attention to natural specimens, classical ruins, and fossil remains became the basis for an appeal to enlightened Venetian connoisseurs. The resources of Dalmatia, its "useful or curious products," were both scientifically collectible and economically exploitable according to Fortis's sense of enlightened imperial mission, formulated on behalf of the Republic of Venice and the Republic of Letters. The Adriatic empire could no longer be merely rhetorically represented by such poetic Goldonian formulas as "the glorious name of the Venetians" and the "valor of the Slavs." Fortis proposed not only to reform the administration of the province, as Foscarini recommended in the previous generation, but also, more philosophically, "to reform the ideas" about Dalmatia that prevailed in Venice.[3] Foscarini in 1747 seized upon Dalmatia as the occasion for investigating Venice's contemporary political condition; Goldoni in 1758 chose his Dalmatian heroine as a dramatic subject suitable for presenting the Adriatic empire to the Venetian public. Fortis in 1774 managed to discover in Dalmatia a cultural correlation between Venice's imperial preoccupations and the philosophical concerns of the Enlightenment throughout Europe.

Venetian Neutrality, Adriatic Turbulence, and Caminer's History

Domenico Condulmer came to Zadar as Provveditore Generale in 1768, the year that the Russian-Ottoman war began; in addition to his regular dispatches to the Senate, he also maintained an occasional correspondence with the State Inquisitors concerning matters of security. In 1768 accounts from Kotor, the administrative center of Venetian Albania, reported unrest in neighboring Montenegro, where an impostor Stephen Mali was claiming to be the Russian Tsar Peter III (who was actually killed in 1762 when Catherine, his wife, seized the Russian throne). Venice received warning about the possibility of related unrest in its own trans-Adriatic territories, since "the populations, unfortunately ill-disposed by recent turbulences and revolutions, could become even more alienated." Condulmer wrote to the State Inquisitors in 1769 about Catherine's manifesto, which appealed to Orthodox Slavs and Greeks to fight on her behalf against the Ottomans. "If this incitement should spread, agitations would increase," worried Condulmer, and those agitations might affect Dalmatia, with its "numerous subjects conforming to the Serbian rite, and maybe of a not dissimilar character, ferocious by nature and in such proximity to the borders of Bosnia."[4] At the Dalmatian-Bosnian border, the neutral Venetian republic adjoined the belligerent Ottoman empire. Orthodox Dalmatians of the *nuovo* and *nuovissimo acquisto* had been formerly Ottoman subjects, religiously ruled by the Serbian patriarchate, and throughout the eighteenth century Venice resisted the hierarchical claims of that patriarchate regarding Dalmatia, for fear of foreign influence over Venetian subjects. As much as a fifth of the population of Dalmatia was Orthodox—of the Serbian rite—and in spite of Venetian neutrality, this religious minority was susceptible to Catherine's call for a war of Orthodox liberation.

With the coming of war, Venice could not help being concerned about agitation, alienation, and turbulence in Dalmatia. Condulmer wrote to the State Inquisitors in 1769, further confirming their apprehensions: "It was almost impossible that the universal revolt of the peoples of Montenegro in favor of Russia should not have provoked also within the Republic some troublesome humor, considering the proximity, the character of the mixed interests, and the uniformity of rite between this nation and that nation."[5] The problem of disaffected Orthodox subjects was evidently upsetting to Condulmer, and his excessive reactions revealed the measure of his anxiety. In 1769, at the time of the election of Pope Clement XIV, the apostolic nuncio in Venice, Bernardino Honorati, was gratified to hear that Condulmer had punished "those Greeks refusing to join the official celebrations for the most felicitous exaltation of Our Lord." Condulmer was reported to have gone so far as to "oblige them by force, having put many of the chiefs in chains." Those "Greeks" were Orthodox Slavs, and Venice was as sensitive as Rome to their Orthodox and Slavic affinities; the nuncio reported, later in 1769, the rumor from Dalmatia "that Venetian villages and communities, adjoining Montenegro, are in a great ferment of rebellion against the government."[6] The research of Paolo Preto has shown that the secret services of the Republic were especially active in Dalmatia in the eighteenth century and that Venetian spies attentively monitored agitations along the borders of the province in the 1760s.[7] The outbreak of the Russian-Ottoman war, followed by the arrival of the Russian fleet in the Mediterranean, provoked evident unrest in Venetian Dalmatia and serious Adriatic apprehensions in Venice itself.

Franco Venturi has argued that the "first crisis" of the *ancien régime* and the origins of its collapse "are to be sought not in the great capitals of the West, in Paris and London, or in the heartland of Europe, in Vienna and Berlin, but on the margins of the continent, in unexpected and peripheral places." Venturi, in fact, began his own account with Catherine reviewing the fleet that was about to depart upon the Mediterranean expedition, while her representative in Venice, Pano Maruzzi, awaited the eventual arrival as the prinicipal agent of military and political preparation for an unprecedented campaign. In addition to encouraging the Greek revolt, Catherine intended to take advantage of anti-Ottoman sentiment among the Slavs of southeastern Europe; Nikita Panin, as minister of foreign affairs, wrote to Maruzzi as early as 1768, to mention "on the frontiers of Dalmatia, near the border of the Montenegrins, little stores of munitions and provisions that could be seized and used against the Turks." Venetian neutrality was the major obstacle to such a scheme, but, clearly, from St. Petersburg the frontiers of Dalmatia already appeared as one of those "peripheral places," where little stores of powder could pay off in significant political explosions. Dalmatian sailors, moreover, could be found in many ports of the Mediterranean, and in 1769 Russian agents successfully recruited in Livorno some Slavic deserters from the Venetian navy.[8] Such desertion was a blow to the Goldonian ideal of the loyal Dalmatian sailor.

The anticipated arrival of the Russian fleet in the Adriatic created a Dalmatian dilemma for Venetian neutrality. The Russians would want to provision their ships in Venice's Dalmatian ports. The papal nuncio in Venice, Honorati, hoped to learn the contents of official reports from Dalmatia in order to appreciate properly the Adriatic crisis and inform the Vatican about the Venetians: "Here they preserve deep mystery so as to keep their intentions secret and to conceal the news they receive from the Provveditore Generale of Dalmatia."[9] He had no doubt that the most pertinent information concerning the arrival of the Russians in the Adriatic depended upon the dispatches from Dalmatia. The gazettes of Italy, in 1769, were aware that the Russian naval presence meant "Dalmatia could become a theater of war." Honorati kept an eye on the Arsenal, where Venice refurbished its own Adriatic fleet, and he reported to Rome in 1770 that five Venetian galleys were "ready to set out for the waters of Dalmatia." He knew that Venetian neutrality would be tested in those waters, according to the showing of "the Venetian fleet which was to be put in order so as to render respectable the neutrality of this Republic between the Ottoman Porte and Muscovy."[10] Venice dispatched its galleys to Dalmatia not to fight, but to keep from fighting.

"Let's go, Venetians," wrote Voltaire in 1769, in a letter to Catherine, "equip your vessels, help the heroine of Europe." By May 1770 he was somewhat sarcastic about Venice's persistent neutrality, writing to Catherine that "as for the Venetians, they will play your game, but only when you have already won the contest." In August he reported, "I still have little attacks of fever when I see that the Venetians are not deciding," and in September he declared, "I do not love the Venetians, who wait so long to make themselves Greeks."[11] Venice, however, after having gone to war against the Ottomans so many times in past centuries, this time judged that there was more to be lost than gained. It was not only a matter of maintaining relations with the sultan, but also of resisting the insurrectionary forces that Russia sought to provoke in the Mediterranean; the Venetians could never make themselves Greeks, for the Greek uprising was already causing unrest on the Ionian islands of Venice's own Adriatic empire. Nevertheless, Venturi's research suggests that through Maruzzi's operations "a large part of the Russian armament around Greece was controlled from Venice," while Russian agents also engaged in the "recruitment of Slavs and Greeks, without paying much attention to whether they were Turkish or Venetian subjects."[12] Such inattention was thoroughly subversive of Venetian sovereignty. At the same time the common recruitment of Slavs and Greeks underlined their potential relation to each other, and thus undermined their respective allegiances to Venice. Goldoni represented Slavs and Greeks as mutually antipathetic, but also recognized a certain affinity inasmuch as a Greek could pass for a Slav. For the purposes of Russian recruitment in 1770, Greekness was not only a national but also a religious quality, justifying a joint appeal to Greeks and Slavs in the name of Orthodoxy. Though the Venetians could not make themselves Greeks, even to please Voltaire, the Slavs of Dalmatia lived along a slippery slope of uncertain identity and allegiance. Goldoni's rhetorical resolution of the paradoxes of Dalmatian patriotism began to come undone with the arrival of the Russian fleet in the Adriatic.

Voltaire cheered for Russia from Ferney, but there was also support for Russia within Venice. A Greek publisher in Venice, Demetrio Teodosio, published in 1772 a celebratory book about Peter the Great, written "in the Slavic language," probably intended for Dalmatian readers. In 1773 there was published in Venice an Italian translation of a French tribute to Catherine, *Elogio di Catterina II*, in honor of her military victories; the French author was Ange Goudar, who resided in Venice, while the translator was the enlightened Venetian economist Francesco Griselini.[13] Thus, enthusiasm for Russia came from Greeks and Slavs who were subjects of the Venetian republic and from French and Italian members of the enlightened Republic of Letters.

Venturi has followed the crises of the old regime through the public record of eighteenth-century Italian journalism, arguing for the historical importance of that particular perspective on the news of the day. Venetian news was especially attentive to the issues and ramifications of the Russian-Ottoman war, and Venice's perspective was defined by the factors of geographical proximity, diplomatic neutrality, political susceptibility, ideological engagement, and generally sophisticated standards of journalism. News of the war in the eastern Mediterranean was often first received in Venice for transmission around the rest of Europe, so that Voltaire at Ferney reported to Catherine in St. Petersburg in 1770, "The most recent letters from Venice say . . ." In Venice itself such news engaged the concerns of an emerging modern public, nourished on an evolving sphere of journalism. News was received and assimilated so promptly that in 1770 there appeared a publication of ambiguous genre, combining the journalistic imperatives of the gazettes with the philosophical commitment to universal history. This was the *Storia della guerra presente*, of which the first volumes were already published in Venice in 1770, two years after the outbreak of the war, in an "edition adorned with geographical maps, portraits, and the plans of fortresses." In 1776, two years after the conclusion of the war, the work was republished in a complete edition as the history of the conflict just concluded, *Storia della ultima guerra*. The very contemporary nature of the work was also appreciated elsewhere, and the 1770 edition in Venice was quickly followed by an edition in Naples in 1771, as well as the German translation that also began to appear in 1771; this last was so rapidly brought to press as to cause some uncertainty over which was the original and which the translation.[14]

The *Storia della guerra presente* was published anonymously, but the author has been identified as Domenico Caminer, a leading figure of the Venetian Enlightenment. As a young man in the 1750s he tried to write comedies in the manner of Goldoni, whom he much admired, but in the 1760s Caminer turned to journalism and began to make his mark on its modern development in Venice. In 1762 he was involved in editing a Venetian gazette; in 1763 he conceived of a new journal to be called *Curiosità*, which failed to get off the ground in spite of Goldoni's encouragment: "I too would like to be able to contribute to your pages some curiosities."[15] For three months in 1765 he published Venice's first daily newspaper, *Diario veneto*. In 1768, working together with his seventeen-year-old daughter Elisabetta and with the enlightened abbé Alberto Fortis, Caminer launched the literary monthly, *Europa Letteraria*. The first issue included an extract from Voltaire's *Princesse de Babylone*, only just published in French, a token of Caminer's intention to keep the public of Venice up to date in the literary affairs of the Enlightenment.[16] For Caminer, *Europa Letteraria*, intitiated in the same year that the war began, proceeded on a parallel track to that of the *Storia della guerra presente*. The extracts and reviews from the world of the Enlightenment seemed to belong to a separate journalistic sphere from that of the dispatches and reports from the various fronts of the Russian-Ottoman war.

The tenth volume of the *Storia della guerra presente* commenced with the heading, "Fermentazione generale della Europa," and anxiously reflected upon the ominous political ramifications of war in every country, inasmuch as "fervid fermentation" could lead to the most dangerous consequences. Caminer went on to describe "discord" in Poland and "tumult" in Turkey. There were even "perturbations" in Ragusa on the eastern Adriatic coast, for the Ragusans were resisting heavy pressure from Russia to abandon their neutrality in the war, while paying large sums in Constantinople to preserve their eastern commerce. Venetians might take some rivalrous satisfaction in the predicament of Ragusa, but above all they had to recognize their parallel position with its consequent perturbations. Caminer, however, declined to make the parallel explicit, and when he came to speak of Venice it appeared as the most placid lagoon in such a sea of fermentations. The Serenissima Repubblica, he wrote, "pursued the fulfillment of its wise decrees on the regulation of religious orders, and made in this time a most curious and interesting discovery in Dalmatia." There at Salona a peasant, while working in the fields, had accidentally come upon an underground opening that led to a subterranean Roman ruin, perhaps public baths, "marvelous" especially for the quantity of columns.[17] Such a story hardly fit into an account of fermentations and perturbations, and emphasized all the more clearly the purposeful effacement of Venice within the framework of Caminer's history. At the same time, the author permitted his readers to palpate discreetly that sensitive and vulnerable region of the republican body and to hope devoutly that nothing more disturbing than Roman ruins lay lurking beneath the provincial surface.

Though Venetian anxieties about Dalmatia were not openly aired in Caminer's account of the Russian-Ottoman war, there occurred at this time not just discoveries in Dalmatia, but really the discovery of Dalmatia itself on behalf of the public of Venice. In 1770, the same year that Russian ships appeared in the Adriatic, Alberto Fortis crossed the Adriatic from Venice to undertake the century's most comprehensive scientific exploration of Dalmatia. In 1768 Fortis was Caminer's collaborator on *Europa Letteraria,* his fellow philosophe in the forefront of Venice's Enlightenment; in 1769 Fortis was jettisoned from the journal, judged by Caminer as too outspoken in print: "I am tired of blushing over the inopportune things that he introduces without saying a word about them to me."[18] Fortis, as an eighteenth-century priest, was particularly anti-clerical, too irreverent for the cautious policy of Caminer, who also worried about such an influence on his precociously intellectual daughter. After the end of the collaboration, each man invested his enlightened efforts during these years in dramatically different but plausibly complementary concerns. While Caminer's work of contemporary history ranged over the map of Europe, analyzing the causes and consequences of war in every state except Venice, Fortis ignored the war almost completely to compose a work of natural history that would illuminate every angle of the most misunderstood province in Venice's vulnerable empire.

Foreign Personages and Venetian Patricians

Fortis's work was structured on an elaborate scaffolding of multiple dedications, so that every aspect and district of Dalmatia seemed to be assigned to an honorary sponsor from either the Republic of Venice or else the Republic of Letters at large. This notably contrasted with the ecclesiastical courtesies of Farlati's *Illyricum Sacrum* in the 1750s and 1760s, whose various volumes concerning different Dalmatian dioceses were dedicated to reigning Roman pontiffs. For Fortis in the 1770s, the accumulation of dedications not only recognized enlightened patronage received in the course of his researches, but also commended Dalmatia to the specific attention of eminent men who might otherwise overlook its newly enhanced scientific significance. At the same time, the reading public of Venice, taking up the book, discovered Dalmatia as a subject of national urgency and international erudition; the province was explored and explicated in correspondence between the author and his learned circle of friends and patrons, designated in the dedications. Publishing the book in 1774, the year of the peace, when Dalmatia was no longer a site of concern for Ottoman incursion or Russian subversion, Fortis proposed to Venice a revised imperial ideology, not just a matter of administrative imposition, but also a project of scientific exploration. Witnessed by the intellectual authorities of the Enlightenment, as invoked in the dedications, Fortis's work made Dalmatia into an operational domain of modern imperial discourse.

In 1774 *Viaggio in Dalmazia* appeared before the Venetian public at a moment full of promise for enlightened reform. Proposals for the economic reform of the "corporations" were under consideration, aimed at the privileges and monopolies that frustrated economic development, and the possibility of political reform, raised in the "correction" of 1774, seemed more serious than at any time since the crisis of 1761. Controversy encompassed a wide range of matters from postal services and gambling casinos to the fundamental financial and constitutional procedures of the Republic. In fact, both the economic and political impulses toward reform would give way to more conservative currents in 1775, but Fortis in 1774 addressed the patriciate and the public in a spirit of enlightened enthusiasm. He commenced with Venetian obeisances, naming three most illustrious and most excellent senators, Andrea Quirini, Girolamo Grimani, Sebastiano Foscarini; these worthies were the Riformatori of the University of Padua. The Riformatori, chosen by the Maggior Consiglio in Venice, constituted a supervisory body for the university, playing an important part in choosing professors and also in censoring publications. Fortis was himself Paduan by birth, the most proximate and least exotic sort of provincial subject under the rule of the Republic, and he hoped to be rewarded for his work on Dalmatia with an academic chair at the university in his native city. Because the Venetian patriciate served in such an elective variety of political positions, it was no mere coincidence that all three illustrious senators came from families whose names were already associated with government in Dalmatia in the eighteenth century. Fortis moved on immediately to another acknowledgment: "I had already glanced over part of Dalmatia, profiting by the learned company of a most notable foreign personage *(Personaggio Straniero)*, and I was getting ready to pass into more remote regions, pressed by the desire to acquire new lights, when the elevated genius of the most generous senator Giovanni Ruzzini fervidly promoted my second expedition into that kingdom, following the much repeated and sustained example of the most enlightened sovereigns of our age." For Fortis, it was not just the sponsorship of science in general, but the scientific challenge of Dalmatia in particular, that became the measure of the Enlightenment in Venice. After naming Ruzzini he went on to thank for their "generous efficacy" Filippo Farsetti and Carlo Zenobio.[19] With these names Fortis sought to make of his voyage in Dalmatia a native Venetian expedition, but this was to some extent a purposeful revision of the project's real history, involving the unnamed "foreign personage," barely noted in spite of his superlative notability.

In fact there were two earlier expeditions in the company of several different foreign personages. Fortis's first trip across the Adriatic in 1770 took him to the threshold of Dalmatia, to the island of Cres (Cherso), and also to the nearly connected island of Osero (Losinj); he traveled in the company of an historian from England, John Symonds, and a botanist from Naples, Domenico Cirillo. In 1771 Fortis published his essay of observations about the island, *Saggio d'osservazioni sopra l'isola di Cherso ed Osero,* which touched upon many of the scientific and economic concerns that he would later pursue through the rest of Dalmatia. This work was published in Venice but dedicated to John Stuart, Lord Bute, the former minister of George III and Scottish sponsor of Fortis's Adriatic researches. By 1771, however, Fortis was already recrossing the sea to visit Dalmatia together with Frederick Hervey, the bishop of Londonderry in northern Ireland, like Fortis a cleric of passionate scientific preoccupations. Finally, a third voyage was sponsored by generous personages of Venice, just in time to be generously acknowledged by Fortis with the publication of *Viaggio in Dalmazia* in 1774. Not only Bute and

Hervey, but also John Strange, an English patron of the arts and sciences in Venice, all received dedications within the work; Ruzzini, Farsetti, and Zenobio, however, were prominently recognized in the preface. In the Venetian edition of 1774, Fortis naturally preferred to underplay the preponderant importance of British participation in his project, which then received more frank recognition in the English edition of 1778. Yet the shadow of the "foreign personage" was sufficent to remind the public of Venice that this project, so properly Venetian in view of Dalmatia's political condition, was very nearly appropriated by foreigners, whose interest and support were actively engaged. At the same time that the Russian fleet was establishing its intrusive presence in the Adriatic, the British Enlightenment was making intellectual incursions along the shores of Dalmatia. In 1770, when he was about to set out for Dalmatia, Fortis published a manifesto in Venice, announcing his project in advance; while Caminer recorded the arrival of the Russian fleet in the Mediterranean, Fortis insisted upon the importance of "the natural history and geography of the provinces adjacent to the Adriatic."[20] From the beginning he was determined to summon Venetian attention to the challenge of Dalmatia, to combat ignorance, indifference, and unconcern in the name of enlightened rule.

"The results of the voyage executed under such fortunate auspices," wrote Fortis in the preface of 1774, "form the work that I dare to offer to the wisdom of the most excellent magistrate by whose zeal are protected and encouraged the useful studies in the supremely happy estates of the Venetian dominion." The emphasis on "useful studies" was fundamental for Fortis, as he justified his work before the Riformatori, expressing "the hope that Your Excellencies may kindly receive the homage of a devoted subject," whatever the imperfections of the work.

> If from the publication of this work of mine one obtains no other present advantage than the substitution of Dalmatian marbles (which served the Romans in architecture no less than in the nobler uses of statuary) for those that foreigners sell to us at an expensive and ever more unreasonable price, I would think that my most noble patrons could feel satisfaction, for the discovery of those ancient quarries, at having rendered not a slight service to the nation. If then . . . by the news of the natural products of that vast country, and by the directions aiming to augment and improve them, to render them more useful to the state . . . may be derived some noticeable advantages to the public patrimony and the national commerce and the arts, then the generous promoters of my expedition would enjoy by irrefutable title the

qualification of optimal patriots, and I would fully taste the internal content that floods the soul of the useful subject *(Suddito utile)*, to which every well-born man must aspire, more than to the fame of a scholar and scientist.[21]

Fortis, who was himself preeminently a scholar and a scientist, preferred to pursue a rhetoric of patriotism in which his own proposed identity as a "useful subject" was inseparable from the published presentation of Dalmatia as a useful province.

In the elaborate network that Fortis constructed between himself and his patrons—the illustrious senators who kindly received his publication and the enlightened patricians who generously supported his expedition—there emerged the idea of an imperial patriotism based on the discovery and deployment of provincial resources. Yet Fortis also put his case for Dalmatia before the public, because he feared that the patrons he invoked would only reluctantly deign to take notice of Dalmatia, inclined by patrician inertia to avoid the trouble of extraction and exploitation. When he remarked that Dalmatian marble served the mineral needs of imperial Rome, it was to emphasize the worthiness of the province to supply the same needs in imperial Venice. Fortis did not only appeal to ancient precedent, but also to the modern standard of the Enlightenment, when he concluded the preface by expressing his "desire to penetrate with views to the public utility into the secrets of natural science," whose value was "recognized by all of civilized Europe *(l'Europa colta)*."[22]

So prominent were the dedications within the body of the work that the individual sections commenced in the format of letters to esteemed correspondents. Thus, the first section, concerning the district of Zadar, was addressed to Jacopo Morosini, "Patrizio Veneto"—and began with the conceit of Fortis in Dalmatia posting a letter to Morosini in Venice. "The distance from Venice depriving me of the honor of being near you often," wrote Fortis, "and on account of the interposition of the sea, taking from me the means to send you news of me frequently and with security, this still will not make me neglect to write to you. Your Excellency will probably receive this letter rather late . . ." Late indeed—though not because Dalmatia was really so remote from Venice, but rather because the letter was conceived as part of the published account of the voyage. In thus emphasizing his acknowledgments through the pretense of posted letters, Fortis attributed to the project a precisely elaborated sponsorship, as a work "undertaken under the auspices of the most noble patrician patrons *(Mecenati Patrizi)*, and that small number of illustrious amateurs or of famous professors, with whom I kept in correspondence by the strongest chain of common studies." Correspondence constituted the metaphor for a common interest in matters of science, and epistolary form made Fortis's individual adventure into a collective scientific undertaking. The first dedication was assigned to a Venetian patrician in a spirit of patriotic priority, though within the context of clearly articulated criticism of Venice: "Beginning by writing to you," wrote Fortis to Morosini, "seems to me all the more a precise duty inasmuch as the cultivators of the good and useful science of facts and the productions . . . of nature (in a century of such light for the rest of Europe), which are disesteemed and unfortunately badly known among us, find a good welcome and reception uniquely with Your Excellency."[23] In truth, Morosini was the unique member of the Venetian patriciate to merit a dedicatory letter within the work, after the names that were mentioned in the preface; Fortis's criticism of Venice's scientific indifference, delivered in the name of the Enlightenment, paralleled his concern that indifference to Dalmatia would compromise the reception of his work. He worried about sluggishness in Venice, demanding of his readers both scientific attention to natural history and imperial interest in provincial economy. At the same time he appealed to patrician patrons and the reading public, calling the patrons to account before his readers, encouraging the readers to rally by advertising his patrons. The Morosini family was, of course, a legend of imperial history, since it was Francesco Morosini who had to surrender Crete to the Turks in 1669 but later made compensatory gains in Greece and even in Dalmatia.

"With my Dalmatian voyage I am quite content," wrote Fortis in an authentic letter of 1773 to Lazzaro Spallanzani, the celebrated scientist of biological reproduction at the university of Pavia. "I hope that foreigners will want to read it: but I do not promise for the Venetians. Here one is expecting a universal physical-ancient-political-moral history of Dalmatia from a man who has passed six months there."[24] Fortis's worries about the Venetians' reception of his book fluctuated between the conviction of their indifference and the fear of their disappointment. In the hope of provoking interest based on considerations of commerce and utility he had to forego the traditional academic ambition toward universal erudition; he would appear principally as a "useful subject" of Venice. When Fortis addressed himself to Morosini within the work itself, he offered a further defense of incompleteness in his account of Dalmatia.

> The extension of Venetian Dalmatia is too vast, the number of islands in this sea too considerable, for naturalists to be able to expect something complete from brief peregrinations. There are audacious men who, transported by the thoughtless fervor of youth, and persuaded that they can impose upon the literary world, promise to give in a few months the botany, the zoology, the paleontology of the vastest provinces: but whoever is accustomed to contemplating with philosophical composure the immense variety of things understands all too well that the life of one man alone is not enough (even if he may have generous assistance) to weave the complete natural history of the smallest island or of the narrowest territory.[25]

Fortis's invocation of the vastness of Dalmatia—as if it were Venice's America—was fundamentally a matter of philosophical perspective. Dalmatia might loom large across the Adriatic, or it might seem trivially unimpressive within the dismissive metropolitan consciousness of the capital; Fortis himself purposefully enlarged his readers' sense of Dalmatia, the better to insist upon its imperial importance. In fact, though it was hardly one of the "vastest provinces"—compared, for instance, to the empire that England was about to lose in America—neither was Dalmatia "the narrowest territory," though narrowness seemed to designate its geographical form of extension along the coast. As Foscarini discovered in 1747, when he finally obtained a current map, Venice had, since the seventeenth century, greatly enlarged the interior depth of Dalmatia, and Fortis's idea of its vastness comprehended that still unfamiliar interior.

Natural Resources and National Collections: From Art to Zoology

The historian Krzysztof Pomian has written about Fortis and Venice in the context of an emerging eighteenth-century concern with assembling collections, of both works of art and objects of natural history. In 1773, while Fortis was preparing his manuscript of the *Viaggio in Dalmazia,* the Council of Ten approved a proposal to undertake the state protection of paintings in public places, on the principle that "the precious body of paintings is, perhaps, the rarest ornament of this powerful republic." In 1774, the year of Fortis's publication, a catalogue of paintings was completed for the government by Antonio Maria Zanetti. The catalogue of 1774, according to Pomian, proceeded from an unprecedented conception of public paintings displayed in different churches and schools as "pieces of a single collection," so that the whole Republic of Venice became "a sort of dispersed art gallery." When in 1779, the Senate considered assembling an actual public gallery for the purpose of better conservation, the proposal was framed not only in terms of ornament but also utility in Venice: "contributing to the instruction and industry of its subjects, to the embellishment of the town, and the national genius for this art." Assembling works of art for the advantage of Venice and its national genius was related to the assembling of a scientific collection—in botany, mineralogy, or ichthyology—in the name of natural resources and national economy. "Before the first half of the eighteenth century, nobody had asked the state to become the owner of a natural history collection," writes Pomian. "Similarly, nobody had asked the state prior to the 1770s to assume responsibility for the protection of pictures or even for the creation of a public art gallery."[26] In the context of these newly conceived state responsibilities, Fortis outlined an agenda for collecting in Dalmatia according to a sense of the state's imperial opportunities and obligations.

In 1766 Francesco Griselini published in Venice an open letter on "practical methods to render a nation rich and powerful." Griselini, who started out as a humble artisan, undertook an intellectual career as the protégé of Marco Foscarini, and together they explored the Venetian legacy of Paolo Sarpi. After Foscarini's death in 1763, Griselini gave greater priority to economic concerns, establishing in 1764 an organ intended to bring together the study of economy and natural history, *Giornale d'Italia*—a journal of Italy "with respect to natural science and principally to agriculture, arts, and commerce." It was here that he published his open letter of 1766, announcing that the first imperative of any government seeking to enrich the nation was knowledge of natural resources, "to know what products or primary materials are abundant, are scarce, or are lacking." He further specified the necessary information in such a way as to emphasize its relation to the study of natural history. It was necessary to ascertain:

> I. A balance of the actual condition of the state itself with regard to its natural riches, and those riches that derive from its physical constitution.

II. Another balance regarding the number of the most useful quadruped animals, the human population, and the quality and quantity of the arts exercised in the state itself, objects which form its artificial riches.[27]

That the state should take an interest in natural history collections was fully consistent with a new awareness of its sovereign concern with natural (and national) resources. The pursuit of scientific knowledge toward the purpose of enriching the nation was precisely the motivation of Fortis, who recognized the need to calculate a bicoastal balance of resources across the Adriatic. Griselini proposed such pursuit as the challenge of the Enlightenment in Venice: "We have the satisfaction of being aware that this is the actual study of the most enlightened governments of our Europe; a study that, if it well considers its object, will bring honor forever to our century." He hailed the philosophical triumph of "beneficence and humanity" over "ignorance, fanaticism, and barbaric customs."[28] These were the grand values of Voltaire, though pursued by the prosaic means of counting cattle, or maybe sheep, that is, "the most useful quadruped animals." Fortis would have considered himself included in Griselini's declaration in the name of "our Europe" and "our century," the possessive pronoun designating the men of the Enlightenment.

In 1768 the Russian-Ottoman war began, with its worrisome implications for Venice's diplomatic neutrality, imperial stability, and Adriatic security. It was also the year that Caminer and Fortis began to publish *Europa Letteraria,* offering a pacific alternative vision of Venice happily integrated into the Enlightenment's international community of letters. At the same time, in 1768, Griselini published in Venice a dictionary of arts and trades, *Dizionario delle arti e de' mestieri,* in which the peaceful pursuit of economic development was described encyclopedically for enlightened readers who preferred to contemplate commerce rather than combat. In fact, he too was engaged in combat, a philosophical war against poverty and its cultural consequences. In the dictionary's preliminary discourse Griselini warned that wherever "commerce lacks or languishes, there is only penury, misery, and poverty, and instead of cultivation, instead of gentle and humane customs, instead of knowledge, there triumphs ignorance, roughness and barbarism." To frustrate the triumph of barbarism through economic advancement required a knowledge of natural history, conceived in the spirit of Linnaean classification:

The mineral kingdom gives us the materials that serve for our habitations, for our public and private edifices, and for a quantity of manufactures and uses . . . The animal kingdom offers us furs, wools, horns, bones, hides, silk, honey, wax, fat, meat, etc . . . The vegetable kingdom brings us grains, crops, oil, wine, wood, fruit, hemp, flax, and a thousand other sorts of products . . .[29]

Clearly there was a role for the naturalist to play in identifying natural resources, and there was also a role for the state to play in conserving each raw material. "To let it leave the country in this condition," warned Griselini, "means losing not only the profit that could come from processing it, but also the advantages to the country of an industry that gives a living to the inhabitants."[30] Both the commercial conception of natural history and the philosophical principle of national economy made Griselini's dictionary in 1768 the appropriate reference for Fortis's approach to Dalmatia in 1770.

While Fortis was voyaging in Dalmatia, other naturalists, including foreign amateurs, explored Venice's mainland Italian territories. Lady Anna Riggs Miller, an Englishwoman in Italy in 1771, enjoyed looking for fossils near Verona, and took home her souvenirs: "We have employed the evening in viewing some cabinets of natural history. Amongst many rare and curious articles of the fossil kind, the petrified fish are the most surprising. I have packed up some to travel with us." Antonio Carlo Dondi Orologio was also pursuing research in the Euganean Hills around Verona in the 1770s; publishing his work at the end of the decade in 1780, he warned that "foreigners come and collect the fossils in our hills," while "we travel in foreign lands but do not know our own." He advocated the creation of a "national cabinet" of natural history: "I simply regret that nobody should yet have had the useful idea of assembling exclusively the products of our hills which offer very fine and varied examples of every sort, and of classifying them carefully and methodically in order to form a Gabinetto Nazionale."[31] Such an approach to natural history was clearly consistent with Griselini's emphasis on the national knowledge of natural resources. Fortis in Dalmatia operated according to the same principle, with the further innovation that his trans-Adriatic explorations implicitly indicated the importance of a fully imperial Venetian collection, Gabinetto Imperiale.

The idea of the collection was important for these public projects on a number of levels. If a collector's catalogue of every individual region of the Republic constituted a part of the complete national representation of natural resources, then the state could be conceived as a master

FIGURE 6. "A Country Woman of the Canal of Zara." From *Travels into Dalmatia* by Alberto Fortis, English edition of 1778. Fortis was not only attuned to the folkloric details of costume in Dalmatia, but appreciated them in the context of the natural history of the province. Here the country woman appeared in an illustration together with a fig branch (A) and a gall (B) which grew on the fig branch. Fortis was interested in whether the galls might produce a profitable red dye; such a dye, perhaps, could have been used in the coloring of the country woman's costume. Natural history, national economy, and folkloric anthropology came together in Fortis's voyage. *(By permission of the Department of Printing and Graphic Arts, the Houghton Library, Harvard University.)*

collection of its aggregate regional cabinets. In this sense, the imperial state was defined by its possession of component colonial collections, and national economy appeared as the curatorial integration of varying regional resources. Fortis took this principle a step further when he presented the province of Dalmatia divided into a number of regional accounts, all dedicated to particular patrons, of whom a significant number were noted natural history collectors. At the same time Fortis pursued the ordinary business of collecting in several spheres, from fish fossils to ancient inscriptions, so that the representation of Dalmatia could be completed in the cabinet as well as in the catalogue, in material as well as metaphorical form. In a somewhat different domain, his collection of the folk poetry of the South Slavs was received with considerable cultural interest all over Europe. Pomian has proposed that the essense of the early modern collection was its semiotic mediation between the domains of "the visible and the invisible."[32] In the case of Fortis in Dalmatia, his collections and accounts represented a transmarine province—out of sight, across the Adriatic—to the metropolis of imperial curators in natural history and national economy.

Adriatic Researches: Collecting Shells and Catching Fish

"Our stay on the island was not long enough," wrote Fortis of the first voyage to Cres, "to make a good collection of plants." In any event he appended a list of plants compiled by the botanist Cirillo, the catalogue for an uncollected collection, to satisfy "the amateurs of that part of natural history." Botany, by studying "useful and harmful shrubs and herbs," would not only serve the interests of science, but "could bring advantages to the people of Cres." Fortis insisted on this aspect of his scientific research, "holding thus to my principal purpose, which is to be of use *(giovare)* in all possible ways to that population by which I have been so well treated and received," the population of the island. He remarked upon the botanical prevalence of Salvia (sage), noting that "everyone knows its medical virtues." Since the Dutch traded Salvia from the Mediterranean to the Chinese for tea, Fortis proposed that Venice also seek to profit from its Dalmatian resources.[33] Thus, along with the scientific importance of making a botanical collection, and the philanthropic concern to serve the local population, Fortis ultimately emphasized matters of national economy, to argue that the better knowledge of Adriatic herbs would benefit the Venetian balance of trade. Fortis's purpose was consistent with the economic policy pursued in Sweden by the century's most famous naturalist, Carl Linnaeus. In the 1740s Linnaeus had high horticultural hopes of making tropical herbs and spices adapt to the Swedish climate. "Let us bring the Tea-tree here from China," he proposed, even pitying the "poor Chinese" who would thus lose their profits from the tea trade. In the 1750s, less optimistic about such transplants, Linnaeus sought indigenous substitutes for tea and for herbal medicines. Regretting that "a poor man here can hardly be given a purgative without it being prescribed from the East or West Indies," he offered botanical suggestions for local alternatives in his *Purgantia indigena* in 1766.[34] Fortis in Dalmatia sought to apply the lessons of natural history toward the end of economic advantage for Venice in the same enterprising spirit as the great Linnaeus in Sweden.

It was on Cres that Fortis also began to contemplate the economic importance of fishing. There he found the fishermen rewarded with "an infinity of sardines, which are salted there, and distributed in barrels through the various lands of the state, forming a most considerable article of internal commerce." Natural history could nevertheless improve upon this trade by studying the seasonal movements of the sardines in the sea:

> It would be worth doing some particular researches on these voyages of the fishes, which show something still more surprising than the voyages of the quails, of the swallows, etc. Also under the waters of the sea there are customs *(costumi)* analogous to those of the terrestrial animals, and there must occur from year to year some very curious emigrations and pilgrimages. The regularity, as well as the variations, of these voyages seem to me the more worthy of observation as they have been little observed in our seas, where the short distance from one shore to the other, and the frequency of the islands, invite an examination of the works of nature, which in the subaqueous kingdom has spread marvels far more prodigious, relative to us, than in the terrestrial kingdom. Nor should this examination be believed to be uniquely an object of curiosity, since there may result the greatest advantages to commerce.[35]

Fortis's vision of a natural history of the Adriatic, comprising the inhabitants of both land and sea, reflected an imperial vision in which fish were an integrating force of nature, passing between the opposite shores of the sea, which were bound together by underwater routes of passage. Foscarini in the Maggior Consiglio in 1747 was concerned about the economic consequences of human migrations from Dalmatia into the Ottoman empire, and Fortis was keen to emphasize the economic importance of understanding the amazing migrations of fish. Foscarini had also sponsored Griselini's early studies of Adriatic natural history, and Fortis, in the next generation, explicitly formulated the economic and ecological integration of the Adriatic domain, terrestrial and marine. Beginning with these reflections on the "customs" of the Adriatic fishes, Fortis later became famous for studying the customs of the Morlacchi.

Fortis recognized the earlier efforts of his recent scientific predecessors who had also studied the Adriatic. Luigi Marsigli of Bologna was the towering Italian naturalist, as well as an insatiable collector, of the late seventeenth and early eighteenth century. He combined the vocations of soldier and scientist, especially in the service of the Habsburgs and in the study of the Danube, but in 1715 he worked for the pope along the Adriatic coast around Rimini, giving attention to fortification and defense against the Ottomans, on the one hand, and the science of the sea, on the other.[36] More recent and even more relevant was the work of Vitaliano Donati who, like Fortis, was from Padua, and whose essay on the natural marine history of the Adriatic, *Saggio della storia naturale marina dell'Adriatico,* was published in Venice in 1750. Both natural historians discovered in Dalmatia a complementary perspective on the Adriatic, compared to the more usual approach from the Italian coast. "I turned my eye to Illyria," wrote Donati, "almost completely neglected by others, because of the roughness of its regions, the barbarism of its peoples, and the danger of researches." He was perhaps inclined to live dangerously, since he survived Dalmatia and went on to explore the Nile and the Middle East, where he died in 1763. It was Donati who, "with the greatest possible attention observed the depths of the Adriatic," and provided both information and inspiration for Fortis.[37] However, it was Fortis, with most of his attention focused well above sea level, who gave the natural history of the Adriatic a patriotic and economic message.

Fortis further suggested to the enlightened amateur in Dalmatia various courses of study, from aquatic insects to marine polyps and testaceous shellfish: "They would form a long, assiduous, and no less useful than delightful occupation for a traveler driven from rock to rock, by genius and by eagerness to acquire new knowledge in Natural History." Such an appeal made its impact upon a public for which science had

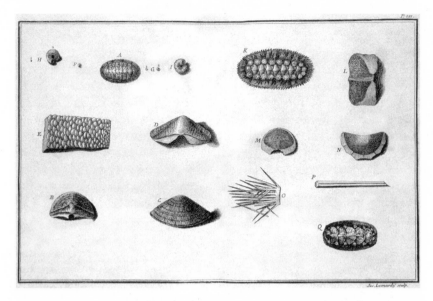

FIGURE 7.   Natural History Specimens. From *Travels into Dalmatia* by Alberto Fortis, English edition of 1778. Fortis's principal vocation was natural history, and in Dalmatia he collected and depicted specimens, like these marine creatures with their shells, found around Trogir. The comprehensive investigation of natural history in Dalmatia was also a mark of Venetian imperial mastery, and Fortis further contemplated the possible economic implications of studying natural resources. *(By permission of the Department of Printing and Graphic Arts, the Houghton Library, Harvard University.)*

become a "fashionable" subject of interest. Later, Fortis himself would lead small parties of ladies from Verona in search of fossils. On Cres, when he envisioned the studious traveler along the Adriatic coast, Fortis considered the inevitable issue of collecting. He regretted that "the museums of our amateurs, who buy shells, crustaceans, and exotic lithophytes at a high price, are completely unprovided with our own, something which rightly shames them, but also does most unjust wrong to the country, which produces, like any other, an abundance of natural curiosities, and ought to be preferred to any other by those among us who love to make such collections."[38] This patriotic imperative to establish specifically Adriatic shell collections was consistent with Dondi Orologio's scientific concern to create a Gabinetto Nazionale. There was even an element of national economy in disparaging the purchase of exotic shells from distant seas and preferring Adriatic shells, which were freely collectible by anyone with the energy to roam from rock to rock.

Fishing was the particular concern for which Fortis received the sponsorship and support of the Senate in Venice. The enlightened patrician Andrea Memmo, in his efforts to achieve a broad reform of corporative economic restrictions, attempted to make use of Fortis's expertise, and charged him in 1773 to report upon fishing in Dalmatia. Gianfranco Torcellan has commented that Memmo, in sponsoring Fortis, "was seeking to impose cautiously upon the political class the talents and merits of a man who, usefully employed, could have brought great advantages to the state."[39] In this sense, Memmo's ambitions to make use of Fortis's middle class merits in a campaign of Venetian revitalization paralleled Fortis's own program for exploiting the provincial economy of Dalmatia to the advantage of Venice. In both cases the challenge was to overcome the conservative inhibitions of a patrician and metropolitan preserve. Fishermen of the Enlightenment, Memmo and Fortis were angling for the future of Venice.

"The advantageous use that could be made of Lake Vrana," Fortis declared, "is for fishing. The eels, which are found there in the greatest quantities, and are abandoned to the poorly understood art of the fishermen of those areas, would supply a not indifferent number of barrels to our internal commerce." In Fortis's explicit concern for "our" commerce, he presented not only the natural history of marine life, with its implications for salted seafood, but also, even more vividly, the anthropology of labor among the fishermen of Dalmatia. At Pacostiane, a "poor and ignoble place," he disapprovingly witnessed the unproductive method by which the inhabitants fished the waters of Lake Vrana:

> They commonly feed on the fish from the lake, and eels in particular.
> . . . The manner employed there for fishing them, when they group together to mate, is singular. Two men advance, wading through the lake in the shallow places, and with a thick cord, which each holds by one of the two ends, they beat on the bodies of the eels; they kill some, and put the others to flight; they gather the dead, and eat them.[40]

Such a principle—"kill some, and put the others to flight"—was obviously antithetical to any ambitious commercial sense, though it may have made sense for the subsistence fishing of the Dalmatians, killing only as many eels as they cared to eat. Fortis proposed more effective technology of fishing—reed pens, called *lavorieri,* to trap the eels—as practiced around Venice, and suitable to be transferred to Dalmatia for the advancement of Venetian commerce.

> It would not be bad advice to send there some fishing boats used for taking eels in our lagoons subject to the doge, so the inhabitants of Pacostiane and the neighboring places might learn a better method. The nation annually spends a lot of money for the provision of eels salted and marinated at Comacchio; why should we not sooner value the lakes and lagoons of the state? One of the principal objects of my observations along the shores of Dalmatia has been fishing, how to systematize it, or introduce it anew where it has not been practiced properly; it can and should be a source of savings and national income. Lake Vrana is the most extensive of all those which are found not far from the sea, and therefore the most worthy to be particularly contemplated by the magistrature that presides over our commerce and the cultivation and increase of our domestic products.[41]

For Goldoni the Dalmatians were naval heroes; for Fortis they were fishermen, and not very skillful even at that. While Goldoni treated Dalmatia as a subject of national glory, Fortis regarded it in terms of national economy.

Fortis reminded his readers of the very fundamental fact that Dalmatia was within the Venetian state, and he looked for the modern economic meaning of that relation. The proverbial valor of the Dalmatians at war against the Ottoman enemy counted for less than their inefficient efforts against the eels. Fortis, however, did not hold the Dalmatians responsible for their own backwardness, but rather charged the Venetians to teach a better method and enjoy the benefit in barrels of salted eels, all from within the state. The eels of Comacchio, at the delta of the Po River, came conveniently from the western coast of the Adriatic, but their cost could only benefit the economy of the Papal State. In the name of national economy—"our commerce" and "our domestic products"—Fortis enjoined the Venetians to look across the Adriatic and discover the eels of Dalmatia.

His section on the Primorje littoral was addressed to Hervey, bishop of Londonderry, who had accompanied Fortis on one of the voyages. It was natural, therefore, for Fortis to recommend state promotion and protection of fishing in Dalmatia with reference to the celebrated economic success at sea of the British isles.

> Your most noble nation, Mylord, supplies a luminous example of the influence of the art of fishing on maritime forces. It is true that we do not have whales to combat in the Adriatic, nor the great quantity of polar fishes that abound in the seas of the North; but it is also true that our navigation is not ordinarily directed toward America or China, and therefore the fisherman used to beating our sea in whatever condition becomes a most fit mariner for the needs that we have.[42]

The association of fishing with maritime power indicated the emphasis of Fortis on the economic rather than the military basis of the Adriatic empire. If his imperial model was Britain, he clearly recognized that Venice could only aspire to a microcosmic version of the worldwide commerical domain that brought Chinese tea to the Boston harbor. Indeed the dumping of Chinese tea into that harbor in the Boston Tea Party took place in 1773, as Fortis was writing, so he would have had reason to wonder whether the supplies and demands of transoceanic commerce were as manageable as a more modest marine domain.

The adaptations of Dalmatian fishermen made for fit mariners within the context of Adriatic natural history. Some local fishes, like the conger eels, could be caught by night from illuminated boats, and Fortis recorded that the local fishermen were "marvelously dexterous in catching them with the Foscina, which is a long lance of wood, armed at the end with an iron comb, that has teeth in the shape of hooks." His regard for their technology as an Adriatic adaptation was tempered by an intimation of their primitive character. Fortis did not hesitate to censure the Dalmatian fisherman for superstitious customs, which seemed to work against full economic exploitation of marine resources. There may not have been whales in the Adriatic, but there were dolphins.

> They wander freely in these waters, and until now no one has given a thought to drawing advantage from this small species of the Cetacea in our sea. The Dalmatian fishermen feel a sort of friendship and gratitude for the dolphins, giving them credit for chasing the fish to the illuminated boats, whether they fish with nets or with the Foscina. In this last case the fishermen do not fail to throw from the boat to the dolphin some large fish as if to divide the booty with him. If I had had the time and the necessary opportunity, I would have tried to establish for some fisherman less irrational than

the others the damage which these voracious animals cause to fishing, and
the advantage that can be obtained from their flesh salted and their fat
melted.[43]

This unsentimental attitude toward dolphins, taken together with a
rather critical perspective on Dalmatian economic customs, suggested
that for Fortis the crucial concern was to refine the relation between
human arts and natural resources and to build a more modern provincial
economy. Illuminated boats counted for less than enlightened minds.
Fortis obviously felt that local superstition was a drag on economic development, which might be advanced by the scientific lessons of natural
history.

Fortis paid tribute to Hervey as an "indefatigable researcher of nature's secrets" and also thanked him for "your generous proposals to
pass to the contemplation of greater things, in more remote and still
unknown lands." This allusion let the public know that Fortis had been
invited to undertake even more adventurous voyages, but, in the end,
science and circumstances brought him back to Dalmatia: "I recrossed
the Adriatic, instead of navigating the ocean."[44] In fact, the years of
Fortis's travels in Dalmatia were precisely the years of great oceanic exploration, notably of Captain Cook's voyages in the South Pacific.
Cook returned from the first voyage in 1771, having visited Tahiti, New
Zealand, and Australia, and he set out on the second voyage in 1772,
proceeding to explore the Antarctic. Fortis could hardly have helped
being aware that his own explorations were of less sensational interest
to the public than the oceanic adventures of the *Endeavour* and the
Resolution. Nevertheless he persisted in his own Adriatic ambitions to
combine regional natural history with national economy in the service
of the Venetian republic.

While Fortis was in Dalmatia, Andrea Memmo in Venice prepared his
proposal for economic reform, which could incorporate the results of
Dalmatian research. In Memmo's report to the Senate of 1772, fishing
was saluted as "the mother art, which merits being regarded with equal
predilection as agriculture, especially in a Catholic state." Fortis, though
a priest, did not address the Catholic question of whether, for instance,
the supply of salted eels was sufficient for Lenten consumption. He
seemed less concerned about Catholicism than about the Papal State as
an economic rival, and he viewed Dalmatia as crucial for any attempt to
seek Venetian economic advancement through fishing. Memmo pro-

posed as possible strategies the awarding of prizes for "whoever can best succeed in experimenting with that which is publicly taught in many books," or the deputizing of someone to go abroad "to learn that which is no longer a secret among the nations who do the most commerce in the various kinds of dried fish," or even the recruiting of a foreign expert to prescribe policy based on "practical knowledge of our seas and of nature and the quantity of fish that could be gathered."[45] Fortis, who had some sponsorship from the Venetian state through Memmo's interest, proved that the necessary knowledge had to be acquired within the Republic itself, and the best of all possible books was that which, like his own, was inspired by local research and patriotic purpose. It was in this spirit that he advocated and pursued the collection of native shells and native shellfish, outlining a new natural history of the Adriatic, while traveling "from rock to rock" along the coast of Dalmatia.

Collecting Antiquities: Roman Remains in Venetian Dalmatia

Fortis's interest in collecting on the eastern Adriatic coast was not only for specimens of natural history, but also for the Roman remains of classical antiquity in Dalmatia. "Your Excellency," he wrote to Jacopo Morosini, concerning Zadar, "will easily find among the collectors many inscriptions that were conserved there up to the beginning of this century. They prove that this city and colony were regarded with particular affection by many Roman emperors, and signally by Augustus and the optimal Trajan." That optimal emperor "had built or restored an aqueduct that carried water there from far away, which one discovers from the fragment of an inscription still existing in the city." To emphasize the presence of Roman remains and to cite the concern of the Roman emperors was, for Fortis, an implicitly political matter, reminding his readers of Dalmatia's ancient status as a subject colony and challenging Venice to live up to the optimal imperial standard of Rome. Every collectible inscription was thus an archaeological admonishment toward responsible imperial rule, conceived according to the pervasive classicism of the Enlightenment. Such responsibility also included the curatorial care of the province's ancient remains, either in collections or on the original sites. In fact, among Venice's significant eighteenth-century collections of antiquities, that of the Nani family prominently included inscriptions removed from Dalmatia. Fortis encouraged the predatory acquisitions of antiquarian connoisseurs, but he also observed the more careless consequences of Venetian rule. The Roman ruins of Zadar were but "miserable vestiges," on account of the "the modern fortifications having been made there at the expense of the ancient remains."[46] This regret at the archaeological indifference of military concerns was particularly appropriate as a message for Jacopo Morosini, since it was his own supremely illustrious family hero, Francesco Morosini, whose maneuvers accidentally resulted in blowing up the Parthenon in 1687, in the course of war against the Ottoman empire.

In the late seventeenth century the ancient remains of Dalmatia had been visited and described by foreign personages, preempting the imperial priority of Venice. Jacob Spon of Lyon and George Wheler, an Englishman, traveled to Dalmatia in the 1670s, a century before Fortis, and they published in Lyon in 1678 *Voyage d'Italie, de Dalmatie, de Grece, et du Levant.* Traveling as they did, for "the love of antiquity alone," Dalmatia became the intermediary stage of their geographical and antiquarian progress from Italy to Greece. They looked for inscriptions in Zadar from the age of Augustus and inspected at Trogir the recently discovered manuscript of the *Satyricon* of Petronius. After being "badly lodged" in the only hotel in Zadar, they took rooms in the lazaretto at Split, "a stage for the caravans of Turkey, which there discharge their merchandise for Venice." Split also presented to the travelers Dalmatia's most impressive ancient remains, the palace of Diocletian.[47]

In the eighteenth century, there were other foreign personages who visited Dalmatia to study, sketch, and eventually publish engravings of Diocletian's palace. Robert Adam, the Scottish architect, whose fame lay still before him, and the French architect Charles-Louis Clérisseau came to Split in 1757 and spent five weeks sketching the Roman ruins. Adam then published in London in 1764 his *Ruins of the Palace of the Emperor Diocletian at Spalatro in Dalmatia.* The foreigners were given no official encouragement in Split, and the Venetian authorities, according to Adam, "began to conceive unfavorable sentiments of my intentions, and to suspect that under pretense of taking views and plans of the Palace, I was really employed in surveying the state of the fortifications." Fortunately, he received support from a Dalmatian amateur, "Count Antonio Marcovich, a native of that country, and an officer of rank in the Venetian service, who has applied himself with great success to the study

View of the Inside of the Temple of Jupiter

FIGURE 8. "View of the Inside of the Temple of Jupiter." From Robert Adam, *Ruins of the Palace of the Emperor Diocletian at Spalatro in Dalmatia,* published in London in 1764. A visiting artist sketches the temple from one side, while a drama ensues between powdered, bewigged foreigners and tufted, shaved Dalmatians, the tonsorial encounter between civilized Western Europe and exotic Eastern Europe. An outstretched arm implies the prevalence of beggarly contemporary misery amidst the magnificence of ancient architectural monuments. *(By permission of the Fine Arts Library, Harvard University.)*

of Antiquities." Venetian resentment was expressed as concern for military security, but Adam also invaded Venice's cultural preserve, and the publication of the engravings of the palace was dedicated to George III and the glory of the British empire. "I beg leave to lay before Your Majesty the Ruins of Spalatro, once the favorite Residence of a great Emperor," wrote Adam. "At this happy Period, when Great Britain enjoys in Peace the Reputation and Power she has acquired by Arms, Your Majesty's singular attention to the Arts of Elegance promises an Age of Perfection that will compleat the Glories of your Reign." Adam's visit to Split coincided with the earliest excavations at Pompeii, in the kingdom of Naples, while, from the 1750s, Roman ruins excited increasing artistic interest in Europe with the dramatic etchings of the Venetian Giovanni Battista Piranesi. The subscribers to Adam's publication in 1764, in addition to numerous great names of the English aristocracy, included David Hume, Joshua Reynolds, and Horace Walpole, as well as the Venetian doge, the library of San Marco, and several Venetian patricians, such as Filippo Farsetti, Fortis's future patron.[48] Ten years later Fortis's *Viaggio in Dalmazia* put the province's ancient remains before the Venetian public of connoisseurs and at the service of a Venetian ideology of empire.

In Zadar, as "civilized" as the cities of Italy, Fortis witnessed the rewards of collecting in Dalmatia.

> I was received at Zara with generous hospitality in the beautiful habitation of Dr. Antonio Danieli, learned Professor of Medicine. It is adorned with various pieces of ancient sculpture, among which may be distinguished four colossal statues of saline marble, that this zealous lover of antiquity had transported from the ruins of the nearby city of Nona at his own exorbitant expense. A lot of stone tablets are to be seen, brought there from various places in Dalmatia. . . . With this optimal friend and host one also finds an abundant collection of ancient Roman coins and a good number of Greek ones splendidly preserved.[49]

If, when Fortis went to Nona (Nin) himself, he found nothing to evoke "the greatness of Roman times," this was evidently because collectors like his host had already pounced upon even the colossal monuments and carried them off to the civilized city of Zadar. Fortis published his *Viaggio in Dalmazia* for a Venetian public that, over the course of the eighteenth century, continued to appreciate the special collectibility of precious antiquities. Statues, inscriptions, and coins were acquired, displayed, and catalogued by connoisseurs, and, as it happened, Farsetti, whom Fortis thanked for generous support of the Dalmatian expedition, was also Venice's most celebrated collector of plaster casts of ancient statues. In the 1760s Farsetti assembled a collection that included casts of such masterpieces from Rome as the Laocoon and the Apollo Belevedere, which could then be studied in Venice by artists like the young Canova.[50] Farsetti died in 1774, the year that Fortis acknowledged his patronage in the published book, but the account of antiquities in Dalmatia was clearly aimed at other such collectors in Venice, who would value the province all the more for its Roman remains and might even be tempted to cross the Adriatic themselves in search of precious pieces. Just as the natural resources of Dalmatia, like eels and herbs, offered an economic incentive to imperial attention, cultural commodities, like ancient coins and inscriptions, could also inspire and sustain the interest of Venetians.

Inland from Zadar and Nin, Fortis found an even more promising site for collecting antiquities, the ancient city of Asseria, mentioned by Ptolemy and Pliny, near the contemporary village of Podgraje. Until the site passed to Venice as part of the more recent acquisitions in Dalmatia, "the ruins of Asseria were still subject to the Turks, and therefore could not be easily observed." A diagram of the remains of the ancient walls was artfully decorated with an attractive illustration of broken columns, tumbled together with the relief of a pointed pediment, set against an arboreous backgound in the evocative style of Piranesi; the scale of distance was inscribed on a chipped classical pedestal. This picturesque appeal was supplemented with a more explicit verbal invitation to knowledgeable parties in Venice, that they might consider making a visit to inland Dalmatia. The ancient fortifications were deemed by Fortis to be of great interest for "modern military architecture," a field in which he himself, for all his astonishingly diverse academic concerns, was far from professionally expert. He promised that Asseria offered much that was "worthy of the particular attention of a professor in that most noble art." Fortis, however, did not invite only the professors of military engineering, but also those who would take an interest in the Roman past for its own sake.

> The antiquarian, or even the simple amateur of fine arts and of good erudition, when he finds himself at Podgraje, will not be able to help wishing that some powerful hand, "Quicquid sub terra est in apricum proferat." He will

be moved to this desire especially by seeing that in the ruin of that city, until then, no one has searched deeply there with the will to extract something. Those walls surround a deposit of antiquities falling to pieces within, who knows by what cause; maybe by an earthquake, or by some sudden inundation of barbarians which is even worse. The buried gate, the considerable height of the walls, seen from without in more than one place, some thick walls, that one still sees on the ground among the bushes, are all circumstances that give cause for the highest hope of a quantity of valuable monuments, that might be gotten there.[51]

With a Latin line for the eager antiquarians, Fortis urged that they hasten to depart for Dalmatia, there to bring to light what lay underground, for they were sure to be rewarded with precious acquisitions for their classical collections.

The diagram of the walls of Asseria appeared as a sort of treasure map, marking for adventurous Venetians the perimeter of the presumptive hoard. Indeed, at the very center of the map was one single structure, with a steeple surmounted by a cross, whose presence Fortis now explained in his continued address to the interested amateurs: "In the middle of the open space, which covers the remains of Asseria, one finds an isolated parish church of the little village, that was built of ancient wreckage excavated on the spot. There may be seen ill-used inscriptions, and pieces of grand cornices."[52] The enlightened abbé Fortis would, in his general conclusions about the backwardness of Dalmatia, critically ascribe a certain pernicious influence to the ignorance of the parish clergy, incapable of assuming an enlightening role among the benighted flocks. In the case of the parish church within the Roman walls, he offered an image of comic incongruity, thus encouraging the connoisseurs of Venice to come sort through the unappreciated ancient wreckage of Dalmatia.

Treasure hunting in Dalmatia, however, ran the risk of resulting in serious damage to the antiquities if the local population was not tactfully reconciled to the venture. Above all, Fortis feared that the Morlacchi, feudally drafted to perform forced labor in transporting the colossal monuments of the ancient world, would take their revenge upon the marbles rather than the masters.

> The Morlacchi inhabitants of Podgraje did not in the past do any injury to the tablets that they encountered while plowing and digging the earth for their needs. But since they have been obliged to haul, without pay, several sepulchral columns all the way to the sea with their oxen, they have sworn enmity against all the inscriptions; and they ruin them as soon as they are dis-

interred with blows of the pick-axe, or else they inter them again more deeply than before. It would certainly be wrong of anyone to want to accuse them of barbarism for this. The way to make them into researchers and preservers of the ancient monuments would be to have them hope for a prize for discoveries and labors. I have found, by a rare accident, in the house of the Morlacco Jureka, a sepulchral piece, which I acquired for little money, and will carry back to Italy along with some others. By captivating the confidence and friendship of the Morlacchi, one could reasonably hope to get useful indications. I flatter myself that I know how to do it, knowing the character of the nation; and therefore I left Podgraje with a great will to return there armed with the necessary faculties to excavate.[53]

Where once the Romans ruled over Dalmatia, the Venetians now not only ruled in their own right, but also exercised a special curatorial imperialism over the Roman remains. Indeed, Fortis made his antiquarian ambitions into part of the general project of imperial conciliation, benevolently articulated as "captivating the confidence and friendship of the Morlacchi."[54] He himself indicated the political implications of knowledge when he advertised his own expertise in "knowing the character of the nation."

Caminer, in the *Storia della guerra presente,* took momentary refuge from the complications of war in the Roman ruins of Dalmatia at Salona. His account of the peasant who accidentally discovered an ancient subterranean structure was consistent with Fortis's advertisement of Dalmatia as an unexplored domain where archaeological discoveries were just waiting to happen. When Fortis traveled from Split to nearby Salona, he saw "a wretched village which preserves little that is recognizable of its ancient splendor," not only on account of the comparative wretchedness of contemporary Dalmatia, but also because the ancient ruins were subject to modern depradations. "The two last centuries have destroyed that which escaped the barbarism of the northern nations," wrote Fortis, thus positing a continuity of vandalism between the Goths who overran the ancient Roman empire and the more recent recurrence of barbarous destruction. He clarified his accusation with reference to the kind of local discovery that Caminer described in his mention of Salona, but Fortis saw such discovery as less completely serendipitous:

> The inhabitants of the village that arose from the ruins of Salona unfortunately often bring up inscriptions from underground, and other works of ancient carving, but their greed is so proportional to their barbarism that they prefer to break and wreck everything rather than receive a moderate price. I

have tried to save some beautiful tablets newly discovered by the sad hands of
a peasant, who had already wrecked many others of which we saw the pieces,
by making himself frames for windows and doors: but his avidity smashed my
designs at that time and I had to be content with copying.[55]

Here the continuity of barbarism was explicitly stated; the new Goths
were none other than the local inhabitants. At inland Podgraje Fortis's
offer of "little money" was readily accepted, and he gloated over the bar-
gain; at Salona, however, barbarism was not tempered by need but aggravated by greed and, to his outrage, the "moderate price" was declined.

Fortis warned his cultivated readers that "the daily danger of being
destroyed threatens all things of that kind that are found spread around
Dalmatia, and it is also for that woeful reason that I believe I am obliged
to speak of this." His obligation to speak—of this as well as every other
aspect of Dalmatia—implied a reciprocal public obligation to respond in
a spirit of civilized responsibility. In this sense, his voyage in Dalmatia
was also an invitation to Dalmatia, and that invitation had to be construed as an imperial imperative. For anyone who found the marbles of
Salona insufficiently enticing Fortis hastened to add that in the little river
that ran through the site there was to be found "in the mossy grottoes an
exquisite species of trout." Fortis's public charge was to report on fishing
in Dalmatia for the Venetian government, and he noted the satirical legend that Diocletian put aside his imperial power to better enjoy the deli-
cious local fish. The most famous Roman ruin in Dalmatia was Diocletian's palace at Split, but Fortis expressed reservations about the "bad
taste" of the late third century.[56] He referred antiquarians to Adam's
book of engravings and recommended to architects and sculptors that
they skip Split and study the ruins in Rome.

Near Zadar at Nin he hoped to discover ancient ruins but found himself more impressed by the fish. "I brought myself there with the hope of
seeing something worthy to be noted, but found myself disappointed,"
wrote Fortis. "Not only does nothing remain that indicates the greatness
of Roman times, but not even any residue of barbarous magnificence
that recalls the centuries when the kings of the Slavi Croati resided
there." He consoled himself with the hope of harvesting "a considerable
quantity of fish and especially eels," even envisioning an important industry in salted eels "that would serve our internal commerce."[57] It would
not have occurred to Fortis to consider the contemporary inhabitants of

Dalmatia as Croatians; the Slavi Croati were, to his mind, a name from the historical roll call of ancient barbarians.

Along the Primorje littoral Fortis took an interest in Slavic as well as Roman antiquities. He reported finding at Tucepi "many ancient Slavic tombs, without any inscription, but with various bas-reliefs," including one that featured "a warrior strangely dressed who wore on his head a kind of cap upon which rose a most pointed cone." There was even a legend that this marked the resting place of a Venetian doge who fell in fighting against the Narentani. Fortis made a drawing of the relief, *per curiosità*. He could not do the same for the classical antiquities from that area: "Greek and Roman inscriptions have been found, and have passed into Italy." Even inscriptions that had not yet been collected and dispatched were sometimes inaccessible. "We stopped at Drasnize to see a Roman tablet that was supposed to be there, but was kept hidden by the rude curate of the place for the usual reasons of suspicion and ignorance," wrote Fortis. "We had to be content with copying two Slavic inscriptions."[58] Here he seemed to set out his antiquarian priorities, with Slavic inscriptions ranked as lesser, though sometimes copied for the sake of curiosity when Roman remains were unavailable for inspection. In this he certainly conformed to the values of contemporary Venetian collectors, but, ironically, the general European interest in Fortis's voyage put greater emphasis on his altogether original collection of Slavic songs from the oral tradition. Fortis was the first to present the poetry of the South Slavs to the public of Europe; it was perhaps his most important "discovery" in Dalmatia. Considering the Slavic archaeological remains in Dalmatia, however, Fortis, as he wrote his account, seemed almost to apologize for taking the time to attend to antiquities that were neither Greek nor Roman.

If he returned to Venice with more Slavic songs than Roman tablets, the most material reason, regardless of cultural priorities, was that stone was so heavy. He only dared to imagine the collection that he could not possibly pursue, the sampling of marbles that would engage all his various interests in geology, antiquity, and the economic deployment of natural resources.

> I gathered some stray pieces of the finest marble for statues, evidently detached from superior strata not very far from the sea, and a noble red marble of a fine and most uniform grain, worthy of being employed in any ornament

for sacred places or noble rooms. If the naturalist traveler (*viaggiatore Natu-ralista*) ever had the necessary means to carry back to our country (*Patria*) some speaking proofs of the utility (*utilità*) of his observations, I would have returned to Venice with slabs or pieces of the most beautiful littoral marbles, that might have made sculptors and stone-masons fall in love with our own domestic productions (*produzioni nostrali*) of this kind.[59]

Fortis once again proposed a collection of raw materials, in the spirit of Griselini's dictionary, to be established in the name of national economy. The power of the principle was all the more evident from the fact that the collection itself was completely impracticable, its items too weighty to assemble; in fact, the sum of the raw materials of the Republic consti-tuted just such a theoretical collection of actual uncollectibles, the Patria conceived as Gabinetto Nazionale. Fortis's fantasy of carrying home a collection of marble slabs was also intended to justify himself as *viaggia-tore Naturalista*, proving the essential ring of relations that linked the ur-gent concerns of national economy, raw materials, and domestic produc-tions, to the scholarly study of antiquity, geology, and natural history. His ultimate flourish was to endow his fantasy with elements of grandeur and gorgeousness from the tradition of Venetian art, appealing to the values of Veronese, emphasizing color and texture, in the reddish beauty, fine grain, and ornamental splendor of Dalmatia's noble marbles.

Fossil Remains and Geological Reflections

Fortis's interest in antiquities in Dalmatia not only offered marble entice-ments to the connoisseurs who read his account, but also served as a sort of decorative erudition in the context of the book as a whole. If marble samples and antique columns were too heavy to carry back to Italy, the discussion of antiquities made for comparatively light reading alongside the scientific and economic issues that Fortis addressed. The section on Split was dedicated to John Strange, the British minister in Venice, who pursued parallel passions for geology and art. He was a collector and dealer who acquired the works of Titian and Veronese, of Tiepolo and Canaletto, but he offered his patronage not only to a painter like Francesco Guardi for his views of the Venetian lagoon but also to Al-berto Fortis for his researches in Adriatic geology. Strange, Fortis sup-posed, would appreciate the balance of the book, its range of concerns from eels to antiquities. "I hope that you," wrote Fortis to Strange, discussing the age of Diocletian in Dalmatia, "far from condemning me, will approve my diligence in spreading perhaps some not disagreeable variety in my writing, rendered unfortunately tedious by the aridity of the paleontological matters."[60] Fortis and Strange both cultivated an enlightened Venetian variety, in which the spirit of empirical observation and curatorial collection brought together art and science, antiquity and geology, ancient history and natural history. This integration of interests reflected the comprehensive intellectual curiosity of the European Enlightenment, an ideal that found its monumental expression in the encyclopedic project of Diderot and d'Alembert.

The perceived relation between fossils and antiquities was formulated in a rhetorical appeal from Giovanni Arduino (Fortis's geological colleague in Padua) to Johann Jakob Ferber (Fortis's geological correspondent in Sweden): "Illustrious Ferber, quit those Greek and Roman medals, monuments to transient episodes in history, and leave their study to the indolent antiquary. . . . Observe and enrich your already abundant collection with those which Vulcan and Neptune, those two eternal and powerful rulers, have liberally dispersed throughout the Earth's stratified entrails." Fossils were thus conceived as the most truly ancient antiquities, so that "he who wishes to learn the true version of the great history of our planet, as well as the many periods of tremendous catastrophes and changes it has undergone, has no choice but to study these signs and medals attentively." Fortis and Strange, who together with Arduino constituted a sort of Venetian school of geology, would have appreciated this view of fossils as the ultimate antiquities, as monuments to the most ancient history of the earth. Luca Ciancio, writing about Fortis's geology, has observed that Fortis, Strange, and Arduino "believed in the possibility of reconstructing a history of the most recent phases in the life of the planet thanks to the integration of mythological sources, ancient testimonies, and fossil evidence."[61] His interest in fossils brought Fortis to the brink of current evolutionary concerns in natural history, and, at the end of the century, he would go to Paris to the Muséum d'Histoire Naturelle, to consider such issues in the scientific company of Georges Cuvier and Jean-Baptiste Lamarck. In Dalmatia, however, Fortis's interrelated attentions to geology and paleontology, as well as antiquarian studies, were also politically implicated in the Adriatic imperial mission.

"Fossil bones, which are so frequently found in Dalmatia," wrote Fortis, in his initial work on the island of Cres, "were the principal object of our voyage." Griselini, to be sure, had emphasized the political importance of knowing "what products or primary materials are abundant, are scarce, or are lacking," but an abundance of fossils was unlikely to be commercially profitable to the Republic. As in the case of antiquities, however, fossil remains had acquired a special value in the eighteenth century from their place in the collections of connoisseurs, and Fortis appreciated both the material importance of fossils as collectible objects and also their more abstract significance for the advance of science. Local inhabitants knew where to find the fossils: "The fishermen and sailors, who coast along those shores in small barks, know where to indicate, and the shepherds know where on land and in the caverns." Fortis, however, invited further exploration by scientists and amateurs of the public, whose researches would be rewarded with a trove of collectibles. "Chance could reveal new things to observers, as it did to us," he declared, "if, from now on, the amateurs of natural marvels came with some frequency to those shores." Fortis mentioned that some fossils of "Illyrian bones" were already in the care of the Venetian patrician Jacopo Morosini, saluted as a "diligent collector of marine curiosities and fossils."[62] To direct the interests of other such collectors toward Dalmatia, Fortis illustrated his invitation with the grim engraving of a human jaw, marking the pirate treasure of precious fossils.

Human bones made the fossil troves of Dalmatia particularly interesting, and Fortis seemed to see the quantity as a matter of patriotic pride, while casting doubt on the fossils of other nations:

> Even if all the fossil bones mentioned by various writers were truly human, our Illyrian bones would, on that account, be no less worthy of particular consideration, for in conservation, in frequency, and in quantity they surpass all the others known until now by the paleontologists. In our rather hurried voyage across the island of Cherso and Osero, in more than one place we had them excavated under our own eyes.[63]

Direct eyewitnessed demonstration was essential to Fortis's scientific method, but though he testified to the stratum of fossils that was unearthed before his own eyes, he could only speculate about how far that stratum extended, and his scientific suppositions traveled well beyond the range of his own vision. The "extraordinary supply of bones" and the "position of the various heaps observed by us" suggested to Fortis the "conjecture" of a vastly extensive geological stratum that reached all the way from the Adriatic islands to the Aegean islands—which was, as it happened, the very domain of Venice's receding maritime empire. These "heaps of Illyrian bones" might not extend continously along the coast, Fortis remarked; that was, however, no reason to deny the existence of "such a portentous stratum," since the long passage of time would have had a disruptive effect. If Fortis's geological geography looked to distant horizons, his geological chronology presupposed an immensely ancient history for the fossil remains:

> How many centuries would have been needed to render them so frequent, and how many more to raise from their level the mountains and hills, in whose bases or bowels the heaps of bones are interned? And in what century would we want to believe that there dwelled in these regions the nation that preexisted the formation of the marine mountains and the islands that rise in our own times from the Adriatic? I am far from offering an opinion of my own about the origin of such a strange phenomenon . . .[64]

Fortis's caution was both politic and scientific, for his heaps of fossils inevitably pointed toward the dangerously controversial geological issue of deep time, indicating a chronology of the earth's history that made nonsense out of Genesis.

By the end of the decade, in 1780, Fortis would have to respond to an accusation, published in a journal in Rome, of insufficient respect for religion "in speaking of the age of the world." As a priest, he seemed to think it prudent to answer politely, though evasively: "It is true that I tend to give the world the oldest age that I can: but it is equally true that my desire to make it old has been accompanied by the respect due to the Sacred Documents." There was perhaps an element of irony in the unspecified amount of "respect due" (*rispetto dovuto*), for Fortis was not enthusiastic about having to reconcile every finding of fossils with the biblical history of Noah and the Flood. Back in 1767, in an anonymous article, Fortis had named his heroes, hailing "the great Galileo" and "the immortal Bacon" as "the fathers of modern knowledge," while in 1769, in a satire on the baptism of abortions, he had written ironically about the popes who "decided that Galileo was of infirm mind, and proved that the earth stood still." Toward the end of his life, publishing in Napoleonic Paris in 1802, Fortis had no need to temper his contempt for the "superstition"—which meant Christianity according to the code of the Enlightenment—that insisted on "the absurd doctrine of the youth of the world." Faced with the fossils of Cres, Fortis dismissed the past objections of religious apologists: "They were certainly wrong to call religion to the assistance of their favorite hypothesis, trying to combat and overturn the observations of the most learned naturalists with arbitrary interpretations of sacred texts. Religion never gains on such occasions, as is proved by the abjuration of Galileo which does such dishonor to Italy."[65] Fortis, crossing the Adriatic and removing himself from Italy, was all the more ready to articulate a modern and enlightened perspective on the unedifying former relations between Roman religion and Italian science.

"As for myself," wrote Fortis, "I am too demonstratively convinced that I do not have the necessary data to hit the truth, and therefore I do not defend as reasonable any conjecture about the ancient origin of the Illyrian fossil bones." Far from feeling impelled to offer any definitive conclusion, Fortis much preferred to invite the attentions of other researchers and bring them to Dalmatia by attracting them with heaps of bones: "These are certainly, to my belief, among the most important objects that may exercise the educated curiosity of the naturalists; and it would be desirable that some of them, disposed by genius, might be able to give us an account of how far, precisely, these extend throughout Dalmatia and the islands of the Levant." Without insisting on his own conjectures, he nevertheless permitted his scientific imagination to play over the particular geographical regions of greatest historical interest to Venice; the invocation of Dalmatia and the Levant could hardly fail to inspire in his readers some patriotic associations with Venice's imperial past. He believed that the maritime domain of Venice possessed its own distinctive geological history, for the islands off the coast of Dalmatia, like Cres and Losinj, were formed "by a most ancient sea," much older than the "new sea," that is, the modern Adriatic.[66] Science thus had something to offer to the Venetian tradition of historiography, looking back far beyond the accounts of Pietro Bembo and his successors to identify the geological stratum on which the history of Venice found its geographical base.

Fortis supposed that the effects of ancient seas and volcanoes had transformed the landscape of the Adriatic, "that the most ancient protuberances of our globe were much more vast and more regular, and completely different in structure from those that we see today." The undulating hills of Cres and Losinj seemed "the work of a most vast ocean," for the island, according to Fortis, was so old and so altered that nothing remained of its ancient surfaces. Inspecting the hills along the Adriatic he articulated his hypothesis of ongoing geological transformation, an altogether unbiblical interpretation of dynamic negotation between land and sea through the many millennia of deep time.

> With the passage of centuries those hills, the roots and interiors of which were inclined toward the dismantling sea, have been reduced by half, and therefore show outwardly their inclination toward the land. And the hills which in our days are thus half demolished, will be destroyed with the passing of years; their roots will become hidden quicksands; and the sea continuing to press, and gaining more every day on the land from that side, will swallow up again, little by little, that stretch of country, which perhaps it has abandoned little by little, and covered over again, in alternation, who knows how many times. This kind of prophecy is not based on intellectual chimeras, but properly on visible facts.[67]

The gaining of the sea upon the land was annotated by Fortis with reference to Venice itself, where every Venetian could see that the sea was rising and the city sinking, where the reinforcement of the dikes was "today no longer enough to keep the sea away from us." This was not to be ascribed to the providential destiny of Venice, but rather to the simple fact that "the sea sometimes loses and sometimes gains," in accordance with the "revolutions" of the earth. In 1765, in Istria, Fortis was inspired by the Adriatic to propose an imaginative experiment, which came to him as a "geological dream." One had to imagine the waters of the Adriatic gulf suddenly dropping to the point where the bottom was exposed as a rolling landscape, domesticated and inhabited, and then imagine that landscape suddenly submerged again under the sea. "It would take a great turning of centuries to cause, or gradually to conduct, such a remarkable revolution," Fortis admitted, but he was unintimidated by deep time.[68]

In Dalmatia Fortis found confirmation of his geological dream, and the underground presence of Roman antiquities—like the ruins at Salona, announced by Caminer—offered further evidence of changing geological levels. In fact, not only collectors of inscriptions and fossils, but also researchers of scientific truth, needed to be sent to Dalmatia for their own enlightenment:

> It might be necessary to send up there all those who, remaining at ease and taking shelter in their rooms, pronounce magisterially that our earth is now

precisely in the same state in which it was sixty centuries ago, and who believe they have proved it sufficiently when they adduce in confirmation of their opinion, not based on observation, the remains of remote antiquity that are still exposed in elevated places, forgetting all those that are found completely buried.[69]

Crossing the Adriatic from Italy to Dalmatia offered a more reliable scientific perspective for those benighted souls who could not face the hard facts of geology, who remained subject to the pernicious influences that once forced Galileo to his knees. Dalmatia appeared as the touchstone of the Venetian Enlightenment. Appropriately, it was the subterranean ruins of antiquity which demonstrated the religiously problematic truths of geological history, that the earth was immensely old and always changing.

"Tutto, tutto si cangia," chanted Fortis in his "geological poem" of 1768: "Everything, everything changes." In 1802, in his natural history memoirs, he elegantly articulated the same principle in almost poetic French prose. Nature was eternal, each century passing like a moment ("la nature éternelle, devant qui les moments et les siècles sont égaux"); nature's laws were forever forming and reforming different combinations of matter ("composant, décomposant, recomposant sans cesse et sans relache les différentes combinaisons de la matière"). The geological formations of the eastern Adriatic coast confirmed Fortis in this principle in the 1770s, and he affirmed that there, in Dalmatia, "the thought of the observer can not but pursue conjectures about the revolutions endured by our globe, and about the different aspects that its parts must have had in remote times."[70] While Caminer's *Storia della guerra presente* ranged widely over the international scene to create the genre of up-to-the-moment contemporary history, Fortis's *Viaggio in Dalmazia* focused on only one strictly delimited provincial space to discover the principles of supremely ancient geological history. Caminer's register of rapidly evolving "perturbations" in contemporary politics was in marked metronomic contrast to Fortis's notion of the staggeringly slow-paced "revolutions" of the earth.

To Reform Ideas about Dalmatia

In 1765, at the conclusion of his triennial term as Provveditore Generale of Dalmatia, Pietro Michiel reported to Venice on the incongruity of the province's economic backwardness, considering that "it abounds in lands that in other regions serve to render the subject comfortable, to give a considerable increment to commerce, and to bring noticeable utility to the state." He enumerated its products—from animals and almonds to salt and sardines to wine and wax—and he put the blame for backwardness on the laziness of the Dalmatians.[71] At the same time, in 1766, Griselini in Venice emphasized the importance of studying natural resources as part of any program "to render a nation rich and powerful." Fortis, in his *Viaggio in Dalmazia*, sought to apply his understanding of natural history to the imperial purpose of making Dalmatia economically useful to Venice; in the matter of fishing he actually entered into the service of the state, commissioned by Memmo who presided over a special deputation. In 1773 the Senate adopted the deputation's "useful suggestion" to take advantage of Fortis's researches in Dalmatia, inasmuch as "together with the scientific knowledge that adorns him, the practice of various languages including Illyrian is very much adapted to the present need."[72] Fortis, however, was disappointed later in the decade when he did not receive the official recognition that he most coveted in the form of a chair in natural history at the University of Padua. Though eager to be useful to the Republic of Venice in the 1770s, he sought to make himself useful to the Kingdom of Naples in the 1780s, in a project that concerned the exploitation of resources of saltpeter for gunpowder in southern Italy. His dedication to integrating natural history and economic development was such that in 1791, after his return to the Republic, he was credulously enthusiastic about the performances of a supposed diviner who seemed possibly useful for divining the presence of mineral deposits.[73]

While the exploitation of natural resources could make Dalmatia useful to Venice, the collection of fossils and antiquities could be internationally useful to the advancement of science. "On one of these little islands," wrote Fortis, exploring around Cres, "we stopped to dig up most of the fossil bones, with which we returned, and which are now distributed among the most considerable museums of England." One particular Adriatic fossil specimen, illustrated in the *Viaggio in Dalmazia*, was announced as having "passed to England, into the rich collection of Lord Bute, the most celebrated patron of natural history in that kingdom."[74] The dispatch of Dalmatian fossils to England was an incentive to Venice to pay greater attention to a province whose products and artifacts were valued abroad. Indeed, with the passing of decades Fortis would come to feel that he too was valued more abroad than in Venice, and he was finally elected to the English Royal Society in 1795, though he could never obtain a proper university position at home in Padua. English patronage and scientific companionship were crucial to his research in Dalmatia; he traveled together with Symonds and Hervey and received financial sponsorship from Bute and Strange. Fortis was probably not fully aware of the fact that his British collaborators came to regard his manifold enthusiasms with some reserve, as indicated by a letter from Hervey to Strange in 1778: "What a misfortune to the Publick that a man endowed with almost every requisite for the pursuit of Physical truths should from the mere redundance of genius and fire want the essential. Years perhaps may calm him and give him to us with less wind in his sails, but more ballast in his bottom."[75] Hervey spoke for the international scientific public of the Enlightenment, while Fortis's more volatile genius also addressed the political and economic concerns of the Venetian public.

Fortis's patriotic emphasis on Dalmatia's utility to Venice served partly to mask the fact that his trans-Adriatic project was so substantially an English scientific concern. "I have for these ten years past, on and off," wrote Strange about Fortis in 1781, "employed him in various peregrinations, in Italy, Sicily, Dalmatia etc., chiefly for the purpose of Physical Geography, Antiquities, and Philology in general for which he has an admirable turn." While Fortis might have hesitated to see himself as an English employee, in the *Viaggio in Dalmazia* he dedicated different sections to Bute, to Hervey, and to Strange, and the whole book was published in London in 1778, only four years after the original Venetian edition. The dedication to Strange of Fortis's section on Split offered gratitude for the "precious friendship" of a "true philosopher." Strange himself had recently returned from a voyage of paleontological research in the Alps, and Fortis sought to emphasize the different quality of his own voyage: "What a difference from Germany and France to Dalmatia!" A report from Dalmatia was of special value to the cause of science precisely because it was remote from the more familiar scientific itineraries:

> I have traveled through a vast country where the sciences are little cultivated, and natural history is barely known by name. My expeditions have been made by chance; I often went wandering like a blind man through vast deserts, and wild mountains, with the hope of encountering something that would repay my labors, and unfortunately often finding myself disillusioned. I could know nothing about the useful or curious products of those regions except what I could see with my own eyes.[76]

Fortis's sense of himself as a scientific pioneer, making his way through an unknown landscape, was proportional to the emphatic difference that he formulated between Dalmatia and the rest of Europe.

The real reward of his labors, for his scientific colleagues and correspondents in the Republic of Letters, was an acquaintance with a region that none of them knew at all. Dalmatia offered scientific and economic opportunities as yet unexplored and unexploited, but because the province was subject to Venice it was accessible to the Venetian investigator in search of "useful or curious products." Whatever he discovered there, in spite of inconvenience and obstruction, was guaranteed to be empirically pure, because, in a province where science had been hitherto unknown, every discovery was made by direct observation—"what I could see with my own eyes." He affirmed his expertise as one who "has extended his own observations along the beaches and the coasts of the Adriatic, and after long examinations knows the nature of the marble strata of Dalmatia."[77] Thus he appeared as an authority on the province, putting before the public of Venice his claim to know Dalmatia by direct observations better than any previous visitor.

Earlier authorities on Dalmatia were casually dismissed: "One can only laugh when one reads, in the first volume of the *Illyricum Sacrum* of the Jesuit Father Farlati . . . that the waters of the rivers Narenta and Cetina come together against those of the river Kerka. The mouth of the Narenta is a good eighty-five miles away from this place." In fact, Farlati's first volume had appeared not long ago in 1751, with sacred concerns taking priority over rigorous geographical observations. Fortis was all the more ready to correct the important Dalmatian authorities of the seventeenth century, like Simone Gliubavaz of Zadar, who wrote a manuscript, *De situ Illyrici,* and especially Joannes Lucius of Trogir, author of *De regno Dalmatiae et Croatiae,* published in Amsterdam in 1666 and republished in Vienna as recently as 1758. Observing the remains of Roman aqueducts, Fortis declared, "I am in a position to assert positively that the Dalmatian historians," notably Gliubavaz and Lucius, "have made a great blunder in this matter, having written that Trajan conducted water from the river Tizio or Kerka all the way to Zara, taking it from the waterfall at Scardona." In the spirit of enlightened criticism Fortis investigated and laughed at the blunders of previous authorities, one at a time, or all together. "Simone Gliubavaz wrote, Giovanni Lucio published, and Father Farlati repeated, on faith, that in other times there was an aqueduct," noted Fortis, at the waterfall. "They were led into error by the remains of an ignoble brick canal."[78] As a scientist Fortis set himself to correct these errors on the basis of direct and accurate observations.

The accessibility of Venetian Dalmatia to such scientific study appeared in clear contrast to the case of Ottoman Bosnia, just across the border. Though Pliny advertised gold in Dalmatia in ancient times, Fortis, even without a diviner, regretfully ruled out the likelihood of either gold or silver among the natural resources of the province. Bosnia, he thought, might be more happily endowed with precious metals, "to the extent that one can conjecture from the relations of our men who do business there." Srebrenica, for instance, took its name from the word "*Srebro,* which signifies silver in all the dialects of the Slavonic language." Second-hand reports and erudite etymologies, however, were not the same as direct observation with one's own eyes, and Fortis respected the distinction between Dalmatia which he had personally explored and Bosnia about which he had only heard reports. "Many other things relevant to the fossil history of Bosnia were recounted to me," he remarked, "but I do not think it proper to give an account of them on the word of others."[79] The borders of Dalmatia remained, for the moment, the Adriatic frontier of European paleontology.

Fortis was keen to advertise the virtues and values of Dalmatia, its economic utility for Venice and its scientific significance for Europe. However rich in minerals Bosnia might be, Dalmatia was not to be despised. Fortis reported on the antiquities that he saw with his own eyes, not only to excite the interest of antiquarians, but also "to reform the ideas (*riformare l'idee*) that are commonly held among us with regard to Dalmatia, where so many Roman colonies would not have been planted if it was such a horrid country as portrayed." If Rome had thought it worthwhile to colonize Dalmatia, then the same province would surely repay the imperial attentions of Venice. Fortis's campaign to burnish and refurbish the image of Dalmatia before the public, to rediscover the province with his own eyes and confirm its colonial value for a modern empire, was crucial to the purpose of demonstrating that natural history was truly useful. The book was intended not just to inform, but more generally to "reform" ideas about Dalmatia. He went on to define and confide his personal commitment, addressing Antonio Vallisnieri, professor of natural history at the University of Padua, Fortis's godfather, his early scientific mentor, and now the elderly occupant of the chair that Fortis hoped to obtain for himself in succession.

> Although I know well enough the small strength of a book, and the very great strength of prejudices and circumstances, I will confess to you that I secretly feel a sort of satisfaction in thinking that it is possible that my voyage will cause some benefit to the Dalmatian nation, if not now immediately, at least with the passing of years. I would believe myself to be the most fortunate of all voyagers, if before I ceased to exist upon our earth I could be convinced that I existed usefully.[80]

This invocation of the Dalmatian nation (*Nazione Dalmatina*) in 1774 echoed the verses of Goldoni's *La Dalmatina* of 1758, but whereas the drama celebrated the glory of that nation, Fortis's work advertised utilitarian values. He sought to prove himself ultimately useful by demonstrating the unanticipated utility of Dalmatia. The textual web of dedications to patrons and colleagues, like the interspersed invitations to collectors and connoisseurs, were designed for the purpose of involving and engaging an inner circle of the enlightened public in the reformed idea of Dalmatia.

Conclusion: Magnificent Monuments of the Adriatic Empire

In the mountains Fortis visited the fortress of Clissa, identified it by a reference to Pliny, and reflected, for a moment, on military matters:

> Now Clissa is in fact a small distance from Salona, constructed upon an inaccessible cliff, surrounded by canyons and ravines, dominated by the peak of the mountain. Pliny speaks of Mandetrio as a place ennobled by actions of arms. Clissa has also been that, unfortunately, in times near to us; and it would be again whenever the scourge of war should desolate Dalmatia ("ogniqualvolta il flagello della guerra desolasse la Dalmazia").[81]

This tentative, grammatically subjunctive, reference to the possibility of war was one of the few to be found in Fortis's *Viaggio in Dalmazia*. Such reticence seems hardly incidental, considering that the fundamental fact of contemporary politics was the ongoing Russian-Ottoman war. In 1770, the year that Fortis first crossed the sea to visit Dalmatia, the Russian fleet also made its astonishing appearance in the Adriatic; in 1774, the year that Fortis published his book in Venice, St. Petersburg and Constantinople reached their public peace accord with the treaty of Kuchuk Kainardji.

In spite of Voltaire's impatience, Venice maintained a nervous neutrality throughout the conflict, and Dalmatia, with its vulnerability to Ottoman incursions along the Bosnian border, fortunately escaped the desolations of war. Fortis's voyage depended upon Venetian neutrality, since he could hardly have undertaken such a project of comprehensive research in an armed and active arena of military conflict. At the same time, his attention to Dalmatia at that particular moment in the history of Venice was conditioned by heightened concern about the proximity and susceptibility of the province to the ongoing war in southeastern Europe. Furthermore, Fortis's whole program for economic development and scientific study in Dalmatia, for making the province useful, profitable, and interesting to Venice, was only consistent with the maintenance of peace. The scourge of war would mean the end of his imperial project.

Just as Caminer, in the *Storia della guerra presente,* permitted himself to contemplate Dalmatia for a moment, announcing the discovery of the underground ruins at Salona, so Fortis, in the *Viaggio in Dalmazia,* could not repress an occasional reference to the contemporary war, formulating his anxieties not far from Salona at the mountain fortress of Clissa. Otherwise the mountains there inspired him with his more usual sort of reflections on science and resources. "The isolated cliff upon which Clissa rises," he remarked, "is for the most part of marble breccia, whose origin is submarine, so that between one pebble and another there are caught isolated little marine bodies." Here was more Dalmatian evidence of the geological transformations of the earth. In the nearby mountains he admired the marble for its gorgeous coloring—"marked with purple and other most beautiful colors"—and he imagined it put to splendid use. "Superb columns and magnificent monuments could be worked from it," he suggested, "if the place were less far from the sea, or the connecting roads more passable." Yet, if it was possible to imagine the monuments, it was also possible to envision the roads, and Fortis permitted himself a moment of hypothetical history: "Who knows if in past centuries a country, so inhabited by Roman colonies and frequented by armies, might not have had comfortable roads, of which we have now lost both the vestiges and the memory?"[82] In such speculation, as in the geological dream of rising and falling seas, Fortis spun a fantasy of both the past and the future.

Without those roads from the mountains to the sea, Venice could not easily transport across Dalmatia either great blocks of marble or large armies of men. Yet, whether or not the Romans ever really built the roads that Fortis imagined—"who knows?"—Venice might still undertake to build them someday soon, and proudly witness the rewards in purplish marble monuments, lustrously reflected in the Venetian canals. When Fortis published *Viaggio in Dalmazia* in 1774, Venice had managed to preserve its neutrality through the conclusion of the peace and, having averted the desolations of war in Dalmatia, could contemplate a program of modern imperial economy to take advantage of the natural resources across the Adriatic.

~ CHAPTER THREE

The Character and Customs of the Morlacchi: From Provincial Administration to Enlightened Anthropology

Introduction: Ferocious Morlacchi

"Several times, during your sojourn among us," wrote Fortis, addressing himself to Lord Bute within the *Viaggio in Dalmazia*, "you will have heard talk of the Morlacchi as a race of ferocious men, unreasonable, without humanity (*d'una razza d'uomini feroce, irragionevole, priva d'umanità*), capable of any misdeed; and maybe it will have seemed to you that I have been rather more temerarious than one ought to allow to a naturalist, choosing the country inhabited by them as the object of my peregrinations."[1] In fact, the choice of Dalmatia as an object of study was determined by its political relation to Venice, for the Morlacchi, like Fortis himself, were subjects of San Marco. If the ferocious reputation of the Morlacchi gave Fortis's voyage an air of reckless danger, this only underlined the imperial asymmetry between Venice's metropolitan perspective and Dalmatia's provincial status. Fortis, as a full-fledged philosophe of the Enlightenment, found further reason for his voyage to Dalmatia in rebutting the unenlightened disparagement of its inhabitants as irrational and inhumane. Though his principal scientific purpose may have been the search for fossils, and his official economic assignment the study of fishing, it was his account of the Morlacchi and his collection of their Slavic folk poetry that made *Viaggio in Dalmazia* a work of immediate sensational renown, not only in Venice but all over Europe. Though travel among the Morlacchi might have appeared to be a reckless choice for a naturalist—and indeed he found them, if not actually dangerous to

126

himself, still unhelpful, and even obstructive, in his collection of fossils and antiquities—the choice was nevertheless serendipitous for revealing in Fortis yet another vocation among his vast diversity of researches; for thus he played the part of a pioneering figure in the modern study of folklore and anthropology.

"The inhabitants of the coastal cities of Dalmatia recount a great number of cruel deeds of these people," wrote Fortis. He recognized the distinction between urban coastal society and the pastoral people of the mountainous interior, but he also appreciated that this distinction was a matter of perspective, the supposedly "civilized" coastal Dalmatians regarding with horror and apprehension the Morlacchi, who allegedly committed "the most atrocious excesses of murder, arson, and violence." Fortis declared himself in defense of the Morlacchi against such imputations, which he thought were "out of date" (*d'antica data*) and "rather to be ascribed to the corruption of a few individuals than to the bad universal character of the nation" (*all'universale cattiva indole della Nazione*). Goldoni in 1758, in *La Dalmatina,* recognized a distinct Dalmatian "nation" within the Venetian empire, and Fortis in 1774 seemed to distinguish a Morlacchi "nation" within the province of Dalmatia. Indeed, like Goldoni with the Dalmatians, Fortis declared himself the champion of the Morlacchi: "I believe that I owe to the nation, by whom I was so well received and humanely treated, a most ample Apologia, writing about that which I personally saw of their inclinations and customs."[2] The apparent ascription of distinct nationhood to the Morlacchi, among the Dalmatians, was in part a matter of geography, the distinction between the coastal cities, ruled by Venice for centuries, and the interior villages, added only recently to the Venetian empire with the *nuovo* and *nuovissimo acquisto.* Fortis, however, also indicated that this was not merely a geographical matter, for whereas every other section of the *Viaggio in Dalmazia* was geographically specified, by region or by river—for instance, "Del Contado di Zara" or "Del Corso della Kerka"—this one alone was anthropologically labeled: "De' Costumi de' Morlacchi."

In Dalmatian documents the Morlacchi were first mentioned in the fourteenth century, when they visited the market of Zadar to obtain salt for their flocks. From the fifteenth century, after the Turkish conquest of Bosnia, these Morlacchi appeared as part of the Ottoman population, across the border from Venetian Dalmatia. In the seventeenth century,

Jacob Spon and George Wheler encountered the Morlacchi, also in the marketplace of Zadar, and found them ferocious in appearance: "They have a terrible look, and, bringing their goods to the market, they also bring their sabers and muskets. They speak Slavic, and for the most part they follow the religion of the Greeks."[3] Fortis, a century later, was aware that the name of the Morlacchi implied some relation to the Vlachs, the linguistically Latinate, pastoral population of southeastern Europe, but he also recognized that these contemporary Morlacchi were, by language, unequivocally Slavs. In the early twentieth century the Serbian ethnographer, Jovan Cvijić, discussing the Adriatic variety of the Dinaric type, identified in a footnote "the Slavicized Vlachs or Morlachs," seen as "the most primitive population," and already "very rare."[4] They could still be found, however, in the early twentieth century in the marketplace of Zadar where they were noted by foreign tourists as a rare and remarkable attraction. Alice Moqué described the Morlacchi as "strange, uncouth-looking people," and Maude Holbach heard them speak "the strangest tongue that ever assailed my ears." Frances Hutchinson identified them as "swarthy Slavs," admiring their "barbaric costumes" and general "picturesqueness."[5] Fortis, in the eighteenth century, made the Morlacchi famous throughout Europe, as a subject for anthropological and philosophical reflection; by the twentieth century, in spite of their picturesque appeal, they were well on the way to ethnographic oblivion.

Spon and Wheler noted that "for the most part" the Morlacchi were Greek Orthodox in religion, though some were Roman Catholic; in the nineteenth and twentieth centuries, the Morlacchi were sorted out as Serbs and Croats, according to the categories of modern national identity. For Fortis those modern designations were irrelevant to Venetian Dalmatia and more plausibly referred to the populations of foreign provinces, Ottoman Serbia and Habsburg Croatia. Though Venetian and also Vatican documents, in the eighteenth century, sometimes specified that the Orthodox Morlacchi belonged to the Serbian rite, referring to their problematic affiliation with the Serbian patriarchate, this was a religious designation whose national implications lay largely in the future. By the same token, when Fortis mentioned the "barbarous magnificence" of the ancient kings of the "Slavi Croati," he referred to a Croatian presence in Dalmatia that seemed to him to lie largely in the past. The designations of "Croatian" and "Serbian" were present among a range of competing and overlapping identifications in Dalmatia in the eighteenth century, but it would be anachronistic to interpret them according to their modern national significance. Historical and anthropological scholarship has also indicated the related identities of the populations called Morlacchi in Venetian Dalmatia and more often called Vlachs in Ottoman Bosnia and the Habsburg Military Frontier region.[6] The designation and signification of the name Morlacchi must be considered in the political and cultural context of Venetian rule in Dalmatia, articulating an Adriatic perspective on the imperially problematic arena of the Triplex Confinium, the Ottoman-Habsburg-Venetian frontier. Fortis was aware that the people he was studying often referred to themselves as Vlachs, but he made them famous under the name of Morlacchi. The eighteenth-century celebrity of the Morlacchi illuminates the ascribed and constructed aspects of identity—national and anthropological—in an internationally recognized people whose name has now been completely forgotten.

In the Venetian Enlightenment, the Morlacchi nation appeared not so much as a division, but rather as an aspect of the Dalmatian nation, conceived as anthropologically alien to Italy and emphatically backwards in customs and economy. The character of the Morlacchi, while far from universally violent according to Fortis, was still the less "civilized" aspect of Dalmatia, which made the province appear as part of "Eastern Europe," according to the values of the Enlightenment. The inhabitants were conceived as Dalmatians when Goldoni composed his drama in celebration of their glory, but they were known as Morlacchi when Fortis offered his Apologia for their alleged misdeeds. Marco Foscarini, in his speech of 1747, invoked the name of the Morlacchi when he pointed to the economic misery of the province; it was the "unhappy Morlacco" (*infelice Morlacco*), unhappy on account of extreme indigence, who might well starve to death without the assistance of the Republic. These were the "villagers of Dalmatia, a people crafty from need and ferocious by nature."[7] The Dalmatians were characterized as Morlacchi when they were seen as unhappy and ferocious, victims of poverty and perpetrators of violence, their condition inspiring in the Venetians either pity or fear. Goldoni had no need to denominate his Dalmatians as Morlacchi since they were altogether noble and valorous, taken totally out of the social and economic context of their native province. The Dalmatians whom Goldoni put on the stage in 1758 could never have been confused with the Morlacchi whom Fortis presented to the public in 1774. Goldoni's Dalmatians needed no apology.

Fortis's Apologia for the Morlacchi was formally addressed to Lord Bute in England, but it was, of course, read by the public in Venice. In the Venetian edition of *Viaggio in Dalmazia*, the first section on Zadar was dedicated to Jacopo Morosini, "Patrizio Veneto," and the second section on the Morlacchi to Bute. For the English edition of 1778 Fortis reversed the priority, dedicating Zadar to Bute and the Morlacchi to the Venetian Morosini. In this case, Fortis forthrightly challenged Morosini to acknowledge his prejudice: "You have, no doubt, often heard the Morlacchi described as a race of men, fierce, unreasonable, void of humanity."[8] Thus, by the ordering and layering of the dedications in the different editions, the English public was invited to view the matter of the Morlacchi as a Venetian controversy, while the Venetian public was put on notice that Fortis would take the case of the Morlacchi before the bar of international opinion.

It was, ultimately, foreign admirers of Fortis who would make the Morlacchi into a European phenomenon; already in 1775 Goethe was writing German poetry, rendered "aus dem Morlackischen," while Herder in 1778 and 1779, in his collections of *Volkslieder*, included German versions of South Slavic poetry based on Italian translations by Fortis. All at once, the Morlacchi, with their Adriatic reputation for ferocious violence, came to possess an international renown for fascinating folk poetry. Such celebration, of course, did little for the socioeconomic condition of Foscarini's *infelice Morlacco*, but Fortis's Apologia, without emphasizing issues of economic misery, nevertheless served to reframe the reputation of the Morlacchi so as to spur Venetian interest in ameliorative reform. Foscarini in 1747 learned about the Dalmatian economic crisis from the reports of the Provveditori Generali in Zadar: "That the unhappy Morlacco was often subject to such scarcities the Provveditori Generali themselves bear witness, they who several times moved by compassion for that mendicant but loyal people have interceded with the Senate for liberal loans of fodder, so they would not die of hunger."[9] During the last half-century of the Venetian republic, from 1747 to 1797, the administration in Zadar continued to analyze, address, and bear witness to the social and economic problems of the Morlacchi.

In the official reports of the Provveditori Generali, the Morlacchi first appeared as a problem of disciplinary administration and then, especially with the advent of Fortis before the literary public of the Enlightenment, as a problem of imperial civilization. Fortis's ideology of empire, based on principles of national economy, received philosophical legitimation from the articulation of a civilizing mission, tempered by the anthropological appreciation of primitive customs. The modulating emphasis from discipline to civilization reflected the different priorities of administration and anthropology, with their convergent interests in the Morlacchi. While the Provveditori Generali, before Fortis, wondered whether the Morlacchi could be disciplined, the reformulated dilemma, after Fortis, was whether the Morlacchi should be civilized. By posing the civilizing dilemma, Fortis guaranteed that their customs and conditions would remain at the center of public concern in Venice, as an issue of imperial responsibility and enlightened authority, right up to the abolition of the Republic itself.

Incapable of Discipline

In the first decades of the eighteenth century, after the settlements of Carlowitz and Passarowitz, Venetian Dalmatia achieved its deepest inland territorial extent and its largest subject Morlacchi population. This inaugurated a new level of Venetian official concern about the administration of the Morlacchi. In the early 1730s Zorzi Grimani served as Provveditore Generale and completed his term with a relation to the Senate, formulating the new problem of governing the Morlacchi in peacetime. He began by distinguishing them from the coastal Dalmatians, who had "devotion and loyalty already rooted in them," after centuries of Venetian rule.

> The Morlacco too, who is not of very ancient subjection (*sudditanza*), shows himself of optimal heart toward his prince. He is by nature ferocious, but not indomitable (*indomito*). He is accustomed to being treated without excess. Too much gentleness makes him impertinent, and extraordinary rigor renders him fierce and harsh. He does not love working the land; he is inclined rather to pillage, and succeeds best at arms.[10]

Grimani emphasized the fact that the Morlacchi were new subjects of Venice in the eighteenth century. Though they appeared to be already devoted to the Republic, he obviously regarded that devotion as volatile and unreliable, not "rooted" in centuries of habituated subjection. His calculus for governing them—not too gentle, not too rigorous—was aimed at taming and training them to a condition of docile loyalty that matched the temper of the coastal Dalmatians. Along these lines, the Morlacchi could be seen as Dalmatians in the making, or the Dalmatians could be seen as already domesticated Morlacchi.

When Foscarini addressed the Maggior Consiglio in 1747 he rhetorically invoked the figure of the "unhappy Morlacco" who lived in poverty as the victim of an exploitative and corrupt administration. Foscarini alluded to the reports of the Provveditori Generali, but the contemporary occupant of that office, Giacomo Boldù, when he made his final relation to the Senate in 1748, offered a considerably more detailed and less sympathetic account of the Morlacchi. While Foscarini judged the character of the administration from the economic condition of the inhabitants, Boldù evaluated the economic potential of the province according to the character of its people.

> Agriculture and the arts are the principal if not the only sources of commerce, which certainly can not flourish where human labor and industry languish. Here is the invincible defect of these peoples of Dalmatia. . . . Agriculture in this province, if it is not totally absent, is at least languid and unattended. . . . Obstinate is the aversion of even the coastal subjects to every other application except that of the flocks, and the labor of arms, which are then devoted by most of them to pillage, blood, and other human disorders. . . . Also lazy by nature, especially the Morlacco. . . . and incapable of discipline . . .[11]

Boldù emphasized that the coastal Dalmatians and inland Morlacchi were closely related, inasmuch as "even" the former were averse to labor, while the latter were simply "especially" lazy. The particular figure of the Morlacco thus presented the most marked features of the general Dalmatian character. The "invincible defect" was economic inaptitude, a matter of character rather than circumstance, perceived as languor, laziness, disorder, and indiscipline. During the term of Boldù's predecessor in Zadar, Girolamo Quirini, the national character had actually been represented in performance by Carlo Gozzi, appearing as Luce, the impoverished but ridiculous Dalmatian servant girl.

Boldù was scathing in his summation of the Morlacchi, as "rough and lazy people, of a different rite, equally slothful in religion, but all by nature ferocious and vindictive, more or less avid for blood and prey, troublesome to their neighbors across the border and to their own compatriots." There followed naturally, as an economic consequence, the "total defect of industry, the lack of every art, and the scarcity of agriculture."[12]

Fortis in 1774, when he offered his Apologia on behalf of the character of the Morlacchi nation, was challenging a prejudicial opinion that was already fully articulated within the Venetian administration by the middle of the century. Boldù in 1748, however, represented an administration which had faced serious criticism the previous year in the Maggior Consiglio, for alleged abuses and corruption, for failing to "enamor the peoples." It was natural enough for Boldù to offer an implicit justification of his administration by replying with criticism of the peoples themselves. Indeed, his denunciation seemed to offer something for everyone in Venice, a comment on Greek Orthodoxy in Dalmatia to provoke the suspicion of Catholic conservatives, an indictment of violence and inertia to rouse the indignation of enlightened reformers.

Boldù was not even fully enthusiastic about the military valor of the Morlacchi, though he conceded their aptitude for arms. Because of the War of the Austrian Succession in the 1740s, regular troops had been recalled from Dalmatia to Italy to defend Venetian neutrality. There was even a mobilization of Morlacchi soldiers, who were assembled at Zadar to embark for Italy. Gozzi, serving under Quirini, remembered the event: "I was present at the review of this species of anthropophagi, which took place at the harbor of the city of Zara before the Provveditore Generale." Gozzi watched them doing "strange dances" as they boarded the ships. Furthermore, once transported to Italy, the Morlacchi provoked violent disorder, because, according to Gozzi, they could not heed "the commands of discipline or subordination."[13] In the meantime, the administration in Dalmatia was left with no other force but the territorial militia, known as the Craina (Krajina). "But one soon discovered the bad service of this Craina," commented Boldù, "in substance Morlacchi with the insignia of soldiers, without military discipline, likely to abandon their posts to go home, called there by the spirit of family, and likely besides to collude with criminals rather than arrest them."[14] The ideal of discipline, which Michel Foucault has seen as essential to the concerns of the Enlightenment, was repeatedly invoked by the Venetians in the eighteenth century as the standard by which to evaluate the Morlacchi.

Collusion with criminals was a merely modest statement of Boldù's most pressing problem with the Morlacchi, the difficulty of reconciling their propensity for violence to the forms of law and requirements of public order. Every effort to govern them by the routines of legal administration was frustrated by "the ferocious character of the nation, the multiplicity and gravity of the crimes that occur, and the serious disorders that derive from the strength of a barbarous custom." That custom was the vendetta of the South Slavs, the private family revenge by which the Morlacchi took the law into their own hands, and Boldù in a special supplement to his general relation to the Senate provided an account of the vendetta that constituted an early contribution to Venice's anthropological study of the Slavs of Dalmatia, a concern that would culminate in Fortis's "Customs of the Morlacchi." Fortis wrote of the Morlacchi in a spirit of apology and appreciation, while Boldù, one generation earlier, from his position as Provveditore Generale, described the "barbarous custom" of the vendetta as an obstacle to civilized administration.

> The Morlacchi, by their own instinct, easily determine to commit homicide, so a brief dispute and a few words precipitate the resolution to attack for every trifling cause or suspicion. Considerable is the number of subjects who perish in the province in such a manner from year to year, but the harm to the population from this loss would not be so serious if it were not aggravated by the vendettas that are immediately undertaken by the relatives of the victim. As soon as they receive the news of the misfortune of the killing, they all rise up tumultuously, and, with arms in hand, coming to the house of the killer, they carry off the effects and animals they find there, and with indomitable furor lay waste to all that they can not easily carry, often even setting fire to the house, the granaries, the stables and whatever is found in the possession of the unhappy family. . . . It sometimes happens that some families that have been subjected to such misfortune have closed up their own homes and abandoned entirely the Venetian state. However vigorous are the orders and dispositions of the penitentiary office . . . it has never been possible to eradicate in the nation this barbarous custom of reprisals.[15]

If the Morlacchi character was repeatedly designated as "ferocious," Morlacchi customs were, correspondingly, conceived as "barbarous." The observation that vendettas sometimes drove the Morlacchi out of the Venetian state addressed Foscarini's concern about emigration from Dalmatia—"to return as tattered beggars under the Ottoman tyranny"— but the fundamental problem with private revenge was that it subverted the legal administration of the province.[16] While in Venice the administration of Dalmatia faced criticism as allegedly corrupt and oppressive, Boldù believed that it was merely ineffective in the face of the character and customs of the nation. Therefore, he argued for the eradication of the barbarous customs of the Morlacchi as the necessary precondition for more effective provincial government.

Since his objection to the vendetta was that it removed the administration of justice from the courts, Boldù was neither edified nor gratified by the private arbitration and resolution of such cases. This too was described in detail as a barbarous custom of the Morlacchi:

> They gather in a place determined by all the relatives of both the victim and the murderer together with the arbiter judges elected by both sides. The murderer appears in this gathering with a meek and submissive air, presenting himself to the closest relative of the victim, and throws himself at the other's feet, lowers his head, and offers voluntarily his own life to the other's judgment. The offended relative shows himself enraged, and drawing his scimitar, which he keeps ready at his side, holds it hanging over the neck of his adversary. . . . But finally at the renewed instances and energetic clamor of that gathering he desists from his resolution, gives life to his enemy by the grace of the communal intercessions, declares himself satisfied and content; he puts away his scimitar in its sheath, then embraces the murderer, who rises; they kiss each other as a sign of peace. . . . Finally, this gathering is never dissolved except after a sumptuous meal according to Morlacchi custom with abundant consumption of wine, often repeated for several days.[17]

The Venetian account was attuned to the dramatic aspects of this staged reconciliation, with its Oriental accent marked by the curved blade of the scimitar, but Boldù could hardly approve the reconciliaton and restoration of order, when both the murderer and the vigilantes thus eluded the provincial administration of justice.

He was no more sympathetic to the Morlacchi when, in cases other than homicide, they sought to take advantage of the courts with "incredible insistence," whether their cause was right or wrong.

> Few are the memorials in which the truth is not masked, in which first place is not held by the malignity and calumny to which the Morlacchi incline by their own instinct. . . . They display such animosity and fervor in their suits, that if the judge were ignorant of the character of the nation, he would only with difficulty be induced to believe that a subject could have so much audacity as to present himself so frankly before the court with plain lies. . . . If then one reflects upon the copious congeries of disorders that encumber these improper provinces (*provincie scorrette*), and especially the depraved and ferocious character of the nation, it will not be difficult to recognize that it is not possible among peoples who abhor the method of the courts, and

know no other law than that which they learn by the extravagance of their customs, to be able always to observe in criminal cases the legal method as it is observed in other parts of the state and especially in Italy.[18]

Boldù thus concluded with an argument for administrative asymmetry, replying to Foscarini's denunciation of official abuses by insisting on a different standard of administration for Dalmatia. The rhetoric of reform might ring out powerfully in the Maggior Consiglio, among the Venetian patricians, beneath celestial allegories of Venice by Veronese and Tintoretto, but the conclusions of the council, Boldù believed, would be inevitably compromised by the application of an Italian perspective to circumstances that could not be compared to those of Italy.

"I have sweated under the weight of incessant labors," wrote Boldù at the conclusion of his long relation. "I have stayed up whole nights to prepare the orders and attend to the endless correspondence." If there were defects in the administration of the province, he seemed to imply, they were not to be attributed to any failure of conscientiousness in his own character; he was a dedicated servant of the state, concerned only "to fulfill the obligations of my own office for the best service of my country (*Patria*)."[19] The obligations of his office as Provveditore Generale concerned Dalmatia, but the "country" that he served was Venice. Boldù's final relation of 1748, summing up the situation at the time of the arrival of Foscarini's inquisitors, raised within the government the controversial issues of relating Venetian rule to Morlacchi character and customs, issues which Fortis would finally reformulate according to the anthropological values of the Enlightenment to put before the public in the *Viaggio in Dalmazia*.

Inquisitors, Ineptitude, and Inertia

The true precursors of Fortis in Dalmatia were the inquisitors dispatched from Venice after Foscarini's appeal in 1747 and Boldù's departure in 1748. They issued their final report in 1751, at the end of their investigation in Dalmatia. Fortis's interests in the province were far more wide-ranging, from fish to fossils to Roman ruins, while the inquisitors concentrated on issues of provincial government, but in both cases the Morlacchi were central as subjects of study. For Fortis they offered an anthropological case study, while for the inquisitors they appeared as a problem in provincial administration. The audience for these studies was also very different, with the inquisitors addressing themselves to the Senate on an issue of state which concerned the "public" interest only in the narrow official sense of the term, while Fortis presented his subject to the broader "public" sphere of civil society. The three inquisitors, Giovanni Loredan, Nicolo Erizzo, and Sebastian Molin, began their final report in 1751 with a declaration of their own dedication, "returned from the most heavy and thorny office of Sindici Inquisitori, sustained through the long course of almost three years in the provinces of Dalmatia and Albania." Service in Dalmatia, across the Adriatic from metropolitan Venice, was conventionally considered to be a "thorny office" (*spinoso carico*), though the inquisitors did not feel the need to moisten their manuscript with sweat and tears as Boldù had in his more vivid evocation of official martyrdom. "Always the inseparable companions of our spirits," wrote the inquisitors, "were the purposes of paternal charity, of justice, and of public service and interest in the commissions that were the object of the decree instituted by the Serenissimo Maggior Consiglio on 17 December 1747."[20] It was the date of Foscarini's speech from which they derived their mandate.

"There appears at the first stroke as worthy of emendation," they wrote, "the corruption of customs which we have found prevailing among these populations." After the opening formalities of thorny office and public service, the very first concern of the report was the customs of the Morlacchi:

> Considerable and ruinous we have discovered among the Morlacchi the custom of solemnizing annually their saints' name days, the celebration of the anniversaries of their deceased, as well as the deaths of the moment, the solemnity of weddings, the celebrations of wedding masses, the confirmation of their peacemakings: all occasions on which, for the course of several consecutive days and nights, they lavished with excessive intemperance and squandered in costly debauches with a copious number of guests, in such a manner as finally to convert their solemn days of consecration not only into profane use but into an outlet for vice, with revelry and indecent bacchanals right in the face of the church.
>
> With such ruinous formalities houses were destroyed in excessive behavior, and, fomented by prodigality and intemperance, their native ferocity sparked brawls and awakened dormant quarrels; nor did the arrangements ever finish ordinarily without scandalous enormities and without the shedding of blood.[21]

Boldù had mentioned the celebratory meals after reconciliation, "with abundant consumption of wine," but only as a sarcastic endnote to the description of the vendetta. The inquisitors made such occasions into the centerpiece of their criticism of the customs of the Morlacchi, with bloodshed perceived almost as an incidental consequence of excessive celebration. The terms of their denunciation perfectly fit the campaigns of reform against popular culture, as Peter Burke has treated the subject, campaigns promoted by the reformed churches and the early modern state throughout Europe since the sixteenth century.[22] The Morlacchi, only recently redeemed from the Ottoman empire, received such attention belatedly in the eighteenth century, in the name of enlightened administration.

The imprint of the Counter-Reformation was evident in the moralistic phrases of the inquisitors, though they represented the Venetian state even as it sought to adapt to the values of the Enlightenment. The Morlacchi appeared as a Rabelaisian race, characterized not only by ferocity, but intemperance, prodigality, debauchery, and the blasphemous perversion of religious observance. Their "ruinous" appetites for food and drink fit their natural inclination to violence and even, by implication, to some sort of bacchanalian sexuality. This utter condemnation of the customs of popular culture also contained an element of economic criticism with an emphasis on the squandering of time, wealth, and resources. Sent to investigate administrative abuses, the inquisitors first found fault with the character and customs of the inhabitants themselves. With the authority of the Senate behind them, they proscribed excessive celebration for some occasions (name days), limited the number of guests for others (weddings), and prohibited "indecent revelry" at all times. The inquisitors also condemned the vendetta, described as a "barbarous custom of all these populations," by which "for a homicide, sometimes even accidental and not culpable, whole numerous families are exterminated," with consequences "prejudicial to the most jealous concerns of the principate." An attempt was made to involve the local Morlacchi leaders, the chiefs (*Capi*), assigning to them some responsibility for forestalling such "violent oppressions."[23] Through a policy of stringent prohibition and ongoing vigilance, the inquisitors ultimately claimed a measure of success in the suppression of private vengeance.

The inquisitors further noted the unfortunate effects of "greed and malice" in some officials, who arbitrarily raised court fees whenever the Dalmatians were involved in civil or criminal cases. Such abuses "reduced to extreme misery and desperation those poor populations." Foscarini orated rhetorically, hypothetically, on behalf of the Dalmatians—"if they could speak"—for they could not speak in the Maggior Consiglio of the Venetian patricians. The inquisitors, however, listened to those voices of protest in Dalmatia:

> In fact copious complaints of subjects have been directed mostly against the unprecedented oppressions that they experienced from the avarice of the chancelleries concerning criminal costs, complaints deploring the fatal effects that derive from their arbitrary and intolerable exactions. . . . By the excess of the costs of a trial the poor Morlacchi (*poveri Morlacchi*) are destroyed, since to obtain the payments. . . . even their arms, agricultural instruments, and the plowing animals themselves are illegally violated; so that desperate at seeing themselves denuded of everything, either they join with criminals or they are forced to give up being Venetian subjects.[24]

The noting of these grievances was fully in accordance with the mandate that the inquisitors received from Foscarini's speech. They specified the forms of administrative oppression which he only generally indicated, and set beside his figure of the *infelice Morlacco* a whole population of *poveri Morlacchi*. In this formulation their misery and poverty were not altogether of their own making, and the inquisitors set about to reform the administration by establishing fixed costs for all judicial instances.

They also understood, however, that the poverty of the Morlacchi, though aggravated by an avaricious administration, was fundamentally determined by agricultural issues and especially the distribution of land. This too could be conceived as a matter of character: "If we were disturbed by the depravities and disorders in which we found these provinces immersed, our spirit was especially distressed at seeing the ineptitude (*dappocaggine*) and inertia (*inerzia*) of its peoples, which, as due to the laziness (*pigrizia*) of their ancestors, leaves the lands desperately idle (*perdutamente oziosi*)." Without purposefully playing on words the inquisitors set the "laziness" of the people to be meaningfully associated with the "idleness" of the land. There would have been no escape from the damning implications of this simple equation if the inquisitors had not also credited the structural significance of land distribution as a relevant variable. They declared themselves committed "to impose salutary rules toward an equitable and charitable distribution of lands, for upon this, we frankly can not keep from repeating, depends uniquely the true redemption of these provinces, the true well-being of the peoples, and the interest of the principate."[25] While it was only natural for the inquisitors to assume an identity of interests between the peoples of Dalmatia and the state of Venice, the analysis pointed toward another potentially contradictory set of assumptions. On the one hand, the character of the Morlacchi was sweepingly supposed to be the source of all political and economic troubles in Dalmatia; on the other hand, the regulatory power of the government was confidently invoked as the salutary solution to them all, from bloody vendettas to uncultivated fields.

The inquisitors were most struck by an uncertainty of property rights in the *nuovo* and *nuovissimo acquisto* in Dalmatia. "Such lands of new conquest were discovered by us in a general disorder, confusion (*sconvolgimento*), and chaos," they declared, "most of them occupied, invaded, possessed without title, against every right and reason, and by arbitrary violence." The conquered territories were claimed by Venice as the property of the state, but the Morlacchi who lived there treated the land as if it belonged to them.

> This serious affair having proceeded without system, and without appropriate rules, the Morlacchi, guided by their improper abuses, according to custom, presumed to sell the lands of Vostra Serenità, to mortgage them, to assign them, to donate them, to give them as dowries, to divide them, to bequeath them, and to make of them whatever most prodigal and arbitrary disposition, as if they were of their own right and free dominion.
>
> Accustomed to invade, not only reciprocally among themselves the seeded land, the vineyards, the pastures, the plants, to expel whomever they think unable to resist their violence; but also to cut into and occupy the communal lands destined for the pasture of plow cattle, and to usurp the meadows reserved for the hay of the Public Cavalry.
>
> From such serious and violent causes are derived the mournful effects of brawls and homicides and innumerable criminal cases, and above all, very obscure and involved confusion of the public accounts: in which turbulence, the most powerful hold on to the greater part, in oppression of the poor.[26]

The inquisitors made themselves again the advocates of the "poor Morlacchi," while ultimately attributing their poverty to their failure to recognize the full proprietary prerogatives of the state over the lands Venice acquired by war. The Morlacchi would be compelled to concede the nullity of their own property rights before the claims of the state, so that the state might make use of its acquisitions to impose an equitable distribution of land on behalf of the inhabitants. The inquisitors perceived a chaos of unclarified property arrangements, in which the Morlacchi illegitimately maneuvered by violence, invasion, and usurpation, according to their character. The distribution of land according to law would vindicate the state's right to impose such an order while submitting the Morlacchi to the ultimate discipline of property.

Violence and irregularity of national character were to be countered by the imposition of discipline on social and economic structures. "We believed it essential above all," remarked the inquisitors, "to give a methodical form to the village, where houses are dispersed and widely distant one from another." Patterns of settlement and habitation were to be modified in conjunction with the reformed distribution of land, so that economic and administrative order could be pursued simultaneously. "It was our precaution," warned the inquisitors, "to concede to the Morlacchi the investiture of confirmation or addition of lands only in those villages where they were planted with their families, so they might not escape from the observation of their leaders and from their contributory obligations." Observation and obligation were invoked as basic principles of administration, and the redistribution of land was conceived as a strategic measure toward the countering of customs and character, the transformation of the Morlacchi into disciplined subjects. "We have thought to propose," reported the inquisitors, "as most sufficient, just and proportionate to the sustenance of the Morlacco, were he to wish to employ himself at his labors and the required work, two fields per person, and these in perpetuity in the masculine line."[27] The formula of two fields to each Morlacco, unalienable and indivisible, was to be the basic principle of the Grimani law in 1755.

The ferocious Morlacco was to be invested with his fields by the state, from the lands of the *nuovo* and *nuovissimo acquisto,* thus binding him in recognition of the Republic's prerogative. This mid-century land reform, with its ambitious social, political, and economic expectations, could only address the fundamental problem of character in hypothetical subjunctive clauses. The Morlacco, "were he to wish to employ himself" (*quando volesse impiegarsi*), might perhaps make something of his two fields; the proposal for reform created the possibility of economic amelioration but only on the condition of an essential change in character. The decrees and proposals of the inquisitors sought to restrict the customs and transform the circumstances of the Morlacchi, but the question of their character— ferocious, violent, lazy, intemperate, indecent, barbarous—hovered over the attempted reform and eluded its structural prescriptions.

When Francesco Grimani left Dalmatia in 1756, a year after the promulgation of the land law that carried his name, he wrote with some satisfaction about the state of the province to his successor as Provveditore Generale, Alvise Contarini. "By duty of office I have the obligation to give you an accounting of emergent affairs, and I will do it briefly," wrote Grimani to Contarini, "because, praise be to God, there are no developments which might essentially disturb the internal or external tranquillity of these states." This was very far from the spirit of crisis which Foscarini had fostered in the Maggior Consiglio less than ten years before, and closer to the air of innocuousness which Goldoni seemed to assume when he made Dalmatia the subject of his drama just two years later. Writing to Contarini, Grimani presented the crisis of land, the "chaos" decried by the inquisitors, as something that he had personally confronted and resolved.

> Entering into civil affairs, of which the urgent character may merit being explained before the illumination of Your Excellency, I present first of all the agrarian matter.
>
> Upon my coming to the province I found it in circumstances so murky (*torbidi*) and contumacious that I was overcome (*soprafatto*), considering the tenuousness of my talents . . .
>
> With a topographical plan of every village on the desk I reviewed the villagers, family by family, and in this way came to know the truth of things.
>
> Satisfying thus their honest conveniences, even to the point of bringing them to call themselves spontaneously content, I fixed by my own hand the detail of the assignments. With this guide, the consignments of two fields per person were executed on the spot. . . . Thus the cadaster was formed, that is, the register in two large volumes, each of which corresponds to the topographical plans.[28]

With remarkable confidence Grimani presented agrarian affairs as a crisis past, which he once had feared would overcome him, but which he himself overcame through the rational procedure of enlightened administration.

In the previous decade Foscarini claimed he could only with difficulty obtain a decent map of Venetian Dalmatia, but Grimani now ordered detailed topographical plans of every village, to study at his desk, so as to review the situation of each inhabitant and adjudge each assignment of land. Furthermore, while the inquisitors had found the Morlacchi full of grievances, a people of "copious complaints," Grimani now claimed the extraordinary achievement of "bringing them to call themselves spontaneously content." Thus Grimani affirmed his own satisfaction with the agrarian settlement, assuring his successor Contarini that he need only attend "with equal care and commitment to its inviolable fulfillment."[29] Such excessive confidence in the future of the one-year-old reform was based not only on the distribution of land but also and especially on the triumphant management of the Morlacchi, whose coordinates were now precisely marked on the topographical maps and definitively inscribed in the volumes of the cadaster.

His faith in agrarian reform and administrative efficacy was such that Grimani sought to play down the significance of the "character" of the Morlacchi.

> I will not stop here to say anything new in describing the character of these subjects. Speaking about the Morlacco, all the observations of my predecessors combine to characterize him as ferocious, intemperate, inertial, and devoted to theft. Yet since it is a most well-known principle that population is the substance of the principate, and that the most healthy policy teaches to procure the increase in number, I have studied every expedient to eliminate any necessity for the Morlacchi to take refuge in foreign states. And I reflected that for every family that the prince loses here, he loses the seed (*semenza*) of able soldiers . . .[30]

Grimani refused to contribute to the already well-established discourse on character, reciting the various attributes from ferocity to criminality as if they were tired and irrelevant clichés. The Morlacchi, whatever their character, remained nevertheless the inhabitants of the province, and therefore the state had no choice but to value them, to seek to preserve them, and to render them more content there than elsewhere. Grimani's vision of their value was also evident from the remark that every Morlacco lost to Venice took with him the "seed of able soldiers," depleting the spermatic supply of Venice's military prospects. He urged Contarini to govern the Morlacchi "with maxims of tolerance and gentleness," even toward the end of "keeping them in discipline and moderation."[31] Disciplined subjects constituted one of the state's valuable resources, and, anticipating the concerns of Fortis, Grimani then proceeded to discuss the management of other resources, such as fishing for sardines.

Intemperance, Indiscipline, and Alienation

Pietro Michiel, completing his term as Provveditore Generale in 1765, also saluted the "precious fishing for sardines, from which the people and the public coffers profit." This remark, however, came in the context of general frustration at the economic debility of Dalmatia, in spite of such natural resources as fish, flocks, wine, wax, honey, oil, figs, almonds, and salt. Particularly regrettable was the province's agricultural inadequacy, even after the enactment of the Grimani reform. With the government having done its legislative best, Michiel had no hesitation about restoring the economic blame to the character of the inhabitants. When he conventionally lamented the difficulties of his office, he mentioned the "unusual and fatal combinations of plague, famine, and rivalrous military aggravations in neighboring Bosnia, that kept me occupied almost through the entire triennium," but he also cited as a chronic problem of the province "the indocile nature of its inhabitants, different in customs and in rite of religion." This latter theme received elaboration within the established contours of the official discourse. The population of Dalmatia, estimated by the administration at 270,000, was denounced by Michiel in formulas of sweeping generalization: "people moreover not at all industrious . . . but lazy and profligate in the extreme, although abounding in lands that in other regions serve to render the subject comfortable, to give notable increment to commerce, and to bring appreciable utility to the state."[32] Michiel's sense of economic purpose was already attuned to the commercial concerns of the *Giornale d'Italia,* founded by Griselini in Venice in 1764, which also pointed toward Fortis's future focus on public profit from natural resources.

"The true character of the Morlacco is intemperate to excess, lazy, inclined to theft and vendetta, restless, and violent," wrote Michiel, recycling older observations. Such a catalogue also inevitably mentioned that the Morlacco was "ferocious" and "inclined to arms," which was of some military value to Venice. On the conventional question of discipline Michiel offered a hopeful formula for the future of the subject Morlacco: "Although he appears to be without discipline, he is not incapable of receiving it, and if the chiefs (*Capi*) of the territories were to use (*usassero*) the prescribed diligence, it would not be difficult to impress it upon him (*imprimergliela*)." Such subjunctive and conditional language reflected the still uncertain disciplinary status of the Morlacchi as subjects. The suggested reliance on local leaders implied that Michiel was less optimistic about the direct application of administrative discipline by Venetian officials. The same subjunctive spirit undercut any confidence in agricultural prospects, even with the apportionment of lands according to the Grimani law: "The Morlacco would be wealthy if he wished (*se volesse*) to apply the labor to the cultivation of lands, and if he felt (*sentisse*) the utmost temperance." This issue of temperance pointed toward a particular emphasis within the economic discourse on the Morlacchi. Michiel faulted them for refusing to cultivate beyond their immediate needs:

> They only want to sow what will serve to feed themselves, and to pay the public tithe; nor do they care about extracting a greater yield that could permit them to live in greater comfort. Intemperance, as I said, is one of the vices that dominates the Morlacco. However abundant is the harvest of grapes, he consumes all the wine in a few months, and is content to drink water or milk from January until the new harvest.[33]

Intemperance, thus described, was not only a matter of alcoholic indulgence but an incapacity for economic foresight. Unable to store their crops over the course of the year, the Morlacchi were obviously not the sort of modern economic actors who would be able to produce an agricultural surplus toward an increase in wealth. The implicit equation of temperance with discipline suggested that the absence of discipline among the Morlacchi could have economic, as well as military and administrative, ramifications.

Furthermore, Michiel returned to the issue of discipline concerning other important aspects of imperial government. Having mentioned the "fatal" problem of plague in Bosnia, his relation later specified the risk factors in Dalmatia. "The danger of infection always hangs over the province when neighboring Bosnia has been struck," he wrote, and singled out the Turkish caravans as the carriers of contagion. The caravans, when crossing from Bosnia into Dalmatia, were supposed to deposit their goods in quarantine in the lazaretto of Split, but "they collude with the undisciplined (*indisciplinati*) Morlacchi and especially with the citizens of that city."[34] This association of the coastal Dalmatians with the inland Morlacchi suggested a consistency of character that made it possible to generalize about the whole population of the province. The character of the Morlacchi was further compromised by their indisciplined collusion with the Ottoman caravans. Such collusion had clearly pernicious consequences in time of plague, and the disciplinary aspects of public health would become cataclysmically evident at the time of the great outbreak of plague in Split in 1783.

The *cordon sanitaire* between Bosnia and Dalmatia, which also separated the Ottoman Balkans from Adriatic Italy, was often casually
breached, according to Michiel, by Morlacchi with family on both sides
of the border. "They pass into neighboring Bosnia and Hercegovina and
live on the lands that the Ottomans give them to cultivate as farmers,"
he remarked. "It is not that lands are lacking within Dalmatia, if they
wanted to take note of the disposition of public properties to their advantage, but the Morlacco neither seeks it nor wants it." The incapacity
to recognize and pursue advantage was consistent with a conception of
the Morlacchi as irrational economic actors, but their alleged indifference to whether they farmed, after their own intemperate fashion, on
the Ottoman or Venetian side of the border represented a much more
alarming disciplinary failure. When Foscarini addressed the Maggior
Consiglio in 1747 he attributed Dalmatian desertions to poverty and
poor administration, but by 1765, after the inquisitors had accomplished
their mission, and after agricultural reform had been implemented, the
abandonment of Venice reflected all the more troublingly on the character of the Morlacco. "Improper and violent as he is, the one state or the
other serves as a refuge for perpetrating crimes," remarked Michiel,
"and with the insurgence of plague, freedom of passage renders impossible, as I mentioned, the custody of health."[35] Living on the border between Moslem and Christian Europe, between the Ottoman and Venetian empires, between Bosnia and Dalmatia, the Morlacchi, with their
problematic character, appeared all the more menacing to the purposes
of enlightened administration. From the perspective of the Provveditore
Generale, their inability to apply themselves economically to agriculture
was paralleled by an unwillingness to commit themselves politically to
Venice. This latter concern was to become all the more urgent in 1768,
with the outbreak of the Russian-Ottoman war, when the possibility of
Russian allegiance made the Morlacchi seem all the more volatile.
Michiel, in his relation of 1765, emphasized the diverse aspects of indiscipline that characterized them, and with the label *indisciplinati Morlacchi* he consolidated the discourse at a level that summed up and transcended the more conventional attributions.

Domenico Condulmer arrived in Zadar as Provveditore Generale in
1768, the year the war began, and he worried about the "agitations"
across the border in Bosnia where Ottoman troops were on the move. As
an indication of good will, he ordered from Venice as a gift for the pasha

of Bosnia a large armchair upholstered in gold velvet with gilded carvings *alla turca*. He had no doubt that Venice would be able to come up with something sufficiently in the Turkish style to give satisfaction in Turkey. In Dalmatia, however, the luxury of gold velvet was frivolously irrelevant to the worsening crisis of drought and famine, such that, according to Condulmer, "these miserable people in their natural poverty are constrained either to flee the state or remain victims of starvation." There was furthermore the danger that they would "in desperation" follow their natural criminal inclination and take up "the infamous exercise of pillage." The issue of economy raised the related issue of emigration with its corollary question about the level of loyalty in Dalmatia.

> The extreme misery of the Morlacchi, which becomes every day greater, has already constrained many thousands to go away either to the Ottoman or to the Austrian empire. . . . Usually the Morlacco, when the necessity that pressured him has ceased, returns to his native domicile, but each time many remain over there, and Vostra Serenità suffers the greatest damage from the loss of its subjects.[36]

Economic hardship revealed the tenuousness of allegiances in Dalmatia, and as Condulmer received reports of "the universal weeping of these most loyal subjects," he urged Venice to approve the dispensation of grain from the public reserve to provide relief. In 1769, he declared that "the hunger and universal misery in this too wretched and downcast province surpasses and exceeds this year all the memories of times past." He even reported "some cases of death which occurred from the sole effect of starvation."[37]

Russian incitement and Orthodox enthusiasm made Condulmer all the more anxious about the Morlacchi, living along the Bosnian border and, after all, "ferocious by nature."[38] It was Condulmer who put some Orthodox subjects "in chains" when they refused to participate in the public celebration of the election of Pope Clement XIV in 1769. With increasing unrest in Montenegro, there were further reports of "a great ferment of rebellion" in the adjoining region of Dalmatia.[39] Ferocity of character, by now an old cliché, dating back half a century to the time of Venice's own military involvement against the Ottomans, made the Morlacchi appear as an all the more volatile element, at a moment when the Republic was seeking to preserve neutrality. War and famine together created a crucible for testing the character of the Morlacchi, just as Fortis was about to cross the Adriatic in 1770.

Moral and Domestic Virtues of the Morlacchi

Giacomo Da Riva, who succeeded Condulmer in 1771, still received reports about "the secret seduction of subjects for the service of Russia." He also still faced the crisis of famine that occupied his predecessors in the previous decade, and advised that in view of "the straits of the poor Morlacchi in the scarcity of the harvests," it would be "opportune" to provide public assistance to those who were starving.[40] These crises of war and famine could not be considered altogether separately, since the likelihood of foreign "seduction" was obviously greater when the subjects were on the point of starving to death. Marko Jačov has counted more than six hundred families who emigrated from Venetian Dalmatia into Bosnia or into the Habsburg lands during the years from 1771 to 1774 and has attributed their flight to Orthodox religious sentiment as well as social and economic misery. At the death of Matteo Karaman, archbishop of Zadar, in 1771, the Vatican nuncio in Venice worried about finding the right episcopal successor for a diocese that seemed "most difficult on account of the Schismatic Greeks."[41] Even in peacetime the circumstance of famine undermined Morlacchi allegiance to Venice by provoking them to emigrate; in time of war, when the Russian army was recruiting soldiers in the region, hunger made the issue of loyalty appear all the more urgent.

Dositej Obradović, born among the Habsburg Serbs of the Banat of Temesvar, later a leading figure in the Orthodox Enlightenment and a literary pioneer of Serbian national culture, was preaching in Zadar in 1771 to the "Schismatic" Orthodox community there. "I knew that a fairly large number of Serbian officers and merchants lived in the place," he wrote in his memoirs, "and that if I got acquainted with some of them there was a chance that they would keep me there." The heterogeneous Orthodox society of Zadar included Montenegrin officers and Sarajevo merchants, and Obradović also found friends who came from Corfu and Crete. He had already spent time on Venetian Corfu, where he moved in a similarly mixed Adriatic society, encountering "some captains and majors in the Venetian service, Dalmatians and Montenegrins by birth, who took me to the archpriest of the town, showed him my certificate of identity and explained it to him, and obtained his permission for me sometimes to conduct a service in the Church Slavic language in the Church of St. Catherine." Obradović took advantage of his time on Venetian Corfu to study ancient and modern Greek, Latin, and also Italian. He was hoping to settle himself as a preacher at Skradin in Dalmatia, but this plan was forestalled by the local Roman Catholic bishop, "since I was not a Venetian subject nor would I agree to become one." Though Obradović actually traveled to Venice to try to appeal to the Senate against the bishop, permission to settle in Skradin was ultimately refused.[42] Not only the Vatican in Rome, for religious reasons, but also the Senate in Venice and the Provveditore Generale Da Riva in Zadar, for political reasons of state, were concerned to reduce foreign influence on Orthodox Dalmatians, including the Morlacchi.

Da Riva would eventually go on to literary immortality, albeit under his initials, in Casanova's memoirs; Casanova was in Da Riva's service on Corfu in the 1740s, when the latter was a naval officer and the former was madly in love with Mme F.[43] Dalmatia in the 1770s may have offered less in the way of romantic intrigue, and, at the beginning of 1772, Da Riva as Provveditore Generale offered Venice a realistic review and troubling diagnosis of the situation of the Morlacchi under Venetian rule.

> Vostra Serenità has lavished immense treasures in three consecutive wars to expand your dominion in Dalmatia, the nearest bulwark (*propugnacolo*) of state liberty. To the glory of the acquisitions was joined that of conciliating the blessings of the very numerous rustic peoples by the sweetness of civil government. . . . As in the earliest times of their new subject status, they would be always truly happy, if the conduct of their respective national chiefs (*Capi*) always conformed to the divine law, the natural law, the piety of public maxims, and the delicate views of the principate. . . . One would have saved serious and extraordinary expenses to the public economy, in order to promote the better fortune of these subjects by restoring the decline of discipline.[44]

The Morlacchi, previously regarded as being altogether "without discipline," were now supposed to have declined to an even lower level of indiscipline, perhaps under the stresses of war and famine. Da Riva's diagnosis of decline, however, emphatically denied that Venice was to blame for the misery of the Morlacchi; instead he blamed their chiefs for abusing the impoverished mass of the population. "The chiefs themselves," wrote Da Riva, "although generously salaried by Your Excellencies, rather than cooperating in the work of relief, are only venal ministers of the oppression of the Morlacchi." Those victims of oppression remained, in Da Riva's opinion, "a numerous population of good people truly affectionate and loyal to San Marco."[45] Da Riva's denunciation of the chiefs achieved at one blow the rhetorical redemption of both the Venetian government in Dalmatia and the Morlacchi subjects.

Da Riva presented his analysis of the situation in a dispatch to the Senate and took action upon his views with a proclamation in Dalmatia. "Our spirit is sensitively struck by the detailed accusations of extortion, imposition, and violence that the Morlacchi suffer," he declared, "from those very figures who are employed to direct them and treat them with humanity conforming to the most sweet character of the state." Under threat of the galleys, the proclamation forbade the chiefs to seek any agricultural services for themselves from the Morlacchi, whether to sow, to hoe, to harvest grain, or to gather grapes. The chiefs were to pay for their own private service, "with their own purse, not with the sweat and free labor of the poor subjects." Again under threat of the galleys the chiefs were forbidden to extract from the Morlacchi arbitrary contributions, neither grain nor oil, neither calves nor lambs.[46] Such stipulations suggested that Da Riva recognized the limits of his own office, in matters of administrative efficacy, and especially in the regulation of agriculture, even after the Grimani reform. In 1751 the inquisitors returned from Dalmatia with the suggestion that the administration make use of the chiefs in order to reform Morlacchi customs. By 1772 Da Riva had concluded that the chiefs were not the means, but rather the obstacle, to more effective government of the Morlacchi.

The final point of his proclamation concerned the provocative issue of corporal punishment for the Morlacchi, which was evidently relevant to their noted need of discipline.

> Indubitably, however courageous and loyal to San Marco the Morlacchi of this country may be, they are just as much combative and obstinate by nature, and thus they have often resisted the execution of the orders of their natural chiefs, so that they are corrected with the stick. Such punishment however is highly injurious to them, though practiced also among the state troops, as well as among the most polite Christian nations. It may be furthermore that this sort of punishment is not always the consequence only of disobedience, but becomes also colored by the brutal venting of the passions of the chiefs themselves, or for not having been able to require service of the unhappy Morlacchi, especially in the fields, or in order to extort misconceived contributions, or to impose subjection upon those who threaten to have recourse to justice against the extortions. . . . For whatever motive, it

remains absolutely forbidden to beat or have beaten the contumacious ones, so as not to humiliate their spirit, much less then for private causes, since divine and human laws, public order, and other regards of the principate all declaim against such vexations.[47]

Though the "violence" of the Morlacchi character had long been noted and regretted by Da Riva's predecessors, he now formulated a new perspective on violent behavior as systematically and oppressively practiced among the Morlacchi in subversion of the supposed "sweetness" of Venetian administration. Much as their obstinacy might require discipline, Da Riva invoked a higher discipline in forbidding them to employ corporal punishment among themselves. Thus he reserved to the state the disciplinary prerogatives of administration, noting that "jails and galleys stand ready."[48] The "unhappy Morlacchi" were to be rendered happier by protecting them from the abuses of their own leaders, so that they might recognize the beneficent principles of Venetian rule.

Da Riva's proclamation in January 1772 against the chiefs was followed by another in July against the bandits. Once again he focused on violence among the Morlacchi and sought to stop it: "Bandits and criminals disturb the tranquillity of the border with the murder and pillaging of Turks as well as fellow Christian subjects." Da Riva proposed an appeal to violence in order to restore tranquillity: "To extirpate this worst sort of men one sole expedient was put into use with an entirely good outcome by the perspicacity of my predecessors. That was the promise of the punctual payment of four zecchini for each bandit or criminal head."[49] Evidently, Da Riva's hesitations about corporal punishment by the chiefs did not mean that he was inveterately tender about penal consequences. Indeed, in the unstable circumstances created by war and famine, Da Riva sought all the more urgently to preserve for the imperial administration an absolute and ultimate authority over the deployment of violence. At a moment when general issues of discipline were aggravated by inklings of ambivalent allegiance, Da Riva pointedly insisted on the loyalty of the Morlacchi in general, while targeting as figures of oppression and transgression the chiefs and the bandits. Da Riva's tense triennial term from 1771 to 1774 was also precisely the period of Fortis's exploration of Dalmatia and revaluation of the Morlacchi. Responding to "talk of the Morlacchi as a race of ferocious men, unreasonable, without humanity," Fortis centered his anthropological Apologia upon a sympathetic account of the bandits and the chiefs.

"Travelers ordinarily try to magnify the dangers they encountered and the discomforts they suffered in remote lands," remarked Fortis, addressing Lord Bute in the Venetian edition. "I find myself far from such charlatanry, and Most Noble Lord, you will observe from the detail that I will give you about the manners and usages of the Morlacchi, how securely and with what slight discomfort I traveled through their regions." Fortis's scientific accounts of fossils, specimens of natural history, and ancient remains of Roman Dalmatia invariably involved an implicit or explicit invitation to readers to visit the province, investigate its resources, and claim its collectibles. The chief obstacle to such visits was not that Dalmatia was so geographically "remote" from Venice, but rather that the legend of the ferocious Morlacchi made the voyage seem so dangerous. Like Da Riva, Fortis was well aware that there were bandits in Dalmatia.

> The greatest danger that could be feared comes from the quantity of Haiduks, who customarily find refuge in grottoes, rough woods, and the desolate mountains of the border. There is no need however to feel excessive fear of them. The expedient, for traveling with security in mountainous places, is precisely that of taking as an escort a couple of these gentlemen (*galantuomini*), who are incapable of betrayal. Neither must one feel horror to know that they are bandits: for laying hands on the causes of their miserable situation, one ordinarily finds cases more likely to arouse compassion than mistrust. Woe to the inhabitants of the maritime cities of Dalmatia if the unfortunately exorbitantly multiplied number of Haiduks had a nature of wicked character![50]

Fortis responded directly to the discourse on the character of the Morlacchi when he refused to attribute a bad character even to the bandits among them. At the same time that Da Riva was calling for the heads of the Haiduks, Fortis recommended them to the public as gentlemen, as trustworthy guides, and as objects of compassion.

An allusion to "the causes of their miserable situation" indicated the economic situation in Dalmatia during these years of drought and famine. According to Fortis, the Haiduks were hungry:

> They lead the life of wolves, wandering among rocky and inaccessible precipices, hanging on from stone to stone, in order to uncover dangers from a distance, agitated by continuous suspicion, exposed to the intemperate weather of the seasons, often deprived of the necessary food, forced to risk their lives to procure it, languishing in the most horrid and uninhabited curves of the caverns. It would not be surprising if frequently one heard of

strokes of atrocity by these men grown wild *(insalvatichiti),* and irritated by the always present sentiment of such a miserable situation; it is quite amazing that, far from undertaking anything against the people to whom they think they owe their own calamities, they ordinarily respect the tranquillity of inhabited places, and are loyal escorts for wayfarers.[51]

Fortis offered a geologist's account of bandit life, with its setting of caverns and precipices, its progress from stone to stone. He argued that it was only natural for men leading such hard lives, aggravated by hunger, to turn to crime. On the issue of character, he played upon the proverbial "loyalty" of the Dalmatians when he insisted that the Haiduks would act as "loyal" guides to visitors from Venice like himself.

Fortis admitted that the Haiduks might feel some murderous sentiment toward the Turks, but this too he was able to explain and excuse according to the calculus of the Enlightenment. "A spirit of misunderstood religion, combined with natural and acquired ferocity, brings them to violent molestation at the border," Fortis reasoned. "For this their priests are often to blame, full of the national impetus and prejudices that they maintain, and often they incite the ferment of hatred against the Turks."[52] Fortis's anti-clericalism would not let him miss an opportunity to ascribe the alleged crimes of the Morlacchi to the supposed fanaticism of their priests. In the folk poetry of the South Slavs the Haiduks played an heroic role as enemies of the Turks, and Fortis, who collected that poetry in Dalmatia, was obviously aware of the positive aspects of such a reputation. The "ferocity" of the Morlacchi meant that "four Haiduks do not fear to assault a caravan of fifteen or twenty Turks." Fortis did not altogether deny the conventional discourse on the character of the Morlacchi, but rather he accepted some of its terms at an inverted value, valorizing violence and ferocity even while invoking compassion for the bandits. Emblematic of the Morlacchi in their ferocity, the Haiduks also seemed to be typical in their fears. Fortis regarded with enlightened amusement the local "superstitions," remarking upon the ready belief in witches, fairies, and vampires among the Morlacchi. "The most audacious Haiduk," commented Fortis, "would flee at full speed at the apparition of some specter, spirit, phantasm, or other such demon, which never fail to be seen by the heated fantasies of credulous and prejudiced men."[53] In this regard, as well, the Haiduks were only typical Morlacchi, bound by their customs, and, as Fortis implied, too fearful to be truly feared.

Da Riva put a price on the heads of the Haiduks and denounced the Morlacchi chiefs as abusive oppressors of their people. Fortis, on the other hand, was as sympathetic to the chiefs as to the bandits and introduced a fine figure of a chief to his readers in the section on "Moral and Domestic Virtues of the Morlacchi." Fortis did not hesitate to praise "the sincerity, faith, and honesty" of the Morlacchi, noting that they were often victimized in commerce with Italians and coastal Dalmatians. Indeed, the "bad faith" of the Italians was proverbial among the Morlacchi. "This negative prejudice against us could be uncomfortable for the unfamiliar traveler," Fortis reasoned, "but it is not so at all. In spite of this, the Morlacco, born hospitable and generous, opens his poor hut to the foreigner." Generous hospitality was the principal moral virtue that a foreign traveler would come to recognize in the Morlacchi, and Fortis experienced this especially as the guest of a chief.

> I will never forget as long as I live the reception and cordial treatment of me by the Voivod Pervan at Coccorich. My only merit was to be the friend of a family of his friends. He sent servants and escorts to meet me, and heaped me with all kinds of exquisite national hospitality. . . . After I departed from the lodging of such a good host, he and all his family followed me with their eyes, and did not return to the house till the moment when I was lost to sight. This affectionate farewell awakened in my spirit an emotion that I have never experienced till now, nor do I hope to experience it often traveling in Italy. I carried away with me the portrait of this generous man, principally to have the pleasure of seeing him again even at a distance, in spite of the sea and the mountains that separate us, as well as to be able to give an idea of the splendor of the nation in the clothing of its chiefs *(Capi)*.[54]

Just when Da Riva, the Provveditore Generale, attributed the misfortunes of the Morlacchi to coercions and exploitations perpetrated by their chiefs, Fortis was bringing back to Venice a very different portrait with the finest moral features. Inverting the conventional balance of morality between the supposedly savage and presumptively civilized, in this case between Morlacchi and Italians, Fortis made the chiefs into ideal figures of Dalmatian virtue. His sentimental representation of the chief under the heading "Moral and Domestic Virtues of the Morlacchi," in 1774, would serve as the literary model for the creation of a fictional village chief of simple Rousseauist virtue, in 1788, in the novel *Les Morlaques,* by Giustiniana Wynne.

FIGURE 9. Morlacchi Triptych: "The Voivod Pervan of Coccorich, A Noble Young Lady of Coccorich, A Young Lady of the Kotar." From *Travels into Dalmatia,* by Alberto Fortis, English edition of 1778. This image first appeared in the Italian edition of 1774, as Fortis praised Morlacchi hospitality, declaring, "I will never forget as long as I live the reception and cordial treatment of me by the Voivod Pervan at Coccorich." Fortis further noted, "I carried away with me the portrait of this generous man, principally to have the pleasure of seeing him again even at a distance, in spite of the sea and the mountains that separate us." The two female images illustrated Fortis's observation that "the dress of the Morlacchi women is different in the different districts, but always equally strange to the eyes of the Italians," clothing accessorized by "whimsical and barbarous ornaments." The figure of Pervan would later appear in the novel *Les Morlaques* by Giustiniana Wynne. *(By permission of the Department of Printing and Graphic Arts, the Houghton Library, Harvard University.)*

"It is enough to treat the Morlacchi with humanity to obtain from them all possible courtesies and make them cordial friends," wrote Fortis. "Hospitality among them is as much a virtue of the wealthy as of the poor." He found that the wealthy offered him meat, while the poor offered him milk. Furthermore, he insisted that such generosity was not only reserved for the foreign traveler, but functioned as a social principle of the community: "As long as there is something to eat in a village in the house of the wealthy, who today are reduced to a small number, the neighboring poor do not lack for necessary sustenance."[55] Fortis here alluded to the economic misery of these years, though he never made that an emphatic part of his account; in general, his reporting of folk songs and customs stood in stark contrast to the dispatches of the Provveditori Generali concerning famine and starvation.

"Domestic economy is not at all commonly understood among the Morlacchi," remarked Fortis, in another such allusion. "In this particular they resemble the Hottentots, and use up in a week what ought to suffice for many months." In the celebration of weddings and saints' days, "one drinks and eats intemperately as much as is in the house."[56] Michiel, as Provveditore Generale, had made much the same observation in 1765, citing "intemperance" as "one of the vices that dominates the Morlacco," noting that all the wine was drunk within a few months after the harvest. Fortis fully agreed about the evident lack of economic foresight and further emphasized the aspect of barbaric backwardness with his far-fetched comparison to the Hottentots. For Fortis, however, such intemperance appeared under the noble signs of generosity and hospitality, which were rather to be seen as excessive virtues than national vices. With his compassion for the bandits and admiration for the chiefs, Fortis overturned the moral balance that had hitherto prevailed in official accounts of Dalmatia. Though the Hottentots might still remain a proverbial point of reference for comparing primitive peoples, Fortis offered his readers a directly observed anthropological account of the customs of the Morlacchi.

Uncorrupted Customs and Civilized Society

Voltaire's *Essai sur les moeurs,* published in 1754, made manners or customs into the essential philosophical principle of universal history, and Fortis's discussion, "De' Costumi de' Morlacchi" in *Viaggio in Dalmazia* in 1774, pursued that same principle in studying a contemporary people. Voltaire tried to trace the course of progress through the centuries, as Europe became "more inhabited, more civilized, more wealthy, and more enlightened." He mentioned Dalmatia, together with Poland and Ukraine, as lands of Europe that offered opportunities for new cultivation and colonization; when he considered the subject of "savages," he casually cited "the Morlaque, the Icelander, the Lapp, the Hottentot" as recognizably representative figures of that category.[57] Although Dalmatia and the Morlacchi were of only the most incidental interest to Voltaire, they came up in contexts that left little doubt about their lowly place in an enlightened ordering of customs and civilization. Fortis—setting out from Voltaire's assumptions, preserving even the casual comparison to the Hottentots, but reversing the valuation of savagery in the spirit of Rousseau—established the Morlacchi at the center of discussion in the European Enlightenment. In addition to the complete translations of *Viaggio in Dalmazia* into German in 1776 and into French and English in 1778, special editions of the section on the Morlacchi appeared in German in 1775 as *Die Sitten der Morlacken* and in French in 1778 as *Lettre de M. l'Abbé Fortis à Mylord Comte de Bute sur les moeurs et usages des Morlaques, appelés Montenegrins*. This last identification of the Morlacchi as Montenegrins, a correspondence also noted with concern by the Venetians during the Russian-Ottoman war, suggested that the sudden emergence of the Morlacchi into international celebrity in the 1770s provoked speculative curiosity about their classification. The regional resemblance to the Montenegrins was already considerably more plausible than any remote comparison to the Hottentots.

Voltaire's emphasis on "customs" in 1754, together with Rousseau's treatment of the "savage" in the *Discours sur l'origine de l'inégalité* of 1755, guaranteed that Fortis's account of the Morlacchi would be of general interest to the philosophes of the Enlightenment. Michèle Duchet has traced the intellectual history of anthropology as the study of "the savage world" by the French philosophes, leading to the adoption of the term with its modern meaning in a work titled, *Anthropologie ou science générale de l'homme,* published by Alexandre-César Chavannes in 1788. Duchet argues that in the eighteenth century, prior to the denomination of the discipline, "the anthropological discourse did not exist except inside the general philosophical discourse."[58] Fortis studied the Morlacchi within that philosophical discourse of the Enlightenment, but Venice's imperial rule in Dalmatia through the eighteenth century drove the development as well of an administrative discourse about the Morlacchi with political and economic implications. The relations and dispatches of the Provveditori Generali created a discursive context for Fortis's investigations, which were for that reason less purely philosophical. Furthermore,

Fortis's anthropological knowledge of the Morlacchi was based on direct observation during his voyage, which clearly differentiated his study of their customs from the fictional or philosophical figures of Montesquieu's Persians, Voltaire's Hurons, Rousseau's Caribs, or Diderot's Tahitians. The Slavs of Dalmatia, just across the Adriatic from Venice, offered the Enlightenment its most accessible savage subjects for pioneering the principles of anthropology.

Fortis's scientific interest in the revolutions of the earth was also accompanied by some attention to the possible transformations of species, including humans. Franco Venturi has emphasized "the passage from the primitive to the civil world which was evidently at the center of Fortis's preoccupations." Dating back to the period when he was a young priest in Rome in the 1760s, discussions about Vico led Fortis to consider the question of primitive peoples. In contemporary politics, the rising of the Corsicans against Genoa inspired in 1767 an admiration for "an indomitable nation" of "ferocious strength" nourished in "inaccessible mountains"—noted by Fortis before he ever encountered the Morlacchi. At the same time he expected Pasquale Paoli to reform his Corsican nation, following "on a small scale the example of Muscovy under the immortal Tsar Peter." Such enlightened faith in the transformation of men received scientific formulation after Fortis went to Napoleonic Paris at the end of the century to work at the Muséum d'Histoire Naturelle in the circle of Lamarck. Fortis, addressing evolutionary issues in natural history, proposed that humans were capable of "degeneration and perfectibility without limit, with respect to the physical as well as the moral."[59] Scientific interest in the transformation of the species, conditioned by enlightened optimism about the perfectibility of man, was also relevant to the political stakes of Venice and the administrative frustration of the Provveditori Generali as they evaluated the character of the Morlacchi.

Having considered the "Moral and Domestic Virtues of the Morlacchi" and found in their favor, Fortis turned to their "Talents and Arts." Here too he issued a favorable judgment: "Alertness of intelligence and a certain natural spirit of enterprise render the Morlacchi apt *(atti)* to succeed in any sort of employment." This emphasis on aptitude suggested that the talents of the Morlacchi still awaited development, that their "spirit of enterprise" was a sort of "natural" resource that might be cultivated and exploited in an imperial context. Fortis stressed the importance of guidance for the Morlacchi on the path toward perfectibility:

> In the profession of arms, when they are well directed, they provide optimal service, and at the end of the last century they were usefully employed *(ad-operati utilmente)* as grenadiers by the valorous General Delfino who conquered an important stretch of land subject to the Porte, especially by the service of these troops in various uses *(vari usi)*. They succeed marvelously in the direction of mercantile affairs, and even adults easily learn to read, to write, and to keep accounts.[60]

On the one hand, they had to be well "directed" to serve in the army; on the other hand, they could be educated to the point of assuming "direction" themselves in commercial matters.

Fortis did not imagine the Morlacchi serving always in absolutely subordinate positions, but believed that their usefulness as subjects could be realized by both the application of discipline and the encouragement of enterprise. His most serious reservation about their talents concerned the most economically important matters of agriculture and animal husbandry:

> In spite of their optimal natural dispositions to learn everything, the Morlacchi have the most imperfect notions of Georgica and Veterinaria. The tenacity of ancient usages singularly of the nation, and the little care taken until now to conquer it by showing them by evidence the utility of new methods, must necessarily lead to this consequence. Their cattle and sheep often suffer from hunger, and from cold exposure. The plows they use, and the other rural instruments, seem to be of the oldest invention, and are just as dissimilar from ours as would be the other modes of the times of Triptolemus from the usages of the present age.[61]

Fortis presented an interplay between the "natural dispositions to learn" and the "tenacity of ancient usages," which acted as opposite forces along the course of economic development. He thus insisted on an analysis of the Morlacchi that considered character in the context of customs. At the same time, he outlined the time frame of progress, dating from the mythological age of Greece, when Triptolemus supposedly invented the plow, to the modern moment of enlightened agriculture. Fortis suggested that any effort to reform or transform the Morlacchi, to push them along the path toward economic modernity, had to come to terms with the tenacity of their customs.

Though Fortis recognized custom as a possible obstacle to progress, he also recorded customary practices in a spirit of descriptive sympathy.

He viewed the customs of the Morlacchi as a notable aspect of natural history and more often praised their primitive virtues than condemned their proverbial barbarism. Beginning with the subject of "Friendships and Enmities" ("Amicizie e Inimicizie"), he presented the customs of the Morlacchi in a manner implicitly intended to counter the official discourse of the provincial administration. The subject of enmities naturally referred to the notorious custom of the vendetta among the Morlacchi, which, according to Fortis, was "so identified *(immedesimata)* with the spirit of this nation, that all the missionaries in the world would not suffice to eradicate it." He had heard that the vendettas were even more "atrocious" in Albania and offered as an anthropological paradox the theorem that "the man of the most gentle character is in these regions capable of the most barbarous vengeance." Such an observation clearly indicated Fortis's readiness to reformulate the relation between character and customs. Detailed denunciations of the vendetta in official accounts dated back to the mid-century description of that "barbarous custom" by Giacomo Boldù in 1748, and Fortis's remarkable contribution to the discourse in 1774 lay in balancing the familiar story of enmities with a sympathetic discussion of friendships among the Morlacchi.

> Friendship, so subject to change among us, even for the smallest motives, is most constant *(costantissima)* among the Morlacchi. They have made of it almost a point of religion, and this sacred bond is formed at the foot of the altars. The Slavonic ritual has a particular benediction for solemnly conjoining two male friends, or two female friends, in the presence of all the people. I found myself present at the union of two girls, who made themselves *posestre* in the Church of Perussich. The contentment that shone in their eyes, after having formed that sacred bond, proved to those present how much delicacy of sentiment may be found in unformed spirits, or, to say it better, spirits uncorrupted *(non corrotte)* by the society that we call civilized *(colta)*. The male friends thus solemnly united are called *pobratimi,* the women *posestrime*.[62]

Thus Fortis reported upon the South Slavic custom of blood brotherhood, *pobratimstvo,* which demonstrated to him that the Morlacchi, however bloody their vendettas, were also capable of great "delicacy of sentiment" in their friendships.

He compared friendship among the Morlacchi to friendship among the Italians ("among us") and pronounced in favor of the former for their superlative constancy. In a verdict altogether conditioned by the values of Rousseau, he reversed the conventional hierarchy of manners to praise the primitive Morlacchi for remaining "uncorrupted by the society that we call civilized." Fortis reconsidered the terms of the imperial relation between Venice and Dalmatia, as he presented a new perspective on the "primitive" customs of the Morlacchi, addressed to a reading public of supremely "civilized" Venetians.

The injunction "to treat the Morlacchi with humanity" in order to "make them cordial friends" suggested that their friendship was something to be sought strategically. Fortis was evidently aware of the implications for imperial policy, inasmuch as he encouraged collecting antiquities in Dalmatia, "by captivating the confidence and friendship of the Morlacchi," based on knowledge of "the character of the nation."[63] In this instance, knowing the character of the nation also required some appreciation of customs concerning friendship among the Morlacchi. To captivate them as friends could be, for a foreigner like Fortis, a means toward making them "useful" to himself, and such a scheme was fully consistent with the larger purpose of making the Morlacchi useful to Venice. Finally, Fortis's emphasis on the constancy of their friendship also reflected on the proverbial loyalty of the Dalmatians, somewhat uncertain in the stressful context of famine and war. Da Riva, for all his concerns in 1772, still clung to the certitude that the Morlacchi were "truly affectionate and loyal to San Marco," echoing Goldoni's Dalmatian declarations of 1758. By presenting the Morlacchi as supremely constant friends, Fortis offered a context in anthropological custom for the axiom of their ultimate loyalty to Venice.

Innocent Kisses and Sexual Customs

Fortis's discussion of friendship pointed toward the subversive implication that in some aspects of character and custom the Morlacchi were actually more admirable than the supposedly civilized Italians. His sentimental susceptibility to the ritual bonding between boys and between girls made him all the more philosophically reflective about what happened between the sexes among the Morlacchi.

> The innocent and natural liberty *(libertà naturale)* of the pastoral centuries are maintained still in Morlacchia; or at least there remain the greatest vestiges in the places most remote from our establishments. The pure cordiality of sentiment is not restrained there by considerations, and gives clear exterior signs without distinction of circumstances. A beautiful Morlacchi girl *(bella fanciulla Morlacca)* meets a man of her village in the street, and kisses him affectionately, without thinking of mischief. I have seen all the women and girls, and the young and old men, from more than one village, kiss each

FIGURE 10. "Map of the Territories of Trau, Spalatro, and Makarska, the Primorje and Narenta, with the Adjacent Islands." From *Travels into Dalmatia* by Alberto Fortis, English edition of 1778. The principal islands were Brazza (Brač), Lesina (Hvar), and Curzola (Korčula). The map represented the mountainous terrain and showed the Ottoman border; a tiny notation indicated the home of Pervan of Coccorich, Fortis's host among the Morlacchi. The comprehensive mapping of Dalmatia was an important part of Venice's imperial rule in the eighteenth century. Foscarini appreciated the political significance of geography when he included in his speech to the Maggior Consiglio of 1747 an account of his search for an up-to-date map of Dalmatia. *(By permission of the Department of Printing and Graphic Arts, the Houghton Library, Harvard University.)*

other as they arrived in the squares of the churches for festival days. It seemed that this people was all of one sole family.[64]

Fortis's treatment of the "Customs of the Morlacchi" was an exception to the otherwise geographical organization of his *Viaggio in Dalmazia,* every other section corresponding to a designated region. The Morlacchi, however, were to be found throughout Dalmatia, as soon as one ventured inland from the coastal towns. Though the place name "Morlacchia" (or, in French, "Morlaquie") could be found on eighteenth-century maps, it did not necessarily possess a precisely delineated location but occurred generally around the region of the Triplex Confinium. When Fortis referred to "Morlacchia," he seemed to suggest a philosophical as well as a geographical domain. Morlacchia was another name for Arcadia: the land of "the innocent and natural liberty of the pastoral centuries."

If this mythological Morlacchia had real geographical coordinates, they followed from the rule of inverse remoteness: "the places most remote from our establishments." The administrative and commercial centers of Venetian domination were the philosophical antithesis of the natural landscape of Morlacchia. There, the constancy of same-sex friendship was matched by the purity of sentiment between the sexes, recognized anthropologically by Fortis in the public gesture of the innocent kiss. Jean Starobinski has emphasized the importance of "transparency" for the philosophical values of Rousseau, and Fortis put the same premium on the frank and transparent expression of feeling among the Morlacchi, identifying their kisses as "clear exterior signs" of inner sentimental innocence.[65] Such supposed transparency, of course, also confirmed his own virtuosity in interpreting their customs and discerning their character.

Fortis put before his Venetian readers the alluring innocence of the *bella Morlacca,* as Goldoni had offered his public the virtuous charms of the *Dalmatina.* Beginning with innocent kisses, Fortis moved toward a discussion of the South Slavic custom of romantic abduction. He emphasized, however, that this was neither an expression of primitive Dalmatian ferocity nor the counterpart of rococo Venetian libertinism.

> In times of festival and commotion, besides the kiss there occurs some other
> liberty *(libertatuccia)* of the hands, that we would find improper, but among
> them it does not pass as such; if they are taken up on it, they say, "it is a joke
> that amounts to nothing." From these jokes, however, their loves often
> begin, which frequently end in abductions *(ratti)*, when the two lovers have
> found themselves in accord. It is a rare case (and certainly does not happen in
> the places more remote from commerce) when the Morlacco abducts a non-
> consenting girl, or dishonors her. If this happens, the young girl would cer-
> tainly make a good defense, since the robustness of the women in this coun-
> try concedes little to the males ordinarily. Almost always the abducted girl
> herself fixes the hour and the place of the abduction.[66]

In passing from the Rousseauist ideal of *libertà naturale* to the more
equivocal sense of *libertatuccia*, Fortis recognized that his readers would
respond to the custom of abduction either with moral reprobation or with
libertine titillation. Insisting upon the fully consensual nature of the custom, he argued that the *ratto* was not a rape, and therefore the Morlacchi,
even in this seemingly barbarous aspect, merely manifested their natural
liberty. Diderot, in the *Supplément au voyage de Bougainville*, written at
the same time as Fortis's *Viaggio in Dalmazia*, explored the alien sexual
customs of the Tahitians by mocking the moral scruples of Europeans.
Like Diderot, Fortis was ready to recognize that impropriety was a matter
of cultural perspective, while consent and accord made abduction among
the Morlacchi more civilized than seduction among the Italians.

The figure of the *bella Morlacca* exercised an ambivalent sexual fascination even on Fortis himself, and he went to some literary lengths to at-
tenuate her textual appeal.

> The Morlacchi women keep themselves somewhat in order before they marry,
> but after they have acquired a husband, they abandon themselves totally to
> filth *(sudiciume)*; it is almost as if they wished to justify the contempt *(dis-
> prezzo)* with which they are treated. It is not, however, that the girls send forth
> pleasant effluvia; for they are accustomed to greasing their hair with butter,
> which easily becomes rancid, and exudes even from afar the most disagreeable
> stench that could ever wound the nose of a gentleman *(galantuomo)*.[67]

No sooner had Fortis begun to represent the charms of the Morlacchi
women than he suddenly repressed the spirit of literary titillation, changing over to a tone of emphatic repulsion. Though he expressed no moral
censure of their innocent kisses or even their consensual abductions, his
ambivalence took the form of a powerful olfactory objection to their un-

pleasant effluvia. The evocation of filth and stench guaranteed that any Venetian *galantuomo* would think twice about responding to the text with erotic enthusiasm, while Morlacchi men appeared far from fastidious in their sexual susceptibility to the scent of rancid butter. Fortis further undermined the appeal of Morlacchi women with the report that their breasts were of such "prodigious length" that "they can give milk to babies over the shoulders and under the arms." This pretzel presentation of Morlacchi maternity caused enough of a sensation to call forth public rebuttal, as in the work of the Dalmatian author Giovanni Lovrich, whose reply to Fortis was published in Venice in 1776. Lovrich denied the possibility of such feats of nursing and expressed particular surprise that a natural historian like Fortis could accept such a thing. "I would not dare to deny, however," admitted Lovrich, concerning Morlacchi women, "that there are breasts of immense size in the eyes of foreigners, but in the same country one may also observe some of mediocre size, similar to those of many women of the other European nations."[68] With regard to this issue, Fortis was evidently determined to emphasize the difference between the Morlacchi and the other nations of Europe.

"The greatest difference between us and the Orientals is the manner in which we treat women," wrote Voltaire at the end of the *Essai sur les moeurs*, seeking to sum up the balance of customs which made Europeans civilized. "In general it seems," remarked Fortis, "that Morlacchi women, and even the women of the islands, but excluding the inhabitants of the cities, do not mind some beating by their husbands, and often even by their lovers."[69] At the very same time that Da Riva was denouncing the chiefs for abusively beating the poor Morlacchi, Fortis was discovering that beating was a casual occurrence among them, almost too casual to be construed as ferocious. Such beating was more a matter of custom than abuse and appeared fundamental to relations between the sexes. Thus Fortis identified a complex of sexual customs that expressed the difference between the Morlacchi and the Italians, from generally approved public kissing, to mutually consensual sexual abduction, to casually accepted conjugal violence. Such were the customs of the Morlacchi, coherent and consistent, however different they might be from Europe's civilized standard.

Contempt for women appeared to Fortis as an essential principle of these customs, though he himself was torn between censuring such contempt as uncivilized and sharing it himself. Indeed it seemed to impress itself upon him as he contemplated the circulation of innocent kisses among the Morlacchi.

> In the surroundings of Dernish new brides, during the first year of marriage, are obliged to kiss all their acquaintances of the nation, who arrive at the house; after this term, usage excuses them from such a compliment: as if the intolerable dirtiness to which they ordinarily abandon themselves rendered them unworthy to practice it. Maybe their filth is at the same time the cause and effect of the humiliating manner in which they are treated by their husbands and relatives. . . . The most civilized Morlacco (*il piu colto Morlacco*), having to mention his wife, always says, "da prostite, moia xena," ("pardon me, my wife"). Those few who possess a bed, upon which to sleep in the straw, do not there put up with their wives, who must sleep on the floor. I have slept several times in a house of the Morlacchi, and I saw almost universally practiced this contempt of the female sex, which is merited over there, where the sex is not at all lovable or gentle, bur rather deforms and spoils the gifts of Nature.[70]

Fortis thus advertised his intimate opportunity for direct anthropological observation of marital relations, though he did not specify whether he was sleeping in the bed with the husband or on the floor with the wife. Evidently, he fully shared the "contempt" of Morlacchi men for their women and pronounced it fully merited by the degree of female filth. Yet Morlacchi men and women both were faulted for their reciprocal offenses, contemptuous men and contemptible women, with Fortis still uncertain which was cause and which was effect. The remark that even "the most civilized Morlacco" was subject to such customary conduct suggested that the level of civilization altogether failed to meet Voltaire's standard for the treatment of women among Europeans. The quoted ritual apology for mentioning one's wife—"da prostite, moia xena"—was a reminder that even the most civilized Morlacco spoke an alien Slavic language, the spoken expression of his alien customs and altogether incomprehensible to Venetian readers.

Fortis's ambivalence about the filthy figure of the *bella Morlacca*, characterized both by allure and effluvia, found further expression in his detailed description of women's clothes. "The dress of the Morlacchi women is different in the different districts," he observed, "but always equally strange *(strano)* to the eyes of the Italians." He himself made sure that his Italian readers would receive that impression of strangeness, since, after all, they were unlikely to set eyes on the Morlacchi in any more direct observation. "Bizarre *(bizzarro)* in its ornaments," he commented on the dress of young girls, not failing to mention, with anthropological prurience, the veil which was "the sign of their virginity." Their scarlet caps might be decorated with "exotic shells" *(conchigliette esotiche)*, he remarked, though such an attribution of exoticism was hardly typical of his serious scientific approach to natural history; presumably the exotic impression was more a matter of the girls than the shells. Not only shells, but snails and feathers, adorned the caps and met the natural historian's eye as he stared at the strangeness of such "whimsical and barbarous ornaments." In the collector's spirit, he also noted among the ornaments some silver coins that appeared to be "ancient and valuable." Though Fortis was not altogether unadmiring and was even willing to concede "a sort of genius" in the decoration, the variation of the verdict from "strange" to "exotic" to "barbarous" followed a course of aesthetic alienation that undercut his appreciation of Morlacchi customs. The Provveditori Generali had no hesitation about labeling the Morlacchi as generally barbarous, but Fortis brought forward the word in more elliptical contexts, as when he noted necklaces with "glass beads of various sizes and colors barbarically confused."[71] He seemed confident that the Venetians, with their famous refinement in the art of glass beads, would readily accept that the Morlacchi could not measure up to the civilized standard of Murano.

These implications of barbarism focused upon the female figures among the Morlacchi, who exercised such fascination and repulsion upon the enlightened Italian observer. To put their ornaments in a broader context of anthropological barbarism he cited the coins and beads in their braided hair "according to the Tartar and American usage."[72] When he compared the *bella Morlacca* to the American Indian, Fortis's anthropology followed the same casual associative principle as Goldoni's theatrical exoticism, which celebrated alternatively the heroines of *La Dalmatina* and *La Bella Selvaggia*, the beautiful savage of Guyana. Fortis included in the *Viaggio in Dalmazia* an illustration of figures, including the hospitable chief Pervan of Coccorich, as well as two fully costumed and ornamented girls of different districts—intended to appear "equally strange" to the eyes of the public in Venice.

Conclusion: Food and Famine

"Morlacchi eating much resembles Tartar eating," remarked Fortis, "and therefore would not please all those people who are accustomed to the table of the French and the Italians." Yet Fortis, even as he emphasized this primitive unfamiliarity, declared himself satisfied with the food of the Morlacchi on the occasions when he enjoyed their hospitality. In an account of marriage customs, he described the wedding feasts that had appeared to the mid-century Venetian inquisitors as wasteful debauches, "fomented by prodigality and intemperance." Fortis agreed that "the most overflowing abundance reigns in these banquets," but did not regard them as disorderly manifestations of intemperate character. Rather, he saw such feasting as the carefully ordered ritual observance of national custom:

> The fruit and the cheese open the meal; the soup concludes it, precisely the opposite of our usage. Among the foods prodigally prepared they have all species of domestic birds, the meat of goats, lambs, and sometimes game: but rarely is veal to be found there, and perhaps never among Morlacchi who have not been ruined by foreign society. This abhorrence of calf's meat is most ancient among the nation.[73]

Even in their prodigality the Morlacchi appeared to Fortis as strictly governed by custom, incapable of tempering their national abhorrence for veal unless previously corrupted by foreign influence.

Tastes and taboos concerning food were customs of special relevance to an economic situation of recurring famine, and though a taste for veal would hardly bring any broad improvement in conditions of subsistence, there were other dietary items that appeared to be of more considerable consequence. Fortis, for instance, observed that "in general all the Morlacchi have a mortal aversion to frogs," so that "in times of famine (which are unfortunately frequent in Dalmatia, both because of misunderstood agriculture and the greatest constitutional defects) no true Morlacco *(niun vero Morlacco)* would eat frogs even at the cost of letting himself die of hunger." When Fortis went so far as to ask a local curate "why instead of bad cheese he did not eat frogs," the man responded with "indignation" *(sdegno)*.[74] Fortis only rarely mentioned the contemporary crisis of famine, and the issue of the frogs illustrated the "tenacity" of customs as an obstacle to any alleviation of economic misery. In this case some corruption of custom would have been desirable, if a foreign taste for frog would have permitted starving men and women to survive. Yet, Fortis was not without some positive appreciation of the indignant national tenacity that characterized the "true Morlacco," who would hold to his customs even unto death.

Just as their aversion to eating frogs appeared as an economic inconvenience under conditions of famine, so their preferences in food also seemed to make no sense in the economic situation of the Morlacchi. Fortis observed that "garlic and shallots are the food most universally pleasing to the nation, after roast meat," such that "every Morlacco sends out many paces ahead of him the effluvia of this his ordinary aliment, and announces himself from afar to unaccustomed nostrils." This somewhat derogatory remark was balanced by Fortis's conviction that garlic helped to keep the Morlacchi "robust and vigorous" into old age. The main problem with their taste for garlic was not the offense to foreign nostrils but rather the failure to grow it for themselves.

> It seemed extremely strange *(stranissimo)* to me that the Morlacchi, consuming so many onions, shallots, and garlics, should not put them in their vast and fertile fields, but are forced to acquire them from year to year, for many thousands of ducats, from the people of Ancona and Rimini. It would be certainly a salutary violence *(salutare violenza)*, or, to say it better, a stroke of paternal charity *(paterna carità)*, to force them to cultivate these products.[75]

As in the case of eels, identified as an improperly managed natural resource of Dalmatia, Fortis worried about losses to the national economy of Venice through purchases made in the Papal State. In the case of garlic and onions, he purposefully proposed the manipulation of the provincial economy to correspond to the customs of the native inhabitants. This was the point at which his economic priorities met his anthropological purposes, for by knowing the customs of the Morlacchi he could more knowledgeably counsel appropriate economic measures. The purpose of provincial administration, informed by anthropology, was to seek a corresponence between customs and economy. Fortis mentioned the Provveditori Generali as the most likely agents of such administrative adaptation, citing a previous effort to encourage the cultivation of hemp.[76] With his equation of "salutary violence" and "paternal charity" Fortis summed up the dilemma of imperial government faced with the competing concerns of tenacious custom and economic misery.

Fortis's anthropological explorations took place in the philosophical context of the Enlightenment, conditioned by Voltaire's emphasis on customs and Rousseau's interest in savages, but the *Viaggio in Dalmazia* was also a voyage undertaken in the political context of Venice's Adriatic empire. The problematic issue of the Morlacchi was already well developed within the discursive channels of the Venetian administration when Fortis redirected the discourse to put it before the public of Venice as conceived according to the values of enlightened anthropology. In fact, he helped to define those values as he insisted on the importance of empirical observation, in the spirit of natural history, and therefore sought to describe the Morlacchi according to their observable customs rather than presuming to sum up the essence of their national character. Since the beginning of the century the Provveditori Generali had reported to the Senate on the character of the Morlacchi with special emphasis on their ferocity. For Giacomo Boldù in 1748 it was axiomatic that "the ferocious character of the nation" naturally corresponded to the "barbarous custom" of the vendetta. Francesco Grimani in 1756 was already impatient with "all the observations of my predecessors" that described the character of the Morlacco in such terms as "ferocious, intemperate, inertial." He pointed out that the Morlacchi were the inhabitants of Dalmatia, and Venice could not afford to lose them, "the seed of able soldiers," whatever their character. In 1774 Fortis rejected the reputation of the Morlacchi as "a race of ferocious men, unreasonable, without humanity," and he rejected more generally pronouncements upon "the bad universal character of the nation." His anthropological research refocused the whole controversy over the Morlacchi from the ascription of character to the description of customs.

"The customs of a community, taken as a whole," wrote Claude Lévi-Strauss in *Tristes Tropiques,* "always have a particular style and are reducible to systems." Lévi-Strauss saluted the anthropological heritage of the Enlightenment and the writings of Rousseau in particular, "the most anthropological of the philosophes: although he never traveled to distant lands."[77] Fortis did not travel to very distant lands himself, but, with Dalmatia just across the Adriatic and the Morlacchi just inland from the coast, he did not have to go far to find the sort of primitive society that Rousseau only speculatively imagined. Fortis claimed to have discovered "the innocent and natural liberty of the pastoral centuries" in Dalmatia, or rather in Morlacchia. Dalmatia was the name of the province, ruled by Venice as a part of the Republic; Morlacchia was the anthropological domain of the inhabitants, ruled by the customs of the Morlacchi. Fortis sought to describe "the customs of the community, taken as a whole," recognizing that the systematic summation of those customs would constitute a knowledge of the Morlacchi surpassing all epithets of character. Though Fortis was aware of the customary correspondences between the inland inhabitants of Dalmatia and the Slavic or Vlach populations across the Habsburg and Ottoman borders, along the triple frontier or Triplex Confinium, he purposefully presented the Morlacchi subjects of Venice as a whole and coherent community. For it was precisely within the imperial context of Venetian Dalmatia that knowledge about the Morlacchi could be useful; just as Fortis's observations on natural history had some economic significance, his observations on national customs had administrative implications. The Provveditori Generali cherished the ideal of discipline for the management of the Morlacchi, but Fortis's comprehensive account of customs envisioned the "salutary violence" of more strategic interventions.

"What results from this tableau," wrote Voltaire, at the end of the *Essai sur les moeurs,* "is that all that relates intimately to human nature shows resemblance from one end of the universe to the other; and all that may depend upon custom is different." He proclaimed an "empire of custom," which gave "variety" to the universe.[78] Fortis followed this enlightened principle when he refused to countenance general condemnations of the character of the Morlacchi, for he had no doubt of their humanity and human nature. To identify the meaningful difference that made the Morlacchi a distinct nation within the Venetian republic, he proposed to study their customs, and in the domain of uncorrupted customs he claimed to recognize the "true Morlacco." Such recognition made it possible to formulate clearly the civilizing mission of the Adriatic empire, and, at the same time, Fortis further refined that mission by articulating an ambivalent anthropological view of civilization itself. For he admired the moral and domestic virtues of the Morlacchi and relished the innocent and natural liberty of Morlacchia. He even sometimes himself assumed the identity of the Morlacchi, when, for instance, he was climbing in the mountains:

> My own savage self-esteem *(selvaggio amor proprio)* was much flattered by the surprise of those men, born and hardened to the effort, at my agility in climbing and descending the cliffs. I heard one of them exclaim with extreme

satisfaction: "Gospodine, ti nissi Lanzmanin, tissi Vlah!" "Sir, you are not a cowardly Italian *(Italiano-poltrone)*, you are a Morlacco!" I confess to you that I was more appreciative of that peroration than I could ever be of the mostly insincere praises of men in the great world.[79]

Fortis, freely refashioning identity, unhesitatingly translated Vlach as Morlacco and enthusiastically accepted the latter term as the highest and most sincere compliment. From an epithet of disparagement that desig-nated Dalmatian savagery, Fortis revaluated the reference so that the sav-age self-esteem of a self-proclaimed Morlacco became an implicit criti-cism of the customs of the great world beyond the mountains of Dalmatia.

CHAPTER FOUR

The Morlacchi and the Discovery of the Slavs: From National Classification to Sentimental Imagination

Introduction: Slavic Resemblances

"The origin of the Morlacchi," wrote Fortis, "is involved in the darkness of barbarous centuries, together with that of so many other nations resembling them in customs and in language in such a manner that they can be taken for one sole nation, vastly extended from our sea to the glacial ocean." This "one sole nation," from the Adriatic to the Arctic, could only have been the nation of the Slavs, for certainly it was the resemblance of the Slavic languages that provided the basis for generalizing over this geographical area. Fortis's career in natural history, in the century of Linnaeus, made him always alert to issues of classification. If he did not simply state that the Morlacchi were Slavs, but offered instead a more circuitous reflection on resemblances, it was because the category of Slavdom had not quite acquired its modern ethnographic significance at the moment when he was writing in 1774. That occurred in the following decade, when Herder in Weimar began to publish his reflections on the philosophy of history, *Ideen zur Philosophie der Geschichte der Menschheit,* with the first part appearing in 1784. The fourth part was published in 1791 and identified the "Slavic peoples" (*Slawische Völker*), living in an area "from the Don to the Elbe, from the Baltic to the Adriatic," which constituted "the most monstrous region in Europe which *one* nation for the most part inhabits still today." Migrating into the Byzantine empire in the seventh century, the Slavs, according to Herder, were spreading "farther and farther till the Emperor Heraclius received them even in Dalmatia."[1] Herder and Fortis participated in the same fundamental project of intellectual discovery as each, from his opposite perspective—Herder gazing south toward the Adriatic, Fortis looking north toward the Baltic—perceived the cultural coherence of the Slavs across the whole of Eastern Europe.

"The emigrations of the various tribes of the Slavic peoples (*Popoli Slavi*)," wrote Fortis, "who under the names of Scythians, Geti, Goths, Huns, Slavini, Croats, Avars, and Vandals inundated the Roman provinces, and particularly the Illyrian province, in the times of the decline of the empire, must have strangely intertwined with the genealogies of the nations who lived there."[2] Fortis's category of *Popoli Slavi* seemed to anticipate Herder's denomination of *Slawische Völker*. Writing about the Slavs as the barbarians who overran the Roman empire, Fortis, like Gibbon, recognized them as related tribes from ancient history. Like Herder, however, Fortis also appreciated the Slavic resemblances of customs and language that made them a common nation of contemporary anthropology, still living between the Don and the Elbe, the Baltic and the Adriatic. Fortis, exploring Dalmatia on behalf of the Venetian Enlightenment, altered the anthropological frame of analysis when he gave the category "Slav" a general signification, across space and time, over the map and through the centuries.

Although the Enlightenment inaugurated a general European recognition of Slavic ethnographic relations, the issue of a common Slavic identity had been earlier addressed in the sixteenth and seventeenth centuries from across the Adriatic by writers such as Vinko Pribojević from Dalmatia, Mauro Orbini from Dubrovnik, and Juraj Križanić from Habsburg Croatia. Pribojević lectured at Hvar in 1525 and published in Venice in 1532 on the origins and advances of the Slavs, *De origine successibusque Slavorum,* and in 1601 Orbini published in Pesaro his book about the kingdom of the Slavs, *Il regno degli Slavi;* Križanić traveled to Russia in the seventeenth century in pursuit of the Slavic connection. On the threshold of the eighteenth century, in 1700, Pavao Ritter Vitezović published in Zagreb a book about Croatian revival, *Croatia rediviva,* arguing that all the Slavs should be considered Croatian. Ivo Banac has observed that "*Croatia rediviva* was also a polemic against Venetian territorial pretensions, and a legitimist entreaty for Habsburg support" and, further, that this reflected a Croatian emphasis on "Slavic reciprocity."[3] Inasmuch as Venetian rule in Dalmatia, aggrandized at the time of the treaty of Carlowitz in 1699, was precisely the target of Vitezović in his expansive reflections, the Slavic resemblances of Dalmatia were rendered politically problematic in Venice, while any proposed connection to Habsburg Croatia appeared diplomatically dangerous. From a Serbian perspective, Dositej Obradović would affirm the linguistic unity of the South Slavs in his "Letter to Haralampije" of 1783:

> The part of the world in which the Serbian language is employed is no smaller than the French or the English territory, if we disregard very small differences that occur in the pronunciation—and similar differences are found in all other languages. Who is ignorant of the fact that the inhabitants of Montenegro, Dalmatia, Herzegovina, Bosnia, Serbia, Croatia (except for the peasants of the district around Zagreb), Slavonia, Srem, Bačka, and the Banat (except for the Rumanians) all speak the same language. When I write of the peoples who live in these kingdoms and provinces, I mean the members both of the Greek and of the Latin Church and do not exclude even the Turks of Bosnia and Herzegovina, inasmuch as religion and faith can be changed, but race and language can never be.[4]

All of these alleged similarities encompassing Dalmatia could only be troubling to Venice, inasmuch as they implied cultural and political connections to peoples beyond the borders of the Republic.

Goldoni, in *La Dalmatina,* spoke of the Slavs (*Schiavoni*) in a purely provincial context, as simply another name for Dalmatians or Illyrians; the kingdom of the Slavs did not extend beyond the Adriatic empire in the ethnographic mythology of the drama. Yet, at the same time, Venetian sensitivity to issues of Slavic identity, meant that the question could not be altogether ignored in Dalmatia. In the eighteenth century, with the new and newest acquisitions, Venetian officials had the opportunity to recognize resemblances across the border between Dalmatia and Bosnia and along the Habsburg Military Frontier. At the time of the Russian-Ottoman war, between 1768 and 1774, concern over the recruitment of Dalmatians into Russian military service made Venice even more nervous about Slavic resemblances.

Fortis benefited from an acquaintance with earlier Dalmatian perspectives on the Slavs. When he traveled to the island of Hvar (which he called Lesina), he did not fail to cite Vinko Pribojević (whom he called Vincenzo Pribevio) for his oration, *De origine successibusque Slavorum.*[5] Though Fortis came close to making the categorical generalization of Slavic identity, he was perhaps too sensitive to the subtleties of natural history to insist that the resemblance of customs and languages was sufficient to define, comprehensively, "one sole nation." In fact, the fractured history of the modern nations of Eastern Europe has vindicated his hesitation to attribute absolute national unity to the Slavic peoples. His enumeration of the many ancient barbarians, whose names fell under the Slavic rubric, could certainly be matched by a long list of insistently distinct modern nations, under the same rubric, in the twentieth century.

One nation that did not appear among the ancient Slavic barbarians was the Morlacchi; nor would they appear among the contemporary Slavic nations today. The recognition as a nation that they received from Fortis, based on their distinctive customs, followed from the special historical circumstances of the eighteenth century, when Venice's new inland acquisitions in Dalmatia made the Morlacchi the objects of public interest and concern. Through the nineteenth and twentieth centuries they were ethnographically effaced to the point of virtually vanishing in Habsburg Dalmatia and independent Yugoslavia. In the nineteenth-century Habsburg censuses the Morlacchi, along with most other Dalmatians, were identified as "serbisch-kroatisch" by language, and in twentieth-century Yugoslavia the Dalmatians were generally considered Serbs or Croats, according to their Orthodox or Catholic religious affiliations.[6] The early modern significance of the Morlacchi, and especially their eighteenth-century celebrity, can only be appreciated by looking back beyond modern national categories to the political and cultural matrix of the Adriatic empire, in which the Venetian Enlightenment encountered the Dalmatian Slavs.

Fortis, though he made the Slavs of the Dalmatian interior famous under the name of Morlacchi in the eighteenth century, was sensitive enough to issues of identity to record that this was not necessarily the name they used themselves. "The Morlacchi generally call themselves Vlassi in their idiom," he noted. "The denomination of Moro-Vlassi, corrupted to Morlacchi, which the inhabitants of the cities use to name them, could perhaps point to their origin, coming by forced marches from the Black Sea to invade these distant kingdoms." The meaning of "Moro" might refer to the Black Sea, going back to the "barbarous centuries" of Slavic emigrations and inundations, while the identification as "Vlassi" or Vlachs might indicate some sort of Romanian affiliation to Wallachia, though the Morlacchi spoke a Slavic and not a Latin language. Fortis's etymological explorations of the name Morlacchi, looking for evidence of their origins, ended in frustration due to the difficulty of unraveling the "strangely intertwined" genealogies of the region. "The conjecture perhaps would not be ill founded to suspect that even in the last in-undation of Tartars," wrote Fortis, "many families may have remained to populate the deserted valleys that lay between the mountains, and left those Calmuck offspring that still continue to develop there, especially in the area around Zara."[7] The heterogeneity of ethnographic influences, including Tartar and Romanian peoples, as well as all the Slavic tribes of ancient history, made the origin of the Morlacchi both mysterious and miscegenetic, an emblematic summation of the idea of Eastern Europe.

When the Enlightenment discovered Eastern Europe, it appeared as an intermediary domain where Oriental influences (like the Tartars) pen-etrated into Europe, and barbarous peoples (like the Morlacchi) were present in close proximity to civilized societies. From the western per-spectives of Paris or London, of Weimar or Venice, Eastern Europe ap-peared as an indeterminate balance between identity and difference, fa-miliar features and alien accents.[8] Though it seemed plausible to Fortis that the Morlacchi might have come from farther east around the Black Sea, he knew very well from his own observations that the etymology of "Moro" did not mean the Morlacchi were black Moors. In spite of their reputation for alien customs and savage ferocity, they looked like Euro-peans. "Our Morlacchi may be perhaps whiter than the Italians," he commented sharply, though in the English translation Italian sensitivities were spared by making the Morlacchi only "as white as the Italians," not more white.[9] In fact, Fortis could not come up with a racial or physiog-nomic formula to sum up the national distinctness of the Morlacchi.

> The various populations of Morlacchi are even different among themselves, in consequence of the diverse regions from which they come, and the multi-ple mixings that their families had to undergo during repeated changes of country in times of invasions and wars. The inhabitants of Kotar are generally blond, with blue eyes, a broad face, and a crushed nose; characteristics which also fit commonly enough the Morlacchi of the plains of Sinj and of Knin; those of Duare and of Vergoraz are of chestnut hair, long face, olive color, and fine stature. The character of the two varieties is also various. The Mor-lacchi of Kotar are for the most part of gentle manners, respectful, and docile; those of Vergoraz rough, proud, audacious, and enterprising.[10]

Such Linnaean delineations appeared to rule out any general classifica-tion of the nation according to physical characteristics. Furthermore, Fortis's insistence on variations of character seemed to defy the efforts of the Provveditori Generali to sum up the Morlacchi according to an essential character of the nation; indeed, one would never suppose from the official dispatches that it was possible to find among the Morlacchi any part of the population with gentle manners and docile temper. The variations in their appearance and character made it all the more evident to Fortis that the Morlacchi, for all their distinctive aspects, were not absolutely different from other European peoples. Venice's minimal remove from Dalmatia, just across the Adriatic, permitted a pioneering perspective on the balance of difference and identity between Western Europe and Eastern Europe.

In the sixteenth century, Sebastian Münster of the University of Basel already mentioned in his Renaissance cosmography the related "Sclavonian languages," spoken by many peoples, including the Dalmatians, and Konrad Gessner of Zurich, writing about the differences between languages, also remarked upon the broad Slavic domain. In 1601 Mauro Orbini, in *Il regno degli Slavi,* enumerated the peoples of "the Slavic nation and language," beginning with the Dalmatians, and then extending from the Serbs, Croats, and Bosnians all the way to the Russians.[11] Following these Renaissance intimations, Fortis, in the age of Enlightenment, observed on the island of Cres that the people spoke the "Slavic language, which is the most extensive of all the European languages." He noted that "from Carniola to the last frontier of the Russian empire one can travel far and wide speaking this language alone." Fortis had never made such a voyage, but he had only to cross the Adriatic to find himself looking still farther east in a spirit of sweeping generalization. When Fortis described Morlacchi marriage customs, mentioning for instance that the consummation of the marriage was marked with pistol shots by the wedding guests, he pursued a general comparison to Ukraine: "They do not, however, make the noise made in similar cases by the Ukrainians, who in this respect are a little different from our Morlacchi, though on the whole they have the greatest conformity of clothing, customs, dialect, and even orthography." A footnote mentioned that "these usages are common to the entire Russian land."[12] A footnote to the footnote might have remarked that Fortis never visited either Russia or Ukraine.

If resemblances of customs and language were what linked the Morlacchi of Dalmatia to the vast domain of Eastern Europe, Fortis also recognized that speaking a Slavic language did not absolutely separate them from the world of Western Europe. "One can not deny," he wrote, "that

many words of Latin origin may be found in the dialect of the Illyrians."
He compiled a list of examples, comparing Slavic and Latin words, but
cautioning that such similarities of language did not necessarily tell anything about origins; he did not conclude that the Morlacchi were likely
to be the descendants of the Romans. "I am most persuaded," he wrote
"that the examination of languages can lead to discovering the origins of
the nations that speak them, but I am then also convinced that it requires
a most acute judgment to distinguish adventitious words from primitive
ones."[13] For Fortis the question of national origins was like a problem in
paleontology, with words as fossils from past epochs and uncertain
chronology a factor in each hypothesis.

As a theology student in Rome in the 1760s Fortis acquired a sensitivity to linguistic issues from his teacher and mentor Agostino Antonio
Georgi, a master of Oriental languages and author of the *Alphabetum
Tibetanum* in 1763. Fortis would not have presumed to conduct research
in Dalmatia without learning the local language, and by 1773, when Andrea Memmo assigned him on behalf of the government to investigate
fishing in the province, the official commission specified his qualifica-
tions: "joining to the scientific knowledge that adorns him the practice of
various languages, including the Illyrian." Fortis himself casually remarked that his voyaging in Dalmatia taught him "to babble tolerably
enough in Slavic."[14] It was perhaps a modest attainment compared to
learning Tibetan, but Fortis thereby gained not only the ability to inter-
rogate the Morlacchi about their customs but also the key to evaluating
their family relation to the other nations of Europe.

In the 1780s William Jones went to colonial Calcutta, where his Sanskrit studies revealed resemblances to Greek and Latin, suggesting the
family relation of the Indo-European languages. Fortis in Dalmatia in the
1770s, pursuing his Slavic studies, discovered resemblances among European languages, which led him to speculate about a common Scythian
origin. Not only did he observe Slavic similarities to Latin and Greek, but
he also noted related terms in Slavic and English. The British readers of
the English edition of 1778 might have been surprised to discover their
relation to the Morlacchi: "For the words *stina, meso, med, biskup, brate,
sestra, sin, sunze, mliko, snigh, voda, greb,* are not unlike the English,
stone, flesh, mead, bishop, brother, sister, son, sun, milk, snow, water, grave."
Fortis reserved judgment about whether such correspondences came
from a common origin or only from accidental ancient contact. His own

language—"our Italian"—had its share of "exotic" words: "Does it not have also a very great number of Slavonicisms?" Furthermore, there were "innumerable words of our Venetian dialect" that "came to us from the Illyrian."[15] Though the Morlacchi were related by language to Slavic peoples from the Adriatic to the Arctic, the Slavs were not altogether alien to the Venetians. Fortis's special linguistic informant was the Dalmatian Matteo Sović, who was born in St. Petersburg, where his father was in the service of Peter the Great. Returning to Dalmatia, Sović applied his knowledge of Slavic languages to the study of Glagolitic codices and breviaries. In 1745 Pope Benedict XIV accepted the validity of the Glagolitic Slavonic liturgy in Dalmatia, where it had been maintained, controversially, since the tenth century. Both Vinko Zmajević and Matteo Karaman, archbishops of Zadar, were interested in the Slavonic liturgy, partly because it offered the possibility of attracting the Orthodox Morlacchi to Roman Catholicism.[16] The Glagolitic rite, like the poetry of the Morlacchi, invited the rediscovery in Dalmatia of a common Slavic cultural heritage.

Fortis's identification of the Morlacchi in relation to the Slavs, and the Slavs in relation to Europe as a whole, transformed an imperial discourse that, up until then, had been focused more narrowly on the inhabitants of Dalmatia as subjects of Venice. After Fortis, the Morlacchi could be recognized more clearly in the context of Eastern Europe, as conceived by the Enlightenment, classifiable according to their Slavic character. Up until his voyage the subject of the Morlacchi had been the official preserve of the Provveditori Generali. Fortis presented the Morlacchi not only in a more sympathetic light but also before a broader public. They now received the attention of the public of Venice, where readers were appropriately interested in Dalmatian affairs, and more generally, Fortis also introduced the Slavs of Eastern Europe to the public of the Enlightenment in Italy, England, France, and Germany. "Morlacchismo," the abstract term that was coined at the end of the eighteenth century to sum up the essential character of the Morlacchi, could also describe, in historical retrospect, the intellectual interest they provoked.[17] Fortis discovered the folkloric key to the Slavic character of the Morlacchi in their Slavic poetry, which then received further European recognition in the collections and translations of Goethe and Herder. Ultimately, the ethnographic investigation of the Morlacchi as Slavs received its most complete and compelling literary expression in 1788, in the novel *Les Morlaques,* written in French by the Venetian writer Giustiniana Wynne. Informed and inspired by Fortis, she managed in her unique anthropological novel to transmute Venice's nervous sensitivity to the Slavic affiliations of its Dalmatian subjects into a philosophical study of primitive customs, folk poetry, and national identity among the Morlacchi. With the injunction, "You are a Slav," addressed to a child within the novel, Wynne took Fortis's work to its implicit conclusion, enunciating the Enlightenment's intellectually triumphant ascription of national identity to the peoples of Eastern Europe.

Poetry among the Morlacchi

"I have put into Italian some heroic songs of the Morlacchi," wrote Fortis, applying his linguistic skills to the appreciation of South Slavic poetry and publishing side by side a sample of verse transcription and translation, Slavic and Italian, as a sort of appendix to his discussion of the customs of the Morlacchi. This sample, the "Hasanaginica" or "Mourning Song of the Noble Wife of Asan Aga," appearing in *Viaggio in Dalmazia* in 1774, brought South Slavic poetry to the attention of enlightened literary circles all over Europe. Ultimately, Fortis also contributed to the nineteenth-century national literary movement of the South Slavs, led by the Serbian Vuk Karadžić, who collected folk poetry and published a landmark volume in Vienna in 1814, *Mala prostonarodna pjesnarica,* a small volume of simple folk poems. Fortis, in keeping with his geological and paleontological concerns about the past eras of the earth, was naturally interested in such popular poems as the literary fossils of remote times. "I would not pretend to make a comparison with the poems of the celebrated Scottish Bard," wrote Fortis, addessing himself to the Scottish Lord Bute.[18] Graciously Fortis deferred to the poetic supremacy of Ossian, whose works had been recently "discovered" in 1762 by James Macpherson and even more recently translated into Italian by Fortis's friend Melchiorre Cesarotti. Those poems were still then considered authentically ancient Celtic creations; not until the nineteenth century would it be demonstrated that they were largely the work of Macpherson himself. In 1768 the Austrian Jesuit poet Johann Michael Denis, who was also translating Ossian, wrote to the German poet Friedrich Gottlieb Klopstock, "Should one not be able to find among our Slavic nations, but especially in Bohemia, Dalmatia, and Croatia, the survivals of poetic antiquity preserved in just this way?" Klopstock replied with enthusiasm for "Illyrian bards" and requested samples in translation: "Take the best from among the most ancient, leave the Illyrian text in Latin characters to one side, and write a complete literal translation on the other."[19] This was precisely what Fortis achieved in publishing the poetry of the Morlacchi, poetry which he regarded as an oral artifact of the ancient Slavs, illuminating the distant past of Dalmatia. Fortis's anthropology proposed a continuity of primitive customs between the ancient Slavs and the contemporary Morlacchi, and though he "discovered" their poetry for the public of the Enlightenment, he also recognized that the poems had never really been lost, but survived and circulated continuously within the oral culture of the inland inhabitants of Dalmatia.

Fortis hoped that Lord Bute would concede, perhaps more readily than the public of Venice, that in the songs of the Morlacchi lay the dignity of a venerable descent and the virtue of an aural appeal.

> I flatter myself that the finesse of your taste will find therein another kind of merit, recalling the simplicity of Homeric times, and relative to the customs of the nation. The Illyrian text, which you will find after my translation, will put you in a position to judge how well disposed to serve music and poetry would be this language, most sonorous and harmonious, which is yet almost totally abandoned even by the civilized nations that speak it. Ovid, while he lived among the Slavs of the Black Sea, did not disdain to exercise his poetic talent composing verses in their idiom, and obtained praise and applause from those savages; although, in a return of Roman pride, he was then ashamed of having profaned the Latin meters.[20]

The example of Ovid seemed to address Fortis's own ambivalence about the poetry of the South Slavs, for he too, though he could partly appreciate the harmonies of the language, nevertheless held some reservations about the literary quality of his discoveries. Fortis accepted that the same imbalance of civilization between Rome and the savage Slavs at the time of Ovid was preserved in the contemporary condescension of Venice with respect to the ferocious Morlacchi. Though Fortis's bilingual presentation of the "Hasanaginica" seemed to bid for a more equal literary footing between Italian and Illyrian rhythms, in fact the appeal to foreign finesse for a favorable verdict had to come up against the paradoxical impossibility of registering sonorities and harmonies from the printed page while reading the verses in probable incomprehension. Lord Bute could hardly do more than defer to Fortis's own opinion, just as Fortis generously rendered Italian recognition to Ossian.

The reference to "the simplicity of Homeric times" was intended to explicate the creative context of the primitive customs of the Morlacchi. Fortis was familiar with the writings of Vico, which were discussed not only among enlightened men in Venice but also in papal Rome within the academic circle of Giorgi, Fortis's professor in the 1760s. Vico's urgent reflections in the *Scienza nuova* on ancient poetry, barbaric peoples, and the elusive legend of Homer then influenced Fortis's appreciation of the songs of the Morlacchi in the 1770s. With the statue of Homer in the famous frontispiece to the *Scienza nuova,* Vico set out upon the "search for the true Homer." His point of departure was the barbarism of Homeric times: "Let us concede to Homer what certainly must be granted, that he had to conform to the quite vulgar feelings and hence the vulgar customs of the barbarous Greece of his day." Vico's emphasis on this barbarous context was clearly revelant to Fortis's remark on Morlacchi poetry: "recalling the simplicity of Homeric times, and relative to the customs of the nation." These customs, preserved in song, were both contemporary and ancient at once, transcending history, since the Morlacchi, having preserved their barbarous customs, were presumed to be living still in the simplicity of Homeric times. Vico ultimately concluded that there was no historic Homer as poetic composer of the *Iliad* and the *Odyssey,* but rather that "the Greek peoples were themselves Homer," creating the epic over generations and across centuries.[21] This too was fully consistent with Fortis's assumptions about the anonymous composition of the Morlacchi songs, which gave him no individual name to set alongside that of Ossian. In applying Vico's reflections on Homer, formulated in the first half of the eighteenth century, to his own discovery of the poetry of the South Slavs, Fortis anticipated the fundamental principles of modern scholarship in the field of folklore.

The poetry of the Morlacchi, according to Fortis, "perpetuates the memory of the national histories of ancient times," in the course of repeated recitations. "There is always some singer," he noted, "who, accompanying himself on an instrument called *guzla,* which has only one string composed of many horsehairs, is heard repeating, and often confecting (*impasticciando*) anew the old *pisme* or songs." Fortis recognized that the songs were subject to oral evolution in the mouth of every singer, but believed that they nevertheless preserved from their ancient origins elements of the historical past. In this sense the perseverance of the songs reflected the tenacity of customs among the Morlacchi, and Fortis even used the songs as a sort of fossil evidence. When he wrote about marriage customs, for instance, he mentioned that on the wedding day the groom would come to the bride's house at the head of an armed party as a precaution against the violent disruption of the marriage. Fortis supposed that "such surprises happened often in times gone by when (inasmuch as one gathers from the heroic songs of the nation) it was the custom that various claimants to the hand of a girl would earn the preference with valorous actions."[22] This attempt to apply the subjects of oral poetry to understanding the customs of primitive people indicates Fortis's intellectual significance at the intersecting origins of modern folklore and anthropology, as influenced by natural history, within the Enlightenment.

The Venetian historiographical tradition, dating from the Renaissance, still offered a model for historians like Diedo and Sandi in the eighteenth century to write the history of Venice, including the political and diplomatic aspects of imperial rule over coastal Dalmatia. Fortis, however, looking to Vico for inspiration, conceived of a completely different sort of history of Dalmatia, the natural history of the customs of the inland inhabitants. The "Hasanaginica" or "Mourning Song" was chosen by Fortis for translation and inclusion with his account of the customs of the Morlacchi, and its interest for him was surely related to his own observations on those customs, especially concerning the mistreatment of women. The poem tells of a woman cruelly renounced by her husband, brutally bullied by her brother, and tragically separated from her children, until she finally expires from grief.

The "Hasanaginica" has been recognized and confirmed as a true specimen of oral folk poetry. The poem was probably first transcribed in Split, where it came to the attention of Fortis's friend Giulio Bajamonti.[23] Some of the Morlacchi poems translated and circulated by Fortis, however, were not authentically oral or ancient, but came from the almost contemporary pen of Andrija Kačić-Miošić, who composed his own verses on the history of the Slavs, modeled on the oral epics; his *Razgovor ugodni naroda slovinskoga* was published in Venice in 1756. Albert Lord, collecting folk songs in Yugoslavia two centuries later, noted that Fortis—"collector of the famed Hasanaginica"—also erroneously accepted the work of Kačić as true oral poetry. Thus, by way of Fortis's Italian translations, the poems of Kačić ended up in Herder's collections of folk songs.[24] For instance, in his essay on Cres in 1771 Fortis appended the Italian translation of a poem from Kačić, "The Song of Milos Cobilich and Vuko Brankovich," which Herder then published in German in his *Volkslieder* of 1778. In Fortis's translation the names became Italianate, Vuko di Branco and Milosso Cobilizio: "So as not to torture Italian ears I have sought to remove the harshness of Brankovich and of Cobilich, dividing the first and giving the second our sort of termination."[25] Herder, in the German version, restored the Slavic names. Such translations and republications also involved reclassifications that illustrated the fluidity of early modern national labels in the denomination of folk poetry. The "Slavic" poems of Kačić, published in Italian by Fortis, eventually became "Morlackisch" in Herder's collection. Poetry that Fortis and Herder attributed to the Morlacchi would later be labeled as Serbian by Vuk Karadžić in the early nineteenth century.

For all his sympathetic interest in the Morlacchi, and although he publicized their poetry all over Europe, Fortis was neither sentimentally nor aesthetically enthusiastic about the recitations that he observed. Indeed, the reserved character of his response, his frank admission of his own alienation, indicated how fully he was a man of the Italian Enlightenment rather than a forerunner of German Romanticism.

> These poems have strong strokes of expression, but scarcely a flash of imagination, and even that not always felicitous. They have a great effect on the souls of the listeners who, little by little, learn them by memory; I have seen some of them crying and sighing at some stroke that did not awaken any feeling in me. Probably the value of the Illyrian words, better understood by the Morlacchi, produced this effect; or maybe, as seems reasonable to me, their simple souls, little enriched by refined ideas, need only little impact to be shaken up. The simplicity and disorder, that are often found combined in the ancient poems of the Provençal troubadours, form the principal character of the poetic tales of the Morlacchi, generally speaking. There are some, however, that are well-ordered: but it is always necessary for the listener or reader to supply for himself a great number of the little details of precision, which can not be omitted without making a sort of monstrosity of narrations in the prose or verse of the civilized nations of Europe.[26]

To witness a recital of Morlacchi poetry was, for Fortis, to reinforce the anthropological sense of distance that separated him from the subjects of his study, between his own "refined" perspective and their "simple souls."

Their extreme susceptibility to their own poetry, manifested in sighing and crying, seemed to set the Morlacchi psychologically apart from the enlightened Italian observer, though such emotional responses may have seemed less strange when reported in German translation in the decade of *Sturm und Drang*. Fortis, remarking upon the "monstrosity" of Morlacchi poetry in its literary details, formulated his own "refined" alignment with "the civilized nations of Europe," collectively, in enlightened contrast to the Slavs of Dalmatia. Indeed, by putting the customs of the Morlacchi before the public, not only of Venice and Italy, but also of England, France, and Germany, Fortis's *Viaggio in Dalmazia* structured a distinctive relation between the readers and the subjects of the book, between civilized nations and simple souls, between the evolving domains of Western Europe and Eastern Europe.

Barbarous Modulations

Though Fortis recognized resemblances across the geographically extensive Slavic domain of language and customs, his folkloric focus conjured an image of the Morlacchi in mountainous isolation, singing their primitive songs to one another.

> The Morlacco, traveling through deserted mountains, and especially at nighttime, sings about the ancient deeds of the Slavic kings and barons or some tragic happening. If it occurs, that upon the peaks of a nearby mountain, another traveler is walking, he repeats the verse sung by the first; and this alternation of singing continues until distance divides the two voices. A long howl (*urlo*), which is an *oh!* barbarously modulated, always precedes the verse; the words that form it are rapidly pronounced almost without any modulation, which is then entirely reserved for the last syllable, and finishes with a prolonged howl shaped as a trill.[27]

In presenting this lonely scene, as if these were the last two Morlacchi on earth, Fortis evoked a moment of pure communion, between the Morlacchi, free of all possible external influences, and with their ancient Slavic ancestors whose deeds formed the subject of the song. There was a certain element of prurient literary perversity in imagining such a secluded moment of Dalmatian isolation only to dramatize it before the reading public of Venice, but it was that very counterposition of the "civilized nations" and the "simple souls" that formed the philosophical framework of Fortis's representational strategy.

The precision of the scrupulously described alternation of parts and modulation of voices clearly indicates Fortis's claim to be considered among the earliest folklorists. However, the attribution of howling barbarism made such a style of singing seem consistent with a social complex of primitive customs. The howls of the Morlacchi travelers would have recalled to readers Fortis's preceding discussion of Haiduks, who "lead the life of wolves." At the same time Fortis's account fit with Rousseau's ideas about the origins of language, adumbrated in the essay on inequality and fully developed in an unpublished piece, "Essai sur l'origine des langues." There Rousseau argued that language developed as a social phenomenon, so that "as soon as one man was recognized by another as a sentient, thinking being similar to himself, the desire or need to communicate his feelings or thoughts made him seek the means to do so." In this same sense, Fortis's scenario was also a sort of study in the social origins of language, the Morlacchi singing responsively to one another in the mountains. For Rousseau, language developed according to the human passions, as "nature dictates accents, cries, lamentations," such that "the first languages were singable and passionate." The singing and howling of Fortis's Morlacchi matched such a vision of primitive language, and Rousseau's conclusions about the original relation of song, poetry, and language were also relevant to the case: "Verse, singing, and speech have a common origin. . . . The periodic recurrences and measures of rhythm, the melodious modulations of accent, gave birth to poetry and music along with language. Or rather this was the only language in those happy climes and happy times." This speculative anthropology, typical of Rousseau's approach to the origins of society as well as language, provided a philosophical context for appreciating the priority of oral poetry among primitive peoples. "Writing, which would seem to crystallize language, is precisely what alters it," argued Rousseau. "It changes not the words but the spirit, substituting exactitude for expressiveness." With reference to Rousseau's reflections on language, Jacques Derrida, in *Of Grammatology*, would develop the deconstructive concept of writing as the "supplement" to language.[28] Fortis's folkloric interest in the howls and modulations of the Morlacchi songs should thus be considered in the context of the Enlightenment's attention to the origins of language. The discovery of Slavic poems like the "Hasanaginica" in the mountains of Dalmatia empirically confirmed that which was philosophically presumed, the primitive priority of oral poetry, before the "supplementary" advent of scriptive and corruptive civilization.

In 1770, the year that Fortis first went to Dalmatia, Herder entered an essay contest on the origins of language, sponsored by the Berlin Academy of Sciences. His winning effort was published in 1772 and began with the reflection that "while still an animal, man already has language," inasmuch as "all strong passions of his soul express themselves directly in screams, in sounds, in wild inarticulate tones."[29] By the end of the decade Herder would be publishing in his collections of *Volkslieder* South Slavic poetry, designated as "Morlackisch" and provided by Fortis. With their related themes and concerns, Herder, Rousseau, and Fortis seemed almost to be singing to one another from their respective peaks in the landscape of the Enlightenment.

"Traditional songs contribute very much to maintaining ancient usages," wrote Fortis. "Like their rituals, so also their games and dances are from the most remote times." Oral poetry was not only customary in its recitation but also, by sustaining the themes of past performances and previous generations, preserved the primitive customs that constituted Morlacchi society. Fortis's anthropological perspective emphasized this interrelated structural totality of tenacious customs, mutually reinforced and aggregately preserved into the eighteenth century. Folklore belonged to this complex of customs, not only song but also dance. "To the singing of the songs, and to the sound of the bagpipe," he noted, "the Morlacchi do their favorite dance which is called *Kolo*, or circle, and which then degenerates into *Skocci-gori*, that is, high leaps." This degeneration was, of course, the progress of the dance, described by Fortis in precise folkloric detail:

> All the dancers, men and women, taking each other by the hand, form a circle, and they begin first to turn slowly, swaying, to the rough and monotone notes of the instrument, which is played by someone skillful in the art. The circle goes on changing forms, and becomes now an ellipse, now a square, accordingly as the dance becomes animated; and finally it is transformed into most excessively high leaps. . . . The transport that the Morlacchi feel for this savage dance is incredible. They undertake it often, in spite of being tired from work, or from long walking and ill nourishment; they are accustomed to devoting many hours with small interruptions to such violent exercise.[30]

As when listening to the songs, Fortis's principal response was a sense of his own alienation from the participants in the dance, their strange "transport," which appeared "incredible" to him. The attributes of Morlacchi character, so often reiterated in the relations of the Provveditori Generali, here appeared in Fortis as folkloric description. The dance was "savage" and "violent," while the dancers still received his general sympathy for their hard work and malnourishment. The degeneration of the dance was described as a sort of failure of geometric discipline. The Morlacchi in their closed circle experienced the excesses of the dance in primitive relation to one another, while Fortis, with all his readers among the "civilized nations of Europe," maintained an anthropological perspective from outside the circle of the dance.

International Fascination: Morlacchi, Morlackisch, Morlaques

Fortis's section on the "Customs of the Morlacchi" concluded with his bilingual Slavic transcription and Italian translation of the "Hasanaginica," the "Mourning Song of the Noble Wife of Asan Aga." The opening lines, describing the white tents of Asan Aga, were then presented in three more versions, so that Fortis could demonstrate the three forms of Slavic writing in Dalmatia: liturgical Glagolitic, ancient Cyrillic, and "the Cyrillic cursive of the Morlacchi which much resembles the cursive of the Russians." The supreme incomprehensibility of these alphabetic forms for the Venetian public only emphasized the alien exoticism of the Slavs and the almost cryptological achievement of Fortis in cracking their folkloric code. "The Serbian capitals of the caloyer monks and the cursive used in the interior of Bosnia, which is almost in Arabic style (*arabizzato*), are also curious," remarked Fortis, in a further display of scriptive erudition, though he declined to impose upon his readers with these additional variant versions. In fact, any Arabic flourishes would have suited the subject of the poem, for the story of the rejected wife of Asan Aga took place among Moslem Slavs.[31] The Morlacchi included Orthodox and Catholic subjects of Venice, but they were also closely culturally related to some Moslem Slavic communities across the Ottoman border in Bosnia.

In 1774 or 1775, just after Fortis published the Venetian edition of *Viaggio in Dalmazia,* Goethe took up the wife of Asan Aga and created a German version of the poem:

> Was ist Weisses dort am grünen Walde?
> Ist es Schnee wohl oder sind es Schwäne?
> Wär es Schnee da, wäre weggeschmolzen,
> Wären's Schwäne, wären weggeflogen.
> Ist kein Schnee nicht, es sind keine Schwäne,
> 's ist der Glanz der Zelten Asan Aga. . . .

> > What is white there in the green woods?
> > Is it snow or is it swans?
> > If it were snow it would have melted away,
> > If it were swans, they would have flown away,
> > It is not snow, it is not swans,
> > It's the gleam of the tents of Asan Aga. . . .

Goethe's work effectively transformed the folk poem of the Morlacchi into a literary work of lyrical poetry. He became famous as the author of *Werther* in 1774, and, perhaps in deference to the anonymous folk authorship of the Morlacchi, Goethe preserved his own anonymity when the poem was published in Herder's *Volkslieder* in 1778. Fortis was cited as the source of the poem, and since Herder specified the national origin of each selection, "Klaggesang von der edlen Frauen des Asan Aga" was labeled as "Morlackisch," which thus ranked as a cultural category alongside "Deutsch" or "Spanisch" or "Englisch."[32] The "Klaggesang" was the concluding selection of the first part of the *Volkslieder,* directly preceded by Ophelia's lament at the death of her father, from *Hamlet.*

Fortis named the Morlacchi as a "nation" within Venetian Dalmatia, and Herder, who referred to Fortis, indicated by the label "Morlackisch" that they could be considered among the nations of Europe. Clearly the concept of the nation or people, whether invoked by Fortis, Herder, or Kačić—*Nazione, Volk, Narod*—still lacked the cultural and political implications of modern nationalism, but, by the late eighteenth century, early modern notions of the nation were already on the verge of modern revaluation. In the 1770s Herder had not yet reached the point at which *Slawische Völker* became his fundamental classification, though he and Fortis were moving together toward the anthropological discovery of the Slavs. In the first part of the *Volkslieder,* along with the "Klaggesang," the one other poem marked as "Morlackisch" was the "Song of Milos

Cobilich and Vuko Brankovich," about medieval Serbia and the coming
of the Ottomans, the song that Fortis had taken from the collection by
Kačić. In the second part of the *Volkslieder,* Herder included two more
poems contributed in manuscript by Fortis, each designated as "eine mor-
lackische Geschichte." These were followed by a Bohemian selection—
"eine böhmische Geschichte"—to form an implicitly Slavic grouping.
The first of the Morlacchi poems was titled "Radoslaus" and concerned a
Dalmatian king unthroned by his wicked son; the second, "Die schöne
Dolmetscherin" ("The Pretty Translator"), told of a girl from Grahovo
in Montenegro, at the time of the Ottoman invasions, who could speak
Turkish and, tragically, preferred a pasha to her own husband.[33]
Through Fortis's folkloric interest in the poetry of the South Slavs, their
songs were included in Herder's landmark collections, and the Morlacchi
themselves thus received international recognition as ranking among the
poetic peoples of Europe.

Goethe designated his "Klaggesang" as a translation "aus dem Morlackischen," though he himself, as he admitted, knew "none of the Slavic
dialects," and could only translate from translations. The young Walter
Scott, in 1797, made his translation of the "Hasanaginica" into English
from Goethe's German version: "What yonder glimmers so white on the
mountain?" Georgii Ferrich published a Latin translation in Ragusa in
1798, citing Fortis, working from the "Illyrian" language: "Quid viridi in
silva candens elucet?" By the time Vuk Karadžić decided to include the
"Hasanaginica" in his collection in 1814, it was almost obligatory to recognize Goethe's role in publicizing the poem, and Karadžić inscribed accordingly a copy of his book for Goethe: "A Slav sends to the greatest
German, alongside the original of the 'Mourning Song of the Noble
Wife of the Hero Asan Aga,' also the first publication of Serbian folk
songs." Goethe went on to take a lifelong interest in the poetry of the
South Slavs, enthusiastically endorsing the work of Karadžić. When
Goethe reflected on the subject later in the 1820s, the basic cultural classification was no longer "Morlackisch" but rather, in a modern national
attribution, "Serbische Lieder," Serbian songs.[34] The nineteenth-century
national effacement of the Morlacchi had begun.

Karadžić claimed the "Hasanaginica" as a Serbian song, but its origin
in Venetian Dalmatia, among the Morlacchi, meant that in the nineteenth century Croatian national culture could also exercise a claim to
this most celebrated piece of South Slavic poetry. Karadžić, who never

found a singer to sing him the song, made alterations in Fortis's transcription that had the effect of creating a more Serbian version. Camilla
Lucerna, from Habsburg Zagreb, wrote about the "Hasanaginica" at
the beginning of the twentieth century, emphatically rejecting the
nineteenth-century Serbian pretensions of Karadžić, on the grounds that
the dialect of the poem was Croatian while its subject concerned Moslem
Slavs. "So it is incorrect to designate the poem as Serbian, as in Vuk's
misleading procedure," concluded Lucerna. Yet, equally emphatically,
she rejected the notion that the poem could be attributed to the Morlacchi: "There is no Morlacchi language, no Morlacchi people." The identity that Fortis had ascribed in the eighteenth century was now emphatically denied, a casualty of disjunction between the early modern
classifications of Venetian Dalmatia and the modern national names of
the Habsburg Slavs. Lucerna, in 1905, decided to denominate "Croatian
poetry" as "South Slavic"—and regretted that it was no longer possible
to employ "the beautiful, good, old name Illyrian."[35] Thus, on the
threshold of the twentieth century, the "Hasanaginica" continued to
provoke classificatory concern, following from its discovery in the age of
Enlightenment as a masterpiece of the Morlacchi.

Looking back to the 1770s, Goethe recalled in the 1820s: "It is already fifty years since I translated the 'Klaggesang der edlen Frauen Asan
Agas,' which was to be found in the *Reise* of the abbé Fortis, and also in
the *Morlackische Notizen* of the Countess Rosenberg. I translated it from
the accompanying French, with a notion of the rhythm and attention to
the word order of the original." Goethe must have been misremember-
ing here, for Giustiniana Wynne, Countess of Orsini-Rosenberg, did not
publish her novel, *Les Morlaques,* until 1788, and in any event she did not
include the "Hasanaginica." The error in attribution by Goethe, however, underlined her particular importance in drawing international attention to Fortis's account of the customs of the Morlacchi. Goethe was in
Italy in 1787, and distinctly not interested in traveling across the Adriatic:
"The Prince of Waldeck made me uneasy by suggesting . . . I should
accompany him to Greece and Dalmatia."[36] Having evaded that voyage,
Goethe was still in Italy at the beginning of 1788, when *Les Morlaques*
was published there; in 1789, back in Weimar, he finally published the
"Klaggesang" in a collection of his own poetry under his own name.
Whatever the coincidences and inaccuracies of chronology, when Goethe
looked back on a lifetime of interest in the poetry of the South Slavs, he

significantly associated his own poem "aus dem Morlackischen" with the fictional rendering of *Les Morlaques* by the literary countess.

Giustiniana Wynne, in spite of her English father, her German title, and her French novel, lived most of her life in and around Venice and was more Venetian than anything else. *Les Morlaques* was therefore a novel of Dalmatia composed from the Venetian perspective but conceived for the cosmopolitan public of Europe. Like Fortis, whose account she frankly acknowledged as her source and inspiration, Wynne was aware that the importance of the Morlacchi involved not only the state interests of Venice but also the intellectual interests of the European Enlightenment. The philosophical influence of Rousseau was evident in the preface of the novel, which presented Dalmatia as a model for studying the state of nature.

> The islands, the shores, and the towns experience the advantages of civilization, which commerce and populous society attract in their wake; everywhere else this vast country, although so close to Italy and in great part subject to the Republic of Venice, offers the image of nature in primitive society, such as it must have been in the most remote times, and such as it has been found among the inhabitants of the most unknown islands of the Pacific.[37]

The word *civilisation* was only just acquiring its modern meaning in French and English during the second half of the eighteenth century. Fortis in the 1770s used *colto* in Italian to signify "civilized"; Wynne in the 1780s, writing in French, applied the new word *civilisation* to indicate the "advantages" of proximity to Italy and subjection to Venice.

The oceanic isolation of the Pacific islands allowed for a purely geographical explanation of their exemption from "civilization," but the paradox of Dalmatia's presence in Europe and proximity to Italy suggested an all the more interesting case of cultural immunity to progress: "What force, what art can apply against the irresistible and continuous action of time, against the revolution of the centuries?" Fortis's explanation was the "tenacity" of customs, and Wynne constructed, accordingly, an anthropological novel of customs, virtually inventing the genre, in order to explore the persistence of primitive society:

> The natural course of ordinary events in a Morlacchi family will make us acquainted with the customs and usages of the nation in a manner more sensitive than the cold and methodical relation of the voyager. It has not been thought necessary to have recourse to the romantic or marvelous. The facts are true and the national details faithfully exposed . . . . This is perhaps the

most agreeable way to give an accurate idea of a people who think, speak, and act in a manner very different from ours.[38]

She thus proposed a novel in which the characters were fictional but the customs accurately described. The realism of the eighteenth-century novel depended upon representing to readers the familiarity of characters and circumstances, but *Les Morlaques* was composed according to the opposite principle of portraying an alien sphere, "very different from ours." This was a novel of sensibility intended to inspire in its readers an "agreeable" feeling of difference from the anthropological realm of the subject.

Wynne's hasty dismissal of the "cold and methodical relation of the voyager" seems almost ungrateful in view of her own heavy reliance on Fortis as a source. From his fifty pages on Morlacchi customs she found most of the material that she needed to elaborate into a novel of 350 pages. In fact, if she had no need of recourse to marvels, she seems to have felt no more need of recourse to travels. Though she acknowledged Fortis's book, as well as personal informants who had served the government of Venice in Dalmatia—"those whom public employments and particular affairs have caused to reside in that country"—she made no mention of any voyage to Dalmatia on her own part. Indeed her geography of *Morlaquie* suggested that it was perhaps too imprecise a space for a regular travel itinerary: "This same *Morlaquie* in the time of the Romans was a portion of flourishing Dalmatia, of redoubtable Illyrium. . . . At present it forms a part of that country which is generically named *Esclavonie* or the country of the Slavs, whose vast extent from Albania ascending all the way to Hungary can only with difficulty be marked by fixed and constant limits." Even more than Fortis, Wynne was interested in the Slavic character of the Morlacchi and their relation to a larger Slavic domain that far overran the boundaries of Venetian Dalmatia. The absence of "fixed and constant limits" gave all the more freedom to the author's imagination, as she mentally traversed the "country of the Slavs" with reference to the eighteenth-century idea of Eastern Europe: "The nations who inhabit it are a confused melange of indigenous peoples, of Latin colonies, of Scythians, Goths, and Vandals, of all those who overwhelmed Europe at the fall of the Roman Empire. But the peoples of the interior *Morlaquie* may be regarded as the true indigenes or at least as the most ancient inhabitants."[39] Writing at the same time that Herder was composing his *Philosophie der Geschichte,* Wynne also made the imaginative connection between the barbarians of ancient history and the primitive peoples of contemporary anthropology. She claimed for the Morlacchi a special significance, based on their ultimate autochthony, as the ethnographic key to Eastern Europe. The plot of the novel would turn on their emerging consciousness of themselves as belonging to a larger nation of Slavs.

Writing after Fortis, Wynne could not present to the public a novel about the customs of the Morlacchi without including their songs, the cultural artifacts that testified to their ancient national lineage. *Les Morlaques* included ten such songs, whose importance was emphasized by a separate enumeration, "Table des Chansons." There were songs for weddings, songs for deaths, and songs of ancient Slavic heroes, like the "Chanson de Pecirep":

> Pecirep détruisit ses ennemis. . .
> Les croissants de Klivno tremblaient devant lui: puissent-ils
>   disparaître devant nous!
> Les ombres des anciens Morlaques massacrés le suivaient
>   dans ses courses rapides. . .
> Les Turcs tombent sous les coups d'un Haiduc,
>   comme les fruits mûrs du pommier secoué par le jeune
>   Morlaque.
> Pecirep foudroyait les hordes infidèles. . .
>
> Pecirep destroyed his enemies. . .
> The crescents of Klivno trembled before him: may they
>   disappear before us!
> The shades of ancient massacred Morlaques followed
>   him in his rapid courses. . .
> The Turks fall beneath the blows of a Haiduk,
>   like the ripe fruits of the apple tree shaken by
>   the young Morlaque.
> Pecirep struck the infidel hordes. . .[40]

Though the singing of such songs was one of the true "national details" of Morlacchi custom in the novel, the songs themselves appear to have been the French literary improvisations of the author, posing as translations from the authentic poetry of the South Slavs. In the age of Ossian such dissimulation was hardly unprecedented, and Wynne's "Chansons" demonstrated the imaginative appeal of such poetry for contemporary writers and readers. Though she did not include a French version of the "Hasanaginica" in the novel, the song was sufficiently famous already in 1788 to be casually mentioned as the specialty of a particular singer: "He will still sing to you, with the *guzla,* of the death of the beautiful wife of Asan Aga."[41] Wynne's contribution to the literary cult of Slavic songs may be judged from the fact that Goethe would confusedly remember her, together with Fortis, for having inspired his own poetic interest in matters *Morlackisch.*

Imagining Dalmatia: The Fictional Morlacchi of Giustiniana Wynne

Giustiniana Wynne, also known as Justine, was born in Venice, the daughter of a Protestant Englishman abroad and a Venetian woman, devoutly Catholic, from a family of Greek origin. The date of birth, in the 1730s, remains uncertain and was intentionally obfuscated since it apparently preceded the parents' marriage. Lady Mary Wortley Montagu reported on the family history from Venice in 1758: "He was introduced by his Gondolier . . . to this Greek . . . and had three daughters by her, before her artifices prevailed on him to marry her. The eldest daughter speaks English." Giustiniana Wynne's earliest romantic entanglements involved Casanova, who wrote about her appreciatively in his memoirs under the name of Mlle X. C. V. Casanova greatly admired her: "Although she was only fifteen, she was a perfect beauty, all the more ravishing in that the charms of her figure were joined to all the advantages of a cultivated spirit."[42] He made the conquest some years later, in Paris, when Wynne was already pregnant with someone else's child; Casanova persuaded her that sex with him would help to bring about an abortion. In fact her great love at this time was Andrea Memmo in Venice, himself a friend of Casanova and later of Fortis. Through her romance with Memmo she was, from her earliest years, in contact with the new generation of the Venetian Enlightenment. In 1761 she married the Austrian ambassador in Venice, Count Philip Orsini-Rosenberg, then in his 60s, a union that met with disapproval at the Habsburg court of Maria Theresa. The count conveniently left his wife a young widow in 1765, and since he had great family estates in Carinthia, she spent some years living in Klagenfurt. There, on the ethnic border between Germans and Slovenes, she would certainly have had some reason to reflect upon the Slavs, and in *Les Morlaques* she claimed to have benefited from "conversations with the Slavs of neighboring regions."[43] Her return to Venice in 1770 coincided with Fortis's announcement of his departure for Dalmatia.

In Venice she held an enlightened salon, somewhat overshadowed by the more celebrated contemporary salon of Caterina Dolfin. Casanova was also in Venice in the 1770s and was able to report in his memoirs on Wynne's respectable widowhood. "She lives today in Venice, the widow of Count Rosenberg," he reported. "There she shines by her sage conduct and by all the social virtues with which she is adorned. Nobody finds any fault in her except that of not being rich enough."[44] That single fault, however, made her vulnerable to the temptations of gambling in Venice, and she ended up retiring from the city in the 1780s, to live as the guest of Angelo Querini at the villa of Altichiero near Padua. Querini, whose political aspirations in Venice had been blocked by Marco Foscarini in the constitutional crisis of 1761, created at Altichiero a villa retreat, adorned with busts of Voltaire and Rousseau, celebrating the values of the Enlightenment. Querini's important collection of antiquities provided the marble statues for the gardens at Altichiero. There, Wynne became a writer, encouraged by Querini and by her romantic companion, Bartolomeo Benincasa from Modena. She composed an appreciative description of Altichiero itself, as a tribute to her host. She also wrote a collection of "moral and sentimental pieces," which were praised by Fortis in 1785 as the work of "a lady endowed with superior talents and solid culture, and therefore very far from all that gives rise to the ridicule of women of letters in our times." Wynne saw herself as embarking upon a new stage of life in the 1780s, negotiating the appropriate roles permitted to an eighteenth-century woman. "When I was a pretty woman," she wrote in one of the essays, "I at least had enough intelligence to understand that I would have a long life beyond the brilliant life of youth. Happily, I did not love animals then; I love them at present and now give my dogs the time I used to give to my admirers. Books always remain to me. . ."[45] One of the books that remained with her in her retirement at Altichiero was Fortis's *Viaggio in Dalmazia,* ready at hand as she set out to write a novel about the Morlacchi.

"At the foot of the mountain of Crisiza the beautiful valley of Dizmo spreads its fertile fields and rich pastures to the banks of the Cetina," wrote Wynne, setting the scene. "In all of the vast *Morlaquie* it is the most agreable canton because of its fortunate position and the gifts of nature." The place names emphasized the exoticism of Dalmatia, almost as if they belonged to the fictional world of the novel, but Wynne took them directly from the pages of Fortis. "At the foot of the mountain of

Crisiza lies the beautiful valley of Dizmo," he recorded, "which has good pastures and not infertile terrain." Thus Wynne followed in the footsteps of Fortis's voyage, setting her novel from the pages of his book. That she herself never saw the scene did not prevent her from rendering its picturesque appeal for her readers: "The errant flocks, the scattered cottages, the inhabitants who ramble in passing from one to another, form the most enchanting tableau."[46] In its pastoral aesthetics, featuring sheep rather than dogs, as well as in its anthropological assumptions, *Les Morlaques* elaborated upon the details from Fortis in a spirit of literary fantasy evidently influenced by Rousseau. In addition to her reading of *Viaggio in Dalmazia*, Wynne also received additional assistance from the author, as witnessed by a letter that Benincasa wrote to Fortis in 1786: "I thank you on behalf of the countess for the papers so readily and so kindly sent; they will be kept by us until you return or arrange for them, and, meanwhile, will be of much use for our need."[47] Fortis was thus personally involved in the project of writing the novel, while Wynne herself waited at Altichiero for his papers concerning Dalmatia to come to her.

"It seemed that this people was all of one sole family (*una sola famiglia*)," wrote Fortis, describing the Morlacchi who casually kissed one another in greeting. "Each village is one sole family (*une seule famille*)," echoed Wynne. "It conserves the same name, the spirit of filial and fraternal attachment; the society never breaks the bonds of nature." She then introduced a particular family village, that of the Narzevizca, and named its paternal leader as one of the principal characters in the novel:

> The respectable old man Pervan is the Starescina or old chief. . . . The name and charge of Starescina makes him the common father of all the inhabitants, among whom his great age, the memory of his valor, his justice, and his gentleness have merited the sole distinction that occurs in the society of the Morlaques. . . . In the middle of a profound peace Pervan by his wisdom preserves order, union, and comfort among the Narzevizca.[48]

Readers who had casually read the *Viaggio in Dalmazia* in the 1770s might not have remembered the name Pervan when they came to *Les Morlaques* in the 1780s. Fortis himself, however, had declared: "I will never forget as long as I live the reception and cordial treatment of me by the Voivod Pervan at Coccorich." Fortis kept a portrait of Pervan "to have the pleasure of seeing him again even at a distance," and that portrait was published in the *Viaggio in Dalmazia*. In a strange sort of cartographical tribute, Fortis actually located Pervan's house—"Casa del

Pervan"—on one of the maps in the book, as if to assist other travelers who sought hospitality among the Morlacchi.[49] If Fortis put Pervan on the sentimental map of Dalmatia, it was Wynne who found him there and removed him to a more imaginative realm of fantasy.

Fortis's fond appreciation of his host Pervan was formulated at a time when Giacomo Da Riva, the Provveditore Generale, had denounced the chiefs for the "oppression" of their fellow Morlacchi. Wynne went further than Fortis in representing the chief as an almost utopian paragon of village leadership, who "by his wisdom preserves order, union, and comfort." The influence of Rousseau's discourse on inequality was evident in her vision of a society whose "sole distinction" was that of the "common father." That influence was all the more unmistakable as Pervan addressed the villagers—"*Oh mes enfants*"—heralding the communal harvest:

> The time of the harvest approaches, the time of joy, the recompense of labor, the restoration of strength, the renewal of life. The animals roam in the pastures, their products fill our stores with everything necessary for our continual needs and for the necessary exchanges with our neighbors. This soil is ours, like the air we breathe, like the day we enjoy, like the beneficent warmth of the sun that animates nature. Can one partition the air, the day, the warmth among those who thus receive life? Can one partition this soil that nourishes and sustains us all, that responds so abundantly to our labors, that presents its fruit equally to the robust arms that farm it, and to the weak and timid hands of the child and the young mother?[50]

Wynne's insistence on the natural necessity of communal property came after a generation of Venetian agricultural reform in Dalmatia, ever since the Grimani law, which instituted the principle of state assignment of fields to individual farmers among the Morlacchi. Her fantasy reverted to an anterior anthropological scenario that followed the speculative logic of Rousseau concerning the economic life of happy savages:

> The first person who, having enclosed a field, thought to say, "This is mine," and found people simple enough to believe it, was the true founder of civil society. What crimes, wars, murders, miseries, and horrors might have been spared the human race by someone who could have cried out to his kind, "Beware of listening to this impostor; you are lost if you forget that the fruits belong to everyone, and the land belongs to no one."[51]

Wynne made Pervan into Rousseau's hypothetical hero, speaking out eloquently against any individual claims on the common property of all.

Pervan reminded the villagers that their sense of community was founded on common descent. "Always remember that we are all brothers," he declared, "that we have the same name, the same blood, the same father, the glorious Pecirep Narzevizca. The song that preserves among us the memory of his exploits is always in your mouths, that his story may be in your hearts." Wynne clearly appreciated from reading Fortis the important anthropological connection between the social solidarity of customs among the Morlacchi and the oral transmission (*dans vos bouches*) of a common heritage through the singing of songs. The history of their ancestor Pecirep, however, offered not only an inspirational model to the villagers but also a cautionary injunction. For Pecirep began as a bandit Haiduk, committing dauntless acts of pillage and violence against the Ottomans. At the age of fifty, he gave up his bandit life, and descended from the mountains, determined to live usefully in the valley of Dizmo: "After having been feared like thunder by the traveler lost in the mountains, he ended by being beloved like the rainbow that restores serenity."[52] The career of Pecirep was a parable of social progress among primitive people, commemorating the moment at which this population of Morlacchi became more civilized than they had been before, giving up banditry to live in agricultural and pastoral peace. This condition did not bring "the advantages of civilization" as known to the Venetians, but it brought about that elevation from barbarism that enabled the Morlacchi to achieve "the image of nature in primitive society," to live according to the laws of nature.

In 1788, when Wynne published her fictional celebration of justice, gentleness, and serenity among the Morlacchi, Obradović also penned his impressions of settling in inland Dalmatia, where he served as a schoolteacher in the region around Knin in the 1760s. "The very name of Dalmatia delighted me," recalled Obradović, "just as if I had had a premonition in my heart that there I should spend several quiet and happy years." The local population turned out to be "industrious, good, truthful, and honest," generously compensating him for his teaching with wheat, butter, and cheese, while the Orthodox clergy were exemplars of "frankness, simplicity, kindness, and gentleness."[53] This leading figure of the Enlightenment in southeastern Europe matched in his memoirs the sentimental appreciation of Dalmatia cultivated within enlightened Venetian circles by Fortis and Wynne.

Wynne also took care to adjust Fortis's general observation of contempt for women among the Morlacchi. She admitted that the "savage warrior" would have regarded women with contempt, as "every pacific and gentle being is ignominious to him," but the Morlacchi were no longer utterly savage or totally bellicose: "The Slavs were formerly like that; then their customs began to soften (*s'adoucir*) through a long peace and the influence of a moderate government." Venetian Dalmatia in the eighteenth century, according to Wynne, marked an epoch in the customs of the Morlacchi, rendering conceivable an equality of the sexes hitherto unknown among the Slavs or, for that matter, among the other peoples of Europe. "The family of Pervan Narzevizca," declared Wynne, "spread over all the others by its example this spirit of a gentle social equality."[54] Since in any event her fiction required no empirical research, Wynne allowed herself the liberty of imagining a hypothetical household in which the Morlacchi conformed to the philosophical fantasy of an enlightened woman.

Romance among the Morlacchi

The plot of *Les Morlaques* involved a tragic romantic triangle, which centered on the female figure of "la belle Jella Toposnich," the fictional characterization of Fortis's *bella Morlacca*. Indeed the beautiful Jella stepped out of the pages of the *Viaggio in Dalmazia*, wearing the exotic headdress described by Fortis and copied by Wynne in a spirit of literary sensitivity to female adornment: "The cap of red cloth, with the virginal veil visibly attached behind, was surmounted and surrounded by a thousand different ornaments that hung all around and fell upon the forehead: medals of gold, silver, and copper, mixed with little crosses, with glass beads, with shells . . ."[55] Of course Jella made a considerable noise as she moved, attracting favorable male attention. "The noisier it is, the more it indicates the quantity of ornaments, a sign of her taste and opulence," commented Wynne, who had some experience in attracting the interest of men. She pronounced Jella's appearance *magnifique*, and certain to appeal to Jervaz, the son of Pervan: "Jervaz could not look at her without examining her avidly, and without desiring to possess the attractions that she displayed in such a rich and substantial manner." The

202 Venice and the Slavs

occasion was the ceremony of sworn brotherhood, described in Fortis as evidence of the faithful friendship sustained among the Morlacchi; Jervaz saw Jella for the first time "in the church of Perussich, the day that Jervaz and the brother of Jella swore indissoluble fraternity at the foot of the altar, becoming *pobratimes*."[56] After the ceremony Jervaz, exercising what Fortis saw as the "natural liberty" of the Morlacchi, took the opportunity to kiss Jella on the mouth.

At the banquet that followed, Jervaz discovered that he was not the only admirer of Jella's charms. The women were serving wine to the men, and Jervaz saw that Jella was constantly being summoned by "the valiant Marcovich," recently returned from service in the Venetian fleet, marked by "a ferocious air that was natural to him." Wynne constructed a triangle in which the two suitors of Jella illustrated contrary aspects of the Morlacchi character, with Marcovich representing their reputation for ferocity and Jervaz their gentler aspect as pastoral people close to the state of nature. Wynne, setting the two men face to face, had evidently read of the excitablity of the Morlacchi at their festive banquets.

> Already the fumes of the wine were beginning to rise to the heads of the guests; they were bursting out in cries of cheer that one would have taken for howls. . . Jervaz became indignant at seeing that the indiscreet Marcovich gave no rest to poor Jella, making her always serve the drinks, and preventing her from going to dine with her companions. "Answer me, Marcovich," said Jervaz, "have you bought Jella in some Caravanserai of Bosnia, or is she your wife that you make her serve you like your slave?" "What do you presume to tell me, rash son of Pervan," replied Marcovich, turning up his moustache, and fixing Jervaz with a ferocious eye. "The host who invited us here spares neither his women nor his other animals to do us honor."[57]

Marcovich had already drawn his saber, when the two elders, Pervan and Toposnich, intervened to prevent bloodshed. Marcovich and Jervaz were ready to fight, not just over their interest in the same woman, but over the general issue of the status of women in society. Wynne, as a woman herself, may have taken a personal interest, but Fortis had already identified the issue of contempt for women among the Morlacchi, while Voltaire, in the *Essai sur les moeurs,* had made the treatment of women into an enlightened measurement of civilized manners. Jervaz espoused the "gentle social equality" that prevailed only in the household of Pervan, while the misogyny of Marcovich was interpreted in terms of the

Ottoman influence from neighboring Bosnia. His service in the Venetian fleet could hardly civilize Marcovich in this regard, offering scant opportunity to learn the chivalrous refinements due to the opposite sex. In 1758 Goldoni made the seafaring Radovich fully worthy of the Dalmatian heroine, but in 1788 Wynne insisted that the unenlightened valor of Marcovich was an insufficient credential. Actually, there was a dramatic revival of *La Dalmatina* in Venice in 1788, so the public could have made the comparison.[58] The tragedy of *Les Morlaques* followed from the conflict between barbarous ferocity and more civilized inclinations among the Morlacchi.

Fortis devoted considerable attention to the courtship and marriage customs of the Morlacchi, and Wynne made good use of his account, with further elaborations of her own, to describe at length the course of romance between Jervaz and Jella. Wynne herself had been unable to marry Memmo, the great love of her early life, because of his grand patrician status, and her eventual marriage to the elderly Orsini-Rosenberg was evidently an unromantic arrangement of convenience for her. If she had reason to be cynical about love and marriage in Venice, she was all the more enthusiastic about romance in Dalmatia:

> The absolutely savage barbarian does not attach any importance or solemnity to the choice of a companion, to the sweetest bond by which nature brings us together. The entirely civilized man most often makes of marriage only an affair of convenience and of interest. . . . But the peoples equally remote from these two states, or a little closer to that of simple nature, regard marriage as the most interesting and remarkable epoch among all the events of life. It is on the occasion of marriage that their imagination is deployed in ingenious allegories and expressive ceremonies. . . . This beautiful moment was approaching for the family of the Narzevizca.[59]

Wynne's conception of the Morlacchi as living in a condition "equally remote" from absolute barbarism and complete civilization fit the formulas of the Enlightenment for the idea of Eastern Europe in the 1780s. The French diplomat Louis-Philippe de Ségur saw St. Petersburg as a city that brought together "the age of barbarism and that of civilization," while the Russians appeared to him as "demi-savage figures." The English traveler William Coxe observed that in Russia "their progress towards civilization is very inconsiderable and many instances of the grossest barbarism fell under our observation." The German naturalist Georg Forster in Poland remarked upon the "half-wildness and half-civilization of the

people," and the American explorer John Ledyard, traveling east across
Russia and Siberia, noted "the nice Gradation by which I pass from Civilization to Incivilization."[60] Thus Wynne's idea of Dalmatia between barbarism and civilization was entirely consistent with the context of contemporary comments about the eastern lands of Europe in the 1780s, but
it was her original contribution to envision that intermediary status as offering the ideal social circumstances for romance and matrimony.

When Jella accepted the proposal of Jervaz, he jumped for joy and
presented her with peacock feathers: "Jervaz, at the height of joy, jumps,
dances, embraces Jella, utters cries of oh! oh! with all his might, and in
poetic ecstasy compares her beauty to a beneficent fairy." Wynne discovered in Fortis's account of the improvised oral poetry of the Morlacchi an
element of romantic interest to appeal to the readers of novels. She imagined Jervaz composing poetry, as naturally as breathing, out of his love
for Jella:

> He abandons himself to this last sentiment and seeks to exhale it in love
> songs, which resound along the silent shores of the peaceful river Cetina.
> From the other side of the river, a traveler on his way home takes up the last
> verse of the stanza completed by Jervaz and adds one of his own invention.
> Jervaz interrupts him and, full of the love that inspires him, makes up new
> stanzas on the spot. . . . It is often thus that the Morlaque, child of nature,
> exempt from cares, occupies the sensibility of his soul, and does not torment
> it by desires without limits; his imagination and his poetic verve cause him to
> relish the tranquil and pure enjoyments. . . . The Morlaque, born a poet
> and a musician in his fashion, makes and sings his verses of love according to
> the sweet need that excites love itself.[61]

Though Goethe may have taken an interest in *Les Morlaques,* Wynne
seemed to offer her poet-hero as a sort of antidote to the tormented poetic passions of Werther, which took Europe by storm in the 1770s.
Wynne presented her own "child of nature" to the public as a model
lover for the 1780s, transmuting his tranquil love into improvised poetry.
"Extraordinarily sensitive for a Morlaque, his soul elevated by love," Jervaz, according to Wynne, "glimpsed a rather more delicate sort of happiness: that which simple and innocent nature indicates in the union of
two hearts that suit one another, that which brute and barbarous nature
seeks in vain to degrade, that which corrupted nature really degrades by
a false and irregular course."[62] Thus even the sexual sensibility of Jervaz
was balanced between the poles of barbarism and civilization, the latter

named as "corrupted nature" according to the values of Rousseau. Indeed Wynne, who surrendered to Casanova under the most false and irregular pretenses, had reason to doubt the delicacy of civilized sex. In the natural utterances of Jervaz—oh! oh!—and in his poetic expression of "the sweet need that excites love itself," Wynne sought to discern among the Morlacchi a more natural relation between sex and sentiment than that which prevailed in the rococo arrangements of super-civilized Venetians.

Catherine the Great à la Morlaque

The marriage of Jella and Jervaz faced the obstacle of the militantly virile Marcovich. Pervan worried that Marcovich would actually disrupt the wedding with violence; Wynne knew from Fortis that "such surprises happened often in times gone by." Jella's father, Toposnich, informed Pervan that the problem was resolved, that Marcovich had gone off to war again. This departure introduced the most important political theme of the novel, the fraternal feeling of the Morlacchi for their fellow Slavs. If the gentle Jervaz was capable of greater romantic delicacy, the warlike Marcovich demonstrated a more emphatic fraternity.

> I believe I have heard the trumpet of war: the Russians, our ancient brothers, are going to fight the Turks. Their immense vessels have departed from the river Neva, which winter stops with ice: they are traversing infinite spaces, they are approaching our waters: and they are the friends of our sovereign. My courage is roused with a start: I burn, I am going to join them. . . . I will return laden with the spoils of the vanquished, and perhaps then, if destiny shall have marked it thus, your Jella will comb my hair and wash in the waters of the Cetina my linens colored with the blood of the infidels.[63]

Still, while Marcovich was away killing the Turks, the marriage of Jervaz and Jella could take place without fear of disruption. Furthermore, as Toposnich confided in Pervan, "it is not certain that the war will finish so soon, or that Marcovich will return to us."[64] The departure of Marcovich set the action of the novel in historical time, during a precise period that would have been easily recognized and clearly remembered by readers all over Europe. It is true that when the novel was published in 1788 Russia was again at war with the Ottoman empire, but the amazed account of Catherine's fleet circumnavigating Europe, as well as other details of the fighting, indicated that Marcovich was going to fight in the Russian-Ottoman war of 1768 to 1774. Just as the anthropological details of *Les Morlaques* came from Fortis's *Viaggio in Dalmazia*, the historical circumstances could have come from Caminer's *Storia della guerra presente*.

Wynne looked back to the years of nervous Venetian neutrality, when the Russian-Ottoman war made an issue of Dalmatian loyalty, when the Provveditore Generale Giacomo Da Riva, in 1772, was worried about the "seduction" of Dalmatians by Russian recruiters.[65] The fictional case of Marcovich, who joined the Russian army along with a band of fellow Morlacchi—"among our compatriots sixty of the most brave"—addressed the tensions and insecurities of Venice in the previous decade. Even though Marcovich remarked in passing that the Russians were "friends of our sovereign," it was hardly reassuring to sovereign Venice to see its subjects, even in a novel, aflame in fraternal solidarity with the soldiers of a foreign power. Fortis's emphasis on the factors that made the Morlacchi identifiable as Slavs, taken up by Wynne in a novel that attributed to them an extravagant intensity of sentiment, addressed an important imperial issue of Venetian vulnerablity during the final decades of the Republic.

In preparing for the wedding of Jervaz and Jella, Pervan supervised the polishing of the family weapons, not only daggers and pistols, but also bows and arrows: "the ancient arms of the nation were preserved with veneration by the Narzevizca," including even the great saber of Pecirep. This attention to these weapons, however, inspired in the peaceful Pervan a sad nostalgia for the warfare of the past. Through Pervan, Wynne posed the problem of Morlacchi discontent with Venetian neutrality:

> Oh my children, why does our Lion at present seem to have wet wings? Why does he not seek to attack the unworthy Ottoman? . . . Wouldn't the valiant Slavs hasten with joy to gather around the flags of their good sovereign? The arms that you see here uselessly displayed, and that I would so gladly see in your hands, would be polished rather differently if they were steeped in the blood of the infidels.[66]

Even expressed in a spirit of sympathetic loyalty, such Dalmatian disparagement of the winged Lion of San Marco would have alarmed the Inquisitors of State, and Wynne thus spotlighted what was most worrisome about the warlike Morlacchi in the context of Venice's Adriatic insecurity.

When Pervan learned that Marcovich had gone to join the Russians, he himself was intrigued and pressed Toposnich for further news of the international situation: "But what do you tell me about our brothers the Russians, about their wars and their power? You understand the language of paper; you know all our ancient songs; you have traveled in your youth in distant lands; you have been to Venice on the one hand, and Bosnia on the other." Toposnich, however, was uninformed about current events, and he referred the matter to a caloyer, an Orthodox monk, who had just returned to Dalmatia from Russia. While a lamb roasted on the spit, the caloyer told the two venerable Morlacchi that their ancestors had come from the north, from the land of the Russians, migrating south, across the Sava River, over the mountains of Bosnia, to settle in Dalmatia. "You see, my friends," he said, "that our origin is the same, and that the Russians are our brothers."[67] Fortis saw Slavic resemblances from the Adriatic to the Arctic, and Wynne discovered, accordingly, an imagined fraternity between Russians and Morlacchi.

Within the world of the Enlightenment there was a well-established political wisdom concerning the redemption of Russia in the eighteenth century, which Wynne now introduced into her fictional world of the Morlacchi. The caloyer seemed to speak for the philosophes of the Enlightenment when he narrated the history of Russia:

> God, the protector of the Slavs, regarded them with a propitious eye and gave them a sovereign destined by him to operate prodigies of creation and omnipotence. His name was Peter, and the astounded universe always called him Peter the Great. As soon as he mounted upon the throne he saw all the evils that covered the immense face of his empire. . . . From the bottom of a marsh he brought forth an immense and magnificent city, and there he placed his throne. The splendor of victory surrounded him, the love and union of his subjects strengthened him, and the most vast empire that ever was, received from the superior genius who governed it, the beginning of a new and glorious existence.[68]

The Enlightenment's celebration of Peter the Great dated back to his death in 1725, when Bernard de Fontenelle presented the eulogy before the French Academy of Sciences. The fullest formulation of the flattering legend was in Voltaire's *Histoire de l'empire de Russie sous Pierre le Grand,* published in two volumes in 1759 and 1763.

Wynne's choice of the caloyer to represent a Russophile perspective within the novel was also consistent with the suspected role of the

Orthodox monks in Dalmatia during the Russian-Ottoman war of 1768 to 1774. In 1775 the Provveditore Generale Giacomo Gradenigo reported to the Venetian Inquisitors of State concerning the recent activities of the caloyers as agents of "seduction" in Dalmatia:

> The caloyers themselves and especially a certain Spiridion Simich insinuated to the Morlacchi alienation from the government of the Republic, passing from family to family, and saying that this was not their legitimate kingdom, that it only aimed at making them apostatize to the Latin Church, that they should pass over to Muscovy, the legitimate sovereign of all the Greeks in the world.[69]

This sort of seditious sentiment, as reported to the Inquisitors concerning the political danger of Orthodox religious solidarity, was transmuted in *Les Morlaques* into the national sentiment of Slavic fraternity, no less imminently menacing to Venice. Wynne did well to choose the caloyer as the fictional representative of Russia, for there had indeed been monks who went "from family to family," making similar speeches to the Morlacchi while the spit turned with the roasting lamb.

The fictional caloyer explained that at Peter's death his great work of reformation in Russia was not quite complete, but awaited still the magnificent genius of another ruler on the throne of St. Petersburg:

> Catherina, Catherina, she alone has brought the power and glory of the empire to a degree that the greatest of men would not have dared to envisage. The dew of dawn, the warmth of the afternoon, the cool of the evening are not more beneficent than Catherina. The dense darkness that enveloped that vast portion of the world dissipated at the apparition of a luminous dawn. . . . Catherina appeared like the sun. At her appearance, vast infertile lands and deserts have been able to nourish new inhabitants. She has taught them to pass tranquil days, in submitting to the laws that she herself has designed for their happiness. Enlightened, conducted by her, directed by her maternal attentions, they have marched rapidly along the traces that she has indicated to them; they have perceived and tasted the sweet enjoyments of a well-regulated society; they have known the riches of nature and the arts. The inexhaustible source of light and of life-giving warmth, Catherina carries her happy influence to the extremities of the earth.[70]

The rapturous effusions of the caloyer were couched in the metaphors of the Enlightenment, with Catherine as the source of light, dissipating darkness. Almost from the moment that she seized the throne in 1762 Catherine had carefully cultivated the good will of the foreign philosophes, and her most ardent fans among them included such lead-ing lights as Voltaire and Diderot.[71] With some self-delusion, they be-lieved that Catherine offered the most convincing contemporary model of enlightened monarchy, and Wynne transposed their enthusiasm into the mountains of Dalmatia.

The caloyer himself did not doubt that the glory of Catherine was ul-timately relevant to the Morlacchi of Dalmatia. He ecstatically saluted her, from the valley of Dizmo to the palaces of St. Petersburg:

> Live, Catherina, if only you could be immortal like your glory! Live and be as happy as you are great. Bring your victorious arms to meet the rising sun: hunt the barbarians who soil by their impiety, by their cruelties, the beautiful countries that the sun illuminates by its first rays: spread our religion, our lan-guage, and your good deeds up to the mountains of Starnazza; we are guard-ing the passages against the enemy. We will cross them one day to salute our brothers in the opposite plains. We will exchange our daughters; they will renew our bonds. Sitting by the fires of our cottages, we will sing together the old songs of our valiant fathers. We will be taught those that celebrate your name, and all our brave Morlaques will cry out, Long live the immortal Catherina, the love of her peoples, the terror of the barbarians, the admira-tion of the earth.[72]

Thus the Morlacchi seemed to encourage Catherine to liberate the Balkans from Ottoman rule, that is, to conquer the lands of "the rising sun," to the east of Dalmatia. Wynne attributed to them a merely poetic sense of geography, but there was nothing unequivocal about their political impulse to join with the Russians in a spirit of national fraternization. Al-ready religiously and linguistically related—"our religion, our language"— the Morlacchi and the Russians would confirm their common Slavic identity in the exchange of daughters and the singing of old songs. Wynne could not have failed to be aware that what seemed most inspira-tionally sentimental among the Morlacchi would also seem most subver-sively sinister to the Venetians.

Those implications became even more evident when the caloyer had finished his effusion, and the impact of his enthusiasm registered upon his Morlacchi interlocutors:

> After a moment of silence, Pervan cried out as if inspired, "Great Catherina, divinity of the Slavic nation, receive also my vows and homages. I am too old to make the pilgrimage from here to the great city where you reside: but I will see you, I will throw myself at your feet (I swear it by that eternal God

LES MORLAQUES

Par J. W. C. D. U. & R.

V O L . I.

1788.

FIGURE 11. *Les Morlaques,* title page, by J. W. C. D. U. & R. (Justine Wynne Comtesse des Ursins & Rosenberg), published in 1788. The winged allegorical figure appears to represent history, inscribing on a shield the words "magnae invictae," of the "great invincible," possibly with reference to Catherine the Great, to whom the book was dedicated. Wynne's novel described the moment at which the Morlacchi, living in the ahistorical world of primitive anthropological custom, entered into the historical narrative of the eighteenth century, discovering their Slavic identity in the context of Catherine's contemporary war against the Ottoman empire. *(By permission of the Houghton Library, Harvard University.)*

who has given you to so many nations for their happiness); yes, I will see you on the road that you will have marked out, in marching to the great city of the infidels, where your dazzling light will make the pale crescent disappear."[73]

Pervan's enthusiasm for paying homage to Catherine when she conquered Constantinople echoed the earlier acclamations of the philosophes. At the outbreak of war in 1768 Voltaire wrote to Catherine, "I ask of your imperial majesty permission to come place myself at your feet, and to pass several days at your court, as soon as it is established in Constantinople."[74] Voltaire, like Pervan, considered himself too old for the northern voyage to St. Petersburg, but the philosophes generally agreed that a journey to visit Catherine, like that of Diderot in 1773–1774, constituted a "pilgrimage" of the Enlightenment. Of course Catherine's triumphal route from St. Petersburg to Constantinople was most unlikely to pass through Dalmatia. The notion of the triumphal procession itself, however, was extremely timely, inasmuch as *Les Morlaques* appeared just one year after Catherine's celebrated voyage to the conquered Crimea in 1787, a year that also witnessed the Russian renewal of warfare against the Ottomans. In 1788 Domenico Caminer was once again publishing an instant history of the current war, *Storia della guerra presente,* with a frontispiece illustration of Catherine. In that same year, Vincenzo Formaleoni published in Venice a book about commerce and navigation, enthusiastically advocating Venetian trade with Catherine's empire by the way of the Black Sea.[75]

Pervan's enthusiasm for Catherine entered into Wynne's concern about regard for women among the Morlacchi. When Pervan and Toposnich gathered the women of the household around them for a toast to Catherine, "the glory of your sex," there was some puzzlement. "The astonished women could not understand how these transports of acclamation could have for their object a woman," Wynne explained. "They believed it must concern a saint, and they crossed themselves before drinking." Pervan's consciousness was raised to a new level of sensitivity about Morlacchi contempt for women, for "the actions of Caterina had inspired in him a greater idea of the sex than he had until then."[76] It was no doubt the remarkable position of the tsarina as an illustrious and enlightened female contemporary that made her so interesting to Wynne, who retired to Altichiero while Catherine was actively ruling an empire. Wynne's first attempt to attract Catherine's attention came in 1782, when her son and heir, the Grand Duke Paul, made a visit to Venice. Wynne composed a pamphlet describing his reception in the city, which went through several editions in French and Italian. Then, in *Les Morlaques*, Wynne made Catherine a central subject of the novel, enjoying the most flattering admiration of the Morlacchi; furthermore, the whole book was dedicated to the tsarina and sent to St. Petersburg for her appreciation. Catherine, however, was a busy woman, then at war with the Ottomans, and the novel was 350 pages long. She noted receipt of the book in 1788: "Tell Count Chernyshev, that I beg him to thank Countess Wynne Rosenberg for her letter, for her sentiments toward me, and for her book: *Les Morlaques*. If I can find the time, I will try to read it. Presently I am too much occupied."[77] Certainly Catherine would have found the book gratifying.

After the wedding of Jervaz and Jella, Pervan had more time to contemplate the glory of Catherine, which became his "favorite subject." He was thrilled to learn that her war with the Ottomans might eventually bring the Russian army right up to the border of Venetian Dalmatia. At this point Wynne had to reassure her readers that Pervan was truly loyal to Venice: "Pervan recognized his own sovereign and felt all the ancient attachment of his nation. The protection, the defense, the assistance which his people enjoyed, cost them nothing but a little tax that each family paid to the commissary of the Provveditore Generale of Zara who came to collect it once a year." To be sure, this had the air of a somewhat perfunctory loyalty to a government that barely touched the lives of the Morlacchi, living as they did in the state of nature. Pervan's emotional attachment to Catherine was of an altogether different character and intensity: "In the middle of the description of the marvelous enterprises of Catherina he could not persuade himself that she was only a woman. He believed she was a fairy . . . and worthy of the cult that genies and fairies receive in the spirit of the Morlaques."[78] One day, Pervan led the people of Dizmo into the woods, to a round clearing where he had set up the statue of a woman.

> She was dressed à la Morlaque and in the most magnificent fashion. A long veil hung from her head over her back: upon her chest fell great tresses in which one saw sparkling a silver cross studded with stones. The neck, the hair, the belt were ornamented with every kind of jewel à la Slav, that is, with silver coins, glass beads, corals, and chains. She had on one side the great saber of Pecirep; two beautiful pistols and a rich dagger came out of her belt. This proud attire showed that the heroine was a warrior. . . . The whole population of Dizmo remained for several minutes immobile with surprise

and admiration, until the moment when the sentiment of devotion unani-
mously prevailed and made everyone fall to their knees before the statue that
was then invoked. "Stay," cried out the Starescina, standing at the foot of the
mound, extending his arms toward the kneeling people, "Yes, on your knees,
my good children, adore the image of the great Catherina."[79]

Catherine herself, in St. Petersburg, would have had to read 120 pages of
Les Morlaques to arrive at the clearing in the woods, but there she would
have discovered that Wynne had created a cult of the tsarina among the
Morlacchi, dedicated to the worship of her beaded and bedizened image.

Pervan explained to the Morlacchi their national relation to Catherine: "She speaks our language. Her innumerable subjects have our customs, our religion; they sing our songs, they recognize our same ancestors, they are Slavs like us." The caloyer had hoped the Morlacchi would
one day learn songs to celebrate the name of Catherine, and Pervan composed just such a song, now offered in prayer to the statue. The first
stanza invoked Catherine on behalf of Pervan's grandson, Demetry Jer-
vavich, the child of Jervaz and Jella: "Powerful Catherine, it is under
your protection that I am going to give the first marks of virility to my
grandson so that the recitation of your great virtues and manly courage
may inspire in him the worthy qualities of one of your children and of a
brave Slav." Wynne did not hesitate to list this song together with the
other "Chansons" of the Morlacchi included in her novel, her own original French contributions to the folk poetry of the South Slavs. At the
conclusion of the song, which called for the destruction of the infidels,
the child received a haircut, as the promised mark of virility, as well as
Pervan's grandpaternal exhortation: "You are a Slav."[80] This was the
great ethnographic truth that Wynne had taken away from her reading of
Fortis. It emphasized the exoticism of her subject, for just as their "primitive society" made the Morlacchi generally alien to the "civilized"
reader, so their national identity as Slavs made them specifically alien to
the Venetians who ruled over Dalmatia.

The clearing in which the statue presided was surely inspired by the
celebrated gardens of Altichiero where Wynne wrote her novel. At Altichiero there were landscaped woods where one encountered classical
deities and pagan altars. In the villa there was even a bust of Catherine
as a heroine of the Enlightenment.[81] Yet Wynne seemed to recognize
the difference between enlightened appreciation and the rather more
literal worship that she attributed to the primitive Morlacchi with their

susceptibility to superstition. The cult of Catherine, as explained by Pervan to the Morlacchi, was a matter of sentimental fraternity among Slavs, which fundamentally excluded the author and the readers of the novel while at the same time perhaps encouraging some ironic reflection on the parallels between the forms of worship in the village of Dizmo and in the Republic of Letters. Voltaire's letters to Catherine, which were well publicized in his lifetime and partially published after his death in 1778, included numerous homages that corresponded to the style of Pervan. In 1766 Voltaire wrote to Catherine, in the name of the Enlightenment, "We are three, Diderot, d'Alembert, and I who set up altars to you; you make me a pagan. I am in idolatry, madame, at the feet of your majesty." In 1772 Voltaire declared his veneration for "saint Catherine II, the object of my cult."[82] Such effusions from Voltaire were marked by a spirit of ironic play and frank flattery, but Wynne, attributing the same sort of "cult" to the Morlacchi, seemed to seek a higher level of irony in the parodic counterpoint between enlightened enthusiasm and primitive worship. The Morlacchi, as children of nature, seemed to offer homage to Catherine in the spirit of Rousseau, rather than the sophisticated flatteries of the more cosmopolitan philosophes.

Venice and the Curiosity of the Morlacchi

Les Morlaques was apparently published in two small editions, one in Venice and one in Modena, the hometown of Wynne's companion, and perhaps collaborator, Benincasa. One edition was semi-anonymous, with the author identified by the string of initials J. W. C. D. U. & R., while another spelled out the name of J. Wynne Comtesse des Ursins & Rosenberg. The novel appears to have been published privately, outside of commercial circulation, and it is possible that the work's somewhat subversive political content, its affirmation of Morlacchi love for Catherine and indifference to Venice, made it vulnerable to censure and even censorship. The fact that it was written in French meant that its readership, however select, was also inevitably international as well as Venetian. International interest was demonstrated by the prompt translation of the work, including the songs, into German as *Die Morlaken,* which appeared in Breslau in 1790; Goethe could have known the work either from the original French or the German translation. Breslau (Wrocław today, in Poland) belonged to Prussia in 1790, since the province of Silesia was seized by Frederick from Maria Theresa fifty years before, and it may be more than coincidence that the book was published there on the Silesian frontier between Germans and Slavs. The translator Samuel Gottlieb Bürde took the liberty of editing out the most flattering tributes to Catherine. In 1797 there appeared in Leipzig another German edition entitled *Jella oder das Morlachische Mädchen*.[83]

After Wynne's death in 1791, after Catherine's death in 1796, and after the death of the Venetian republic in 1797, an Italian translation of the novel was published in Padua in 1798 under the title *Costumi dei Morlacchi*. Thus emphasizing the anthropological character of the work, the anonymous translator attempted to correct details of the customs of the Morlacchi, based on published works and personal study: "in part the observations that the translator made of the places he had visited, in part the live testimony of the Morlacchi themselves who, as soldiers in our companies, frequent our mainland towns." He cut out all of Wynne's Morlacchi songs, suppressed the tributes to Catherine, and insisted that the Morlacchi were so loyal that "they would defend Dalmatia against whatever incursion, acting for the preservation of the honor of their sovereign." By the time this was published, however, sovereign Venice no longer existed as an independent republic to defend. Though the name of the translator remains unknown, there has been some Croatian academic debate on the subject; Marijan Stojković proposed in 1929 that the anonymous pen was wielded by none other than Fortis's Dalmatian friend, Giulio Bajamonti, but Rudolf Maixner emphatically rejected that hypothesis in 1955. Another attempted Italian translation of the 1790s never appeared, the work of the Dalmatian churchman, poet, and philosophe, Giandomenico Stratico, the Roman Catholic bishop of Hvar. His concern for the economy and society of Dalmatia made him naturally interested in the Morlacchi, and his native familiarity with the region made it possible for him to undertake the correction of Wynne's inauthentic Slavic names, such as Narzevizca instead of Narcevizza or Narcevica.[84] Though hardly a bestseller, *Les Morlaques* enjoyed an international circulation and reputation in French, German, and Italian during the last decade of the eighteenth century.

Wynne delivered to her readers in the concluding chapters a satisfyingly tragic denouement, rich in blood and tears. Marcovich returned from the wars and was furious to find Jella married to Jervaz. More ferocious than ever, Marcovich hoped to have the opportunity to kill his more civil rival: "I myself will bring his head to Jella." Marcovich met up with Jervaz in Zadar, killed him in bloody combat, and died a violent death himself, leaving Jella to sing her lamentation, Slavic style, in the "Chanson de la mort de Jervaz." In a footnote Wynne insisted that the fatal encounter between the rival Morlacchi was based on a true incident that took place in Venice on the Riva degli Schiavoni. "This tragic event excited my curiosity and my interest in that nation," she commented, revealing that she had found some of her inspiration in Venice itself.[85] It was not necessary to go to Dalmatia to discover the ferocity of the Morlacchi, when they themselves came to demonstrate that character along the embankments of Venice.

In these concluding chapters, Venice came to loom larger and larger in the minds of Wynne's Morlacchi. Jervaz and his brother visited the coastal city of Split and came home to Pervan in high excitement: "Oh my father, what marvels we have seen! How the city is admirable!" Pervan was immediately concerned about his sons. "As their hearts are enflamed for objects that were unknown to them," he reflected, "I fear that they may despise their cottages, that they may desire things which it is not in my power to procure for them, and that they may be unhappy." In Split Jervaz had heard that Venice was a still more amazing city, and he was impatient to see for himself. He urged Pervan to lead the whole family on a Grand Tour à la Morlaque:

> Come with us, dear father, to Venice, to bring back to our tribe industry and comfort. You will choose better than we, that which could augment our happiness. We will not leave you for a moment. You will bring back with you the statue of Velika Catherina, the object of your desires that you will order to be made before your eyes; and we will celebrate the festival of our return before the statue, with new games that we will teach to our friends and to all the Narzevizca.[86]

Like Rousseau, Wynne would hardly have believed the Morlacchi capable of augmenting their happiness by anything they brought back from civilized Venice. Surely she was amused at the idea of ordering a bigger and better statue of Catherine the Great (Velika Catherina) in the art world of Venice (from the young Canova perhaps) and bringing it back to Dalmatia to worship in the woods. As for the "new games" that might be learned in Venice, Wynne may have been thinking of her own unlucky inclination to gambling.

"All the usages of the city may not suit the Morlaques," warned the wise Pervan, declining the delights of Venice, defending the values of village life based on the customs of the Morlacchi.

> Go to the city and may God bless you there. Examine before all else whether the people who inhabit it love one another more than we do, if they respect their fathers more than we do, if the fathers cherish their children, if they repel with greater courage the outrages of their enemies, if they take a just vengeance. See if they open their arms and their homes to the stranger as we do, if they help the unfortunate neighbor.[87]

The young Morlacchi set out on the voyage but never arrived at their ultimate destination; tragedy struck at Zadar on the way to Venice. Wynne, whatever the balance of her ambivalence about Venice, evidently did not relish the literary work of establishing her Morlacchi characters in the city and putting them through the predictable paces of depravation and disillusionment. The death of Jervaz at Zadar followed from the village drama of ferocious rivalry, and Pervan, his forebodings fatally vindicated, died of grief upon receiving the news. In Dizmo old Toposnich attributed the tragedy to restless discontent excited by the illusionary charms of urban civilization. To enjoy the riches of nature, he moralized, the Morlacchi did not need to look any further than the banks of the Cetina. This was also the author's moral: Only by clinging to their customs and foregoing "the advantages of civilization" could the Morlacchi preserve their society from corruption and hold out "against the irresistible and continuous action of time, against the revolution of the centuries." Toposnich concluded the novel by warning the villagers to resist the insidious consequences of "curiosity," which somehow was seen as the agent of tragedy: "It has been fatal to us, and our children shall renounce it forever."[88] The incident among the Morlacchi on the Riva degli Schiavoni in Venice, Wynne noted, "excited my curiosity and my interest in that nation," and she counted on a corresponding public curiosity when she published her novel. Paradoxically, however, she was convinced that at the very moment when Venice was most curious about the Morlacchi, they themselves had no hope but to suppress all reciprocal curiosity about Venice.

The measure of the novel's success among the enlightened public of Venice may be taken from its most important reviewer, Melchiorre Cesarotti, professor at Padua, translator of Ossian, friend of Fortis. He reviewed *Les Morlaques* in July 1789 in the *Nuovo giornale enciclopedico;*

the journal was published in Vicenza, within the Republic of Venice, and was the descendant of *Europa Letteraria,* which Fortis and Caminer had created in 1768.[89] Cesarotti began by focusing on the literary "curiosity" of *Les Morlaques,* its resistance to conventional classification by genre, which would have condemned the work in the judgment of a more traditional critic.

> The title and the nature of it, the class in which it had to be placed would have produced a crowd of persistent questions, and professorial pedantry would have relegated it to a place among those bizarre and heterogeneous productions that serve to entertain the curiosity more than to increase the patrimony of nature. Is this a history or a romance? Prose or poetry? . . . We would tranquilly reply that this is an original work. . . . We believe that just because it does not belong precisely to any one genre, it unites the values of all, and merits collectively the separate praises that are due to each species of the productions of genius.[90]

Cesarotti's appreciation would have been influential enough within the contemporary circles of the late Venetian Enlightenment to count *Les Morlaques* as an unusual, even bizarre, literary masterpiece. He wholeheartedly accepted that the novel's "principal object was to make known the usages and ideas of the Morlacchi," and he praised its originality as an anthropological fiction by comparison with the artifices of French exoticism:

> Unfortunately the poets of France have been reproached for the fact that their heroes, whether they be Turks, Chinese, or Americans, are at bottom nothing but masked Frenchmen. Here on the contrary, whatever one sees or feels, everything is Morlacco, everything is fitting, everything in custom and in truth.[91]

Indeed, the Venetian Goldoni, as much as the poets of France, invented heroes and heroines from Persia to Peru who were recognizably European in their manners and motivations. *Les Morlaques* was actually set in Europe, in the differentiated domain of Eastern Europe; the characters costumed themselves not so much in the robes of geographical exoticism but rather according to the customs of anthropological primitivism.

For Fortis the customs and poetry of the Morlacchi constituted their coherence as a nation within Venetian Dalmatia, though he recognized that they existed in relation to a broader domain of Slavic peoples across Eastern Europe. Wynne's Morlacchi came to see themselves essentially as

Slavs during the course of the novel, with their fraternal relation to the Russians becoming even more sentimentally important than their regional Dalmatian identity. "You are a Slav," declared Pervan to his grandson, before the statue of Catherine. This attribution of identity was precisely what Wynne accomplished before the public, classifying the Morlacchi as Slavs in a spirit that combined enlightened Linnaean taxonomy with early Romantic nationalism. Noting the Slavic resemblances suggested by Fortis, Wynne, with her imaginative and sentimental insights, arrived at the philosophical discovery of the Slavs at just the time that Herder was formulating the classification of *Slawische Völker*. As in Benedict Anderson's conception of the nation as an "imagined community," the Venetian discovery of the Slavs of Dalmatia in the eighteenth century demonstrated an imperial literary imagination at work in the designation of a national community, presumptively imagined from outside itself. While the Morlacchi of Dalmatia, according to Fortis, still called themselves Vlachs, Wynne was already able to imagine them as Slavs. Indeed Catherine herself, who presided over the novel's festivals of Slavic fraternity, was born a German princess.

Old-Fashioned Slavs

The Morlacchi became not simply Slavs, but the original, ancient, old-fashioned Slavs in Camillo Federici's dramatic comedy, *Gli Antichi Slavi,* performed in Venice in the Teatro Sant'Angelo during the carnival of 1793, five years after the appearance of *Les Morlaques.* The preface to Federici's published edition remarked that at the performance "the national customs and character were exactly maintained," and the setting was a scene from Fortis, mountain cliffs, caverns, and streams, in the region of the Cetina River. The character and customs of the ancient or old-fashioned Slavs were those of the Morlacchi, as investigated by the Venetians during the eighteenth century. The protagonists were romantic rivals: an old-fashioned Slav named Dusmanich, from the mountains, with his sword in hand, and a new-fashioned Slav named Serizca, from the Adriatic coast, in Italian clothes with Italian manners. Both were in love with the same Dalmatian heroine, Elena, costumed in a red cap as a token of her virginity. The old-fashioned Slavs, like Dusmanich, despised foreign customs and were even proudly illiterate: "This is the science of the Morlacchi. (*Indicates sword.*) There is none other among us, except to obey our sovereigns and defend our country." Dusmanich thus combined the Dalmatian patriotism of Goldoni's Radovich with the primitive customs of Fortis's Morlacchi. The latter did not actually call themselves Morlacchi, as Fortis frankly reported, but when they appeared upon the stage in Venice, they could proudly proclaim the identity under which they were recognized by the Venetians. Federici himself was from Liguria, but he triumphed in the theaters of Venice and Padua during the 1780s and 1790s.[92] The obligatory patriotic flourish naturally referred to San Marco, when it was recited on the Venetian stage in 1793; by the time the play was published in Venice in 1819, however, Dalmatia was ruled by a Habsburg prince in Vienna, and the unelaborated reference could be interpreted accordingly.

Arturo Cronia has described *Gli Antichi Slavi* as "the boldest interpretation of Fortisian *morlacchismo*," appealing for its success to the *morlaccomania* of the Venetian public. Dusmanich proclaimed himself an old-fashioned Slav from the very beginning of the play by his ungallant attitude toward women, the same attitude that Fortis diagnosed among the Morlacchi twenty years before. The old-fashioned Slav had never set eyes upon the woman he was supposed to marry and explained himself to his friend: "You, Slav, you who are like me of noble descent from the Geti and the Scythians, you ask me if I have lowered myself to the weakness of contemplating a woman?" Just to want to see his promised spouse would make him "effeminate," and, when told that all other men gaze upon their brides before the wedding, he declared them all "degenerate." *Morlacchismo* was most emphatically *machismo*, as Dusmanich defined himself on the Venetian stage:

> Shall I imitate the custom of the Italians and the French, who make idols of their women, who basely bend the knee and adore their own slaves? For me it is enough to know that she is the daughter of a robust and fertile mother and of a valorous father. I marry to immortalize my posterity. If not for that I would live free, friend only of my name and my sword. The daughter of such parents will perpetuate the heroes of my descent, with arms always in hand in the service of my prince.[93]

While Fortis philosophically called into question the customs of "the society that we call civilized," Federici ultimately flattered the Venetian public by representing their own civilized gallantry from the perspective of a primitive Morlacco. Of course, it is possible that Venetian men and

Venetian women interpreted the misogyny of Dusmanich differently, according to the divergent perspectives of the gendered public.

The female public, at least, must have sympathized with the heroine, Elena, in her reluctance to marry Dusmanich, in spite of the recommendation of her father, Marcovich:

> Marcovich: You are near to becoming the wife of the most valorous man of our nation. Our country (*patria*) is proud of his name, and its enemies tremble within.
>
> Elena: That means I shall be the slave of a ferocious man.
>
> Marcovich: No, love will make him gentle and humane with you. I told you he was valorous, not barbarous (*valoroso, non barbaro*).[94]

Thus the Goldonian ideal of the valorous Dalmatian encountered the ferocious reputation of the Morlacchi in philosophical argument on the Venetian stage. This was Wynne's sentimental assumption as well, that love might bring about a transformation of the ferocious male Morlacco, civilize him, endow him with humanity. Federici brought Dusmanich face to face with his civilized coastal counterpart, Serizca, a Dalmatian with Italian manners and clothes. Dusmanich first supposed, or pretended to suppose, that his rival was a foreigner, but Serizca replied, "Your country is my country. I was born here, and I too share the honor of your nation."[95] Such were also the words of Lisauro, the perfidious Greek who pretended to be a Dalmatian, in Goldoni's *La Dalmatina,* and now Federici, in the next generation, staged a public debate about what constituted a true Dalmatian, between the old-fashioned Slav and the newly fashionable Slav. Both parts were, presumably, taken by Italian actors.

Dusmanich spoke first, making the case for the primitive virtues of the Morlacchi, comparing his own stage costume to that of his rival:

> Look at you and me, from head to toe. Where are your native clothes, the glorious insignia of a valorous people? . . . Oh my country, look upon a son who disfigures you, who renounces the hair that nature gave him and adorns his head with ornaments of women, of barbarous and dishonest habits. His hair, his countenance, announce the softness and slavery of pleasure. The heavy, shining sword no longer hangs at his side . . . Oh my prince, shining star, my defense, my deity, remove if you can this shame from my country; make the degenerate sons put on again the insignia of their elders, and strike down these rebels. I pray you with my head prostrate in the dust, in the name of your justice and the glory of my nation.[96]

The old-fashioned Slav was thus recognizable on stage by his old-fashioned costume, and he presented the case for clinging to old customs in the face of modern fashions. He sustained the ideology of Adriatic empire by his insistent synthesis of the glory of his Slavic nation with reverent loyalty to Venice. Indeed, he appealed to his Venetian prince on behalf of the nation, just as he presented his case to the Venetian public in the audience.

Serizca, however, was unintimidated by the insults of Dusmanich and defended his own Dalmatian identity by affirming his extravagant loyalty to Venice.

> I will not blush before you at such an accusation. I want to have the strength to pity you, because you, restricted within the confines of these horrible crags, do not know that this respectable uniform is dedicated like yours to the service of the same government. . . . Ask the most courageous enemies of my country, and they will tell you that they have seen me the first in every intrepid encounter to oppose my own breast to their desperate blows, in defence of my just and beloved prince.[97]

In an age of Venetian neutrality it might have been difficult to determine just when Serizca found the opportunity to engage in such valiant combat against the enemies of San Marco. Federici, however, clearly affirmed before the Venetian public that Venice still commanded the absolute loyalty of both primitive Morlacchi and civilized coastal Dalmatians. Indeed, the speech of Serizca seemed to suggest that Venice could confidently decide to civilize the Morlacchi without fear of attenuating their ferocious patriotism. Federici proposed the formula of "valorous-not-barbarous" to sum up Venice's civilizing mission in Dalmatia.

"If you call yourself a Slav, put your valor to the test," cried Dusmanich, challenging his rival and, at the same time, addressing the fundamental issue of identity concerning Venetian Dalmatia. Wynne wondered what it might mean for the Morlacchi to call themselves Slavs, to discover a Slavic identity that transcended the borders of the Republic. Federici explored divergent representations of Slavdom, but limited his reflections to Venetian Dalmatia, virtually insisting that loyalty to Venice was the defining characteristic of the Slav. Elena, the heroine, did not call them Slavs, but gave them another name, as they prepared to fight each other for her sake: "Ah, barbarians!" The occasion of the rivals' combat, however, offered an opportunity to an evil Bosnian Moslem, Orcano, who had been lurking and plotting since the beginning of the drama and now kidnapped Elena with the intention of delivering her to his master, Osman Ogly, "the richest and most effeminate Moslem in Bosnia." Dusmanich and Serizca had to bury their quarrel to rescue Elena from "a troop of Bosnians," in the name of "Illyrian glory," but she ultimately killed Orcano with her own hand. "Let's massacre them all (*trucidiamoli tutti*)," cried Marcovich, Elena's father, in pursuit of the Bosnians, but this was the eighteenth century, not the twentieth century, and the play was a comedy, so, in the end, the Moslem prisoners were spared: "Morlacco valor knows how to pardon even the enemy."[98] The Bosnians, after all, were also Slavs, though the play did not take note of that. As in Goldoni's *La Dalmatina,* so in Federici's *Gli Antichi Slavi,* the drama of Dalmatia lay in its Oriental relations, the danger of Dalmatians exposed to Moslem depradations, the prurient redemption of Illyrian glory from the menacing shadow of the harem.

As in Wynne's novel, so in Federici's drama, the plot turned on the romantic rivalry between more and less civilized Slavs over a red-capped Dalmatian heroine: Jervaz and Marcovich competing for Jella in the novel, Serizca and Dusmanich dueling for Elena in the drama. In presenting these Slavic alternatives, violent primitives versus more refined fellows, the authors posed the dilemma of Dalmatia within the Adriatic empire; that same dilemma—between barbarism and civilization—defined the domain of Eastern Europe as a whole, according to the philosophical values of the Enlightenment. Federici, like Wynne, had no doubt about which of the brave deserved the fair, and, at the end of the comedy, he had Dusmanich concede the hand of Elena to Serizca: "Enjoy the prize of your virtue, and may you have children who emulate the heroism of their parents, increase the number of loyal subjects of our good prince, and crown the glory of this fortunate nation." Serizca accepted the prize with a gracious nod to his rival: "Generous friend, worthy Dusmanich, you are the hero who honors these climes. Your friendship is dear to me and completes my happiness."[99] Thus Federici represented the friendly reconciliation of the more and less civilized Slavs, and reaffirmed the Goldonian ideal of Dalmatian loyalty on the basis of Venice's civilizing mission among the Slavs.

In 1802, the year of Federici's death in Padua, *Gli Antichi Slavi* was performed there as a comic opera about marriage among the Morlacchi, under the title *Le Nozze dei Morlacchi,* with libretto by Giulio Artusi and music by Vittorio Trento.[100] In that same year the work was staged as a ballet, also called *Le Nozze dei Morlacchi,* with choreography by Giacomo Serafini and presumably exotic costumes by Francesca Piatoli. The ballet was performed in Bergamo, another city of the former Venetian republic, and, with the subtitle "The Kidnapping of Elena," appeared on the same program with an opera by Domenico Cimarosa. The corps de ballet were specified, female and male, as "Morlacche" and "Morlacchi," though the program gave no intimation of the savage dances by which they would have expressed their barbarous natures. The denouement of the plot, however, was reversed from the Federici play, and the civilized suitor from coastal Split generously surrendered the hand of Elena to the primitive Morlacco, whose leading role was danced by the choreographer Serafini himself.[101] The Venetian revaluation of primitive virtues among the Morlacchi was consummated in the spirit of early Romanticism, when the civilized Dalmatian thus recognized the superior merit of the barbarous Morlacco. For several decades into the nineteenth century the ballet continued to be performed.[102] In the aftermath of anthropological discovery and sensation, the Morlacchi became a folkloric curiosity, an exotic entertainment, an exercise in the choreography of barbarism, on the way to eventual effacement and oblivion.

Conclusion: The View of Dalmatia from San Marco

In 1805 there was published in Rome a play by Carlo Federici, the son of Camillo, offering an extraordinary new variation on the formula of *Gli Antichi Slavi*. The heroine of the play, Elena again, was now Italian, and she was confronted with the choice between an Italian suitor, approved by her father, and an Illyrian Slav, regarded as a barbarian. The barbarism of the Slav made him susceptible to savage jealousy, and the play was thus a reworking of Shakespeare, titled *Otello ossia lo Slavo,* (*Othello, or The Slav*). Shakespeare's hero, of course, fought in the service of Venice, so nothing could have been more dramatically apt than to make him a loyal Dalmatian. Federici's play in its published form was actually set in the Republic of Genoa, but the publisher thought this was probably not the author's original version; indeed, with a doge and a senate already written into the drama, just the change of a name would have sufficed to restore Othello to Venice for any particular performance. Elena's father denounced Othello before the doge as a "vile Slav" born in "barbarous climes," which were then specified as the "Illyrian cliffs." Othello pointed out that in spite of his "barbarous descent" he had been loyal in combat: "Look at my wounds, the blood that I have shed for my country (*per la patria*)." He had "come down from the Illyrian mountains" to fight as a soldier, with "no other inheritance but my honor and my sword." At the happy ending, when jealous Othello was stopped just in time from murdering Elena, he spoke the unmistakable language of the proverbial Slavic devotion to Venice: "Elena will always have/the most tender part of my heart,/but my country will have my arm and my sword."[103] It is important to note that Carlo Federici's Dalmatian Othello did not hail from the Adriatic coast, but rather from the Illyrian mountains and cliffs. In other words, Shakespeare's Moor was recast as a Morlacco.

In 1804 Madame de Staël sent a note to Goethe: "Je suis ravie de la *Femme morlaque*." She was delighted by his German version of the "Hasanaginica," translated thirty years before "aus dem Morlackischen," representing a cruelly mistreated woman of the Morlacchi. Herself harassed and persecuted by Napoleon, indeed banished from Paris the previous year, Madame de Staël was perhaps ready to embrace the wife of Asan Aga as an unhappy heroine in the name of European Romanticism. She would later praise Goethe particularly for his poetic capacity to interpret the national character of the Morlacchi: "When he transports himself into completely new lands, customs, and situations, he grasps with unique talent that which pleases in the national songs of each people; he becomes, as he wishes, a Greek, an Indian, a Morlaque."[104] Voltaire, in the 1750s had listed the Morlacchi as prototypical savages—"the Morlaque, the Icelander, the Lapp, the Hottentot"—but, half a century later, after receiving the attentions of Fortis and Goethe, the Morlacchi appeared in more dignified company, together with the Greeks and the Indians. The Morlacchi now evoked that measured degree of exoticism by which the Enlightenment, and then Romanticism, recognized the Slavs of Eastern Europe.

In Madame de Staël's novel *Corinne*, published in 1807, the heroine went to Venice and ascended to the top of the Campanile in Piazza San Marco. From there she enjoyed a view—an optically impossible view—of Dalmatia, all the way across the Adriatic. From the perspective of San Marco, Corinne declared herself bored with "the civilized world," and artistically intrigued by the improvised poetry of the Dalmatians, of "peoples who remain close to nature," remote from civilization. "Let us give another moment to Dalmatia," said Corinne, "for when we go down from this height, we will not be able to make out even the vague delineation of that country, as indistinct in the distance as a recollection in the memory of men."[105] By the illumination of the late Enlightenment, Fortis let Europe see the Morlacchi in distant Dalmatia more clearly than ever before, delineated from the imperial perspective of San Marco. The vivid play of light in Venice, however, was both illusionary and illuminating; the optical refractions and philosophical reflections across the Adriatic refocused the remote image of the Morlacchi according to the values of the viewer. Fortis's empirical observations inspired collateral imaginative visions, from the gardens of Altichiero to the ducal court at Weimar. Corinne's vision of Dalmatia from the Campanile in 1807, ten years after the extinction of the Republic, offered a final metaphorical summation of the Venetian perspective, as it receded into indistinct memory.

In 1827 there was published in Paris a collection of Slavic poetry in French, *La Guzla,* named for the instrument on which the Morlacchi accompanied their songs. This was specified as a collection of "Illyrian" songs, supposedly collected in Dalmatia, Bosnia, Croatia, and Hercegovina. The anonymous collector declared himself to be half-Italian and half-Morlaque ("my mother was a Morlaque from Spalatro"); he had spoken "Illyrian" since childhood and knew from his travels every corner of the Adriatic coast and much of Bosnia and Hercegovina. The poems were transcribed from the recitations of a particular poet, Hyacinthe Maglanovich, who lived among the Morlacchi around Sinj, associated with Haiduks, and sang his songs for the collector in Zadar in 1816; Maglanovich was then sixty years old, with a shaved head, a nasty scar, and, of course, a long moustache.[106] *La Guzla* created a literary sensation in 1827 for its remarkable folkloric discoveries; in 1828 it was revealed as an artistic imposture. Not only the Morlaque Maglanovich, but also the anonymous half-Morlaque collector, and almost all the Illyrian poems, were the fictional inventions of Prosper Mérimée; twenty years later he would tell the compelling tale of Carmen among the gypsies, but now his French Romantic imagination played upon the *guzla* among the Morlacchi.

The collection included a melancholy ballad that seemed to consummate the cultural preoccupations of the Venetian Enlightenment: "Un

Morlaque à Venise." Through Maglanovich Mérimée reached back into the history of the Adriatic empire to transcribe the lament of a Slavic soldier who found himself serving in Venice, having left the mountains of Dalmatia, having crossed the Adriatic Sea.

> The women laugh at me when I speak the language of my country, and here the people of our mountains have forgotten their own language, as well as our old customs: I am a transplanted tree in summer, I wither and die.[107]

Mérimée's Morlaque sang his nostalgia in French, but Alexander Pushkin provided appropriately Slavic flavor when he reworked Mérimée in Russian, and Adam Mickiewicz permitted the transplanted Slav in Venice to express himself in Polish: "Jestem jak drzewo przesadzone w lecie."[108] It was Fortis who had defined the Morlacchi as Slavs, according to the resemblances of their language and customs, according to the rhythms of their songs and dances. Fortis discovered their Slavic character by his anthropological observation, while Wynne attempted to imagine their own sentimental sense of Slavic identity by fictional intuition. It needed a non-Venetian perspective, however, to become imaginatively a "Morlaque in Venice," singing of his own sense of strangeness, as manifested in his Slavic language and customs. Mérimée imagined the Morlacchi dying in Venice a death by alienation, but, in fact, the effacement of their identity in the nineteenth century followed from the end of the Venetian Enlightenment and the death of the Venetian republic. "Let us give another moment to Dalmatia," said Corinne, as French Romanticism contemplated the poetry of the South Slavs, of "peoples who remain close to nature." By then, the moment of the Morlacchi in the spotlight of the Enlightenment had already passed into history along with the Adriatic empire of Venice.

CHAPTER FIVE

Public Debate after Fortis: Dalmatian Dissent and Venetian Controversy

Introduction: The Importance of Empirical Inspection

Giacomo Gradenigo, concluding his triennial term as Provveditore Generale in 1777, introduced his final relation by politely declining to present a comprehensively detailed portrait of Dalmatia. "I would not want to abuse the most humane clemency of the most excellent Senate by extending myself to geographical descriptions of that region," he insisted, refusing further to account for the "population in full or their habits."[1] He claimed to defer to the previous relations of his predecessors, but, in fact, Gradenigo, who came to Dalmatia in 1774, the year of publication of Fortis's *Viaggio in Dalmazia,* had to recognize that public knowledge concerning the province was more generally pervasive in Venice than ever before. The privileged cognizance that constituted the official discourse created by his predecessors would never again monopolize information and debate about Dalmatia, which now escaped into the public sphere of the Venetian republic, to make the province a subject of critical interest and controversy. Fortis had provided a sufficiently engaging geographical description of Dalmatia so that members of the reading public could feel that they had voyaged along with him, while his sensational account of the customs of the Morlacchi gave Venice a vivid image of the "habits" of the population. Gradenigo had good reason to feel that general description would be a superfluous formality in 1777, and, from the moment of Fortis's publication in 1774, the administration of Venetian Dalmatia had to respond to the agenda of issues and imperatives that had been put before the public. Furthermore, Fortis inspired an additional dimension to the discourse by encouraging and provoking reactions from Dalmatian writers and reformers, beginning with the rather hostile "observations" of Giovanni (or Ivan) Lovrich, who mounted a native assault on Fortis's supposed expertise. Thereafter, the Provveditori Generali, like Gradenigo, had to contend with and respond to the publicly elaborated perspectives of Venetians and Dalmatians concerning the conditions of the province.

Gradenigo declared his own dual dedication to both the "treasury" of fiscal potential in the province and the "well-being of that most loyal (*fedelissima*) population." He reminded the government in Venice that when he began his term, in 1774, Dalmatia was in crisis. The Russian-Ottoman war had just concluded, and the Morlacchi faced a combination of famine and foreign pressure—"occult insidious seductions"—which made them inclined to emigrate from Venetian Dalmatia. Hundreds of families emigrated into the Habsburg and Ottoman empires between 1771 and 1774, during the preceding term of Giacomo Da Riva, and Gradenigo, with the waning of war and famine, faced the challenge of halting this hemorrhage of the population. Šime Peričić has described the Habsburg pressures and pretensions that arose on the border between Venetian Dalmatia and Austrian territory during the period of the Russian-Ottoman war and intensified in 1774 with the settlement of peace. In that year, with every interested reader in Venice following the itinerary of Fortis's travels among the Morlacchi, Gradenigo would have found it awkward to insist upon handling the provincial crisis at a distance, from his gubernatorial court at Zadar. "I saw the necessity of visiting personally the regions," he reported, and "submitted myself therefore to the hardships of horrid roads, the most uncomfortable lodgings, and the tedious tolerance of listening to innumerable petty questions that were greatly disturbing the peace of the Morlacchi."[2] Fortis's account did not include any whining about roads and lodgings, nor any manifest irritation about having to listen to the Morlacchi; he was obviously a more enthusiastic traveler than the Provveditore Generale. On the other hand, Fortis did not have to deal with problems of famine, emigration, and foreign provocation; indeed, he barely seemed to notice the crisis conditions of the early 1770s.

Gradenigo, however, serving in Dalmatia after Fortis's voyage, could not forego the personal visitation of the province, in spite of the alleged hardships and his evident distaste for the whole experience. His relation echoed Fortis's scientific tone in emphasizing the empirical evidence of his own eyes. "With these most burdensome applications, with moderate aid that was contributed to the most indigent before my eyes," wrote

Gradenigo, "I succeeded in maintaining that canton of the state without further losses." This empirical policy, following the arduous principle of directly witnessed assistance, was, Gradenigo seemed to suggest, the key to his success. There could be no proper administration without personal observation:

> I had to visit village by village the vast regions of Zara, Knin, Scardona, and Sebenico, and I was therefore given reason to recognize from close up (*d'avvicino*) the inconveniences that, obstructing the increase of the public patrimony, maintain the Morlacchi and the townsmen in poverty and desolation, and render squalid a province that ought to be significant both for its vastness and for its natural position.[3]

This visit to the enumerated regions was almost a recapitulation of Fortis's voyage, while Gradenigo's "village by village" progress stood in striking contrast to the work of his most distinguished predecessor Francesco Grimani. Preparing for the great agrarian reform of the 1750s, Grimani reported: "With a topographical plan of every village on the desk, I reviewed the villagers, family by family, and in this way came to know the truth of things."[4] After Fortis it was no longer plausible to seek "the truth of things" in Dalmatia without leaving one's desk, without visiting the villages and observing for oneself.

After the publication of *Viaggio in Dalmazia* in 1774, the Venetian administration had to confront the challenges that Fortis had posed, both in his empirical method of observation and in his anthropological perspective on the importance of customs. Furthermore, the central concerns of Venice's imperial agenda in Dalmatia, the economic development of the province and the disciplinary civilizing of its inhabitants, especially the Morlacchi, became public issues defined by Fortis's enlightened formulations. Yet, if the subject of Dalmatia no longer remained an entirely official preserve, neither was Fortis able to maintain any intellectual monopoly on the concerns of the province. By the time he returned to Dalmatia in 1780, to put forth his own policy proposal in an address to the Economic Society of Split, he was already defending himself against hostile currents of native Dalmatian dissent as well as conservative Venetian disapproval. The resentments of Giovanni Lovrich testified to Fortis's literary triumph in appropriating the subject of Dalmatia, even at the expense of interested Dalmatians, while the reflections of Carlo Gozzi clearly articulated the conservative Venetian rejection of Fortis, which made it ultimately impossible for him to apply his expertise to the service of the Republic. When Paolo Boldù came to Dalmatia as Provveditore Generale in 1780, his administration could respond to and benefit from a broad range of public perspectives on the province, reflecting not only political controversy among the metropolitan Italian parties of Venice, but also the emergence of a trans-Adriatic dialogue between Venetians and Dalmatians. After Fortis the Venetian ideology of empire was adapted and contested according to subaltern strategies, provincial priorities, enlightened prescriptions, and metropolitan presumptions, which all combined within a public discursive crucible.

Physiocratic Reflections of the Provveditore Generale

When Gradenigo first came to Dalmatia in 1774, he applied himself with particular attention to the territory bordering the Habsburg military frontier province of Lika; he was concerned about further emigration along the border, where bad harvests and Habsburg pressures combined to cause "this most pernicious effect." Gradenigo sought to provide for the "relief and comfort of the Morlacchi" and excused himself to Venice for not visiting the border area immediately. "I would have made the tour of the territory in person," he wrote at the end of October, "if the grave season which is now beginning did not oppose by indispensable exigencies the movement of this office."[5] By the spring of 1775 the Vatican nuncio in Venice already reported the arrival from Dalmatia of "a map which exactly describes the situation on those frontiers, the precise determination and number of villages, and the definite enumeration of the reciprocal bordering inhabitants."[6] The map was to serve as a guide to the Venetian Senate in negotiating the disputed frontier issues with Austria. Foscarini in the 1740s regretted the difficulty in obtaining a map of Dalmatia. Gradenigo in the 1770s recognized the importance of empirically informed mapping as an essential imperial procedure.

In 1774 Gradenigo learned from local officials about the crisis developing along the border on account of the traditional transhumance by which the flocks of Venetian Dalmatia sometimes pastured over the border on Habsburg land. That summer the Austrians had seized several hundred sheep and goats, and by the fall they were claiming possession of the shepherds as well as the sheep. The soldiers from Lika came to the village of Triban to demand that the villagers acknowledge themselves as Austrian subjects. Gradenigo was gratified to learn that "the rustics protested that they were born in Venetian vassalage and wanted to die in submission to the republican name." The Austrian soldiers then targeted the four houses of the Vuchich family, which lay along a disputed border tract of territory, where sheep and goats freely grazed. The family was told that unless they submitted as Austrian subjects, their houses would be destroyed, a threat which the soldiers promptly carried out by torch.[7] Gradenigo had to address the urgent issue of emigration in the context of Venice's rhetorical claims to the supreme loyalty of the Dalmatians. Yet, after Fortis, it became increasingly important to try to decipher the conditions and connotations of that loyalty in terms of economic factors and pastoral circumstances and within the context of the customs of the Morlacchi.

The villagers of Triban insisted that "they wanted to die under San Marco." The Vuchich family affirmed the same loyalty in their appeal to Gradenigo after the burning of their houses. "Born Venetian subjects, we wished also to die submissive to our prince," they wrote. "We find ourselves with our houses burned and deprived of what we need to live and feed ourselves. Constant as we are in living as subjects of our prince, in these dolorous circumstances we have come to appeal to His Excellency the Provveditore Generale." Yet Colonel Marco Luchich, in the service of Venice along the border, also reported to Gradenigo that three years ago the Vuchich family had declared themselves Austrian subjects on account of their houses, "in spite of their later reconsideration in returning to submission to their natural sovereign." Evidently, loyalty was not a simple and straightforward proposition among the Morlacchi, who could be born as Venetian subjects, intend to die in the same condition, but sample other sovereignties in between. Gradenigo received a letter from the eighty-year-old patriarch of the Vuchich family to declare that any insinuations that the family had accepted Austrian sovereignty were "totally false." The old man declared, "Although I am old and infirm, I have come to reaffirm my submissive subjection, and that of all my family, to the republican name." He too wanted only "to die in submission to my prince." The Vuchich family's Venetian loyalty took precedence even over their religious affiliation: "We are of the Greek rite, but we conform to the custom of our fellow villagers and frequent the functions of the church in the village in the only Latin parish."[8] In the aftermath of the

Russian-Ottoman war, after Catherine's appeal to the Orthodox population of southeastern Europe, a declaration of Venetian loyalty could include an effacement of religious affiliation, rendered suspect in the preceding years. Once again Gradenigo had to contemplate the "custom" of the Morlacchi and what it meant for loyalty at the local level.

By December 1774 Gradenigo had arrived at an understanding of the emigration problem considerably more complicated than his initial assumption of supreme perniciousness. He recognized that, given the interplay of economic and political pressures, the customs of the Morlacchi did not necessarily recognize any absolute liminal significance within state borders. Gradenigo could therefore see that loyalty and alienation were not absolute alternatives but permitted some fluctuation of back and forth. He proposed an adaptation of Venetian law to suit the irregularity of Morlacchi customs, since, as with the oscillating loyalty of the Vuchich family, the temporary determinants of emigration might eventually, under altered circumstances, bring the emigrants back to Venetian Dalmatia.

> I have reason to suspect that some Morlacchi may have seen as profitable to themselves the removal of their fellow villagers, in order to occupy the lands the emigrant families possessed. Seeming necessary to me in the meanwhile to provide immediately for lands belonging to subjects who have abandoned the country, I have determined . . . that the lands should not be absolutely disposed of for the benefit of other subject families except after the period of two years, the property always reserved for the possessor, if in this interval he should return to his native soil.[9]

Gradenigo proposed, with the consent of the Senate, to append this reservation to the Grimani law of 1755, which remained the fundamental law on the assignment of lands.

Gradenigo thus recognized that emigration was not a definitive disaster or even a permanent loss for Venice, but rather a chronic and temporary circumstance inherent in the economic and political situation; it was also consistent with some of the customs of the Morlacchi. Accordingly, he had to admit that the problem of loyalty was not as self-evident and clear-cut as had been previously supposed. The Morlacchi, he suggested, had fallen from that "pristine constancy and loyalty toward the republican name" and so had to be "observed from close up." Therefore the whole region required "a more immediate inspection."[10] From an administrative perspective, observation and inspection, aimed at the irregularities of loyalty, defined a dual imperial strategy of study and surveillance.

"One would be pleased to contemplate," wrote Gradenigo in his final relation of 1777, "a change in the squalid configuration of Dalmatia, truly capable of maintaining a greater population, with a notable augment in tithes and duties."[11] These "treasury" concerns were tied to the issue of population according to the economic wisdom of the 1770s. Gradenigo's term in Dalmatia coincided with Turgot's ascendancy in France between 1774 and 1776, the temporary political triumph of the physiocrats. Gradenigo's assumption of a natural relation between increase in population and enriching the treasury was the perfect expression of that physiocratic moment, but in Dalmatia the issue of population was inevitably linked to the longstanding concern about emigration. His stoical acceptance that emigration would ebb and flow along the Habsburg border, according to inconstant economic factors, led Gradenigo to propose that Venice seek to attract population along its other borders with the Ottoman empire and the Ragusan republic.

> Bordering with Bosnia and the state of Ragusa, and in the upper province [Venetian Albania] with Turkish Albania, there would occur daily emigrations of families (to escape the oppression they suffer under the tyrannical yoke of the Ottomans and the hardness of the oligarchic government of Ragusa), coming to establish themselves in Dalmatia, and in the sweet subjection to Your Excellencies: whenever the civil economy of the territories appears to be systematized, and the lands offer work and sustenance, lands that now stand miserably occupied by waters that generate with their impure influences pernicious effects on the health of the neighboring inhabitants . . . and when republican wisdom recognizes as appropriate to the service of the state that it should give some attention to attracting population to Dalmatia, one would not hesitate to affirm frankly the ease of the enterprise in the fortunate circumstances of current times. It would however be necessary to have greater vigilance in the regions so that the laws of public order may be observed, provisions that are now scandalously neglected.[12]

This was a veritable manifesto of the Enlightenment in the spirit of physiocracy, optimistically applied to the longstanding Venetian concerns in Dalmatia.

There was no time like the present for changing Dalmatia's "squalid configuration," attracting population by taking advantage of "fortunate circumstances," which were outlined by allusion to Montesquieu's *L'Esprit des lois;* Venice could only benefit from the less pleasant political forms of neighboring states, the tyranny of Turkey, the oligarchy of Ragusa. If Venice could not altogether stop the outflow of emigrants on the Habsburg border, there were other borders at which the inflow could restore a favorable balance of population. While some inhabitants of Dalmatia, like the Vuchich family, might declare that they were born Venetian subjects and wanted to die under San Marco, Gradenigo was more pragmatic in his perspective on population. Most of the Morlacchi had come to Venice with the *nuovo* and *nuovissimo acquisto* in the eighteenth century, and however many remained were regarded by Gradenigo not as a closed set of subjects by descent, but rather as the critical mass for attracting more.

Gradenigo was interested in the drainage of lands for reasons of reclamation and public health. From Fortis's first voyage to Cres in 1770 he too was troubled by stagnant ponds; he complained that people generally believed that it required "a great marsh to corrupt considerably the air, and they pay little attention to small ponds." Returning to Cres the following year, he announced triumphantly, in a public letter to his English friend and fellow traveler John Symonds, that "two fetid pools" had already been drained, thanks to the "paternal attention" of the Venetian official Giambattista Cornaro, demonstrating his "zeal for agriculture, for commerce, for civil peace, and for the civilizing (*raddolcimento*) of customs."[13] Fortis seemed to assign some of the credit to himself, for having noted the problem, and he also wrote about issues of drainage elsewhere in Dalmatia as challenges to the Venetian administration. Following the course of the Cetina River from the Ottoman border, near the fortress of Sinj, Fortis expressed concern about inundations creating marshland. "It would be a useful and worthy thing," he thought, "to seek the remedy to this evil, that brings about the infecundity and insalubriousness of a beautiful province." He also thought it would be possible to employ the local inhabitants in this work, for "the Morlacchi of the district of Sinj understand very well the utility which would be gained by public and private interest from this operation." Fortis insisted that they "would offer themselves willingly" for the labor and "would exult in finding themselves employed for the glory and real advantage of the prince whom they adore."[14] Gradenigo, then, could have looked to Fortis for drainage proposals, but he could have looked beyond Dalmatia as well in the 1770s. Pius VI was elected to the papacy in Rome in 1775 and would dedicate himself to the largely unsuccessful land reclamation project of draining the Pontine marshes. Although Gradenigo believed there was too little population for the land in Dalmatia, he nevertheless proposed

the reclamation of new land to attract more inhabitants. With the Morlacchi of Venetian Dalmatia already avidly at law over the land assignments under the Grimani law, Gradenigo had to go beyond the *nuovo*
and *nuovissimo acquisto* to envision an even newer acquisition, established by drainage.

Whether or not the Morlacchi would loyally exult in the service of
Venice seemed increasingly irrelevant to Gradenigo, who hoped to improve "public order" by relying on supervision and surveillance. The ap-
pointed local chiefs and colonels, like Marco Luchich, required "accurate
investigation" by the government precisely because it was their reponsi-
bility, in turn, to "watch over from close up (*vegliar d'avvicino*) the bad
and undisciplined Morlacchi." Administrative supervision was the key to
Venice's civilizing mission in Dalmatia: "The Morlacchi will always remain in the barbarism in which they now appear, if the vigilance of their
immediate inspectors is not efficacious and faithful, to observe immediately their lapses and make candid reports to the primary office."[15] That
office, of course, was that of the Provveditore Generale, Gradenigo himself, who stood at the panoptic center of this elaborately conceived network of informants and information. Beginning from Fortis's empirical
principle of direct observation in Dalmatia, Gradenigo constructed a theoretical model of administration that related the methods of surveillance
and the purposes of discipline in a manner that plausibly illustrates
Michel Foucault's historical hypothesis on the deployment of power in
the age of Enlightenment.

This monitoring of the Morlacchi involved particular attention to
their customs. For Gradenigo issues of economy and administration had
to be adapted to an anthropological appreciation of customs, though this
also sometimes inspired a reciprocal attempt to adapt and revise the customs under investigation. Gradenigo, in his final relation, focused on the
common pastures of the Morlacchi:

> Following an ancient custom, there stands still now in practice the Gaj, for
> each village, for the pasture of the animals of the community. This is a very
> extensive space that, if well administered, could bring true benefits. The at-
> tention that I have paid has made me recognize it, however, as of little
> utility.[16]

After Fortis, every Provveditore Generale had to be an amateur anthropologist, paying attention to the customs of the Morlacchi. Fortis himself, determined to make Dalmatia useful, freely applied the utilitarian

standard to almost everything except those customs, and Gradenigo, less sentimental about primitive society, pushed that standard to its logical conclusion. His own study seemed to indicate that the wealthier Morlacchi managed to take advantage of the poorer ones in the common pastures, and therefore he proposed instead "a new system, more simple and more natural," by which those pastures were partitioned among individual families, each taking responsibility for the upkeep of its own portion. Fortis's account of the Morlacchi had created a European sensation precisely because it seemed to present a primitive people who lived by simple and natural customs, in something like the state of nature envisioned by Rousseau. It was therefore a bold gambit for Gradenigo to propose a reform of customary Morlacchi arrangements in the name of something "more simple and more natural."

Gradenigo thus employed the philosophical phrases of enlightened anthropology. He argued that "when the Morlacco was attached to the simplicity of his customs, the promiscuity of the Gaj worked easily without individual charge," but, nowadays, "dissipation" caused "inconveniences" in such established customs. "Each individual, then, in the hope that the Gaj may provide pasture to his own animals," wrote Gradenigo, "neglects in the good season any concern to gather forage, and therefore it occurs that many animals perish in the winter."[17] The priorities of economy, utility, and reform made the Provveditore Generale ready to reevaluate Morlacchi customs, but, following Fortis, Gradenigo articulated his concerns within the context of an already established anthropological discourse.

The Dalmatian Condemnation of Fortis

"The errors of certain illustrious writers," observed Giovanni Lovrich, at the outset of his *Osservazioni,* "often obtain such dominion over the minds of many men, that it takes centuries, and not years, to eradicate them. This everyday prejudice made me tremble every time I thought of having to publish some small observations about the *Viaggio in Dalmazia* of Signor Abate Alberto Fortis."[18] Such supposed timidity did not prevent Lovrich from frankly announcing at the very beginning of his book his unabashed animosity toward Fortis, the illustrious writer who had made such a literary success and public sensation out of his voyage in

Dalmatia. Only two years after the publication of *Viaggio in Dalmazia,* Lovrich in 1776 already felt himself compelled to launch an assault upon the alleged errors of Fortis, lest they secure the lasting dominion of un-challenged truths.

Fortis managed to make some remarks about almost every aspect of Dalmatia, thus staking out a total authorial hegemony over his chosen subject, all the more daunting to a challenger, like Lovrich, who trembled with resentment as he surveyed the literary scope of his nemesis:

> Fortis in his *Viaggio,* so hasty as he was, spoke of almost every one of the well-known places of Dalmatia. Besides natural history, which was his principal purpose, he added a sprinkling of antiquities, of national history, of popular customs previously little known, from time to time political and economic reflection, and even some erudition in the Illyrian language. If to the force of his genius he had added accuracy, and if he had contented himself to speak only of natural history, his work would be one to hold in the highest consideration.[19]

The problem, of course, was that Fortis did receive such consideration, altogether unmerited according to Lovrich, who promised an unremitting attack on the grounds of superficiality and inaccuracy. The more brilliantly Fortis extended himself across diverse arenas of investigation, the more broadly he exposed himself to the fiercely pedantic criticism of his resentful rival.

Naturally, Lovrich was angriest about the specific subject that gave Fortis his greatest renown. "Regarding the customs of the Morlacchi," Lovrich remarked, "though many things were said with precision, nevertheless there reigns such great disorder in their description, and there are such gross (*madornali*) errors, that national spirit obliges me to remark upon them, so that concerning this completely new subject readers should not trust blindly."[20] The "national spirit" that obliged Lovrich to write and publish was Dalmatian pride. He came from Sinj, in the inland region where Fortis identified marshlands to target for reclamation, claiming that "the Morlacchi of the district of Sinj understand very well the utility" of such an endeavor. Lovrich had left Dalmatia to study medicine at the University of Padua, in Fortis's own city. A young man in his early twenties, Lovrich wrote his observations in a spirit of almost adolescent outrage. This was to be his one and only work, for he died of tuberculosis in 1777, the year after publication.[21] He wrote in Italian and published in Venice under the Italian name of Giovanni, but his perspective was distinctly Dalmatian. As a native of the province, with some experience of Italy, Lovrich was motivated by "national spirit" to reclaim not the Dalmatian marshlands, but the public discourse on Dalmatia, which Fortis had so stunningly preempted as his own dominion.

The Provveditori Generali, beginning with Gradenigo, found that they had to learn from and respond to the public controversy created by *Viaggio in Dalmazia*. For educated Dalmatians, like Lovrich, the challenge of Fortis was differently disconcerting. Venetian rule in Dalmatia was, all at once, partly accountable to the public sphere, but it was the metropolitan public sphere of Venice; the Dalmatians themselves, whether devoted or discontented, were in danger of being left out of the discursive loop. Lovrich, who published his *Osservazioni* in the name of "national spirit" in the spring of 1776, while the American continental congress was meeting in Philadelphia, was outraged that Fortis had ingeniously invented and triumphantly dominated the colonial discourse of Dalmatia. The aggressive pedantry that attacked every petty point of Fortis's presumed erudition constituted a sort of declaration of intellectual independence. Thus, the challenge of Fortis's *Viaggio in Dalmazia* immediately energized the emergence of Dalmatian spokesmen for the social and economic concerns of the province. They had little choice but to publish their work on the Italian side of the Adriatic, since there was no effectively established printing press in Dalmatia until 1792, when Antonio Bobolin opened a press in Zadar.[22] Until then, the absence of publishing facilities in the province compelled Dalmatians and Italians to confront one another directly, discussing Dalmatian issues in the Italian language, within the metropolitan public sphere of the Adriatic empire.

The development of this discourse of the Dalmatians in the shadow of Fortis's triumph meant that they felt inevitably obligated and encouraged, as well as preempted and inhibited, by his Italian precedence. They included his devoted friends as well as his envious enemies. Chief among Fortis's friends was Giulio Bajamonti of Split, a prominent member of the agricultural academy there. In October 1774, the year that Fortis's book was published in Venice, Bajamonti presented to the academy in Split an address on the economic condition of Dalmatia, affirming that "whoever applies himself to discovering the defects and suggesting improvements in this province would render one of the most important services to the nation." Employing the model of development that served to distinguish Eastern Europe from Western Europe in the eighteenth century, Bajamonti saw the Dalmatians at fault for the "imitation of the most uncivilized European peoples," when they should have been following "the more cultivated and awakened nations." According to Franco Venturi, Bajamonti's address to the academy in 1774 was "his *Viaggio in Dalmazia,* parallel and coeval to that of Fortis."[23] When that address was published, the following year, in the *Giornale d'Italia,* Bajamonti put his own Dalmatian perspective before the Venetian public.

More critical of Fortis was the work of another Dalmatian, also published in 1775, *Riflessioni sopra lo stato presente della Dalmazia,* by Pietro Nutrizio Grisogono, a lawyer who came from Trogir. It was published in Florence, but dedicated to a Venetian senator of the Grimani family and publicized in Venice in 1776 with a review in the *Giornale enciclopedico,* which saluted the author for his "enlightened patriotism." Grisogono remarked upon the errors of a certain "modern traveler," who had surveyed "like a flash some small stretch of Dalmatia." The central emphasis of Grisogono's reflections was Dalmatia's miserable poverty, which Fortis really did underplay in his account, as he sought to excite interest in the province's useful natural resources and curious social customs. Grisogono affirmed that the inhabitants of Dalmatia were "confused, uncivilized, degraded, and poor." The province was in the unfortunate condition of a "convalescent who seeks only to live, waiting for a more opportune season to apply himself to caring for his own interests." There could be no question of formulating grand imperial schemes to make Dalmatia "useful" to Venice, when, for the moment, poverty and survival were the only issues that mattered. Grisogono, in the historical evaluation of Venturi, was a "conservative" man of the Enlightenment, "capable of multiplying criticisms of detail in Fortis's *Viaggio,* and suggesting to the Venetian government a series of modifications of local legislation, but not of promoting new and original initiatives."[24] Criticizing Fortis, however, was evidently an end in itself, as Dalmatian writers sought to publish their own perspectives on Dalmatia. In 1780 Grisogono offered a work on the natural history of Dalmatia, another challenge to Fortis. Later in the 1780s Grisogono again explored the misery of Dalmatia with a work on the outbreak of plague in the province. In 1790 he put before the public of Venice a proposal concerning the cultivation of silkworms. His career as a writer about Dalmatia, dating from just after the publication of *Viaggio in Dalmazia,* was indebted to Fortis for creating public interest in the subject, but that was not a debt that all Dalmatians could comfortably acknowledge.

No one illustrated that principle more emphatically than Lovrich, whose "observations" of 1776 singled out Fortis for sarcasm, insinuation, disparagement, and denunciation, lavishly administered by turns throughout the book's 260 pages. The outrage of Lovrich indicated the urgency of his underlying need to reclaim the discourse that Fortis had so successfully hijacked. The book began by retracing a portion of Fortis's voyage, along the river Cetina, in the native region of Lovrich. The course of the river he announced as "among the most important and delightful objects that could merit the reflections of a naturalist," but its natural delights were clouded for him by the shadow of his rival: "I will take the liberty for now, at the same time as I go about observing the inaccuracies of Fortis, to describe and mention that which appears to me more interesting for a natural historian." Lovrich's book was more of an angry voyage through Fortis's book than an exploration of Dalmatia itself. If Fortis remarked upon the flooded marshlands near Sinj, Lovrich objected to the suggestion that there was anything "insalubrious" about his own native region. "That certainly is not permitted to be said by anyone except Fortis," remarked Lovrich, sarcastically.[25] He objected to many particular points, but especially resented Fortis's general freedom to pronounce upon every aspect of the province.

Lovrich objected most strenuously concerning the matter on which Fortis had pronounced most successfully, that is, on the customs of the Morlacchi. The bulk of Lovrich's reflections addressed that same subject, though he worried that after Fortis no one would care about Dalmatian contributions: "It would seem superfluous, since Fortis has done the description of the customs of our Morlacchi, that now I should set about the same work; but whoever likes order, accuracy, and the entire notion of the customs of a people, will find my labor necessary." Wrestling with the disheartening sense of his own intellectual superfluousness, Lovrich assumed possession of "our Morlacchi" on behalf of his fellow Dalmatians. Fortis could also claim the Morlacchi as "ours," along with the rest of Dalmatia, as a component possession of Venice's Adriatic empire. For Lovrich the possessive was based on a sense of national relation and regional proximity to the Morlacchi, but though he himself came from inland Dalmatia, he made it clear that he did not actually identify himself as one of them; they were always *nostri Morlacchi*, rather than *noi Morlacchi*. In fact, Lovrich

242 Venice and the Slavs

was, on the whole, inclined to take a more negative view of them than Fortis did, precisely because he recognized that the success of *Viaggio in Dalmazia* was partly due to its favorable perspective on primitive customs. Concerning the supposed "talents" of the Morlacchi, Lovrich insisted that they lived "in a most perfect ignorance and Fortis certainly wanted to praise them too much."[26] Lovrich obviously resented the praise that Fortis received for praising the Morlacchi.

The particular reflections of Lovrich tended to support the general conviction that Fortis was wrong about everything. "It is amazing that so many Illyrian authors, copying one from another, have always believed that the name Morlacchi is pure Illyrian, and never knew its true etymology," wrote Lovrich, "but it is even more amazing that Fortis, pretending to correct them, has substituted an even more chimerical conjecture." The tone of mock amazement was sustained throughout the work as Lovrich uncovered ever more astounding instances of Fortis's perfect ignorance. Concerning the supposition that Morlacchi women could acrobatically nurse an infant over the shoulder, Lovrich remarked: "This opinion which foreigners invented as a fable, I would never have suspected that a natural historian like Fortis would have embraced it." In general Fortis was taken to task for making extreme and categorical statements about the customs of the Morlacchi. Fortis had cited as a point of refinement that the Morlacchi under no circumstances ever relieved themselves indoors, and Lovrich was not squeamish about arguing that his rival was as wrong in excremental as in etymological affairs:

> Fortis says that even the moribund are carried outside to perform in the open that function, but this may be said and believed only by one who lets himself be persuaded that whoever dirties the cottages of the Morlacchi by relieving himself of the excessive load of his intestines would run the risk of losing his life. The Morlacchi do not reach this excess of brutality.[27]

Fortis's point of refinement became, in Lovrich's reading, an excess of brutality, the Morlacchi murdering the moribund for failing to control their bowels.

Similarly, Lovrich sought to reduce to absurdity Fortis's supposition that the Morlacchi would rather die than eat frogs.

> I would not dare to affirm, like Fortis, that no true Morlacco would eat frogs, even at the cost of letting himself die of hunger. But if hunger has induced men at other times and other places in this universe to feed upon that which human nature most abhors, how could it escape from the mouth of a reason-

able man that the Morlacchi would sooner die than eat frogs? And what would happen if I were to say that many true Morlacchi, without any necessity, for some time have begun to eat frogs, and maybe it will not be long before the whole nation discards the prejudice against eating them? One can not say the same about Morlacchi of the Greek rite. The chain of religion constrains them not to eat frogs, and whoever eats them, they believe, can not be saved.[28]

Lovrich saw the Morlacchi as not eternally bound by the laws of custom, but moving gradually toward a condition of frog-eating civilization, in spite of the obstacles of Orthodox superstition. Above all, he sought to engage in debate with Fortis, casting himself as someone who would only speak with the greatest circumspection, casting his rival as someone who could not keep stupidities from popping out of his mouth. Thus Lovrich affirmed his higher claim to pronounce the truth about Dalmatia and to describe the character and customs of the "true Morlacco."

Dalmatian Ambivalence and the Customs of the Morlacchi

Nothing was more infuriating to Lovrich than Fortis's linguistic erudition that permitted the Paduan to claim some knowledge of the language of the Slavs:

> Fortis acting as usual as the Maestro of the Illyrian language says that *osveta* signifies both vengeance and sanctification. He would have been worthy of being forgiven much if he had cited the author from whom he copied such a pretty piece of erudition. But probably they were all in error without being aware of it. *Osveta* in Illyrian signifies vengeance and *posveta* sanctification.[29]

Lovrich made much of his Slavic linguistic edge in competition with Fortis and contemptuously accused him first of plagiarizing his knowledge and then of getting it wrong anyway. Furthermore, linguistic inadequacy supposedly resulted in travesties of meter and meaning in Fortis's already widely celebrated transcriptions and translations of Morlacchi poetry. Lovrich found it preposterous for Fortis "to pretend to such minute notions of Illyrian versification," or even "to pretend that he possesses the language perfectly." With sneering condescension Lovrich showed how Fortis might have better transcribed some of his least felicitous verses.[30]

Lovrich wrote in Italian to dispute Fortis's expertise on Dalmatia before the public of Venice, but advertised his own superior Slavic fluency as a decisive reason for reclaiming the discourse.

Fortis made much of his contacts and conversations with the Dalmatians, and Lovrich aggressively insinuated that these were not as intimate as they were made to seem. "I will never forget as long as I live the reception and cordial treatment of me by the Voivod Pervan at Coccorich," wrote Fortis, in praise of the hospitality of the Morlacchi. Lovrich gratuitously suggested that Fortis, in spite of his sentimental memories, was actually an unwelcome guest.

> Fortis says that while he was eating with his honored Voivod Pervan at Coccorich, the daughters of the house were watching through the crack of the door. But if none of them served him at table, it is not because they hide from foreigners . . . but because sometimes the Morlacchi take umbrage against certain subjects without any reason.[31]

With nasty satisfaction Lovrich implied that though Fortis may have liked the Morlacchi, the Morlacchi did not reciprocate his fond feelings but rather disliked him especially. Lovrich not only sought to turn Fortis's own account against him, but also claimed the authority to represent with greater interpretive sensitivity the sentiments of the Morlacchi.

Since Fortis included a lengthy discussion of marriage customs among the Morlacchi, Lovrich had to have a section on that subject as well. He particularly wanted to reconsider the role of the Kum, or best man, at a Morlacchi wedding.

> I remember once having told an Italian, as a joke, that the Kum must deflower the new bride, and has the privilege of sleeping with her on the first night. He asked me immediately how he could become the best man of a Morlacco; but thinking about it seriously a little he realized that I was joking. So I marvel that Fortis, whom I believe to be more intelligent, let himself be persuaded that the Kum still undoes the girdle of the maiden, just because in past times he used to deflower her completely.[32]

Lovrich allowed himself the amusement of suggesting that Fortis was taken in by a joke, that the Slavs of Dalmatia took pleasure in telling tall tales about the Morlacchi to Italians just for fun. The moral seemed to be that all Italians, including Fortis, were less intelligent than they seemed and that the *Viaggio in Dalmazia* had to be read with the reservation that its author was the gullible victim of his snickering informants. Lovrich did not, however, claim to speak for the Morlacchi as one of them, but rather as a Dalmatian with better knowledge of the Morlacchi than any Italian could hope to have.

Lovrich was particularly critical of a story related by Fortis about climbing in the Biokovo mountains, near Makarska along the Primorje coast. "My sweetest friend Signor Giulio Bajamonti consented to keep me company," recalled Fortis, and they brought along two armed local guides, "without whom my prudent companion would not have come, not thinking it well to expose himself to an encounter with Haiduks, of whom many, secure in the roughness of the site, dwell like wolves in the grottoes of the Biokovo." The travelers encountered, however, neither Haiduks nor wolves, but only a snake, which the guides insisted on stoning to death, superstitiously supposing it to be a demon.

> Signor Bajamonti, having said many things to them that they might recognize the extravagance of this thinking, removed from the ground the dead beast, which was being watched by them from a distance with a fearful eye, and he went toward them that they might see that truly it was dead. Those two brutes at once put themselves in position to discharge their two firearms against him, breaking out into the most decisive insults and threats: and it was truly a stroke of good fortune that our friend did not throw the dead snake at them, as he indicated he would; in which case indubitably he would have been killed on the spot.[33]

This story of violence, irrationality, and superstition among the Morlacchi emphasized the friendly solidarity of the enlightened naturalists, Fortis and Bajamonti, though they came from opposite coasts of the Adriatic.

Since Fortis had a section on superstitions of the Morlacchi, Lovrich had to have such a section as well, and within it he addressed the subject of snakes. "If the Morlacchi are plunged in an abyss of ignorance, as we have remarked elsewhere," wrote Lovrich, showing himself no great admirer of the Morlacchi, "it will be no surprise that they are also superstitious." He recounted a Morlacchi myth of a snake that once tried to swallow the sun, so that the sun now shined favorably upon people who killed snakes.

> This fable is somewhat Oriental, and it is admirable that it has been traditionally preserved among some of our Morlacchi. But serpents also stand guard over treasures. When one encounters many serpents it is a sign of good fortune, according to the opinion of the Morlacchi. I remain greatly stupefied, that the Primorje guides who conducted Fortis in the Biokovo mountains, wanted to kill his companion because the latter pretended to throw a snake at them, since it is common opinion that it is good luck to encounter snakes

while traveling. One of those very guides told me that neither he nor his companion had committed such an action, and that the complaints were all wrong. But in confrontation with the Morlacchi one must sooner believe Fortis.[34]

In tracking down and interviewing the guide, Lovrich outdid himself in his dedication to expose Fortis as a dupe and a fraud; the initial statement of mock stupefaction was modified by testimony that made Fortis out to be not only completely wrong but willfully dishonest. Lovrich was particularly pleased to set up a "confrontation" between Fortis and the Morlacchi, and the sarcastic concluding dilemma—whom to believe?— summed up the essential intention of undermining Fortis's credibility concerning Dalmatia.

The observations of Lovrich offered an ambivalent Dalmatian conception of the Morlacchi. He too took his lead from Rousseau in setting up an opposition between civilization and the state of nature as the fundamental framework of analysis: "The principle of the education of the Morlacchi, which will seem strange to the civilized (*colte*) and polished (*polite*) nations, is barbarous and distant by only a very few degrees from the original state of nature."[35] When Fortis counterposed the Morlacchi to the civilized nations of Europe, he might have sympathized with the former, but he had no doubt that he belonged to the latter. In the case of Lovrich this alternative was more troubling, and his ambivalence about the Morlacchi followed partly from an uncertainty about his own relative status as an educated Dalmatian.

Writing about the education of the Morlacchi, Lovrich began by discussing their earliest infancy.

> Mothers, being certain that the infants do not lack the means of sustenance for life and health, leave them to cry or be silent according to their inclination; meanwhile, the mothers apply themselves to domestic affairs, from which it follows that their little creatures, who cry by nature, learn to be silent from exhaustion . . . Each mother with her own breasts (unless necessity opposes) nurses her own child.[36]

Thus the child rearing of the Morlacchi became an enlightened anthropological demonstration of Rousseau's principles in *Emile* and even a reproach to "civilized" women who failed to follow the fashion for nursing their own babies. Nursing among the Morlacchi was not, as Fortis suggested, an acrobatic stunt, but rather a perfectly natural practice. Lovrich insisted that an upbringing in accordance with nature was healthy for the children of the Morlacchi:

> They expose the nude chest equally to the excessive boiling heat of summer and the most insufferable rigor of winter. Therefore it comes about that they acquire that valuable health and robustness that is rendered very desirable and very rare in the civilized and delightful cities, notwithstanding the most delicate attentions and every possible diligence.[37]

Under the influence of Rousseau, Lovrich looked for positive advantages in the primitive customs of the Morlacchi to set pointedly before the public of Venice, that most civilized and delightful of cities.

The Morlacchi, thought Lovrich, "make us recall the memory of the enviable though rough usages of the first men." He invoked the Enlightenment's conventional notion of the changelessness of China: "Just as the Chinese want no other laws than those of Confucius, so the Morlacchi are constant and do not want any other customs but their ancient ones." Yet, Lovrich recognized that such fidelity to custom could be an obstacle to the economic advancement of the Morlacchi, and so, for the sake of their own "felicity," he thought it would be desirable to "extirpate" such Chinese "prejudices" in Dalmatia.[38]

Lovrich was himself evidently ambivalent about how to evaluate the merits of primitive life in the state of nature. Love among the Morlacchi, Lovrich warned, might seem "scandalous" to foreigners, though he himself believed that "the Morlacchi with their loves recall to memory the sincerity of ancient times." They did not indulge in the affectations of rococo Venetian romance: "Amorous languors, panting, convulsions, sighs, sobbing, and other such tedious gallantries, are things that would require quite a number of years before they might mingle in the rough breasts of the Morlacchi. They have no preliminaries of any sort to their loves." The backwardness of the Morlacchi in expressing their sexual impulses was presented in ironic contrast to the supposed sophistications of civilized lovers. Yet Lovrich sometimes seemed to apply his irony in the reverse direction, upon the Morlacchi themselves. Considering the marital rights of Morlacchi men, he explained: "When they have satisfied their own passion, they forget the wife until the next time that she excites them. I have heard some people, accustomed to gallantry, accuse them on this count of brutality, but who does not see that such is man in the state of nature?" Lovrich hesitated to endorse wholeheartedly the life of men, and especially women, in such a state of nature, however uncomplicated and unconvulsed their sexual encounters. "The Morlacchi are filthy and dirty in the extreme," he remarked, fastidiously. "That depends upon the natural state in which they live."[39] Lovrich's sense of his own Dalmatian difference from the Morlacchi nourished in him a certain distaste for their primitive condition, however true to nature.

The mutual perceptions between Morlacchi and Italians were similarly problematic for Lovrich who could not really identify with either camp. He took for granted that the Morlacchi were naturally antagonistic:

> They do not trust the Italians, and view them with an eye of contempt just because almost all nations mutually despise one another. Therefore they give the same force to the word Lazmanska-Virro, the faith of an Italian, that the Italians attach to the word Morlacco. Both believe they rebuke one another in speaking thus. Fortis, who here and there was gathering notions of the customs of the Morlacchi, is not blamable for not having understood the force of the word Lazmanska-Virro.[40]

Lovrich would not have missed an opportunity to make a sarcastic remark about Fortis's linguistic misapprehensions as a supposed "Maestro of the Illyrian language," and the Dalmatian would also have relished reminding Fortis that the Morlacchi "do not trust the Italians." Fortis, of course, was familiar with such disparagement and flattered himself that he transcended the gulf of mistrust between the nations. He actually quoted and translated the approval of the Morlacchi at his agility in the mountains: "Gospodine, ti nissi Lanzmanin, tissi Vlah!" "Sir, you are not a cowardly Italian, you are a Morlacco!" Clearly, Fortis recognized the negative connotations of *Lanzmanin,* as well as *Lazmanska-Virro,* though he saw himself as exempt. Lovrich allowed for no such exemption. He argued that mutual contempt was to be found between all nations, not only between the civilized and primitive peoples. In fact, Lovrich mentioned that the Morlacchi had a parallel term for "faith of a Greek," which they applied to Orthodox Slavs even though "the Greeks among us are of the same nation as the Morlacchi of the Latin rite."[41] The ambiguous usage of "us" suggested the awkwardness of his personal relation to these pejorative distinctions.

Lovrich made a similar point about the mutual perceptions of dress between Morlacchi and Italians. He began by remarking upon the "excessive" attachment of the Morlacchi to their style of clothes: "They think there is no clothing in the world more noble. The Morlacco who changes clothing receives the opprobrium of the nationals." Lovrich even included a poem about "the contempt that the Morlacchi have for the clothing of the Italians," translated into Italian. "I detach myself somewhat perhaps from the words," remarked Lovrich, reserving the issue of his personal identity. The poem was actually composed by Filip Grabovac fifty years before in 1729, published in his *Cvit razgovora* in 1747, and dedicated to the Venetian Zaccaria Vallaresso, the author of *Baiamonte Tiepolo in Schiavonia.* Quoting the poetry of Grabovac, without attribution, in Italian translation, Lovrich sought to define an educated Dalmatian perspective on the balance between Slavic and Italian culture in the province. The poem mocked Dalmatians in Italian clothes: "Who having just arrived from Italy on our shores/Made themselves Italians, and blushed/To call themselves Slavs."[42] Lovrich represented this as a contemptuous Morlacchi perspective on Italian clothes, though, in fact, it defined the dilemma of his own Dalmatian identity between the customs of the Morlacchi and the customs of the Italians. Federici represented this same sartorial issue on the stage in *Gli Antichi Slavi,* when Dusmanich denounced the Italianate costume of his coastal Dalmatian rival.

Lovrich evidently felt himself to be closer to some Morlacchi than to others, when he remarked that "Morlacchi women of the Greek rite adorn their clothing more bizarrely than ours do." However, his account of reciprocal observation between Morlacchi and Italian women, witnessed in his native Sinj, recognized the importance of perspective. He first introduced an Italian perspective, probably intended as an ironic reflection on the philosophical Fortis studying women's clothes among the Morlacchi.

> For an Italian, who has never seen it before, and observes with every diligence when the occasion presents itself, this becomes philosophical curiosity. I once happened to see at the fair at Sinj some Morlacchi women observing with admiration, seen for the first time, the clothes of some Italian women, and these Italians began to laugh and mock them; so that which appears as philosophical curiosity in an Italian, passes for simplicity and foolishness in the Morlacchi.[43]

The Italian women seemed not to be laughing at the clothes of the Morlacchi, but rather at the fact that the latter were staring at their first sight of foreign finery. When Italians observed Morlacchi, the study counted as enlightened anthropology; when Morlacchi observed Italians, it was considered gaping ignorance. The aggrandizing gaze of the Enlightenment did not admit reciprocity. In undercutting its pretension to "philosophical" perspective, Lovrich administered his most intellectually significant criticism of Fortis's work.

Lovrich attempted to formulate a philosophical balance of perspectives, mediating between the Venetian public and the Morlacchi. "Italian music bores them greatly," he remarked, "in just the same fashion that Morlacchi music bores an Italian." It was Fortis, of course, who remarked that the Morlacchi songs showed "scarcely a flash of imagination" and "did not awaken any feeling in me."[44] Lovrich could not miss the opportunity to allude sarcastically to that and to conjure up the striking counter-instance of ferocious Morlacchi condemned to listen to the four hundred concertos of Vivaldi. Though far from admiring the Morlacchi, Lovrich could not altogether accept that they were utterly different from other nations.

Lovrich recognized the invidious distinction by which primitive Morlacchi were made into anthropological entertainment for the supposedly civilized public of the Enlightenment, but he found himself appearing before that same public with the obligation to offer some of the same literary bait. His reflections concluded with the biography of an authentic eighteenth-century Haiduk, Stanislavo Socivizca, once the terror of the Turks, now comfortably retired from murder and pillage; Lovrich actually went to interview him in person in order to write about his life. "He deserved to be called more ferocious than a wolf," reflected Lovrich, thrilling the public by appealing to the conventional legend of the Morlacchi, "but there were Haiduks even more ferocious and stronger without however managing to murder as many Turks as Socivizca." His exploits, according to Lovrich, were similar to those "that the Morlacchi sing about the ancient champions of the nation." Here Lovrich had something to offer the public that went beyond Fortis's literary wares, an interview with a true and contemporary Haiduk. The frontispiece for the book was a print of Socivizca, armed with a rifle, a curved sword, and numerous daggers at the belt, looking appropriately ferocious. Yet such a frontispiece was far from apt for the work as a whole, unless of course Lovrich liked to imagine his Haiduk cutting to bits the body of Alberto Fortis. There was some irony in the fact that the short account of Socivizca was the only part of Lovrich's book to be translated for an international audience, published in French by the Société Typographique in Bern—"avec le portrait de Socivizca"—in 1777, the year of the author's

Stanislavo Socivizca

Vox fera trux vultus verissima mortis imago,
Quamque lupi sęve pluſ feritatis habet.
Ovid

FIGURE 12. "Stanislavo Socivizca." Frontispiece of Giovanni Lovrich, *Osservazioni*, published in Venice in 1776, his critical observations on Fortis, also including an account of the life of the Haiduk bandit Socivizca. The Latin epigraph from Ovid emphasized the ferocity, the wolflike savagery of the Haiduk, though such character was often attributed more generally to the Morlacchi. "He deserved to be called more ferocious than a wolf," wrote Lovrich, who was concerned to distinguish himself as a "civilized Dalmatian" from the supposedly barbarous population of inland Dalmatia. This account of Socivizca appealed to an international fascination with the Morlacchi and, like Fortis's book, was translated into French, German, and English. *(By permission of Widener Library, Harvard University.)*

premature death. Meanwhile, the story of Socivizca was translated into German in 1778 and published anonymously in Leipzig as *Leben des berüchtigten Haiducken Sotschiwizka*. An English edition of *The Life and Adventures of Captain Socivizca* appeared around the same time.[45] Lovrich only achieved this small success by peddling to the "civilized" public the literary entertainment of lupine ferocity among the Morlacchi. He himself would have been the first to consider critically the "philosophical curiosity" with which such a work was consumed by the international public of the Enlightenment.

Lovrich wrote approvingly of Dalmatians who "are not ashamed of the Slavic family name and do not Italianize it." He himself published his reflections under the Slavic name of Lovrich (though he appeared under the Italian first name of Giovanni, rather than Ivan), and the issue of Slavic pride recurred often enough in his book to indicate its personal importance to him. The song that he cited about Dalmatians who "made themselves Italians" and "blushed to call themselves Slavs," was relevant to Lovrich, as a student in Padua, at a time when the Slavs of Dalmatia had achieved a dubious fame for their primitive customs. Praising the poetry of the Morlacchi, Lovrich regretted that "the most civilized (*colti*) Dalmatians today do not deign to employ their talent in national poetry, and for fear of being considered barbarians some of them claim (foolishly thinking it a virtue) to be ignorant even of the language."[46] This was the dilemma of the youthful Lovrich, seeking to define his national identity at a moment when even the most civilized Dalmatians, with whom he presumably associated himself, were nervous about being perceived according to the provincial reputation for barbarism.

It was Fortis who had made the issue of civilization and barbarism in Dalmatia of such compelling "philosophical" interest to the public of Venice, and it was against Fortis's mastery of the discourse that Lovrich turned his own outrage, all the more furious for the uncertainty and insecurity of his Dalmatian identity. He criticized Fortis for having praised too highly the talents of the Morlacchi, failing to recognize their "most perfect ignorance," but Lovrich was more personally preoccupied with the unappreciated talents of "the most civilized Dalmatians, who can not be virtuosos equal to Italians, by whom they are reputed to be stupid by nature." He consoled himself with the thought that there were Dalmatians who "have merited the praises of the most civilized nations"—like the seventeenth-century heretical theologian, Marcantonio de Dominis of Split, and the eighteenth-century Jesuit astronomer and mathematician, Ruggiero Boscovich of Dubrovnik. Such celebrated figures "prove sufficiently how much it is possible to perfect the natural dispositions of Dalmatians, unfortunate in not having the necessary means to give proof of their talent."[47] The misfortune of Lovrich was that Fortis not only preempted the discourse by his sensational discovery of Dalmatia, but also publicized so successfully the primitive customs of the Morlacchi that their barbarism reflected upon even the most civilized Dalmatians. Yet, in provoking the responses of Dalmatians like Bajamonti, Grisogono, and Lovrich, whether friendly or hostile, Fortis decisively stimulated the concurrent articulation of Dalmatian and Venetian perspectives on the province during the final decades of the Adriatic empire.

Pietro Sclamer: The Invented Dalmatian Identity of Alberto Fortis

Fortis promptly replied to Lovrich's hostile attentions, publishing in Modena in 1777 a pseudonymous "sermon" by an invented Dalmatian, "Pietro Sclamer" of the island of Cres. By assuming this pseudo-Slavic identity to administer his counterblast, Fortis seemed to recognize that the larger concern of Lovrich was to reclaim the discourse on behalf of the Dalmatians. At the same time that he published the fictional perspective of Pietro Sclamer, Fortis also issued in his own name a response to Lovrich, which appeared as an open letter in Brescia. "Although almost all my friends believe that I should respond to your productions with nothing but silence," began Fortis, haughtily, before modulating into sarcasm, "and with an intimate sense of gratitude for the honor that you do to me and to my voyage in Dalmatia, I am inclined to believe . . . that it would be a failure of duty toward you, who treat me so kindly, not to communicate a few reflections." The first reflection was a direct accusation of "literary calumny," and Fortis trumpeted his own empirical principles as the appropriate reply to "a calumnious accusation against a man who tells the public that he has seen what he has seen, and no more." The pedantic disputations of Lovrich were rejected as "chattering, inconclusive, and puerile." In fact, Fortis's affirmation of his own empiricism raised the difficult issue of how the public was to judge critically different representations concerning relatively remote lands. The reader in Venice, constituting a part of the public sphere, could not knowledgeably judge competing empirical testimonies about Dalmatia without actually visiting the province whose aspects were under dispute. "That the Morlacchi women have the longest, most disgusting breasts," remarked Fortis, "I said it, because I saw it, and because many honest people, incapable of ridiculing anyone, have confirmed it."[48] The discursive mastery of Dalmatia was a matter of empirical fact, but there was evidently also an element of personal prejudice. Fortis's distaste for Morlacchi women seemed to intensify in proportion to his indignation at Lovrich.

Fortis was not above boasting about his own scientific celebrity in order to establish the credentials that made his observations more credible than those of Lovrich: "My fortunate circumstances, beyond my own merits, are such that I frequently find myself mentioned with honor in the acts of various illustrious academies, and in the immortal works of many famous writers, Italian and foreign." Fortis not only celebrated himself to minimize the importance of Lovrich but also cited the example of Bajamonti as a model Dalmatian man of letters: "who, by everyone except you, is respected, loved, and esteemed, who has a large dose of true merit, who writes with golden elegance and singular robustness, who does honor to and loves the honor of the Dalmatian nation."[49] Bajamonti, of course, also possessed the supreme merit of being Fortis's personal friend and intellectual ally. In a Goldonian flourish Fortis made himself and his friends into the true guardians of the "honor of the Dalmatian nation," while the Dalmatian Lovrich was implicitly accused of dishonoring his own homeland. Fortis fully recognized that what was at stake was control of the discourse, as Lovrich attempted "to impose upon a herd of good people who believe that a Dalmatian must know his country's affairs, even without having studied them, better than a foreigner who has thus occupied himself with them for some time." Yet Fortis felt himself in need of Dalmatian endorsement and so introduced the public to a new character in the controversy. "Do you know who was laughing a little maliciously after having read your book of observations?" wrote Fortis, challenging Lovrich, in a rhetorical formula that echoed the mocking pseudonymous polemics of Voltaire. "A young man from Cres was laughing . . . "[50] Not coincidentally, the island of Cres was made famous by Fortis in his essay of 1771, and the laughing young man, of course, was Fortis's own literary invention, Pietro Sclamer.

The *Sermone Parenetico*, or "exhortative sermon," of Pietro Sclamer was published in Modena, just outside the Venetian republic, for Fortis, typically, had found himself controversially engaged over the manuscript. Sclamer began by summing up the polemic between Fortis and Lovrich as a familiar sort of literary encounter: "It has always been usual, young Signore Lovrich, for writers of some fame to be attacked by obscure men who desire to make a name for themselves; but it has also been usual, for the most part, for the writers molested by such a contemptible race of troublesome people not to deign to respond to their detractors." Such a formulation suggested that the polemic between Fortis and Lovrich reflected the disparity of position between established authors and aspiring writers of the Enlightenment, as described by Robert Darnton.[51] In this case, the rivalry between the angry young man and the famous philosophe was complicated by the additional factor of national difference, across the Adriatic, within the imperial framework of the Venetian republic. That was precisely the reason for introducing Sclamer to pretend to mediate the controversy. He described himself as initially neutral in the controversy, indeed inclined to favor his fellow Dalmatian:

> Fresh from reading the voyage of the abbé Fortis, I was curious to read also your so-called observations; and knowing something about the usages and history of our common country, I set myself to compare his work with your censures, for the purpose of weighing, on the one hand, the inaccuracy of the Italian traveler, and, on the other, the justice of the corrections of a Dalmatian critic.[52]

Sclamer thus put himself forward to face the same judgmental dilemma that confronted the public, the comparative evaluation of the discordant empirical testimonies of Fortis and Lovrich. "I therefore wanted to note one by one your critical observations," declared Sclamer to Lovrich, "and with surprise I found them all badly founded, badly supported, and frivolous." Sarcastically, Sclamer even suggested that if Lovrich really wanted to make plausible criticisms of *Viaggio in Dalmazia*, he might look in the forthcoming English and French translations of the work, where Fortis would openly acknowledge corrections to the original edition.[53] It was merely a reminder of Fortis's international stature as an expert on Dalmatia, compared to the provincial insignificance of Lovrich.

Sclamer did rebut Lovrich point by point concerning the factual criticisms of *Viaggio in Dalmazia*, but also aggressively addressed the evident sensitivity of Lovrich to his own standing among "the most civilized

Dalmatians." He was denounced for "inurbane, insidious, and hostile modes" of attack against Fortis, a man admired by "our nation collectively." Sclamer spoke for the Dalmatian nation, reprimanding Lovrich:

> I confess that I was scandalized and embittered by your scarcely civil manners; it seemed to me that you caused dishonor to the nation, which fully ought to be, and certainly is, grateful to the abbé Fortis, the first foreigner who thought to make our provinces illustrious.[54]

Sclamer thus attacked Lovrich as an unpatriotic Dalmatian, but also as an uncivilized Dalmatian with uncivil manners and inurbane modes. The literary style of the *Osservazioni,* written by Lovrich in Italian, was cited with particular ridicule, the better to remind him that he looked hopelessly provincial within the metropolitan public sphere. "From now on I hope you will write in Illyrian," remarked Sclamer, "because you have too often abused Italian." Sclamer disparaged Lovrich as one Dalmatian to another: "Now for what purpose do you use a contemptuous and insulting mode, exposing yourself to the accusation of being badly educated, my dear fellow countryman (*mio caro Connazionale*)?" Sclamer, like Lovrich, subscribed to the scale of more or less civilized Dalmatians, determined by manners, modes, literary style, and formal education. The sermon, however, assigned Lovrich to a lesser status, according to that scale, with the barely concealed intention of insulting his sense of civilized Dalmatian self-esteem. Sclamer, predictably, proposed Bajamonti as an example of the civilized Dalmatian at the other end of the scale: "Signore Giulio Bajamonti of Split, for his application to scholarship, for his prudence, customs, and manners, should serve as a model for Dalmatian youth."[55] Lovrich himself was only in his early twenties, and his observations could be dismissed as "puerile," so he could be condescendingly encouraged to model himself on Bajamonti.

The charges of incivility, inurbanity, immaturity, inadequate education, and literary "barbarisms" pointed inevitably toward another epithet which Sclamer eventually supplied. It was already implicit on the title page of the sermon, which addressed the exhortation to Giovanni Lovrich, native of Sinj, "in Morlacchia." Sinj lay inland from the Adriatic coast, but Morlacchia was as much a philosophical as a geographical attribution. From one Dalmatian to another the epithet of "Morlacco" was certainly intended as an insult, but Sclamer applied it to Lovrich with a full sense of the ironic inversions invested in the term. "I am your countryman," declared Sclamer, with the difference that he himself was from the island of Cres. As an islander, Sclamer pretended to defer to Lovrich: "I feel myself to be inferior to you, who are a Morlacco, and therefore more noble, more valorous, and more virtuous than I am."[56] In his own *Osservazioni* Lovrich had carefully distinguished himself from the Morlacchi, even written about them disparagingly, so Fortis, writing in the persona of Sclamer, took aim at the insecurity of the youthful Dalmatian critic, and called him a Morlacco. Of course Fortis cheerfully considered it a compliment when the Morlacchi accepted him as one of themselves ("Sir, you are not a cowardly Italian, you are a Morlacco!")—but he knew that the label could only be mortifying when applied by an islander like Sclamer to an inlander like Lovrich. Some years later, in 1785, Fortis deployed the same insult in a private letter about the proud patricians of Dubrovnik, remarking that "although they have shorter moustaches than the Morlacchi, those Senators are no less barbarous in some regards."[57] In fact, Fortis must sometimes have contemplated applying the same comparison to the unappreciative patricians of the Venetian Senate.

The epithet of Morlacco summed up the charge of incivility that Sclamer was making against Lovrich. This was formulated as a sort of ethics of civilized literary controversy:

> I am convinced that a well-born writer has the duty to use the most civil modes possible. Insult, malicious sarcasm, and impertinent mockery make a few people laugh, but nauseate the greater number, and do not prove anything. Whoever wants to make known the imperfections of a book should not insult or bite the person of the author, and can not do it without dishonoring himself. You have undertaken to bite and insult the abbé Fortis, and he certainly will not bite or insult you, as I have not, for I have only attended to the errors of your writing.[58]

This strategy for occupying the higher ground, by claiming more "civil" and "civilized" polemical manners, would have been more convincing if Fortis himself, writing as Sclamer, had been better able to resist his own inclinations toward irony, sarcasm, and mockery. For instance, the accusation of "biting" became particularly nasty in discussing the endlessly interesting subject of the breasts of Morlacchi women. Sclamer remarked that the length of their breasts was related to the fact that they nursed their children to the age of four or five. "You deny it," said Sclamer to Lovrich, "and I have the discretion to wish to believe that this usage does not occur in the region around Sinj, where if all the children resemble you, the mothers might find themselves obliged to remove them rather early so as not to be bitten."[59] Sclamer was far from adhering to the judicious and civil literary standard that he enjoined upon Lovrich. Fortis was obviously unable to maintain the philosophical composure of an international celebrity irritated by a literary mosquito, any more than he was able to preserve a dignified and indifferent silence. His evident need to absolutely annihilate his young critic seems excessive, especially in view of the fact that Lovrich anyway died of tuberculosis in November 1777, at the end of the year of Sclamer's sermon.

Sclamer concluded with some words of advice, as a "good friend and fellow countryman," suggesting that if Lovrich sought "fame" through "literary war," he would do better to employ "the honesty and urbanity that are customarily used by well educated men." In fact, Lovrich, during that last year of his short life, did achieve a certain fame by countering Fortis as a Dalmatian critic before the Venetian public. The ferocity of Fortis's response only confirmed the importance of the challenge and further circulated the name and fame of Lovrich. Had he lived, he would surely have replied again and compounded the polemical intensity. His contribution was not a matter of superior knowledge of Dalmatia or the Morlacchi, but rather his commitment to articulating a distinctly Dalmatian perspective, as a matter of "national spirit." Fortis seemed to concede the point when he made his reply to Lovrich under the pseudonymous Dalmatian name of Pietro Sclamer. Having discovered Dalmatia for Venice, Fortis now found himself compelled to conjure Dalmatian confirmation of his discovery. In 1932 Marijan Stojković published in Zagreb an article, written with national spirit, rediscovering Lovrich in the context of Croatian historiography as a protagonist of the Enlightenment in Dalmatia—"who unfortunately did not write in Croatian." Lovrich considered himself Dalmatian; Fortis mocked him as a Morlacco. The term Croatian was alien to the eighteenth-century controversy between them, but its deployment in twentieth-century historiography was consistent with the national dimension of the trans-Adriatic self-assertion of Lovrich. Interestingly, Stojković hesitated to accept conclusively that Pietro Sclamer was Fortis's invention.[60] After all, Sclamer could also be considered a "fellow countryman," articulating an indigenous Dalmatian perspective within the Adriatic Enlightenment.

The Patriotic Importance of Chestnuts

When Fortis returned to Dalmatia in 1780 to address the Economic Society of Split, he was aware that his preeminence as an authority on the province, established in the 1770s, had created angry controversy among Dalmatians like Lovrich. Accordingly, Fortis considered it an endorsement of his own expertise to be invited to address an audience of Dalmatians about Dalmatia. "The Venetians make the greatest case of the Dalmatians," remarked Goldoni in his memoirs, with reference to writing *La Dalmatina*. "I make the greatest account of the honor accorded to me by you," declared Fortis to the Dalmatians in Split, envisioning the vindication of his *Viaggio in Dalmazia* by virtue of their approval. "It much increases the personal sense of satisfaction that I experience the flattering hope of being able to be a not unproductive collaborator in your patriotic applications." Indeed, he almost gloated over the evidence of "your good opinion which is confirmed for me today by the numerous concourse of notable persons gathered to listen to me." He declared himself "all the more grateful" in view of the fact that there were also other Dalmatians, "some ill-considered spirits who make efforts to cause me all possible trouble," and thus also "cause dishonor to their country."[61] Fortis thus insisted that true patriotism in Dalmatia allowed for the inclusive collaboration of imperially concerned Italians like himself.

"You, most civilized (*coltissimi*) listeners," Fortis addressed his audience, "are the sole literary tribunal that legally represents the learned part of the Dalmatian nation, ever glorious and friendly to guests and studies." The attribute of superlative civilization was not a casual courtesy by Fortis, since the issue of who was civilized, more civilized, and most civilized was fundamental to the whole discourse of Dalmatia in the eighteenth century. Lovrich had sought to speak on behalf of "the most civilized Dalmatians," outraged that they were "reputed to be stupid" by Italians. Fortis seemed to respond directly when he presumed to decide who among the Dalmatians was most civilized, who was qualified to represent the nation. Those Dalmatians who showed themselves most sympathetic to Fortis himself in Split were the only ones he recognized as the proper "tribunal" for exercising critical judgment upon literary contributions concerning Dalmatia. This tribunal, in its civilized, critical, and representative character, was evidently conceived by Fortis as an institution of the public sphere, corresponding to the formulations of Jürgen

Habermas. Having already put the subject of Dalmatia before the public in Venice, Fortis presumed to denominate the public in Dalmatia as well. With his appearance in Split he encouraged a dual discourse concerning Dalmatia that henceforth developed before the bar of a dual public, Venetian and Dalmatian, through the final decades of the Adriatic empire. Indeed, he almost constituted that duality within his own person, when he created Pietro Sclamer as the Dalmatian aspect of his public literary life. "Approved, protected, and praised by the wisdom of the most excellent Venetian Senate," pronounced Fortis, adding imperial ratification to his own personal approval of the Economic Society of Split, "your patriotic body need not fear the evil influences of the tenebrous attempts of its censurable detractors."[62] Fully aware of the furious insinuations of his own detractors, Fortis thus invoked the authority of Venice to determine who was legitimately entitled to speak for the Dalmatians.

"Although for my past labors and cares I have not always been by chance well compensated by all those Dalmatians who aspire to praise for having a civilized spirit," declared Fortis, in ironic reply to Lovrich and his aspirations, "far from being exacerbated or made in the least lukewarm in my friendship toward this respectable nation, I avidly seize the opportunity to give public proofs of the constancy of my sentiments." This was an elegant rhetorical inversion of the most fundamental axiom of the discourse on Dalmatia: instead of affirming the loyalty of the Dalmatians to Venice, Fortis declared his own Italian loyalty to them and to their nation. There was even in this gesture perhaps a hint that Fortis was turning his back on Venice, for it was above all the Venetians who had failed to give him fitting compensation for his *Viaggio in Dalmazia*. Through the 1770s he awaited his reward in the form of the chair in natural history at the University of Padua, and the moment of truth arrived in 1777 with the death of the incumbent professor, Antonio Vallisnieri, to whom Fortis had dedicated a part of his book. "The name of my competitor makes people laugh," commented Fortis on his academic rival Angelo Gualandris. "I have reasons to hope. The voice of the public is in my favor." He counted too much on public opinion, however, for conservatives in the Senate, led by Pietro Barbarigo, disapproved of Fortis as a freethinking priest and an enlightened protégé of patrician reformers like Andrea Memmo. In 1777, the year of Fortis's academic disappointment, conservatism advanced its cause in Venice with the imposition of new economic restrictions on Jews. The opposition to Fortis also occurred in the context of political tensions that culminated in the crisis of 1780, when Zorzi Pisani advocated "correction" and reform, and conservatives, like Barbarigo, successfully checked the enlightened current. Barbarigo was especially irate at the committee of Riformatori of the University of Padua for failing to censor effectively the "universal inundation of pernicious books in every corner of the state."[63] The committee had, of course, approved the publication of *Viaggio in Dalmazia*.

Fortis, deeply disappointed and exacerbated at being denied the chair at Padua, recrossed the Adriatic in 1779 to find more sympathetic appreciation in Dubrovnik and in Venetian Dalmatia. In 1780, after presenting his address in Split to the friendly tribunal of Dalmatians, he proceeded to Naples in the hope of finding better patronage there at the Bourbon court than he had obtained at home in the Venetian republic. His speech in Split was therefore published in Naples in 1780 and thus became Fortis's last significant contribution concerning Dalmatia, even though his *Viaggio in Dalmazia* remained at the center of discussion and controversy in the 1780s and 1790s, as the public in Venice and in Dalmatia reevaluated the imperial Adriatic relation.

The polemical significance of the address at Split was Fortis's triumphant confirmation of his success in the "good opinion" of the Dalmatians, in spite of the "censurable detractors," like Lovrich, already prematurely deceased by 1780. The actual substance of the speech could be summed up in one word: chestnuts. From the vantage point of his own celebrated expertise in affairs of the province, he had determined upon the ideal solution to its ecological and economic problems, the planting of chestnut trees. In fact, Fortis had earlier contemplated the possibilities of chestnuts, going back to his essay on the island of Cres in 1771, which remarked upon the dangers of deforestation and proposed the introduction of chestnut trees.[64] He was also interested in other new crops for Cres, such as potatoes, and then in the *Viaggio in Dalmazia* he seemed to survey not only all the products of the province but all the possible products that could be usefully encouraged there. The address at Split in 1780 stood out by its focus on a single solution to the multiple problems in Dalmatia.

The most politically pointed aspect of the proposal for chestnuts was that Fortis seemed ready to give up on land reform as the agricultural

remedy for Dalmatia's economic misery, after a full generation of unsuccessful efforts based on the Grimani law of 1755.

> Among all the means from which one may hope for the resurgence of Dalma-
> tian agriculture, the first place must belong not to the reform of actually
> seeded and planted lands, but rather to the reduction of rough, despoiled,
> and abandoned places, and the well conceived renovation of the woods. To
> this end I shall propose to you the cultivation of the chestnut . . . and I will
> try to prove to you that it is more opportune than any other to the character
> of the mountains, the climate, and your peasants, and the most apt to give a
> source of real, enduring, and progressive wealth to the province, unfortu-
> nately poor and desolate at this time, and menaced by the still frequent hor-
> rors of famine and the consequent damages of emigration.[65]

Famine and emigration had been cited for decades as the recurrent crises
of the province, dating back to Foscarini's oration of 1747, and Fortis
now suggested that Venice's whole approach to these problems had been
misguided in its priority of means.

The problem of "rough, despoiled, and abandoned places" was presented as a visual exercise in the appreciation of landscape, as it appeared
from both foreign and native perspectives: "Among all the mountainous
lands that surround the Adriatic and the Mediterranean there is none
that presents a more horrid aspect, a more ungrateful spectacle to the
eyes of the foreigner, an object of greater affliction to the good patriot,
than the rough and bare sterility of the littoral mountains of Dalmatia."
Without specifying the responsibility for deforestation, whether of
Venice's shipbuilding industry, in need of timbers, or of Dalmatia's domestic prodigality, in need of kindling, Fortis recognized that Venetian
rule had failed to find a remedy, that the initiative now fell to the Dalmatians. He invited them to contemplate an alternative vision of the landscape, to imagine the picturesque mountain ranges of Italy as they might
appear from a visitor's perspective: "Instead of causing horror to voyagers (*viaggiatori*), those wild regions awaken in them an agreeable surprise, appearing majestically from high to low covered with magnificent
trees, planted once by the industry of the poor inhabitants, and then
raised by nature."[66] Fortis, who had made his literary career as a voyager
in the *Viaggio in Dalmazia,* now made the traveler's impressions into the
measure of civilized landscape, which further reflected the progress of
economic development.

It was this simple formula—planted by industry, raised by nature—
that made chestnut trees the most apt solution to Dalmatia's economic

misery. Because of the "laziness" of the population, the only promising projects were those that required little labor, like planting chestnut trees, which "has the double advantage of being the least needy of long attentions and the most opportune for the circumstances of the country." There would also be multiple rewards, rendering the landscape beautiful, preventing soil erosion, improving the air, offering shade to the flocks, and, finally, providing food for the population in time of need. The chestnut, wrote Fortis, "either serves as nutriment for poor rustic families, or one sells it to advantage in the market, or in the case of great abundance one destines it for maintaining and fattening the swine." If it was food for the pigs in the best of times, however, it was fit for human consumption at least in times of famine. Fortis wrote that in the Italian Alps and Apennines, "mountain families rarely or never find themselves afflicted by horrid hunger; and they lead a healthy life in their poor cottages, nourishing themselves on polenta and focaccia made with the flour of ground chestnuts."[67] The contrasting visions of mountain landscapes, between Italy and Dalmatia, corresponded to disparate economic circumstances. Fortis proposed to balance that asymmetry across the Adriatic divide.

As Fortis reached his peroration he recalled that not everyone in Dalmatia was sympathetic to him and his projects, and he warned the Economic Society to beware of negative influences.

> May heaven protect and may wicked men not thwart the attempts that you certainly will not fail to undertake; after which the felicity of the first experiments may summon all Dalmatia to cultivate that sole product which can bring about the prompt resurgence of its agronomical decline! Your children and grandchildren will perhaps remember with a sentiment of gratitude that an Italian, led to these regions by not prejudicial curiosity, sought to prove his friendship for the whole nation by rousing it to promote a branch of agriculture by whose progressive influence the Morlacco may be insensibly removed from the plow that he does not know how to handle, and restored to the pastoral life, the only one that suits his nomadic origin and character; by which the littoral peasant, who is now made brutish and undisciplined, may be rendered more intelligent and more docile; and by which finally might be changed in the brief course of half a century even the horrid exterior aspect of the province, and the material wealth of the nation might be increased.[68]

A tangle of subjunctive verbs attended Fortis's uncertain conjuring of the future, the next half century with its generations of children and grandchildren, more time than actually remained to the Venetian republic.

Venice, however, had already almost vanished from view in Fortis's peroration, which focused on Dalmatia alone, set to achieve its agricultural resurgence by the enterprising projects of its own patriotic elite, with perhaps the acknowledged assistance of one single Italian.

Fortis spoke directly to the Dalmatians in this address, with only token allusions to the Venetian state and without any attentions to the Venetian public; he then published the piece in Naples. At the same time, he ultimately justified his proposal by asserting his own particular expertise, for which he was famous in Venice and throughout Europe, concerning the customs of the Morlacchi. The Venetian policy of agricultural reform, ever since the Grimani law, was fundamentally misguided, according to Fortis, because it rested on the false premise that the Morlacchi could be made into farmers. Only by recognizing and respecting their true character, as Fortis did, by removing them from the plow and restoring them to pastoral life, could Dalmatia aspire at last to economic success. With this indirect indictment of Venice and in direct defiance of his Dalmatian detractors, Fortis in 1780 set out to demonstrate that an Italian could employ his expertise on behalf of Dalmatia and turn his mastery of the discourse to the good of the nation.

Gozzi Against the Anthropophagi

Carlo Gozzi, writing his *Useless Memoirs* in 1780, noted in a spirit of pointed irony the recent proliferation of writings about Dalmatia, with facetious praise for Fortis as the principal expert before the public. Gozzi recounted his own adventures in Zadar back in the 1740s, including his theatrical impersonation of a Dalmatian servant girl, but he also allowed himself some brief general reflections on the Morlacchi in response to the contemporary discussion initiated by Fortis in the 1770s.

> Many have already written and published relations of greater consequence, and the abbé Alberto Fortis, a man of vast intellect, of equal presumption (*ardire*), and indefatigable in his reportedly solid and useful observations and discoveries, has made the most useful and considerable discoveries among the inhabitants, in the seas, the mountains, the lakes, the rivers, and the fields of those provinces. They have been published, and everyone can read them and believe them, as they have read and believed some others.[69]

There is no doubt that Gozzi's intentions were entirely ironic as he paid mock tribute to Fortis's vast intellect, indefatigable research, and most useful discoveries; this was mere mimicking of the general public acclaim for the *Viaggio in Dalmazia,* which Gozzi regarded as rather over-praised. There was an odd convergence between the perspectives of Lovrich and Gozzi, the young indignant Dalmatian and the old derisive Venetian, in their respective disrespects for Fortis. Lovrich in 1776 had begun his book with a sarcastic reflection on how little remained to be said about Dalmatia when Fortis had already made himself the expert in not only natural history, but also "a sprinkling of antiquities, of national history, of popular customs previously little known, from time to time political and economic reflection, and even some erudition in the Illyrian language." Lovrich would have been gratified to see Gozzi designate "presumption" as the basis of Fortis's manifold erudition. Though Gozzi's memoirs remained unpublished until 1797, the work reflected conservative Venetian aversion to the *Viaggio in Dalmazia* in the 1770s, the negative opinion that probably cost Fortis the chair at Padua.

Gozzi's contemptuous tribute to Fortis was intended as general disparagement of the Enlightenment with its eager engagements on behalf of fashionable projects for reform and improvement.

> I am told that he has inventoried some great marvels and projected some manners of products and barrels of goods that may be extracted from that piece of the world, which he judges abandoned in disgusting neglect. Such projects have an attractive image, which please some who are enamored by the novelty of discoveries, and it does not matter that they may be in great part false and in great part impracticable, since in every age there is a science dictated by a phantasm called fashion, which has always found amusement in human volubility, human avidity, and human caprice.[70]

From Gozzi's conservative perspective, the Enlightenment was no more than "a phantasm called fashion," dreaming up projects for the distraction of those "enamored by the novelty of discoveries." Fortis, as the enlightened spokesman for the phantasm, had discovered the novelty of Dalmatia, which had become the momentary entertainment of the public in Venice. Indeed, Fortis was in Split in 1780 proposing the "project" of chestnuts, even as Gozzi was writing his memoirs.

Gozzi doubted that Dalmatia could be of any economic use to Venice, as Fortis had so optimistically envisioned in his book, with its central theme of imperial profit and provincial utility. Furthermore, Gozzi's splenetic disapproval also touched upon the aspect of Fortis that conservative Venice found most offensive: his enthusiastic projects for Dalmatia amounted to an implicit indictment of Venice for having left the province in "disgusting neglect." It was one thing for Foscarini to denounce the abandoned condition of Dalmatia before the patricians of the Maggior Consiglio in 1747; it was something else again for Fortis to suggest such criticisms before the broader public in 1774. Gozzi's dubious perspective on projects for improvement in the province gave an implicit vindication of Venice's imperial performance.

The conservative solution that Gozzi proposed for the problems of Dalmatia was simply "moral education," a nice contrast to Fortis's prescription, that same year, for the comprehensive efficacy of chestnuts.

> I do not believe that the abbé Fortis, for whose intellect one must have much esteem, has deigned to recall that to bring Venetian Dalmatia and Albania to all the good that they could give with industry, it would be necessary to begin, little by little, with insistence, to spread an effective good morality over custom and thought. With this preliminary and indefatigable effort, after the course of a century and a half, one could perhaps fulfill a tenth of the promising projects.[71]

Fortis's enlightened outlook, which looked for economic success in half a century, was three times as hopeful as Gozzi's conservative perspective, anticipating improvement only after a century and a half. Teaching morality would take more time than planting chestnut trees, and the harvest would be much longer delayed. Fortis proposed chestnuts as the simplest solution to the problems of Dalmatia, requiring the minimal amount of effort and attention, while Gozzi insisted on the more rigorously demanding program of moral improvement.

In proposing morality as an antidote to "custom and thought," Gozzi indicated the philosophical core of conservative objections to the *Viaggio in Dalmazia*. The enlightened public had embraced Fortis's anthropological account of the customs of the Morlacchi, his Rousseauist sympathy for their primitive virtues, his contextual explanation even of the banditry of the Haiduks and the violence of vendettas. Gozzi failed to appreciate the sentimental appeal of primitive customs and saw Fortis's anthropology as the exculpation and even celebration of mere immorality. To make his case Gozzi cited his own experience in Dalmatia forty years before, when Morlacchi from the interior were mobilized and brought to Zadar; from there they were to embark for Venice as reinforcements at a time of tense Venetian neutrality during the War of the Austrian Succession in the 1740s. The Morlacchi obstinately resisted being sent to Venice and refused "to abandon their burrows (*tane*) to pass into Italy." Gozzi denounced such men, who sought "to reconcile being subjects with being able to steal and murder," including bandits known for "frequent misdeeds of theft, homicide, arson, and other similar heroisms." Gozzi called a crime a crime in the language of conventional morality and was anything but anthropologically indulgent in his account of the Morlacchi. To him they appeared as a "species of anthropophagi"; thus he made the unsentimental association between barbarians and cannibals, "these Laestrygones," like those who almost ate Odysseus. Gozzi noted that when the Morlacchi received their advance pay, upon which they had insisted, they "barked" (*abbaiavano*) out their songs, and performed "strange dances" before boarding the ships.[72] Writing after Fortis, Gozzi was well aware that those songs and dances of the Morlacchi were celebrated all over Europe as fascinating manifestations of folkloric culture, and his account of the military review of the "anthropophagi" in the harbor at Zadar was clearly intended to undermine such misplaced sentimentality.

Much as he deplored the Morlacchi reluctance to serve in Italy, he was even more disgusted by the consequences of their sojourn there.

> I venerated creation even in these barbarians, but I pitied their education, and I had a passing desire to penetrate into paradise by sight to see how the Morlacchi would camp out in that place of eternal beatitude. It is certain the piazzas of Italy possessed by our clement government were more disturbed than defended by those brutes. Especially in Verona, without paying attention to the commands of discipline or subordination, they followed their systems of theft, murder, violence, tumult, and pertinacious disobedience; and a few months later they were remanded to their caverns to liberate Venetian Italy of an intolerable vexation.[73]

The providential place of the Morlacchi in God's creation was not a mystery that Gozzi proposed to contemplate anthropologically. He could not imagine them coming closer to paradise than the piazzas of Italy, and there they clearly demonstrated an unsuitability to any environment beyond their native burrows and caverns. Their conduct in Italy was described as a modern descent of the ancient Goths, and the encounter between Morlacchi and Italians, as star-crossed nations in Verona, suggested that the Adriatic empire of San Marco had to maintain the separation of its peoples on their respective shores of the sea.

Though this particular contingent of Morlacchi troops may have been soon sent back to Dalmatia—"to liberate Venetian Italy"—there remained a significant presence of overseas militias (*milizie oltremarine*) from Dalmatia stationed in Italian garrisons during the following decades. In 1760 two regiments with 896 soldiers from Dalmatia were stationed at the garrison of the Lido di Venezia, with another regiment of 448 around the Venetian Terraferma. In 1774, the year that Fortis published his *Viaggio,* there were 520 Dalmatians soldiers on the Lido and 430 elsewhere in Venetian Italy.[74] The Morlacchi were therefore not as absolutely alien to Italy as they appeared in Fortis; neither was the episode of the 1740s the single disastrous occasion of cannibals in paradise, as Gozzi seemed to suggest. A regular presence of Slavs from Dalmatia in the army and navy of Venice, as well as among the population of the capital, meant that public debate about the Morlacchi in the 1770s could play upon unfocused peripheral perceptions of their longstanding presence in the garrisons of Venetian Italy.

Writing after Fortis, Gozzi also had to justify himself by citing his direct experience and observation in Dalmatia, albeit some forty years out of date.

> I have seen all the fortresses, many lands and many villages of those provinces. In several cities I found educated persons of good faith, cordial and liberal. In those places farthest from the court of the Provveditore Generale, I found rough and barbarous customs. The villagers are all fierce and cruel, superstitious, insensible to reason. They perfectly preserve in their marriages, their funerals, their games, the usages of ancient heathens. Whoever reads Homer and Virgil finds the image of the Morlacchi.[75]

The marriages, funerals, and games of the Morlacchi were among Fortis's principal subjects, and Gozzi also claimed to have studied them in Dalmatia, at least well enough to label them as barbarous. The allusion to Homer seemed at first glance to follow the formulations of Fortis, who, in the spirit of Vico, had suggested that the poetry of the Morlacchi recalled "the simplicity of Homeric times."[76] Gozzi's ironic intention, however, was to subvert that bardic resemblance by discovering the "image of the Morlacchi" in Homer's anthropophagi.

The diagram of the degree of civilization in Dalmatia followed the reliable rule of inverse proportion to distance from the center of Venetian

administration at Zadar. When the Morlacchi appeared before the officials there, the Venetians received some idea of the level of barbarism in
the more remote districts. "I saw a woman of about fifty years prostrate
herself before the Provveditore Generale," Gozzi recalled, "to draw out
from a gamebag a parched skull, deposit it at his feet, weep copiously,
and ask for mercy and justice. For the last thirty years she had preserved
that skull of her mother, who had been killed."[77] That the woman's savage sense of vengeance survived for thirty years with this grisly souvenir
of her mother made such an impression on Gozzi that he himself preserved the memory of the occasion for another forty years to include it in
his memoirs.

Gozzi's moral indictment of the Morlacchi included charges of sexual
vice as well as savage violence. "The climate of those provinces," he remarked, "makes the men and women supremely libidinous, and the legislators who know that it is impossible in those lands to curb the fury of
lust, have established a tariff on the defloration of a Morlacchi virgin little more than the payment given by a liberal depraved man in Venice to
the female merchant in sin on the ground floor." This observation fit
with Gozzi's personal memoirs of losing his own youthful Venetian virginity to a libidinous Dalmatian woman and then becoming one of the
several lovers of a depraved thirteen-year-old Dalmatian girl. His greatest
triumph in the role of Luce, the Dalmatian servant girl, was his mockery
from the stage of the notorious Tonina of Zadar for her meretricious immorality.[78] The political message of Gozzi's conservatism was that sensible legislators realized it was "impossible in those lands to curb the fury
of lust," and he applied the same principle of intractable unregeneracy to
issues of economic and agricultural reform. The Venetian government in
Dalmatia could never hope to achieve anything by the proliferation of
"promising projects" as long as there was no moral formation of character among the Morlacchi.

Following Fortis, Gozzi noted that the Morlacchi did not even grow
their own "favorite foods," onions and garlic: "Reproached and corrected
for this harmful inertia, they respond that their ancestors did not plant garlic and onions, and they do not alter the direction of their grandfathers."
The indolent inertia of the Morlacchi, like their libidinous lust, made it impossible for legislators in the Venetian Senate to bring about reform.

> I asked the most civilized (*colte*) persons of those lands the reason for the general
> rural lazy indolence of Dalmatia. People replied to me that it was impossible,

without risk of one's life, to oblige the Morlacchi to do more than they do, or to introduce the smallest innovation to reform their labors in the fields. I said that the owners of the lands could summon Italian farmers and make this country become like Puglia. I saw my confabulators laugh coarsely at my project, and when I asked the reason for their laughter, they answered me that many Dalmatian gentlemen had tried to bring industrious peasants from Italy, and that a few days after their arrival they were found killed across the country, without anyone able to get to those guilty of their deaths. I was promptly persuaded that I was a bad projector (*progettante*), and I marveled that these gentlemen laughed instead of weeping when they gave me this information.[79]

His point was the incurable indolence and inertia of the Morlacchi, which rendered all "projects" impracticable, and the account of the fatal encounter between Italians and Morlacchi in Dalmatia reinforced his message that those nations needed to remain on their separate coasts of the Adriatic.

Gozzi's disparagement of the Morlacchi turned into the corollary censure of even "the most civilized" Dalmatians, who knew no better than to laugh when they should have wept. This was precisely the class in which Fortis placed his highest hopes, when he addressed them in the Economic Society at Split, and Gozzi's negative insinuations underlined his conviction of the hopelessness of Dalmatia. "My preaching, writing, printing, and proving," noted Gozzi, fully aware of the public dimension of the discourse on Dalmatia, "that the first indispensable agriculture should be upon the heads and hearts of the people, to have the consequence of good effects in submission and subordination, has made many projectors choleric against me."[80] In the rising temperature of choleric controversy over Dalmatia in 1780, Gozzi suggested not the planting of chestnut trees in mountainous terrain, but the cultivation of moral sentiments in the hearts and minds of the Morlacchi.

Conclusion: The Microphysics of Empire

Paolo Boldù came to Dalmatia in 1780 as Provveditore Generale, scion of a patrician family that had already produced a previous Provveditore, Giacomo Boldù, in the 1740s. Giacomo Boldù had identified as the "invincible defect of these peoples of Dalmatia" the economic inaptitude expressed in their "aversion" to work and resistance to discipline: "lazy by nature, especially the Morlacco" and "by nature ferocious and vindictive." Paolo Boldù, forty years later, faced a similar problem of economic inactivity, but, considering Dalmatia after Fortis, he evaluated the crisis less in terms of the "nature" of the inhabitants and more as a matter of their customs. The mission of Venice, he proposed, in his official relation of 1783, was "to render homogeneous and coherent so many parts made dissimilar and disconnected by ruinous bad habits (*ree abitudini*), and to compose those maximal physical and moral disorders that are the causes of depopulation." Such work, he warned, might require "the attentions of centuries" when dealing with "rough and barbarous peoples." In fact, the most dramatic disorder of Boldù's term in Dalmatia was the famine of 1782, caused by frost in February followed by drought in the summer, which resulted in the distressing emigration of several thousand Dalmatians across the Habsburg and Ottoman borders.[81] The even greater crisis of plague in 1783 had only begun to exercise its terrible toll at the time of his departure from Dalmatia. In spite of climatic and medical catastrophes Boldù maintained an enlightened vision of Venice's imperial project; the civilizing process of social homogenization was to make the machinery of administration run smoothly over the rough irregularities of custom. Like Gozzi he could not be sentimentally enthusiastic about primitive customs, but recognized them rather as "bad habits" in need of moral reform.

Like Fortis, however, Boldù refused to accept that either the land or its inhabitants were inherently unfit for economic development and social progress. He too delineated a picturesque perspective on the landscape of Dalmatia: "everywhere spacious fields, mountains, and hills, delightful and all susceptible to cultivation such that it seems Providence has taken particular care to form with partisan effort that extended province." This image was, however, displaced by its negative image, "the contrary aspect," whenever Boldù contemplated "the inertia and the bad habits of those peoples," who were "contaminated by idleness and averse by ancient custom (*antico costume*) to procuring by labor the many goods of fortune." The whole province suffered from a "passive ruinous commerce," illustrated by the now familiar complaint that the Morlacchi did not even grow their own onions and garlic. Custom became the culprit for economic backwardness, and Boldù further refused to implicate nature in the faults of the Morlacchi; their inertia and idleness were in no way natural.

> All these reflections, however, though unfortunately true, make one recognize what these peoples are, not by nature, but by circumstance; for in fact, examined in their external and inner qualities, they appear to be born precisely for industry and labor. Large stature, elegance of form, robustness of body, agility of movement . . . everything in conclusion that liberal nature can give to a man that he might be useful with the work of his hands and his intelligence for whatever use . . .[82]

The Morlacchi may have been elegantly endowed by provident nature, but they were ruinously influenced by the circumstance of custom.

Boldù sought to dissuade the Senate from "total desperation" in Dalmatian affairs, after "the paternal attentions of Your Excellencies have sought to redeem Dalmatia from so many calamities and from extreme misery, but always until now without fortunate success." He found himself compelled to demonstrate that the disciplinary transformation of primitive populations was indeed a possible outcome of policy.

> Leaving apart the histories which are full of examples of savage and rough peoples made useful with constant good discipline, we have, I would say, before our eyes the Austrian Morlacchi of Lika, who were, little more than thirty years ago, similar and maybe worse than those of Dalmatia. . . . They were brought to such perfection of cultivation (*coltura*), of condition, and of mind that, to someone who knew them before, such a surprising metamorphosis seems almost impossible. Educated in arms, and with the same rigors of military discipline in civil life and in the labors of the fields, they became farmers, soldiers, and stewards.[83]

Boldù paid tribute to the Habsburg program of the recently deceased Empress Maria Theresa, without knowing, of course, that the Habsburgs would have all of the next century to exercise their efficacy upon the Morlacchi of Dalmatia. Whereas Fortis was ready to restore the Morlacchi to the freedom of pastoral life, according to their customs, Boldù endorsed the forceful application of administrative discipline toward a complete metamorphosis of the Morlacchi. Boldù's conception fits Foucault's history of discipline and docile bodies in the age of Enlightenment: "By the late eighteenth century, the soldier has become something that can be made; out of a formless clay, an inapt body, the machine required can be constructed; posture is gradually corrected; a calculated constraint runs slowly through each part of the body, mastering it, making it pliable, ready at all times, turning silently into the automatism of habit." The making of the soldier was also to be the remaking of the Morlacchi. Foucault describes an age that "discovered the body as object and target of power"; Boldù paid close attention to the bodies of the Morlacchi, their stature, elegance, robustness, and agility. "A body is docile that may be subjected, used, transformed, and improved," writes Foucault; for Boldù this was the formula for the civilizing metamorphosis of the Morlacchi.[84] The purpose of policy was to apply "good discipline" to "bad habits."

Fortis, in 1780, recommended the planting of chestnut trees in order to adapt economic policy to social customs, while Boldù proposed to target customs as the site of human susceptibility to a program of social transformation.

> Glancing over the notions of all the centuries, among the general causes of depravation and disorder two are notable, which more than any others have always influenced toward corruption, that is, inertia and the perversion of customs, and both occur in this province even to excess. The most essential laws are those that regard customs in detail (*in minuto*).[85]

The proposed regulation of customs "in detail" is again suggestive of Foucault's model of the "microphysics of power" in the age of Enlightenment. The two cited problems of inertia and the perversion of customs were, in fact, interrelated inasmuch as the constraints of custom were considered a cause of inertia. Gozzi too had noted the inertia of the Morlacchi, while Fortis had observed a corruption of customs, though not in the same sense as Boldù. Fortis, more or less admiring the primitive customs of the Morlacchi, regretted corruptive foreign influence, but Boldù, though he denounced the perversion of customs, had no intention of restoring them to their pristine primitivism. The modern metamorphosis that he envisioned was precisely what Fortis would have considered complete and total corruption. Boldù thus manipulated the discourse created by Fortis, inverting the value of ancient customs in order to condemn their perversion and promote their transformation.

Boldù noted a "deformed morality" among the Morlacchi, saw them as living "almost in the state of barbarians," and regretted that Dalmatia was in "universal disorder," but he saw none of these problems as beyond the ultimate efficacy of enlightened administrative reform. The first step, he thought, was to select several villages and "introduce there gradually good order and discipline," with the expectation of eventually extending the program to the entire province. He advised the Senate to take a long view of reform, "contemplating the duration of centuries."[86] Boldù, like all those who addressed themselves to the profound problems of Dalmatia, had no idea of how little time actually remained to Venice. He supplemented his relation with a comprehensive survey of the situation in Dalmatia, a "compendium," to serve as a point of departure for future planning, and he offered an unusually abrupt criticism of past administrations in Dalmatia.

> The Dalmatian nation was supposed to be only suited to war, and therefore, on this false basis, the peoples were almost abandoned to themselves. A legislation ill-adapted; a confused distribution of lands; no provisions for removing the causes of depopulation; no constitution to humanize the men with religion; no encouragement to agriculture; enormous tax burdens as needed, and distributed without equity, are causes that render the people unhappy and miserable.[87]

Boldù formulated this indictment as an agent of imperial authority, but his enumeration of the ways in which Venice had failed the "Dalmatian nation" over the course of the eighteenth century was consistent with the patriotic perspective of Dalmatians who sought to claim a place for themselves in public discussions concerning the future of the province.

From Gradenigo's arrival in Dalmatia in 1774, when Fortis's book was published in Venice, to Boldù's arrival in 1780, the year of Fortis's address in Split, the administration of Dalmatia had to face the challenges posed by the celebrated traveler when he put his own perspective on the province before the enlightened public. Gradenigo with his empirical inspections and his physiocratic calculations, Boldù with his comprehensive compendium and envisioned metamorphosis, responded to the philosophical challenges of Fortis, while wrestling with the ramifications of his special emphasis on the customs of the Morlacchi. These Provveditori Generali could not conduct their administrations within purely official channels, indifferent to the public interest aroused by the *Viaggio in Dalmazia*. The public sphere, however, as Habermas has conceived it, functioned as an arena for critical inquiry and divergent views, so Fortis, though his work inaugurated public discussion, could not thereafter monopolize public opinion. If his published concerns posed a public challenge to the Venetian administration, he himself was almost immediately challenged from rival perspectives within the public sphere. Gozzi's moral disapproval of the Morlacchi reflected a divergent Venetian view of the subject, while Lovrich's Dalmatian ambivalence about the Morlacchi was articulated in the context of his emphatic excoriation of Fortis. Lovrich's *Osservazioni* demonstrated the viability of putting a Dalmatian perspective before the Venetian public, while Fortis's lecture on chestnuts before the Economic Society of Split constituted the reciprocal presentation of a Venetian perspective before the Dalmatian public. By the time Boldù wrote his final relation in 1783, the year that England recognized by treaty America's independence, the Adriatic empire was being discussed, debated, criticized, challenged, justified, and vindicated before a newly constituted imperial public. The contours of that public included readers, writers, journals, and academies on both shores of the sea, while its controversies explored the imperial responsibilities as well as the provincial dissatisfactions that reinforced and undermined the political relation between Venice and Dalmatia.

CHAPTER SIX

The End of the Adriatic Empire: Epidemic, Economic, and Discursive Crises

Introduction: Professors and Prescriptions

"This epidemic inertia has not only extended its malignant influence over the Morlacchi, and over all those who form the rough and vulgar people," reported the Provveditore Generale, Paolo Boldù, in 1783, "but it has been communicated through a compendium of fatalities also among the most civilized persons who (excepting some individuals) are certainly in the same indolence, lovers of idleness and inaction." At a time when the educated elite in Dalmatia, meeting in the academies, was seeking to address the problems of the province, Boldù insisted on attributing the alleged faults of the Morlacchi to even "the most civilized" Dalmatians. The medical metaphor of "epidemic inertia" infecting the entire population was further elaborated as Boldù diagnosed a "disease (*malattia*) of inertia," one which was "very difficult to cure," because the correct prescription was not easy to discern.

> The principal difficulty is precisely that which the professors of medicine encounter in serious illnesses, that is, not always being able to reconcile the various wills and the many circumstances that have a part in a difficult cure, optimally represented as a machine of multiple parts in which, if all the means do not work, if a perfect harmony in their movements does not occur, it will never be able to succeed.[1]

There was not only a crisis of social and economic circumstances in Dalmatia, but also a crisis of discursive prescriptions as an increasing crowd of experts, Venetians and Dalmatians, variously advanced a concatenation of causes and cures. The bursting of the boundaries of the official administrative discourse on Dalmatia, and its abundant elaboration in the public sphere, rendered it much less possible for a single authority, the Provveditore Generale, to prescribe a cure without having to consider a profusion of second opinions.

In 1783 Boldù's framing of the problem in the medical language of infectious disease occurred in the context of growing concern about a real medical crisis in Dalmatia, the outbreak of plague that came across the Ottoman border from Bosnia. This was to be the central concern of his successor, Francesco Falier, who served from 1783 to 1786, and it temporarily displaced attention from all other programs of improvement in the province. The terrible toll of the plague of 1783 and 1784, especially in Split, but also in the inland areas around Sinj and Knin toward the Ottoman border, tested the limits of administrative discipline in Dalmatia, as life and death depended upon the maintenance of strict quarantines, which were not necessarily suited to the pastoral customs of the Morlacchi. The plague also became the occasion for Dalmatians to seize discursive control of an issue of deadly relevance to the province. Giulio Bajamonti, Pietro Nutrizio Grisogono, and Gregorio Stratico all promptly published books on the epidemic to place the catastrophe of Dalmatia before the public. Boldù's metaphorical diagnosis of "epidemic inertia" among the Morlacchi was even appropriated and reframed by Dalmatian commentators on the plague, who took the medical epidemic as an occasion for the diagnosis of fatal "inaction" on the part of the Venetian administration.

The 1780s and 1790s witnessed a new proliferation of professorial prescriptions for the ailments of the province, with the academies at Split, Zadar, and Trogir taking the lead in Dalmatia, and Andrea Memmo, the grand old man of the Venetian Enlightenment, dedicating his last political energies to composing a program of Dalmatian reform for the Venetian Senate. In the final crisis of the Venetian republic, facing Napoleon's armies in Italy, Venice's interest in Dalmatia focused once again on the issue that Goldoni had dramatized on the stage in *La Dalmatina*, the loyalty of the Slavs. In 1797, it was not Dalmatia looking to Venice for provincial redemption, but Venice seeking imperial salvation by summoning the Dalmatian troops. At the moment of the abolition of the Adriatic empire in 1797, Giulio Bajamonti published an essay in Venice on the "Morlacchismo" of Homer, attributing to the Morlacchi of Dalmatia the primitive virtues of Homeric heroes. This was Venetian Dalmatia's final statement, formulated by Fortis's old friend, addressed to those Venetians, like Boldù, who could only ascribe to the Morlacchi a character of inertia, indolence, idleness, and inaction.

Dalmatia and Bosnia: Epidemic Relations

Francesco Falier's very first shipboard dispatch, on the way to Dalmatia in September 1783, reported the presence of plague in the province, and the new Provveditore Generale declared himself ready for "whatever sacrifice." He was in Zadar at the beginning of October, but before the end of the month he had moved his headquarters to Split, which was to become the center of the epidemic. His dispatches described the military lines of quarantine, along the Ottoman border and between the endangered districts of Dalmatia, and identified the fundamental issue of "discipline" in preserving the integrity of those lines. By January, he was alarmed at the infractions against the quarantine, by "these incorrigible Morlacchi," who "give no regard to risking life with guilty concealments or with thefts." He reported the "insane audacity" of these "untamed peoples," and he declared "guilty transgressions" to be punishable by death. His only hope of containing the epidemic was "to instill in these undisciplined peoples the spirit of subjection."[2] This was an old complaint about the Morlacchi, which was made by the Provveditori Generali throughout the eighteenth century and which now, in the context of the plague, acquired a newly intense and imminently catastrophic significance.

The lesson that Falier claimed to have learned, by the time he finished his term in 1786, was that of Dalmatia's intimate geographical relation to Bosnia, mediated by the Morlacchi who lived and served along the border.

> In spite of every vigilance and remedy, whenever the plague is ignited in Bosnia, it will always be impossible to keep it from penetrating into Dalmatia, as much on account of the border places—which being nothing other than a series of the roughest mountains, of thick woods, of violent torrents, and of horrible precipices, are made rather difficult to guard—as on account of the character of the Morlacchi.[3]

It was their lack of discipline that made them unreliable guards in the militia along the Bosnian border. Falier's perspective on the Dalmatian mountainous landscape offered a new valuation, based not on its promise for economic or agricultural development, but rather on the rough irregularities that rendered impossible an effective quarantine. For Falier, it was the features of the landscape combined with the character of the inhabitants that determined the condition of the province.

Falier, though disheartened by his experience of the plague, remained all the more committed to addressing the social and economic problems of the Morlacchi in the context of the security of Dalmatia.

> The population is scant, and also little attached by nature to the cultivation of the land, or to any other sort of industry, without arts, and with a commerce of little account, barely capable of according a stunted sustenance, it suffers between languor and misery. That notwithstanding it merits the distinct predilection of Vostra Serenità, inasmuch as those subjects, full of loyalty toward the August Name, form the Adriatic littoral, and can be counted without doubt as the Antemurale of Italy, of liberty, and of state security.[4]

The horror of the plague, which reached to the Adriatic coast at Split, had offered Falier a vision of Dalmatia as a bulwark against Oriental infections that menaced even the civilization of Italy. If the line of quarantine could not be reliably held in the mountains of Dalmatia, it had to be maintained along the shores of the Adriatic. Medical infections were obviously most on his mind, but the Antemurale that Falier invoked also seemed to include unspecified spiritual insinuations that might threaten the liberty and security of Venice from the Oriental depths of Ottoman Bosnia. Falier's relation broached the subject of a new office of "bearer of gifts" to the pasha of Bosnia, the better to preserve his good will, and advocated attention to the fortresses at Knin and Sinj, "that front the Ottoman state and serve as a barrier to the maritime places."[5] In time of plague, Venice could not fail to appreciate the Morlacchi of Dalmatia in terms of geographical contiguities that went beyond the borders of the Adriatic empire: the immediate adjacency of Bosnia and the broader contextual significance of the Balkan peninsula.

Split was especially hard hit by the plague of 1783 and 1784, which was not only transmitted across the mountainous frontier with Bosnia, but also broke out within the lazaretto of Split, on the coast, where Ottoman caravans were routinely held in quarantine, before their merchandise was shipped across the Adriatic. The city lost some 1,300 lives, more than a third of the plague deaths in Dalmatia as a whole, estimated at 3,500.[6] Considering the importance of Split as a site for the plague, it was fitting that an account of the epidemic should come from one of the city's most prominent figures, Giulio (or Julije) Bajamonti, a medical doctor educated in Padua, a friend and traveling companion of Fortis, and a founder of the Split Economic Society. Bajamonti was also a musical composer of madrigals, motets, and masses, as well as a religious oratorio and a classical symphony. He shared Fortis's folkloric interests, applied his musicality to the transcription of Slavic songs, including the "Hasanaginica," and employed folk melodies in his symphony. Though he composed some church music, he also read the works of irreligious French philosophes and was rumored to be an atheist.[7] Bajamonti was, in short, a Dalmatian man of the Enlightenment. His history of the plague that reigned in Dalmatia, *Storia della peste che regnò in Dalmazia negli anni 1783-1784*, was published in Venice; it appeared in 1786, dedicated to two Venetian senators, in the same year as Falier's final relation to the Senate.

The publisher in Venice, Vincenzo Formaleoni, was himself in the process of compiling a four-volume encyclopedic investigation of the lands of the Republic, *Topografia veneta*, including a discussion of Dalmatia; it was natural for him to take an interest in an account of the plague from the other shore of the Adriatic. Bajamonti began by observing emphatically, as if it might be doubted, that the loss of population in Dalmatia to the plague was a loss to the Republic of Venice as a whole. He took his stand upon the physiocratic platform of population and prosperity, as hopefully heralded by Gradenigo in Dalmatia in the 1770s. A small state like Venice, Bajamonti thought, had all the more reason to count its population:

> Today it is all too evident that the abundance, the flourishing, and the vigor of a state no longer depend upon the vastness of its lands and its seas, but rather on the maximum number of its inhabitants; that the more densely numbered the nation, the more it has the arms to cultivate the products of necessity and arts of comfort . . . that, in sum, where subjects are scarce, everything inspires desolation, languor, and meanness. One no longer believes that social bodies have need from time to time of purging to alleviate themselves by replenishments . . . for healthy policy has found the way to render usefully industrious (*utilmente operosa*) even the most villainous rabble (*scellerata canaglia*).[8]

It might have seemed strangely superfluous to remind the public of Venice that an epidemic loss of lives in Dalmatia was something to be regretted, but Bajamonti's phrasing was clearly keyed to contemporary controversy over the economic "languor" of the province and the unindustrious character of its inhabitants. If he felt the need to argue against public complacency about the purging of the population, it was because he feared that even in the context of rising interest in Dalmatia, after Fortis, there remained some sentiment that its inhabitants were useless and therefore dispensable.

Bajamonti included in his book a map of Dalmatia, with an illustration of two cows, grazing together by the sea, and a ship in the background. In the foreground a young herdsman sat upon a rock, leaning on his staff, apparently fast asleep, as if to illustrate the inertial languor of the Dalmatians. For Bajamonti the character and customs of the Dalmatians, especially the Morlacchi, were fundamental for explaining the outbreak and transmission of the plague within the province. Echoing the contemporary epidemiological conclusion of Falier, Bajamonti regretted that "in spite of all these remedies and fortifications, it is almost impossible that, whenever the plague is ignited in Bosnia, it should not manage to leak (*trapelare*) into Dalmatia." This was partly because of the reticence of the Turks, refusing to alert their neighbors, but also largely to be attributed to the Morlacchi of the border region.

> Our Morlacchi, most alien to anticipating the evils of life with melancholy reflections and fearful warnings, and resolved to seize blindly at whatever minimal interest and present comfort, as long as they hear there is doubt about plague in the vicinity, they remain tranquil about crossing the border, and though barely fit for the most foolish and cheap commerce, they return to their own homes with stuff susceptible to contagion, and with no other concern than to evade the eye of official vigilance. These same Morlacchi, under the name of Panduri, form the body of the rustic militia and are employed to garrison the fortresses of the quarantine lines, together with however many soldiers of the regular national militia: all people who are little or not at all moved by the importance of the object that they are made to serve, and therefore easily inclined to assist in transgressions. Even if the character of these peoples were the most wide-awake (*svegliato*), and the most punctilious, it would still turn out too hard and uncertain to guard the borders, which are nothing other than a series of the roughest mountains, of thick woods, of violent torrents, and of horrible precipices, and always offer to the transgressor a thousand unobserved and unguardable transits and subterfuges.[9]

The verbatim resemblance to Falier's relation, concerning the border terrain, suggests an unusual discursive convergence between the public

FIGURE 13. "Carta Geografica della Dalmazia." From Giulio Bajamonti, *Storia della peste che regnò in Dalmazia,* his history of the plague in Dalmatia, published in Venice in 1786. The map showed the geography of Dalmatia in the 1780s, in the context of an epidemic crisis for which it was necessary to establish quarantine lines along the inland Bosnian border. The sleeping herdsman with his cattle illustrated contemporary concern about the economic inertia of Dalmatia and also perhaps Bajamonti's frustration with the failure to respond alertly to the menace of medical infection. *(By permission of Widener Library, Harvard University.)*

presentation by the Dalmatian doctor and the official version of the Venetian Provveditore Generale. Though *Storia della peste* was published in Venice in 1786, the dedication was dated March 1785 in Split, so it was presumably Falier, in his relation of November 1786, who borrowed the violent torrents and horrible precipices from Bajamonti's manuscript. In other words, the official accounts of the Provveditori Generali, which had held a virtual imperial monopoly on discussion of Dalmatia before Fortis's publication of 1774, were now in the 1780s open to the influences and formulations of Dalmatian writers addressing the issues of their own national condition and topographical terrain.

Bajamonti's hypothetical invocation of "the most wide-awake" Morlacchi seemed to allude by contrast to the sleeping herdsman on the border of the map, suggesting a scale of unenlightened languor. From their incapacity to anticipate future evils, to their foolish commerce and transgressive evasions, the Morlacchi appeared as dangerously unenlightened and undisciplined Dalmatians, suited by their character and customs to become the agents of fatal infectious transmission. "But those who most boldly despise the regards of public health, as well as the other sacred rights of peoples," wrote Bajamonti, "are the Haiduks or assassins, induced by desperation to become ferocious against their own kind." To invoke the fearsome reputation of the Haiduks was to conjure up for the public of Venice the whole legend of the ferocious Morlacchi, in their most transgressive aspect: "These wretched (*sciagurati*) heroes, having the courage to undertake such excursions even when the contagion caught fire in Bosnia, and at the cost of becoming themselves the first victims of the scourge, put the state at continual risk of becoming infected."[10] In Bajamonti's account all the familiar faults of the Morlacchi appeared newly alarming for making Dalmatia susceptible to the plague.

The plague compelled public awareness of the permeability of the border between Bosnia and Dalmatia. Falier's insistence on Dalmatia as the "Antemurale of Italy" was all the more urgent for the realization that the frontier between the Venetian and Ottoman empires was marked by constant, casual, and dangerous interchange. Bajamonti explained the social circumstances that created such danger:

> Not only do ours enter freely into Bosnia and return in spite of prohibitions to their homes; but the Bosnians as well—sure of dissimulation and a good reception on our side, or sure of the impossibility in which we find ourselves, on account of the local temperament, to oppose their clandestine passage—come among us whenever they are drawn by interest or whatever other motive. The mountaineers and the plebeians of Bosnia, especially the Christians, who are tolerated in notable quantity, can easily be confused with our Morlacchi. By gait, by voice, by face, by clothes; therefore they do not appear universally recognizable when, having arrived among us, they remain freely for as long as it pleases them. It is a most common thing for those same Bosnian operators who on one day enter in custody the lazaretto of Split, a

few days later to participate in our markets and roam around everywhere confused with the Morlacchi.[11]

Gradenigo, as Provveditore Generale in the previous decade, had recognized the ebb and flow of emigration among the Morlacchi as a regular demographic response to economic circumstances, but Bajamonti went further in appreciating that the Morlacchi of Dalmatia and the mountaineers of Bosnia seemingly constituted one sole population, virtually indistinguishable to the point that borders were rendered irrelevant. Bajamonti, like Lovrich, as an educated Dalmatian, regarded the Morlacchi as "ours," though distinct from "us," and that distinction was underlined in their resemblance to the Bosnians across the border—especially, though not exclusively, the Bosnian Christians. Bajamonti emphasized the anthropological aspects of resemblance on the frontier, and there was even an element of implicit theatrical masquerade in his account, as if the Bosnians purposefully assumed the gait, the voice, the face, and the clothes of the Dalmatian Morlacchi, who reciprocally assisted the deception by their own "dissimulation." Such confusion was singularly sinister in a time of plague, subverting the effectiveness of the quarantine, but the noted resemblance was also more generally provocative inasmuch as it called into question the fundamental political affiliations of the Morlacchi of Dalmatia.

Pietro Nutrizio Grisogono, from Trogir, also composed an account of the plague, *Sopra il morbo pestilenziale insorto nella Dalmazia Veneta l'anno 1783*. He too emphasized the Balkan significance of Venetian Dalmatia, as construed from its adjacency and resemblance to Ottoman Bosnia. Though Bajamonti had no doubt that the plague was strictly infectious and came to Dalmatia from Bosnia, Grisogono proposed an alternative epidemiology by which the plague might have arisen independently in both Bosnia and Dalmatia, due to the similarities between the two provinces. He wondered whether poverty, poor nutrition, and unsanitary conditions were sufficient reasons to account for the outbreak of plague in either province without a necessary vector of infection across the border:

> Bosnia and Dalmatia can be considered under the same degree of latitude. The lands of the one and the other are of the same character. One notes the uniformity of climate, as well as of life, complexion, color, and figure of the respective inhabitants, for size and form depend upon climate's influence. The nature of the Bosnians is similar to that of the Morlacchi, and so their customs are also similar, if religion is excepted, and the different maxims it

prescribes. Therefore if in Bosnia the pestilential disease sometimes has developed by itself, evidently there is a climate suited to producing it, altogether notably different from that of Asia; and for the same reason it can be generated by itself also in Dalmatia.[12]

While Grisogono, a Dalmatian lawyer not a doctor, was medically mistaken in doubting the significance of infection for the dissemination of the plague, he argued from the plausible premise of the geographical and ethnographical resemblances of Bosnia and Dalmatia. Reasoning from the miserable social conditions of Dalmatia and the primitive customs of the Morlacchi, he undermined the Venetian conception of an Antemurale by arguing that plague was not necessarily an alien Oriental intrusion but might just as well have incubated within the Adriatic empire. Both Bajamonti and Grisogono, as Dalmatians contemplating the catastrophe of the plague epidemic, came to recognize that their native province of Venetian Dalmatia and its inhabitants could not be considered in isolation—in conceptual quarantine—from the context of neighboring lands and peoples, beyond the dominion of San Marco.

Medical and Imperial Responsibility

"Plague is an evil that rightly induces fear," wrote Bajamonti, "and fear leads to superstition." As a man of modern science he was outraged when the superstitious attribution of the plague to divine intervention obstructed the implementation of medical measures. In this regard too he saw striking resemblances across the border between Bosnia and Dalmatia.

> The fatalism of the Turks concerning the plague is founded on the conviction that it was sent expressly by God, and that man should not and can not get out of its way; and our Morlacchi, no less fatalist than the Mohammedans, whenever they are interrogated as to whether they know how they were infected, reply that it occurred only by the will of God; and they never think of having contracted the infection by stealing, as they do, contaminated goods, or dealing in some other way with infected persons or places. And besides the stupid mountaineers, there are also in the province among the townspeople those who, to cut off any investigation into the introduction of the contagion, attribute its cause to the direct and immediate divine will . . . and go to sleep indolently (*addormentarsi indolentemente*) in the face of evils that threaten their country and the state, with the pretext of not being able to resist divine dispositions.[13]

Superstitious fatalism marked the convergence of character between Moslems and Morlacchi, witnessed from the scientific perspective of an enlightened Dalmatian in a moment of medical crisis. In fact the accusation of fatal indolence in the face of the plague perfectly fit the conventional vocabulary of the Venetian view of the Morlacchi. The charge of falling asleep when danger threatened also matched the image on the map of the sleeping herdsman. In further disparagement of religious fatalism, Bajamonti attributed the same spirit of useless resignation to the Jews, who formed a presence in both the Venetian and Ottoman empires.[14] The medical problem posed by the customs and character of the Morlacchi in time of plague was thus framed, according to the values of Voltaire, within an enlightened denunciation of superstition in all its religious forms.

Bajamonti regretted that it took too long to recognize in Dalmatia that there was plague in neighboring Bosnia, and he included in his book notices from the network of informants along the frontier. Greek Orthodox monks in Bosnia composed a letter to the authorities on the Dalmatian border to let them know that there was plague in Sarajevo in 1782. A doctor in Sarajevo wrote to a surgeon in Zadar that Moslems, Christian, and Jews were dying in the Bosnian city. Antonio Surich of the Dalmatian militia at Sinj had reports of plague across the border in Bosnia; Pietro Covacevich in Mostar wrote to inform the Dalmatian authorities that there was plague all over Bosnia, but not yet in Hercegovina. A letter from the monk Angelo Glavas in Bosnia, to the vicar of a monastery in Dalmatia, urgently reported: "Regarding the plague, brother, definitely believe me; I am not mistaken about the plague, as you know me, brother, certainly. . . . In Sarajevo itself some say that there are eight thousand dead, others say fifteen thousand: this I can not definitely tell."[15] Bajamonti's point was that there was enough firm information to have warranted a faster response in Dalmatia and a more unequivocal verdict in medical opinion. Though he claimed to have been thoroughly convinced himself that the problem in Bosnia was plague, other doctors in Dalmatia were more hesitant to take a definitive stand during the course of 1782. That was a year of famine in Dalmatia, when some of the Morlacchi emigrated into Bosnia, following the "vagabond inclination of their Scythian race," instead of awaiting the "unfailing charity and munificence of their own sovereign." Then, as rumors of the epidemic reached them in Bosnia, "the fear of disease was one more strong motive determining the expatriates to return," and "this return exposed the state to the most serious danger of infection."[16] Thus, even as reports of the plague were coming over the border in military, medical, and monastic correspondence, the plague itself was also crossing into Dalmatia with the returning Morlacchi, whose irregular emigrations had already troubled the Venetian administration for decades as a demographic disorder.

Boldù did order a quarantine line at the border with Bosnia during the summer of 1782, but then, when a medical commission delivered an inconclusive report, the order was withdrawn. Bajamonti was obviously more comfortable blaming the doctors (excluding himself) than doubting the wisdom of the Provveditore Generale. Though Bajamonti enumerated the various plausible excuses for inaction, there was no way around the conclusion, with the benefit of hindsight, that the provincial administration responded too slowly. It finally faced the seriousness of the crisis when Falier came to Dalmatia to replace Boldù in the fall of 1783, and promptly established himself in Split instead of Zadar, in order to supervise personally the management of the epidemic.

The Venetian Senator Angelo Diedo was also sent to Dalmatia on a special mission to deal with the plague, and, according to Grisogono, "as the little wandering clouds flee and dissipate at the appearance of the sun, so at the arrival of this cavalier the plague seemed dispelled."[17] In other words, by the time Diedo arrived, the plague was over; he would return to Dalmatia at the end of the decade as Provveditore Generale. Bajamonti further celebrated Paolo Emilio Canal, the Venetian commander who took charge of public health in the border region around Sinj. The Dalmatians, "recognizing in Canal a liberator, a defender, a father, a deity (*nume*), paid him tribute with ingenuous transport and the most passionate signs of gratitude and veneration." They presented him with a medal, which Bajamonti copied as an illustration in his book, noting that Canal's name, "engraved in indelible characters in the hearts of those people will have there eternally a glorious and tender cult." Bajamonti, as a composer, produced many religious pieces, including masses, requiems, a Miserere, and a Te Deum; his book on the plague suggested aspects of Miserere and Te Deum, conceived in enlightened literary form.[18] His effusive account of the Dalmatians' grateful devotion to their Venetian "deity" refurbished the formulas of loyalty in the aftermath of disaster. It was now a "civilized" Dalmatian who spoke for the "ingenuous transport" of the general population, addressing the public of Venice, promising eternal veneration of an Adriatic empire that was soon to be eternally dissolved.

Falier, in his relation of 1786, urged the importance of the Adriatic empire in designating Dalmatia as "the Antemurale of Italy, of liberty, and of state security." Bajamonti's account of the plague in 1786 also emphasized the importance of Dalmatia as Antemurale, as a bulwark of public health, separating Italy from the epidemics of the Ottoman empire. Smuggling goods across the border from Bosnia into Dalmatia, without waiting the proper period of quarantine in the lazaretto of Split, "could not only become fatal to the province, but could also carry danger into the bosom of the *Dominante*." Such goods were all too likely to end up as "the cargo of ships going to Venice." The restless Morlacchi, moving around without regard to public health, were a menace to the whole Venetian republic, "which by a generous stroke of public confidence in the nation does not ordinarily hold itself in reserve with respect to this province." Dalmatia could be the defensive bulwark of Venice, but could also, by virtue of its position, become a conduit for foreign infections.

> Dalmatia, in spite of its mingling and contiguity with the Ottomans, and in spite of the frequency with which it becomes contaminated, to the serious harm of the state, except in the most suspect circumstances enjoys the privilege of free dealing with the other lands of the Venetian dominion. The sovereign clement purposes toward this province are too ill repaid by what occurs; and too serious are the violations by which the devastating pestilences of the province originate.[19]

Bajamonti wrestled with the difficult question of reciprocal interests between Dalmatia and Venice, arguing that the province owed greater regard to the beneficent metropolis; at the same time, he clearly implied that the Venetians were too intimately involved with the trans-Adriatic Dalmatians to risk disregarding the challenges of imperial responsibility. "May heaven keep the pestilential scourge always far from the civilized nations," wrote Bajamonti, on the last page of his book.[20] Writing about the plague in Dalmatia for the public of Venice, he indicated to his readers that the risk of infection corresponded to the imbalance of civilization within the Adriatic empire.

Andrea Memmo Immersed in Dalmatia

The final decade of the history of Venice began in 1790 with the most important political figure of the Venetian Enlightenment, Andrea Memmo, dedicating the last efforts of his long career to a senatorial study of Dalmatia. Educated by the enlightened Franciscan Carlo Lodoli, Memmo as a young man in the 1750s was the friend of Casanova and the lover of Giustiniana Wynne, while receiving the dedication of a drama from Goldoni. In the early 1770s Memmo commissioned Fortis to put his Dalmatian investigations at the service of the Senate, where Memmo led a special deputation for the economic reform of the corporate restrictions on industry. Through the 1770s and 1780s he served as the Provveditore of Padua, the Venetian ambassador in Constantinople, the ambassador to the Vatican, and the Provveditore of San Marco; he was almost elected doge in 1789, the very last election before the abolition of the Republic. It was thus with tremendous political and international experience—and connections to every significant figure of the Venetian Enlightenment who had ever contemplated Dalmatia—that Memmo at sixty, defeated in his dogal campaign, fixed his attentions upon the opposite shore of the Adriatic. "I have begun to immerse myself in the great Dalmatian chaos," wrote Memmo in 1790 to a Dalmatian correspondent in Zadar, Gregorio (or Grgur) Stratico, who supplied him with reports about the province. Fortis had enjoyed Stratico's company in Zadar, twenty years earlier, and praised him in print as "most civilized" (*coltissimo*).[21] In 1790 Memmo had only three years to live, and his death in 1793 was soon followed by the expiration of Venice in 1797, but his last enlightened engagement for the reform of the Republic was dedicated to ordering the chaos of Dalmatia.

The early 1770s, when Memmo's deputation took an interest in Dalmatia, was the period of Venice's delicate neutrality in the Russian-Ottoman war; two decades later Memmo's interest also coincided with Venetian neutrality in another Russian-Ottoman war. At the beginning of that war, in 1787, the Inquisitors of State in Venice received reports from Dalmatia about "suspect individuals" in Russian service, like a certain Zuanne Voinovich; Orthodox monks were also being monitored, under suspicion of allegiances to Russia. Still concerned in 1790, the Inquisitors learned about a certain Marco Julich, enrolled in the Russian army, and worried about the foreign recruitment of more Dalmatians by another "presumed seducer."[22] In 1790, as in 1770, the international complications of a Russian-Ottoman war, menacing the stablility of Venetian Dalmatia, made the administrative and economic reform of the province appear all the more urgent in Venice.

Memmo immersed himself in the archive of official relations and dispatches composed by the Provveditori Generali during the course of the century, "which we have attentively read." It was not one of the many offices that Memmo had held himself, but his perusal of the relations took him back through the chronology of his own political career, dating even as far back as the year of his birth in 1729, when Pietro Vendramin organized Venice's military establishment in Dalmatia. Memmo followed the official reports of the inquisitorial team dispatched after Foscarini's speech in 1747, the relations of Gradenigo in 1777 ("after having visited the whole province with his supreme and well-known diligence"), of Boldù in 1783 ("the most detailed relation, containing the most opportune lights as well as wise advice"), and, most recently, of Angelo Memmo, a member of his own patrician family, who served as Provveditore Generale from 1786 to 1789. Andrea Memmo in 1790 headed his own team of inquisitors, "Inquisitorato ai Pubblici Rolli," commissioned to investigate Dalmatian affairs. Though ten years before he was serving in Constantinople, by 1790 he was already ailing and undertook his study of Dalmatia without any intention of seeing everything for himself; he relied on the official relations of those who had served there in the past and reports from Dalmatian correspondents, like Gregorio Stratico in Zadar. Memmo's archival immersion in the records of the Provveditori Generali made him almost a modern historian of Venetian Dalmatia, coming away from his reading with an impression of the province's obdurate resistance to reform and improvement. To read the historical progression of official relations in the eighteenth century was to recognize that "they detect continually the same evils that predominated before."[23] After studying half a century of efforts at enlightened reform, his own half century of the Venetian Enlightenment, Memmo concluded that nothing was changing in Dalmatia.

"As the care of subjects is committed by God to respective sovereigns," reflected Memmo in his report to the Senate, "the regulation of custom must depend upon their vigilance and wise provisions." Immersed as he was in the relations of the Provveditori Generali, he could hardly help commenting on the "natural ferocity" of those subjects, but, writing twenty years after Fortis first crossed the Adriatic in 1770, Memmo almost automatically identified "custom" as the crucial factor for reform in Dalmatia. He manifested, however, no anthropological reverence for custom as the conduit of venerable tradition; custom was rather the accessible arena in which an enlightened sovereign state was to exercise its social and economic interventions. Fortis had described how custom was elaborated in detail within a primitive community; Memmo argued that it had to be regulated in detail within a modern state. He was optimistic about the prospects for "happy metamorphoses" and cited the history of the Dalmatian islands, where refugees from the mainland had come "to find just the same asylum that our first fathers found in these fortunate lagoons." There on the islands, the Dalmatians "sweetened custom little by little," thus recapitulating the civilizing process that had achieved its sweetest manifestation of refinement in the lagoons of Venice. Such insular examples were essential to Memmo's argument, as "proof in fact that even the peoples of Dalmatia are susceptible to changing character and customs."[24] Though Memmo certainly read *Viaggio in Dalmazia* in the 1770s and probably read *Les Morlaques* when it was published in 1788, his approach to reform in Dalmatia was uninfluenced by Rousseauist sentiment for the preservation of primitive customs.

He remained in friendly contact with Giustiniana Wynne in the 1780s, long after their passionate love affair of the 1750s; it could not have ended in marriage on account of his exalted patrician status but did result in an illegitimate child, born and abandoned in Paris, perhaps altogether unknown to the father. In 1787 she published a little fable about love, and dedicated it to Memmo, on the occasion of his legitimate daughter's marriage.[25] The appearance of *Les Morlaques* in 1788, followed by Memmo's report to the Senate on Dalmatia in 1790, indicated a convergence of trans-Adriatic interests in the two former lovers during the last years of their lives, but in their attitudes toward primitive customs they demonstrated radically opposed perspectives.

Memmo accepted the responsibility of the state for subjects committed to its care by God, but he also blamed some of the problems of Dalmatia on the inadequacy of parish priests. "Themselves full of ignorance and the most miserable popular superstitions, they do not instill in individuals that reverence which is so necessary toward priests," commented Memmo, "that they might be better able to insinuate the solid principles of our holy religion and of true Christian morality." The survival of the vendetta, for instance, might be attributed to the failure of Christian education: "Those subjects, believing themselves (even without malice) to be largely independent, not fearing either divine or human punishments, may be vindictive in excess, to the last drop of blood, pardoning neither old people, women, or children." Memmo's conception of custom was sufficiently anthropological for him to accept that the Morlacchi practiced bloody vengeance without malice, and his view of moral education sufficiently functional to envision it as an instrument for the reform of custom. Such moral modification was, in fact, the precondition for a more important social and economic metamorphosis. This was the lesson of the archival accounts about the inhabitants, thought Memmo, "concluding with the Provveditori Generali that unless they become civilized (*si civilizzino*) . . . one will never achieve the great object." Memmo, by 1790, could comfortably translate into Italian the new English and French senses of the verb that pointed toward the enlightened ideal of "civilization": civilize, *civiliser, civilizzare*.[26] Yet, in the pragmatically minded Venetian Enlightenment, it was possible to see the civilizing of the Dalmatians as a merely preliminary modification of customs, delegated to the clergy, for the purpose of achieving a greater object of state in economy and administration.

At the same time, consistent with Venice's longstanding insistence on state prerogatives in church affairs, Memmo did not hesitate to recommend intervention in "the essential subject of religious education, relative to the Latin church as well as the Greek Serbian, of which there are more than 40,000 subjects."[27] In Memmo's ecumenical mind those churches, in spite of their religious divergence, could provide the same instruction toward the reform of custom in the service of the state. He proposed not only that a less ignorant clergy should provide basic elementary education "in the Illyrian idiom," but also "that parish priests should be obliged to explain with patience, and by the best instructions, an agricultural catechism." Since the 1740s, Dalmatian churchmen, like Matteo Karaman and Matteo Sović, had encouraged Slavic religious publications; in 1768, for instance, there appeared in Venice a Slavic-language religious catechism ("prineseno v jesik slovinski"), translated on the island of Korčula for use among the Dalmatians. In 1790 Rados Michieli-Vitturi, secretary of the Economic Society of Split, became state inspector for agriculture in Dalmatia, responsible also for commissioning an agricultural catechism, as proposed by Memmo in his report to the

Senate.[28] Memmo himself credited his own education to Lodoli, an enlightened priest, and had no hesitation about entrusting the civilizing instruction of the Dalmatians to the church, as long as the quality of the clergy could be supervised and improved by the state.

As for the greater object, it could not remain altogether in abeyance, pending the reform of custom through the long-term effects of educational catechism. Memmo proposed beginning immediately upon "the regulation of one sole territory or county, almost in an experimental way, which if it had a happy outcome, could serve as the simplest norm for the rest."[29] The empirical observations of the previous decades were now to form the basis of scientific experimentation upon an administrative sample of Dalmatia, the county of Zadar, the region around the center of the provincial government. The idea of establishing a model district for experimental reform was not unprecedented in the Enlightenment's approach to Eastern Europe; Diderot in the 1770s, returning from Russia, thought that it would be impossible "to civilize all at once such an enormous country," that Catherine should begin with a single district "to execute a plan of civilization."[30] Dalmatia, of course, was very small in comparison to the enormity of Russia, but, since the Venetians over the course of the century had failed to reform the whole, Memmo proposed to experiment upon a part.

Memmo envisioned the landscape of Dalmatia as desperately in need of some sort of civilizing intervention: "These peoples in greater number are inhabitants not of houses or huts, but dens (*spelonche*), and dwellings in the woods and crags, worse than those of wild beasts, and such as to cause horror at seeing them several miles distant from one another."[31] Far from Wynne's infatuated fantasy of the home of Pervan in idyllic Dizmo, Memmo played upon an almost Gothic sense of horror at the imagined isolation of these remote and atrocious residences. In fact, it was the distance from den to den that Memmo most wanted to emphasize since the central principle of his model territory was to be the consolidation of dwellings into model villages in the interest of administrative and economic rationalization. As far back as 1751 the mid-century inquisitors in Dalmatia had recommended that something be done "to give a methodical form to the village, where houses are dispersed widely distant one from another." Memmo knew this was not a "new idea" in 1790; the reports of past Provveditori Generali indicated an interest in "inviting the Morlacchi to descend from their burrows (*tane*)."

Now was the time to push for the relocation of those dens or burrows, in which Memmo took a detailed structural interest: "The habitations with their annexes are not for the most part built with solid walls or roofs, but only little enclosures of stones, without any cement, placed one upon another, with covers of tree branches and marsh grasses at barely the height of a man, in such a fashion that every Morlacco is the architect and builder of his own house."[32] There was therefore little reason to be sentimental about consolidating villages, if it merely meant persuading or pressuring the Morlacchi to abandon such simply and crudely constructed homes. In 1786 Memmo had brought out his most serious published contribution to the Venetian Enlightenment, *Elementi dell'architettura lodoliana,* in which he presented Lodoli's functional principles of architectural criticism. It was natural for Memmo in 1790 to consider principles of architecture as an index of civilization and to emphasize the backwardness of the Morlacchi according to the primitive construction of their houses.

The envisioned model district consisted of model villages, with new houses for the relocated Morlacchi, "as well as sufficient space for the church, the piazza," and even residences for the newly improved priests. Fortis at Split had invited his audience to imagine Dalmatia covered with chestnut trees, so that "instead of causing horror to voyagers, those wild regions awaken in them an agreeable surprise," an embellished landscape with the picturesque appeal of Italy. Memmo had in mind the same Italian standard of comparison when he imagined model villages, each with its church and piazza. This formula, he supposed, would appear so perfectly plausible to the Venetian senators, that they should be cautioned not to expect too much too soon, as they pictured Dalmatia in the mind's eye:

> Certainly the new villages will not at the beginning achieve a beautiful appearance, like those of Italy, because for the most part too rustically composed; but that being the work of time, and the clement official dispositions, for now one must not aim at any other object than to render these subjects more reasonable in a more concentrated society.[33]

These Dalmatians would no longer live in isolated dens like wild beasts. The model villages, though they might not immediately resemble the Italian ideal, would not only rationalize administration and economy in Dalmatia, but also, through the civilizing effect of society, make their inhabitants more rational as well.

Dalmatian Academicians

The model villages of the model district were to be located in convenient communication with one another, as well as the administrative center, lest they suffer the frightful effects of remote isolation. Memmo proposed a project of improvement for the roads of the district and nominated a Dalmatian engineer to supervise the work:

> This official is Captain Francesco Zavoreo, native of that province . . . who combines with the appropriate expertise a practical knowledge almost foot by foot of the roads of the county of Zara (which would be the first to be undertaken), and who has been suggested to us by several respectable subjects who have had the opportunity to test his distinct ability and precision.[34]

Francesco (or Frane) Zavoreo was from Šibenik and had just published in Venice in 1787 a topographical map of Dalmatia, which testified to his detailed knowledge of the province. Memmo's recommendation of Zavoreo indicated a general appreciation of such empirical knowledge and also the new importance of the Dalmatians themselves as experts on their own province, supplying pertinent information to the public of Venice as well as to the Venetian state.

Memmo prepared his report in correspondence with Gregorio Stratico in Zadar, who supplied a copy of a lecture he had delivered at the Economic Society of Split in 1783. "I read it immediately," wrote Memmo to Stratico in 1790, "and all the more willingly for I found in it those precise lights that are lacking in the relations of the Provveditori Generali." There could hardly have been a clearer statement of the new importance of Dalmatian perspectives on Dalmatia than Memmo's readiness to concede that they complemented, if not surpassed, the offical accounts of the Venetian administration. Memmo further cited Giandomenico (or Ivan Dominik) Stratico, the bishop of Hvar, "who has published various economic and agrarian pamphlets this year in Venice, which in order to be easily understood in the country in which they were composed, would merit being translated into Illyrian, and sent in intelligible characters into the interior of that country."[35] Memmo, preparing an official report for the Senate, was well aware that prominent Dalmatians were making their own cases concerning the province before the public of Venice.

After remarking on the inefficacy of the Grimani agricultural reform of 1755, Memmo further noted that there had been no recent ameliorations in spite of "all the agrarian academies established on the coasts for the cultivation of the land, and for the revival of pastoralism as well as fishing."[36] If Memmo needed to remind the Senate that the Dalmatian academies alone were not able to bring about the reform of the provincial economy, it was precisely because those academies had recently risen to a new level of prominence, bidding to dominate the public discourse in Venice as well as in Dalmatia. In 1768 the Senate had authorized the institution of economic societies or agricultural academies throughout the Republic, for the diffusion of modern agronomical notions and methods; the intellectual impetus came from the University of Padua where the brothers Giovanni and Pietro Arduino formulated and advocated such a system from their respective chairs of geology and agrarian science. During the following decades sixteen academies were created, including three in Dalmatia, at Split, Zadar, and Trogir.[37] Though sponsored by the state, and partly subsidized, these academies functioned as institutions of the public sphere within their own cities, while also participating through their publications in the enlightened culture of metropolitan Venice.

Franco Venturi, in the final volume of his *Settecento riformatore*, has presented the Dalmatian academies as important manifestations of the Venetian Enlightenment. While Zadar was always the center of Venice's administration, the residence of the Provveditore Generale, the public spirit of Dalmatian academic life first developed at some distance in Split. Already in 1767 an agricultural academy was established there; it received the Senate's official sponsorship in 1771, was named the Economic Society in 1774, and welcomed Fortis back to Dalmatia in 1780 for his speech on chestnuts. The founder of the Split academy was Giovanni Moller, who encouraged the planting of potatoes in Dalmatia; Giulio Bajamonti gave the society its economic program in his address of 1774, which was then published in Venice in the *Giornale d'Italia* as "Prospetto di studi economici per la Dalmazia." Fortis further publicized the society in *Viaggio in Dalmazia:* "It is to be hoped that such a noble and praiseworthy foundation will not be dissolved inopportunely. The province has too great a need for Georgic studies to gain a footing, since the cultivation of the earth as well as the management of animals is very poorly understood by the Morlacchi and the littoral peasants." Edward Gibbon, writing about Diocletian's palace at Split in the *Decline and Fall of the Roman Empire,* cited Fortis in a footnote to spread the news "that a taste for agriculture is reviving at Spalatro" under the auspices of "a society of gentlemen." In 1775 the *Giornale d'Italia* reported that in Split "the zeal of the academy is notably electrifying the entire nation." In 1790, while Memmo was reviewing Venice's record in Dalmatia, Bajamonti could already look back on several decades of academic life in Split, and he addressed the Economic Society on its own history, then published in the *Nuovo giornale d'Italia* as "Dell'origine e dei progressi della pubblica Società economica di Spalato." He recalled how "our society began to make itself not unfavorably known in civilized Europe," and was even in 1776 "honorably mentioned by the celebrated signor Gibbon in his learned work on the causes of the decline of the Roman empire."[38] When Fortis focused the international attention of the Enlightenment on Dalmatia, the academy at Split was already nourishing a Dalmatian discourse to share the limelight.

The later establishment of the academies at Zadar in 1787 and Trogir in 1788 belonged to the final decade of the Adriatic empire, and their early efforts coincided with Memmo's inquisitorial study of Dalmatia. Indeed, it was Rados Michieli-Vitturi, the secretary of the Split society and the founding president of the Trogir academy, who received Memmo's commission for an agricultural catechism as well as the state appointment of inspector general for agricultural affairs in the province. Michieli-Vitturi published in Venice in 1788 a proposal for the cultivation of olives in Dalmatia, in the same spirit as Fortis seeking the salvation of the province in chestnuts. Giovanni Luca (or Ivan Luka) Garagnin gave an inaugural address at the academy of Trogir in 1789, urging every Dalmatian to consider the value of olives: "Even you, worthy priests, who with such ardor have come together in this gathering, you shall achieve glory by employing your sacred hands in the cultivation of olives." Like Memmo, Garagnin, the nephew of the bishop of Split, envisioned a prominent agricultural role for the clergy. In 1792 Giovanni (or Ivan) Banovaz addressed the Zadar academy as the advocate of a different crop, urging the cultivation of grapes for wine in Dalmatia. His proposals for "practical methods and means that ought to be used in this province to make good wines" was also published in the *Nuovo giornale d'Italia*.[39] Thus, the Dalmatian academies were not only supported by the Venetian state, but they presented their prescriptions for Dalmatia to the Venetian public.

Michieli-Vitturi, in addition to his prominent positions in the academies of Split and Trogir, boasted correspondent affiliations with the academies in Bergamo, Brescia, Conegliano, Udine, Verona, and Vicenza, and was therefore well-placed to appreciate the ways in which the academic network constituted a trans-Adriatic public sphere. In an article published in the *Nuovo giornale d'Italia* in 1790, he insisted on the importance of public criticism "in an enlightened century" within the Republic: "Under a wise and enlightened prince it is not a crime to make manifest the evils of which the abuse, the inconvenient application, and the disorder of some laws are the unhappy cause." Michieli-Vitturi faulted the Grimani law for not functioning strongly enough to counter the customs of ordinary Dalmatians, "rough, superstitious, unsociable, and without education." He thought the province needed to be transformed by a "happy revolution" like that of Peter the Great in Russia.[40]

In 1788 Leonardo Crussevich, addressing the Economic Society at Split, also betrayed a Petrine perspective on reform, when he regretted that "gentle Venetian dominion" was too inclined to preserve the "ancient uses and customs" of Dalmatia. Indeed for such reformers the primitive customs of the Morlacchi, as described by Fortis in 1774, were simply evidence of Venice's failure to transform the population of the province according to the standards of modern economy and society. In 1789 Luca Chialetich, one of the "worthy priests" who belonged to the academy of Trogir, noted the evident gap between educated Dalmatians like himself and the general population of the province, "where civilized persons speak one language and the people another, as the former discourse in Italian and the latter in the maternal Illyrian language." The Italian language played a leading role in the Dalmatian academies, and it was especially important for presenting their views before the Venetian public in Italian journals, but agricultural projects had to be ultimately aimed at the population of the province. Chialetich reflected that "to instruct then the common people in the practices of well-adapated cultivation, seeking that they should abandon the ancient inherited prejudices, is the highest good for every nation and especially for Dalmatia."[41] Like Memmo in Venice, the contemporary academicians in Dalmatia looked to education for the ultimate transformation of custom.

Memmo's report alluded to Giandomenico Stratico, the bishop of Hvar, "who has published various economic agrarian pamphlets this year in Venice," and, in fact, the publication of Stratico's *Opuscoli economico-agrari* in 1790 reflected the new importance of Dalmatian perspectives, challenging the imperial expertise of the Venetian Enlightenment. Born in Zadar in 1732, just three years after Memmo was born in Venice,

Stratico received his ecclesiastical education in Rome, before proceeding to professorships of theology in Florence, Siena, and Pisa. His experience as a churchman in the enlightened Tuscany of the Grand Duke Leopold remained an important influence when he came home to Dalmatia in 1786 as bishop of the island city of Hvar, known as Lesina in Italian. Giulio Bajamonti was also working at Hvar in the 1780s, and the generally anticlerical doctor issued a manifesto of enlightened Dalmatian solidarity in his welcoming address to the bishop, which was then published in Padua. Bajamonti refused to accept that it was inappropriate for an enlightened "man of the century" like himself to celebrate a bishop like Stratico: "I consider him principally a philosopher bishop, a citizen bishop, a bishop of the society, which is as much as to say, of nature." This enlightened conception of the episcopacy was accompanied by an appeal for Josephine reforms on Hvar. Bajamonti called upon Stratico, in the name of medical hygiene, to remove cemeteries from the churches in the city center and to curtail the ringing of church bells, indeed to replace them with useful lightning conductors. "Thus at last we cease to be barbarians," exclaimed Bajamonti. "The time of lights (*lumi*) has come. Stratico is at Lesina. Let us profit for once from the felicitous courage of the century."[42] This was a neat summation of what the Enlightenment meant to educated Dalmatians, the reform of barbarism, and an escape from the stigma of barbarism, as perceived from the Venetian or Paduan perspectives. Bajamonti's book on the plague, also published in 1786, hailed the Venetian commander Canal as "a liberator, a defender, a father, a deity." The welcoming address to Stratico, however, apotheosized a luminously enlightened Dalmatian.

"Most Illustrious and Reverend Monsignore," declared Bajamonti, "you shall promote the mother arts of agriculture and fishing."[43] These were, in fact, Stratico's own social and economic concerns. He came to Hvar in time to participate in the founding of the Trogir academy in 1788, and his addresses to the academy were regularly published in the *Nuovo giornale d'Italia*. At Trogir he upheld Tuscan standards of agricultural reform, based on his own experience, and he regretted in 1789 that Fortis's project for planting chestnut trees in Dalmatia remained unfulfilled. In that year Stratico declared his refusal to accept as impossible to achieve in Dalmatia all that "which is most easy in every corner of neighboring Italy, almost as if it were another sky, other elements, and another nature." In an address to the Trogir academy, also in 1789, he

conceded and calculated the degree of backwardness: "Dalmatian agriculture is one century behind that of Italy." He insisted, however, on
considering Tuscan strategies to make up the difference, arguing, as
Memmo did, that the clergy had to play a prominent educational role.
He cited priests in Tuscany who were willing and able "to explain in
church, after the catechism, how to cultivate new plants," such as the po-
tato. The idea of an agricultural catechism was obviously plausible to
him, but Stratico also proposed the composition of agricultural poetry
for the Dalmatians. In view of their famous affinity for poetry, which
Fortis had noted among the Morlacchi and brought to international attention, Stratico wondered if agricultural precepts could be made into
"beautiful Illyrian songs."[44] Just as Giustiniana Wynne embroidered
upon the South Slavic folkloric tradition by inventing French songs for
her Morlacchi characters to sing, so Stratico proposed to extend that tradition artificially by the invention of pseudo-folkloric Slavic poetry on
agronomical subjects, poems about chestnuts, olives, grapes, or potatoes.

Chialetich observed in 1789 that agricultural reform depended
upon the education of the common people, who were further removed
from educated Dalmatians by the linguistic gulf between literary Italian and "the maternal Illyrian language." Stratico was sympathetic to
this concern and even published in Venice in 1790 a trilingual collection of his religious writings in Latin, Italian, and Illyrian. He was full
of appreciative enthusiasm for "the most beautiful Illyrian language,
which is the most extended in Europe," but he himself, with his Italian education and ecclesiastical career, was an enlightened Dalmatian
who required, as Memmo suggested, translation into Illyrian. His
great literary project at Hvar was to try to translate *Les Morlaques* from
French into Italian, certainly not to create an Illyrian version.[45] Indeed
his fascination with the novel suggests that he himself, an educated
Dalmatian, was somewhat susceptible to the sentimental exoticism of
the Morlacchi, as conceived according to the foreign imagination of
Giustiniana Wynne.

While Giulio Bajamonti welcomed Stratico to Dalmatia in 1786, it
was the doctor's brother who saluted Memmo on the completion of his
Dalmatian study in 1791. In that year Girolamo (or Jerolim) Bajamonti
addressed the Economic Society at Split on "various methods to promote agriculture in Dalmatia," and dedicated the address to Memmo.
The speaker recalled that it was now more than ten years since Fortis had

come to Split to advocate the cultivation of chestnuts, and yet, in Dalmatia, "that most convenient plant is still almost unknown." The address saluted the importance of the academies for reforming agriculture in Dalmatia, but the dedication to Memmo underlined the still essential role of the state for the prospect of such reform. Memmo was praised "for the indefatigable commitment, for the provident attentions, for the paternal solicitudes, for his profound studies and applications all tending toward the object of energizing and rendering happy this beautiful, extensive, fertile, but also miserable province, that recognizes in Your Excellency one of its most committed and loving protectors (*patrocinatori*)."[46] In 1774 Fortis had dedicated the different parts of his Dalmatian voyage to his own various patrons, hoping to interest them in the province; now the Dalmatians could speak for themselves, but still similarly sought to flatter and confirm the patronage of powerful patricians in Venice. Franco Venturi has remarked that "up until the end, for Stratico, as for the men of his generation, the hope of reform remained tied to Venice, to the tradition and to the vision of the Serenissima."[47] It was also reciprocally true that for Memmo and the men of his generation, up until the end, a commitment to redemptive reform of the Venetian republic meant ongoing efforts to meet the crises and challenges of imperial rule in Dalmatia.

Penultimate Imperial Prescriptions

The Provveditore Generale in 1790 was Angelo Diedo, and therefore it fell to him to try to implement Memmo's proposals for reform. In a competitive discursive climate, Diedo was doubtful about the economic efficacy of the Dalmatian academies. "Till now they have restricted their studies to mere writings, which distinguish the spirit of individuals," wrote Diedo about the academies at the end of his term in 1792, "but if they do not join instructive practice to theory, they remain without result, reduced to pure formalities, useless to the Morlacco." Stratico was capable of being similarly concerned about the academies, lest "inundated with beautiful dissertations, applauded memorials, doctrines, catechisms, and every genre of scholarly labor, one would not see how to plant an asparagus or a cabbage better than before."[48] Diedo offered the Senate "some of my reverent reflections" on the prospects for the proposed reform in the county of Zadar. That county, he reflected, was "inhabited by ferocious and sanguinary people," while the provincial military institutions were inadequate to sustaining a sufficient central authority for the task of imposing the "discipline" of comprehensive administrative reform. In pursuit of ferocious bandits Diedo announced a raise in the bounty reward from twelve to twenty-four zecchini for each Haiduk head.[49] While the academies urged the cultivation of chestnuts and olives, and Memmo suggested the composition of an agricultural catechism, Diedo countered with the traditional concerns of the Provveditori Generali, citing the ferocity of the inhabitants and the imperative of discipline. Without more extensive military means attached to his own office, he doubted the practical efficacy of any reform.

By July 1790 Diedo had circulated throughout the county of Zadar the proclamation of Memmo's inquisitors, approved by the Senate, and announced his readiness to have Zavoreo undertake the improvement of the roads. Diedo was dubious, however, about the consolidation of villages, envisioning "not minor difficulties on account of the natural resistance of the rough Morlacco to the spontaneous abandonment of his own houses and huts, gardens, stables, pastures, woods." Various incentives and exchanges were to be offered, but Diedo, the practical Provveditore Generale, reminded Venice that nothing could be accomplished, in any event, until the current harvest was completed. Memmo's enlightened diagnosis was rhetorically subsumed within Diedo's more negative view of Dalmatia: "The ameliorative arts unknown, the people immersed in the darkness of ignorance, everything still indicates the stupid barbarism which is the consequence of privation, the discomfort of impassable roads, the disunion, distance, and disconnection of the villages, the lack in every sense of religious and civil education, and of the rule of well-ordered internal discipline."[50] Sandwiched between the familiar diagnosis and prescription of "barbarism" and "discipline," Diedo managed to sum up the substance of Memmo's report; barbarism became the "consequence" of bad roads and remote villages, rather than the condition that accompanied, or even caused, such phenomena.

In the interest of internal discipline, Diedo was virtually at war against the Haiduk bandits of Dalmatia, and in October he reported a shoot-out between his own Panduri militia and the outlaws led by Ante Marsich, "the most ferocious among his criminal companions." Marsich was fatally wounded in the exchange of fire, and his companions performed a last service for their leader: "Half alive, recognizing the wound as mortal, he himself encouraged his accomplices to cut off his head and carry it off with them, rather than see it exposed on the infamous scaffold . . . in the piazza of Sebenico." Diedo had promised a bounty of twenty-four zecchini for a head, and, even without the head, he made a public presentation of the reward to the Panduri.[51] Certainly he did not feel he could indulge in the sentimental luxury of sympathy for the Haiduks, as expressed by Fortis in the *Viaggio in Dalmazia*. Rather, Fortis's perspective was taken up by Giandomenico Stratico, who wrote in 1791, perhaps in response to Diedo's campaign, "My spirit is horrified in seeing so many heads of valorous Morlacchi cut off as those of assassins and bandits, led into that condition by pure desperation and sad hunger." Stratico recalled with strong disapproval a certain Dalmatian colonel, "who used to glory in having achieved fifty or sixty heads of bandits, and then lamented that his merit was poorly remunerated." The bishop further remarked, concerning bandits: "I myself knew a tenant farmer of my family, a most honest young man, reduced by persecution to that unfortunate profession. With as much horror as I saw the head of that man affixed to a stake, with that much delight I would have seen the head of the worst official."[52] Stratico's outlook may have remained bound to the Venetian tradition, but he was certainly capable of voicing strong criticism, however theoretical, of the provincial administration.

By the end of 1790 Diedo had arrived at the predictable conclusion that the Morlacchi were to blame for the failure of Memmo's reform. They were not eager to cooperate in the consolidation of villages, which meant moving their homes and exchanging their fields; they gave no indication of any readiness "to conform to the due obedience to the salutary views of their sovereign tending to civilize their customs." Diedo, who had doubled the bandit bounty, found the incentives to reform insufficient to move the Morlacchi:

> The commended methods of sweetness and clemency have little influence on the spirit of the Morlacchi. . . . I can not foresee other than ever new oppositions to put off the desired accomplishment. . . . The simple path of gentleness is not able to eradicate from their hearts the seeds of stupid inertia. . . . The fear of seeing their lands dismembered . . . would render them less indolent in the fulfillment of the state objects.[53]

He had had reservations from the beginning about putting the program into effect and seemed to find some satisfaction in concluding that

schemes elaborated in Venice, even by the most distinguished of statesmen, were likely to prove unrealistic in Dalmatia.

In April 1791, Diedo informed the Senate that, so far, seven families
in the county of Zadar had taken advantage of the opportunity to exchange their lands in accordance with the desired consolidation. He
himself seemed to regard this aspect of the reform as a definitive failure
and turned his attention to the other principal aspect of Memmo's program, the educational role of the clergy. "This is perhaps the most interesting article of the contemplated reform," he remarked, suggesting that
he had given up on the consolidation of villages. He could imagine
working through the seminary at Zadar to try to ameliorate the "crass
ignorance" and oppressive poverty of the Dalmatian clergy, so that the
priests might "serve usefully the objects of their institution, and also to
instruct youth in reading, writing, accounting, and agrarian catechism."
An improved clergy could have a positive influence: "to render docile
the Morlacchi and to civilize their barbarous customs." This was the conventional perspective of the administration in Dalmatia, dating back
through the eighteenth century, and, in fact, Memmo was influenced by
reading the relations from Zadar concerning the Morlacchi: "concluding
with the Provveditori Generali that unless they become civilized . . . one
will never achieve the great object."[54] For Diedo the great object in civilizing the Morlacchi was to render them administratively docile, the
same object pursued by other means with the capture and display of
Haiduk heads.

Nevertheless, Diedo, for all the severity of his pronouncements, was
willing to concede some regard for "these peoples, who in the midst of
their roughness and natural ferocity of character, do not fail to feel the
most desirable sentiments of subjection toward their prince, for whom
they would, without incitements, give their blood and substance."[55] In
spite of his general view of the force of interests and incentives, Diedo
conceded the disinterested nature of Dalmatian loyalty. In formulating
the paradox of sentimental subjection to the prince, unaccompanied by
"due obedience to the salutary views of their sovereign tending to civilize
their customs," Diedo also identified the crux of the discursive controversy that had developed ever since Fortis set his enlightened anthropology alongside the official perspective of the Provveditori Generali. As a
monument to his own commitment to Dalmatia, Diedo left behind the
municipal portico that still stands in the main square in Zadar, inscribed

with his own name and dated 1792, the year of his departure. The time for the Dalmatians to offer blood and substance to their prince was almost at hand.

In October 1793 a popular revolt erupted on Korčula, in response to the imposition of new taxation; this was, according to Marino Berengo, "the most serious insurrection that occurred in Dalmatia during the last twenty years of Venetian government." Yet the spirit of insurgency was directed more against the local nobles than against San Marco, and, influenced by reports of the contemporary French revolutionary terror, the people of Korčula "went hunting noble wigs, saying they wanted to cut them all off as in France."[56] The Provveditore Generale, Alvise Marin, also dealt with much smaller disputes, as, for instance, when the Republic of Ragusa protested in 1794 the theft by Dalmatian sailors of two mules and a horse. Later that same year Ragusa reported to Marin that two steers and a donkey had been carried off, and that the thief, identified as Stefan Zvietanovich, from near Makarska, was said to have already butchered one of the steers. In Marin's final relation of 1795, upon leaving Dalmatia, he declared himself fully committed to the Senate's intention "to civilize the nation."[57] Thus, in the last years of Venetian Dalmatia the concerns of the Provveditore Generale encompassed the most ambitious enlightened purposes, the most serious insurrectionary crisis, and the pettiest pursuit of crime and compensation.

Andrea Querini, the last Provveditore Generale, came to Dalmatia in 1795, at a moment of renewed medical menace, with plague again on the other side of the border in Bosnia. "The first object of my applications," reported Querini in December, was "to discipline effectively the quarantine lines." Like Diedo, Querini followed a formula for disciplinary success based on interests and incentives: "The certainty of reward and the vigor of prompt punishment are the fundamental bases of good order and useful provisions, but the one can not be separated from the other." This time Dalmatia was spared, and in 1796 there was published in Ragusa, and then reviewed in Venice, a tribute to Querini, "on the occasion of the tour, undertaken by him last December, of the lines at Sinj, Knin, the triple border, Vergoraz, Makarska, Narenta, etc. etc., and the great provisions established by him in order to defend the province of Dalmatia from the plague that was desolating Bosnia." Querini was saluted for the successful quarantine, which was taken as a fine omen for the anticipated triumph of dynamic reform in the province: "Everything is in motion. Almost in a breath the aspect of things are changing, the ancient systems are disappearing, abuses are being abolished. . . . Oh, fortunate epoch! Oh, days of Dalmatia!"[58] The days of Venetian Dalmatia were numbered in 1796, and the tribute to Querini underlined an urgent attitude toward the transformation of the province, which prevailed right up to the very last moment. In the Republic of Ragusa there was equal concern with containing the plague in Bosnia, and in 1796 a special envoy was sent from Dubrovnik to salute Querini, in the "great hope of seeing perfectly founded the mutual tranquillity and common peace of both our subjects."[59] Thus both doomed republics nourished their false hopes for the future.

No one could have appreciated Querini's efforts on behalf of the quarantine more than Giulio Bajamonti, medical doctor, who also celebrated the Provveditore Generale in Italian verse. Just as he had welcomed Stratico to Hvar in the previous decade, the doctor now saluted Querini for his enlightening presence in Dalmatia. Bajamonti extravagantly imagined the rocky crags, the wild beasts, and the human barbarians of Dalmatia responding to the civilizing voice of Querini:

> Al nuovo suon di sua signoril voce
> Fremono di sacro orror gli alti dirupi:
> Turchi e Morlacchi si fanno la croce
> Per maraviglia, e ammiranlo anche i lupi. . .

> At the new sound of his lordly voice
> The high cliffs tremble with sacred horror:
> Turks and Morlacchi cross themselves
> In wonder, and even the wolves admire him. . . [60]

In fact, Bajamonti was aware that some Dalmatians regarded with irony this poetic celebration of Querini.[61] What was most notable about the poem, however, was not simply its hyperbolic enthusiasm, but rather Bajamonti's imagery of a savage province overwhelmed by the voice of Venetian imperial rule. Clearly, enlightened Dalmatians remained susceptible to the Adriatic empire's civilizing mission.

In May 1796, just one year before the Maggior Consiglio voted to abolish itself in Venice, Querini forwarded to the Senate an appeal from the city of Zadar, concerning the municipal misfortune of the broken clock in the main square. The spokesmen for the city graciously recalled that Venice had undertaken to pay for the care of the clock at the time when Zadar's adherence to the Republic was definitively resolved in the early fifteenth century. "In the first fortunate moments in which the city of Zara became a subject of the Venetian dominion," stated the appeal, "it pleased the sovereign greatness of the Principe Serenissimo to assume to itself the incomes peculiar to the city, with the sacred commitment to supply the needs of the same." This arrangement of 1409 included a stipulated salary for a clockmaker, to be reponsible for the town clock in the piazza, and that salary had not been increased since then.

> At that time the stipend of the artisan was proportionate to the circumstances, but it is certain that after the course of almost four centuries these have greatly changed. Because of such scantness it was not possible to invite anyone to lend himself to the enterprise with his own personal labor. For this reason the mechanism was ruined, because it was entrusted to bad and dishonest hands. . . . So this city came to be completely without a public clock. . . . We the councillors and procurators, the heads of the city, have made a commitment of honor to arrange with an able artisan for the construction of a new mechanism.[62]

They needed the Senate, however, to agree to raise the official salary of the city clockmaker to a respectable modern amount, to revise the archaically scant stipend that dated back to the establishment of Venetian Dalmatia. No one in Zadar, not even Querini who endorsed the appeal, seemed to realize that time was running out for the Adriatic empire.

The Mobilization of the Dalmatians

Napoleon entered Milan in May 1796, and in June Querini was already dispatching Dalmatian soldiers to Venice for the imminent encounter with the French army in Italy. Diedo had promised that the Dalmatians would give their lives for Venice, and now Querini offered "visible proofs" of "their uncorrupted loyalty to the principate." The mid-century Goldonian rhetoric of Slavic loyalty was about to be put to the test, after decades during which Venetian neutrality had kept the Dalmatian troops from demonstrating their devotion in battle. Querini was confident that now, in the moment of crisis, it was only necessary to "reinvigorate in these populations the sentiment of subject loyalty, and conduct them to ready service." The ships were setting sail from the Dalmatian coast, bringing to Venice the provinical militiamen of the Craina, while the regular Venetian infantry already included a heavy proportion, as much as a third, of overseas soldiers, *milizie oltremarine,* from Dalmatia. On June 12 Querini reported good weather—"the winds are favorable for navigation along the coast"—and hoped that a recently dispatched contingent of the Craina "may already have arrived at our country's shores (*ai patrii lidi*)." Thus the history of Venetian Dalmatia moved toward its conclusion with phrases from the final scene of Goldoni's *La Dalmatina:* "Torniamo ai patrii lidi."[63] Querini's own patriotic sentiments seemed to be sailing along with the Dalmatians, wafted by favorable winds, but it was to be his patrician class that capitulated without resistance and surrendered the Republic to Napoleon in the following year.

On June 17, 1796, Querini announced the dispatch of two great galleys and 1,929 men of the Craina.

> The subjects concur voluntarily in the eminent public purposes, and dedicate themselves to serve loyally the sovereign exigencies of the state. . . . While I do not omit any efforts by which to draw out willingly the inborn (*ingenita*) devotion of these loyal subjects for ready service, and while their respectful concurrence is authenticated by indubitable proofs in their own punctuality, I spend the whole day in the most embarrassing distress at the censurable lack of opportune embarcations. And such is the vivacity of their subject enthusiasm to hasten to meet the public exigencies that, impatient with the purpose of the ships that are not fit for an immediate transport, they compete to hasten their shipping from these shores with little boats, lest remaining behind they should have imputed to them the charge of being subjects without courage and attachment to Vostra Serenità. But this frenzy (*smania*) which emphasizes the character of loyal subjection increases my apprehension at having exhausted the possible resources for their most speedy embarcation.[64]

The enthusiasm of the Dalmatians to fight for Venice was such that Querini had to describe it, with some reserve, as a "frenzy." Such extreme sentiment seemed not only to outdo his own more appropriate sense of patriotism, but, more materially, to outrun his resources for shipping them all to Italy. There were isolated contrary cases, like that which came to Querini's desk in 1796 concerning four Morlacchi military deserters, accused of highjacking a Dalmatian boat in Venice to take them home; it turned out that the owner of the boat, a certain Giuseppe Lovrich, had accepted all their money in payment for the supposedly coerced transport, so he too was imprisoned.[65] In spite of this particular instance of unpatriotic connivance, in 1796 almost all the transport of Dalmatians was moving in the other direction, toward Venice, in a triumphant achievement of mass mobilization. It was a magnificent demonstration of Dalmatian loyalty, but a wasted military endeavor; the Dalmatians would all be sent home as soon as Venice surrendered, lest their bellicosity give cause for offense to the victorious Napoleon.

In July 1796, Querini announced a total of 7,327 soldiers shipped to Venice from Dalmatia and another 880 from Kotor in Venetian Albania, "besides those enrolled in the overseas companies (*compagnie oltremarine*)." This was merely consistent with the longstanding, almost legendary, reputation of the Dalmatians, "the devotion to the government of these most loyal (*fedelissime*) subject populations." At the same time, he reminded the Senate, that the mobilization itself was unprecedented; in the "course of centuries" Dalmatians had often demonstrated their "uncorrupted (*incorrotta*) loyal subjection" by fighting for Venice, generally against the Ottoman empire, but they had never fought in Italy to defend the metropolis.[66] In Fortis's *Viaggio in Dalmazia* and in Wynne's *Les Morlaques,* Italy and Venice were seen as corrupting influences on the primitive and natural customs of the Morlacchi. Now the Dalmatians, specifically on account of their "uncorrupted" loyalty, were being sent to Venice, the source of sophisticated corruption, there to witness the ultimate demonstration of impotent political decadence.

With the work of embarcation largely complete, Querini admitted to further reasons for his "apprehension." He had stripped the province of its own defense, abandoned the borders, emptied the garrisons, and demolished the local militias, to send all the Dalmatians to serve "the more glorious object" of fighting for Venice. "Only five companies of the nation still remain available," he reported in July, "and at this point a dutiful reflection of prudence counsels me to invoke the most wise provision of sovereign instructions." Diedo had already complained, back in 1790, that the military resources of the Provveditore Generale were inadequate to his administrative responsibilities; now Querini waited to learn whether the Senate would summon to Italy his last five companies. He warned of the dangers of social unrest under the circumstances: "The people, disquieted and inclined to perturbations, taking advantage of the absence of armed ships, confusedly practice aggressions, and bring the tranquillity and security of the subjects to orgasm (*orgasmo*)."[67] Registering popular temperament in strong terms, like "frenzy" and "orgasm," Querini reflected his own patrician disquiet at a moment when the armies of revolutionary France were moving toward Venice. The problems of social disorder would become all the greater in 1797, after Venice fell in May and before the Austrians arrived in July; during that interim Querini continued as Provveditore Generale in a sort of political vacuum. When loyalty to Venice had lost its leonine object, the perturbations of politics in Dalmatia confusedly pitted Habsburg against French sympathies, and Catholic conservatives against revolutionary democrats. Michieli-Vitturi thought the social distress in Split in 1797 was worse than during the plague in the previous decade; an anonymous June manifesto in that city, blaming the fall of Venice on "Jacobins and Jews," incited new frenzies of agitation, to be composed only with the coming of the Habsburg army.[68] Querini's troubled diagnosis in the summer of 1796 of an orgasm in the social body of Dalmatia anticipated by a year the full climax of unrest.

In November 1796 Querini was hearing new reports about plague in Bosnia, but, of course, the quarantine line was supposed to be manned by military force, and the Dalmatian troops had all been sent to Venice. Querini assured the Senate that he would do what he could, considering "the deficiency of means."[69] With Napoleon in Italy, unrest in Dalmatia, and plague on the Bosnian border, in February 1797 the bishop of Makarska presented to Querini an ecclesiastical analysis of the causes of the contemporary crisis. "Unrestrained licentiousness infallibly compromises and dashes the foundations of faith, public and private felicity, as well as the security of sovereigns," declared the bishop. "The grievous catastrophe that is about to conclude this century completely owes its origin, in my devout opinion, to impurity and an inundation of lust." He therefore appealed to Querini to rescue the century from catastrophe by banishing from the town of Makarska three prostitutes, named as Girolama Lallich, Petronilla Grubissich, and Mattea Covacich, all noted for their "incorrigibility." This was a measure that did not require much military manpower, and Querini readily acquiesced in the request. The bishop was further concerned about a certain Antonio Marinovich, a notorious blasphemer in a village near Vergoraz, within the diocese; Marinovich had recently given new cause for scandal by blaspheming even on Christmas day. The bishop's "appeal against scandalous libertines and blasphemers" can hardly have seemed particularly urgent to Querini in 1797, especially since the number of sinners was so small, but he too had reason to be troubled by the coming catastrophic conclusion to the century.[70]

February was, in fact, the last month of the syncopated Venetian calendar, which began in March, so that February 1797 was still recorded as February 1796 m. v. (*more veneto*), by Venetian custom. It was thus the last month of the last year before the abolition of the Republic in 1797, the lapsing of Venice's political and calendrical independence. That February Querini was less preoccupied with the three prostitutes in Makarska than with the shocking arrival of 112 refugees from the Papal State, fleeing from Napoleon's invasion. They arrived on the shores of Dalmatia in badly rigged boats, "not fit for navigation," from across the Adriatic, seeking asylum, including pregnant women and nursing children. "Humanity does not know how to resist such a moving spectacle of desolation," declared Querini in his dispatch to the Senate, where the news must have seemed all the more alarming in the conviction that Venice was next on Napoleon's calendar of conquest.[71] Actually, after Venice surrendered in May, the last doge Ludovico Manin, elected instead of Memmo in 1789, was himself advised to seek refuge in Dalmatia and to reestablish the Republic there. In the end, Venetian Dalmatia did outlive the Republic of Venice, with Querini presiding as Provveditore Generale over the transition to Habsburg rule.[72]

"In those first moments," remembered Michieli-Vitturi, "when my spirit was oppressed by an extreme affliction caused by the fall of Venice, I saw no other means to obtain security in Dalmatia and spare it the sad vicissitudes of the rest of the Venetian state, than to restore it to subjection to His Imperial Majesty . . . as it had already been before the year 1420." The Dalmatian academicians of the previous generation became themselves political refugees within their own province, looking for a sympathetic asylum, recalling the historical memory of the old claim by the Hungarian crown. The Dalmatians too created moving spectacles, as they ritually lamented the loss of their long affiliation with the Venetian republic. In July the flag of San Marco was finally lowered at Zadar, and brought to the cathedral for a solemn "Te Deum." So many loyal Dalmatian mourners wept over the flag that it was supposedly wet with their tears. As they covered it with kisses in the cathedral, according to one account, "the people emitted cries, howls, and sighs, and it was a touching spectacle to see this church full of a crowd in tears."[73] The great Goldonian moment, however, came in August with the lowering of the flag in the small town of Perasto near Kotor, when Captain Giuseppe Viscovich addressed the assembled Dalmatians: "In sto amaro momento, in sto ultimo sfogo de amor, de fede al Veneto Serenissimo Dominio." In this bitter moment, in this last outpouring of love, of loyalty, he perorated dramatically, looking back over four centuries of Venetian dominion:

> For 377 years our loyalty and our valor have always protected you by sea . . . . For 377 years our substance, our blood, and our lives have always been for you, and we have considered ourselves supremely happy. You with us, we with you ('ti con nu, nu con ti'), we have always been victorious, always illustrious and virtuous.[74]

The scene was intensely theatrical, with "a deluge of weeping," and the recitation was delivered in the language of valor and virtue that Goldoni attributed to his stage Dalmatians forty years before; the Venetian drama of 1758 and the Dalmatian oration of 1797 celebrated the same ritual discourse of loyal devotion. In Viscovich there was perhaps even a resemblance to Pervan, Wynne's literary creation in *Les Morlaques,* the old man who addressed his fellow villagers in a spirit of uncorrupted simplicity. Wynne would certainly have appreciated the moment when Viscovich supposedly turned to a child in the gathering, and, in Venetian dialect, commanded him to kneel, to kiss the flag of San Marco, and to remember the moment all his life: "Inzenocite anca ti, basile, e tientele a mente per tuta la vita."[75] The scene was preserved in historical memory long enough for Attilio Tamaro to revive it again, in all its pathos, when he published his history of Dalmatia in 1919 for presentation to the Versailles peace conference, arguing the Italian case against the Yugoslav case for possession of Dalmatia. One might as well have staged *La Dalmatina* at Versailles. In 1997, two hundred years after the collapse of Venice, a commemorative stone tablet was installed on the Riva degli Schiavoni in Venice: "On this bank the valorous Slavic soldiers, determined to defend Venice, but forced by foreign injunction to abandon the city, expressed publicly the bonds of loyalty which for many centuries united Dalmatia and the Venetian republic."

In Venice in March 1797, the *Nuovo giornale enciclopedico d'Italia* published an article entitled "Il Morlacchismo d'Omero," that is, "The Morlacchismo of Homer." It was signed only with the letter "B," but the author was Giulio Bajamonti, with his very last public contribution to the discourse of Dalmatia before the public of Venice. He began by remarking that Homer was a divinity, a divine poet, whom "the translators have variously transformed and even deformed," and who was thus poetically reinterpreted and reconceived. Bajamonti himself proposed to take this sort of creative liberty with Homer:

> Have we not seen the venerable old man (to say nothing of versions in other foreign languages) travestied variously in Florentine, in Lombard, in Venetian? Now the thought has come to me to make him become a Slav (*farlo diventare schiavone*). I see no other means by which to understand that this divine genius belongs to me. I thus want to make myself related (*imparentarmi*) to him in a certain manner.[76]

This was a peculiar point of pride for Bajamonti, refashioning Homer as a Slav, to claim Homer as someone related to himself; it also involved decisively identifying himself as a Slav, even as he presented his views in Venice, written in Italian, his own literary language. "It is not that I propose to transport his works into the Slavic language," Bajamonti hastened to explain, without adding that such a task might have challenged his literary capacities.[77] Bajamonti meant to make Homer a Slav without setting him to Slavic verse.

It was fitting for Bajamonti to have the final word on the Morlacchi in the Adriatic imperial discourse, for no one more thoroughly embodied the multiple and ambivalent aspects of Dalmatian identity during the final decades of Venetian rule. Because of his friendship with Fortis, he stood closer than any other Dalmatian to the Venetian intellectual discovery of the province; he participated in that discovery, exploring the Biokovo mountains together with Fortis, but was also the object of that discovery when Fortis held up Bajamonti to the Venetian public as a "model" Dalmatian—"for his prudence, customs, and manners." They were bound together both as enlightened readers of the most irreverent French philosophes and by a common Italian culture, indeed Paduan culture, for Bajamonti studied medicine in Fortis's home town. "I knew him rather well," recalled a Dalmatian acquaintance, long after Bajamonti's death. "He read with passion the works of the unbelieving Frenchmen; he was the intimate friend of the misbelieving abbé Fortis." Yet, for all their French and Italian correspondences, Fortis and Bajamonti were also united in a common fascination with Slavic matters; for Fortis such matters were entirely foreign, but for Bajamonti they evidently touched a chord of identity, perhaps ultimately made him feel "related" to the Slavs. Like Fortis he was interested in Slavic folk poetry, and it was very probably Bajamonti who first obtained in Split the transcription of the "Hasanaginica," passing it on to his friend who made it famous.[78] Bajamonti was also a composer and used musical material from folk songs in his compositions; he was a more adventurous collector than Fortis and traveled into Bosnia in 1780, transcribing Slavic songs in Travnik. Though Fortis and Bajamonti spoke and corresponded in Italian, they had some sense of being bound in Slavic friendship, for Fortis sometimes began his letters with a Slavic salutation: "Moj dragi prijatelu!" My dear friend! Fortis claimed to find "completely cold" (*tutto freddo*) those friendships without "a little Slavic character"(*un po di slavonismo*).[79] It was only natural that Bajamonti should think of himself in relation to the Slavs of Dalmatia.

Bajamonti celebrated Venetian rule when he paid poetic tribute to the Provveditore Generale Andrea Querini and praised the commander Paolo Emilio Canal for his efforts in time of plague. Yet he also advocated economic reform in Dalmatia, working through the Economic Society of Split, even corresponding with Andrea Memmo.[80] Bajamonti did not venerate only Venetians; he celebrated Stratico, welcoming him to Hvar in 1786, as an indigenous personage of the Dalmatian Enlightenment. Slavic enthusiasm was almost subversively vocalized when Bajamonti wrote an ode on the Russian capture of the Turkish fort at Ochakov in 1788, deifying Catherine as the "Russian Juno." This was close to the Russophile Slavic sentiment of Wynne's *Les Morlaques,* and, in fact, it has been debated whether Bajamonti might have been behind the anonymous Italian translation of the novel that was published in Padua in 1798. There is no doubt, however, that Bajamonti was the "B" who wrote "Il Morlacchismo d'Omero." In the Venetian journal he explored his own Dalmatian identity, and he ordered his Latin translations of the *Iliad* and the *Odyssey* from the publisher in Venice.[81] Furthermore, Bajamonti's perspective on the Morlacchi was profoundly influenced by the explorations of the Venetian Enlightenment.

"I intend to establish that the Homeric poems are in Morlacchi taste," Bajamonti explained, "and that the Morlacchi would find in them the manners and customs of their country." At this particular moment in history, when the Morlacchi had been dispatched to the shores of Venice, to give their blood and substance in its defence, Bajamonti was ambivalent about what country, what *patria,* could appropriately be attributed to the Morlacchi. He offered them an honorable anthropological heritage, in "the manners and customs of their country," to replace the imperial political affiliation that was about to lapse.

> Although I do not believe that Homeric things are of the Morlacchi alone, still I sustain that today the Morlacchi nation and, no less, Morlacchi poetry are the most analogous to Homeric taste; since other peoples, for the most part, either are mannered according to what is called civil cultivation; or if they are savages and barbarians, as we say, they have tastes and customs rather different from those of the Morlacco and from those of Homer.[82]

By making Homer not simply a Slav, but actually a Morlacco, Bajamonti, the distinguished academic Dalmatian, suggested a revision of his own previously ambivalent perspective on the Morlacchi; he recognized them now as related to him, through their common family connection to Homer. It was Bajamonti, traveling with Fortis in the 1770s, who threatened to throw a dead snake at the Morlacchi guides, to demonstrate his contempt for their superstitions. It was Bajamonti, writing about the plague in the 1780s, who blamed the Morlacchi for their obliviousness to the risks of contagion. Now, in the 1790s, in appreciation of Homer, Bajamonti was ready to reconsider the customs of the Morlacchi, and even to imply that it might not be altogether bad to be barbarous.

Vico could certainly have served as a philosophical guide to the anthropological understanding of primitive poetry through Homer. Fortis, who also read Vico, had noted the relation between Homer and the Morlacchi in a passing remark in the *Viaggio in Dalmazia;* Morlacchi poetry suggested "the simplicity of Homeric times, and relative to the customs of the nation." Gozzi too had made the connection, considering the "rough and barbarous customs" of the Morlacchi: "Whoever reads Homer and Virgil finds the image of the Morlacchi."[83] Following Vico's argument that "the Greek peoples were themselves Homer," Bajamonti pointed out that Morlacchi poems were also oral, ancient, collective, and anonymous in their original authorship. "And even today," he observed, "there are, though more rare, some Illyrian Homers, who on the occasion of some duel or abduction, or other similar event, enrich the national muse with these productions." He might have suggested the possibility of contemporary Homeric poetry in the story of the Haiduk Ante Marsich who, in 1790, had encouraged his companions to cut off and carry away his head, rather than leave it to be dishonored on the scaffold.

Like Homer's poetry, that of the Morlacchi was "the product of vivid sensation and robust imagination." Like Homer the Morlacchi made use of frequent repetition of verses and the constant reiteration of personal epithets.[84] Bajamonti went far beyond Fortis and Gozzi in pursuing the formal and stylistic comparison between Homer and the Morlacchi.

"Up to this point we have seen in Homer a species of poetic Morlacchismo; now we will see in him the moral Morlacchismo," wrote Bajamonti. "Certainly those sublime outpourings of wrath and zeal are all in the Morlacchi taste." From morality he moved on to the crucial subject of customs, beginning with banquets: "The Morlacchi in truth are always big eaters and big drinkers." Furthermore their taste in food matched that of the heroes in Homer: "roast meat and wine, precisely as on the Morlacchi tables." Bajamonti cited the story of Achilles at the funeral of Patroclus, offering as prizes to the athletes a tripod worth twelve oxen and a female servant worth only four. "Can you imagine anything more Morlacco?" asked Bajamonti, assuming familiarity with the subject on the part of his Venetian readers. He reminded them, in case they had forgotten from reading Fortis years before, that the status and value of women among the Morlacchi was generally low.[85]

Bajamonti himself meant to make at least one point that was not altogether gallant toward women. Having appreciated the poetic productions of the primitive Morlacchi, he inevitably found himself taking Rousseau's inverted view of the value of civilization. "Attenuated and softened by our cultivation, by our refinements," he remarked, here aligning himself with the civilized Venetians rather than the barbarous Morlacchi, modern literature was inevitably inferior to the *Iliad* and the *Odyssey*.

> Our enervated productions are of ephemeral taste, and seem to be intended precisely to pass the time, and for the studies of frivolous and superficial minds, and especially for women, who, to tell the truth, are a great good in this life for men, but oh how rare are those, speaking of these times, who can guide a poet to immortality![86]

Bajamonti's gendered conception of *morlacchismo* was conditioned by a certain Slavic *machismo,* and the Homeric virtues that he celebrated were those of roast meat and muscular masculinity. For anyone who could read the writing on the walls of Troy, however, in March 1797 it was evident that the enervated Venetians would never withstand a French siege, no matter how many loyal Morlacchi crossed the sea to come to the defense of San Marco. Bajamonti's tribute to the Homeric heroism of the Morlacchi, whose identity he ambivalently considered adapting for himself, was published just as their heroic moment was about to arrive, and then pass forever from the epic of Venetian history.

Epitaph: Morlacchismo

The end of Venice meant, in another sense, the end of the Morlacchi, for their official importance as undisciplined subjects and their public reputation as fascinating and ferocious primitives belonged to the particular historical epoch of their presence in the Venetian empire during the eighteenth century. The Morlacchi were the civilizing project of Venice in the age of Enlightenment, the crucial component of the Venetian ideology of empire in Dalmatia. Under Habsburg rule in the nineteenth century, alongside other Slavic populations, the distinct classification of the Morlacchi began to dissolve, as they were sorted out into Serbs and Croats according to region and religion. Thus, Bajamonti was writing the epitaph of the Morlacchi in 1797, when he remarked upon their heroic spirit:

> In establishing this Homeric Morlacchismo it is too evident that I shall have procured an honor to the Illyrian nation; but I would not want it attributed to me that at the same time I have thus procured any dishonor to Homer. By noting in his poems the taste and the customs of the Morlacchi I do not intend to infer that such taste is bad, nor that such customs are bad. Rather I thus claim to adduce a new proof of their heroic character, as by analogy I wish to demonstrate the same heroic character of the Morlacchi. In such a manner one may demolish some critics who found something obscene, boorish, absurd, and atrocious in the inimitable poet.[87]

By demolishing the literary critics of Homer, of course, Bajamonti also rebutted those social critics who found the same negative qualities in the character and customs of the Morlacchi.

At the same time, in making himself the public spokesman for the honor of the "Illyrian nation," Bajamonti made the case, one last time, for Dalmatian preeminence in the discourse on Dalmatia. After the epidemic crisis of plague in the 1780s, when Bajamonti himself had weighed the balance of imperial responsibility between the heedless Morlacchi and the temporizing Venetian administration, there was new impetus for an Adriatic public forum of competitive prescriptions for the province.

Between enlightened Venetian patricians like Memmo and enlightened Dalmatian academicians like Bajamonti there was often common political purpose in the context of an imperially inflected discursive rivalry. The Morlacchi, targeted by the Provveditori Generali as the crucial problem for administrative discipline and economic development, also became the focus for the rivalry inherent in Venetian and Dalmatian public debate. Because the Morlacchi did not speak for themselves, every entrant in the competitive discourse on Dalmatia spoke about them: defining their character, explaining their customs, explicating their interests, criticizing their inaptitudes, revealing their virtues, and claiming the prerogative to pronounce on their behalf. Discovering the Morlacchi, Venetians and Dalmatians together created the concept of *morlacchismo*.

Bajamonti's recognition of contemporary ambivalence about the poetic qualities of Homer made this subject the perfect vehicle for coming to terms with decades of ambivalence about the Morlacchi, ever since the publication of *Viaggio in Dalmazia*. Bajamonti traveled with Fortis for parts of that voyage, twenty-five years before, and now made peace with his own ambivalence at the moment of the imminent annihilation of Venice. Fortis himself was in Paris in 1797, in the enemy capital, pursuing his paleontological researches in the Muséum d'Histoire Naturelle. Surely he gave a sympathetic thought to vulnerable Venice, his own country after all, though the Republic had never properly appreciated his efforts on its behalf in Dalmatia. "I will never forget as long as I live the reception and cordial treatment of me by the Voivod Pervan at Coccorich," he had written in 1774.[88] After Fortis, right up until the end of Venice, a whole generation of the Enlightenment had been unable to forget his discovery of the Morlacchi, sympathetically conceived as "spirits uncorrupted by the society that we call civilized."

Conclusions and Continuities: The Legacy of the Venetian Enlightenment in Napoleonic Illyria, Habsburg Dalmatia, and Yugoslavia

The Ideology of Adriatic Empire: From Discipline to Civilization

The sovereign state of Venice remained most serenely republican, the Serenissima Repubblica, right up until the moment of its abrupt political annihilation in 1797, but when Goldoni presented *La Dalmatina* in 1758 he celebrated the state in an alternatively imperial aspect, as the Adriatic empire. It was precisely the Dalmatian subject of the drama that evoked and vindicated the imperial designation at the very moment when England and France were fighting the Seven Years' War, engaged in a world-wide struggle for empire in Canada, in India, in the Caribbean. Measured by those imperial models, Dalmatia was unimpressive, territorially slender and relatively unremote; the Adriatic empire could hardly compare to the Atlantic powers with their disputed possessions in Asia and America. The model of empire, however, with its political prestige and economic incentives, proved irresistible to Venice as well, and Dalmatia became the base for fashioning a modern "ideology of empire," analogous to the intellectual concerns that Anthony Pagden has noted in the imperial cases of Spain, England, and France.[1] Goldoni thus dramatized Venice's ideological bid for an imperial identity, celebrating what amounted to an empire in miniature over the Slavs of Dalmatia. In 1755 the Provveditore Generale Grimani had sponsored agricultural reform in recognition of Venice's imperial responsibility to the Dalmatians, "bringing them to call themselves spontaneously content." In 1758 Goldoni added ideological luster to the recent reform, when he scripted the Italian lines by which his invented Slavs saluted "the fortunate peoples of the Adriatic empire."

In 1763, the year of the peace of Paris, concluding the imperial contest between England and France, Goldoni published *La Dalmatina* in

Venice, five years after the first performance, with a dedication alluding "to the well-being, to the splendor, to the tranquillity of the Adriatic empire." Dramatic form was better suited to celebrating than defining the political character of empire, but Goldoni designated the special significance of the play as a matter of almost enigmatic imperial conjunction: "It concerns a nation loyal and worthy of the Serenissima Repubblica; it concerns in some fashion the glorious name of the Venetians, the valor of the Slavs, and the respect that they both command principally upon the sea." The Serenissima Repubblica could be thus conceived as an Adriatic empire, analogous to the seafaring Atlantic powers, and the intellectual labors of the Venetian Enlightenment would seek to fathom in what fashion precisely the Slavs of Dalmatia might imperially magnify the glory of Venice. In 1765 the Provveditore Generale Michiel already adumbrated a modern economic perspective on the problem, when he wondered how Dalmatia might be made "to give notable increment to commerce, and to bring appreciable utility to the state." Fortis in 1774 made this a matter of public concern when he evaluated the resources of the province "to render them more useful to the state," when he advocated "the utility of new methods" in agriculture, and even when he insisted upon the "utility" of his own observations.

The principles of "loyalty" and "utility" were to be the provincial themes from which the Venetian Enlightenment composed its imperial vindication in the discursive discovery of Dalmatia. Administrative and literary perspectives, in the official domain and in the public sphere, converged in their concern with these themes and produced an ideology of empire all the more intricately coherent in intellectual structure for the diminutive dimensions of its geographical base. That structure depended upon an unstable ideological balance involving a fundamental insistence upon the identity of interests between Venice and Dalmatia and an equally important articulation of difference and asymmetry. Goldoni testified to a shared sentiment of loyalty when he averred that the Lion in the breast of his Dalmatian hero was identical to "that glorious Lion that I too cherish jealously in my breast, that animated me to write this comedy." The loyal playwright, of course, invented the leonine Radovich and wrote the patriotic verses to be pronounced upon the stage. Yet beyond this structural asymmetry between the scriptive Venetian and the scripted Slav, there was clearly a sentimental distinction between Venetian loyalty to Venice and Slavic loyalty to Venice. The latter loyalty was the subject of ritually recurring comment and remark throughout the eighteenth century, as Venetians found reassurance in Slavic "acclamations." Such loyalty was both excessively celebrated and attentively monitored under the awkward circumstances of irregular emigrations into the Ottoman and Habsburg empires and even disloyal enlistment in Russian military service. In *Les Morlaques* Giustiniana Wynne staged the nightmare scenario of asymmetrical allegiances when she imagined the Morlacchi kneeling in worship before the statue of Catherine, discovering a Slavic sentimental devotion that overwhelmed a merely perfunctory Venetian loyalty. In the novel Pervan lamented Venetian neutrality in war—"Why does our Lion at present seem to have wet wings?"—and discovered an inspirational Slavic icon: "Great Catherina, divinity of the Slavic nation, receive also my vows and homages."

The imperial asymmetry of "utility" was made explicit in Venice's system of economic restrictions on Adriatic commerce, intended to benefit the metropolis at the expense of provincial initiatives and exigencies. Thus the mutual utility of economic development could also appear under the alternative aspect of imperial exploitation. When Fortis made his earliest voyage to Cres in 1770, he invoked natural history in the name of utility, studying, for instance, "useful and harmful shrubs and herbs," but he dedicated their use to the local inhabitants. Botanical resources "could bring advantages to the people of Cres," and Fortis formulated his own utility accordingly: "holding thus to my principal purpose, which is to be of use in all possible ways to that population by which I have been so well treated and received." By 1773 he was visiting Dalmatia under the auspices of Andrea Memmo, with a senatorial commission to study fishing, and Fortis's sense of utility underwent a meaningful modulation. In the *Viaggio in Dalmazia* he studied the natural resources of the province "to render them more useful to the state," and declared his "desire to penetrate with views to the public utility into the secrets of natural science." Now he invoked the formula of "our gulf," proclaimed the priority of "our commerce and the cultivation and increase of our domestic products." The first-person plural pointed to the systematic economics of empire, betraying the imbalance between the Venetian state and the Dalmatian inhabitants. Even in the first-person singular his priorities were plain, as he proposed to bring "sensible advantages" to "national commerce" for his own personal satisfaction: "I would fully taste the internal content that floods the soul of the useful

322 Venice and the Slavs

subject." Utility, like loyalty, could appear as a principle of mutual relation between Venice and Dalmatia, but ultimately both themes emphasized the underlying asymmetrical structure of empire.

The theme of imperial loyalty could be adapted from the Venetian
Renaissance rhetoric of civic patriotism, while the theme of imperial utility could be improvised upon the economic writings of the Venetian Enlightenment concerning national economy. However, the most important element of Venice's ideology of empire, the crucial articulation of
difference and vindication of asymmetry, was the civilizing mission discovered especially for the case of Dalmatia. This followed from the study
of primitive customs among the Morlacchi, first undertaken as an administrative matter by the Provveditori Generali but then reformulated by
Fortis as a founding field study in the new and undenominated discipline
of modern anthropology. Whether censured as barbarism or celebrated
as the state of nature, the customs of the Morlacchi became the cultural
counterweight to what appeared, by implicit contrast and counterpoint,
as the civilization of Venice. Over the course of the eighteenth century
the administrative issue of instilling "discipline" in the subject Morlacchi
was increasingly infused with the new philosophical purpose of civilizing
them. The Provveditori Generali addressed the disciplinary susceptibility
of the Morlacchi, from Giacomo Boldù in the 1740s who thought them
"incapable of discipline," to Michiel in the 1760s who thought them
"not incapable of receiving it," to Gradenigo in the 1770s who prescribed attentive inspection of the "undisciplined Morlacchi," to Paolo
Boldù in the 1780s who cited "examples of savage and rough peoples
made useful with constant good discipline." This last formulation already
revealed the new importance of the civilizing mission, with discipline
conceived as the antidote to savagery and roughness. By 1790 Memmo,
the leading political figure of the Venetian Enlightenment, was framing
the imperial problem of the Morlacchi according to the most recent
French and English usage of the civilizing verb: "unless they become civilized," he warned, the promises and purposes of empire would be
empty. Angelo Diedo, as Provveditore Generale, followed Memmo's lead
on the Morlacchi but made the verb active rather than reflexive; in 1790
he pronounced the need to "civilize their customs," and in 1791 he
demonstrated the administrative and ideological amalgam of the civilizing mission with the formulated purpose "to render docile the Morlacchi
and to civilize their barbarous customs." By 1795 the Provveditore Gen-

erale Marin could affirm, almost casually, Venice's commitment to "civilize the nation," as if the formula had already become conventional.

The turning point in this programmatic evolution from discipline to civilization, between the 1740s and the 1790s, was unquestionably the publication of *Viaggio in Dalmazia* in 1774. Fortis, writing about the customs of the Morlacchi, had little use for the concept of "discipline," and had not yet adopted the new vocabulary of "civilization." For "civilized" he wrote *colto,* or "cultivated," eschewing those forms of the modern verb *civilizzare,* which Memmo, Diedo, and Marin would later apply. Furthermore, Fortis regarded the "civilized" or "cultivated" aspects of society with philosophical ambivalence. On the one hand, he saluted the scientific concerns of "civilized (*colta*) Europe" and compared the poetry of the Morlacchi to the standards of "the civilized (*colte*) nations" of Europe; on the other hand, he admired the "delicacy of sentiment" in the Morlacchi, "uncorrupted by the society that we call civilized (*colta*)." In his anthropological account of their customs he relished precisely this uncorrupted aspect of their mountain society, noting the "bizarre" or "barbarous" ornaments of the Morlacchi women, which called to his mind images of Tartars or American Indians. Fortis censured the wasteful domestic economy of the Morlacchi—"in this they resemble the Hottentots"—and endorsed the "salutary violence" of forcing them to cultivate the garlic and onions they consumed; he was, however, far from desiring to "civilize" their customs, and thus transform their society, as a matter of imperial policy.

Fortis's account made the uncorrupted customs of the Morlacchi into a public sensation and powerfully influenced the further formulation of administrative aims in Dalmatia, though not necessarily as he would have wished. The customs that he had so sympathetically described became the targets for Venetian intervention, as anthropological knowledge was incorporated into the technology of imperial power. The "delicacy of sentiment" that he admired in the Morlacchi was taken up by Giustiniana Wynne, as she pursued the philosophical implications of Fortis's voyage and played upon the sensibilities of the reading public. Her Morlacchi presented "the image of nature in primitive society," located conceptually somewhere between the social poles of "the absolutely savage barbarian" and "the entirely civilized man." As for their geographical location, they might as well have been on an island in the South Pacific, as Wynne suggested. They were, however, just across the

Adriatic from Venice, and while Wynne in 1788 was full of sentimental appreciation for the social virtues of the village of Dizmo—where the Morlacchi lived as "one sole family"—Memmo in 1790 was proposing the drastic consolidation of farflung dwellings—"worse than those of wild beasts"—into new and modern model villages. The concept of custom, anthropologically analyzed by Fortis, became the key to adumbrating an imperial metamorphosis in the name of civilization. The anthropological representation of difference indicated the asymmetry of civilization and barbarism and became the capstone of the Venetian ideology of empire in Dalmatia.

Venice, Dalmatia, and the Slavs of Eastern Europe

The philosophical stipulation of an intermediary stage of social development in Dalmatia, balanced between civilization and barbarism, served as the vindication of Venice's Adriatic empire, but that same developmental dilemma was also ascribed to other lands, most notably Russia and Poland, as the philosophes of the Enlightenment invented the distinction between Eastern Europe and Western Europe. The Enlightenment's legend of Peter the Great and Catherine the Great, so enthusiastically sustained by Voltaire, was also relevant to Venice's civilizing mission in Dalmatia. A people poised between barbarism and civilization was supposed to be influenced and elevated from the former toward the latter by the enlightened intentions of its sovereign. In *Les Morlaques* Peter and Catherine were actually cited as models for the Morlacchi, in spite of the fact that Venice regarded Russia suspiciously as a force for the alienation of loyalties in Dalmatia. Precisely because of Venetian sensitivity to such political concerns Venice guided the European Enlightenment toward the idea of Eastern Europe, through the crucial project of classification that produced the discovery of the Slavs. Not only could certain eastern regions of the continent, including Dalmatia, be sorted together between civilization and barbarism, but it was also possible to identify an ethnographic key to the resemblances among those regions. The Venetian Enlightenment, beginning with the *Viaggio in Dalmazia,* recognized the cultural, anthropological, ethnographic, and linguistic unity of the Slavs and appreciated the importance of the Slavic factor for mapping Europe into eastern and western domains. From across the Adriatic, the Renaissance and Baroque insights of Pribojević, Orbini, Križanić, and Vitezović had already indicated elements of what Ivo Banac has called "Slavic reciprocity"; Fortis returned from his voyage in Dalmatia to formulate this conception according to the values of the Enlightenment.[2] Enunciated by Fortis in 1774 and later elaborated by Herder in 1791 in the fourth volume of the *Philosophie der Geschichte,* the conception of the Slavs as a single ethnographic category, even a unified nation, consolidated the Enlightenment's invention of Eastern Europe.

Goldoni sometimes identified his Dalmatians as Slavs or Illyrians, but these were epithets from the ancient world, decorous denominations of the Dalmatian drama, employed without any seeming awareness of a broader relevance beyond the Adriatic arena. Fortis on Cres already recognized that relevance, when he wrote about "the Slavic language which is the most extensive of all the European languages," reaching "to the last frontier of the Russian empire." Later, after voyaging in Dalmatia, he considered whether such an extensive language should be considered as the basis of a coextensive nation, and he introduced the Morlacchi in the context of "so many other nations resembling them in customs and in language in such a manner that they can be taken for one sole nation, vastly extended from our sea to the glacial ocean." This detection of resemblances, in language and customs, was for Fortis a work of Linnaean natural history, of classification according to the similarities of species, very different from Gozzi's denigration by classical allusion, in which the Morlacchi appeared as a "species of anthropophagi." Fortis noted similarities in contemporary populations, such as the Morlacchi and the Ukrainians, who demonstrated "the greatest conformity of clothing, customs, dialect, and even orthography." In Fortis the construction of Eastern Europe thus appeared as an intellectual labor, the systematic matching of patterns and alignment of resemblances. In 1788 Wynne already assumed the validity of such a construction, when she imagined Catherine as the "divinity of the Slavic nation," worshipped beyond the frontiers of Russia, in the mountains of Venetian Dalmatia. This Slavic nation claimed its members from all the lands of linguistic and customary resemblance, including the Morlacchi, so that Pervan could welcome his grandson into a newly conceived anthropological community: "You are a Slav."

Not every Dalmatian would have been gratified at having a Slavic identity so emphatically assigned. Giovanni Lovrich, in 1776, spoke for "the most civilized Dalmatians today" and observed that "for fear of being considered barbarians some of them claim (foolishly thinking it a virtue) to be ignorant even of the language." Lovrich was writing—in Italian—at the moment when Dalmatia had become a sensational subject in the aftermath of Fortis's publication. By publicizing the intriguing presence of the Morlacchi in Dalmatia, classifying them as Slavs, and detailing their primitive customs, Fortis posed a dilemma of identity for those who considered themselves "the most civilized Dalmatians." The denomination of Slav was no longer just a decorous epithet, but rather a classification by language and customs, with uncomfortable associations for those who did not recognize themselves in the bizarre and barbarous ornaments of the Morlacchi, for those who did not feel any connection to the farthest frontiers of the Russian empire.

Fortis's *Viaggio in Dalmazia* was published in Italian, German, French, and English, the languages of the public sphere of Western Europe, and even *Les Morlaques,* written in French, was accessible to the cosmopolitan public of the Enlightenment. These works, however, made their first and greatest impression within the more restricted public sphere of the Venetian republic. As a consequence of Fortis's discovery of Dalmatia, the Dalmatians themselves were thrust before the public, and some, like Lovrich and Bajamonti, actively seized the opportunity to participate in the public representation of their province. The Venetian public sphere thus developed a Dalmatian dimension, with bases on both shores of the Adriatic, including the agricultural academies of Split, Trogir, and Zadar, as well as the journals, publications, and academic contributions of Venice, Vicenza, and Padua. Thus the evolution of an Adriatic public sphere, corresponding to the map of the Adriatic empire, suggested a measure of symmetry, qualified by the predominance of Italian as the language of discussion and the focus on Dalmatia as the subject of discussion. Yet, in the years after Fortis's landmark publication, there did develop an Adriatic discourse concerning Dalmatia in which Dalmatians also participated in addressing the problems of the province.

Fortis's attention to the Morlacchi made it possible for "the most civilized Dalmatians" to join in the public discussion, along with the Venetian patricians and Paduan professors, by establishing the civilized negative identity of not being Morlacchi. The appropriate relation was one of proprietary concern—"our Morlacchi"—rather than any admission of resemblance or community. Thus the bicoastal encounter across the Adriatic was premised upon the very principles of "civilization" and "barbarism," which vindicated the Venetian empire in Dalmatia and determined the distinction between Eastern Europe and Western Europe. Lovrich was perfectly prepared to concede the barbarism of the Morlacchi, even as he deplored the "fear of being considered barbarians," which preoccupied the self-affirmed "civilized" Dalmatians like himself. Fortis reassured his audience in Split in 1780, addressing them as "most civilized listeners," saluting them as the public "tribunal" that represented "the most learned part of the Dalmatian nation." He joined them in an Adriatic public sphere, a Paduan before the Economic Society of Split, and sealed their civilized compact with the anthropological proposal that the Morlacco be "restored to the pastoral life, the only one that suits his nomadic origin and character."

Bajamonti, from the most civilized Dalmatian perspective, echoed this sentiment in 1786 when he regretted the medically irresponsible nomadism of the Morlacchi during the time of plague, noting the "vagabond inclination of their Scythian race." He hoped that "the civilized nations" would be spared the scourge of plague. Yet, the Adriatic public sphere, shadowing the Adriatic empire, seemed to transcend the formulated frontiers of civilization by which the Enlightenment demarcated the domains of Western Europe and Eastern Europe. "From the Don to the Elbe, from the Baltic to the Adriatic Sea," wrote Herder in 1791, denominating the eastern lands of the Slavs. Between Venice and Dalmatia, however, the Adriatic Sea could be conceived both as a binding sphere and a sundering border; the administrative mechanics of empire emphasized relation and proximity, while the ideology of empire explored the cultural implications of primitive exoticism. Adriatic adherence to the principles of civilization and barbarism preserved a philosophical distinction that ordered the regional elements of imperial geography. Only in 1797, with the empire on the point of permanent dissolution, did Bajamonti publicly compromise his own identity as a "most civilized Dalmatian," arguing for the "Morlacchismo" of Homer, making Homer a Slav in order "to make myself related to him." Fortis boasted of his friendship for the Morlacchi, and claimed to know how to "make them cordial friends," but he never had to consider the possibility of a closer relation. Dalmatians like Lovrich and Bajamonti were inevitably aware that the Morlacchi were their near neighbors within the same slender province. Furthermore, though the term "Morlacchi" had a geographical and anthropological significance with reference to a pastoral people of the mountains, the most civilized Dalmatians knew that the label could be more generally employed to designate the least civilized Dalmatians.

Dalmatian National Identity and Venetian Imperial Ideology

The issue of national designations was essential, but also ambiguous and unresolved, in Venice's discovery of Dalmatia and in the formulation of an ideology of Adriatic empire. In particular, the problem of national denominations and identities within an imperial context reflected the political and cultural concerns of early modern Europe, just on the verge of the controversial developments of modern nationalism. Goldoni in 1758 did not doubt that there was a Dalmatian "nation" within the Adriatic empire, though he also employed the designations Illyrian and Slav. Fortis in 1774 wrote with similar conviction about a Morlacchi "nation," though he also proposed that it might better be classified as part of the "one sole nation" of the Slavs, based on common language and customs. Yet, in 1780 in Split he addressed his audience as "the learned part of the Dalmatian nation," and in 1783 Paolo Boldù concluded his term as Provveditore Generale with reflections on Venice's unfulfilled imperial responsibilities to the "Dalmatian nation." Bajamonti in 1786, discussing the failure of the quarantine lines at the Ottoman border, observed that the Bosnians "can easily be confused with our Morlacchi," fully comparable "by gait, by voice, by face, by clothes." Stratico in 1789 wrote of Dalmatia's "beautiful Illyrian songs," while Memmo in 1790 named the Slavic language of Dalmatia as "the Illyrian idiom." Bajamonti in 1797 made Homer a Slav by discussing his relation to the "Morlacchi nation," in order to bring "honor to the Illyrian nation."

This proliferation of national labels, applied to Dalmatia, illustrates the multiple imaginings of community. Benedict Anderson has explored the origins of nationalism within the communal imagination, and he has also suggested that imperial structures, with their component administrative units, became the incubators of "anti-metropolitan" sentiment, nascent nationalism, in the warming ideological climate of the Enlightenment.[3] The case of Dalmatia shows that the process of imperial imagination could be implicated in the ascriptive national denomination of a subject community. Within the public sphere of the Adriatic empire, the national aspect of Dalmatia was formulated by foreign forces in the age of Enlightenment, with the participation of the most civilized Dalmatians joining in an imperially framed discourse. Thus the imaginative ascription of national identity in Dalmatia was conditioned by the imperial values of Venice and the philosophical concerns of the Enlightenment. From the Venetian perspective the denomination of a Dalmatian nation was politically convenient, for such a nation was naturally tailored to fit the imperial frontiers of the province. The Illyrian alternative could be similarly measured to match the dimensions of the province and was indeed even more imaginatively versatile than the Dalmatian designation, since the historical frame of reference was altogether ancient, almost mythological, without any correspondence to the modern map. At the same time, the invocation of the Morlacchi nation was philosophically valuable to Venice, since that label was richly invested with the aspects of ferocity and barbarism, an implicit justification of Venice's civilizing mission in Dalmatia.

With the mountains so close to the Adriatic coast, the label "Morlacchi" was always slipping down the slopes of signification to indicate a general provincial condition of backwardness, excepting only those "most civilized Dalmatians" who ratified the stigmatic sense of the term by insisting on their own exemption. In 1783 Boldù perceived the "epidemic inertia" of the Morlacchi as a problem of national character, "communicated" by a sort of organic infection "among the most civilized persons who (excepting some individuals) are certainly in the same indolence." Wayne Vucinich has suggested that the names "Vlach" and "Morlacco" were often flexibly applied to populations, "regardless of their ethnic background," while Predrag Matvejević has indicated the "polysemantic quality" and "multifarious uses" of those terms.[4] The Morlacchi nation could thus include anyone not specifically excepted from it and emerged as a sort of alternative aspect to the Dalmatian nation envisioned by Goldoni. The Dalmatian nation was celebrated for its loyalty and valor, while the Morlacchi nation was characterized by its primitive customs, whether positively associated with moral virtues in the state of nature or negatively diagnosed as ferocious barbarism and economic inertia.

The overlapping significations of these differently denominated nations meant that each could embrace the province as a whole, each with its own exceptions. The Morlacchi nation was the barbarous aspect of the Dalmatian nation, as recognized by the Enlightenment. The Dalmatian nation belonged to the early modern Mediterranean arena; the Morlacchi nation belonged to Eastern Europe. Though Bajamonti in 1797 was almost ready to acknowledge his own implicit relation to the Morlacchi, the evolution of the national label was remarkable for the fact that there was no constituency to claim the name. Fortis admitted that the so-called Morlacchi sometimes identified themselves as Vlassi, or Vlachs; he knew that the name "Morlacchi" actually came from the Adriatic coast, from those who considered themselves more civilized Dalmatians. The Morlacchi were the silent subalterns of the Adriatic empire, a nation empirically observed, ascriptively imagined, and philosophically defined, always "our Morlacchi" (*nostri Morlacchi*), never "we Morlacchi." Bajamonti's concept of "Morlacchismo" must be considered in relation to the later evolution of what Maria Todorova has called "balkanism," defined as "a discourse about an imputed ambiguity," addressing the lands and peoples of southeastern Europe.[5]

The philosophical convenience of the Morlacchi nation, affirming the civilizing mission of the Adriatic empire, was countered by its problematic political implications. The issue of Morlacchi emigration across the Habsburg and Ottoman borders had been frankly recognized as a political problem since Foscarini's speech of 1747, an awkward empirical counterstatement to the presumption of exemplary Dalmatian loyalty to Venice. Fortis further discerned the Slavic resemblances that might make the Morlacchi susceptible to a national affiliation that went beyond the limits of Venetian sovereignty. This problem appeared all the more acute in the context of the Russian-Ottoman war, between 1768 and 1774, when Russian military recruitment and appeals for support posed the question of Slavic resemblances in its most subversive form. Bajamonti in 1786 noted empirically the regional similarity between Morlacchi and Bosnians, across the Ottoman-Venetian border, but Wynne in 1788 conceived of a much more extensive extra-Adriatic affiliation when she imagined a "Slavic nation," inspiring profound sentimental allegiance that focused more intensely on St. Petersburg than San Marco. The ascriptive conception of a Slavic nation by the Venetian Enlightenment meant putting a name to the potential political phenomenon that Venice deeply desired to prevent in Dalmatia. Imperial apprehension thus helped to formulate the very subversions it sought to discourage.

Ernest Gellner argues that "nations are not inscribed into the nature of things," that modern nationalism comes from the "crystallization of new units" derived from previously "overlapping, interwined" cultures.[6] By the same token, nations are not ascribed according to nature, but rather by the crystallizing of distinct national meanings around formerly overlapping labels. The constellation of national names deployed within the discourse of Dalmatia, as the Venetian Enlightenment attempted to denominate the imperial subjects of the Adriatic empire, indicated the unassorted and unstable status of the "nation" in eighteenth-century Dalmatia. The publication in Venice in 1747 of the *Cvit razgovora* by Grabovac concerned the "Illyrian or Croatian" nation and language; in 1756 the *Razgovor ugodni* by Kačić-Miošić preferred to specify the "Slavic" nation or people. These overlapping designations indicated a similar absence of national consensus in these works, written in a language that could be alternatively identified as Illyrian, Croatian, or Slavic. In the much denser discourse pursued in the Italian language by Venetians and Dalmatians during the later eighteenth century, the label "Croatian" was most notable for its absence, neither affirmed nor refuted, but barely mentioned. In Fortis it occurred as a designation from ancient history, as he hunted for antiquities in Dalmatia and failed to find "any residue of barbarous magnificence that recalls the centuries when the kings of the Slavi Croati resided there." The designation of "Serbian" for the Orthodox Morlacchi was similarly rare, occurring, for instance, in a strictly religious context when Memmo proposed improving religious education in Dalmatia, "relative to the Latin church as well as the Greek Serbian." The designations "Slavi Croati" and "Greek Serbian" clearly illustrate the phenomenon of overlapping labels. Writing about nationality in Transylvania within the imperial framework of the Habsburg monarchy, Katherine Verdery has noted a "fluidity of self-conception" in the early modern centuries, which began to become less permutable with the consolidations of modern ethnicity and nationalism.[7] In the case of Venice and Dalmatia the early modern imperial matrix also conditioned the ascription, affirmation, and fluctuation of still volatile identities. Goldoni's political formulation of a "Dalmatian nation" within an "Adriatic empire" posed the question of who actually lived in Venetian Dalmatia, dramatizing a discourse of analytical national ascription that contributed to the controversial crystallization of modern nationalism.

Civilization and Barbarism:
From Venetian Dalmatia to Napoleonic Illyria

Dalmatia largely belonged to the Habsburgs through the long nineteenth century from 1797 to 1918, with the brief interlude of Napoleonic
rule from 1805 to 1813; the "Illyrian Provinces," after 1809, included
Dubrovnik as well as Dalmatia, with an administrative capital at Ljubljana
in Slovenia. After the Congress of Vienna in 1815 the Habsburgs re-
gained both Venice and Dalmatia, together again in common subjection
to the Austrian empire. After 1866 Venice severed the Austrian attachment to enter into independent Italy, but Dalmatia remained subject to
Vienna and was purposefully kept apart from Croatia after the Austro-
Hungarian compromise of 1867. With the resolution of Zadar in 1905
Dalmatia emerged as a political base for encouraging the common cause
of the South Slavs, Serbs and Croats, within the Habsburg monarchy. In
the twentieth century Dalmatia became the Adriatic coast of the kingdom of Yugoslavia, as established by the peace of Versailles, though competing Italian claims successfully preserved the prize of Zadar for the rule
of Rome. The Italian occupation of Dalmatia during World War II was
followed by the incorporation of the coast into the republic of Croatia
within Communist Yugoslavia after the war. After the dissolution of Yugoslavia in 1991 Dalmatia remained a geographically distended and mili-
tarily vulnerable region of independent Croatia, governed from Zagreb,
but uncomfortably close to the violence of the civil war across the border
in Bosnia.

The course of two centuries has thus politically redefined Dalmatia
from a province of Venice to an integral region of Croatia, after a variety
of imperial authorities and allegiances. As for the Dalmatians themselves,
the same two centuries since the end of Venetian rule have witnessed the
national elaboration of provincial identity according to the stringent and
strident claims of modern nationalism. The nineteenth-century Habsburg censuses, surveying nationality by language categories, found that
Dalmatia consisted not of Dalmatians or Illyrians, let alone Morlacchi,
but rather a Serbo-Croatian majority of 96 percent and an Italian minority of 3 percent. By religious affiliation it was possible to analyze that
Serbo-Croatian majority into components of roughly 80 percent Croatian Catholics and 20 percent Serbian Orthodox, almost the same confes-
sional proportions that characterized Venetian Dalmatia. By the logic of

modern nationalism such statistics brought most of Dalmatia into Yugoslavia after World War I, and into Croatia within Yugoslavia after World War II. Though the Serbs of the inland Dalmatian Krajina sought to secede from independent Croatia in 1991, the region was reconquered by the Croatian army and the Serbian population was expelled in 1995. Dalmatia today is a region of almost entirely Croatian nationality, pending the unfulfilled stipulations of the Dayton accords by which the Krajina Serbs might claim the right of repatriation. The intertwined and overlapping designations of the eighteenth century have succumbed before the uncompromising competitive presumptions of modern nationalism. As for the Morlacchi, banished from the statistical categories of the census, they have vanished from the catalogue of nations, persisting into the early twentieth century only in the anecdotal record as a folkloric curiosity. Such a fate was, in some sense, phenomenologically appropriate, since their eighteenth-century celebrity involved a chimerically ascribed identity, sustained by the interplay of administrative and philosophical perspectives. Eventually, the forces of modern economy and administration—of "civilization," as envisioned by the Venetian Enlightenment—made the Morlacchi less and less distinguishable among the Dalmatians. At the same time, the population of Dalmatia was nationally redefined by the competing claims of Serbian and Croatian identity, which left no place for the Morlacchi.

The international reputation of the Morlacchi in the late Enlightenment, however, was such that Marshal Auguste-Frédéric-Louis Marmont, who governed Napoleonic Illyria, was well aware of their presence in the province. He employed the Morlacchi both in building roads and in constructing an Illyrian ideology of empire for French Dalmatia. Attentive to the military concerns of the Napoleonic enterprise, Marshal Marmont initiated projects to build roads in Dalmatia, connecting the coastal towns from Zadar to Split and leading inland along the Cetina River to the Bosnian border. His justification for imposing forced labor on the Morlacchi was formulated as a fundamental principle of imperial responsibility: "When an enlightened government possesses a country of poor and barbarous peoples, it must hasten to have executed, by corvée, the great works of public utility. It thus advances the epoch of their wealth and civilization." France reframed the Venetian civilizing mission in Dalmatia, vaunting the values of the Enlightenment, clarifying the relation between "civilized" government and "barbarous" peoples. The construction of roads not only met the military imperatives of Napoleon, but also matched the ideological agenda of empire among the Morlacchi, promising "a more precocious civilization" in Dalmatia: "for to civilize barbarians it is necessary to bring them together."[8] Roads would bring the barbarians together and civilize them in the service of France.

The same agenda appeared in the work of an anonymous French traveler who visited Napoleonic Illyria and published in Turin his *Souvenirs d'un Voyage en Dalmatie,* giving only his initials C. B. on the title page. He was especially interested in the Morlacchi and recycled the observations of Fortis and Lovrich, for instance, on the incomprehensible language ("the Illyrian language which is, as one knows, the most extensive of any language of Europe"), on the songs and dances ("the Morlaques sing thus, or rather, to say it better, they howl"), on the red caps of Morlacchi girls ("the symbol of virginity"), as well as the familiar subjects of friendship and vengeance, love and marriage.[9] The Venetian Enlightenment had already created an arsenal of conventional observations concerning the Morlacchi, and the anonymous Frenchman only needed to adapt the civilizing mission of Venice to that of Napoleonic France. His catalogue of the defects of Morlacchi character was similarly familiar from the epithets of the Enlightenment: "Brigands by heroism and by superstition, declared enemies of economy, of agriculture, of laws, of subordination, of order, and of all that could hinder the indolent and unbridled life in which they love to wallow: in a word, savages."[10] Yet C. B. relished the barbarism of the Morlacchi sufficiently to hope that they would preserve their customs and their costumes, that they would not become, in an original French coinage, *démorlaquisé.* Rather, a beneficient government would have to try "to tame them little by little, to render them susceptible to a more refined civilization." In fact, he thought that only French government could manage to "operate this miracle" in Dalmatia, and he particularly praised Marshal Marmont for building such "superb" roads.[11] The anonymous traveler tried to reconcile the sentimental and civilizing perspectives of the Venetian Enlightenment regarding the Morlacchi when he proposed a policy of civilization that would nevertheless preserve them from the condition he insightfully discerned as *démorlaquisé.* This was, in fact, precisely the condition that awaited the Morlacchi, destined gradually to disappear as a recognizable community.

While Marmont in the 1830s was writing his memoirs, remembering the past glory of Napoleonic Illyria, Ljudevit Gaj in Zagreb was contemplating the future glory of Illyria as the national destiny of the South Slavs. His modern Illyrian movement naturally looked to Dalmatia, which was so closely associated with the ancient name of Illyria. In 1835 Gaj published a Croatian translation of Herder's account of the Slavs— "from the Don to the Elbe, from the Baltic to the Adriatic Sea"—and then gave his own view of the Slavs, with his own geographic coordinates and organic imagery:

> A huge giant lies across half of Europe. The top of his head is bathed in the blue Adriatic. His immense legs reach across the northern ice and snow to the walls of China. In his strong right hand, stretched through the heart of the Turkish Empire, he carries the Black Sea, and in the left, extended through the heart of the German lands, he holds the Baltic. His head is Central Illyria. . . . This giant is our nation, the Slavic nation, the largest in Europe.[12]

The concept of Slavdom, as outlined by Fortis and Herder in the Enlightenment, was deployed on behalf of romantic nationalism by Gaj in the 1830s. Dalmatia, by the blue Adriatic, was thus essential to his Illyrian movement, which proposed to include all the lands of the South Slavs within one Illyrian nation. When Gaj went to Dalmatia in 1841, however, he was disappointed to discover that Italian cultural influence in the coastal towns made them unreceptive to his Slavic Illyrianism. The exception was Dubrovnik, which was never part of the Venetian empire and gave Gaj a warm welcome.[13] Vuk Karadžić was also in Dalmatia in 1841, and he too was disappointed in his visit. He was preparing the third and definitive edition of his collection of Serbian songs, and he hoped to find among the Dalmatians an authentic oral version of the "Hasanaginica." He was always dissatisfied with Fortis's version, suspecting that it had lost its popular Slavic character as it passed into the hands of a foreign Italian author.[14]

While Gaj and Karadžić were in Dalmatia in 1841, pursuing their related Croatian and Serbian national purposes, both wrestling with the intellectual legacy of Fortis's *Viaggio in Dalmazia,* Fabio Mutinelli published in Venice a history of the city, *Annali Urbani di Venezia.* The book was dedicated to the Dalmatians:

> AI DALMATI: To you who for so many centuries in the armies and navies of the Venetians shared with them their victories and defeats; to you who alone among all others, in the extremity of Venice, when handing over the flag of San Marco, kissed and embraced it, sighing, breaking into bitter weeping, to

you this book properly belongs. Receive it therefore with benign spirit, while we will not cease to repeat: happy the prince who supports such a generous nation, and in the day of danger can rely upon its unshaken loyalty.[15]

Mutinelli, in the text of his book, recorded the role of the Dalmatian troops in Venice in 1797, recalling that "when the patricians retreated to their homes weeping and saying 'San Marco is no more,' some Slav soldiers, whether in anger, whether in affection for their republic, vigorously exclaimed to the contrary, 'Viva San Marco.' " This was an episode from Venice's "urban annals," whether as history, whether as legend, but the dedication made clear that for Mutinelli the relation between Venice and the Dalmatians was still sentimentally alive. The principles of the Adriatic empire could still be publicly articulated in a spirit of profound nostalgia, whether as ideology, whether as mythology. The cry of 'Viva San Marco' would be heard again in 1848, in the Venetian revolutionary republic of Daniel Manin, and there were Dalmatians, like Niccolò Tommaseo, hero of the Italian Risorgimento, who crossed the Adriatic to fight for liberty in Venice. In November 1848 Lord Palmerston cautioned Venice that England would not permit the Republic to reestablish its rule in Dalmatia.[16] By that time the historical memory of the Adriatic empire had persisted for half a century after the folding of the flag of San Marco.

In 1848 Matija Ban came from Serbia to Dalmatia to study the state of national sentiment there. He reported that "only the people in the mountain regions are not infected by alien ideas, but they have no common national consciousness outside of speaking their own language, adhering to their own customs, and resenting townspeople."[17] The Morlacchi in 1848 thus appeared still immune to the various national appeals of the nineteenth century, and in England in that year, J. Gardner Wilkinson published an account of the Morlacchi that recognized them as an anthropological community, bound together by common customs. "I had an opportunity of observing the manners and customs of the Morlacchi," he wrote, and strongly contrasted them to the coastal Dalmatians, who appeared to him "mostly of Venetian extraction." The customs of the Morlacchi seemed all the more "singular," but Wilkinson's account leaned so heavily on Fortis and Lovrich that the implied persistence of custom was partly explained by the evident persistence of literary authority.[18]

French awareness of the Morlacchi in the nineteenth century derived from the same eighteenth-century sources; the Venetian legacy was studied in Marshal Marmont's Illyria and disseminated in post-Napoleonic France. In 1813, the last year of the Illyrian episode, Charles Nodier was working in Ljubljana, writing for the official journal of the province, the *Télégraphe*. His articles on "Poésies illyriennes" and "Coutumes des Morlaques" were largely based on Fortis and Lovrich. Fortis's remarks about vampire beliefs among the Morlacchi became the basis for Nodier's vampire tale, *Smarra,* in 1821. Mérimée, publishing *La Guzla* in 1827, took the material for his mock Morlacchi poems from Fortis, with an emphasis on vengeance, violence, and vampires.[19] After fifty years, Fortis remained fundamental for representations of Dalmatia in France, but, under the influence of French Romanticism, the Morlacchi were now conceived as dwelling somewhere between the domains of the anthropological and the fantastic.

Provincial Economy and National Identity in Habsburg Dalmatia

In 1892 there was published in Vienna a large, handsome, heavily illustrated book about Dalmatia, as part of a series entitled *Die österreichisch-ungarische Monarchie in Wort und Bild,* the Austro-Hungarian monarchy "in word and image." The diverse provinces received their respective volumes, and the whole project was imperially sponsored, with an acknowledgment of the patronage of the Archduke Rudolf, who had actually committed suicide at Mayerling three years earlier. The book was published by the official press of the court and state ("Druck und Verlag der kaiserlich-königlich Hof- und Staatsdruckerei"), thus imperially and royally presenting Dalmatia as a province of the Habsburg monarchy. As a collaborative work of scholarship, including Dalmatian contributors, the perspective involved provincial views integrated into an overall imperial representation.

Tullio Erber, for instance, professor at the Gymnasium of Zadar, had researched and published during the preceding years a history of Dalmatia between 1797 and 1814, that is, of the transition from Venetian to Austrian rule, including the Napoleonic Illyrian interlude; his work had appeared in serial periodical installments in Zadar, written in Italian, and now, in 1892, he summed up his subject in German for the official Habsburg account. From the perspective of the nineteenth-century

Austrian empire, the superseded eighteenth-century Venetian empire
could hardly be celebrated. Venice, as Erber recounted more in sorrow
than in anger, was not capable of bringing about economic development
in Dalmatia.

> Venice, in a condition of decline, was no longer able to cope with such cir-
> cumstances, and even when the Senate proclaimed some decrees to improve
> agriculture and forestry, still everything remained as before because of the
> lack of energy and proverbial corruption of the officials. At the same time the
> Morlacchi were numbed (*abgestumpft*) by sufferings and deprivations, and
> the clergy was too ignorant to lift the peasants out of their moral decline. Of
> roads, schools, and other beneficent establishments there was not a trace in
> the countryside. . . . And yet the people (*das Volk*) adhered to the Venetian
> dominion with touching loyalty and love, grateful for their liberation from
> the Turkish yoke. When Bonaparte's troops menacingly drew near to Venice,
> and the cry for help from the doge Ludovico Manin reached Dalmatia,
> 12,000 men of the Dalmatian provincial militia hastened to the defense of the
> lagoons.[20]

Erber's historical vision of Venice in decline, lacking the energy to govern its Adriatic empire, was evidently intended to vindicate the Viennese
takeover in 1797 but also matched other images of Venice in fin-de-siècle
Vienna. Hugo von Hofmannsthal's verse drama of 1892, "The Death of
Titian," evoked the decadence of late Renaissance Venice in an artistic
circle of reclusive and enervated aestheticism, the Venetians waiting at
Titian's deathbed for the inevitable end of an epoch. Erber, though he
criticized the rule of Venice in Dalmatia, could not resist the recitation of
the ultimate end of the Adriatic empire, complete with the almost legendary drama of Dalmatian loyalty.

That loyalty was represented in all its sentimental resplendence,
even devoted to the corrupt and ineffective sovereignty of Venice, because Erber was about to make over that same treasury of Dalmatian
loyalty to the Habsburgs. Thus he described the conclusion of the
Napoleonic wars:

> Even if the sacrifice which the Dalmatians made in Austria's favor was great,
> so the beneficences of the ensuing peace corresponded to all legitimate ex-
> pectations. Taxes were lowered and a regulated administration cared for the
> well-being of the land. Trade and industry gradually blossomed, seafaring re-
> ceived a rapid stimulus, and numerous schools contributed no small amount
> to the education of the people (*des Volkes*). The grateful Dalmatians consid-
> ered it henceforth an honor to be subjects of Austria, and their demonstrated

bravery in the wars of the past decades gave the best proof of the prevailing loyalty and attachment in the land. "Property and Life (*Gut und Blut*) for our Emperor" is the motto of the Dalmatians, relative to which the passions of the political parties disappear.[21]

The rhetorical achievement was not only to displace completely eighteenth-century Dalmatian loyalty to Venice, but also to insist on the contemporary displacement of any political platforms—whether Italian irredentism or Illyrian solidarity—that went beyond Habsburg loyalism.

Erber's contribution generalized about the Dalmatians under the German concept of *Volk*, which had received its particular national and anthropological meaning from Herder in the age of Enlightenment. Following Erber in the volume, there began a long essay on the *Volkskunde* or folklore of Dalmatia, written collaboratively by a team of contributors, including Dalmatians. The first page of this essay was adorned with pictures of Morlacchi, a traditionally dressed couple from the region around Zadar, and a group of women working in the fields. They were specified as Morlacchi—*Morlakenpaar* and *Morlakenweiber*—but the text then promptly undermined the whole concept of the Morlacchi as a meaningful designation. "With the exception of a small percentage (6%) of Italians on the coast and the islands," the essay began, already exaggerating the percentage of Italians, "the whole population of Dalmatia is united in the Serbo-Croatian language community." This was, in fact, the crucial classification in the Habsburg census. The essay went on to consider the special case of the Morlacchi:

> In a natural history of the Dalmatians descent is all the less acceptable as a basis for classification, as with regard to the Morlacchi the scientific struggle still fluctuates, since some want them to be viewed as Romans (Mavro-vlachos, that is, black Latins), and others as true Serbs. Since, however, the Morlacchi conform almost completely (*nahezu vollkommen übereinstimmen*) to the Serbo-Croatian majority of the inhabitants of Dalmatia, in body size, as well as in eye, hair, and skin color, and no less in the form of the skull, here the more notable differences between the inhabitants of the Dalmatian mountains and the coast will be incidentally (*gelegentlich*) indicated.[22]

With that introduction the authors made almost no further mention of the Morlacchi, who thus virtually vanished before the reader's eyes; within the volume the classification was thus reconceived in complete conformity to the Serbo-Croatian majority, specified as the Dalmatian *Volk*.

The essay on literature and folk poetry cited Fortis for his pioneering contribution: "In the book *Viaggio in Dalmazia* (Venice 1774) Fortis published several specimens of Morlacchi (that means Serbo-Croatian) songs."[23] The parenthetical redefinition—"einige Proben morlackischer (das heisst serbischkroatischer) Lieder"—effectively eliminated the Morlacchi from the anthropological equation. It was impossible to mention Fortis without mentioning the Morlacchi, but they were named only to be dismissed as an anachronistic folkloric classification, irrelevant to the official *kasiserlich-königlich* account of Dalmatia.

In 1905 Camilla Lucerna, from Zagreb, wrote about the "Hasan-aginica" and took the opportunity to put in historical perspective the eighteenth-century discovery of the Morlacchi, rejecting emphatically the whole concept.

> Fortis's "Morlacchi" came into fashion. Though he was not the first to use this dubious designation, it was really launched with the success of his work. It is misleading and should therefore be given up. Ethnographic relations among us are under the influence of political tendencies and have become sufficiently entangled. There is no Morlacchi language, no Morlacchi people. ("Es gibt keine morlakische Sprache, keinen morlakischen Volksstamm.")[24]

For those who believed in the objective character of ethnography and nationality at the beginning of the twentieth century, the Morlacchi did not really exist. They were merely an imaginary community.

Habsburg Zagreb in the late nineteenth century was also the site for Croatian discussion concerning the national character of Dalmatia as a whole. Charles Jelavich, in his research on textbooks and nationalism, found one text by Petar Matković in the 1870s describing Dalmatians as "almost exclusively of Croatian-Serbian origin," and another by Vjenceslav Mařik in 1876 making them "almost all Croats and Serbs," while those texts of Ivan Hoić and Vjekoslav Klaić in the 1880s insisted that the population of Dalmatia was more strictly Croatian. Hoić wrote regretfully about "the Croatian coastal inhabitants" who had to become sailors for "the glory and greatness of arrogant Venice," but he held that "throughout all of Dalmatia, Croatian customs and language prevailed." In counterpoint, Jelavich found that contemporary Serbian textbooks, published in Belgrade, affirmed that Dalmatia was inhabited entirely by Serbs, whether Catholic or Orthodox. Serbian perspectives emphasized linguistic similarity to Dalmatia, based on the štokavian dialect, as distinct from the kajkavian dialect spoken around Zagreb; Croatian perspectives stressed a common heritage coming not only from Roman Catholicism, but also from historical unity in the medieval triune kingdom of Croatia, Slavonia, and Dalmatia. In Habsburg Slovenia textbooks were much more likely to compromise in characterizing Dalmatians as Serbo-Croatian. Interestingly, the eighteenth-century poems of Kačić-Miošić were widely anthologized in the nineteenth century, and, in a reader published in Zagreb in 1875, his work was considered representative of "the entire people, be they called Croats or Serbs."[25] On the threshold of the twentieth century there remained considerable ambivalence about the national character of both the Morlacchi and the Dalmatians.

In the 1860s and 1870s another Bajamonti, Antonio, the mayor of Split, advocated Dalmatian autonomy and a distinctive Dalmatian identity within the Habsburg monarchy, resisting administrative unification with Croatia. In 1910, when Josip Smodlaka, the deputy representative of Split, stood up in the Austrian Reichsrat in Vienna to speak on behalf of his Dalmatian constituents, he affirmed "the national cause of the Serbo-Croats, to whom Dalmatia belongs as one of their noblest provinces." The officially sponsored Habsburg account of 1892 still made Venice responsible for the economic backwardness of Dalmatia, but in 1910 Smodlaka held the Habsburgs accountable. The social and economic concerns of the eighteenth-century Dalmatian academies, of the Venetian Provveditori Generali, of Andrea Memmo in 1790, even of Marco Foscarini in 1747, were echoed in Smodlaka's appeal on behalf of "the desperate condition of Dalmatia." He was voting against the state budget in 1910, on account of "the neglect of Dalmatia on the part of all Austrian governments, including the present, the way in which my native land's most vital needs are ignored."[26] Smodlaka presented Dalmatia as both the challenge and the responsibility of the Habsburgs.

Smodlaka had high hopes for hydroelectric power in Dalmatia, but Austrian capital had failed to materialize and Italian capital was blocked by Vienna, for political reasons, from making the investment. "And for Dalmatia a question of life and death is at stake," declared Smodlaka. He called for imperial officials who would govern the province in a spirit of modern enterprise: "Have you an Austrian Cecil Rhodes, a Cromer, a Curzon? If you have, or even men of lesser calibre, then send them to Dalmatia. But give the man to whom you entrust the fate of the province, and the task of its regeneration, also the power to effect something." Citing the recent period's legendary leaders of the British empire—like Lord Curzon in India, Lord Cromer in Egypt, and Cecil Rhodes in South Africa—Smodlaka seemed implicitly to consider Dalmatia as comparable to such remote colonial domains. As in the eighteenth century, it was still England that set the standard for imperial government, and Smodlaka almost taunted the Habsburgs with the comparison. "If you do not care to learn from the English," he commented sarcastically, "give us proconsuls, propraetors, like those of the ancient Romans." He invoked "the greatness of Roman Illyria," regretting the present circumstances: "Today—I am ashamed to admit it, but it is the sad truth—Dalmatia has become a land of beggars, through no fault of its own."[27] Foscarini in 1747 thought that the moment of life and death—"either salvation or desperation"—had already arrived, as he heard of Dalmatians abandoning the Venetian for the Ottoman empire, emigrating "as tattered beggars." The discourse of the Enlightenment on Dalmatia produced rhetorical forms for political discussion of the province which echoed even in the beginning of the twentieth century.

Smodlaka in 1910 was particularly apprehensive about the political significance of folkloric appreciation:

> Dalmatia is regarded as something exotic; it is only regarded from the standpoint of archaeology and tourist traffic. We have no wish to play the part of an archaeological cemetery or an "Indian reservation" with the authentic Dalmatian Red Indians in their gay costume. No, gentlemen, we want to be able to live and work, to earn our living honestly by agriculture, trade, and industry and thus serve the interests of the state as a whole.[28]

Smodlaka's criticism of such folkloric condescension was a response to the legacy of the Enlightenment, as he put the Habsburgs on notice that the Dalmatians of the twentieth century would no longer sing the songs, dance the dances, or wear the costumes of the primitive Morlacchi. Instead, they demanded hydroelectric power, to be developed under the modern imperial management of someone like Rhodes, Cromer, or Curzon.

That same year, in 1910, an academic conference on Dalmatia was held at the University of Vienna, with a variety of experts surveying every aspect of the province, from the flora and fauna of the Adriatic, to the folk art and folk songs of Dalmatia. The lectures were published in 1911, in Vienna and Leipzig, and the discussion of economy in Dalmatia, by an official of the imperial ministry for trade, seemed almost an official response to Smodlaka's grievances.

When people speak about the economic situation in Dalmatia, as a rule this happens in direct conjunction with complaint about the neglect and backwardness of the land. The cause of this backwardness is sought by preference . . . in the sins and omissions of the administration. The reproach is not completely to be denied, but also not completely fair.[29]

Rather than focus on the controversial assignment of blame, the official perspective preferred to emphasize the ongoing effort to discover practical remedies for economic backwardness in Dalmatia.

In the same publication the article on folk art, which included handsome illustrations of provincial embroidery, addressed the relation between folkloric and economic issues.

The land is poor, the people all too much oppressed by harsh necessity. Dalmatia is far richer in folk art, and generally in folkloric respects, for which the causes are to be adduced in the first place from the economic peculiarity and seclusion of the land from large trade. The great primitiveness and antiquity of its inhabitants in their form of life and type of spirit, their economic poverty, which in many ways keep them in a pure natural economy, their seclusion and their particularism are the hitherto strong and undisrupted roots, from which folk artistic qualities of the first rank have flowered.[30]

The direct causal relation between economic poverty and folkloric wealth was explicitly formulated; modern economic development, by implication, was not necessarily consistent with the preservation of primitive folk culture. The Enlightenment had discovered in Dalmatia both of these important problems of modernity, the challenge of economic development and the fascination of folkloric persistence in the survival of customs. The disappearance of the Morlacchi as a recognizable community based on the preservation of customs must partly be attributed to the pressures of modern economic development upon folkloric particularism in the mountains of Dalmatia. The elimination of their name, however, followed from the discursive innovations of modern nationalism.

Between East and West: Tourist Travel in Modern Dalmatia

The agricultural academies of Venetian Dalmatia had contemplated a variety of economic remedies to backwardness, pinning their hopes for prosperity upon such diverse alternatives as chestnuts and olives, grapes and potatoes, eels and sardines. No one in the eighteenth century, however, was sufficiently prophetic to foresee that Dalmatia's most profitable modern commodity would be its Adriatic beaches. Smodlaka in Habsburg Dalmatia in 1910 still refused to accept that "tourist traffic" was an honorable route to economic salvation, but the revolution was already under way, and in twentieth-century Yugoslavia the development of the Dalmatian coast would be accepted without compunction. In 1909 Hermann Bahr published the account of his voyage in Dalmatia, *Dalmatinische Reise*, celebrating Austria's Adriatic coast, "everywhere the blue sea, rejoicing in the sun." Bahr had been the presiding literary figure of Young Vienna in the 1890s, and he continued to encourage the public to follow him in his own shifting intellectual enthusiasms. As he had once discovered and celebrated the poetic teenage genius of Hugo von Hofmannsthal, so now Bahr discovered Dalmatia, another Austrian treasure for which he commanded public appreciation:

> I am a true heliotrope. I must turn toward the sun. As the sun shines, accordingly I gain strength. This draws me every year again to the land of sun, to Dalmatia. It is like a pilgrimage, coming from anxiety and affliction to recover in light and warmth. But Dalmatia is not simply a land of sun, a land of fairy tales, a land of magic (*Sonnenland, Märchenland, Zauberland*), but also a province of the Austro-Hungarian monarchy.[31]

Fortis had suggested a great variety of reasons why Venetians might want to voyage in Dalmatia, but neither he nor any of his enlightened contemporaries anticipated the twentieth-century enthusiasms of Bahr's invitation to travel in Dalmatia—*Sonnenland, Märchenland, Zauberland*—the province reconceived as a paradise for Viennese vacationers. The travel fever that Bahr so excitedly proclaimed, the hyperbolic longing for the south and the sun, would be echoed a few years later in Thomas Mann's literary masterpiece *Death in Venice*. Gustav von Aschenbach, the troubled protagonist, found decadence and disease in Venice, in contrast to the healthy holiday that Bahr recommended in Dalmatia.

A traveler's guide to Dalmatia, published in 1912 in Vienna and Leipzig, advertised the therapeutic charms of the Adriatic climate, according to Bahr's formula, as the antidote to "anxiety and affliction." The island of Lesina (that is, Hvar), where Stratico presided as an enlightened bishop and Bajamonti practiced medicine in the 1780s, was now, in the early twentieth century, represented as a curative resort for neurotic Viennese vacationers:

> The moist, warm island climate of Lesina corresponds roughly to that of Ajaccio (Corsica), Palermo, and Corfu. This climate with its sedative character is good for the respiratory organs and the nervous system. For this reason a sojourn there is recommended for a great number of medical symptoms. Especially recommended for neurasthenics and generally for those with nervous ailments. But also as a recovery place for convalescents and finally for general recuperative needs, Lesina offers, thanks to its southern dustfree situation and its attractive surroundings, a pleasant sojourn. In recent times it has been more and more visited for seabathing, for which its southern climate is most conducive.[32]

The resort hotel *Kaiserin Elisabeth,* named for the Austrian empress who was assassinated in 1898, was particularly cited as a likely place on Lesina to recover from anxieties and afflictions. The existence of a "Hygienic Union," already in 1912, reflected the heliotropic health agendas that would bring groups of Germans to Hvar, and to Dalmatia in general, for enthusiastic nudist sunbathing in the later twentieth century.

In 1912 the particular concern with nervous illnesses suggested that the Viennese patients of Sigmund Freud, wrestling with their repressions, were those most in need of a voyage to Dalmatia. When Rebecca West traveled to Yugoslavia in 1937, she met Germans in the train compartment, taking a vacation from Nazi Germany, and one woman explained that "they were travelling to a Dalmatian island because her husband had been very ill with a nervous disorder affecting the stomach which made him unable to make decisions." The Germans felt nothing but contempt for Yugoslavia, nourishing a sense of "German superiority to all non-German barbarity," and Rebecca West could not help asking, "But why are you going to Yugoslavia if you think it is all so terrible?" They told her, "We are going to the Adriatic coast where there are many German tourists and for that reason the hotels are good."[33] The development of tourism since the turn of the century made Dalmatia into a sort of extraterritorial entity, *Sonnenland,* which German tourists with nervous disorders approved and appropriated as their own.

Rebecca West was not, however, the first twentieth-century traveler to appreciate Dalmatia in English; indeed her reflections purposefully sought to transcend the conventions of an established tourist itinerary.

Already before World War I, when Bahr was traveling from Vienna to Dalmatia, women from England and America made a much longer voyage to the same destination, and some wrote the accounts of their travels. In 1908 Maude Holbach published *Dalmatia: The Land Where East Meets West;* in 1910 Frances Kinsley Hutchinson reported on the new automobile tourism in *Motoring in the Balkans: Along the Highways of Dalmatia, Montenegro, the Herzegovina and Bosnia;* in 1914 Alice Lee Moqué enthusiastically contributed *Delightful Dalmatia*. Moqué, like Gibbon in the eighteenth century, was first struck by the obscurity of Dalmatia as a proposed destination: "For I was trying my very best to remember *where* on earth it was—and most unsuccessfully."[34] Hutchinson was entranced by her sense of Dalmatia's exoticism. "Dalmatia!" she exclaimed. "What strange magic in the name! How remote and Asiatic it sounded! What visions of mountain fastnesses and landlocked harbors, of curious buildings and primitive peoples, danced before my excited fancy!"[35] Holbach located Dalmatia in Eastern Europe, according to the vague geography of touristic impressions: "Today Dalmatia dwells apart, in a borderland somewhat off the highway of the world's traffic, like a shadow left by the receding tide between the sea and shore, belonging more to the East than to the West—more to the past than to the present."[36] Like the German traveler whose nervous disorder made him unable to make decisions, Maude Holbach remained undecided about the status of Dalmatia, but the idea of Eastern Europe prevailed in the end. Dalmatia was declared to be less western and less modern, not altogether of the twentieth century.

All three travelers cited as their cicerone in Dalmatia the three-volume guide to its architectural monuments by Thomas Graham Jackson, published in 1887, and all had some recourse to Professor Frane Bulić, the director of antiquities at Split, who also contributed to the Habsburg volume on Dalmatia in 1892. Jackson emphasized the incongruity between the splendors of Venetian architectural style in Dalmatia and the Slavic population, whose splendors did not go beyond embroidery. He described "country people," whose appearance "may perhaps smack slightly of semi-barbarism, but they are not the less interesting on that account to those who like to see civilization in the making."[37] He did not hesitate to name these interesting semi-barbarians as Morlacchi and thus guaranteed that the travelers who followed his guide would also discover the Morlacchi as part of their touristic experience of Dalmatia.

"The huts in which the Morlacchi live are the same as those described by Fortis," wrote Jackson, more than a hundred years after the publication of *Viaggio in Dalmazia*. He went on to describe the Morlacchi women as "half-savage looking creatures," wearing "embroidered leggings that give them the appearance of Indian squaws." Alice Moqué encountered the Morlacchi women in the market at Zadar, squatting "in oriental fashion," bedizened in "barbaric gorgeousness." She was reading Jackson closely enough to note "their embroidered leggings, which are worked in colored thread and adorned with many beads like the leggings and moccasins of an American Indian."[38] Frances Hutchinson also admired "the barbaric costumes of the Morlacchi" in the market at Zadar ("Such bravery of color! Such gorgeous raiment! Such charming caps and kerchiefs!"), and she could not help regretting that "civilization is about to encroach upon picturesqueness." One member of her party exclaimed, "How monotonous a world entirely civilized would be!" Maude Holbach included a photograph of the Morlacchi women in the Zadar market, remarking that "at the first glance they seemed to me more like North American Indians than any European race."[39] Smodlaka had good reason to fear that Dalmatia was being visited as an Indian reservation, for in the eyes of these visitors the Morlacchi were already Indians.

All three travelers had such a similar experience in the marketplace at Zadar that this "first sight" of the Morlacchi appears as almost a piece of packaged tourism, the requisite encounter with picturesquely primitive people in Dalmatia. The encounter was schematically outlined for them in the English guidebook, by Jackson, who even gave the Americans the cue to think of American Indians. It was as if the public really had followed Fortis into Dalmatia, accepting his rhetorical invitation, eager to enjoy the gratifications of amateur anthropology. Just as the "Customs of the Morlacchi" constituted Fortis's sensational discovery in the eighteenth century, so at the beginning of the twentieth century the observation of customs still permitted travelers to recognize that Dalmatia belonged to the different domain of Eastern Europe. Yet, the perceived degree of difference did not diminish from the eighteenth to the twentieth century, for the articulation of that difference within the Venetian Enlightenment remained discursively valid—indeed, became cliché—for the centuries that followed the fall of the Adriatic empire. Jackson was actually citing Fortis in the guidebook.

If the Morlacchi could be categorically identified as Serbo-Croatian, the Serbo-Croats could still be occasionally identified as Morlacchi. It was thus that the eleventh edition of the Encyclopedia Britannica in 1910 counted the Morlacchi as 96 percent of the Dalmatian population. The Encyclopedia thus deployed "the name of Morlachs, Morlaks or Morlacks commonly bestowed by English writers on the Dalmatian Slavs."[40] As a byword for barbarism, or perhaps semi-barbarism, the term could be casually invoked to emphasize that aspect of Dalmatia, as it appeared in "Western" eyes. Jackson in 1887 recognized "degrees among these Slavs," with the term "Morlacchi" denoting the lowest degree of civilization, "the wildest and rudest figures imaginable." He observed, sinisterly, that "they stare at you from under wild shocks of unkempt hair," and he reported their beliefs "in witches, fairies, enchantments, nocturnal apparitions, and vampires or spirits of dead persons who suck the blood of infants."[41] Such was the mythology or anthropology of the Morlacchi, known as Morlacks to English writers. It was natural for modern English and American travelers at the beginning of the twentieth century to see these Morlacks as relics of the primitive past, destined for extinction by the inevitable course of civilization, which would iron out the differences in customs and the "degrees" among the Slavs, as the world advanced toward the monotony of modernity. It required the genius of science fiction for an English writer to imagine a different course of development, as H. G. Wells did in 1895, envisioning the distant future in *The Time Machine*. When the narrator sees a "queer little ape-like figure" disappear down a shaft into the subterranean world, he realizes that human evolution has not produced a uniformly civilized society: "The truth dawned on me: that Man had not remained one species, but had differentiated into two distinct animals: that my graceful children of the Upper World were not the sole descendants of our generation, but that this bleached, obscene, nocturnal Thing, which had flashed before me, was also heir to all the ages."[42] The graceful and refined beings of the Upper World were called the Eloi, and they were preyed upon by the sinister figures of the subterranean world, who only came out by night as nocturnal apparitions. These creepy creatures had regressively evolved away from civilization, and every science fiction aficionado knows that H. G. Wells named them the Morlocks.

Dalmatia and Yugoslavia

During the years before World War I, as tourism developed in Dalmatia, R. W. Seton-Watson also traveled there from England, becoming a forceful foreign political advocate of the South Slavs. In friendship and correspondence with Smodlaka, as well as the Dalmatian journalist Ivo Lupis-Vukić, Seton-Watson publicized the political aspirations of Serbo-Croatian nationalism, urged the "trialist" reorganization of Austro-Hungarian dualism, and eventually endorsed the independent statehood of Yugoslavia, including Dalmatia. In advance of his later political celebrity and importance, Seton-Watson's early encounters with Dalmatia were arranged with attention to the details of tourist travel. Lupis wrote to him from Korčula in 1909, in somewhat awkward English:

> I read with pleasure of your intentional coming to Spalato. I am of the opinion that choice is good, and that your sojourn at Spalato will be pleasant. . . . Hotel Belvue is very good. Do you wish me to obtain information for a good teacher of our language? . . . And I look with pleasure on your visit to Curzola. I wish you would prolong it here as much as possible.[43]

In a letter of 1911, urging Seton-Watson to return to Dalmatia, the touristic accommodations of Korčula were advertised in greater detail:

> When you make up your plans, please, allow to Korčula at least one month. The new hotel will have twenty eight rooms, electric light, good kitchen, and a fine caffe. . . . And now you can freely recommend your friends to visit Curzola. The hotel-proprietors have already bought a nice motor-boat for excursions to surrounding places, while the hotel itself will offer them accommodations and comfort which any tourist can desire. . . . Please, recommend me to your lady, whom we will be so delightful to see with you in Dalmatia as early as possible.[44]

Thus, important international exchanges concerning the national aspirations of the South Slavs in Dalmatia took place in the context of the development of modern tourism in "delightful" Dalmatia.

In 1911 Smodlaka urged Seton-Watson to arrange for an art exhibit in London to feature the work of the Dalmatian sculptor, Ivan Meštrović. Such an exhibit had recently been a great success in Rome, and, for the moment, Smodlaka was not concerned about the potentially aggrandizing nature of Italian enthusiasm for Dalmatian matters. In fact, at home in Split (or Spalato), he wrote to Seton-Watson in Italian:

> You can imagine how proud we are! Could one not organize in London an exposition of Serbo-Croatian art, which would present us to the Anglo-Celtic world as *one* nation, showing the progress made by this people on the road of civilization *(civiltà)*?[45]

Smodlaka embraced the ideal of civilization, with nationalism invoked as the vehicle for traveling along that road. At a time when the Encyclopedia Britannica was peculiarly recording that the population of Dalmatia was 96 percent Morlacchi, there was every reason to seek to "present us" to the English as a single Serbo-Croatian nation.

In 1911 Seton-Watson made his own important contribution to representing the aspirations of Serbo-Croatian nationalism, with the publication of *The Southern Slav Question and the Habsburg Monarchy*. Dalmatia was essential to the resolution of that question, inasmuch as "the whole Eastern coast of the Adriatic still remains an unsolved equation in the arithmetic of Europe."[46] His challenge to the Habsburgs to attend to their nationalities problems before it became too late made him a hero in Dalmatia when he returned in 1912.

> Our stay in Dalmatia has been one long series of fêtes, so that we have hardly had time to draw breath. On the quai at Zara we were met by friends, and from that moment we have hardly ever been alone from morning till night. At Zara we were shown over the various sights, a magnificent private collection of embroideries etc., and ended with an official banquet. . . . We were taken in a motorboat round the Riviera di Castelli (between Spalato and Trau) and found at two of the little towns the Mayor's house decorated with Croat tricolours, the population with flags waving on the pier and men firing guns and shouting in our honor. . . . Finally the Mayor . . . and Corporation of Spalato gave us a banquet, at which there were further speeches and I had to try my hand at Croat in replying!![47]

Smodlaka welcomed Seton-Watson to Split, and, in fact, Smodlaka's speech in the Reichsrat in 1910, concerning the condition of Dalmatia, was published in English translation as an appendix to Seton-Watson's book. The celebrity of Seton-Watson in Split in 1912, after the publication of his book on the South Slavic question, was historically reminiscent of Fortis's triumphant return to Split in 1780, to address the Economic Society after *Viaggio in Dalmazia* had brought the province to the attention of the European Enlightenment.

During World War I Seton-Watson began to argue in England for the dissolution of the Habsburg empire and the creation of an independent Yugoslavia, including Dalmatia. "Without Dalmatia there can be no Serbo-Croat Unity, no Jugoslavia," he declared in 1915, aware of the rumors, quite correct, that England was secretly conceding Dalmatia to Italy as an inducement to enter the war. He worked with the Yugoslav Committee, based in London, and through his journal, *The New Europe,* attempted to mobilize European opinion against any such concession. Frano Supilo, the leading Dalmatian member of the Yugoslav Committee, exclaimed in 1916: "Either God (if he exists) or the very nature of Great Britain protests today against the projected consummation of a rape and a blasphemy in London: the proclamation of the *italianità* of Dalmatia!"[48] The Italian historian Gaetano Salvemini, agreeing to work with *The New Europe* in 1917, denounced "our nationalists who, thanks to their stupid pretensions to Dalmatia, and the detestable and dishonest arguments by which they support those pretensions, dishonor Italy, break our beautiful Mazzinian and Garibaldian tradition, and create a deplorable hostility between Italy and the South Slavs."[49] Another of Seton-Watson's Italian correspondents, Antonio de Viti de Marco, was willing to concede in 1918 that "Dalmatia is peopled by a great majority of Slavs," but, precisely on that account, for fear of national violence after the war, "Italy can't abandon the Italian groups living there in the hands of savages."[50] In this revealing remark Italy's international ambitions appeared in the context of the Adriatic anthropology of the Enlightenment. Both Seton-Watson and Smodlaka would be present in Paris in 1919 to try to influence the Versailles peacemakers concerning the future of Dalmatia.

In 1919 Woodrow Wilson went to Paris to adjudicate a peace based on the principle of national self-determination. At the very beginning of the war Wilson's confidant, Colonel Edward House, had written to Seton-Watson, requesting a copy of his book on the South Slavs: "I have more than passing reasons for wishing to be thoroughly informed regarding South-Eastern Europe."[51] At the meetings of the Council of Four in Paris in 1919, Wilson was both informed and resolved, ready to respond emphatically to the Italian prime minister Vittorio Emanuele Orlando: "M. Orlando had then harked back to Zara, Sebenico, and Spalato. President Wilson said that Italy would never get these." The Council of Four was continually discussing Dalmatia:

> Clemenceau. Are we returning to the question of Zara and Spalato?
>
> Lloyd George. I would like another discussion with the Italians, to see if they would accept my plan, with free cities on the Dalmatian coast and a plebiscite at the end of fifteen years.
>
> Clemenceau. You would not place these cities under their administration?
>
> Lloyd George. No, but under that of the League of Nations. President Wilson tells us that the Yugoslavs have a majority in these cities.
>
> Wilson. What I said is that the Italian majority was doubtful, although, certainly, the dominant element at least by culture is the Italian element.[52]

More than a century of Habsburg rule seemed suddenly irrelevant as the discussion reverted to the Italian legacy of Venetian rule. Wilson's conviction was influenced by a powerful sense of Slavdom, as something that went beyond the borders of Dalmatia, a phenomenon of Eastern Europe: "There is a fatal antagonism betwen the Italians and the Slavs. If the Slavs have the feeling of an injustice, that will make the chasm unbridgeable and will open the road to Russian influence and to the formation of a Slavic bloc hostile to western Europe."[53] The division between Italians and Slavs represented to Wilson, an American, the fundamental chasm between Western Europe and Eastern Europe. In fact, it was right here, in Dalmatia, that the Enlightenment first discovered the Slavs, analyzed the resemblances that made them susceptible to Russian influence, and thus contributed to the articulation of the concept of Eastern Europe.

In the spring of 1919, as the Paris peace conference discussed the Adriatic question, the future of Europe seemed to depend upon Dalmatia. Wilson issued a public statement, appealing to Italy to forgo aggrandizement, "to exhibit to the newly liberated peoples across the Adriatic that noblest quality of greatness, magnanimity, friendly generosity, the preference of Justice over interest."[54] Orlando replied indignantly, "It is impossible to qualify as excessive the Italian aspirations toward the Dalmatian coast, Italy's boulevard throughout centuries, which Roman genius and Venetian activity made noble and grand, and whose Italian character, defying for centuries implacable persecutions, still shares the same thrill of patriotism with the Italian people."[55] Invoking Venice to affirm the Italian claim to Dalmatia, Orlando also emphasized the legitimating importance of patriotism, transcending the Adriatic gulf, just as Goldoni had celebrated the common patriotic commitment of Venetians and Dalmatians in the eighteenth century.

After Wilson's public statement in April of 1919, the Italian literary journal *Il Marzocco* replied in May with criticisms of the American president on page one, and an article about Goldoni and *La Dalmatina* on page two. Cesare Levi, a Molière scholar from Trieste, wrote about "Dalmatians on the Stage." Though, in his literary judgment, *La Dalmatina* was "one of the worst of Goldoni," Levi concluded that the Italian tradition was supremely sympathetic to the Dalmatians: "the instinctive good qualities of the race are always put in the best light." Those qualities included courage, as well as "generosity of sentiment, nobility of character, and above all love of country and pride in being associated with the age-old glory of Venice." Indeed, Levi claimed that after 1797 the Dalmatians maintained "almost a nostalgic lament for the greatness of Venice."[56] Thus Goldoni's ideology of Adriatic empire was explicitly inserted into the national confrontation between Italians and Slavs over Dalmatia in 1919.

Attilio Tamaro published his history of Dalmatia in 1919, favorably reviewing the imperial record of Venice, rediscovering the Italian culture of enlightened Dalmatians like Giandomenico Stratico and Giulio Bajamonti, and testifying to the whole province's "profound love" for Venice. Tamaro cited the peroration of Perasto when the standard of San Marco was lowered in 1797: "ti con nu, nu con ti."[57] That same slogan appeared on the title page of Gabriele D'Annunzio's "Letter to the Dalmatians," published in Venice in 1919, and the poet and war hero also revisited the story of Perasto. In his letter he described himself in Venice, alone among the Carpaccio frescoes of San Giorgio degli Schiavoni, "before the Venetian altar of all Dalmatia," in devotional communion with the Dalmatians and utterly dedicated to their reunion with Italy. He denounced the unjust commitment of Wilson at Versailles and issued an extraordinary poetic appeal:

> Loyal Dalmatians (*Dalmati fedeli*), if the injustice is accomplished—and may our God disperse that impending shadow—you will load your boats with the fragments of your glorious stones, and you will embark with them; and you too will go out upon the sea of your desperate love; and you will let them

FIGURE 14. "Ti con nu, nu con ti." From Gabriele D'Annunzio's "Lettera ai Dalmati," letter to the Dalmatians, published in Venice in 1919. The poet D'Annunzio appealed to the Dalmatians from Venice in 1919, in the name of San Marco, when the future of Dalmatia was to be decided by the Versailles conference. D'Annunzio invoked the semi-mythological motto "ti con nu, nu con ti"—"you with us, we with you"—supposedly spoken as a loyal Dalmatian lament for Venice in 1797, when the sovereign standard of San Marco was lowered and the Serenissima Repubblica abolished forever. *(By permission of Widener Library, Harvard University.)*

sink, you and your relics, to rejoin our dead in the depths, no longer nailed down dead but free men among free men. And following my vocation, I will be with you.[58]

This apocalyptic Adriatic vision of Dalmatian loyalty unto death suggests the intensity with which modern Italian nationalism manipulated the imagined persistence of early modern imperial sentiment.

In September 1919 D'Annunzio staged his celebrated occupation of Fiume, or Rijeka, in defiance of Versailles, but, in fact, the Fiume adventure was contemplated in the context of a larger design upon Dalmatia, further down the Adriatic coast. "Brothers of Dalmatia," he declared, saluting the Dalmatians from Fiume, "we have not forgotten you, we can not forget you." He even sailed from Fiume to Zadar in November for a dramatic demonstration of his commitment to Dalmatia, and his appearance in Zadar, according to his followers' official account, was greeted by the Dalmatians with "delirious enthusiasm" and "frenetic acclamations." For D'Annunzio the Fiume adventure pointed toward "the recovery of the lions, the recovery of the Dominante, the recovery of Venetian power and Venetian magnificence on the unpeaceful Adriatic."[59] Nevertheless, Dalmatia went to the kingdom of Yugoslavia at Versailles, though Zadar (Zara) was reserved for Italy, as well as the island of Cres (Cherso) where Fortis made his first Dalmatian explorations in 1770.

D'Annunzio's invocation of "ti con nu, nu con ti" indicated that nostalgia for the Venetian empire was by no means politically benign in the context of the Versailles controversy. Benito Mussolini was also sentimentally engaged in 1919:

> Dalmatia, Italian in its origin, ardent as a saint in its faith, had been recognized to be ours by the pact of London; Dalmatia had waited for the victorious war with years of passion, and holding in its bosom still the remains of Venice and of Rome, was now lopped off from our unity.[60]

This became one of the nationalist themes that he played upon during the following years that led to the triumph of fascism in 1922. In 1920 Mussolini endorsed a Dalmatian parade in Rome, a demonstration of the Dalmatians' "indestructible loyalty to their country," and he denounced the intervention of the police. In 1921 he lamented "the Dalmatian tragedy," that is, its assignment to Yugoslavia, and he vowed, "We will know, love, and defend Italian Dalmatia." Once in power, however, Mussolini resigned himself to a treaty with Yugoslavia in 1924: "We

definitely lost Dalmatia, we lost cities sacred to Italy by the history and
the very soul of the populations."[61] He would occupy the province with
its sacred cities during World War II.

Italian fascist rule in Dalmatia, during the war, offered a last reprise of
familiar imperial themes. The official newspaper of the occupation, published bilingually in Italian and Croatian, evoked Venetian nostalgia in its
exclamatory title: *San Marco!* Athos Bartolucci of Zadar, the civil com-
missioner of the province, envisioned a Goldonian restoration of the "ancient tradition" by which "Dalmatia has always furnished the most valorous soldiers of the Roman empire, the Republic of Venice, and fascist
Italy." Bartolucci also echoed Fortis and Memmo in urging the "total renewal of fishing which could offer a most important contribution to the
Italian food problem and a notable benefit to these coastal populations."
The municipal government of Zadar wrote directly to Mussolini, to remind him of that city's historic role:

> When in the year 1000 the Doge Orseolo with his memorable expedition es-
> tablished the dominion of the Republic of Venice on the Adriatic, it was at
> Zara that he harbored the Venetian fleet, and at Zara that the Doge received
> the submission and homage of all the Dalmatian peoples. . . . When the
> Venetian dominion was restored in 1409 . . . it was at Zara, from then until
> the fall of the Republic, that the Provveditori Generali of Dalmatia resided.[62]

In 1941 the establishment of the occupation was celebrated in Zadar with
a Te Deum at the Duomo of St. Anastasia, and an airplane flew along the
coast dumping fascist manifestoes of "serenity, discipline, and coopera-
tion" in Dalmatia.[63] If the slogan of *serenità* recalled the Serenissima Repubblica, the emphasis on discipline illustrated an uncanny continuity
with the Venetian imperial perspective.

Bartolucci believed that Dalmatia should receive "order and discipline" from Italy, but, as in the eighteenth century, discipline was the
supposed concomitant of civilization. Luigi Arduini, the Italian consul at
Split, recalled that once "Venice had impressed the indelible mark of our
superior civilization" upon Dalmatia, but Giuseppe Bastianini, the governor of Dalmatia, worried that now his Italian administrative personnel
would find it difficult to work "in these lands without the comforts of
civilization and social-hygienic progress." The city of Zadar affirmed its
own Italian superiority by arguing that the other towns of Dalmatia were
"permeated with balkanism (*balcanesimo*)." Outside celebratory Zadar it
was difficult for the Italian occupation to count on enthusiasm from the

Dalmatians, though the most favorably inclined portion of the population appeared to be the Orthodox Serbs; they often preferred Italian fascism to the regional alternative of Croatian fascism, the Ustaša. Alessandro Dudàn of Split advised Mussolini to look to the Serbs of Dalmatia for some support, and characterized them thus: "Orthodox Serbs (for the most part ex-Morlacchi)." In the 1890s the Morlacchi were being parenthetically redefined—"Morlacchi (that means Serbo-Croatian)"— and now, fifty years later in the 1940s, the category had been so successfully dissolved that they could only be parenthetically remembered, in reverse definition, as ex-Morlacchi. The Italian fascist occupation had reason to remember, since *morlacchismo* could still serve the imperial purposes for which it was ideologically created in the eighteenth century. When members of the Yugoslav resistance were condemned to death at Šibenik in 1941, the fascist prosecutor proclaimed the urgent need "to civilize and radically purge, so that this most Italian land need not be trampled by barbarians and Morlacchi."[64] His speech was cited in 1945, in the Titoist newspaper *Slobodna Dalmacija* (*Free Dalmatia*), making the point that the fascists were the true barbarians. Thus early modern *morlacchismo,* merging with the modern noton of *balcanesimo,* played a part in articulating both adherence and resistance to the imperial ambitions of fascist Italy. The titanic ideological currents of the twentieth century, fascism and communism, still responded to some of the conceptual debris of the Venetian Enlightenment.

The soul of the Dalmatians, the inspirational spirit of their proverbial valor and loyalty, entered into the rhetorical armory of political culture in Yugoslavia. In 1944, as the Communist Partisans were fighting against foreign occupations and political rivals, Tito, on the Adriatic island of Vis (or Lissa), saluted his First Dalmatian Brigade. With Goldonian enthusiasm Tito extolled the martial valor of the Dalmatians.

> The celebrated battles of the fifth offensive—when the First Dalmatian Brigade had to wade up to its neck through the Drina River to pierce the enemy encirclement—have shown that there is no task so difficult that the men of Dalmatia can not accomplish it. It was not only the young men but the young women of Dalmatia—on the threshold of life—who lost their lives in the waters of the Drina, their last farewell being the locks of their hair floating on the waves.[65]

Male and female, Dalmatino and Dalmatina, they were cited together as the heroes and the heroines of the Partisan resistance, "true patriots," representatives of "the freedom-loving traditions of the people in Dalmatia." Tito made his Dalmatians Homeric champions, honored for "the epic record of a heroic struggle," that is, "the heroic struggle by the peoples of Yugoslavia for freedom and independence." Tito himself came from the village of Kumrovec in the Zagorje region of Croatia, but he claimed Dalmatian ancestors: "They had come to Kumrovec from Dalmatia in the middle of the sixteenth century, retreating before the onslaught of the Turkish invaders."[66] Thus Tito too was a Dalmatian hero, returning to liberate Dalmatia from Mussolini during the war.

In an illustrated tribute to the "New Yugoslavia," published in Belgrade in 1966 with a portrait of Tito as the solemn frontispiece, a photograph from Dalmatia showed costumed dancers: "A folklore group from Dalmatia (Croatia)—In Yugoslavia there are many excellent folklore ensembles which maintain the rich folklore of the Yugoslav peoples." Communism was ideologically inclined toward popular folkloric forms, and so the dances of Dalmatia were advertised again. Communist Yugoslavia, of course, had industrial priorities as well, and Smodlaka might have been pleased to see the photograph of the "Split hydro-electric power plant (Croatia) which produces about 2,000 million KWh a year."[67] Dalmatia formed part of the Croatian republic in federal Yugoslavia, and parenthetical labels (Croatia) undercut the provincial identity which survived in folklore. Dubravka Ugrešić has recalled the folkloric frenzy of school activities under Tito's regime:

> The songs and dances of the nations and nationalities of Yugoslavia were an integral part of our so-called physical education. Hard-hearted teachers drove us into school folklore groups and choirs. Ethnic identities were forged by stamping, skipping, whirling, twirling, choral singing, pipes, lutes, harmonicas, and drums. And we all knew everything: the sound of the 'bajs' from Zagorje, the tune of ballads from Medjimurje, the songs of Dalmatian groups, the words of Slavonian jigs and Bosnian 'sevdalinke,' the beat of Albanian drums, the sound of the Serbian trumpet, and the rhythm of the Slovene polka . . .[68]

Even with its hydroelectric power plant, Dalmatia (Croatia) remained fundamentally folkloric, integrated into a multicultural Communist festival of singing and dancing identities. The Morlacchi, who had once attracted the attention of all of Europe to the folklore of the South Slavs, were no longer on anyone's dance program.

Of course Dalmatia was also the seashore, and a tourist guide published in Belgrade in 1962 saluted the Adriatic coast as "an internationally known summer vacation land," and "the prettiest touristic region of Yugoslavia." Curiously, the short historical background altogether neglected to mention the long rule of Venice: "Coastal cities have gone through their golden era at the time of the strengthening of the Slav influence and power in these regions, i.e. in the tenth century. This is when some of the coastal cities like Dubrovnik, Kotor, Zadar, and Split have developed into trade and cultural centers known in the whole of the Mediterranean."[69] In the scholarly synthesis of the history of Yugoslavia, first published in Belgrade in 1972, Venetian rule in Dalmatia could not be completely overlooked. The coastal towns of Dalmatia, under Venice, were reported to have been "languishing in poverty and burdened by the obligation to build fortresses and complete public buildings," while, among the Dalmatians, "educated individuals persisted in their literary endeavors to enrich their microcosmic environment and to dispel their own boredom."[70] From the triumphant perspective of Tito's Yugoslavia, the centuries of Venetian rule in Dalmatia appeared as a benighted interlude of burdensome and boring imperial domination.

Imperial Forms and Evolutionary Nationality

Dalmatia was twice liberated in the name of Yugoslavia in the twentieth century, after World War I and then again after World War II. Tito in 1944 had no doubt that Dalmatia was essential to the "heroic struggle by the peoples of Yugoslavia," just as Seton-Watson in 1915 affirmed that "without Dalmatia there can be no Serbo-Croat Unity, no Jugoslavia." Dalmatia was necessary to Yugoslavia for geopolitical reasons, since the province constituted the Adriatic coast, for economic reasons as it attracted foreign tourists and currencies to the coastal beaches, and for ideological reasons as its mixed populations and traditions represented a sort of national unity. Yet the traumatic disintegration of Yugoslavia in the 1990s suggests that Dalmatia's previous liberations under the Yugoslav flag may now be retrospectively reconceived as the impositions of imperial domination by Belgrade. Indeed, inasmuch as Communist regimes in the twentieth century have not been reticent about celebrating the ideological loyalty, model patriotism, and proletarian valor of their comrade citizens, the political status of Dalmatia in Yugoslavia may come to seem rhetorically continuous with earlier provincial incarnations in the Habsburg, Napoleonic, and Venetian empires. Certainly the notion of Dalmatia as the symbol of "Serbo-Croat Unity" already appears as an extravagantly misguided ideological fiction. In this sense the political coinages of the Venetian Enlightenment for the fashioning of an ideology of Adriatic empire, designed to include the Slavs of Dalmatia, may prove particularly relevant for understanding the rhetorical bankruptcy of Yugoslavia with its slogans and ideals of South Slavic unity. Political combinations and recombinations inevitably involve an element of synthetic ideological legitimation, which history retrospectively reveals as intellectual artifice. National loyalties, even imperial loyalties, may have been sometimes sentimentally sincere, but they have also been susceptible to official encouragement, progressive deterioration, revolutionary alienation, and subversive seduction.

In the eighteenth century, the construction of empire in Dalmatia was both an administrative and a philosophical project. The ascription of nationhood was a part of that project, as enlightened observers on both shores of the Adriatic explored the different denominations of Dalmatian, Illyrian, Slavic, and Morlacchi, often overlapping, sometimes seemingly indistinguishable, but signifying alternative solutions to a political equation with multiple variables. The algebra of modern nationalism would prove similarly problematic, as experts inside and outside the province identified the Dalmatians as Illyrians, Serbo-Croats, Yugoslavs, Serbs and Croats, until today when Dalmatia has become emphatically Croatian. The multiplicity of attributions, beginning under the aegis of the Venetian Enlightenment and proceeding through the development of the nationalities question within the Habsburg monarchy, offers a caution against accepting any such labels as natural, essential, definitive, or inevitable identities. Like its several imperial allegiances, Dalmatia's national identities have been susceptible to multiple intimations from inside and outside the province.

The paleontologist Stephen Jay Gould has written about the fossils of the Burgess Shale in the Canadian Rockies and about the scientific realization that these extinct invertebrate creatures, like Opabinia with its five eyes, did not fit into the familiar phyla of Linnaean classification:

"Opabinia was not an arthropod. And it sure as hell wasn't anything else that anyone could specify either. On close inspection, nothing from the Burgess Shale seemed to fit into any modern group." Gould argues that such taxonomical anomalies demonstrate the "multifarious possibilities of historical contingency" in evolution, suggesting that there is nothing inevitable about the contemporary order of natural history, that other paths of evolution were always possible: "The modern order is largely a product of contingency."[71] Gould's evolutionary insights are important for appreciating the discoveries in Dalmatia of that other paleontologist Alberto Fortis, and for reconsidering the evolution of nationality. The Dalmatian Dinaric Alps, like the Canadian Rockies, preserve the fossils of forms whose extinction was never inevitable, whose range of early modern classifications indicate the multifarious possibilities of evolving national identity. The modern order of nations is a product of the contingency of history. The Venetian Enlightenment, discovering the Dalmatians, explored the various ascriptions which rendered them classifiable according to the contemporary concerns of the Adriatic empire.

Dalmatia has never again been as much an object of international fascination as it was in the late eighteenth century, when Fortis's *Viaggio in Dalmazia* made the customs of the Morlacchi famous all over Europe. The sensation of Dalmatia in the age of Enlightenment followed from the Venetian cultivation of an ideology of empire, replete with a civilizing mission among the Morlacchi. Rebecca West, writing about her journey through Yugoslavia in *Black Lamb and Grey Falcon,* was almost eccentric in the context of the 1930s when she insisted on the importance of Dalmatia. Like Fortis she believed that Europe needed to know about Dalmatia, about Yugoslavia, and more generally about the Slavs, because they constituted the continent's complementary other half, which the English, French, Germans, and Italians arrogantly ignored and presumptuously patronized. Russia might be geographically remote, but Dalmatia was Eastern Europe at its most proximate and intimate, just across the Adriatic from Venice. Fortis discovered in Dalmatia an enlightened perspective on his own civilization, contemplating "spirits uncorrupted by the society we call civilized." Rebecca West experienced a comparable epiphany in Dalmatia, similarly calling into question the values of her own civilization and worrying "that Western culture will in the long run overwhelm Dalmatia." In the twentieth century, as in the eighteenth century, it was possible to feel, like Giustiniana Wynne, like Rebecca

West, a fearful philosophical ambivalence about Dalmatia's eventual conformity to the customs of Western Europe.

The legacy of the Venetian Enlightenment reveals the persistence of
early modern forms embedded in the thematic materials of modern history. The structural and ideological forms of the Adriatic empire, crystallizing in the eighteenth century around the discovery and exploration of
Dalmatia, left an historical inheritance to be selectively preserved, exploited, refashioned, refuted, and discarded, according to the diverging
priorities of increasingly distant descendants. Those heirs included not
only the succeeding regimes that ruled along the Adriatic in the modern
age—whether Napoleonic or Habsburg in the nineteenth century,
whether democratic, fascist, or communist in the twentieth century—but
also the posterity of the subject peoples who were ruled from Venice
until 1797. In Dalmatia, the variously articulated South Slavic identities
of the nineteenth and twentieth centuries have descended, not by genet-
ics but in lexicography, through the ongoing definition and revision of
terms, from the Slavs, the Dalmatians, the Illyrians, and the Morlacchi of
the Adriatic empire. In the eighteenth century, the peoples of the
province took their identity in part from the ruling imperial lexicography,
and in part from within the indigenous Dalmatian matrix of discursive
distinctions. Giulio Bajamonti, proclaiming the "Morlacchismo of
Homer," contemplating his own Slavic relation to the Morlacchi, wrote
in 1797 as the Serenissima Repubblica was about to be abolished forever.
His meditation on his own Dalmatian identity was a valedictory to the
Venetian Dalmatia of the *ancien régime*. At the same time, he spoke from
the threshold of modern history to the future generations of South Slavs,
the ex-Morlacchi, for whom the fashioning of national identity would
take place in the succeeding centuries, along the same Adriatic coast that
once attracted the intellectual energies and inspired the imaginative visions of the Enlightenment.

Notes

Introduction

1. Edward Gibbon, *The Decline and Fall of the Roman Empire* (New York: Modern Library, n.d.), volume 1, p. 21.
2. Ibid., p. 21, n. 86; see also Roy Porter, *Edward Gibbon: Making History* (London: Weidenfeld and Nicolson, 1988), pp. 135–57; and J. G. A. Pocock, *Barbarism and Religion:* (Cambridge: Cambridge University Press, 1999).
3. Alberto Fortis, *Viaggio in Dalmazia* (Venice: Presso Alvise Milocco, 1774), re-published by Jovan Vuković and Peter Rehder, eds. (Munich and Sarajevo: Verlag Otto Sagner and Izdavačko Preduzeće Veselin Masleša, 1974), volume 1, pp. 15, 43, 58; Fernand Braudel, *The Mediterranean and the Mediterranean World in the Age of Philip II,* trans. Sian Reynolds (1949; New York: Harper & Row, 1972–73), volume 1, pp. 56–57.
4. Edward Said, *Culture and Imperialism* (1993; New York: Vintage, 1994), pp. 3–14; Anthony Pagden, *Lords of All the World: Ideologies of Empire in Spain, Britain, and France* (New Haven: Yale University Press, 1995), pp. 103–200.
5. Marino Berengo, "Problemi economico-sociali della Dalmazia veneta alla fine del '700," *Rivista storica italiana,* 66 (1954), p. 470; Benjamin Arbel, "Colonie d'oltremare," in *Storia di Venezia: dalle origini alla caduta della Serenissima,* volume 5, *Il Rinascimento: società ed economia,* eds. Alberto Tenenti and Ugo Tucci (Rome: Istituto della Enciclopedia Italiana, 1996), pp. 954, 964, 979.
6. Predrag Matvejević, *Mediterranean: A Cultural Landscape,* trans. Michael Henry Heim (Berkeley: University of California Press, 1999), p. 14.
7. Giuseppe Praga, *History of Dalmatia,* trans. Edward Steinberg (1954; Pisa: Giardini, 1993), p. 204.
8. Attilio Tamaro, *La Vénétie Julienne et la Dalmatie: Histoire de la nation italienne sur ses frontières orientales,* volume 3, *La Dalmatie* (Rome: Imprimerie du Sénat, 1919), p. 309; Fabio Luzzatto, "Scrittori dalmati di politica agraria nel secolo XVIII," *Archivio Storico per la Dalmazia,* year 3, volume 5, numbers 30 and 31 (September and October, 1928), pp. 267–337; Fabio Luzzatto, "Le Accademie di Agricoltura in Dalmazia nel secolo XVIII," *Archivio Storico per la Dalmazia,* year 3, volume 5, number 26 (May 1928), pp. 75–83.
9. Marijan Stojković, "Morlakizam," *Hrvatsko Kolo,* book 10 (Zagreb: Matica Hrvatska, 1929). p. 259; Ivan Božić, "The Yugoslav Peoples under the Hapsburg

Monarchy and the Republic of Venice," in *History of Yugoslavia,* by Vladimir Dedijer, Ivan Božić, Sima Cirković, and Milorad Ekmečić, trans. Kordija Kveder (New York: McGraw-Hill, 1974), p. 197; Marko Jačov, *Venecija i Srbi u Dalmaciji u XVIII vijeku* (Belgrade: Prosveta, 1984).

10. Jovan Cvijić, *La Péninsule balkanique: Géographie humaine* (Paris: Librairie Armand Colin, 1918), p. 363.

11. "Dalmatia," *Encyclopedia Britannica,* 11th edition, volume 7, 1910, p. 773; Alice Lee Moqué, *Delightful Dalmatia* (New York: Funk and Wagnalls, 1914), pp. 58–60.

12. Fabio Mutinelli, *Annali Urbani di Venezia: dall'anno 810 al 12 maggio 1797* (Venice: Tipografia di G. B. Merlo, 1841); Giustina Renier-Michiel, *Origine delle Feste Veneziane,* reprint of 1829 edition, ed. Federico Pellegrini (Venice: Stab. Grafico G. Scarabellin, 1916), pp. 59–60.

13. Marjorie Garber, *Dog Love* (New York: Simon and Schuster, 1996), p. 160.

14. Fortis, *Viaggio in Dalmazia,* volume 2, p. 61.

15. Ibid., volume 1, p. 60.

16. Ibid., pp. 130–31.

17. Gasparo Gozzi, "Marco Polo," *Opere,* volume 11 (Padua: Tipografia e Fonderia della Minerva, 1820), pp. 15–16; Goldoni, *La Dalmatina,* in *Tutte le opere di Carlo Goldoni,* ed. Giuseppe Ortolani, volume 9 (Milan: Arnoldo Mondadori, 1960), p. 953; Giovanni Greppi, *L'Eroe dalmate: ossia Aurangzebbe Re di Siam,* in *Dei capricci teatrali,* volume 2, part 4 (Venice: Giacomo Storti, 1793).

18. Paolo Preto, *Venezia e i Turchi* (Florence: G. C. Sansoni Editore, 1975), p. 506.

19. Stojković, "Morlakizam," pp. 254–73; Arturo Cronia, *La Conoscenza del mondo slavo in Italia: Bilancio storico-bibliografico di un millennio* (Padua: Officine Grafiche Stediv, 1958), pp. 331–35; Mate Zorić, "Croati e altri slavi del sud nella letteratura italiana del '700," *Revue des études sud-est européennes,* volume 10 (Bucharest, 1972), p. 294.

20. Rebecca West, *Black Lamb and Grey Falcon: A Journey through Yugoslavia* (1941; London: Penguin Books, 1982), pp. 208–9.

21. Fitzroy Maclean, *Eastern Approaches* (1949; New York: Time-Life Books, 1964), pp. 375–76.

22. Braudel, *The Mediterranean and the Mediterranean World,* volume 1, p. 17.

23. Ibid., volume 1, pp. 127–32, 287, 336; volume 2, p. 845.

24. Ibid., volume 1, p. 58.

25. Gibbon, *Decline and Fall* volume 1, pp. 337–39; Madame de Staël, *Corinne, or Italy,* trans. Avriel Goldberger (New Brunswick, N.J.: Rutgers University Press, 1987), p. 301.

1. *The Drama of the Adriatic Empire: Dalmatian Loyalty and the Venetian Lion*

1. Carlo Goldoni, *Mémoires,* in *Tutte le opere di Carlo Goldoni,* ed. Giuseppe Ortolani, volume 1 (Milan: Arnoldo Mondadori, 1959), p. 390; Mate Zorić "Croati e altri slavi del sud nella letteratura italiana del '700," *Revue des études sud-est européennes,* volume 10 (Bucharest, 1972), pp. 296–98; see also Arnaldo Momo, *Goldoni e i militari* (Padua: Marsilio Editori, 1973), pp. 397–403.

2. Goldoni, *La Dalmatina,* in *Tutte le opere di Carlo Goldoni,* ed. Giuseppe Ortolani, volume 9 (Milan: Arnoldo Mondadori, 1960), p. 943.

3. Goldoni, *Mémoires*, p. 392; see also Franco Fido, "Le illusioni e i mostri degli anni difficili al teatro San Luca," in *Guida a Goldoni: Teatro e società nel Settecento* (Torino: Giulio Einaudi, 1977), pp. 121–35; and Franco Fido, "Carlo Goldoni," *Storia della Cultura Veneta*, volume 5, *Il Settecento*, part 1, eds. Girolamo Arnaldi and Manlio Pastore Stocchi (Vicenza: Neri Pozza Editore, 1985), pp. 317–20.

4. Goldoni, *La Dalmatina*, p. 953.

5. Carlo Gozzi, *Memorie Inutili*, ed. Domenico Bulferetti, volume 1, in *Collezione di Classici Italiani*, ed. Gustavo Balsamo-Crivelli (Turin: Unione Tipografico-Editrice Torinese, 1928), p. 43.

6. Ibid., pp. 44, 49, 77; Angelo Tamborra, "Problema sociale e rapporto città-campagna in Dalmazia alla fine del sec. XVIII," *Rassegna Storica del Risorgimento*, year 59, Number 1 (January–March 1972), p. 8.

7. Casanova, *Mémoires*, volume 1, eds. Robert Abirached and Elio Zorzi (Tours: Editions Gallimard, Bibliothèque de la Pléiade, 1958), pp. 306–10; see also Mate Zorić, "Casanovini Skjavuni," *Književna prožimanja hrvatsko-talijanska* (Split: Književni Krug, 1992), pp. 196–98.

8. Gozzi, *Memorie Inutili*, p. 50.

9. Ibid., pp. 51, 55.

10. Ibid., pp. 59–61.

11. Zorzi Grimani, Archivio di Stato di Venezia (ASV), *Collegio: Relazioni*, filza 69, March 1732.

12. Marino Berengo, "Problemi economico-sociali della Dalmazia veneta alla fine del '700," *Rivista storica italiana*, LXVI (1954), pp. 478–79.

13. Gozzi, *Memorie Inutili*, pp. 61–63.

14. Ibid., p. 77; Zorić, "Croati e altri slavi del sud," pp. 313–14.

15. Gozzi, *Memorie Inutili*, p. 78.

16. Ibid., p. 79.

17. Ibid.

18. Carlo Gozzi, *Useless Memoirs*, trans. John Addington Symonds, ed. Philip Horne (London: Oxford University Press, 1962), p. 102.

19. Ibid., pp. 107, 111, 114–15.

20. Ibid., pp. 115–19.

21. Larry Wolff, *Inventing Eastern Europe: The Map of Civilization on the Mind of the Enlightenment* (Stanford: Stanford University Press, 1994), pp. 50–62.

22. Gozzi, *Memorie Inutili*, pp. 81–82.

23. Ibid., p. 82

24. Ibid., p. 88.

25. Ibid., p. 92.

26. Giacomo Boldù, ASV, *Collegio: Relazioni*, filza 69, 30 August 1748.

27. Gozzi, *Memorie Inutili*, p. 92.

28. Ibid., pp. 93–94.

29. Ibid., p. 95.

30. Berengo, "Problemi economico-sociali," p. 474; H. C. Darby, "Dalmatia," in *A Short History of Yugoslavia*, ed. Stephen Clissold (Cambridge: Cambridge University Press, 1968), pp. 45–50; see also Marko Jačov, *Le guerre Veneto-Turche del XVII secolo in Dalmazia*, in *Atti e Memorie della Società Dalmata di Storia Patria*, volume 20 (Venice: Scuola Dalmata dei SS. Giorgio e Trifone, 1991), pp. 203–19; Tomislav

Raukar, "Društvene strukture u Mletačkoj Dalmaciji," *Društveni razvoj u Hrvatskoj,* ed. Mirjana Gross (Zagreb: Sveučilišna Naklada Liber, 1981), pp. 103–06; Roberto Cessi, *La Repubblica di Venezia e il problema Adriatico* (Naples: Edizioni Scientifiche Italiane, 1953), pp. 237–59; and Alessandro Sfrecola, "Le Craine di Dalmazia: La 'Frontiera Militare' di Venezia nel primo settecento e le riforme del Feldmaresciallo von Schulenburg," *Microhistory of the Triplex Confinium,* ed. Drago Roksandić (Budapest: Institute on Southeastern Europe, Central European University, 1998), pp. 137–45.

31. Franco Venturi, *Settecento riformatore: Da Muratori a Beccaria* (Turin: Giulio Einaudi, 1969), p. 286.

32. Marco Foscarini, "Degl'inquisitori da spedirsi nella Dalmazia" (Orazione detta nel Maggior Consiglio il giorno 17 dicembre 1747), in *Marco Foscarini e Venezia nel secolo XVIII,* ed. Emilio Morpurgo (Florence: Successori Le Monnier, 1880), pp. 195–97; Franco Venturi, *Da Muratori a Beccaria,* pp. 276–92.

33. Foscarini, "Degl'inquisitori," pp. 211–14.

34. Ibid., p. 215.

35. Luciano Lago, *Theatrum Adriae: Dalle Alpi all'Adriatico nella cartografia del passato* (Trieste: Edizioni Lint, 1989), pp. 213–15, 222–24.

36. Robert and Robert de Vaugondy, *Atlas Universel,* volume 1 (Paris: Chez les Auteurs, 1757), p. 30 and map 91; see also Wolff, *Inventing Eastern Europe,* pp. 144–49.

37. Foscarini, "Degl'inquisitori," p. 215.

38. Ibid., pp. 227–28.

39. Ibid., p. 231.

40. Ibid.

41. Ibid., pp. 231–32.

42. Berengo, "Problemi economico-sociali," pp. 491–92; see also Karl Kaser, *Hirten, Kämpfer, Stammeshelden: Ursprünge und Gegenwart des balkanischen Patriarchats* (Vienna: Böhlau Verlag, 1992), pp. 140–59.

43. Foscarini, "Degl'inquisitori," p. 232.

44. Ibid., p. 235.

45. Paolo Preto, "Diedo, Giacomo," *Dizionario Biografico degli Italiani,* volume 39 (Rome: Enciclopedia Italiana, 1991), pp. 775–76; Gino Benzoni, "Pensiero storico e storiografia civile," *Storia della Cultura Veneta,* volume 5, *Il Settecento,* part 2, eds. Girolamo Arnaldi and Manlio Pastore Stocchi (Vicenza: Neri Pozza Editore, 1986), pp. 78–79; Edward Muir, *Civic Ritual in Renaissance Venice* (Princeton: Princeton University Press, 1981), pp. 119–34.

46. Giacomo Diedo, *Storia della Repubblica di Venezia: Dalla sua fondazione sino l'anno MDCCXLVII,* volume 1 (Venice: Andrea Poletti, 1751), pp. 44–46.

47. Diedo, volume 1, pp. 44–46.

48. Giovanni Lucio, *Historia di Dalmatia: Et in particolare delle Città di Trau, Spalatro, e Sebenico* (Venice: Presso Stefano Curti, 1674; rpt. Bologna: Arnaldo Forni, 1977), p. 10.

49. Filip Grabovac, *Cvit razgovora naroda i jezika iliričkoga aliti rvackoga* (Split: Književni Krug, 1986), pp. 260–66; Tomo Matić "Život i rad Filipa Grabovca," in Grabovac, *Cvit razgovora* (Zagreb: Jugoslavenska Akademija Znanosti i Umjetnosti, 1951) pp. 5–20.

50. Arturo Cronia, *La Conoscenza del mondo slavo in Italia* (Padua: Officine Grafiche Stediv, 1958), pp. 318–20.

51. Sindici Inquisitori in Dalmazia (Giovanni Loredan, Nicolo Erizzo, Sebastian Molin), ASV, *Collegio: Relazioni,* filza 70, 2 October 1751.

52. Berengo, "Problemi economico-sociali," pp. 474–75; see also Gligor Stanojević, *Dalmatinske krajine u XVIII vijeku* (Belgrade and Zagreb: Prosveta, 1987), pp. 100–110; and Fabio Luzzato, "La Legge Agraria Grimani nella critica degli Scrittori Dalmati," *Archivio Storico per la Dalmazia,* year 4, volume 7, number 42 (September 1929), pp. 299–307.

53. Francesco Grimani, "Informazione del Provveditore Generale Grimani al suo successore Alvise Contarini, " ASV, *Collegio: Relazioni,* filza 69, 10 October 1756.

54. Attilio Tamaro, *La Vénétie Julienne et la Dalmatie: Histoire de la nation italienne sur ses frontières orientales,* volume 3, *La Dalmatie* (Rome: Imprimerie du Sénat, 1919), pp. 295–96.

55. Vettor Sandi, *Principi di storia civile della Repubblica di Venezia,* volume 1 (Venice: Sebastian Coleti, 1755), p. 325; Franco Venturi, *Settecento riformatore,* volume 5, *L'Italia dei lumi,* part 2, *La Repubblica di Venezia* (Turin: Giulio Einaudi, 1990), pp. 3–12, 168–71; Piero Del Negro, "Proposte illuminate e conservazione nel dibattito sulla teoria e la prassi dello stato," *Storia della Cultura Veneta,* volume 5, *Il Settecento,* part 2, eds. Girolamo Arnaldi and Manlio Pastore Stocchi (Vicenza: Neri Pozza Editore, 1986), pp. 137–38; Brendan Dooley, *Science, Politics, and Society in Eighteenth-Century Italy: The Giornale de' letterati d'Italia and its World* (New York: Garland, 1991), pp. 172–73.

56. Sandi, *Principi di storia civile,* pp. 329, 331.

57. Bariša Krekić, "On the Latino-Slavic Cultural Symbiosis in Late Medieval and Renaissance Dalmatia and Dubrovnik," in *Dubrovnik : A Mediterranean Urban Society, 1300–1600* (Hampshire: Variorum, 1997), pp. 322–23; Patricia Fortini Brown, *Venice and Antiquity: The Venetian Sense of the Past* (New Haven: Yale University Press, 1996), pp. 33–34; Lucio, *Historia di Dalmatia,* p. 10.

58. Diedo, volume 1, p. 100.

59. Ibid., pp. 51, 57–58, 117; John Fine, *The Early Medieval Balkans: A Critical Survey from the Sixth to the Late Twelfth Century* (1983; Ann Arbor: University of Michigan Press, 1991), pp. 248–91.

60. Giacomo Casanova, *Aneddoti veneziani militari ed amorosi* (Milan: Serra e Riva Editori, 1984), pp. ix–xxx, 37–38, 80–81, 160–61.

61. Antonio Morassi, *Guardi: Tutti i disegni di Antonio, Francesco, e Giacomo Guardi* (Venice: Alfieri, 1975), pp. 91–93.

62. Sandi, *Principi di storia civile,* pp. 326, 334.

63. William Bouwsma, *Venice and the Defense of Republican Liberty: Renaissance Values in the Age of the Counter Reformation* (1968; Berkeley: University of California Press, 1984), pp. 95–231; see also James Grubb, "When Myths Lose Power: Four Decades of Venetian Historiography," *Journal of Modern History,* volume 58 (March 1986), pp. 43–94.

64. Zaccaria Vallaresso, *Baiamonte Tiepolo in Schiavonia: Poema Eroicomico* (Venice, 1770), p. 14; Stanko Skerlj, "Baiamonte Tiepolo (in Schiavonia): poema eroicomico di Zaccaria Vallaresso," *Ricerche Slavistiche,* volume 3 (Rome: Gherardo Casini Editore, 1954), pp. 196–211; Zorić, "Croati e altri slavi del sud," pp. 291–93.

65. Vallaresso, *Baiamonte Tiepolo,* pp. 1–2, 332; Skerlj, "Baiamonte Tiepolo," pp. 196–201; Grabovac, *Cvit razgovora,* p. 290.

66. Vallaresso, *Baiamonte Tiepolo,* pp. 357, 360, 362.

67. Goldoni, *La Sposa Persiana,* in *Tutte le opere di Carlo Goldoni,* ed. Giuseppe Ortolani, volume 9 (Milan: Arnoldo Mondadori, 1960), p. 527.

68. Voltaire, *Essai sur les moeurs,* ed. René Pomeau, volume 2 (Paris: Garnier Frères, 1963), p. 881; see also Larry Wolff, "Voltaire's Public and the Idea of Eastern Europe: Toward a Literary Sociology of Continental Division," *Slavic Review,* volume 54, (winter 1995), pp. 932–42.

69. Goldoni, *Mémoires,* p. 431.

70. Goldoni, *La Dalmatina,* p. 889; see also Pamela Stewart, "Il Labirinto delle Prefazioni," in *Goldoni fra letteratura e teatro* (Florence: Leo S. Olschki, 1989), pp. 7–92.

71. Venturi, *La Repubblica di Venezia,* pp. 12–31.

72. Goldoni, *La Dalmatina,* pp. 889–90.

73. Larry Wolff, "Venice and the Slavs of Dalmatia: The Drama of the Adriatic Empire in the Venetian Enlightenment, " *Slavic Review,* volume 56, (fall 1997), pp. 428–55.

74. Berengo, "Problemi economico-sociali," p. 470.

75. Goldoni, *La Dalmatina,* p. 893.

76. Frederic Lane, *Venice: A Maritime Republic* (Baltimore: Johns Hopkins University Press, 1973), pp. 369, 415; Dennis Romano, *Housecraft and Statecraft: Domestic Service in Renaissance Venice, 1400–1600* (Baltimore: Johns Hopkins University Press, 1996), pp. 122–29; Robert Davis, *The War of the Fists: Popular Culture and Public Violence in Late Renaissance Venice* (New York: Oxford University Press, 1994), pp. 53, 118; Massimo Donà, "Le Milizie Oltremarine nella Terraferma Veneta alla fine del '700" (unpublished thesis, Università degli studi di Venezia, 1993), p. 65.

77. Lovorka Čoralić "La Scuola Dalmata nei testamenti degli immigrati dalla sponda orientale dell'Adriatico," *Scuola Dalmata dei SS. Giogrio e Trifone,* volume 27 (1994), pp. 21–23; see also Daniele Beltrami, *Storia della popolazione di Venezia dalla fine del secolo XVI alla caduta della Repubblica* (Padua: Casa Editrice Dott. Antonio Milani, 1954), Tavola N. 13, "Origine e provenienza dei promessi sposi in Venezia nel sec. XVIII."

78. Goldoni, *Mémoires,* p. 392; Francesco Semi and Vanni Tacconi, *Istria e Dalmazia: Uomini e tempi: Dalmazia* (Bologna, 1992), p. 700.

79. Fra Andrija Kačić-Miošić, *Razgovor ugodni naroda slovinskoga* (Split: Zbornik Kačić 1983), pp. 16–36 and 61; Ante Kadić, "The Importance of Kačić-Miošić," in *From Croatian Renaissance to Yugoslav Socialism: Essays* (The Hague: Mouton, 1969), p. 93.

80. Goethe, *Italian Journey,* trans. Robert Heitner (Princeton: Princeton University Press, 1994), pp. 86–87.

81. Voltaire, *Essai sur les moeurs,* volume 2, p. 156.

82. Paolo Preto, *I Servizi Segreti di Venezia* (Milan: Il Saggiatore, 1994), pp. 503–04; Marko Jačov, *Venecija i Srbi u Dalmaciji u XVIII vijeku* (Belgrade: Prosveta, 1984), pp. 76–83; Donà, "Le Milizie Oltremarine," pp. 136–46.

83. Berengo, "Problemi economico-sociali," pp. 470–71, 503–04, 509–10.

84. Goldoni, *La Dalmatina,* p. 900.

85. Ibid., p. 900.

86. Ibid., p. 901.

87. Ibid., p. 903.

88. Ibid.

89. Ibid., pp. 905, 936.

90. Goldoni, *Mémoires,* p. 391.

91. Goldoni, *La Dalmatina,* p. 907.

92. Ibid.

93. Goldoni, *La Sposa Persiana,* p. 1333.

94. Goldoni, *La Dalmatina,* p. 907.

95. Ibid.

96. Ibid., p. 943.

97. Jean-Jacques Rousseau, *Considérations sur le gouvernement de Pologne,* ed. Barbara de Negroni (Paris: GF-Flammarion, 1990), p. 170.

98. Goldoni, *La Dalmatina,* pp. 942–43.

99. Ibid., p. 943.

100. Ibid., p. 951.

101. Ibid., p. 953.

102. Ibid., p. 952.

103. Goldoni, *Opere Teatrali,* volume 27/28 (Venice: Antonio Zatta, 1792), *La Dalmatina,* pp. 47, 60.

104. Giovanni Greppi, *Dei capricci teatrali,* volume 2, part 4 (Venice: Giacomo Storti, 1793), *L'Eroe dalmata ossia Aurangzebbe re di Siam,* pp. 271–72; Mate Zorić, "Dalmatinski junak Giovannia Greppia, zaboravljeno djelo talijanskog teatra s konca 18. stoljeća," *Književna prožimanja hrvatsko-talijanska,* pp. 151–160.

105. Greppi, *L'Eroe dalmata,* pp. 271–72.

2. *The Useful or Curious Products of Dalmatia: From Natural History to National Economy*

1. Franco Venturi, *The End of the Old Regime in Europe, 1768–1776: The First Crisis,* trans. R. Burr Litchfield (1979; Princeton, New Jersey: Princeton University Press, 1989), p. 57; Voltaire and Catherine, *Correspondence,* in *Documents of Catherine the Great: The Correspondence with Voltaire and the Instruction of 1767,* ed. W. F. Reddaway (1931; New York: Russell and Russell, 1971), Catherine to Voltaire, 29 October/9 November 1769, pp. 39–40; Voltaire to Catherine, 2 January 1770, pp. 42–43.

2. Giacomo Da Riva, Archivio di Stato di Venezia (ASV), *Senato: Dispacci: Provveditori da Terra e da Mar,* filza 625 (Da Riva, 1771–72), 3 June 1772; Domenico Caminer, *Storia della guerra presente tra la Russia, la Polonia, e la Porta ottomana* (Venice: Antonio Graziosi, 1770), republished in *Storia della ultima guerra tra la Russia e la Porta ottomana* (Venice: Antonio Graziosi, 1776), volume 6, chapter 2, p. 19; Marko Jačov, *Venecija i Srbi u Dalmaciji u XVIII vijeku* (Belgrade: Prosveta, 1984), pp. 105–16.

3. Alberto Fortis, *Viaggio in Dalmazia* (Venice: Presso Alvise Milocco, 1774), republished by Jovan Vuković and Peter Rehder, eds. (Munich and Sarajevo: Verlag Otto Sagner and Izdavačko Preduzeće Veselin Masleša, 1974), volume 1, p. 131; volume 2, p. 30.

4. Domenico Condulmer, ASV, *Inquisitori di Stato,* busta 279 (Dispacci dai Provveditori Generali in Dalmazia, 1768–75), 13 November 1768; 1 September 1769.

5. Ibid., 23 October 1769.

6. Bernardino Honorati, Archivio Segreto Vaticano, *Archivio della Nunziatura di Venezia,* register 39, Letters to the Secretariat of State (1767–1775), 1 July 1769 and 7 October 1769; see also Mile Bogović *Katolička Crkva i Pravoslavlje u Dalmaciji za vrijeme mletačke vladavine* (Zagreb: Kršćanska Sadašnjost, 1982).

7. Paolo Preto, *I Servizi segreti di Venezia* (Milan: Il Saggiatore, 1994), pp. 495–504.

8. Venturi, *The End of the Old Regime in Europe,* pp. ix, 3–7; Camillo Manfroni, "Documenti veneziani sulla campagna dei Russi nel Mediterraneo, 1770–71," *Atti del Reale Istituto Veneto di Scienze, Lettere, ed Arti,* volume 72, series 8/15, part 2 (1912–13), p. 1156; Preto, *I Servizi segreti* pp. 503–04; see also Roberto Cessi, "Confidenze di un ministro russo a Venezia nel 1770," *Atti del Reale Istituto Veneto di Scienze, Lettere, ed Arti,* volume 74, series 8/17, part 2 (1914–15), pp. 1575–1604.

9. Honorati, Archivio Segreto Vaticano, *Archivio della Nunziatura di Venezia,* register 39, 21 October 1769 and 11 November 1769.

10. Venturi, *The End of the Old Regime in Europe,* p. 34; Honorati, Archivio Segreto Vaticano, *Segretaria di Stato: Venezia 1768–1776,* register 239, 28 April 1770.

11. Voltaire and Catherine, *Correspondence,* Voltaire to Catherine, 17 October 1769, p. 37; 18 May 1770, p. 53; 11 August 1770, p. 63; 14 September 1770, p. 71.

12. Venturi, *The End of the Old Regime in Europe,* pp. 31–35.

13. Ibid., pp. 62–67.

14. Voltaire and Catherine, *Correspondence,* Voltaire to Catherine, 5 September 1770, p. 68; Venturi, *The End of the Old Regime in Europe,* pp. 21n, 56n.

15. C. De Michelis, "Domenico Caminer," *Dizionario Biografico degli Italiani,* volume 17 (Rome: Enciclopedia Italiana, 1974), p. 235.

16. *L'Europa Letteraria,* volume 1, part 1, 1 September 1768 (Venice: Stamperia Palese, 1768).

17. Caminer, *Storia della guerra presente,* volume 10, chapter 1, p. 1; chapter 7, pp. 145–46; chapter 8, p. 159.

18. Gianfranco Torcellan, "Profilo di Alberto Fortis," *Settecento veneto e altri scritti storici* (Turin: G. Giappichelli, 1969), p. 279

19. Fortis, *Viaggio in Dalmazia,* volume 1, pp. v–vi.

20. Torcellan, "Profilo di Alberto Fortis," pp. 280–81; see also Franco Venturi, *Settecento Riformatore,* volume 5, *L'Italia dei lumi,* part 2, *La Repubblica di Venezia* (Turin: Giulio Einaudi, 1990), pp. 71–84.

21. Fortis, *Viaggio,* volume 1, pp. vi–vii.

22. Ibid., p. viii.

23. Ibid., pp. 1–2.

24. Letter of Alberto Fortis to Lazzaro Spallanzani, 23 January 1773, in *Illuministi Italiani,* volume 7, *Riformatori delle Antiche Repubbliche, dei Ducati, dello Stato Pontificio e delle Isole,* eds. Giuseppe Giarrizzo, Gianfranco Torcellan, and Franco Venturi (Milan and Naples: Riccardo Ricciardi Editore, 1965), p. 368.

25. Fortis, *Viaggio,* volume 1, p. 2.

26. Krzysztof Pomian, *Collectors and Curiosities: Paris and Venice, 1500–1800,* trans. Elizabeth Wiles-Portier (1987; Cambridge, England: Polity Press, 1990), pp. 186–92; Francis Haskell, *Patrons and Painters: Art and Society in Baroque Italy* (1963; New York: Icon Editions, Harper & Row, 1971), p. 345.

27. Francesco Griselini, "Pensieri di Francesco Griselini intorno ai modi pratici di rendere ricca e possente una nazione, esposti dallo stesso in una lettera ad un patrizio

veneziano," *Giornale d'Italia*, 12 July 1766, in *Illuministi Italiani*, volume 7, pp. 144–45; Venturi, *La Repubblica di Venezia*, pp. 51–58.

28. Griselini, "Pensieri," p. 143.

29. Griselini, *Dizionario delle arti e de' mestieri*, in *Illuministi Italiani*, volume 7, pp. 147–48.

30. Ibid., p. 151.

31. Pomian, *Collectors and Curiosities*, p. 219; [Lady Anna Riggs Miller], *Letters from Italy: Describing the Manners, Customs, Antiquities, Paintings, &c. of that Country: In the years MDCCLXX and MDCCLXXI*, volume 2, 2nd ed. (London: Edward and Charles Dilly, 1777), p. 376.

32. Pomian, *Collectors and Curiosities*, pp. 20–25.

33. Fortis, *Saggio d'osservazioni sopra l'isola di Cherso ed Osero* (Venice: Gaspare Storti, 1771), pp. 67–70

34. Lisbet Koerner, "Linnaeus' Floral Transplants," *Representations*, 47, University of California Press, summer 1994, pp. 155–57; see also Koerner, *Linnaeus: Nature and Nation* (Cambridge: Harvard University Press, 1999).

35. Fortis, *Saggio*, pp. 76–77.

36. John Stoye, *Marsigli's Europe, 1680–1730: The Life and Times of Luigi Ferdinando Marsigli, Soldier and Virtuoso* (New Haven, Conn.: Yale University Press, 1994), p. 290.

37. Vitaliano Donati, *Saggio della storia naturale marina dell'Adriatico* (Venice: Francesco Storti, 1750), pp. 3–7.

38. Fortis, *Saggio*, pp. 77–78; Pomian, *Collectors and Curiosities*, p. 218.

39. Torcellan, "Profilo di Alberto Fortis," p. 285; see also Gianfranco Torcellan, *Una Figura della Venezia settecentesca: Andrea Memmo* (Venice and Rome: Istituto per la Collaborazione Culturale, 1963), pp. 101–09; and Aldo Parenzo, "Un'inchiesta sulla pesca in Istria e Dalmazia," *Nuovo Archivio Veneto*, volume 8 (Venice: Fratelli Visentini, 1894), Appendix, pp. 1–72.

40. Fortis, *Viaggio*, volume 1, pp. 25–26, 30–31.

41. Ibid., p. 31.

42. Fortis, *Viaggio*, volume 2, p. 129.

43. Ibid., pp. 129–30.

44. Ibid., p. 105.

45. Provveditori sopra la Giustizia vecchia e Giustizieri vecchi, 18 April 1772, in Luigi Dal Pane, *Il Tramonto delle Corporazioni in Italia (secoli XVIII e XIX)* (Milan: Istituto per gli studi di politica internazionale, 1940), pp. 86–88; Šime Peričić, *Dalmacija uoči pada Mletačke Republike* (Zagreb: Sveučilište u Zagrebu), pp. 77–84.

46. Fortis, *Viaggio*, volume 1, p. 16; Pomian, *Collectors and Curiosities*, p. 243.

47. Jacob Spon and George Wheler, *Voyage d'Italie, de Dalmatie, de Grece, et du Levant*, (Lyon: Chez Antoine Cellier, 1678), volume 1, pp. 1, 86–88, 95–98.

48. Robert Adam, *Ruins of the Palace of the Emperor Diocletian at Spalatro in Dalmatia* (London: Printed for the Author, 1764), pp. iii–iv, 2–3.

49. Fortis, *Viaggio*, volume 1, pp. 16–17.

50. Pomian, *Collectors and Curiosities*, pp. 212–13; Haskell, *Patrons and Painters*, pp. 362–64.

51. Fortis, *Viaggio*, volume I, pp. 33–35.

52. Ibid., p. 35.

53. Ibid., pp. 35–36.

54. Larry Wolff, "The Enlightened Anthropology of Friendship in Venetian Dalmatia: Primitive Ferocity and Ritual Fraternity among the Morlacchi," *Eighteenth-Century Studies,* volume 32 (1998–99), pp. 157–78.

55. Fortis, *Viaggio,* volume 2, pp. 42–44.

56. Ibid., pp. 40, 45.

57. Fortis, *Viaggio,* volume 1, pp. 19–20.

58. Fortis, *Viaggio,* volume 2, pp. 136–39.

59. Ibid., pp. 139–40.

60. Haskell, *Patrons and Painters,* pp. 373–74; Fortis, *Viaggio,* volume 2, p. 45.

61. Luca Ciancio, *Autopsie della terra: Illuminismo e geologia in Alberto Fortis (1741–1803)* (Florence: Leo S. Olschki, 1995), p. 163; Pomian, *Collectors and Curiosities,* p. 238.

62. Fortis, *Saggio,* pp. 90–95.

63. Ibid., p. 97.

64. Ibid., pp. 99–101.

65. Ibid., p. 107; Ciancio, *Autopsie della terra,* pp. 185–88, 269.

66. Fortis, *Saggio,* pp. 103, 107.

67. Ibid., pp. 112–15.

68. Ibid., pp. 117–19; Ciancio, *Autopsie della terra,* p. 123; Fortis, *Viaggio,* volume 1, pp. 18–19.

69. Fortis, *Viaggio,* volume 1, pp. 121–22.

70. Ciancio, *Autopsie della terra,* pp. 102, 269; Fortis, *Viaggio,* volume 2, p. 38.

71. Pietro Michiel, ASV, *Collegio: Relazioni,* filza 70, 25 December 1765.

72. Torcellan, *Una Figura della Venezia settecentesca: Andrea Memmo,* p. 108n; Parenzo, "Un'inchiesta sulla pesca in Istria e Dalmazia," p. 51.

73. Ciancio, *Autopsie della terra,* pp. 220–22.

74. Fortis, *Saggio,* p. 121; Fortis, *Viaggio,* volume 1, p. 174.

75. Rudolf Maixner, *Charles Nodier et l'Illyrie* (Paris: Didier, 1960), p. 41, n.5.

76. Ciancio, *Autopsie della terra,* p. 75n; Fortis, *Viaggio,* volume 2, p. 30.

77. Fortis, *Viaggio,* volume 1, pp. 28–29.

78. Fortis, *Viaggio,* volume 1, pp. 23, 125; *Viaggio,* volume 2, p. 2.

79. Fortis, *Viaggio,* volume 1, pp. 130–31.

80. Ibid., pp. 131–32.

81. Fortis, *Viaggio,* volume 2, pp. 48–49.

82. Ibid., pp. 47, 55; see also Gilberto Pizzamiglio, "Introduzione," in Fortis, *Viaggio in Dalmazia,* ed. Eva Viani (Venice: Marsilio Editori, 1987) pp. xi–xxx.

3. *The Character and Customs of the Morlacchi: From Provincial Administration to Enlightened Anthropology*

1. Alberto Fortis, *Viaggio in Dalmazia* (Venice: Presso Alvise Milocco, 1774), republished by Jovan Vuković and Peter Rehder, eds. (Munich and Sarajevo: Verlag Otto Sagner and Izdavačko Preduzeće Veselin Masleša, 1974), volume I, p. 43.

2. Ibid., pp. 43–44.

3. Branimir Gušić, "Wer sind die Morlaken im Adriatischen Raum?" *Balcanica,* (Belgrade, 1973), p. 460; Jacob Spon and George Wheler, *Voyage d'Italie, de Dalmatie, de Grece, et du Levant,* (Lyon: Chez Antoine Cellier, 1678), volume 1, p. 91; Grga Novak, "Morlaci (Vlasi) gledani s mletačke strane," *Zbornik za narodni život i*

običaje, volume 45 (1971), pp. 579–603; Noel Malcolm, "Serbs and Vlachs," in *Bosnia: A Short History* (1994; New York: New York University Press, 1996), pp. 70–81.

4. Jovan Cvijić, *La Péninsule balkanique: Géographie humaine* (Paris: Librairie Armand Colin, 1918), p. 363n.

5. Alice Lee Moqué, *Delightful Dalmatia* (New York: Funk and Wagnalls, 1914), pp. 58–60; Maude Holbach, *Dalmatia: The Land Where East Meets West* (London: John Lane, The Bodley Head, 1908), p. 31; Frances Kinsley Hutchinson, *Motoring in the Balkans: Along the Highways of Dalmatia, Montenegro, the Herzegovina, and Bosnia* (London: Hodder and Stoughton, 1910), pp. 68–69.

6. Karl Kaser, *Hirten, Kämpfer, Stammeshelden: Ursprünge und Gegenwart des balkanischen Patriarchats* (Vienna: Böhlau Verlag, 1992), pp. 84–101; Nenad Moačanin, "Introductory Essay on an Understanding of the Triple-Frontier Area: Preliminary Turkologic Research," in *Microhistory of the Triplex Confinium,* ed. Drago Roksandić (Budapest: Institute on Southeastern Europe, Central European University, 1998), pp. 125–36; Wayne Vucinich, *A Study in Social Survival: Katun in the Bileća Rudine* (Denver: University of Denver Press, 1975), pp. 13–21; Wendy Bracewell, *The Uskoks of Senj: Piracy, Banditry, and Holy War in the Sixteenth-Century Adriatic* (Ithaca: Cornell University Press, 1992), pp. 25–36; Gunter Rothenberg, *The Austrian Military Border in Croatia, 1522–1747* (Urbana: University of Illinois Press, 1960), pp. 64–75; Novak, "Morlaci (Vlasi) gledani s mletačke strane," pp. 579–603.

7. Marco Foscarini, "Degl'inquisitori da spedirsi nella Dalmazia" (Orazione detta nel Maggior Consiglio il giorno 17 December 1747), in *Marco Foscarini e Venezia nel secolo XVIII,* ed. Emilio Morpurgo (Florence: Successori Le Monnier, 1880), pp. 220–21.

8. Alberto Fortis, *Travels into Dalmatia* (London: J. Robson, 1778), republished as *Travels into Dalmatia* (New York: Arno Press and The New York Times, 1971), p. 44.

9. Foscarini, "Degl'inquisitori," p. 220; Larry Wolff, *Inventing Eastern Europe: The Map of Civilization on the Mind of the Enlightenment* (Stanford: Stanford University Press, 1994), pp. 315–31.

10. Zorzi Grimani, Archivio di Stato di Venezia (ASV), *Collegio: Relazioni,* filza 69, March 1732.

11. Giacomo Boldù, ASV, *Collegio: Relazioni,* filza 69, 30 August 1748.

12. Giacomo Boldù, ASV, *Collegio: Relazioni,* filza 69, 30 August 1748; Josip Kolanović, "Dalmacija prema izvještaju generalnog providura Jakova Boldùa 1748," *Ivan Lovrić i njegovo doba* (Sinj: Kulturno društvo Cetinjanin, 1979), pp. 15–35.

13. Carlo Gozzi, *Memorie Inutili,* ed. Domenico Bulferetti, volume 1, in *Collezione di Classici Italiani,* ed. Gustavo Balsamo-Crivelli (Turin: Unione Tipografico-Editrice Torinese, 1928), pp. 66–67.

14. Giacomo Boldù, ASV, *Collegio: Relazioni,* filza 69, 30 August 1748.

15. Ibid.

16. Foscarini, "Degl'inquisitori," pp. 231–32.

17. Giacomo Boldù, ASV, *Collegio: Relazioni,* filza 69, 30 August 1748.

18. Ibid.

19. Ibid.

20. Sindici Inquisitori in Dalmazia (Giovanni Loredan, Nicolo Erizzo, Sebastian Molin), ASV, *Collegio: Relazioni,* filza 70, 2 October 1751.

21. Ibid.

22. Peter Burke, *Popular Culture in Early Modern Europe* (New York: Harper Torchbooks, 1978), pp. 207–43.

23. Sindici Inquisitori in Dalmazia, ASV, *Collegio: Relazioni,* filza 70, 2 October 1751.

24. Ibid.

25. Ibid.

26. Ibid.

27. Ibid.

28. Francesco Grimani, "Informazione del Provveditore Generale Grimani al Suo Successore Alvise Contarini," ASV, *Collegio: Relazioni,* filza 69, 10 October 1756; Gligor Stanojević, *Dalmatinske krajine u XVIII vijeku* (Belgrade and Zagreb: Prosveta, 1987), pp. 100–110.

29. Francesco Grimani, ASV, *Collegio: Relazioni,* filza 69, 10 October 1756.

30. Ibid.

31. Ibid.

32. Pietro Michiel, ASV, *Collegio: Relazioni,* filza 70, 25 December 1765

33. Ibid.

34. Ibid.

35. Ibid.

36. Domenico Condulmer, ASV, *Senato: Dispacci: Provveditori da Terra e da Mar,* filza 622 (Condulmer, 1768–69), 1 January 1769 (1768 m.v.); 22 August 1769.

37. Ibid., 1 March 1769; 23 March 1769.

38. Domenico Condulmer, ASV, *Inquisitori di Stato,* busta 279 (Dispacci dai Provveditori Generali in Dalmazia, 1768–75), 1 September 1769.

39. Bernardino Honorati, Archivio Segreto Vaticano, *Archivio della Nunziatura di Venezia,* register 39, Letters to the Secretariat of State (1767–1775), 1 July 1769 and 7 October 1769; see also Paolo Preto, *I Servizi segreti di Venezia* (Milan: Il Saggiatore, 1994), pp. 495–504.

40. Giacomo Da Riva, ASV, *Senato: Dispacci: Provveditori da Terra e da Mar,* filza 625 (Da Riva, 1771–72), 22 December 1771; 3 June 1772.

41. Marko Jačov, *Venecija i Srbi u Dalmaciji u XVIII vijeku* (Belgrade: Prosveta, 1984), pp. 105–16; Šime Peričić, *Dalmaciji uoči pada Mletačke Republike* (Zagreb: Sveučilište u Zagrebu, 1980), pp. 20–22; Honorati, Archivio Segreto Vaticano *Archivio della Nunziatura di Venezia,* register 39, 25 May 1771; see also Mile Bogović, *Katolička Crkva i Pravoslavlje u Dalmaciji: za vrijeme mletačke vladavine* (Zagreb: Kršćanska Sadašnjost, 1982), pp. 111–45.

42. Obradović, Dositej. *The Life and Adventures of Dimitrije Obradović.* Trans. and ed. George Rapall Noyes (Berkeley: University of California Press, 1953), pp. 237–38, 253, 258–259.

43. Casanova, *Mémoires,* volume 1, eds. Robert Abirached and Elio Zorzi (Tours: Editions Gallimard, Bibliothèque de la Pléiade, 1958), pp. 342–72, 1139–41.

44. Giacomo Da Riva, ASV, *Senato: Dispacci: Provveditori da Terra e da Mar,* filza 625 (Da Riva, 1771–72), 16 January 1772 (1771 m.v.).

45. Ibid.

46. Ibid.

47. Ibid.

48. Ibid.

49. Ibid., 4 July 1772.

50. Fortis, *Viaggio,* volume 1, pp. 44, 52–53.

51. Ibid., p. 53.

52. Ibid., pp. 53–54.

53. Ibid., pp. 54, 64.

54. Ibid., pp. 54–56.

55. Ibid., p. 56.

56. Ibid., p. 57.

57. Voltaire, *Essai sur les moeurs,* ed. René Pomeau (Paris: Garnier Frères, 1963), volume 1, p, 25; volume 2, pp. 156, 811.

58. Michèle Duchet, *Anthropologie et histoire au siècle des lumières* (Paris: François Maspero, 1971), p. 12.

59. Franco Venturi, *Settecento riformatore,* volume 5, *L'Italia dei lumi,* part 2, *La Repubblica di Venezia (1761–1797)* (Turin: Giulio Einaudi, 1990), pp. 72–73; Luca Ciancio, *Autopsie della terra: Illuminismo e geologia in Alberto Fortis (1741–1803)* (Florence: Leo S. Olschki, 1995), pp. 277–78.

60. Fortis, *Viaggio,* volume 1, p. 61.

61. Ibid., p. 62.

62. Ibid., pp. 58–60.

63. Ibid., p. 36; see also Larry Wolff, "The Enlightened Anthropology of Friendship in Venetian Dalmatia: Primitive Ferocity and Ritual Fraternity among the Morlacchi," *Eighteenth-Century Studies,* volume 32 (1998–99), pp. 157–78.

64. Fortis, *Viaggio,* volume 1, p. 67.

65. Jean Starobinski, *Jean-Jacques Rousseau: Transparency and Obstruction,* trans. Arthur Goldhammer (1971; Chicago: University of Chicago Press, 1988) pp. 22–26.

66. Fortis, *Viaggio,* volume 1, pp. 67–68.

67. Ibid., p. 68.

68. Giovanni Lovrich, *Osservazioni di Giovanni Lovrich sopra diversi pezzi del Viaggio in Dalmazia del Signor Abate Alberto Fortis* (Venice: Francesco Sansoni, 1776), p. 81; Fortis, *Viaggio,* volume 1, p. 81.

69. Voltaire, *Essai sur les moeurs,* volume 2, p. 807; Fortis, *Viaggio,* volume 1, p. 79.

70. Fortis, *Viaggio,* volume 1, pp. 79–80.

71. Ibid., pp. 68–69.

72. Ibid., p. 70.

73. Ibid., pp. 75–76; Fortis, *Viaggio,* volume 2, pp. 74–75.

74. Fortis, *Viaggio,* volume 1, pp. 31–32.

75. Ibid., pp. 83–84.

76. Ibid., p. 84.

77. Claude Lévi-Strauss, *Tristes Tropiques,* trans. John and Doreen Weightman (1955; New York: Atheneum, 1975), pp. 178, 390.

78. Voltaire, *Essai sur les moeurs,* volume 2, p. 810.

79. Fortis, *Viaggio,* volume 2, p. 87.

4. *The Morlacchi and the Discovery of the Slavs: From National Classification to Sentimental Imagination*

1. Alberto Fortis, *Viaggio in Dalmazia* (Venice: Presso Alvise Milocco, 1774), republished by Jovan Vuković and Peter Rehder, eds. (Munich and Sarajevo: Verlag Otto Sagner and Izdavačko Preduzeće Veselin Masleša, 1974), volume 1, p. 44;

Johann Gottfried Herder, *Ideen zur Philosophie der Geschichte der Menschheit,* in *Herders Werke,* volume 4, ed. Regine Otto (Berlin and Weimar: Aufbau-Verlag, 1982), p. 393. Larry Wolff, *Inventing Eastern Europe: The Map of Civilization on the Mind of the Enlightenment* (Stanford: Stanford University Press, 1994), pp. 284–331.

2. Fortis, *Viaggio,* volume 1, pp. 44–45.

3. Ivo Banac, "The Redivived Croatia of Pavao Ritter Vitezović," *Harvard Ukrainian Studies,* volume 10, (December 1986), pp. 502–03; Banac, *The National Question in Yugoslavia: Origins, History, Politics* (Ithaca: Cornell University Press, 1984), pp. 70–75; Zdenko Zlatar, *Our Kingdom Come: The Counter-Reformation, the Republic of Dubrovnik, and the Liberation of the Balkan Slavs* (Boulder: East European Monographs, 1992), pp. 361–81; Ante Kadić, *From Croatian Renaissance to Yugoslav Socialism* (The Hague: Mouton, 1969), pp. 41–92; see also Pavao Ritter Vitezović, *Croatia rediviva,* ed. Zrinka Blažević (Zagreb: Biblioteka Latina and Graeca, Hrvatski Institut za Provijest, 1997); Thomas Eekman and Ante Kadić, *Juraj Križanić (1618–1683) Russophile and Ecumenic Visionary: A Symposium* (The Hague: Mouton, 1976).

4. Obradović, Dositej. *The Life and Adventures of Dimitrije Obradović.* Trans. and ed. George Rapall Noyes (Berkeley: University of California Press, 1953), p. 134–35.

5. Fortis, *Viaggio,* volume 2, p. 174.

6. Grga Novak, "Morlaci (Vlasi) gledani s mletačke strane," *Zbornik za narodni život i običaje,* volume 45 (1971), pp. 579–603; Marko Jačov, *Venecija i Srbi u Dalmaciji u XVIII vijeku* (Belgrade: Prosveta, 1984), pp. 7–9; Mile Bogović, "Tko su Morlaci," *Katolička Crkva i Pravoslavlje u Dalmaciji: za vrijeme mletačke vladavine* (Zagreb: Kršćanska Sadašnjost, 1982), pp. 14–17; Wayne Vucinich, "Katuns and Vlachs," *A Study in Social Survival: Katun in the Bileća Rudine* (Denver, Colo.: University of Denver, 1975), pp. 13–21; Branimir Gušić, "Wer sind die Morlaken im Adriatischen Raum?" *Balcanica,* IV (Belgrade, 1973), pp. 453–64; André Blanc, "Le Problème des Valaques," *La Croatie Occidentale: Étude de géographie humaine* (Paris, Institut d'Études Slaves, 1957), pp. 95–102; Jovan Cvijić, *La Péninsule balkanique: Géographie humaine* (Paris: Librairie Armand Colin, 1918), pp. 363–69; Noel Malcolm, "Serbs and Vlachs," in *Bosnia: A Short History* (1994; New York: New York University Press, 1996), pp. 70–81.

7. Fortis, *Viaggio,* volume 1, pp. 45–46.

8. Wolff, *Inventing Eastern Europe,* pp. 356–74; Maria Todorova, *Imagining the Balkans* (Oxford: Oxford University Press, 1997), pp. 3–20.

9. Fortis, *Viaggio,* volume 1, p. 47; Fortis, *Travels into Dalmatia* (London: J. Robson, 1778), republished as *Travels into Dalmatia* (New York: Arno Press and The New York Times, 1971), p. 47.

10. Fortis, *Viaggio,* volume 1, p. 51.

11. Kiril Petkov, *Infidels, Turks, and Women: The South Slavs in the German Mind, ca. 1400–1600* (Frankfurt: Peter Lang, 1997), pp. 234–35, 249–59; Zlatar, *Our Kingdom Come,* pp. 365, 378, n. 24.

12. Fortis, *Saggio d'osservazioni sopra l'isola di Cherso ed Osero* (Venice: Gaspare Storti, 1771), p. 44; Fortis, *Viaggio,* volume 1, p. 77.

13. Fortis, *Viaggio,* volume 1, p. 48.

14. Luca Ciancio, *Autopsie della terra: Illuminismo e geologia in Alberto Fortis (1741–1803)* (Florence: Leo S. Olschki, 1995), pp. 67–68; Gianfranco Torcellan, *Una Figura della Venezia settecentesca: Andrea Memmo* (Venice and Rome: Istituto per la

Collaborazione Culturale, 1963), p. 108; Torcellan, "Profilo di Alberto Fortis," *Settecento veneto e altri scritti storici* (Turin: G. Giappichelli, 1969), p. 283.

15. Fortis, *Saggio*, pp. *44–45*; Fortis, *Travels*, p. 49; Fortis, *Viaggio*, volume 1, pp. 49–50.

16. Fortis, *Viaggio*, volume 1, pp. 90–91; Matthias Murko, *Das Original von Goethes "Klaggesang von der edlen Frauen des Asan Aga" (Asanaginica) in der Literatur und im Volksmunde durch 150 Jahre* (Brno: Verlag Rudolf M. Rohrer, 1937), pp. 28–29; Bogović, pp. 129–41; Attilio Tamaro, *La Vénétie Julienne et la Dalmatie: Histoire de la nation italienne sur ses frontières orientales,* volume 3, *La Dalmatie* (Rome, 1919), p. 287; Arturo Cronia, *L'enigma del glagolismo in Dalmazia: dalle origini all'epoca presente* (Zadar: Tipografia E. de Schönfeld, 1925), pp. 45–48, 108–111.

17. Giulio Bajamonti, "Il Morlacchismo d'Omero," *Nuovo giornale enciclopedico d'Italia* (March 1797), pp. 77–98; Marijan Stojković, "Morlakizam," *Hrvatsko Kolo,* book 10 (Zagreb: Matica Hrvatska, 1929), pp. 254–73; Arturo Cronia, *La Conoscenza del mondo slavo in Italia: Bilancio storico-bibliografico di un millennio* (Padua: Officine Grafiche Stediv, 1958), pp. 331–33; Andrei Pippidi, "Naissance, renaissances et mort du "Bon Sauvage": à propos des Morlaques et des Valaques," in *Hommes et idées du Sud-Est européen à l'aube de l'âge moderne* (Bucharest: Editura Academiei, 1980), pp. 1–23; Barbara W. Maggs, "Three Phases of Primitivism in Portraits of Eighteenth-Century Croatia," *Slavonic and East European Review,* volume 67 (October 1989), pp. 546–63; Valentina Gulin, "Morlacchism between Enlightenment and Romanticism," *Narodna umjetnost,* 34/1 (Zagreb, 1997), pp. 77–100; Mate Zorić, "Croati e altri slavi del sud nella letteratura italiana del '700," *Revue des études sud-est européennes,* volume 10(Bucharest, 1972), pp. 301–12; Zorić, "Hrvat, Skjavun, Dubrovčanin, Morlak i Uskok—kao stereotipi i pjesnički motivi u talijanskoj književnosti," *Književna smotra,* volume 24 (Zagreb, 1992), pp. 47–55; see also Zorić, *Italia e Slavia: Contributi sulle relazioni letterarie italo-jugoslave dall'Ariosto al D'Annunzio* (Padua: Editrice Antenore, 1989); and Zorić, *Književna prožimanja hrvatsko-talijanska* (Split: Književni Krug, 1992).

18. Fortis, *Viaggio,* volume 1, p. 89; Miroslav Pantić, "Serbian Folk Poetry and Europe in the Late 18th and the Early 19th Centuries," in *The Serbs in European Civilization,* eds. Radovan Samardzić and Milan Duskov (Belgrade: Nova, 1993), pp. 151–58; Zorić, "Croati e altri slavi del sud," pp. 306–07.

19. Camilla Lucerna, *Die südslavische Ballade von Asan Agas Gattin und ihre Nachbildung durch Goethe* (Berlin: Alexander Duncker, 1905), pp. 58–59.

20. Fortis, *Viaggio,* volume 1, pp. 89–90.

21. Ciancio, *Autopsie della terra,* pp. 112–13; Giambattista Vico, *The New Science,* trans. Thomas Goddard Bergin and Max Harold Fisch (Ithaca, N.Y.: Cornell University Press, 1984), pp. 301, 324; see also Albert Lord, *The Singer of Tales* (Cambridge, Mass.: Harvard University Press, 1960), pp. 11–12, 141–57.

22. Fortis, *Viaggio,* volume 1, pp. 72, 88.

23. Murko, *Das Original,* pp. 4, 25–26, 32–39; Ivan Milčetić, "Dr. Julije Bajamonti i negova djela," *Rad Jugoslavenske Akademije Znanosti i Umjetnosti,* book 192 (Zagreb, 1912), pp. 132–49; André Vaillant, "Vuk Karadžić et l'Hasanaginica," *Revue des études slaves,* volume 19 (Paris, 1939), pp. 88–90.

24. Lord, *Singer of Tales,* p. 136; Andrija Kačić-Miošić, *Razgovor ugodni naroda slovinskoga* (Split: Zbornik Kačić, 1983), pp. 12–64; Ante Kadić, "The Importance of Kačić-Miošić," *From Croatian Renaissance to Yugoslav Socialism* (The Hague:

Mouton, 1969), pp, 93–97; Zvane Crnja, *Cultural History of Croatia*, trans. Vladimir Ivir (Zagreb: Office of Information, 1962), pp. 291–93.

25. Fortis, *Viaggio*, volume 2, p. 110; Fortis, *Saggio*, p. 162.

26. Fortis, *Viaggio*, volume 1, pp. 88–89.

27. Ibid., pp. 91–92.

28. Jean-Jacques Rousseau, "Essay on the Origin of Languages," trans. John Moran, in *Two Essays on the Origin of Language*, eds. John Moran and Alexander Gode (Chicago: University of Chicago Press, 1986), pp. 5, 12, 21, 50; Jacques Derrida, *Of Grammatology*, trans. Gayatri Chakravorty Spivak (Baltimore: Johns Hopkins University Press, 1976), pp. 165–94.

29. Herder, "Essay on the Origin of Language," trans. Alexander Gode, in *Two Essays on the Origin of Language*, eds. John Moran and Alexander Gode (Chicago: University of Chicago Press, 1986), p. 87.

30. Fortis, *Viaggio*, volume 1, pp. 92–93.

31. Ibid., pp. 98–105; Murko, *Das Original*, pp. 11–12.

32. Johann Wolfgang Goethe, *Goethes Werke*, volume 1 (Hamburg: Christian Wenger Verlag, 1949), pp. 82–85, 496–99, trans. LW; Herder, *Volkslieder*, in *Herders Werke*, volume 2, ed. Theodor Matthias (Leipzig and Vienna: Bibliographisches Institut, 1903), pp. 275–78, 289.

33. Herder, *Volkslieder*, pp. 186–91, 409–21, 501; Pantić, p. 156.

34. Goethe, "Serbische Lieder," in *Goethes Werke*, volume 12 (Hamburg: Christian Wenger Verlag, 1953), p. 335; W. Macintosh, *Scott and Goethe: German Influence on the Writings of Sir Walter Scott* (1925; Port Washington, N.Y.: Kennikat Press, 1970), pp. 13–14, 206–11; Edgar Johnson, *Sir Walter Scott: The Great Unknown* (New York: Macmillan, 1970), p. 135; Georgii Ferrich, *Ad clarissimum virum Joannem Muller* (Dubrovnik: Andreas Trevisan, 1798), pp. 7–15; Lucerna, *Die südslavische Ballade*, p. 4.

35. Lucerna, *Die Südslavische Ballade*, pp. 65–66; Vaillant, *Vuk Karadžić*, p. 90.

36. Goethe, "Serbische Lieder," p. 335; Goethe, *Italian Journey*, trans. Robert Heitner, in *Goethe: The Collected Works*, volume 6 (Princeton, N.J.: Princeton University Press, 1994), p. 182.

37. Giustiniana Wynne, *Les Morlaques* (Venice, 1788), "Sujet de l'ouvrage" (preface).

38. Ibid.

39. Ibid.

40. Ibid., p. 8.

41. Ibid., p. 177; Rudolf Maixner, "Traductions et imitations du roman *Les Morlaques*," *Revue des Études Slaves*, volume 32 (Paris: Imprimerie Nationale, 1955), p. 70, n. 1.

42. Bruno Brunelli, *Casanova Loved Her*, trans. Alexander McKechnie (1923; London: Peter Davies, 1929), p. 69; Casanova, *Mémoires*, volume 2, ed. Robert Abirached (Tours: Librairie Gallimard, Bibliothèque de la Pléiade, 1959), p. 178.

43. Wynne, *Les Morlaques*, "Sujet."

44. Casanova, *Mémoires*, volume 1, eds. Robert Abirached and Elio Zorzi (Tours: Editions Gallimard, Bibliothèque de la Pléiade, 1958), p. 672.

45. Maixner, "Traductions et imitations," p. 65; Baron Ernouf, "Notice sur la vie et les écrits de Justine Wynne, comtesse des Ursins et de Rosenberg," *Bulletin du Bibliophile et du Bibliothécaire*, (Paris, June and July 1858) p. 1002; Brunelli, *Casanova Loved Her*, pp. 252–81; Krzysztof Pomian, *Collectors and Curiosities: Paris and Venice*

1500–1800, trans. Elizabeth Wiles-Portier (Cambridge: Polity Press, 1990), pp. 254–56; Francis Haskell, *Patrons and Painters: Art and Society in Baroque Italy* (1963; New York: Icon Editions, 1971), pp. 368–72.

46. Wynne, *Les Morlaques,* p. 1; Fortis, *Viaggio,* volume 2, p. 49.

47. Žarko Muljačić, "Alberto Fortis als Berater von J. Wynne und B. Benincasa," *Zeitschrift für Slavische Philologie,* Heidelberg, volume 42, book 2 (1981), pp. 297–99.

48. Wynne, *Les Morlaques,* pp. 1–2; Fortis, *Viaggio,* volume 1, p. 67; see also Jean-Louis Vissière, "Des bons sauvages d'Europe: Les Dalmates," *Revue des études sud-est européennes,* volume 10 (Bucharest, 1972), pp. 335–43.

49. Fortis, *Viaggio,* volume 1, pp. 55–56; *Viaggio,* volume 2, map, "Contadi di Trau, Spalatro, e Macarska, il Primorie, e Narenta, coll'isole aggiacenti."

50. Wynne, *Les Morlaques,* p. 3.

51. Rousseau, *Discours sur l'origine et les fondements de l'inégalités parmis les hommes,* ed. Jacques Roger (Paris: Flammarion, 1992), p. 222.

52. Wynne, *Les Morlaques,* pp. 4–7.

53. Obradović, *Life and Adventures,* pp. 230–31.

54. Wynne, *Les Morlaques,* pp. 9–12.

55. Ibid., p. 13; Fortis, *Viaggio,* volume 1, pp. 68–69.

56. Wynne, *Les Morlaques,* pp. 12–14.

57. Ibid., pp. 16–17.

58. Edgardo Maddalena, "Nota Storica" (*La Dalmatina*), in Carlo Goldoni, *Opere complete,* ed. Municipio di Venezia, volume 25 (Venice: Stamperia Zanetti, 1927), p. 95.

59. Wynne, *Les Morlaques,* pp. 34–35.

60. Wolff, *Inventing Eastern Europe,* pp. 22, 35, 337, 345.

61. Wynne, *Les Morlaques,* p. 24, 38–39.

62. Ibid., pp. 40–41.

63. Ibid., pp. 47–48.

64. Ibid., pp. 48–49.

65. Giacomo Da Riva, ASV, *Senato: Dispacci: Provveditori da Terra e da Mar,* filza 625 (Da Riva, 1771–72), June 1772; see also Paolo Preto, *I Servizi segreti di Venezia* (Milan: Il Saggiatore, 1994), pp. 495–504.

66. Wynne, *Les Morlaques,* pp. 36–37.

67. Ibid., pp. 49–52.

68. Ibid., pp. 57–58.

69. Giacomo Gradenigo, ASV, *Inquisitori di Stato: Dispacci dai Provveditori Generali in Dalmazia,* filze 279/280 (1768–75), 10 August 1775.

70. Wynne, *Les Morlaques,* pp. 58–59.

71. Wolff, *Inventing Eastern Europe,* pp. 195–234.

72. Wynne, *Les Morlaques,* pp. 61–62.

73. Ibid., p. 62.

74. Voltaire and Catherine, *Correspondence,* in *Documents of Catherine the Great: The Correspondence with Voltaire and the Instruction of 1767,* ed. W. F. Reddaway (1931; New York: Russell and Russell, 1971), Voltaire to Catherine, 15 November 1768, p. 20.

75. Domenico Caminer, *Prospetto degli Affari Attuali dell'Europa, ossia Storia della Guerra Presente,* volume 1 (Lugano, 1788; sold in Venice by Antonio Zatta). Franco Venturi, *Settecento Riformatore,* volume 5, *L'Italia dei lumi,* part 2, *La Repubblica di Venezia* (Turin: Giulio Einaudi, 1990), pp. 284–85.

76. Wynne, *Les Morlaques,* pp. 62–64.

77. Maggs, "Three Phases of Primitivism," p. 557, n.12; Brunelli, *Casanova Loved Her,* p. 245.

78. Wynne, *Les Morlaques,* pp. 103–04.

79. Ibid., pp. 118–20.

80. Ibid., pp. 120–23.

81. Brunelli, *Casanova Loved Her,* p. 256; Pomian, *Collectors and Curiosities,* p. 255.

82. Voltaire and Catherine, *Correspondence,* Voltaire to Catherine, 22 December 1766, p. 13; 11 December 1772, p. 177.

83. Maixner, "Traductions et imitations," pp. 69–75; Brunelli, *Casanova Loved Her,* pp. 268–69.

84. Maixner, "Traductions et imitations," pp. 70–76; Marijan Stojković, "Morlak-izam," pp. 271–72.

85. Wynne, *Les Morlaques,* pp. 310, 326–27, 334–36.

86. Ibid., pp. 260–67.

87. Ibid., p. 274.

88. Ibid., p. 353.

89. Venturi, *La Repubblica di Venezia,* pp. 236–56.

90. Melchiorre Cesarotti, "Les Morlaques," in *Nuovo giornale enciclopedico,* Vicenza, (July 1789), pp. 37–38.

91. Ibid., pp. 61–62.

92. Camillo Federici, *Gli Antichi Slavi,* in *Collezione di tutte le Opere Teatrali del Signor Camillo Federici,* volume 16 (Venice: Pietro Bettini Libraio, 1819), pp. 3–5, 20–21; "Camillo Federici," *Biografia degli Italiani Illustri,* ed. Emilio de Tipaldo, volume 5 (Venice: Tipografia di Alvisopoli, 1837), pp. 346–52; Zorić, "Croati e altri slavi del sud," pp. 310–11.

93. Cronia, *La Conoscenza del mondo slavo in Italia,* p. 331; Federici, *Gli Antichi Slavi,* pp. 11–14.

94. Federici, *Gli Antichi Slavi,* pp. 31–32.

95. Ibid., pp. 51–52.

96. Ibid., pp. 52–53.

97. Ibid., p. 53.

98. Ibid., pp. 8, 54–55, 70–71, 78, 84–85.

99. Ibid., pp. 85–86.

100. Cronia, *La Conoscenza del mondo slavo in Italia,* p. 332.

101. *Le Nozze de' Morlacchi, ossia il Rapimento d'Elena,* Ballo eroicomico composto dal Serafini Giacomo, (Bergamo: Stampatore Duci, 1802), Walter Toscanini Collection, *libretti di ballo,* Library for the Performing Arts, The New York Public Library.

102. *I Morlacchi,* Ballo di Carattere in tre atti, composto e diretto da Antonio Biggiogero (Novara: Stamperia Rasario, 1812); *I Morlacchi,* Ballo di Carattere in quattro atti, d'invenzione di Gaetano Gioja, composto da Ferdinando Gioja (Bologna: Stamperia del Sassi, 1830); *I Morlacchi, ossia Le Nozze Interrotte,* Ballo Serio, composto e diretto dal Signor Giovanni Fabris (Milan: Stamperia di Carlo Dova, 1831); Walter Toscanini Collection, *libretti di ballo,* Library for the Performing Arts, New York Public Library.

103. Carlo Federici, *Otello ossia lo Slavo,* in *Capricci teatrali,* volume 3 (Rome: Gioacchino Puccinelli Stampatore a S. Andrea della Valle, 1805), pp. 5–6, 11, 46; see

also Žarko Muljačić, " 'Otello ossia lo Slavo' Carla Federicija," *Radovi Instituta Jugoslavenske Akademije Znanosti i Umjetnosti u Zadru,* volume 20 (1973), pp. 359–66.

104. Madame de Staël, *Correspondance Generale,* volume 5, part 1, *France et Allemagne,* (1803–1804), ed. Béatrice Jasinski (Paris: Hachette, 1982), pp. 236–37 (20 February 1804); Madame de Staël, *Oeuvres complètes,* volume 10, *De l'Allemagne* (Paris: Chez Treuttel et Würtz, 1820), pp. 299–300.

105. Madame de Staël, *Corinne, or Italy,* trans. Avriel Goldberger (New Brunswick, N.J.: Rutgers University Press, 1987), pp. 300–01; Maixner, "Traductions et imitations," p. 76; Zorić, "Croati e altri slavi del sud," pp. 308–09.

106. Prosper Mérimée, *La Guzla,* ed. Antonia Fonyi (Paris: Éditions Kimé, 1994), pp. 21–26; see also Rudolf Maixner, *Charles Nodier et l'Illyrie* (Paris: Didier, 1960); and Goethe, "La Guzla," *Schriften zur Literatur,* volume 3, ed. Horst Nahler (Berlin: Akademie-Verlag, 1973), pp. 259–60.

107. Mérimée, *La Guzla,* p. 38.

108. Adam Mickiewicz, "Morlach w Wenecji," *Wiersze* (Warsaw: Czytelnik, 1972) pp. 266–67.

5. *Public Debate after Fortis: Dalmatian Dissent and Venetian Controversy*

1. Giacomo Gradenigo, Archivio di Stato di Venezia (ASV), *Collegio: Relazioni,* filza 70, 14 December 1777.

2. Gradenigo, ASV, *Collegio: Relazioni,* filza 70, 14 December 1777; Marko Jačov, *Venecija i Srbi u Dalmaciji u XVIII vijeku* (Belgrade: Prosveta, 1984), pp. 105–16; Šime Peričić, *Dalmacija uoči pada Mletačke Republike* (Zagreb: Sveučilište u Zagrebu), pp. 17–23, 182–89.

3. Gradenigo, ASV, *Collegio: Relazioni,* filza 70, 14 December 1777.

4. Francesco Grimani, "Informazione del Provveditore Generale Grimani al suo successore Alvise Contarini," ASV, *Collegio: Relazioni,* filza 69, 10 October 1756.

5. Gradenigo, ASV, *Senato: Dispacci: Provveditori da Terra e da Mar,* filza 630 (Gradenigo, 1774–75), 29 October 1774; Peričić, *Dalmacija,* pp. 182–89.

6. Bernardino Honorati, Archivio Segreto Vaticano, *Archivio della Nunziatura di Venezia,* register 39, Letters to the Secretariat of State (1767–1775), 1 April 1775.

7. Gradenigo, ASV, *Senato: Dispacci: Provveditori da Terra e da Mar,* filza 630 (Gradenigo, 1774–75), 12 November 1774; see also Hannes Grandits and Karl Kaser, "Familie und Gesellschaft in der Habsburgischen Militärgrenze: Lika und Krbava zu Beginn des 18. Jahrhunderts," *Microhistory of the Triplex Confinium,* ed. Drago Roksandić (Budapest: Institute on Southeastern Europe, Central European University, 1998), pp. 27–44; Karl Kaser, *Freier Bauer und Soldat: Die Militarisierung der agrarischen Gesellschaft an der kroatisch-slawonischen Militärgrenze* (Vienna: Böhlau Verlag, 1997), pp. 355–77, 436–48.

8. Gradenigo, ASV, *Senato: Dispacci: Provveditori da Terra e da Mar,* filza 630 (Gradenigo, 1774–75), 12 November 1774; see also Mile Bogović, *Katolička Crkva i Pravoslavlje u Dalmaciji: za vrijeme mletačke vladavine* (Zagreb: Kršćanska Sadašnjost, 1982), pp. 95–98, 146–64.

9. Gradenigo, ASV, *Senato: Dispacci: Provveditori da Terra e da Mar,* filza 630 (Gradenigo, 1774–75), 10 December 1774.

10. Ibid.

11. Gradenigo, ASV, *Collegio: Relazioni,* filza 70, 14 December 1777.

12. Ibid.

13. Alberto Fortis, *Saggio d'osservazioni sopra l'isola di Cherso ed Osero* (Venice: Gaspare Storti, 1771), pp. 50, 151–52.

14. Fortis, *Viaggio in Dalmazia* (Venice: Presso Alvise Milocco, 1774), republished by Jovan Vuković and Peter Rehder, eds. (Munich and Sarajevo: Verlag Otto Sagner and Izdavačko Preduzeće Veselin Masleša, 1974), volume 2, pp. 83–84.

15. Gradenigo, ASV, *Collegio: Relazioni,* filza 70, 14 December 1777.

16. Ibid.

17. Ibid.

18. Giovanni Lovrich, *Osservazioni di Giovanni Lovrich: sopra diversi pezzi del Viaggio in Dalmazia del Signor Abate Alberto Fortis: coll'aggiunta della vita di Socivizca* (Venice: Francesco Sansoni, 1776), p. 5.

19. Ibid., pp. 5–6.

20. Ibid., p. 6.

21. Marijan Stojković, "Ivan Lovrić, pristaša struje prosvjetljenja u Dalmaciji," *Zbornik za narodni život i običaje južnih slavena,* Jugoslavenska Akademija Znanosti i Umjetnosti, book 28, volume 2 (Zagreb, 1932), pp. 1–44; Ivan Lovrić, *Bilješke o Putu po Dalmaciji opata Alberta Fortisa* (Zagreb: Izdavački Zavod Jugoslavenske Akademije, 1948), "Pogovor," pp. 221–29; Mirko Božić, "Ivan Lovrić," *Ivan Lovrić i njegovo doba* (Sinj: Kulturno društvo Cetinjanin, 1979), pp. 9–14; Simeone Gliubich, *Dizionario biografico degli uomini illustri della Dalmazia* (1856; Bologna: Arnaldo Forni Editore, 1974), p. 182.

22. Attilio Tamaro, *La Vénétie Julienne et la Dalmatie: Histoire de la nation italienne sur ses frontières orientales,* volume 3, *La Dalmatie* (Rome: Imprimerie du Sénat, 1919), pp. 350–51; Peričić, *Dalmacija* pp. 210–11.

23. Franco Venturi, *Settecento Riformatore,* volume 5, *L'Italia dei lumi,* part 2, *La Repubblica di Venezia* (Turin: Giulio Einaudi, 1990), pp. 362–64; Ivan Milčetić, "Dr. Julije Bajamonti i negova djela," *Rad Jugoslavenske Akademije Znanosti i Umjetnosti,* book 192 (Zagreb, 1912), pp. 184–86; Arturo Cronia, "Giulio Bajamonti," *Dizionario Biografico degli Italiani,* volume 5 (Rome: Enciclopedia Italiana, 1963), pp. 280–81.

24. Venturi, *La Repubblica di Venezia,* pp. 348–51.

25. Lovrich, *Osservazioni,* pp. 9, 63; see also Bernard Stulli, "Gospodarsko-društvene i političke prilike u Cetinskoj krajini sredinom XVIII stoljeća," *Ivan Lovrić i njegovo doba,* pp. 37–105.

26. Lovrich, *Osservazioni,* pp. 67–68, 168; Peričić, p. 217; Josip Milićević, "Lovrićevi zapisi narodnih običaja," *Ivan Lovrić i njegovo doba,* pp. 309–18.

27. Lovrich, *Osservazioni,* pp. 68, 81, 88–89.

28. Ibid., p. 95.

29. Ibid., p. 108.

30. Ibid., pp. 128–29.

31. Ibid., p. 102; Fortis, *Viaggio,* volume 1, p. 55.

32. Lovrich, *Osservazioni,* p. 157.

33. Fortis, *Viaggio,* volume 2, pp. 113–14.

34. Lovrich, *Osservazioni,* pp. 189–90.

35. Ibid., p. 79.

36. Ibid., p. 80.

37. Ibid., pp. 83–84.
38. Ibid., pp. 82–83, 174.
39. Ibid., pp. 104–06, 136–37, 159, 164.
40. Ibid., p. 103.
41. Fortis, *Viaggio*, volume 2, p. 87; Lovrich, *Osservazioni*, pp. 103–04.
42. Lovrich, *Osservazioni*, pp. 116–19; Filip Grabovac, *Cvit razgovora naroda i jezika iliričkoga aliti rvackoga* (Split: Književni Krug, 1986), pp. 290–92.
43. Lovrich, *Osservazioni*, pp. 121, 126.
44. Ibid., p. 127; Fortis, *Viaggio*, volume 1, p. 88.
45. Lovrich, *Osservazioni*, frontispiece, pp. 258–60; Venturi, *La Repubblica di Venezia*, p. 356; *Leben des berüchtigten Haiducken Sotschiwizka* (Leipzig: Carl Friedrich Schneider, 1778); Ivan Mimica, "Književni značajke Lovrićeva djela 'Život Stanislava Sočivice,' " *Ivan Lovrić i njegovo doba*, pp. 239–51; Andrei Pippidi, "Naissance, renaissances et mort du "Bon Sauvage": à propos des Morlaques et des Valaques," in *Hommes et idées du Sud-Est européen à l'aube de l'âge moderne* (Bucharest: Editura Academiei, 1980), pp. 13–14.
46. Lovrich, *Osservazioni*, pp. 116–17, 131–32, 212–13.
47. Ibid., pp. 168–69.
48. Fortis, *L'abate Fortis al Signor Giovanni Lovrich* (Brescia: Francesco Ragnoli, 1777), pp. 3–5.
49. Ibid., p. 5.
50. Ibid., p. 8.
51. [Fortis], *Sermone Parenetico di Pietro Sclamer Chersino al Signor Giovanni Lovrich, nativo di Sinj in Morlacchia, Autore delle Osservazioni sopra il Viaggio in Dalmazia del Sig. Abate Alberto Fortis* (Modena: Società Tipografica, 1777), p. 3; Robert Darnton, *The Literary Underground of the Old Regime* (Cambridge: Harvard University Press, 1982); pp. 1–40.
52. *Sermone Parenetico*, p. 4.
53. Ibid., pp. 5, 19.
54. Ibid., pp. 4–5.
55. Ibid., pp. 17, 19–21, 24.
56. Ibid., p. 6.
57. Žarko Muljačić, "Iz Korespondencije Alberta Fortisa," *Grada za povijest književnost Hrvatske*, 23 (Zagreb, 1952), 25 March 1785, p. 117.
58. *Sermone Parenetico*, p. 20.
59. Ibid., p. 24.
60. Ibid., p. 28; Marijan Stojković, "Ivan Lovrić," pp. 1–4, 38–41.
61. Fortis, "Della Coltura del Castagno da introdursi nella Dalmazia Marittima e Mediterranea: discorso recitato nella prima sessione della Società Economica di Spalato del MDCCLXXX," in *Illuministi Italiani*, volume 7, *Riformatori delle Antiche Repubbliche, dei Ducati, dello Stato Pontificio e delle Isole,* eds. Giuseppe Giarrizzo, Gianfranco Torcellan, and Franco Venturi (Milan: Riccardo Ricciardi Editore, 1965), pp. 334–35.
62. Ibid., pp. 335–36.
63. Ibid., p. 336; Luca Ciancio, *Autopsie della terra: Illuminismo e geologia in Alberto Fortis (1741–1803)* (Florence: Leo S. Olschki, 1995), pp. 190–92; Venturi, *La Repubblica di Venezia*, pp. 202–05, 214–17.
64. Fortis, *Saggio d'osservazioni*, pp. 62–63.

65. Fortis, "Della Coltura del Castagno," p. 337.
66. Ibid., pp. 337–39.
67. Ibid., pp. 345–49.
68. Ibid., p. 350.
69. Carlo Gozzi, *Memorie Inutili,* ed. Domenico Bulferetti, volume 1, in *Collezione di Classici Italiani,* ed. Gustavo Balsamo-Crivelli (Turin: Unione Tipografico-Editrice Torinese, 1928), p. 73.
70. Ibid.
71. Ibid., pp. 73–74.
72. Ibid., pp. 66–67.
73. Ibid., p. 67.
74. Massimo Donà, "Le Milizie Oltremarine nella Terraferma Veneta alla fine del '700," unpublished thesis, Università degli studi di Venezia, 1993, pp. 65–66, 146.
75. Gozzi, *Memorie Inutili,* p. 68.
76. Fortis, *Viaggio,* volume 1, p. 89.
77. Gozzi, *Memorie Inutili,* p. 69.
78. Ibid., p. 70; Gozzi, *Useless Memoirs,* trans. John Addington Symonds, ed. Philip Horne (London: Oxford University Press, 1962), pp. 102–19.
79. Gozzi, *Memorie Inutili,* pp. 71–72.
80. Ibid., p. 72.
81. Giacomo Boldù, ASV, *Collegio: Relazioni,* filza 69, 30 August 1748; Paolo Boldù, ASV, *Collegio: Relazioni,* filza 70, 5 December 1783; Marino Berengo, "Problemi economico-sociali della Dalmazia veneta alla fine del '700," *Rivista storica italiana,* volume 66 (1954), pp. 489–91; Peričić, pp. 21–23.
82. Paolo Boldù, ASV, *Collegio: Relazioni,* filza 70, 5 December 1783.
83. Ibid.
84. Michel Foucault, *Discipline and Punish: The Birth of the Prison,* trans. Alan Sheridan (1975; New York: Vintage Books, 1979), pp. 135–36.
85. Paolo Boldù, ASV, *Collegio: Relazioni,* filza 70, 5 December 1783.
86. Ibid.
87. Paolo Boldù, ASV, *Collegio: Relazioni,* filza 70, "Compendio," 15 March 1783.

6. *The End of the Adriatic Empire: Epidemic, Economic, and Discursive Crises*

1. Paolo Boldù, Archivio di Stato di Venezia (ASV), *Collegio: Relazioni,* filza 70, 5 December 1783.
2. Francesco Falier, ASV, *Senato: Dispacci: Provveditori da Terra e da Mar,* filza 646 (Falier, 1783–84), 20 September 1783; 13 November 1783; 9 January 1784 (1783 m.v.); 16 January 1784 (1783 m.v.); 27 January 1784 (1783 m.v.).
3. Falier, ASV, *Collegio: Relazioni,* filza 70, 28 November 1786.
4. Ibid.
5. Ibid.
6. Giulio Bajamonti, *Storia della peste che regnò in Dalmazia negli anni 1783–1784* (Venice: Presso Vincenzio Formaleoni, 1786), pp. 167–68, 179; Šime Peričić, *Dalmacija uoči pada Mletačke Republike* (Zagreb: Sveučilište u Zagrebu), pp. 224–26.
7. Franco Venturi, *Settecento riformatore,* volume 5, *L'Italia dei lumi,* part 2, *La Repubblica di Venezia* (Turin: Giulio Einaudi, 1990), pp. 362–63; Ivan Milčetić, "Dr. Julije Bajamonti i negova djela," *Rad Jugoslavenske Akademije Znanosti i Umjetnosti,*

book 192 (Zagreb, 1912), pp. 200–04; Duško Kečkemet, "Julije Bajamonti, Croatian Encyclopaedist," in Duško Kečkemet and Ennio Stipčević, *Julije Bajamonti: Encyclopaedist and Musician* (Zagreb and Split: Croatian P.E.N. Centre, 1997), pp. 9–28; Lovro Županović, "Julije [Giulio] Bajamonti," in *The Symphony in Croatia* (New York: Garland, 1984), pp. xix–xxii; Arturo Cronia, "Giulio Bajamonti," *Dizionario Biografico degli Italiani*, volume 5 (Rome: Enciclopedia Italiana, 1963), pp. 280–81.

8. Bajamonti, *Storia della peste*, pp. 2–3; Venturi, *La Repubblica di Venezia*, pp. 278–82.

9. Bajamonti, *Storia della peste*, pp. 17–18.

10. Ibid., pp. 19–21.

11. Ibid., pp. 21–22.

12. Pietro Nutrizio Grisogono, *Sopra il morbo pestilenziale insorto nella Dalmazia Veneta l'anno 1783*, 2nd ed. (Mantua: Stamperia di Giuseppe Braglia, n.d.), pp. 61–62.

13. Bajamonti, *Storia della peste*, pp. 64–66.

14. Ibid., pp. 184–85.

15. Ibid., pp. 30–52.

16. Ibid., pp. 89–91.

17. Grisogono, *Sopra il morbo pestilenziale*, pp. 15–17.

18. Bajamonti, *Storia della peste*, pp. 118–19; Županović, "Julije [Giulio] Bajamonti," p. xx.

19. Bajamonti, *Storia della peste*, pp. 23–27.

20. Ibid., p. 204; see also Richard Palmer, "L'azione della Repubblica di Venezia nel controllo della peste: Lo sviluppo della politica governativa," in *Venezia e la peste 1348–1797*, Comune di Venezia (Venice: Marsilio Editori, 1979), pp. 103–10.

21. Gianfranco Torcellan, *Una Figura della Venezia settecentesca: Andrea Memmo* (Venice and Rome: Istituto per la Collaborazione Culturale, 1963), pp. 216–25; Andrea Memmo, "A Gregorio Stratico" (11 March 1790), in *Illuministi Italiani*, volume 7, *Riformatori delle Antiche Repubbliche, dei Ducati, dello Stato Pontificio e delle Isole*, eds. Giuseppe Giarrizzo, Gianfranco Torcellan, and Franco Venturi (Milan: Riccardo Ricciardi Editore, 1965), pp. 274–77; Alberto Fortis, *Viaggio in Dalmazia* (Venice: Presso Alvise Milocco, 1774), republished by Jovan Vuković and Peter Rehder, eds. (Munich and Sarajevo: Verlag Otto Sagner and Izdavačko Preduzeće Veselin Masleša, 1974), volume 1, p. 16.

22. Angelo Memmo, ASV, *Inquisitori di Stato,* filza 282 (Dispacci dai Provveditori Generali in Dalmazia, 1783–88), 7 November 1787, 20 November 1787; Angelo Diedo, ASV, *Inquisitori di Stato,* filza 283 (Dispacci dai Provveditori Generali in Dalmazia, 1789–1790), 14 March 1790, 21 September 1790.

23. Andrea Memmo, Inquisitorato ai Pubblici Rolli, ASV, *Senato: Rettori,* filza 389 (1790), 27 March 1790.

24. Andrea Memmo, Inquisitorato ai Pubblici Rolli, ASV, *Senato: Rettori,* filza 390 (1790), 29 May 1790.

25. Bruno Brunelli, *Casanova Loved Her,* trans. Alexander McKechnie (London: Peter Davies, 1929), pp. 262–68; Torcellan, *Una Figura della Venezia settecentesca,* p. 216.

26. Andrea Memmo, ASV, *Senato: Rettori,* filza 389 (1790), 27 March 1790; Norbert Elias, *The History of Manners,* trans. Edmund Jephcott (New York: Pantheon Books, 1978), pp. 44–50; Joachim Moras, *Ursprung und Entwicklung des Begriffs der Zivilisation in Frankreich (1756–1830),* in *Hamburger Studien zu Volkstum und*

Kultur der Romanen, volume 6 (Hamburg: Seminar für romanische Sprachen und Kultur, 1930), pp. 1–61.

27. Andrea Memmo, ASV, *Senato: Rettori,* filza 390 (1790), 29 May 1790; see also Peričić, *Dalmacija,* pp. 55–57.

28. Torcellan, *Una Figura della Venezia settecentesca,* p. 222–24; Mile Bogović, *Katolička Crkva i Pravoslavlje u Dalmaciji: za vrijeme Mletačke vladavine* (Zagreb: Kršćanska Sadašnjost, 1982), pp. 135–45; Mihovilla Tomassa Triali, *Kratko Sabragne: prineseno v jesik slovinski* (Venice: Antonio Zatta, 1768).

29. Andrea Memmo, ASV, *Senato: Rettori,* filza 389 (1790), 27 March 1790.

30. Larry Wolff, *Inventing Eastern Europe: The Map of Civilization on the Mind of the Enlightenment* (Stanford: Stanford University Press, 1994), pp. 231–32.

31. Andrea Memmo, ASV, *Senato: Rettori,* filza 389 (1790), 27 March 1790.

32. Sindici Inquisitori in Dalmazia (Giovanni Loredan, Nicolo Erizzo, Sebastian Molin), ASV, *Collegio: Relazioni,* filza 70, 2 October 1751; Andrea Memmo, ASV, *Senato: Rettori,* filza 390 (1790), 29 May 1790.

33. Andrea Memmo, ASV, *Senato: Rettori,* filza 390 (1790), 29 May 1790.

34. Andrea Memmo, ASV, *Senato: Rettori,* filza 390 (1790), 29 May 1790; Peričić, *Dalmacija* pp. 131–32.

35. Andrea Memmo, "A Gregorio Stratico" (11 March 1790), in *Illuministi Italiani,* volume 7, p. 275; Torcellan, *Una Figura della Venezia settecentesca,* p. 223.

36. Andrea Memmo, ASV, *Senato: Rettori,* filza 389 (1790), 27 March 1790.

37. Piero Del Negro, "La Politica di Venezia e le Accademie di Agricoltura," in *La Politica della scienza: Toscana e stati italiani nel tardo settecento* (Florence: Leo S. Olschki Editore, 1996), pp. 472–75; Brendan Dooley, "Le Accademie," *Storia della Cultura Veneta,* volume 5, *Il Settecento,* part 1, eds. Girolamo Arnaldi and Manlio Pastore Stocchi (Vicenza: Neri Pozza Editore, 1985), pp. 85–90.

38. Franco Venturi, *La Repubblica di Venezia,* pp. 362–66; Fabio Luzzatto, "Le Accademie di Agricoltura in Dalmazia nel secolo XVIII," *Archivio Storico per la Dalmazia,* year 3, volume 5, number 26 (May 1928), pp. 75–81; Edward Gibbon, *The Decline and Fall of the Roman Empire,* volume 1 (New York: Modern Library, n.d.), p. 338, n. 117; Fortis, *Viaggio,* volume 2, pp. 38–39; Peričić, pp. 69–70.

39. Venturi, *La Repubblica di Venezia,* pp. 370–71, 377, 385; Fabio Luzzatto, "Scrittori dalmati di politica agraria nel secolo XVIII," *Archivio Storico per la Dalmazia,* year 3, volume 5, numbers 30 and 31 (September and October, 1928), pp. 325–33.

40. Venturi, *La Repubblica di Venezia,* pp. 372–75; Luzzatto, "Scrittori dalmati," pp. 270–74.

41. Venturi, *La Repubblica di Venezia,* pp. 371, 390; Angelo Tamborra, "Problema sociale e rapporto città-campagna in Dalmazia alla fine del secolo XVIII," *Rassegna Storica del Risorgimento,* year 59, number 1 (January–March, 1972), pp. 3–13.

42. Giulio Bajamonti, *A Monsignore Stratico per il Suo ingresso nella chiesa vescovile di Lesina* (Padua: Stamperia Penada, 1786), pp. 5, 9–10, 14; Venturi, *La Repubblica di Venezia,* pp. 394–97.

43. Bajamonti, *A Monsignore Stratico,* pp. 16, 20.

44. Venturi, *La Repubblica di Venezia,* pp. 401–06.

45. Venturi, *La Repubblica di Venezia,* pp. 398, 407; Rudolf Maixner, "Traductions et imitations du roman *Les Morlaques,*" *Revue des Études Slaves,* volume 32 (Paris: Imprimerie Nationale, 1955), pp. 70–72.

46. Venturi, *La Repubblica di Venezia,* pp. 381–83; Luzzatto, "Scrittori dalmati," pp. 276–77.

47. Venturi, *La Repubblica di Venezia,* p. 411.

48. Angelo Diedo, ASV, *Collegio: Relazioni,* filza 70, 15 November 1792; Marino Berengo, "Problemi economico-sociali della Dalmazia veneta alla fine del '700," *Rivista storica italiana,* 66 (1954), p. 508.

49. Angelo Diedo, ASV, *Senato: Dispacci: Provveditori da Terra e da Mar,* filza 657 (Diedo, 1790–1791), 30 May 1790, 31 May 1790.

50. Ibid., 20 July 1790, 25 August 1790.

51. Ibid., 16 October 1790.

52. Venturi, *La Repubblica di Venezia,* pp. 409–10.

53. Angelo Diedo, ASV, *Senato: Dispacci: Provveditori da Terra e da Mar,* filza 657, 11 December 1790.

54. Ibid., 23 April 1791, 25 April 1791.

55. Ibid., 25 April 1791.

56. Berengo, "Problemi economico-sociali," pp. 503–04.

57. Ragusa, Povijesni Arhiv u Dubrovniku, *Lettere e Commissioni di Ponente,* volume 129 (1794), 3 March 1794, 12 May 1794; Alvise Marin, ASV, *Collegio: Relazioni,* filza 70, 8 December 1795.

58. Andrea Querini, ASV, *Senato: Dispacci: Provveditori da Terra e da Mar,* filza 662 (Querini, 1795–1797), 14 December 1795; Venturi, *La Repubblica di Venezia,* pp. 393–94.

59. Ragusa, Povijesni Arhiv u Dubrovniku, *Lettere e Commissioni di Ponente,* volume 131 (1796), 18 June 1796.

60. Milčetić, "Dr. Julije Bajamonti," p. 116.

61. Ibid., p. 116, n. 1.

62. Querini, ASV, *Senato: Dispacci: Provveditori da Terra e da Mar,* filza 662, 22 May 1796.

63. Ibid., 7 June 1796, 12 June 1796; Goldoni, *La Dalmatina,* in *Tutte le opere di Carlo Goldoni,* ed. Giuseppe Ortolani, volume 9 (Milan: Arnoldo Mondadori, 1960), p. 953; Massimo Donà, "Le Milizie Oltremarine nella Terraferma Veneta alla fine del '700," unpublished thesis, Università degli studi di Venezia, 1993, p. 22.

64. Querini, ASV, *Senato: Dispacci: Provveditori da Terra e da Mar,* filza 662, 17 June 1796.

65. Querini, Povijesni Arhiv Zadar, *Generalni Providur,* box 227 (Querini), 1795–1797), #34.

66. Querini, ASV, *Senato: Dispacci: Provveditori da Terra e da Mar,* filza 662, 25 July 1796.

67. Ibid., 20 July 1796, 25 July 1796.

68. Attilio Tamaro, *La Vénétie Julienne et la Dalmatie: Histoire de la nation italienne sur ses frontières orientales,* volume 3, *La Dalmatie* (Rome: Imprimerie du Sénat, 1919), pp. 323–24; Paul Pisani, *La Dalmatie: de 1797 à 1815* (Paris: Alphonse Picard, 1893), pp. 25–31; Tullio Erber, "Storia della Dalmazia dal 1797 al 1814," *Archivio Storico per la Dalmazia,* year 3, volume 4, number 24 (March 1928), pp. 293–98; Giuseppe Praga, *History of Dalmatia,* trans. Edward Steinberg (Pisa: Giardini Editori, 1993), pp. 207–08.

69. Querini, ASV, *Senato: Dispacci: Provveditori da Terra e da Mar,* filza 662, 11 November 1796.

70. Querini, Povijesni Arhiv Zadar, *Generalni Providur,* box 227, #42.

388 Notes to pages 311–325

71. Querini, ASV, *Senato: Dispacci: Provveditori da Terra e da Mar,* filza 662, 13 February 1797 (1796 m.v.); Michele Neri (Console Pontificio, Zara), Archivio Segreto Vaticano, *Segretaria di Stato: Venezia,* register 252, 18 February 1797.

72. Tamaro, *La Dalmatie,* p. 320; Praga, *History of Dalmatia,* p. 208.

73. Tamaro, *La Dalmatie,* pp. 328–31.

74. Tamaro, *La Dalmatie,* pp. 331–32; Praga, *History of Dalmatia,* pp. 205–06.

75. Tamaro, *La Dalmatie,* p. 333; see also "Il Vessillo di S. Marco deposto nella Cattedrale di Perasto dopo la caduta della Repubblica di Venezia (Cerimonia descritta dal contemporaneo Msgr. Conte Vincenzo Ballovich)," *Archivio Storico per la Dalmazia,* year 1, volume 1, number 3 (June 1926), pp. 13–16.

76. Giulio Bajamonti, "Il Morlacchismo d'Omero," *Nuovo giornale enciclopedico d'Italia* (March 1797), pp. 77–78; Venturi, *La Repubblica di Venezia,* pp. 411–13.

77. Bajamonti, "Il Morlacchismo d'Omero," p. 78.

78. Milčetić, "Dr. Julije Bajamonti," p. 103; Matthias Murko, *Das Original von Goethes "Klaggesang von der edlen Frauen des Asan Aga" (Asanaginica) in der Literatur und im Volksmunde durch 150 Jahre* (Brno: Verlag Rudolf M. Rohrer, 1937), pp. 26–30.

79. Milčetić, "Dr. Julije Bajamonti," p. 233; see also Larry Wolff, "The Enlightened Anthropology of Friendship in Venetian Dalmatia: Primitive Ferocity and Ritual Fraternity among the Morlacchi," *Eighteenth-Century Studies,* volume 32, (1998–99), pp. 157–78.

80. Milčetić, "Dr. Julije Bajamonti," p. 215.

81. Ibid., pp. 132–37; Marijan Stojković, "Morlakizam," *Hrvatsko Kolo,* book 10 (Zagreb: Matica Hrvatska, 1929). pp. 271–72; Rudolf Maixner, "Traductions et imitations," p. 74.

82. Bajamonti, "Il Morlacchismo d'Omero," pp. 78–79.

83. Fortis, *Viaggio,* volume 1, p. 89; Carlo Gozzi, *Memorie Inutili,* ed. Domenico Bulferetti, volume 1, in *Collezione di Classici Italiani,* ed. Gustavo Balsamo-Crivelli (Turin: Unione Tipografico-Editrice Torinese, 1928), p. 68.

84. Bajamonti, "Il Morlacchismo d'Omero," pp. 80–84.

85. Ibid., pp. 85–96.

86. Ibid., p. 98.

87. Ibid., p. 97.

88. Fortis, *Viaggio,* volume 1, pp. 55, 58; Luca Ciancio, *Autopsie della terra: Illuminismo e geologia in Alberto Fortis (1741–1803)* (Florence: Leo S. Olschki, 1995), p. 242.

Conclusion

1. Anthony Pagden, *Lords of All the World: Ideologies of Empire in Spain, Britain, and France* (New Haven: Yale University Press, 1995), pp. 103–200; see also Edward Said, *Orientalism* (1978; New York: Vintage Books, 1979), pp. 31–110; Edward Said, *Culture and Imperialism* (1993; New York: Vintage Books, 1994), pp. 3–19; Homi Bhabha, "Of Mimicry and Man: The Ambivalence of Colonial Discourse," in *The Location of Culture* (London: Routledge, 1994), pp. 85–92.

2. Ivo Banac, *The National Question in Yugoslavia: Origins, History, Politics* (Ithaca, N.Y.: Cornell University Press, 1984), pp. 70–75; Larry Wolff, *Inventing East-*

ern Europe: The Map of Civilization on the Mind of the Enlightenment (Stanford: Stanford University Press, 1994), pp. 284–331.

3. Benedict Anderson, *Imagined Communities: Reflections on the Origin and Spread of Nationalism* (1983; London: Verso, 1991), pp. 1–65; see also Maria Todorova, *Imagining the Balkans* (Oxford: Oxford University Press, 1997), pp. 62–139; and Hans Kohn, *The Idea of Nationalism* (1944; Toronto: Collier Books, 1967), pp. 455–576.

4. Wayne Vucinich, *A Study in Social Survival: Katun in the Bileća Rudine* (Denver: University of Denver Press, 1975), pp. 13–16; Predrag Matvejević, *Mediterranean: A Cultural Landscape,* trans. Michael Henry Heim (Berkeley: University of California Press, 1999), p. 202.

5. Todorova, *Imagining the Balkans,* pp. 3–20.

6. Ernest Gellner, *Nations and Nationalism* (Ithaca, N.Y.: Cornell University Press, 1983) pp. 39–62; see also Liah Greenfeld, *Nationalism: Five Roads to Modernity* (Cambridge, Mass.: Harvard University Press, 1992), pp. 3–26; and Banac, *The National Question in Yugoslavia,* pp. 21–140.

7. Katherine Verdery, *Transylvanian Villagers: Three Centuries of Political, Economic, and Ethnic Change* (Berkeley: University of California Press, 1983), p. 345.

8. Auguste-Frédéric-Louis Marmont, *Mémoires du Maréchal Marmont, Duc de Raguse,* 3rd ed., volume 3 (Paris: Perrotin, 1857), pp. 64–65.

9. C.B. du Département de Marengo, *Souvenirs d'un voyage en Dalmatie* (Turin: Chez Botta, Prato et Paravia, n.d.), pp. 3–5, 53–57, 67.

10. Ibid., pp. 58–60.

11. Ibid., pp. 84–87.

12. Elinor Murray Despalatović, *Ljudevit Gaj and the Illyrian Movement* (Boulder, Colo.: East European Quarterly, 1975), p. 87.

13. Ibid., p. 132.

14. André Vaillant, "Vuk Karadžić et l'Hasanaginica," *Revue des études slaves,* volume 19 (Paris, 1939), pp. 87–88.

15. Fabio Mutinelli, *Annali Urbani di Venezia dall'anno 810 al 12 maggio 1797* (Venice: Tipografia di G.B. Merlo, 1841), dedication.

16. Milorad Ekmečić, "The Revolution of 1848–1849," in *History of Yugoslavia,* by Vladimir Dedijer, Ivan Božić, Sima Cirković, and Milorad Ekmečić, trans. Kordija Kveder (New York: McGraw-Hill, 1974), p. 319; Giuseppe Praga, *History of Dalmatia* (Pisa: Giardini, 1993), pp. 222–27.

17. Ekmečić, "Revolution of 1848–1849," p. 319.

18. J. Gardner Wilkinson, *Dalmatia and Montenegro,* volume 2 (London: John Murray, 1848; rpt. New York: Arno Press, 1971), pp. 152, 164.

19. Rudolf Maixner, *Charles Nodier et l'Illyrie* (Paris: Didier, 1960), pp. 13–32, 68–74; Prosper Mérimée, *La Guzla,* ed. Antonia Fonyi (Paris: Éditions Kimé, 1994), p. 19.

20. Tullius Erber, "Zur Geschichte: Die Neuzeit," in *Die österreichisch-ungarische Monarchie in Wort und Bild: Dalmatien* (Vienna: Druck und Verlag der kaiserlich-königlichen Hof- und Staatsdruckerei, 1892), pp. 105–06; see also Arthur May, *The Hapsburg Monarchy 1867–1914* (1951; New York: W. W. Norton, 1968), pp. 153–54.

21. Erber, "Zur Geschichte: Die Neuzeit," p. 118.

22. Karl Vipauz, "Zur Volkskunde: Physische Beschaffenheit der Bevölkerung," in *Die österreichisch-ungarische Monarchie in Wort und Bild: Dalmatien,* pp. 119–20.

23. Marcell Kusar, "Zur Literatur: Die serbischkroatische Sprache und Literatur," in *Die österreichisch-ungarische Monarchie in Wort und Bild: Dalmatien,* p. 251.

24. Camilla Lucerna, *Die südslavische Ballade von Asan Agas Gattin und ihre Nach-bildung durch Goethe* (Berlin: Verlag von Alexander Duncker, 1905), p. 65.

25. Charles Jelavich, *South Slav Nationalisms: Textbooks and Yugoslav Union before 1914* (Columbus: Ohio State University Press, 1990), pp. 120–21, 150–51, 167–68, 224, 231, 258–59; Banac, *The National Question in Yugoslavia,* pp. 76–81.

26. Josip Smodlaka, "The Condition of Dalmatia," speech of 3 December 1910, in R. W. Seton-Watson, *The Southern Slav Question and the Habsburg Monarchy* (1911; New York: Howard Fertig, 1969), pp. 407–10, 416.

27. Ibid., pp. 412–13.

28. Ibid., p. 415.

29. R. Riedl, "Die wirtschaftlichen Zustände Dalmatiens," in *Dalmatien und das österreichische Küstenland,* E. Brückner, ed. (Vienna and Leipzig: Franz Deuticke, 1911), p. 216.

30. M. Haberlandt, "Die Volkskunst in Istrien und Dalmatien," in *Dalmatien und das österreichische Küstenland,* p. 194.

31. Hermann Bahr, *Dalmatinische Reise* (Berlin: S. Fischer Verlag, 1909), pp. 2, 5.

32. *Illustrierter Führer durch Dalmatien* (Vienna and Leipzig: A. Hartleben, 1912), p. 141.

33. Rebecca West, *Black Lamb and Grey Falcon: A Journey Through Yugoslavia* (1941; London: Penguin Books, 1982), pp. 28–35.

34. Alice Lee Moqué, *Delightful Dalmatia* (New York: Funk and Wagnalls, 1914), p. 15.

35. Frances Kinsley Hutchinson, *Motoring in the Balkans: Along the Highways of Dalmatia, Montenegro, the Herzegovina and Bosnia* (London: Hodder and Stoughton, 1910), pp. 17–18.

36. Maude Holbach, *Dalmatia: The Land Where East Meets West* (London: John Lane, 1908), p. 28.

37. T. G. Jackson, *Dalmatia, the Quarnero, and Istria* (Oxford: The Clarendon Press, 1887), pp. 232–33.

38. Jackson, *Dalmatia,* p. 203; Moqué, *Delightful Dalmatia,* pp. 58–60.

39. Holbach, *Dalmatia: The Land Where East Meets West* p. 31; Hutchinson, *Motoring in the Balkans* pp. 68–69, 78.

40. "Dalmatia," *Encyclopedia Britannica,* 11th ed., volume 7, 1910, p. 773.

41. Jackson, *Dalmatia,* pp. 174, 408–09.

42. H. G. Wells, *The Time Machine* (1895; New York: Dover Publications, 1995), p. 39.

43. R. W. Seton-Watson, *R. W. Seton-Watson and the Yugoslavs: Correspondence 1906–1941* (London and Zagreb: British Academy and University of Zagreb Institute of Croatian History, 1976) volume 1, Ivo Lupis-Vukić to Seton-Watson, 1 November 1909, p. 59.

44. Ibid., volume 1, Ivo Lupis-Vukić to Seton-Watson, 23 September 1911, pp. 87–88.

45. Ibid., volume 1, Josip Smodlaka to Seton-Watson, 29 April 1911, p. 83.

46. Seton-Watson, *The Southern Slav Question and the Habsburg Monarchy,* p. 343.

47. Seton-Watson, *Correspondence,* volume 1, Seton-Watson to George Seton, 22 February 1912, p. 98.

48. Ibid., volume 1, Frano Supilo to Seton-Watson, 14 December 1916, p. 284.

49. Ibid., volume 1, Gaetano Salvemini to Seton-Watson, 10 February 1917, p. 289.

50. Ibid., volume 2, Antonio de Viti de Marco to Seton-Watson, 12 December 1918, p. 11.

51. Ibid., volume 1, Colonel E. M. House to Seton-Watson, 24 August 1914, p. 179.

52. Woodrow Wilson, *The Papers of Woodrow Wilson,* volume 57 (Princeton: Princeton University Press, 1987), Notes of a Meeting of the Council of Four, 22 April 1919, pp. 611–12.

53. Ibid., p. 614.

54. Ibid., volume 58 (1988), Statement on the Adriatic Question, 23 April 1919, p. 7.

55. Ibid., News Report, 24 April 1919, pp. 99–100.

56. Cesare Levi, "Dalmati sulle scene," *Il Marzocco,* 11 May 1919, pp. 2–3.

57. Attilio Tamaro, *La Vénétie Julienne et la Dalmatie: Histoire de la nation italienne sur ses frontières orientales,* volume 3, *La Dalmatie* (Rome: Imprimerie du Sénat, 1919), pp. 309, 332.

58. Gabriele D'Annunzio, *Lettera ai dalmati* (Venice, 1919), pp. 10–14, 40–44.

59. Gabriele D'Annunzio, *La Riscossa dei Leoni: Raccolta degli scritti di Gabriele D'Annunzio sulla Dalmazia italiana,* Eugenio Coselschi, ed. (Florence: R. Bemporad, 1928), pp. 30, 37, 71; Michael Ledeen, *The First Duce: D'Annunzio at Fiume* (Baltimore: Johns Hopkins University Press, 1977), pp. 62, 77, 87, 124–29.

60. Benito Mussolini, *My Autobiography* (New York: Charles Scribner's Sons, 1928), p. 62.

61. Ibid., pp. 106, 130, 253.

62. Oddone Talpo, *Dalmazia: Una cronaca per la storia (1941)* (Rome: Stato Maggiore Dell'Esercito, Ufficio Storico, 1985), pp. 169, 251–2, 283.

63. Ibid., p. 637.

64. Ibid., pp. 245, 271, 281, 285, 739, 747.

65. Josip Broz Tito, *Selected Military Works* (Belgrade: Vojnoizdavački Zavod, 1966), Speech, 12 September 1944, p. 194.

66. Ibid., p. 194; Vladimir Dedijer, *Tito* (New York: Simon & Schuster, 1953), p. 11.

67. *New Yugoslavia 1941–1965* (Belgrade: Mladost, 1966), pp. 142, 228.

68. Dubravka Ugrešić, "Balkan Blues," in *The Culture of Lies,* trans. Celia Hawkesworth (University Park: Pennsylvania State University Press, 1998), p. 132.

69. *Yugoslavia: Economic and Tourist Guide* (Belgrade: Privredni pregled, 1962), p. 215.

70. Ivan Božić, "The Yugoslav Peoples under the Hapsburg Monarchy and the Republic of Venice," in *History of Yugoslavia,* by Vladimir Dedijer, Ivan Božić, Sima Cirković, and Milorad Ekmečić, p. 151.

71. Stephen Jay Gould, *Wonderful Life: The Burgess Shale and the Nature of History* (New York: W. W. Norton, 1989), pp. 131, 288–90.

Index

academies, Dalmatian (at Split, Trogir, and Zadar), 11, 275, 296–299, 301, 341; *see also* Economic Society of Split

Accademia Cosmografica of the Argonauts, 42

Adam, Robert, *Ruins of the Palace of the Emperor Diocletian,* 22, 23 (fig. 2), 28 (fig. 3), 104, 105 (fig. 8), 106, 110

Aegean Sea, 76, 115

Africa, Africans, 65, 68, 69, 72; *see also* Hottentots

agricultural catechism, 292, 297, 300, 304

agricultural reform in Dalmatia, 29, 49, 54, 71, 139–143, 146, 159, 199, 233, 269–270, 274, 295–302; chestnut trees, proposed by Fortis, 261–265; reclamation of land, drainage, 235–236; *see also* Grimani, Francesco: his land reform of 1755

Albania, 160, 194; Venetian, 4 (fig. 1), 5, 15, 30, 41, 42, 44, 137, 234, 266, 309; Ottoman, 15, 16, 234

Altichiero, villa of, 197, 211, 213, 226; *see also* Querini, Angelo

America, 3, 5, 9, 13, 90, 101, 218, 319, 346, 348

American Indians. *See* Native Americans

American revolution, American independence, 3, 239, 275

Ancona, 15, 169

Anderson, Benedict, 71, 219, 328

anthropology, 7, 12, 157–158, 170–171; *see also* Fortis, Alberto: his anthropology

Arbel, Benjamin, 8

Archivio Storico per la Dalmazia, 10

Arduini, Luigi, 356

Arduino, Giovanni, 113, 296

Arduino, Pietro, 296

Arsenal, Venetian, 80

Artusi, Giulio, 223

Ascension Day festival, in Venice, 46

Augustus, Emperor, 53, 103

Austrian Succession, War of, 133, 267

Austro-Hungarian compromise, dualism, 332, 349

Bahr, Hermann, *Dalmatinische Reise,* 344, 346

Bajamonti, Antonio, 341

Bajamonti, Girolamo (Jerolim), 300–301

Bajamonti, Giulio (Julije), 184, 215, 239–240, 245, 253, 254, 256, 296, 297, 326, 344; as composer, 280, 287, 314; on Islam, 285–286; "The Morlacchismo of Homer," 18, 19, 277–278, 312–318, 327, 328, 330, 362; and the plague of 1783–1784, 4 (fig. 1), 280–288, 299, 315, 317, 327, 328, 330; on Stratico, Giandomenico, bishop of Hvar, 299–300, 306, 314

balkanism, 330, 356–357

Baltic Sea, 174, 327, 335

Ban, Matija, 336

Banac, Ivo, 174, 325

Banovaz, Giovanni (Ivan), 297

Barbarigo, Pietro, 260–261

barbarism, perceived, 1, 2, 50, 66, 92, 97,
    109, 110, 177, 186, 203–204, 252, 299,
    302, 324–327, 345; *see also* Morlacchi:
    their "barbarism"
Bartolucci, Athos, 356
Bastianini, Giuseppe, 356
Belgrade, 359
Bembo, Pietro, 47, 116
Benedict XIV, Pope, 180
Benincasa, Bartolomeo, his relationship
    with Giustiniana Wynne, 197, 198, 214
Berengo, Marino, 8, 9, 19, 49, 59, 64
Bergamo, 5, 224, 297
Biokovo Mountains, 245, 313
Black Sea, 176, 177, 182, 211, 335
blasphemy, 310
Bobolin, Antonio, 239
Bohemia, 182
Boldù, Giacomo, Provveditore Generale,
    38, 132–138, 160, 170, 270–271, 322
Boldù, Paolo, Provveditore Generale,
    231, 270–278, 287, 290, 322, 329;
    on "metamorphosis" of the
    Morlacchi, 272–274
Bologna, 97
Boscovich, Ruggiero, 253
Bosnia, Bosnians, 1, 2, 6, 17, 23 (fig. 2),
    122, 127, 129, 144–148, 189, 222,
    223, 226, 306, 310, 314, 330, 346,
    358; its border with Dalmatia, 11, 16,
    40, 79, 124, 175, 203, 234, 305, 333;
    and the plague of 1783–1784,
    277–288, 328
Boston, 101
Bouwsma, William, 533
Božić, Ivan, 12
Braudel, Fernand, 3, 21, 22
Brescia, 5, 253, 297
Bresciani, Caterina, 27, 35, 59, 62, 67
Breslau, Wroclaw, 214–215
Bulić, Frane, 346
Bürde, Samuel Gottlieb, 215
Burke, Peter, on popular culture, 138
Bute, Lord, John Stuart, 86, 119, 120,
    126, 130, 152, 157, 181, 182
Byzantine empire, 5, 17, 22, 50, 51,
    52, 173

calendar, Venetian, 311
Caminer, Domenico, 211; *Storia della
    guerra presente* (*Storia della ultima
    guerra*), 77, 82–84, 87, 109, 117, 118,
    124, 206; *Europa Letteraria*, 83, 84,
    92, 218
Caminer, Elisabetta, 83, 84
Camozzini, Zuanne, 42
Canada, 319
Canal, Paolo Emilio, 287, 299, 314
Canova, Antonio, 107, 216
caravans, Ottoman trade, 16, 17, 22, 23
    (fig. 2), 104, 145, 153, 279
Caribbean Sea, 158, 319
Carinthia, 196
Carlowitz, peace of (1699), 6, 40, 42,
    131, 174
Carniola, 178
carnival, 34, 56, 219
Carpaccio, Vittore, frescoes in Scuola
    Dalmata of San Giorgio degli
    Schiavoni, 14, 61, 353
Casanova, 31, 36, 53, 149, 196, 197, 205
Catherine II, Empress of Russia, 76,
    78–82, 211–214, 233, 293, 314, 324; in
    Wynne's novel, *Les Morlaques,*
    208–216, 219, 321, 324
Cesarotti, Melchiorre, 181, 217, 218
Cetina River, 14, 16, 121, 204, 205, 217,
    219, 235, 241
Chavannes, Alexandre-César,
    *Anthropologie ou science générale de
    l'homme,* 157
Chialetich, Luca, 298, 300
China, 17, 95, 96, 101, 218, 247, 335
Chioggia, 62
Ciancio, Luca, 19, 113
Cimarosa, Domenico, 224
Cirillo, Domenico, 86, 95
civilization, idea of; issue of who is
    civilized, 13, 43, 54, 131, 156–157,
    165–166, 193, 203–205, 225, 269–270,
    276, 292, 293, 298, 303, 304, 322–328,
    333–334, 346–348, 350, 356, 357; in
    Bajamonti, Giulio, 288, 297, 316; in
    Fortis, Alberto, 13, 17, 88, 127,
    160–161, 185–186, 189, 252, 259, 260,

289, 318, 323, 327, 361; in Lovrich, Giovanni, "the most civilized Dalmatians," 252–253, 255–256, 259, 325–327; in Wynne, Giustiniana, 193, 200, 203–205, 323; *see also* civilizing mission
civilizing mission, imperial, 5, 7, 13, 131, 171, 222, 223, 236, 306, 322–324, 329, 330, 333, 361
Clemenceau, Georges, 352
Clement XIV, Pope, 79, 147
clergy, in Dalmatia, 31, 291–293, 297, 298, 300, 304, 338
Clérisseau, Charles-Louis, 104
Cold War, 20
collectors, connoisseurs, 78, 90–93, 95, 97–99, 103–104, 106–108, 111–112, 114, 117, 123
Commedia dell'Arte, 29, 33, 35, 38
Condulmer, Domenico, Provveditore Generale, 78, 146–147, 148
Constantinople (Istanbul), 5, 15, 17, 23 (fig. 2), 31, 50, 53, 124, 211, 289
Contarini, Alvise, Provveditore Generale, 142–143
Cook, Captain James, 102
Corfu, 4 (fig. 1), 5, 31, 76, 148, 149, 345
Cornaro, Giambattista, 235
Coronelli, Vincenzo, 42, 43
corporations, economic reform of, in Venice, 85, 99, 289
Corsica, 158
Council of Ten, 41, 46, 90
Coxe, William, in Russia, 203
Craina, territorial militia in Dalmatia, 133, 307–308
Cres and Losinj (Cherso and Osero), 15, 51, 77, 86, 95, 96, 114–117, 119, 178, 185, 235, 253, 261, 321, 325, 355; Pietro Sclamer from, 253–254, 256–257; *see also* Fortis, Alberto: on Cres and Losinj
Crete, Candia, 5, 40, 44, 89, 148
Crimea, 211
Croatia, Croatian, Croats, 1, 7, 50, 51, 174–175, 178, 182, 226, 331–333, 335, 350, 356–358; Croatia, in Yugoslavia,

10, 12, 14, 332, 333, 358; Croatia, independent in the 1990s, 2, 10, 12, 332, 333; Croatian academic perspectives, modern, 12, 19, 215, 258; Croatian name and identity in Dalmatia, 7, 10, 11, 12, 48, 128, 176, 317, 333, 335, 340–341, 358, 360; Croatians as Slavs, 174–175, 178; Fortis on "Slavi Croati," 110–111, 128, 331; in Grabovac, "Illyrian or Croatian," 48, 61, 71, 331; and the Hasanaginica, 191–192; medieval kingdom of Croatia, 5, 52, 341
Cromer, Lord, Evelyn Baring, 341–342
Cronia, Arturo, 19, 220
cross-dressing, Carlo Gozzi in Zadar, 30, 33–36, 38–40, 45
Crusades, 16, 17, 53
Crussevich, Leonardo, 298
Curzon, George Nathaniel, 341–342
Cuvier, Georges, 113
Cvijić, Jovan, 13, 22, 128
Cyprus, 5, 44

D'Alembert, Jean le Rond, 113, 214
Dalmatian dogs, 14
Dandolo, Andrea, Doge, 47
Dandolo, Enrico, Doge, 53
D'Annunzio, Gabriele, 353, 354 (fig. 14), 355
Danube River, 97
Da Ponte, Lorenzo, *Così fan tutte,* 16
Da Riva, Giacomo, Provveditore Generale, 77, 148–152, 154, 161, 165, 206, 229
Darnton, Robert, 255
Davis, Robert, 60
de Dominis, Marcantonio, 252–253
deforestation, in Dalmatia, 261–263
Denis, Johann Michael, 181–182
Derrida, Jacques, *Of Grammatology,* 187
De Viti De Marco, Antonio, 351
Diario Veneto, 83
Diderot, Denis, 113, 158, 164, 209, 211, 214, 293
Diedo, Angelo, Provveditore Generale, 287, 301–304, 305, 307, 309, 322, 323

Diedo, Giacomo, *Storia della Repubblica di Venezia,* 29, 46–48, 50–54, 63, 184; on the "ferocious nature" of the medieval Dalmatians, 53–54, 63
Dinaric Alps, 3, 9, 15, 16, 361
Diocletian, 22, 23, 24, 110, 113; palace of, at Split, 1, 9, 10, 22, 23 (fig. 2), 28 (fig. 3), 104, 105 (fig. 8), 106, 110, 296
Disney, Walt, *One Hundred and One Dalmatians,* 14
Doge's Palace, 53
Dolfin, Caterina, her salon, 197
dolphins, 101–102
Donà, Massimo, 61
Donati, Vitaliano, *Saggio della storia naturale marina dell'Adriatico,* 97
Dondi Orologio, Antonio Carlo, 93, 99
Drina River, 357
Dubrovnik. *See* Ragusa
Duchet, Michèle, 157
Dudàn, Alessandro, 357
Dürres (Durazzo), 15

Eastern Europe, idea of, 105 (fig. 8), 178–180, 186, 194, 218, 225, 240, 293, 324–327, 330, 346, 347, 352, 361–362; between "civilization" and "barbarism," 203–204, 223; and the ethnographic classification of the Slavs, 7, 173–175, 180, 194, 324–325, 352; and Orientalism, demi-Orientalism 9, 15, 19, 28 (fig. 3); in Voltaire, 62–63; in West, Rebecca, 19–20, 361–362; *see also* Orientalism; *see also* Slavs
Economic Society of Split, 230, 259–264, 265, 270, 280, 292, 295–297, 300, 314, 327; *see also* academies, Dalmatian; *see also* Fortis, Alberto: on chestnuts
economy, development of, in Habsburg Dalmatia, 341–343
economy, national, Venetian ideas concerning, 18, 78, 91–93, 112, 124, 125, 131, 230, 321
emigration, from Dalmatia, 63, 139, 148, 229, 231–235, 262, 271, 284, 321; as concern in Foscarini's speech, 45, 63, 96–97, 134, 146, 262, 330, 342; as concern in time of plague, 286–287; as concern of Provveditori Generali, 134, 143, 147, 233–235, 284
Encyclopedia Britannica, 13, 348, 350
England, Great Britain, 1, 59, 101, 106, 119, 180, 186, 196, 275, 336, 361; British patronage of Fortis, 86–87, 100–102, 112–113, 119–120; British empire, 3, 5, 59, 90, 101, 106, 179, 275, 319, 341–342; British interest in Dalmatia, Morlacchi, and Yugoslavia, 346–352; *see also* Fortis, Alberto: in English translation; *see also* tourism in Dalmatia: British travelers
Erber, Tullio, 337–339
Europa Letteraria, 83, 84, 92, 218; *see also* Caminer, Domenico
exoticism of Dalmatia, 27, 37, 56, 68, 105 (fig. 8), 167, 213, 225, 300, 327, 342, 346

Falier, Francesco, Provveditore Generale, 278–279, 281–282, 287–288; on Dalmatia as Antemurale of Italy, 279, 283, 285, 288
famine, in Dalmatia, 38, 45, 129, 130, 147, 148, 152, 156, 168–169, 229, 262, 263, 271, 286
Farlati, Daniele. *See Illyricum Sacrum*
Farsetti, Filippo, 86, 87, 106, 107
fascism, Italian, 10, 332, 355–358; *see also* Mussolini, Benito
Federici, Camillo, *Gli Antichi Slavi,* 219–224, 249
Federici, Carlo, *Otello ossia lo Slavo,* 224–225
Ferber, Johann Jakob, 113
Ferney, Voltaire at, 82
Ferrich, Georgii, 191
Fiume. *See* Rijeka
folklore, study of, in Habsburg Dalmatia, 339–340, 342–343; its importance in Communist Yugoslavia, 359; *see also* Fortis, Alberto: and folklore
Fontenelle, Bernard de, 207
Formaleoni, Vincenzo, 211, 280
Forster, Georg, 203
Fortis, Alberto, abbé, 2, 6, 13–18, 22, 26, 27, 71, 77, 123, 144, 147, 218, 226, 268,

269, 289, 291, 296, 303, 323, 326, 334, 336, 337, 340, 344, 351; his anthropology, 94 (fig. 6), 99, 127–129, 131, 134, 136, 151, 157–158, 163, 166, 167, 169–171, 182, 184, 185, 188, 227, 236, 266, 304, 322–324; his anti-clericalism, 84, 108, 153; and antiquities, ancient ruins, 78, 103–113, 117–119, 121, 127, 136, 161, 238, 265; his Apologia for the Morlacchi, 127, 129, 130, 132, 134, 151; and Bajamonti, Giulio, 215, 239–240, 254, 256, 313–315, 318; on chestnuts, address in Split in 1780, 230, 259–264, 265, 266, 270, 273–275, 294, 296, 297, 299, 300–301, 327, 328, 350; on Cres and Losinj (Cherso and Osero), 15, 77, 86, 95, 96, 114–117, 119, 178, 185, 235, 254, 261, 321, 325, 355; criticized by Carlo Gozzi, 264–265; criticized by Giovanni Lovrich, 237–239, 241–258, 265; on "The Customs of the Morlacchi," 2, 126–127, 129–131, 134, 136, 151–172, 184, 189, 220, 238, 241, 264, 298, 309, 315–316, 322, 347, 361; Dalmatian response to, 237–243; on eels, 99–102, 107, 110, 113, 169; on "effluvia," the smell of the Morlacchi, 164–165, 169; in English translation, 2, 77, 87, 94 (fig. 6), 98 (fig. 7), 120, 155 (fig. 9), 162 (fig.10), 157, 179, 180, 186, 255, 326; and *Europa Letteraria,* 83–84, 92; on fish and fishing, 95–97, 99, 100, 101, 110, 114, 126, 136, 143, 179, 321, 356; and folklore, 94 (fig. 6), 127, 183, 184, 186–189, 191, 267, 280; in French and German translation, 2, 77, 157, 180, 186, 255, 326; on frogs, 168–169; and geology, 2, 111, 112–118, 121, 122, 124, 125, 181; and natural history, 2, 18, 78, 84, 87, 89, 90, 94 (fig. 6), 95–103, 111, 119, 120, 126, 151, 158, 160, 165, 167, 173, 238, 265, 318, 321; and paleontology, fossils, 2, 16, 90, 95, 98, 112–117, 119, 122, 126, 127, 136, 151, 179, 181, 184, 318, 361; his patrons, his acknowledgments, 77, 84–90, 95, 112–113, 120, 123, 130, 301;

as "Pietro Sclamer," rebutting Lovrich, 253–258, 260; on poetry of the Morlacchi, 181–186, 190–192, 204, 243, 249, 300, 335; and Provveditori Generali, their concerns after Fortis, 228–230, 232, 235–237, 239, 271–275, 323; on rivers of Dalmatia, 121, 127; on shells, shellfish, 97, 98 (fig. 7), 103; and Slavic language, 119, 166, 173, 178–180, 189, 243–244, 265, 325; and Slavic peoples, Slavic resemblances, 173–181, 324–325, 328, 330, 335; on superstition, in Dalmatia, 101–102, 153, 245; utility, usefulness of his studies, 87–90, 119–124, 161, 320, 321; and Wynne, Giustiniana, 192–203, 205–206, 219, 323; in Zadar, 3, 88, 94 (fig. 6), 103, 104, 106, 107, 110

Foscarini, Marco, 29, 41–50, 54, 57, 78, 91, 136, 137, 139, 142, 197, 266, 290, 341, 342; concern with emigration from Dalmatia, 45, 63, 96–97, 134, 146, 262, 330, 342; and the map of Dalmatia, 42–44, 90, 142, 162 (fig. 10), 231; on the "unhappy Morlacco," 129–130, 132

fossils, paleontology, 93, 95, 98, 112–117, 119, 122; *see also* Fortis, Alberto: and paleontology

Foucault, Michel, 133, 236, 272–273

Frederick II, of Prussia, 63, 215

French Revolution, 305, 309–310

French Romanticism. *See* Romanticism

Freud, Sigmund, 345

Friuli, 5

Gaj, Ljudevit, 334–335

Galileo, 115, 116, 118

gambling 85, 197, 216

Garagnin, Giovanni Luca (Ivan Luka), 297

gazettes, journalism, Italian, 80, 82, 83

Gellner, Ernest, 331

gender, 220–221; cross-dressing, 30, 33–36, 38–40, 45; *morlacchismo* as *machismo,* 220, 316; *see also* women, in Dalmatia; *see also* Wynne, Giustiniana: as woman of letters, her views concerning women

Genoa, 158, 224

George III, king of England, 86, 106

Georgi, Agostino Antonio, 179, 183

Gessner, Konrad, 178

Gibbon, Edward, *The Decline and Fall of the Roman Empire*, 1, 2, 3, 5, 6, 22, 23, 174, 296, 297, 346

Giornale d'Italia, 91–92, 144, 240, 296, 297; *see also* Griselini, Francesco

Giornale enciclopedico, 240

Glagolitic rite, 180

Gliubavaz, Simone, 121

Goethe, Johann Wolfgang von, 13, 18, 130, 180, 196, 204, 214; and Hasanaginica,190–193, 225; in Italy, 62, 192

Goldoni, Carlo, *La Dalmatina*, 17, 18, 25–27, 29, 31–35, 39, 40, 43, 45, 46, 48, 52, 55–75, 81, 100, 129, 142, 163, 167, 175, 221, 223, 254, 259, 325, 353, 356, 357; his exotic American dramas (*La Peruviana, La Bella Selvaggia*), 25–27, 68, 167, 218; his exotic Persian dramas (*La Sposa Persiana, Ircana in Julfa, Ircana in Ispaan*), 25, 27, 56, 67, 68, 218; his idea of the Dalmatian "nation," 26, 58, 61, 67, 69, 71, 123, 127, 254, 328, 329, 331; his idea of the "Adriatic Empire," 17, 27, 29, 48, 50, 58, 59, 65, 69, 70, 71, 78, 175, 319–320, 331, 353; his ideal of Dalmatian loyalty to Venice, 64–66, 68, 77, 161, 223, 277, 307–308, 311–312, 319–320, 329; his relation to Domenico Caminer, 83; his relation to Andrea Memmo, 289; his rivalry with Carlo Gozzi, 29; in Paris, 26, 56, 57; Zatta edition of *La Dalmatina*, 72, 73 (fig. 4), 74 (fig. 5); *see also* Radovich, hero of *La Dalmatina*; *see also* Zandira, heroine of *La Dalmatina*

Goudar, Ange, 82

Gould, Stephen Jay, 360–361

Gozzi, Carlo, in Zadar, 18, 29–40, 41, 49, 54, 60, 70, 72, 133; and Commedia dell'Arte, 29, 33, 35, 38; his conservative perspective on Dalmatia, 265–270; his criticism of Fortis, 230,

264–266; cross-dressing as a Dalmatian servant girl, 30, 33–36, 38–40, 45, 60, 70, 72, 132, 264, 269; his dramas (*Il re cervo, La donna serpente, Turandot*), 29, 30; on Morlacchi, 264, 266–270, 271, 274, 315, 316, 325; his rivalry with Goldoni, 29; his sexual relations in Dalmatia, 35–40, 269; his *Useless Memoirs*, 30, 31, 37, 264–265, 269

Gozzi, Gasparo, 17

Grabovac, Filip, 48, 55, 61, 71, 249, 331

Gradenigo, Giacomo, Provveditore Generale, 208, 228–237, 274, 280, 284, 290, 322

Grand Canal, 61

Greece, Greeks, 71, 78, 81, 104, 159, 179, 183, 192, 196, 225, 315–316; in Goldoni, Lisauro in *La Dalmatina*, 66–70, 76, 221; Greek rising of 1770, 76, 78–81; Greek antiquities, 106, 111; Greeks as subjects of Venice, 4 (fig. 1), 5, 27, 51, 66–67, 69–70, 76, 81, 89; *see also* Homer

Greppi, Giovanni, his drama of Dalmatia and Siam, 17, 73–75

Grimani, Francesco, Provveditore Generale, 54, 142–143, 170; his land reform of 1755, 29, 49, 50, 63, 66, 141–145, 150, 199, 230, 233, 236, 262, 264, 295, 298, 319

Grimani, Zorzi, Provveditore Generale, 32, 33, 131

Griselini, Francesco, 82, 91–93, 97, 114, 119, 144; *Dizionario delle arti e de' mestieri*, 92–93; *see also Giornale d'Italia*

Grisogono, Pietro Nutrizio, 240–241, 253, 277, 284–285, 287

Gualandris, Angelo, 260

Guardi, Antonio, 53

Guardi, Francesco, 112

guzla, *La Guzla* (Mérimée), 183, 196, 226–227, 337

Habermas, Jürgen, 27, 259–260, 274

Habsburg monarchy, Austria, 1, 6, 40, 97, 128, 171, 174, 192, 196, 272, 310, 331, 337–346, 349–351; border tensions

with Venetian Dalmatia, 231–232,
234–235; emigration from Dalmatia
into, 45, 147, 148, 229, 234–235, 271,
321, 330; Habsburg Croatia, 1, 128,
174–175, 192, 332, 340–341; Habsburg
Dalmatia, 10, 13, 176, 220, 272, 311,
317, 332, 337–346, 352, 360, 362;
Habsburg gains at Carlowitz (1699),
6, 40; Habsburg Lika, 231, 272;
Habsburg Military Frontier 129,
175, 231
Haiduks, bandits, 151–154, 156, 187, 195,
200, 245, 250, 266, 267, 283, 302–304,
315, 334; Marsich, Ante, 302–303, 315;
Socivizca, Stanislavo, 250, 251
(fig. 12), 252
Hasanaginica, "Mourning Song of
the Noble Wife of Asan Aga," 181,
182, 184, 188–193, 195, 196, 280, 313,
335; Goethe's German version,
190–193, 225
Heraclius, Emperor, 173
Hercegovina, 146, 175, 226, 286, 346
Herder, Johann Gottfried, 13, 18, 180,
188, 339; and the Slavs, 173–174,
194–195, 219, 325, 327, 335;
Volkslieder, 130, 185, 188, 190–191
Hervey, Frederick, 86, 100, 102, 120
history writing in Venice, 29, 41, 46–48,
50–54, 184; *see also* Diedo, Giacomo;
see also Sandi, Vettor
Hofmannsthal, Hugo von, 338, 344
Holbach, Maude, *Dalmatia: The Land
Where East Meets West,* 128, 346–347
Homer, 182, 183, 267, 268, 277, 312–318,
327, 358, 362; "to make him become a
Slav" (Giulio Bajamonti), 313, 327, 328
Honorati, Bernardino, papal nuncio in
Venice, 79, 80, 148
Hottentots, 156, 157, 225, 323
House, Colonel Edward, 351
Hrvatsko Kolo, 12, 19
Hume, David, 106
Hungary, 5, 6, 40, 52, 53, 194, 311
Hutchinson, Frances Kinsley, *Motoring
in the Balkans,* 128, 346–347
Hvar (Lesina), 15, 162 (fig. 10), 175,
298–300, 344, 345

ideology of empire, 3, 5, 7, 9, 27, 54, 77,
85, 106, 130, 222, 231, 319–324, 328,
333–334, 336, 353, 362; *see also*
civilizing mission
Ionian islands (Corfu, Cephalonia,
Zante), 4 (fig. 1), 5, 69, 76, 81; *see also*
Corfu
Illyria, Illyrians, 7, 13, 20, 97, 182, 223,
225, 242, 335, 339, 342; Illyrian
language, 34, 35, 48, 61, 119, 179, 180,
191, 238, 243, 248, 256, 265, 292, 295,
298, 300, 328; Illyrian name and
identity in Dalmatia, 7, 37, 48, 61, 71,
317, 328, 329, 331, 332, 360, 362; in
Bajamonti, Giulio, 315, 317; in Fortis,
Alberto, 114, 174, 180, 182; in Gozzi,
Carlo, 30, 33–35, 37, 72; in Goldoni,
Carlo, 60, 64–66, 70–72, 175, 325, 328;
in Grabovac, Filip, 48, 61, 331; in
Stratico, Giandomenico, 300, 328;
Napoleonic Illyria, including
Dalmatia, 10, 332, 333–334, 337,
360, 362
Illyrianism, of Ljudevit Gaj, 334–335
Illyricum Sacrum, of Daniele Farlati, 48,
71, 85, 121
India, 179, 319
Inquisitors, Sindici Inquisitori, in
Dalmatia (Giovanni Loredan, Nicolo
Erizzo, Sebastian Molin), 41, 43, 48,
49, 136–141, 168, 290, 293
Inquisitors of State, State Inquisitors, 78,
79, 206, 208, 289
Istria, 5, 15, 117
Italian claims concerning Dalmatia,
350–357

Jackson, Thomas Graham, 346–347
Jačov, Marko, 12, 19, 148
Jelavich, Charles, 340
Jesuits, 181–182, 253; *Illyricum Sacrum,*
of Daniele Farlati, 48, 71, 85, 121
Jews, 27, 261, 286, 310
Jones, William, 179
Joseph II, Emperor, 299

Kačić-Miošić, Andrija, 61, 71, 184, 185,
190, 191, 331

Karadžić, Vuk, 181, 185, 191–192, 335
Karaman, Matteo (Mate), archbishop of
  Zadar, 148, 180, 292
Klopstock, Friedrich Gottlieb, 181–182
Knin, 200, 230, 277, 279, 305
Korčula (Curzola), 15, 19, 20, 162 (fig.
  10), 292, 305, 349
Kotor, 4 (fig. 1), 15, 78, 309, 311, 359
Krajina Serbs, 12, 333
Križanić, Juraj, 174, 325
Kuchuk Kainardji, treaty of, (1774), 77,
  85, 124, 229

Lamarck, Jean-Baptiste, 113, 158
landscape, of Dalmatia, 262–263, 271,
  279, 281, 293, 294
Lane, Frederic, 60
Ledyard, John, 204
Leipzig, publications concerning
  Dalmatia, 215, 252, 342, 344
Leopold, Grand Duke of Tuscany, 299
Lepanto, battle of, 60
Levi, Cesare, 353
Lévi-Strauss, Claude, 170
libertinism, Venetian, 163
Lido of Venice, 31, 61, 268
Lika, Habsburg, 231, 272
Linnaeus, Carl, 96, 173, 177, 219, 325, 360
Lion of San Marco, of Venice, 26, 55, 60,
  62, 64, 68, 69, 75, 206, 310, 320, 321, 355
Ljubljana, 332, 337
Lloyd George, David, 352
Lodoli, Carlo, 289, 293, 294
Lord, Albert, 184
Lovrich, Giovanni (Ivan), ambivalence
  about his Dalmatian identity, 246–249,
  252–253, 275, 284, 325–326; attacked
  by "Pietro Sclamer," 253–258;
  criticism of Fortis, 165, 228–230,
  237–239, 241–259, 261, 265, 275; his
  Dalmatian "national spirit," 238, 239,
  258; and Morlacchi, 238, 241–243,
  284, 327, 334, 336, 337; called
  "Morlacco," 256–258; on "the most
  civilized Dalmatians," 252–253,
  255–256, 259, 325–326; on Socivizca,
  250, 251 (fig. 12), 252
Lovrich, Giuseppe, 308

loyalty of the Dalmatians to Venice, 8,
  45, 63–64, 74–75, 206, 212, 215, 224,
  236, 260, 287, 304, 320–322, 324, 329,
  336, 353, 355; in Camillo Federici, *Gli
  Antichi Slavi*, 222–223; in Foscarini's
  speech, 45, 130; in Goldoni, 29, 64–66,
  68, 75, 77, 161, 223, 277, 307–308,
  311–312, 319–320, 329; reconceived as
  loyalty to the Habsburgs, 338–339;
  reconceived as loyalty to Italy, 355; in
  reports of the Provveditori Generali,
  32–33, 131, 147, 150, 161, 279, 304,
  307–309; in the ultimate crisis of the
  Venetian republic (1797), 277,
  307–309, 311–312, 316, 336, 338, 353;
  the villagers of Triban, the Vuchich
  family, 232–233, 235
Lucerna, Camilla, 192, 340
Luchich, Colonel Marco, 232, 236
Lucius, Joannes (Giovanni Lucio, Ivan
  Lučić), 47, 51, 121
Lupis-Vukić, Ivo, 349
Luzzato, Fabio, 11

Maclean, Fitzroy, *Eastern Approaches,* 20
Macpherson, James, 181; *see also* Ossian
Maggior Consiglio, Great Council, 50,
  53, 58, 85, 136, 137, 306; Foscarini
  addresses, 29, 41–46, 97, 132, 133, 136,
  137, 139, 142, 146, 162, 266
Maixner, Rudolf, 215
Makarska, 61, 162 (fig. 10), 245, 305, 310
Malamocco, 31
Manin, Daniel, 336
Manin, Ludovico, Doge, 311, 338
Mann, Thomas, *Death in Venice,* 344
maps, cartography, of Dalmatia, 4 (fig.
  1), 42–44, 90, 142, 162 (fig. 10), 163,
  198–199, 231, 281, 282 (fig. 13), 295;
  see also Foscarini, Marco: and the map
  of Dalmatia
Marchisini, Giovanni, 41
Maria Theresa, Empress, 196, 215, 272
Marin, Alvise, Provveditore Generale,
  305, 323
Marmont, Marshal Auguste-Frédéric-
  Louis, 333–334, 337; *see also* Illyria:
  Napoleonic Illyria

Marsich, Ante, 302–303, 315

Marsigli, Luigi, 97

Marsili, Giovanni, 14, 15

Maruzzi, Pano, 80, 81

Matvejević, Predrag, 8, 329

Mayerling, 337

Memmo, Andrea, 102, 300–301, 311, 314, 318; his report on Dalmatia, 277, 289–295, 297, 298, 300–304, 322–324, 328, 341; his sponsorship of Fortis, 99, 103, 119, 179, 260, 289, 321, 356; his relationship with Wynne, 196, 203, 289, 291

Memmo, Angelo, Provveditore Generale, 290

Mérimée, Prosper, *La Guzla*, 226–227, 337

Meštrović, Ivan, 349–350

Michiel, Pietro, Provveditore Generale, 118–119, 144–146, 156, 320, 322

Michieli-Vitturi, Rados, 292, 297, 298, 310, 311

Mickiewicz, Adam, 226

Milizia Oltremarina, transmarine militia, 61, 268, 308

millennium, the year 1000, in Dalmatia, 5, 46, 47, 50, 51, 356

Miller, Anna Riggs, 93

mobilization, of Dalmatians, for the defense of Venice, 307–309

Modena, 214, 253, 255

Moller, Giovanni, 296

Montagu, Lady Mary Wortley, 196

Montenegro, 15, 78–80, 147, 148, 157, 175, 191, 346

Montesquieu, Charles Louis de Secondat, 158, 234

Moqué, Alice Lee, *Delightful Dalmatia*, 13, 128, 346–347

Morlacchi, 2, 3, 7, 8, 10, 17, 18, 22, 54, 64, 71, 77, 97, 228–230, 296, 298, 301, 306, 309, 326, 332, 336–341, 350, 358, 360–362; abduction, romantic, 163–164; as anthropophagi, 133, 267, 268, 325; and antiquities, 108–109; appearance, 177; and bandits, Haiduks, 151–154, 156, 187, 195, 200, 245, 250, 251 (fig. 12), 252, 266, 267,

283, 303, 304, 334; their "barbarism," 2, 7, 13, 17, 128, 134, 135, 142, 160, 167, 170, 221, 222, 236, 246, 267–269, 273, 302, 304, 322, 323, 327, 329, 330, 333–334, 346–348, 357; their celebrations, 137–138; their character ascribed, 126, 127, 132–134, 136, 139–144, 146, 147, 170, 178, 189, 201, 278, 281; their chiefs, 138, 144, 149–151, 154–156, 165, 199; their children, 246–247; their clothing, 13, 155 (fig. 9), 166–167, 221–222, 248–249, 347; their dances, 133, 188–189, 227, 267, 334, 342; and discipline, as an administrative concern, 8, 130–133, 141, 143–146, 149, 151, 152, 159, 230, 236, 271–273, 278, 283, 302, 318, 322, 356; economy of, 131, 132, 145, 146, 156, 271–272; their ethnographic extinction, 10, 128, 176, 191, 192, 224, 227, 317, 333, 334, 339–340, 343, 357; as ex-Morlacchi, 357, 362; in Federici's drama, *Gli Antichi Slavi*, 219–224; their "ferocity," 126, 129, 131, 134, 135, 137, 141, 143, 144, 151, 153, 163, 165, 170, 202, 216, 221, 250, 283, 290, 302, 304, 329; their foods, 168–169, 242–243, 269, 271, 316, 323; Fortis on "The Customs of the Morlacchi," 2, 126–127, 129–131, 134, 136, 151–172, 184, 189, 220, 238, 241, 264, 298, 309, 315–316, 322, 347, 361; and friendship, *pobratimstvo*, 109, 155, 160–161, 163, 202; and Gozzi, Carlo, 30–31, 264, 266–270, 325; their Homeric aspects, 312–318, 328; their hospitality, 154–156, 168, 199, 217, 244; their hostility toward Italians, 154, 172, 248–249; their houses, huts, 166, 293–294, 302, 303, 324, 347; their "inertia," 139, 143, 170, 269–273, 276–278, 281, 303, 329; their "innocent and natural liberty," 161, 164, 170, 171; and kissing, 161, 163–166; in the law courts, 135–136, 138–139, 140, 236; and Lovrich, Giovanni, 238, 241–258; marriage customs, 166, 178, 184, 203, 206, 244, 268, 334; and morality, 163–164, 266–270, 273, 274, 316; in Napoleonic Illyria, 333–334; as a "nation," 127, 159, 168, 170, 171, 190, 315, 328, 329; pastoralism, 11, 45, 49, 127, 231–232, 236–237, 263–264, 327; religion, 11, 12, 128, 132, 160, 180, 189, 232, 248, 249; and plague, 278–279, 281, 283–288, 315, 317, 327; poetry of, 18, 126, 130, 181–186, 189–192, 204, 213, 225–227, 314–315, 323, 337; in reports of Provveditori Generali, 131–136, 143–151, 154, 157, 158, 171, 180, 231–237, 271–275, 276–278, 293, 304, 318, 322; resemblance to Bosnians, 283–285, 328, 330; and Romanticism, 225–227; and sex, sexuality, 138, 163–166, 204–205, 244, 247–248, 269; as Slavs, 12, 13, 18, 128, 173–181, 207–210, 213–214, 218–219, 222, 227, 321, 325, 330; their superstitions, 153, 245–246, 286, 315, 334; as tourist sight, 346–348; and the vendetta, 134–135, 138, 140, 144, 160, 170, 217, 266, 269, 292, 334, 337; their villages, 141, 142, 293–294, 295, 302–304, 324; as Vlachs, 13, 128, 129, 171, 172, 176, 219, 248, 329, 330; women, 155 (fig. 9), 161, 163–167, 184, 201–202, 211, 220–221, 242, 246, 247–249, 254, 257, 316, 323, 339, 347; in Wynne's novel, *Les Morlaques,* 193–219, 321, 323–325

Morlacchia, 161, 163, 256; the "innocent and natural liberty" of, 161, 163, 164, 170, 171; in Wynne, Morlaquie, 194, 197

Morlacchismo, idea of, 18, 19, 180, 220, 277, 312–318, 327, 330, 357, 362; *see also* Bajamonti, Giulio: "The Morlacchismo of Homer"

Morocco, Barbary, as dramatic setting for Goldoni's *La Dalmatina,* 17, 25, 35, 56, 63, 64, 66–73, 74 (fig. 5), 75, 77

Morosini, Francesco, 89, 104

Morosini, Jacopo, 88–90, 103, 104, 114, 130

Mostar, 286

moustaches, in Dalmatia, 30, 31, 55, 72, 226, 257

Mozart, Wolfgang Amadeus, 16

Muir, Edward, 46

Muljačić, Žarko, 19

Münster, Sebastian, 178

Murano, 167

Muséum d'Histoire Naturelle, Paris, Fortis at, 113, 158, 318

Mussolini, Benito, 10, 20, 21, 355, 356, 358

Mutinelli, Fabio, 14, 335–336

Naples, 82, 86, 106, 119, 261, 264

Napoleon, 15, 115, 158, 225, 277, 307–311, 333–334, 338

Narentani, 47, 50–52, 111

national identity in Dalmatia, 7, 10–12, 48, 67, 69, 71, 72, 128, 129, 181, 190, 328–333, 341–343, 360–362

Native Americans, American Indians, 158, 167, 218, 323, 342, 347; in Goldoni dramas, 25–27, 68, 167, 218

Navagero, Andrea, 47

Nazi Germany, 345

Neretva River, 47

neutrality, Venetian, 79–82, 92, 124, 125, 133, 206, 222, 267, 289, 321

The New Europe, 351; *see also* Seton-Watson, R. W.

Nile River, 97

Nin (Nona), 106, 107, 110

Nodier, Charles, 337

nuovissimo acquisto, newest acquisition, 6, 11, 32, 40, 42, 49, 63, 79, 127, 140, 141, 176, 235, 236

nuovo acquisto, new acquisition, 6, 11, 32, 40, 42, 49, 63, 79, 127, 140. 141, 176, 235, 236

Nuovo giornale d'Italia, 297, 298, 299

Nuovo giornale enciclopedico, 217–218

Nuovo giornale enciclopedico d'Italia, 312

Obradović, Dositej, 148–149, 175, 200

Ochakov, 314

Oltremare, Venetian, 4 (fig. 1), 8

Orbini, Mauro, *Il regno degli Slavi,* 174, 178, 325

Orientalism, demi-Orientalism, 9, 15–17, 19, 28 (fig. 3), 56, 72, 73 (fig. 4), 74 (fig. 5), 135, 165, 177, 179, 223, 245, 279; *see also* Eastern Europe, idea of: and Orientalism
Orlando, Vittorio Emanuele, 352–353
Orseolo, Pietro II, Doge, 47, 50, 52, 356
Orsini-Rosenberg, Count Philip, 196
Orsini-Rosenberg, Countess Justine; *See* Wynne, Giustiniana
Orthodoxy, 11, 71, 175, 357; caloyers, monks, 207–209, 213, 286; in Dalmatia, 11, 12, 63, 76, 79, 128, 133, 149, 176, 180, 189, 200, 208, 232, 243, 248, 249, 292, 331, 332, 340; in Lovrich, Giovanni, 243, 248, 249; and Russia 63, 76, 78, 81, 147, 207–209, 233
Ossian, 181, 195, 217
Ottoman empire, 5, 6, 8, 15, 43, 48, 83, 85, 97, 100, 104, 127, 128, 138, 147, 159, 306, 309, 335, 338; in Bajamonti (Giulio), concerning plague, 281, 285, 288; border with Venetian Dalmatia, 26, 79, 124, 127, 146, 162 (fig. 10), 171, 189, 234, 235, 271, 277, 278, 283, 330; emigration to and from Dalmatia, 45, 146, 229, 234, 321; in Foscarini's speech, 44, 45, 134; Haiduks and the Turks, 151, 153, 200, 250; Moslem Slavs in, 189, 192; in poetry of the Morlacchi, 189–192; in Wynne's novel, *Les Morlaques,* 195, 200, 203, 205, 206, 209, 212; *see also* Russian-Ottoman war of 1768–1774; *see also* Russian-Ottoman war of 1787–1791; *see also* Bosnia, Bosnians
Ovid, 182

Pacific Ocean, 102, 193, 323
Padua, 2, 7, 9, 15, 97, 113, 197, 220, 223, 289, 299, 313, 326, 327; University of, 14, 48, 85, 86, 119, 120, 122–123, 217, 238, 252, 261, 265, 296, 326
Pagden, Anthony, 3, 319
Palmerston, Lord (Henry Temple), 336
Panduri, Dalmatian milita, 281, 302–303
Panin, Nikita, 80
Paoli, Pasquale, 158

Papal State, 15, 97, 100, 102, 169, 235, 289, 311
Paris, peace of (1763), 59, 319
Paris, peace conference (1919). *See* Versailles
Partisans, Yugoslav, 20, 357–358
Passarowitz, peace of (1718), 6, 40, 42, 131
patriciate, patricians, Venetian, 29, 30, 33, 40, 85, 86, 88, 89, 99, 106, 257, 260, 291, 301, 308, 326, 336
Paul, Saint, 20, 61
Peloponnesus, Morea, 40, 44
Perasto, 311–312, 353
Peričić, Šime, 19, 229
Pervan, Voivod, in Fortis's account, 154, 155 (fig. 9), 162 (fig. 10), 167, 198–199, 318; in Wynne's novel, *Les Morlaques,* 154, 155 (fig. 9), 198–202, 205–207, 211–214, 216–217, 293, 312, 321, 325
Peter I, Tsar, Peter the Great, 82, 158, 180, 207, 208, 298, 324
Peter III, Tsar, 78
Petronius, *Satyricon,* 104
physiocrats, 234–235, 274, 280
Piatoli, Francesca, 224
Piranesi, Giovanni Battista, 106, 107
pirates, piracy, 26, 52, 66
Pisani, Gian-Francesco, elected Procurator of San Marco, 56–58
Pisani, Zorzi, 261
Pius VI, Pope, 235
plague, 43, 144, 145, 305, 306, 310; of 1783–1784, 4 (fig. 1), 16, 18, 23 (fig. 2), 145, 271, 277–288, 314, 317, 327; *see also* quarantine; *see also* Split: lazaretto
Po River, 100
poetry of the South Slavs, Morlacchi, 18, 95, 111, 126, 130, 153, 181–192, 225–227, 249, 280, 300, 313–315, 335; in Fortis's account, 181–186, 190–192, 204, 243, 249, 300, 335; in Wynne's novel, *Les Morlaques,* 195–196, 200, 204, 207, 209, 213; *see also* Hasanaginica; *see also* Morlacchi: poetry of

poetry in praise of the Provveditore Generale, 32–33, 49–50

Poland, 62, 63, 69, 83, 156, 203, 227, 324

Polo, Marco 17

Pomian, Krzysztof, 90, 91, 95

Pompeii, excavations at, 106

poverty, in Dalmatia, 38–40, 45, 49, 105 (fig. 8), 129, 132, 139, 140, 147, 230, 240, 284, 342, 343

Praga, Giuseppe, 9, 19

Preto, Paolo, 17, 63, 79

Pribojević, Vinko, *De origine successibusque Slavorum,* 174, 175, 325

Primorje, 111, 245

prostitution, 310

Provveditori Generali; *See* Boldù, Giacomo; Boldù, Paolo; Condulmer, Domenico; Contarini, Alvise; Da Riva, Giacomo; Diedo, Angelo; Falier, Francesco; Gradenigo, Giacomo; Grimani, Francesco; Grimani, Zorzi; Marin, Alvise; Memmo, Angelo; Michiel, Pietro; Querini, Andrea; Quirini, Girolamo

public sphere, 6, 7, 25–27, 44, 56–59, 72, 82, 222, 239, 274, 277, 288, 296–298, 327, 329; reading *Viaggio in Dalmazia,* 85, 88, 130, 137, 161, 170, 180, 228, 326; Dalmatians participate in, 239, 259–260, 270, 275, 283, 296, 297, 298, 317–318, 326

Pushkin, Alexander, 226

quarantine, 305, 310; and plague of 1783–1784, 278–279, 281, 287, 288

Querini, Andrea, Provveditore Generale, 305–311, 314

Querini, Angelo, 57, 197

Quirini, Girolamo, Provveditore Generale, 30–36, 38, 132, 133

race, racial description of the Morlacchi, 177

Radovich, hero of *La Dalmatina,* 26, 60, 61, 65–70, 72, 74 (fig. 5), 75, 220, 320

Ragusa, Dubrovnik, 10, 15, 61, 83, 191, 234, 253, 257, 261, 305, 306, 332, 335, 359

rebellion, in Dalmatia, 33, 52–55, 63, 305

recruitment of Dalmatian soldiers by foreign powers, 63, 64, 76, 77, 80, 81, 175, 206, 208, 289–290, 330

Reichsrat, in Vienna, 341, 356

Renaissance Venice, 46, 53, 57, 60, 72, 184, 338

Renier-Michiel, Giustina, 14

Revolution of 1848, 336

Reynolds, Joshua, 106

Rhodes, Cecil, 341–342

Rijeka (Fiume), D'Annunzio at, 355

Rimini, 97, 169

Risorgimento, 336

Riva degli Schiavoni, 14, 22, 216, 217, 312

roads, in Dalmatia, 295, 302, 333–334, 338

Robert's *Atlas Universel* (1757), 43

Roman Catholicism, 102, 116, 133, 175, 196; in Dalmatia, 11, 71, 176, 180, 189, 208, 232, 248, 292, 310, 331, 332, 340, 341; hierarchy in Zadar, 148, 180, 292; nuncio in Venice, 79, 80, 148; *see also Illyricum Sacrum*

Roman empire, ancient; in Dalmatia, 1, 14, 22, 23, 53, 84, 87, 88, 122, 124, 125, 174, 179, 342, 352, 355, 356; and Gibbon, 1, 3, 5, 22, 23, 297; in Fortis, 14, 87, 88, 103–112, 122, 124, 125, 174, 179, 182; invoked by Italian fascism, 355, 356; Roman ruins, antiquities, 84, 103–112, 117, 121, 136; *see also* Diocletian

Romania, Romanians, 175, 177

Romano, Dennis, 60

Romanticism, 185, 219, 224; French Romanticism, 23–24, 225–227, 336–337

Rome, 59, 60, 79, 80, 85, 107, 110, 115, 158, 179, 235, 332, 349; *see also* Papal State

Rousseau, Jean-Jacques, 54, 69, 158, 170, 187, 197, 246–247, 291, 316; influence on Fortis, 154, 157, 160, 163–164, 170, 237, 266; influence on Wynne, 154, 198, 199, 205, 214, 216

Rudolf of Habsburg, as patron of *Die österreichisch-ungarische Monarchie in Wort und Bild,* 337

Russia, 36, 63, 64, 71, 78–82, 85, 147, 174, 178, 203–204, 227, 314, 324, 325, 352, 361; the Russian fleet in the Mediterranean, 76, 79, 80, 84, 87, 124, 205; in Wynne's novel, *Les Morlaques,* 205–216, 219, 321, 324, 325, 330; *see also* Catherine II; *see also* Peter I; *see also* Russian-Ottoman war of 1768–1774; *see also* Russian-Ottoman war of 1787–1791

Russian-Ottoman war of 1768–1774, 18, 64, 76–84, 92, 123, 146, 148, 157, 175, 229, 233, 289–290, 330; in Caminer's *Storia della guerra presente,* 77, 82–84, 87, 109, 118, 206; in Wynne's novel, *Les Morlaques,* 205–206, 208–209, 210 (fig. 11), 211–212

Russian-Ottoman war of 1787–1791, 205, 211, 212, 289–290, 314

Ruzzini, Giovanni, 86, 87

Sabellico, Marcantonio, 47

Said, Edward, 3

sailors, Dalmatian, 44, 60, 63, 73, 80, 114, 268, 305, 335; *see also* Radovich, hero of *La Dalmatina*

St. Petersburg, 36, 80, 82, 124, 203, 207, 209, 211–213, 330

Salona, 83, 109, 110, 117, 123, 124

Salvemini, Gaetano, 351

San Giorgio degli Schiavoni. *See* Scuola Dalmata

San Marco, Piazza, 23, 225

Sandi, Vettor, *Principi di storia civile della Repubblica di Venezia,* 29, 50–54, 63, 184

Sanskrit, 179

Saracens, 50, 52

Sarajevo, 148, 286

Sarpi, Paolo, 91

Sava River, 207

Sciugliaga, Stefano, 61

Sclamer, Pietro. *See* Fortis, Alberto: as "Pietro Sclamer"

Scott, Walter, 191

Scuola Dalmata of San Giorgio degli Schiavoni, 14, 61; *see also* Carpaccio, Vittore

Scythians, 174, 179, 194, 220, 286, 327

Ségur, Louis-Philippe de, in St. Petersburg, 203

Senate, Venetian, 55, 91, 99, 102, 119, 138, 149, 231, 257, 260, 269, 277, 289–291, 295, 296, 302, 307, 309, 311, 338; and the Provveditori Generali, 78, 132, 150, 170, 228, 272, 274, 280, 301

Serafini, Giacomo, 224

Serbia, Serbs, 51, 71, 148, 189, 317, 335, 336, 357, 358; Krajina Serbs in the 1990s, 12, 333; and the poetry of the Morlacchi, 191–192; Serbian name and identity in Dalmatia, 7, 10–12, 128, 176, 317, 331–333, 339–341; Serbian rite, Serbian Orthodoxy, 79, 128, 331; Serbs as Slavs 175, 178; *see also* Karadžić, Vuk; *see also* Obradović, Dositej

Serbo-Croatian language, identity, 11, 176, 332, 339–341, 348–351, 357, 359, 360

Seton-Watson, R. W., 349–351, 359

Seven Years War, 319

sex, between Venetians and Dalmatians, 35–40, 269

Shakespeare, William, 20, 21, 190, 224–225

shipbuilding, Venetian, 60, 80, 262

Siam, as setting for Greppi's drama, 17, 73–75

Šibenik (Sebenico), 34, 230, 295, 303, 352, 357

Sinj, 177, 226, 235, 238, 241, 249, 256, 257, 277, 279, 286, 287, 305

Skradin, 149

slaves, slavery, 70, 71

Slavonic liturgy, 54, 55, 148, 160, 180

Slavs, Slavic peoples, Slavic resemblances, Slavdom, 173–181, 190–191, 207–210, 213–214, 218–219, 222, 324–328, 330, 335, 352; *see also* Morlacchi: as Slavs

Slovenia, Slovenes, 196, 332, 341, 358

Smodlaka, Josip, 341–342, 347, 349–351

Socivizca, Stanislavo, 250, 251 (fig. 12), 252

soldiers, Dalmatian, 26, 31, 60, 63, 143, 159, 215, 227, 267, 268, 277, 307–310, 335, 356; *see also* recruitment of Dalmatian soldiers by foreign powers

Sović, Matteo, 180, 292

Spallanzani, Lazzaro, 89

Split (Spalato, Spalatro), 3, 7, 15, 22, 66, 109, 162 (fig. 10), 216, 224, 226, 253, 277, 326, 333, 341, 346, 349–352, 359; city of Giulio Bajamonti, 239, 256, 313; Economic Society of, 230, 259–265, 270, 280, 292, 295–297, 300, 314, 327, 350–351; during Italian fascist occupation, 356, 357; lazaretto at, 16, 23 (fig. 2), 104, 145, 279, 283, 288; palace of Diocletian at, 1, 9, 10, 22, 23 (fig. 2), 28 (fig. 3), 104, 105 (fig. 8), 106, 110; and plague of 1783–1784, 16, 18, 23 (fig. 2), 145, 277–280, 282–283, 287–288

Spon, Jacob, *Voyage d'Italie, de Dalmatie, de Grece, et du Levant*, 104, 128; *see also* Wheler, George

Srebrenica, 122

Staël, Madame de, Germaine, 23, 24, 225–227

Stanojević, Gligor, 19

Starobinski, Jean, 163

State Inquisitors. *See* Inquisitors of State

Stephen, Mali, the Small, 78

Stojković, Marijan, 12, 19, 215, 258

Storia dell'Anno, 76

Strange, John, 87, 112–113, 120

Stratico, Giandomenico (Ivan Dominik), bishop of Hvar, 215, 295, 298–301, 303, 306, 314, 328, 344, 353

Stratico, Gregorio (Grgur), 277, 289, 290, 295

Sturm und Drang, 186

superstition, in Dalmatia, 31, 101–102, 153, 245–246, 286, 291, 298, 315, 334; *see also* Fortis: on superstition; *see also* Morlacchi: their superstitions

Supilo, Frano, 351

Symonds, John, 86, 120, 235

Tahiti, 102, 158, 164

Tamaro, Attilio, 10, 21, 312, 353

Tartars, 167, 168, 177, 323

taxation, in Dalmatia, 33, 43, 274, 305, 338

Teatro San Luca, 25, 26, 33, 34, 39, 45, 46, 55, 59, 61, 62, 66, 69

Teatro Sant'Angelo, 219

Teodosio, Demetrio, 82

Terraferma, Venetian, 5, 8, 61, 268

textbooks, discussing Dalmatia, 340–341

Tibet, 179

Tiepolo, Baiamonte, 54, 55; *see also* Vallaresso, Zaccaria: author of *Baiamonte Tiepolo in Schiavonia*

Tintoretto, Jacopo, 53, 136

Titian, 338

Tito, 10, 20, 357–359

Todorova, Maria, 330

Tommaseo, Niccolò, 336

Tonina, of Zadar, in Gozzi's account, 39, 40, 269

Torcellan, Gianfranco, 99

tourism in Dalmatia, 13, 19–21, 128, 342–348, 349, 359, 361–362; American travelers, 13, 128, 346–347; Austrian travelers, 344–345; British travelers, 19–21, 128, 345–347, 349–350, 361–362; German travelers, 345–346

Trajan, Emperor, 103

Transylvania, 331

Travnik, 314

Trento, Vittorio, 223

Trieste, 6, 59, 353

Triplex Confinium, Ottoman-Habsburg-Venetian triple border, 129, 163, 171

Trogir, 47, 98 (fig. 7), 121, 162 (fig. 10); academy of, 277, 296–299, 326

Turgot, Anne-Robert, 234

Tuscany, 299, 300

Udine, 297

Ugrešić, Dubravka, 358

Ukraine, 62, 63, 156, 178

Ustaša, 357

Vallaresso, Zaccaria, 249; author of *Baiamonte Tiepolo in Schiavonia*, 54, 55, 72, 77, 249

Vallisnieri, Antonio, 122, 260

vampires, 153, 337, 348

vecchio acquisto, old acquisition, 32, 33

Vendramin, Pietro, 290

Venetian republic, abolition of, in 1797, 5, 10, 215, 227, 288, 289, 306, 316–318;

mobilization of the Dalmatians, 307–309, 336, 338; aftermath in Dalmatia, in 1797, 310–312, 335, 353, 354 (fig. 14)

Venturi, Franco, 19, 41, 50, 57, 80–82, 158, 240, 296, 301

Verdery, Katherine, 331

Vergoraz, 177, 305, 310

Verona, 5, 63, 93, 98, 267, 297

Veronese, Paolo, 112, 136

Versailles, peace settlement of, 10, 312, 332, 351–353, 355

Vicentino, Andrea, 53

Vicenza, 5, 297, 326

Vico, Giambattista, 158, 183, 184, 268, 315

Vienna, Congress of, 332

Vienna, fin-de-siècle, 338, 344

Vienna, University of, 342

Virgil, 268, 315

Vis (Lissa), 357

Viscovich, Giuseppe, at Perasto in 1797, 311–312

Vitezović, Pavao Ritter, 174, 325

Vivaldi, Antonio, 250

Vlachs. *See* Morlacchi: as Vlachs

Voltaire, 82, 83, 92, 158, 197, 207, 254, 324; *Essai sur les moeurs,* 56, 62–63, 156–157, 165, 169–171, 202, 225; and Catherine, 76, 81, 209, 211, 214, 324

Vrana, Lake, 99–100

Vuchich family, 232–233, 235

Vucinich, Wayne, 329

Wallachia, 176

Walpole, Horace, 106

Weimar, 13, 173, 177, 226

Wells, H. G., *The Time Machine,* Morlocks, 348

West, Rebecca, *Black Lamb and Grey Falcon,* 19–20, 21, 345, 361–362

Wheler, George, *Voyage d'Italie, de Dalmatie, de Grece, et du Levant,* 104, 128; *see also* Spon, Jacob

Wilkinson, J. Gardner, 336

Wilson, Woodrow, at Versailles, 351–353

women, in Dalmatia, 94 (fig. 6); Morlacchi and women, 155 (fig. 9), 161, 163–167, 184, 220–221, 242, 246–249, 254, 257, 316, 323, 339, 347; in Wynne's novel, *Les Morlaques,* 201–202, 211; *see also* Zandira, heroine of *La Dalmatina*

World War I, 10, 332, 333, 346, 349, 351, 359

World War II, 10, 20, 332, 333, 356–359

Wynne, Giustiniana, Countess Orsini-Rosenberg, 18, 154, 155 (fig. 9), 181, 192, 289, 361; her life, 193, 196–197; her novel, *Les Morlaques,* 193–219, 221, 223, 291, 293, 300, 309, 312, 314, 326; influenced by Rousseau, 198, 199, 205, 214; inspired by Fortis, 193–202, 205, 206, 219, 323; on Russia and the Morlacchi, 205–216, 219, 321, 324, 325, 330; on Slavic identity of the Morlacchi, 207–210, 213–214, 218–219, 321, 325, 330; the title page of her novel, *Les Morlaques,* 210 (fig. 11); the translations of *Les Morlaques,* 214–215, 300, 314; as woman of letters, her views concerning women, 197, 201, 202, 211; writes anthropological fiction of primitive customs, 193, 195, 198–205, 213, 215, 218, 323; writes "Chansons," poetry of the Morlacchi, 195–196, 200, 213, 215, 216, 300

Yugoslavia, 10–12, 14, 20, 176, 332, 344, 345, 355, 357–359, 361; creation of, 349–355; dissolution of, 10, 12, 14, 332

Zadar (Zara), 3, 7, 9, 15, 128, 146, 226, 230, 239, 286, 295, 298, 311, 333, 337, 339, 350; academy of, 277, 296, 297, 326; Fortis concerning, 3, 88, 94 (fig. 6), 103, 104, 106, 121, 127, 130, 177; Gozzi in, 29–40, 264, 267, 269; Italian claims to, 10, 332, 352, 355, 356; medieval 47, 51–53, 356, 359; Morlacchi observed in the marketplace, 13, 127–128, 347; Provveditori Generali in, 78, 130, 146, 149, 212, 229, 278, 287, 296, 304, 356; reform in county of Zadar, 293–294, 302, 303, 304; resolution of, (1905),

332; town clock, 306–307; in Wynne's novel, *Les Morlaques,* 216, 217

Zagreb, 174, 175, 192, 258, 334, 340, 341

Zandira, heroine of *La Dalmatina,* 26, 35, 40, 61, 62, 64–68, 70, 74 (fig. 5)

Zanetti, Antonio Maria, 91

Zatta, Antonio, edition of *La Dalmatina,* 72, 73 (fig. 4), 74 (fig. 5)

Zavoreo, Francesco (Frane), 295, 302

Zenobio, Carlo, 86, 87

Zmajević, Vinko, archbishop of Zadar, 180

Zorić, Mate, 19